"In this fourth edition of his already widely admired book on listening, Michael Rost has greatly extended the boundaries of previous work, focusing on new areas such as neuroscience, the use of AI in instruction, and the implementation of research in teacher education. Undoubtedly, researchers, teacher educators and teachers alike will be inspired by such an authoritative resource."

Anne Burns, *University of New South Wales, Sydney, and Curtin University, Perth, Australia*

"*Teaching and Researching Listening* provides a comprehensive, engaging account of listening which updates our understanding of key concepts and issues, and explores the impact of important new developments such as AI. Its focus on both theory and practice makes it an ideal resource for teacher educators, language teachers and researchers."

Neil Murray, *University of Warwick, UK*

"Michael Rost is a proven expert in the field of listening. His latest book is a tour-de-force. It offers a comprehensive and accessible account of listening in a second language from the perspectives of theory, pedagogy and research. This is a must-have book, which I know I will be referring to for years to come."

Rod Ellis, *Curtin University, Perth, Australia*

"The new edition of Michael Rost's book on listening is carefully crafted, addressing crucial issues and presenting innovative ideas in this relatively under-researched area. The author adeptly navigates readers through logically structured chapters, seamlessly blending theory with practice. This approach makes the book a must-read for both teachers and researchers."

Istvan Kecskes, *State University of New York, Albany, USA*

"*Teaching and Researching Listening* is the most comprehensive textbook on second language listening available today. This indispensable resource has something of value for experienced academics, graduate students, and researchers in the field of second language listening given its up-to-date treatment of theory, pedagogy, and research into the complex skill of listening comprehension."

David Beglar, *Temple University, Japan*

"In the fourth edition of this classic, Rost once again authoritatively covers the many dimensions of listening for language teachers, researchers, and app developers. The content ranges from foundations in neuroscience, language processing, and acquisition to the more practical domains of language teaching and assessment. Comprehensive and comprehensible, if you have just one book on listening in a second language, this should be it."

Philip Hubbard, *Stanford U*

"This book has been incredibly important for L2 listening researchers and teachers since the first edition was published over 20 years ago. What's special about it is that it is aimed at both researchers AND teachers, and Rost makes the information in the book accessible and relevant for practitioners, students, and researchers (not an easy task!)."

Elvis Wagner, *Temple University, USA*

"In the fourth edition of *Teaching and Researching Listening*, Michael Rost provides a comprehensive and insightful exploration of the complexities of listening in second language acquisition (SLA) and teaching. This important work integrates research from linguistics, SLA, language teaching and technology, and offers valuable guidance for language educators and researchers. I recommend the book to language educators, researchers, and anyone interested in the intricacies of listening in SLA and communication."

Vahid Aryadoust, *Nanyang Technological University, Singapore*

Praise for the third edition:

"This book is the most comprehensive reference on L2 listening to date and is an invaluable resource for graduate students and academics. Rost offers his interpretation of theories and works that have defined and established the field, along with insights drawn from latest research to move it forward."

Christine C. M. Goh, *Nanyang Technological University, Singapore*

Teaching and Researching Listening

Widely considered to be a foundational work in the field of listening, *Teaching and Researching Listening* is among the most recommended textbooks in applied linguistics oral communication courses, and the most cited reference in current research on second language listening development. Known for its comprehensiveness, clarity, insight, and practical applications, this fourth edition has been substantially revised to reflect the latest research in the areas of linguistics, neuroscience, applied technologies, and teaching methodology, with expanded sections on teaching applications and explorations in social research related to listening.

This completely revised edition includes:

- Detailed overviews of the underlying processes of listening, with additional coverage of decoding processes
- Expansion of sections dealing with artificial intelligence (AI), speech recognition, and input enhancement software
- Emphasis on research of listening in spoken interaction and cross-cultural communication
- Clear templates for instructors and curriculum designers, with an expansive set of practical resources
- Guidance in using observational methods for exploring listening in a range of educational and professional contexts
- Website support, with presentation slides, infographics, and question banks for each chapter

This fourth edition of *Teaching and Researching Listening* serves as an authoritative and comprehensive survey of issues related to teaching and researching oral communication, providing value for language teachers, educational researchers, instructional designers, interpreters, and other language practitioners.

Michael Rost is an independent researcher and instructional designer, and the author of numerous academic articles and books on listening, speaking, interaction, and language acquisition, including *Listening in Language Learning* and *Active Listening*. He is also the author and series editor of several longstanding textbook and courseware series, including *Pearson English Interactive*.

Applied Linguistics in Action

Applied Linguistics in Action is a series which focuses on the issues and challenges to teachers and researchers in a range of fields in Applied Linguistics and provides readers and users with the tools they need to carry out their own practice-based research.

Teaching and Researching Translation
2nd Edition
Basil A. Hatim

Teaching and Researching Speaking
3rd Edition
Rebecca Hughes and Beatrice Szczepek-Reed

Teaching and Researching Reading
3rd Edition
William Peter Grabe and Fredricka L. Stoller

Teaching and Researching Motivation
3rd Edition
Zoltán Dörnyei and Ema Ushioda

Teaching and Researching Writing
4th Edition
Ken Hyland

Teaching and Researching Listening
4th Edition
Michael Rost

For more information about this series, please visit: https://www.routledge.com/Applied-Linguistics-in-Action/book-series/PEAALIA

Teaching and Researching Listening

Fourth Edition

Michael Rost

NEW YORK AND LONDON

Designed cover image: Dusan Stankovic © Getty

Fourth edition published 2025
by Routledge
605 Third Avenue, New York, NY 10158

and by Routledge
4 Park Square, Milton Park, Abingdon, Oxon, OX14 4RN

Routledge is an imprint of the Taylor & Francis Group, an informa business

© 2025 Michael Rost

The right of Michael Rost to be identified as author of this work has been asserted in accordance with sections 77 and 78 of the Copyright, Designs and Patents Act 1988.

All rights reserved. No part of this book may be reprinted or reproduced or utilised in any form or by any electronic, mechanical, or other means, now known or hereafter invented, including photocopying and recording, or in any information storage or retrieval system, without permission in writing from the publishers.

Trademark notice: Product or corporate names may be trademarks or registered trademarks and are used only for identification and explanation without intent to infringe.

First edition published by Pearson Education Limited 2002
Third edition published by Routledge 2016

ISBN: 9781032487915 (hbk)
ISBN: 9781032487908 (pbk)
ISBN: 9781003390794 (ebk)

DOI: 10.4324/9781003390794

Typeset in Times New Roman
by Newgen Publishing UK

Access the Support Material: http://www.routledge.com/9781032487908

Contents

Series Editor Preface	*xv*
Preface	*xvii*
Acknowledgments	*xviii*
Copyright Acknowledgments	*xx*

Introduction   **1**

SECTION I
Defining Listening   **5**

1 Neurological Processing   **7**

   1.1 Introduction: Listening as a Coordination of Networks 7
   1.2 Reception: The Role of Hearing 8
   1.3 Transmission: The Role of the Inner Ear 10
   1.4 Coordination: The Role of the Auditory Cortex 11
   1.5 Orientation: The Role of Attention 12
   1.6 Agency: The Role of Consciousness 14
   1.7 Comprehension: The Role of Language Processing 15
   1.8 Connectivity: The Role of Memory 17
   1.9 Interpretation: The Role of Inferencing and Reasoning 19
   1.10 Complexity: The Role of Individual Differences 22
   1.11 Summary: The Value of Understanding the Neurological
       Basis of Listening 24
   References 25

2 Linguistic Processing   **29**

   2.1 Introduction: Listening as Bottom-Up and Top-Down
       Processing 29
   2.2 The Interdependence of Production and Perception 30

viii   *Contents*

2.3   *Phonological Processing: Integrating the Acoustic Dimensions of Speech 31*
    2.3.1   *Phonological Processing: Psychoacoustic Effects in Perception 33*

2.4   *Morphological Processing: Recognizing Words 35*
    2.4.1   *Recognizing Allophonic Variations of Words 39*
    2.4.2   *Assimilation of Consonant Clusters 40*
    2.4.3   *Vowel Centering and Reduction 40*

2.5   *Syntactic Processing: Parsing Speech 41*
    2.5.1   *Deriving an Argument Structure 42*
    2.5.2   *Sources of Knowledge for Syntactic Parsing 44*
    2.5.3   *Creating Propositional Representations 45*

2.6   *Integrating Multimodal Cues into Linguistic Processing 46*

2.7   *Summary: Merging Bottom-Up Cues with Top-Down Knowledge 48*

References 50

3 Semantic Processing   55

3.1   *Introduction: Top-Down Processing as the Driver of Comprehension 55*

3.2   *Comprehension Building through Lexical Access 56*

3.3   *Comprehension Building through Schema Activation 59*
    3.3.1   *Comprehension Building: The Process of Schema Modification 60*
    3.3.2   *Comprehension Building: Using Heuristic Strategies 62*

3.4   *Interpreting Meaning: Inferencing 63*
    3.4.1   *Explicit vs. Implicit Inferencing 65*
    3.4.2   *Compensatory Strategies in Semantic Processing 67*

3.5   *Listening to Learn 69*

3.6   *Summary: The Role of Semantic Processing in Language Comprehension 71*

References 72

4 Pragmatic Processing   78

4.1   *Introduction: Pragmatic Processing and Pragmatic Comprehension 78*

4.2   *Discourse Framing 79*
    4.2.1   *Contextual Framing 79*
    4.2.2   *Participation Framing 81*
    4.2.3   *Power Framing 81*
    4.2.4   *Community Framing 84*
    4.2.5   *Subjective Framing 86*

Contents   ix

4.3   *Interpreting Intent 88*
    4.3.1   *Deciphering Locutionary and Illocutionary Acts 88*
    4.3.2   *Conversational Maxims 89*
    4.3.3   *Contravening Social Conventions 91*
    4.3.4   *Emotional Signaling 92*
4.4   *Response Weighting 93*
    4.4.1   *Responding 94*
    4.4.2   *Providing Additive Responses 96*
4.5   *Summary: Pragmatic Comprehension and Pragmatic Competence 98*
References 100

5 AI Processing   108

5.1   *Introduction: AI (Artificial Intelligence) and BI (Biological Intelligence) Comparisons 108*
5.2   *Neurological Processing: Neural Networks 109*
    5.2.1   *Linguistic Processing: Automatic Speech Recognition (ASR) 110*
    5.2.2   *Semantic Processing: Natural Language Understanding (NLU) 110*
    5.2.3   *Pragmatic Processing: Natural Language Generation (NLG) 111*
5.3   *Goals of AI Processing 111*
5.4   *Neurological Processing 114*
5.5   *Linguistic Processing 115*
5.6   *Semantic Processing 118*
5.7   *Pragmatic Processing 124*
5.8   *Evolution of NLP and AI 126*
5.9   *Summary: Comparisons of AI and BI Language Comprehension 128*
References 129

6 Listening in Language Acquisition   134

6.1   *Overview: Listening in Language Acquisition 135*
6.2   *Listening in L1 Acquisition: Development of Neurological Processing 135*
6.3   *Listening in L1 Acquisition: Development of Linguistic Processing 137*
    6.3.1   *Acquisition of Phonology 137*
    6.3.2   *Acquisition of Lexical Comprehension 141*
    6.3.3   *Acquisition of Syntax Comprehension 142*

x *Contents*

6.4 *Listening in L1 Acquisition: Development of Semantic Processing 144*
    6.4.1 *The Role of Interaction in Semantic Processing Development 145*
6.5 *Listening in L1 Acquisition: Development of Pragmatic Processing 147*
6.6 *Listening in L2 Acquisition: Development of Neurological Processing 149*
6.7 *Listening in L2 Acquisition: Development of Linguistic Processing 152*
    6.7.1 *Development of L2 Phonological Processing 152*
    6.7.2 *Development of L2 Syntactic Processing 153*
    6.7.3 *Linguistic Processing: Lexis 155*
6.8 *Listening in L2 Acquisition: Development of Semantic Processing 156*
6.9 *Listening in L2 Acquisition: Development of Pragmatic Processing 157*
6.10 *Summary: The Transformative Nature of L1 and L2 Acquisition of Listening 158*
References 160

SECTION II
Teaching Listening
169

7 Approaches to Teaching Listening
171

7.1 *Overview: Integrating Ideas into Teaching Methodologies 171*
7.2 *Historical Approaches to Teaching Listening 172*
7.3 *The Cognitive Revolution 173*
7.4 *Theoretical Models for Teaching Listening 176*
    7.4.1 *The Monitor Model 176*
    7.4.2 *The Interaction Hypothesis 177*
    7.4.3 *The Comprehensible Output Hypothesis 178*
    7.4.4 *Sociocultural Theory 179*
    7.4.5 *Metacognition Approaches 180*
7.5 *Profiling Approaches to Teaching Listening 182*
    7.5.1 *Neurological Processing: Focus on Engaged Listening 182*
        7.5.1.1 *Prototype Activity: Listening Circles 183*
    7.5.2 *Linguistic Processing: Focus on Attention to Bottom-Up Listening Skills 186*
        7.5.2.1 *Prototype Activity: Deliberate Practice 186*
    7.5.3 *Semantic Processing: Focus on Critical Listening 189*
        7.5.3.1 *Prototype Activity: Interactive Problem-Solving 189*

Contents xi

7.5.4   *Pragmatic Processing: Focus on Interactive Listening 193*
      7.5.4.1 *Prototype Activity: Interactive Problem-Solving 193*
7.6   *Summary: Targeted and Balanced Approaches 195*
References 196

8 Input and Interaction   204

8.1   *Overview: Highlighting the Role of Input and Interaction 204*
8.2   *Engaging with Input 205*
    8.2.1   *Interaction Points 206*
8.3   *Input Genres 207*
8.4   *Difficulty and Cognitive Load 215*
8.5   *Strategies for "Easifying" Input 218*
    8.5.1   *Input Simplification 218*
    8.5.2   *Presentation Scaffolding 219*
    8.5.3   *Technology Mediation 220*
8.6   *Summary: Maximizing the Use of Input through Interaction 223*
References 224

9 Designing Instruction   230

9.1   *Introduction: Teaching as Instructional Design 230*
9.2   *Instructional Design Stages 231*
    9.2.1   *Stage 1: Needs Analysis 231*
    9.2.2   *Stage 2: Defining Objectives 232*
    9.2.3   *Stage 3: Content Selection 234*
    9.2.4   *Stage 4: Task Sequencing 236*
    9.2.5   *Stage 5: Technology Integration 237*
    9.2.6   *Stage 6: Assessment and Feedback 238*
9.3   *Sample Instructional Designs 238*
    9.3.1   *Design 1: Linguistic Processing Development 239*
        9.3.1.1 *Linguistic Processing Activity 1: Dictation 239*
        9.3.1.2 *Linguistic Processing Activity 2: Dictogloss 241*
    9.3.2   *Design 2: Semantic Processing Development 243*
        9.3.2.1 *Semantic Processing Activity 1: Selective Listening 244*
        9.3.2.2 *Semantic Processing Activity 2: Note-Taking 244*
    9.3.3   *Design 3: Pragmatic Processing Development 249*
        9.3.3.1 *Pragmatic Processing Activity 1: Collaborative Conversation 249*
        9.3.3.2 *Pragmatic Processing Activity 2: Probing Conversation 250*
9.4   *Summary: Essentials of Instructional Design for Listening 254*
References 256

xii *Contents*

10 Listening Assessment
258

10.1 *Introduction: The Role of Assessment in Language Teaching 258*
10.2 *Identifying the Context for Assessment 259*
10.3 *The Concept of Validity in Assessment 259*
    10.3.1 Construct Validity 263
10.4 *Describing Listening Proficiency 266*
10.5 *Formulating an Assessment Model 271*
10.6 *Content Validity 273*
10.7 *Composing Test Prompts 278*
10.8 *Portfolio Assessment 281*
10.9 *Assessing Interactive Listening Proficiency 282*
10.10 *Uses of AI in Testing Listening 285*
10.11 *Summary: Integrating Assessment into Instruction 287*
References 287

SECTION III
Researching Listening
293

11 Researching Listening Processes
295

11.1 *Introduction: Why Research Listening Processes? 295*
11.2 *Identifying Listener Decisions 297*
    11.2.1 Project: Monitoring Listener Decisions in Interactive Tasks 300
    11.2.2 Research and Teaching Options 302
11.3 *Tracking Listener Judgments 302*
    11.3.1 Evaluating Speaker Impact 303
    11.3.2 Project: Evaluating Speaker Presentations 304
    11.3.3 Evaluating Speaker Comprehensibility 309
    11.3.4 Project: Using Comprehensibility Scales 310
11.4 *Interpreting Listener Filters 312*
    11.4.1 Project: Interpreting Recall Protocols 315
11.5 *Analyzing Listener Misunderstandings 317*
    11.5.1 Project: Collecting and Analyzing Common Misunderstandings, Attributed to Processing Domains 317
11.6 *Summary: The Value of Studying Listening Processes 321*
References 322

12 Researching Listening Outcomes
326

12.1 *Introduction: Posing Questions to Identify Variables 326*

Contents xiii

12.2   *Input Variables 330*
        12.2.1 Input Source Variables 331
        12.2.2 Input Genres 332
        12.2.3 Discourse Types 332
        12.2.4 Project: Making Input Choices 333
12.3   *Intervention Variables 336*
        12.3.1 Project: Comparisons of Instructional Interventions 337
12.4   *Interaction Variables 339*
        12.4.1 Project: Comparing Effects of Interaction Types 344
12.5   *Assessment Variables 345*
        12.5.1 Project: Creating a Formative Assessment for
            Listening 345
12.6   *Course Design Variables 346*
12.7   *Summary: Using Action Research to Enrich Teaching and*
      Learning 351
References 351

SECTION IV
Resources   355

Resources for Teaching Listening   357

Input Sources 357
    Children 357
        Stories 357
        Audio Books and Podcasts 358
        Language Development Activities 358
        Games and Apps 359
        Music 359
        Social Learning 360
        Field Trips 360
    Middle School/High School 360
        Stories and News 360
        Content Learning 361
    University/Adult 362
        Content-Based Listening 362
        Discussions and Debates 363
        Educational Podcasts 363
        Cultural Stories 363
        Conversation 363
        News and Current Events 364
Practice Sources 365
    VR Programs and Platforms 365

xiv *Contents*

AR Programs and Platforms 365
Language-Learning Apps 366
Chatbots for Practicing Listening 366
Practice Ideas from Polyglots 367

Resources for Researching Listening   369

Guidelines for Conducting Qualitative Research 369
Guidelines for Conducting Quantitative Research 371
   Quantitative Research Skills 371
Statistical Procedures for Conducting Research on Listening 372
Tutorials in Applied Statistics 373
Guidelines for Conducting Mixed Methods Research 374

Glossary   *376*
Index   *415*

Series Editor Preface

Applied Linguistics in Action, as its name suggests, is a series that focuses on the issues and challenges to teachers and researchers in a range of fields in Applied Linguistics and provides readers and users with the tools they need to carry out their own practice-related research.

The books in the series provide the reader with clear, up-to-date, accessible, and authoritative accounts of their chosen field within applied linguistics. Starting from a map of the landscape of the field, each book provides information on its main ideas and concepts, competing issues, and unsolved questions. From there, readers can explore a range of practical applications of research into those issues and questions and then take up the challenge of undertaking their own research, guided by the detailed and explicit research guides provided. Finally, each book has a section that provides a rich array of resources, information sources, and further reading, as well as a key to the principal concepts of the field.

Questions the books in this innovative series ask are those familiar to all teachers and researchers, whether very experienced or new to the fields of applied linguistics.

- What does research tell us, what doesn't it tell us, and what should it tell us about the field? How is the field mapped and landscaped? What is its geography?
- How has research been applied, and what interesting research possibilities does practice raise? What are the issues we need to explore and explain?
- What are the key researchable topics that practitioners can undertake? How can the research be turned into practical action?
- Where are the important resources that teachers and researchers need? Who has the information? How can it be accessed?

Each book in the series has been carefully designed to be as accessible as possible, with built-in features to enable readers to find what they want quickly and

xvi *Series Editor Preface*

to hone in on the key issues and themes that concern them. The structure is to move from practice to theory and back to practice in a cycle of development of understanding of the field in question.

Each of the authors of books in the series is an acknowledged authority, able to bring broad knowledge and experience to engage teachers and researchers in following up their own ideas, working with them to build further on *their* own experience.

The early editions of books in this series have attracted widespread praise for their authorship, their design, and their content and have been widely used to support practice and research. The success of the series, and the realization that it needs to stay relevant in a world where new research is being conducted and published at a rapid rate, have prompted the commissioning of this fourth edition of *Teaching and Researching Listening*. This new edition has been thoroughly updated, with accounts of research that have appeared since the previous edition and with the addition of other relevant material. We trust that students, teachers, and researchers will continue to discover inspiration in these pages to underpin their own investigations.

Chris Candlin
David Hall

Preface

Teaching and Researching Listening is designed to be a definitive reference source and guide for teachers and researchers who have an interest in the role of listening in language education and other areas of applied linguistics. In keeping with the intentions of the Applied Linguistics in Action series, *Teaching and Researching Listening* explores issues of ongoing relevance to teachers and researchers of both first and second languages and suggests concepts, principles, approaches, and resources for exploring these issues.

Each of the twelve chapters is designed to stand alone, offering a unique perspective on listening that can be added to the reader's current knowledge. Alternatively, the chapters can be explored sequentially to form a comprehensive course on the topic.

Readers may use the book as a selective reference, focusing on those chapters and sections that may help clarify their current teaching or research goals. Alternatively, because of the wide range of issues introduced, the book may be used as an exploratory text that may impact the teacher's or researcher's work and interests in a broader sense and provide useful points of departure for further professional exploration.

M. R.

Acknowledgments

Due to the ongoing and ever-expanding nature of this project on listening, I have had the good fortune of interacting with and reviewing the work of many researchers, language specialists, and language teachers. Through personal meetings, correspondence, reading, interviews, conferences, conversations, and video chats, I have had the privilege of interacting with many individuals who have made significant contributions to my understanding of listening, teaching, and research. Without their willingness to share their ideas, this present volume would not be possible. In particular, I wish to thank: Todd Beuckens, Graham Bodie, Mike Breen, Gillian Brown, Gary Buck, Karen Carrier, Ron Carter, Jeanette Clement, Richard Day, John Field, John Flowerdew, Irene Frankel, Lee Glickstein, Christine Goh, Jill Hadfield, Doreen Hamilton, Janice Harrington, Greg Kearsley, Ellen Kisslinger, Michal Kopec, Cynthia Lennox, Tony Lynch, Dominic Massaro, Kara McBride, Joseph McVeigh, David Mendelsohn, David Nunan, Sherry Preiss, Brett Reynolds, Mario Rinvolucri, Jill Robbins, Beth Sheppard, Martin Sproul, Leigh Stolle, Eric Tevoedjre, Scott Thornbury, Mary Underwood, and Jef Verschueren.

I would especially like to acknowledge several colleagues who have reviewed early chapter drafts of this current edition and have provided helpful commentary and feedback: Vahid Aryadoust, Collin Baker, David Beglar, Graham Bodie, Charles Browne, Anne Burns, Richard Cauldwell, Rod Ellis, Connie Habash, Yo Hamada, Marc Helgesen, Phil Hubbard, Istvan Kecskes, Curtis Kelly, Kyra Kelly, Claire Kramsch, Josh Kurzweil, John Levis, Nobuaki Minematsu, Neil Murray, Jo Mynard, Noriko Nakanishi, Jonathan Newton, Christopher Plack, Andrea Revesz, Stephen Ryan, Joseph Shaules, Joseph Siegel, Alexa Tanen, Elvis Wagner, and JJ Wilson.

I would also like to thank Scott Iblings for his technical assistance with the illustrations. And a special note of appreciation to my colleagues at Routledge for their vision, expert guidance, and masterful editorial support with this new edition, particularly: Amy Laurens, Bex Hume, Ella MacDonald, Fiona Hudson Gabuya, and Frances Tye.

> **In Memoriam**
>
> In memory of David Brazil, Steve Brown, Chris Candlin, Ron Carter, Wallace Chafe, Craig Chaudron, Anne Cutler, David Hall, Teresa Pica, Steve Ross, and Larry Vandergrift, whose friendship, collaboration, and mentorship have meant so much to me throughout my career. Though they are no longer with us, their guidance and support continues to inspire and guide this project. I am forever grateful for having known and worked with them.

Although I have tried to do justice to my colleagues' work in interpreting and synthesizing selected portions of it, I accept responsibility for any misunderstandings, oversimplifications, omissions, or errors.

I also wish to thank the many inspiring students I have been privileged to work with over the years, particularly at Temple University and University of California, Berkeley, and the many participants I have worked with at live seminars around the world and in online webinars. I've benefited greatly from the interaction, and especially from their feedback on many of the ideas in this volume.

Finally, I wish to express special gratitude to the late Christopher Candlin, series editor and personal guru, for inviting me to undertake this project, with the first edition in 2002. Chris was always extremely generous in providing me access to his broad knowledge of applied linguistic and sociolinguistic realms, and he patiently steered me through the maze of developing this work into its first three editions. Though Chris passed away before this current volume reached publication, it is important to acknowledge that he inspired me to make this volume even more penetrating than the earlier editions. I appreciate his assuring me in our final meeting that he supported continuing this volume and this series. It is a testament to Chris's undying sense of grace that he was able to guide me, through my doctoral work and through this project, to help me achieve things that once seemed so far out of reach. My sincere hope is that this sense of generosity and collaboration will affect the readers of this volume in a positive and generative way.

Copyright Acknowledgments

Figures

All figures are original artwork composed by the author, based on multiple sources. Sources are acknowledged below each figure. In some instances, we have been unable to trace the owners of copyright material, and we would appreciate any information that would enable us to do so.

Tables

All tables are original text composed by the author, with some content based on published sources. Sources that informed or inspired the table are acknowledged in the accompanying text.

In some instances we have been unable to trace the owners of copyright material, and we would appreciate any information that would enable us to do so.

Introduction

Most of us realize the importance of listening in our personal, educational, and professional lives. As someone who has centered my career around exploring the role of listening in education, I often ask other professionals how they define listening and the role listening plays in their own area of specialty. Although each person answers in a unique way, I can usually categorize their focus into one of five domains:

1. Listening is a receptive skill. It is essential to hear a speaker as accurately as possible, without overlaying your own intentions on what they are trying to say. It involves decoding, understanding the exact words and structures used, and finding cohesion.
2. Listening is a constructive ability. It is vital to interpret what the speaker means, to infer what is missing, and to learn something new. It entails reflection, reasoning, and critical thinking.
3. Listening is a collaborative competence. It is imperative to connect to the speaker and build a mutually satisfying communication experience. It includes empathizing, connecting, and supporting.
4. Listening is a transformative experience. It is crucial to feel the flow of consciousness in yourself as you are attending to a person or an event. The experience involves releasing expectations, opening up to potential meaning, and a willingness to integrate diverse stimuli.
5. Listening is an analytic capacity. It is essential to sort vast amounts of spoken data into the proper categories, properties, instances, and axioms in order to generate complete and appropriate responses. The process requires data integration, knowledge representation, and domain modeling.

Teaching and Researching Listening, now in its fourth edition, represents my own efforts to explore these various characterizations of listening, particularly in terms of how they apply to language use and language learning. Similar to numerous peers within the fields of linguistics and education, my specialization

DOI: 10.4324/9781003390794-1

2   *Introduction*

has been a gradual ascent, cultivated over time through immersive experiences in both learning and teaching, allowing my interests to naturally evolve and crystallize.

From the early days of my teaching career, fresh out of university, as a high-school English teacher with the Peace Corps in Togo, I began to sense the undeniable importance of listening. Without access to textbooks, the written language became secondary to oral language: The only written language we employed was whatever I wrote on the chalkboard, which the students dutifully copied into their notebooks. Out of necessity, the spoken language—particularly my students' desire and ability to understand me—became our primary vehicle of connection and learning.

Building on this experience, when I returned to the United States and enrolled in graduate school, I became obsessed with phonology, phonetics, and oral language processing—all of which were relatively undeveloped fields at the time. As a graduate assistant teacher in the language program, I volunteered to teach courses on pronunciation and even initiated a new course on listening, using prerecorded university lectures as course content. I found the whole process of inventing courses and seeing my students succeed very exhilarating—perhaps beginning to find my *ikigai*, that elusive feeling of fulfillment and satisfaction that you experience when you are able to align your personal passions and talents with a purpose that serves a greater good.

Fast forward a few decades, past a doctorate degree with the inspirational Christopher Candlin as my advisor: I consider myself fortunate to have experienced a satisfying career in language education, designing courses and courseware, training future teachers, traveling widely and meeting a diverse group of educators and researchers, exploring an ever-expanding menu of topics in the area of listening in language learning.

Each of the twelve chapters in this book represents an exploratory path that I have taken in my career. I have come to realize that these are paths essentially without a final destination point—contrary to my early expectations that I would somehow solve all of my questions about listening and move on to something else! Quite the opposite has occurred: I continue to find fresh questions and new insights in each of these 12 areas (as well as in related fields such as ecoacoustics, psychoacoustics, musicology, and chakra listening that did not make it into this volume).

I firmly believe that we can all deepen our practice, as teachers and researchers—or just as interested participants in the human experiment—by delving further into each of these 12 areas and discovering ways that specific topical breakthroughs apply to our lives and work.

In this spirit, readers may use the book as a selective reference, referring only to those chapters that may help expand clarify their current teaching or research goals. Alternatively, because of the wide range of issues introduced, the book may be used as an exploratory text that might impact your interests and your work as a teacher or researcher and provide you with takeoff points for further exploration.

The publisher has asked me to provide a series of presentation slides, available at www.routledge.com/9781032487908, to go along with this edition of the book. I would encourage readers to access those slides to supplement their reading, as the slides provide a more vernacular version of selected ideas in each chapter and some expanded visual metaphors. At the publisher's request, I have also supplied review questions and reflection questions (also available at www.routledge.com/9781032487908) to allow you to check your understanding of the concepts presented and to reflect on personal applications.

I do not know how many future editions there will be of *Teaching and Researching Listening*, so I have tried to incorporate some sense of its historical progression through the four editions to date, to reflect my own sense of evolution in the study of listening—an endeavor that I keep pursuing.

I have included more of my personal narrative and (sometimes idiosyncratic) insights in this edition than in previous editions. My hope is that these inclusions will bring some of the more academic points to life and shed some light on my perspective.

In the spirit of this project, I would like to thank you for embarking on this journey with me.

Michael Rost,
San Francisco, February, 2024

Section I

Defining Listening

Listening is a dynamic process involving multiple cognitive operations. This section defines listening in terms of four parallel forms of processing: neurological processing, linguistic processing, semantic processing, and pragmatic processing. A comprehensive understanding of listening needs to account for all four types of processing, indicating how these processes integrate and complement each other. Though there are significant differences between first-language (L1) and second-language (L2) processing, there are important similarities as well.

Chapter 1 describes neurological processing as the basic physical, chemical, and energetic processing underlying listening. Neurological processing involves hearing, awareness, and consciousness attention, and activating an experiential field of cognitive connections that allow the other forms of processing to operate. This initial chapter describes how neurological processing is organized and used in language understanding. The chapter also outlines the essential individual differences in neurological processing as a way of illuminating the personalized nature of the listening experience.

Chapter 2 describes linguistic processing, the aspect of listening that involves perceiving and decoding input from a linguistic source—what is considered the bottom-up aspect of listening to language. This second chapter begins with an analysis of how speech is perceived and proceeds to describe how listeners make sense of spoken language through identifying linguistic units from the smallest to the largest, using prosodic features to group units of speech, recognizing words, parsing speech into grammatical units, and formulating propositions as idea units for further semantic processing.

Chapter 3 details semantic processing, the aspect of listening that seeks both objective comprehension of the messages in the input and subjective interpretation of the significance of the ideas within the messages. Semantic processing revolves around word recognition and activation of the listener's mental lexicon, which contains networked knowledge related to the content words that are recognized in the stream of speech. Semantic processing also

DOI: 10.4324/9781003390794-2

6 Defining Listening

involves schema activation, the initiation of background knowledge links in various memory domains: episodic memory, semantic memory, and procedural memory. In this way, semantic processing integrates memory and prior experience into understanding and interpretation. This third chapter describes comprehension as constructing meaning through conventional reasoning and through inferences that are based on lexical and schema activation. Learning through listening is described as a special form of semantic processing, which includes the intensification of various listening processes.

Chapter 4 focuses on pragmatic processing, that aspect of listening that is embedded in a social and cultural context. While closely related to semantic processing in terms of schema activation and inferencing, pragmatic processing centers around the notion of relevance—the idea that listeners take an active role in identifying relevant factors in verbal and nonverbal input and inject their own agenda into the process of constructing meaning.

Chapter 5 summarizes listening processing from the perspective of artificial intelligence (AI), outlining the ways that AI-driven computing understands language using the same types of neurological, linguistic, semantic, and pragmatic processing that humans employ in biological intelligence (BI).

Chapter 6 serves as a pivotal chapter in the book, delineating the ways that these convergent listening processes are developed, in both L1 and L2 acquisition. The chapter shows how L1 processing development includes an integration of physical, cognitive, and social development, while L2 processing development involves an additive coordination of these previously developed skills.

Taken as a whole, Section I provides a primer in oral language processing that will help the reader understand the cognitive and social processes involved in listening more fully. The concepts explored in Section I will be utilized in the subsequent sections on teaching (Section II) and research (Section III).

1 Neurological Processing

1.1	Introduction: Listening as a Coordination of Networks	7
1.2	Reception: The Role of Hearing	8
1.3	Transmission: The Role of the Inner Ear	10
1.4	Coordination: The Role of the Auditory Cortex	11
1.5	Orientation: The Role of Attention	12
1.6	Agency: The Role of Consciousness	14
1.7	Comprehension: The Role of Language Processing	15
1.8	Connectivity: The Role of Memory	17
1.9	Interpretation: The Role of Inferencing and Reasoning	19
1.10	Complexity: The Role of Individual Differences	22
1.11	Summary: The Value of Understanding the Neurological Basis of Listening	24
References		25

1.1 Introduction: Listening as a Coordination of Networks

Listening is the perceptual and cognitive process of receiving, comprehending, and interpreting auditory information from the environment, including spoken language and nonspeech sounds. It involves actively attending to and processing incoming sounds in order to make sense of the signals conveyed by speakers or the environment.

Listening is supported by coordinated operations within interconnected neural networks throughout the brain. The listening process is initiated when sound waves enter the ear and are transformed into electrical signals sent through the brainstem to the auditory cortex. Language processing involves several interconnected brain circuits branching out from the auditory cortex that work together to decode the linguistic content and create meaning. This processing involves integrating incoming information with existing knowledge and weighing its social and emotional significance. Once the new information is processed, it is encoded into memory (Handel, 2006). Although all humans

DOI: 10.4324/9781003390794-3

8 Defining Listening

possess the same basic neurological structures, there are individual variances in functioning. These variances include processing speed, memory capacity, phonological awareness, and the extent and patterns of neural plasticity.

It is useful for language teachers and applied linguists to understand the nature of neurological processing in order to develop more informed instructional and research approaches. A better understanding of neurological processing allows us to identify and work with natural tendencies and to adapt to individual differences. With a thorough understanding of the neurological processes involved, we can research and implement targeted instructional practices that can enhance listening abilities in learners.

1.2 Reception: The Role of Hearing

Decoding spoken language is the foundation of listening. Even though listening often involves attending to multimodal inputs, the basis of listening is attending to sound. Therefore, a natural starting point for an exploration of listening in teaching and research is to consider the fundamental physical and neurological processes involved in listening.

We all experience hearing as if it were a distinct sense, a self-contained system that we can turn on or off at will. However, hearing is part of an interdependent brain network organization that involves multiple neurological systems, not only auditory stimulation (Gross & Poeppel, 2019; Kayser et al., 2012; Willems & Peelen, 2021). To understand the hearing process, we need to take a wider view of the structural and functional systems that support it.

Hearing, one of several sensory systems in the human brain, is governed by the vestibulocochlear nerve, which is the eighth (of twelve) cranial nerves. Hearing is the physiological channel that allows for the reception and conversion of sound waves into electrochemical signals and their interpretation by the brain.

Hearing begins with the sensation of sound waves, which are experienced through the ear as minute pressure pulses moving through the air and can be measured in **pascals (Pa)**: Force over an Area: Pa = F/A. The normal threshold for human hearing is 20 micropascals—equivalent to the sound of a mosquito flying about three meters away from the ear. Sound intensity is usually measured in decibels (dB), a logarithmic function of pascals.

Normal hearing in an adult ranges from about 0 dB (the sound of a mosquito at one meter) up to about 120 dB (the sound of a jet at takeoff at close range, the maximum sound that can be heard without trauma to the ears), though sustained exposure of several hours to sounds above 85 dB can damage the ear mechanism. (For reference, the maximum measurable sound is known to be 194 dB (as dB is a logarithmic function, this is many orders of magnitude greater than the jet-engine sound). Above this level, the sound waves become distorted, creating a vacuum between themselves, a phenomenon called cavitation.

Sound perception begins with the mechanical process of audition. Perception in any sensory modality creates an internal representation of a distal object, which is a sound source in the case of hearing. This representation occurs through detecting and differentiating properties in the energy field around the listener (Goh et al., 2023; Poeppel et al., 2012). For hearing, the energy field is the air surrounding the listener. The listener detects minuscule shifts in intensity, and small movements in the air, in the form of sound waves and converts these movements to a proximal stimulus in the auditory channel in the ear, detecting patterns through a fusion of **temporal (sequential) processing** and **spectral (holistic) processing**, involving both hemispheres of the brain (Brosch et al., 2010; Emanuel & Eldar, 2022; Mattson, 2014; Murray et al., 2022; Schreiner et al., 2011).

The anatomy of hearing is complex yet elegant in its efficiency. The human auditory system consists of the outer ear, the middle ear, the inner ear, and the auditory nerves connecting to the brain stem, completed by several mutually dependent subsystems (see Figure 1.1).

In addition to this transmission function, the middle ear has a vital protective function. The ossicles have tiny muscles that, by contracting, can reduce the

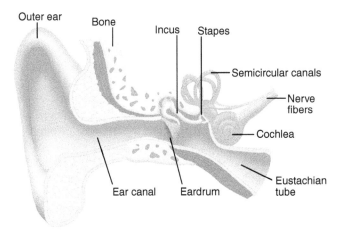

Figure 1.1 The Hearing Circuit

Hearing is a circuit involving the ear, the auditory nerve, and the auditory cortex. Sound waves travel down the ear canal and cause the eardrum to vibrate. These vibrations are passed along through the middle ear, which is a sensitive transformer consisting of three small bones (malleus, incus, and stapes) surrounding a small opening in the skull (the oval window). The major function of the middle ear is to ensure the efficient transfer of sounds, which are still in the form of air particles, to the fluids inside the cochlea (the inner ear), where they will be converted to electrical pulses and passed along the auditory nerve to the auditory cortex in the brain for further processing

10 Defining Listening

level of sound reaching the inner ear. This reflex action, the acoustic reflex or stapedius reflex, occurs when we are presented with sudden loud sounds, such as the thud of a dropped book or the wail of a police siren. It protects the delicate hearing mechanism from damage if the loudness persists.

These pressure pulses are transmitted from the outer ear through the inner ear to the brain stem and then to the auditory cortex of the brain via an electrochemical conversion in the cochlea. Auditory sensations are considered to reach perception only if they are received and processed by the auditory cortex. Although we often think of sensory perception as a passive process over which we have little control, the responses of neurons in the auditory cortex of the brain are strongly modulated by attention (Cohen, 2013; Foley & Bates, 2019; Schreiner et al., 2011).

1.3 Transmission: The Role of the Inner Ear

The cochlea is the focal structure of the inner ear; it is a small, bony structure, about the size of an adult thumbnail, narrow at one end and wide at the other. The cochlea is filled with fluid, and its operation is fundamentally a kind of fluid mechanics. The membranes in the cochlea respond, through a concentrated mass of microscopic fibers, to movements of the fluid, a process called **sinusoidal stimulation**.

The cochlea contains thousands of tiny hair cells, which are connected to the auditory nerve fibers that lead through the vestibulocochlear nerve to the auditory brainstem. These hair cells respond to the minute movements of the fluid in the membrane and **transduce** the mechanical movements of the fluid into nerve activity.

As with other neural networks in the brain, our auditory nerves have evolved to a high degree of specialization. Each auditory neuron has a different **characteristic frequency (CF)** to which it responds, ranging in humans from 20 cycles per second (or Hertz, abbreviated Hz) upward to 20,000 cycles per second. Neurons with high CFs are found in the periphery of the nerve bundle, and there is an orderly decrease in CF toward the center of the nerve bundle. This **tonotopic organization** preserves the frequency spectrum as it passes along the auditory pathway, which is necessary for the accurate processing of sound (Plack, 2018; Ruben, 2020).

The initiation of the neural activity inside the cochlea is called the excitation pattern (Schurzig et al., 2016). How an individual hearer perceives the excitation patterns will be influenced by a wide range of contextual differences, such as the number of overlapping speakers and environmental distractions, as well as by individual listener differences, including language background, familiarity with the context (topic, setting, speaker), and situational expectations. Because of this range of subjective variations, no two listeners are likely to interpret input in precisely the same way (Javel, 2019; Nechaev & Supin, 2013; Sottek & Genuit, 2005).

Neurological Processing 11

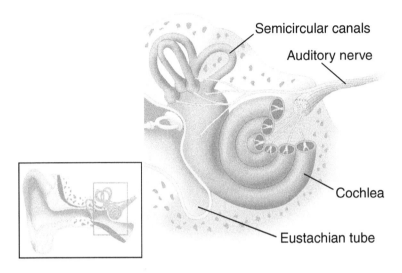

Figure 1.2 The Transmission Process

When sound waves enter the ear, they create vibrations that are transmitted to the cochlea. The cochlea is filled with fluid and has a flexible membrane called the basilar membrane that runs along its length. As the fluid inside the cochlea moves in response to the vibrations, it causes the basilar membrane to flex. This movement causes a conversion of mechanical vibrations into electrical signals. These electrical signals are representations of the specific sound frequencies and intensities that are detected. The electrical signals are then transmitted to the auditory nerve, which carries the signals as neural impulses to the brain's auditory cortex

The electrical signals generated by the hair cells are then transmitted to the auditory nerve, which carries the signals as neural impulses upward to the auditory cortex (see Figure 1.2).

1.4 Coordination: The Role of the Auditory Cortex

When the electrical signals from the auditory nerve reach the **auditory cortex**, the auditory cortex triggers a multidirectional connectivity that rapidly involves multiple areas of the brain.

The primary auditory cortex is a small area located in the temporal lobe in the left hemisphere of the brain. It lies in the back half of the superior temporal gyrus (STG) and the transverse temporal gyri (also called Heschl's gyri).

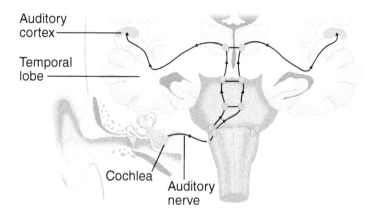

Figure 1.3 The Auditory Processing Circuit
A basic model of dual-stream auditory processing in the human brain. Neural signals from the cochlea undergo complex processing as they travel through the auditory cortex

This is the initial brain structure for processing incoming auditory information. Anatomically, the **transverse temporal gyri** are different from all other temporal lobe gyri in that they run mediolaterally (toward the center of the brain) rather than dorsoventrally (front to back).

While both the cochlea and the auditory brainstem are responsible for perception and sorting of the basic features of sound, the auditory cortex initiates the processing of complex information. The auditory cortex is organized into separate regions for managing specific aspects of acoustic information (see Figure 1.3).

Electrical impulses travel along the auditory nerve and pass through multiple information-processing centers in the auditory brainstem. Signals from the right ear travel to the auditory cortex, which is in the temporal lobe on the brain's left side. Signals from the left ear travel to the right auditory cortex.

The auditory cortices sort, process, interpret, and file information about the sound. The comparison and analysis of all the signals that reach the brain allow you to detect certain sounds and suppress other sounds as background noise.

1.5 Orientation: The Role of Attention

At a neurological level, attention is a process that activates specific brain regions and neurological processes needed for planning, organizing, initiating, and completing tasks.

Attention is essentially a self-serving activation process: when the listener perceives a stimulus that is of value (i.e., it presents a potential reward), the attention mechanism focuses on the stimulus in order to activate parts of the brain that are equipped to process it (Eldar et al., 2013). The effect of attention is to excite neurons and neural pathways (Price & Moncrieff, 2021). Because the listener has some attentional control, attention is considered to be the beginning of involvement in understanding (Taylor & Fiske, 2021). Involvement is the defining difference between simply hearing or auditing input and actively processing it.

In neurological terms, attention is seen as a timed process requiring three neurochemical reactions: arousal, orientation, and focus. Arousal begins with the activation of the **reticular activating system (RAS),** during which the RAS releases a flood of neurotransmitters to fire neurons throughout the brain (Arguinchona & Tadi, 2022). (See Figure 1.4.)

Arousal begins when the reticular formation (RF) in the brain stem becomes activated by ascending impulses through the senses (Helfrich et al., 2018). Once aroused, the RF releases a flood of neurotransmitters to fire neurons throughout the brain. **Norepinephrine** increases alertness and responsiveness to sensory stimuli. **Serotonin** regulates mood and emotions and promotes wakefulness and a positive mindset. **Dopamine** is closely associated with reward and pleasure pathways in the brain, fueling motivation to attend to the input more closely. **Acetylcholine** activates memory, learning, and cognitive functions, helping to maintain arousal and attention.

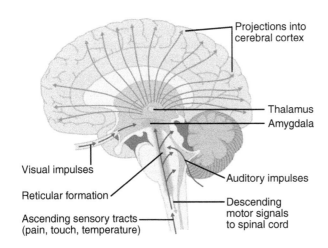

Figure 1.4 The Stages of Attention

Arousal begins when impulses from the senses enter the reticular formation, the lowest area of the brain stem. Orientation is triggered in the superior colliculus area of the midbrain; focus and distribution of attention occur in the thalamus

14 *Defining Listening*

Orientation is a neural organization process performed in the superior colliculus (SC) area of the brain. This process predicts which brain pathways are most likely to be involved in understanding and responding to the perceived object of attention. Activation is simultaneous on both sides of the brain—in the right hemisphere, which functions more as an image-oriented, holistic processor, and in the left hemisphere, which functions more as a temporally oriented, analytic processor.

Focus is achieved by the thalamus in the midbrain. The thalamus selectively activates pathways that are most likely to be involved in processing incoming stimulus, thus allowing for more efficient use of energy (Radonovic & Mansur, 2013; Wijdicks, 2019).

The notion of limited capacity is important in listening. The attentional constraints of the thalamus allow the listener to interact with only one targeted source of information at a time. Selective attention involves a decision, a commitment of our limited capacity to process one stream of information or one bundled set of features. Whenever multiple sources of information are present, selective attention is triggered, deactivating one focus and activating another focus. Selective attention allows our working memory to function efficiently without being overloaded (Gazzaley & Nobre, 2012).

Although attention can be controlled with conscious effort, shifts in attention are not always voluntary. For example, while watching television, a person's baby starts to cry, immediately capturing the attention system of the parent. Detected by the RF, and filtered through the amygdala, the crying has relevance at an emotional level, which overrides less relevant sources of input, an evolutionary phenomenon known as **attentional capture** (Fabio & Caprì, 2019).

The RF receives information from multiple sensory pathways, including visual, auditory, and touch, and can rapidly — some might say intuitively — detect and process emotional information. The RF then sends signals to other brain regions, including the prefrontal cortex and hippocampus, which are involved in regulating emotional responses (Pool et al., 2016; Yiend, 2010).

1.6 Agency: The Role of Consciousness

While attentional processes activate parts of the brain needed for comprehension, the hearer needs to exercise a degree of agency to find relevance in what is being comprehended (Wilson & Sperber, 2012). Agency is achieved when the listener *intends* to interact with the input *for some purpose* (Turner, 2022; Tuuri & Eerola, 2012). Intention is initiated through an acknowledgment of a distal source (recognition), a willingness to be influenced by this source (openness), and a desire to understand its value (discrimination) (Kriegel, 2013; Uithol et al., 2023).

This agency has been described in various ways: awareness (becoming cognizant of something new), mindfulness (being attentive to the current moment), and active listening (making a deliberate effort to understand), all of them emphasizing the act of attending to a stimulus with conscious attention and being aware that you are interacting with the input (Friston et al., 2021; Wallis, 2008).

This conscious attention, or more simply, consciousness, has been described in neurological terms as a confluence and coordination of energy sources in the brain, emerging when two fundamental cognitive processes coincide: (1) the thalamic nucleus, which integrates all sensory signals, identifies a relevant object or event; and (2) the reticular activation system in the brain stem directs the perceiver to interact with this object or event (Baars, 2021; Johnson, 2017). Consciousness is the phenomenon of experiencing this integration as a *subjective* phenomenon, an embodied experience, inclusive of—and not independent of—the object or event (Manzotti & Chella, 2014; Shulman, 2013).

For the purposes of understanding listening, the concept of consciousness is important because it helps to define the notion of context, which is needed to understand any input. The listener's cognitive model of the surrounding world guides them in understanding the nature of the current encounter, including the input (language, sounds, images, movements) associated with it (Manzotti, 2017). Context then becomes a hybrid objective and subjective construct: it is the overlap of the perceptual contact with the exterior event (external context) and the listener's personal experience (internal context) at the time of processing (Dehaene & Naccache, 2001; Lane, 2020).

Conscious awareness is also a neurophysiological motivating mechanism that allows a person to become goal-directed. The listener becomes active, scanning for links in memory that will aid in interacting with and understanding external environments (Bertolero et al., 2018; Chafe, 2000; Meuwese et al., 2013). It is important to note that consciousness emerges from the dynamic interactions among several brain regions rather than being localized in a single area. The complexity of consciousness suggests that it is not solely attributable to any one region or network but instead results from the intricate interplay of multiple neural processes (see Figure 1.5).

1.7 Comprehension: The Role of Language Processing

Once speech sounds have been recognized in the auditory cortices (typically labeled on anatomy charts as B41 and B42), these recognized sounds are relayed for further processing to the anterior superior temporal sulcus (aSTS), which plays a significant role in social cognition and communication processes (see Figure 1.4). **Bottom-up processes** involving phonological decoding and morphosyntactic categorization are performed first, and then **top-down processes** involving analysis of semantic relations (lexical access and background knowledge activation) are activated, integrating prosodic analysis from the right brain. This activation triggers working memory (the phonological loop) (BA47),

16 *Defining Listening*

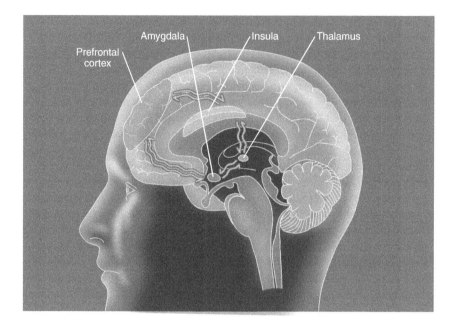

Figure 1.5 Neural Correlates of Consciousness

Consciousness cannot be readily measured, but it involves connections between four regions: the amygdala (emotional processing), the thalamus (relay locus for sensory information,) the insula (interoceptive awareness), and the prefrontal cortex (coordinates cognition and emotions). Emotion and consciousness are closely intertwined, and emotional experiences contribute to conscious feelings

and the involvement of higher-level analysis (Baddeley & Hitch, 2019). (See Figure 1.6.)

Imaging studies have shown that multiple brain areas are recruited in language comprehension through connections within this auditory processing circuit. These neurological findings are consistent with language processing research, indicating simultaneous parallel processing of auditory input in both bottom-up (perception-based) and top-down (comprehension-based) processes (Bullmore & Sporns, 2012; Friederici 2020; Hamilton et al., 2021). Studies across languages have shown that all these areas are involved in aural language comprehension in a cyclical fashion, with certain areas more active while processing particularly complex sentences or disambiguating vague references (MacGregor et al., 2020; Pregla et al., 2021; Vitello, 2014).

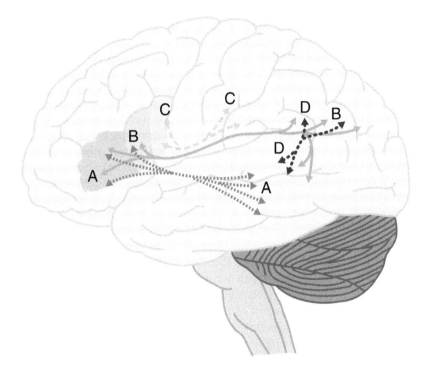

Figure 1.6 Language Comprehension Pathways

Multiple regions of the brain are activated during the listening process. There are four important pathways that are directly involved in listening comprehension. (A) Phonological word forms are detected in the auditory cortex and passed along to the frontal lobe of the brain (Broadman's Area 45) for semantic processing; (B) semantically processed forms (with recognized words and syntactic structures) are networked to the parietal lobe (aSMG, anterior supramarginal gyrus) and posterior part of the brain (pSMG, posterior supramarginal gyrus) for higher-level-comprehension processing; (C) semantic information is processed in the primary motor cortex, which is linked to phonological knowledge and speech production; (D) auditory and visual information is integrated, coordinated through the superior temporal sulcus (STS), which is located in the temporal lobe of the brain

1.8 Connectivity: The Role of Memory

Memory plays a crucial role in listening comprehension, as all incoming information is filtered through various memory networks to connect with prior knowledge and arrive at a coherent understanding (see Figure 1.6).

18 *Defining Listening*

Sensory memory is a brief storage system that holds sensory information for up to a couple of seconds. Each sensory modality has its own sensory memory system; for the auditory modality, this is called echoic memory.

Short-term memory or working memory can hold information for up to 30 seconds without rehearsal. Short-term memory is needed for ongoing listening comprehension in order to provide time to recognize words and calculate syntactic relationships. It involves primarily the prefrontal cortex and parietal lobes. The phonological loop, a component of working memory, is responsible for the temporary storage of verbal information, including speech sounds and language-related information. It consists of two subcomponents: the phonological store, which holds auditory information for a few seconds, and the articulatory rehearsal process, which allows for the subvocal repetition of information to refresh its storage in the phonological store (Baddeley & Hitch, 2019).

Long-term memory is a network of knowledge stores, including declarative memory and procedural memory. Declarative memory consists of semantic memory for general knowledge distributed across the neocortex (the outer layer of the cerebrum). Semantic memory involves storing the vast amount of information we each accumulate over a lifetime, related to general knowledge, concepts, facts, and meanings of words and symbols (Malmberg et al., 2019). It encompasses our understanding of language, objects, people, places, and events. Although triggering links are found in the neocortex, semantic memory is thought to involve a network of brain regions that collaborate in order to process and retrieve information. These regions include brain regions involved in perceptual processing, conceptual organization, and memory retrieval. Semantic memories are often triggered by particular lexical items and are activated as schemas and cognitive frames that encompass various aspects of a concept, such as attributes, roles, relationships, and other associations (Varga et al., 2022).

Episodic memory consists of encoded personal experiences involving people, places, and sequential events, as well as emotional experiences we have encoded as if part of our own lives. Retrieval of episodic memories relies on an interaction of the hippocampus and the amygdala, the emotion center of the brain. Episodic memories are often retrieved during the listening process as scripts, mental frameworks that represent the sequence of events, actions, and emotions that are associated with a particular situation or activity (Alsaeed, 2017; Bulley & Schacter, 2023).

Procedural memory is often considered to be unconscious or implicit memory. Procedural memory refers to the memory for skills, habits, and automatized behaviors that are learned through trial and error, repetition, and practice. Many language skills, including bottom-up listening skills, are considered part of procedural memory. Once procedural memories are acquired as skills or habits, they are typically difficult to articulate or describe.

Procedural memory relies on core brain structures such as the basal ganglia and the cerebellum. This reliance on lower-level brain structures reflects the efficient and automatic nature of procedural memory, which allows individuals to perform tasks and behaviors without having to consciously think about each step (Mochizuki-Kawai, 2008).

Overall, memory is intertwined with various cognitive processes involved in listening comprehension, including attention, comprehension, interpretation, and integration of information (Carter et al., 2019). Effective listening relies on the coordinated operation of working memory, long-term memory, and other memory systems to create a coherent and meaningful understanding of spoken language.

Several parts of the brain are involved in the retrieval and formation of memories during listening. The parietal lobe contributes to spatial memory but is not solely responsible for it. The caudate nucleus, part of the basal ganglia, is involved in procedural learning, habit formation, and procedural memory. The mammillary bodies are primarily associated with episodic memory and spatial memory. (Damage to these structures can lead to deficits in forming new episodic memories.) The frontal lobe is involved in various cognitive functions, including working memory, decision-making, and executive functions. It plays a critical role in working memory, but other regions, such as the prefrontal cortex, are also involved. The putamen, along with other basal ganglia structures, contributes to procedural memory, skill learning, and habit formation. The amygdala is associated with emotional memory processing, especially the formation and storage of emotionally charged memories. The temporal lobe, particularly the medial temporal lobe, is crucial for the formation of new declarative memories, which include general knowledge and facts. The hippocampus, located within the temporal lobe, also plays a central role in this process. The hippocampus is essential for converting experiences into memories, particularly episodic and spatial memories. The cerebellum is primarily known for its role in motor coordination and learning, but it also plays a role in memory for temporal event sequences (see Figure 1.7).

1.9 Interpretation: The Role of Inferencing and Reasoning

Inferencing and reasoning are cognitive processes closely related to listening comprehension. They work in conjunction with comprehension processes during the interpretation of auditory input to build a coherent, relevant interpretation of what the listener is monitoring (Mercier & Sperber, 2020).

Inferencing involves making informed guesses or drawing conclusions based on the information provided in the input. Inferencing allows listeners to fill in gaps in information, connect implicit details, and make predictions about what information is likely to follow. In language comprehension, inferencing helps to construct a coherent and complete understanding of the

20 *Defining Listening*

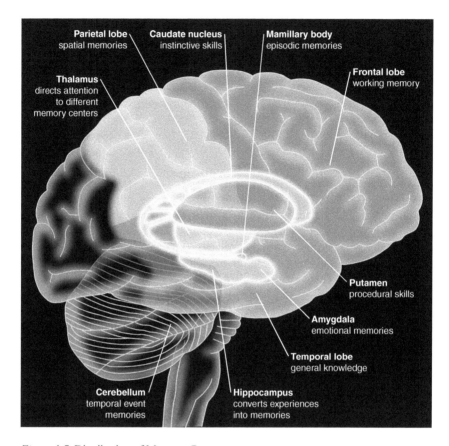

Figure 1.7 Distribution of Memory Centers

Memory connections are distributed throughout the brain and are not technically stored in any one area, though there is often one neural area that is highly activated during the encoding and recall of certain types of memories

message by going beyond the literal meaning of the input. Several types of inferencing, such as causal inferences and elaborative inferences, are used to make connections and provide coherence to the input (Holyoak, 2012; Holyoak & Stamenkovic, 2018).

Reasoning refers to using formal logic and critical thinking strategies to evaluate information, create hierarchies, draw conclusions, and make judgments. Reasoning is often an essential part of language comprehension, especially when interpreting extended discourse or complex concepts. Reasoning helps listeners weigh the information presented, consider different perspectives, and make informed interpretations (Sarafyazd & Jazayeri, 2019).

Neurological Processing 21

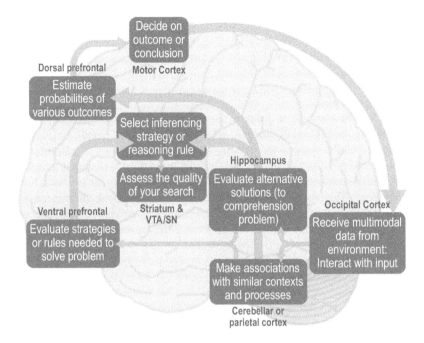

Figure 1.8 Inferencing and Reasoning Processes While Listening

Inferencing and reasoning involve deciding on an outcome or conclusion. The inferencing and reasoning processes consist of making associations with previous problems, evaluating alternative solutions, and deciding on the strategies and rules to use in order to reach conclusions

From a cognitive perspective, inferencing and reasoning are closely related, as both processes involve making sense of evidence and arriving at logical or plausible conclusions. While there are no specific brain regions dedicated solely to inferencing and reasoning, several areas of the brain are involved in these complex cognitive tasks (Goel et al., 2017). (See Figure 1.8.)

The prefrontal cortex, located in the front of the brain, is heavily involved in executive functions such as planning, decision-making, and logical reasoning. It helps us evaluate different options, anticipate outcomes, and make informed choices. Both the frontal and parietal lobes contribute to various aspects of reasoning. The frontal lobe helps control attention, working memory, and cognitive flexibility, all of which are essential for effective inferencing and reasoning.

The anterior cingulate cortex region is involved in critical thinking, for example, detecting discrepancies, fallacies, and deception in information sources. The temporal and parietal lobes are engaged in spatial reasoning, which involves mentally manipulating objects and abstract arguments and understanding their

22 *Defining Listening*

relationships. The dorsolateral prefrontal cortex, meanwhile, is implicated in logical reasoning, abstract thinking, inferencing, and planning. It helps us consider different possibilities, evaluate evidence, and make reasoned judgments (Shuren & Grafman, 2002).

1.10 Complexity: The Role of Individual Differences

Each of the component listening processes—reception, transmission, coordination, comprehension, agency, attention, connectivity, and interpretation—involves multiple areas and pathways of the brain working in harmony. While the neurological processing system has the potential for maximal information-processing efficiency, each individual uses this neurological system differently (Miller & Sherwood, 2023). Because of these individual differences in processing, characterizing the listening experience for any one individual is a complex undertaking, as each individual's processing system is replete with various strengths, weaknesses, and idiosyncrasies.

While all humans process spoken language using the same neural pathways, there are significant individual differences due to variances in age, genetics, inherent cognitive abilities, and personal and cultural experience, as well as education. Below is an outline of specific differences in each of the eight neurological processing areas discussed in this chapter:

- **Reception:** Genetic variations can influence the structure and function of the auditory system. The ability to hear high-frequency sounds tends to decline with age due to changes in the inner ear's hair cells and other components of the auditory system. Prolonged exposure to loud noises can lead to noise-induced hearing loss. Variations in the anatomy of the outer, middle, and inner ear can influence how sound waves are collected, transmitted, and processed.
- **Transmission:** Different individuals may have different sensitivities to different frequencies (pitches) of sound. Some people may have enhanced sensitivity to high frequencies, while others may have better sensitivity to low frequencies. As people age, there can be degeneration of various components of the cochlea, leading to age-related hearing loss. Certain medical conditions, such as diabetes or cardiovascular disease, can impact blood flow to the inner ear and affect hearing. For individuals with severe hearing loss or deafness, cochlear implants can provide an artificial way to stimulate the auditory nerve and restore some degree of hearing (Miyata et al., 2022).
- **Coordination:** Early auditory experiences, such as exposure to different languages and musical training, can shape the development and organization of the auditory cortex. Individuals with extensive musical training or

expertise in sound-related domains may show enhanced activation and connectivity in the auditory cortex. The ability of the brain to reorganize and adapt can lead to individual differences in how the auditory cortex responds to novel stimuli or changes in auditory input. Individual differences in brain connectivity patterns can affect how the auditory cortex communicates with other brain regions involved in language, memory, and emotion. The brain's ability to reorganize and adapt neural networks in response to new experiences, known as neuroplasticity, varies between individuals (Heffner & Myers, 2021). Some individuals exhibit greater neuroplasticity (ability to adapt neural networks in response to new experiences), allowing for faster adaptation to a new spoken language (Bates et al., 2017; Heffner & Myers, 2021). Bilinguals will coordinate their use of language processing centers differently, depending on when they acquired a second language and the degree to which they have become proficient in both languages (Kroll & Bialystok, 2013; Pliatsikas, 2020; Timmer et al., 2019).

- **Comprehension:** People vary in their ability to discriminate between different auditory stimuli, such as distinguishing similar speech sounds or intonation contours. Individual thresholds for detecting faint sounds or changes in sound intensity can differ. Differences in working memory capacity can affect an individual's ability to hold and manipulate auditory information while listening. Some individuals have faster processing abilities, allowing them to comprehend and generate speech more quickly, while others may require more time (Bates et al., 2017; Schmidt, 2012).
- **Agency:** Individuals who have a stronger sense of agency may be more actively engaged in the listening process. These individuals may feel motivated to focus their attention and make more predictive inferences as they listen. Individuals who are more conscious of their own cognitive processes, including their listening strategies and comprehension efforts, may be better equipped to monitor their understanding, identify areas of confusion, and make necessary adjustments to their listening approach.
- **Attention:** Some individuals may have a higher capacity for selective attention, allowing them to focus on relevant auditory information while ignoring distractions. Some individuals will have an attentional bias toward certain types of auditory stimuli. Individuals who are motivated to understand and learn from the listening experience are more likely to allocate their attention effectively.
- **Connectivity:** Individuals with higher working memory capacity can hold and process more information simultaneously, allowing them to better understand and remember complex spoken language. People with robust semantic memory can quickly access the meanings of words and phrases, contributing to better comprehension during listening. Individuals with strong episodic

24 *Defining Listening*

memory can activate knowledge from previous conversations or situations, enhancing understanding during new listening experiences. Individuals with strong phonological memory skills can remember and reproduce spoken language more accurately. Individuals with strong metacognitive skills are more likely to use memory strategies effectively, such as summarizing or self-monitoring during listening.

- **Interpretation:** Individuals with strong logical reasoning skills can effectively identify patterns and infer causal relationships during listening. Individuals with strong critical thinking skills and well-developed executive function can shift between various reasoning strategies and inferencing processes to solve interpretation problems.

1.11 Summary: The Value of Understanding the Neurological Basis of Listening

Spoken language processing is generally regarded as the most complex of all human behaviors (Bickerton, 2016). The neurological processes outlined in this chapter are intricately specialized, yet highly coordinated. At any moment of language processing, we may be engaged simultaneously in attending to new stimuli, auditory perception, vocabulary activation, analysis of syntax, activating multiple aspects of memory, making inferences, monitoring comprehension, combining and recombining incoming information, and storing information for later recall (Chin et al., 2023).

This chapter has surveyed the neurological processes that are involved in listening. The chapter began with an analysis of the hearing process from the outer ear to the inner ear, illustrating its anatomy and functioning. We then looked in detail at the role of the inner ear in transmitting sound to the auditory cortex. This led to an examination of the auditory cortex circuit, the essential coordination center of the listening brain.

The next area we examined was the actual language processing centers of the brain where the comprehension processes of phonological decoding, morphosyntactic categorization and parsing, and semantic activation occur. Following this, we investigated the less tangible roles of agency and attention in organizing and intensifying the listening process.

The last three areas we investigated were connectivity, the role of memory, and interpretation, the role of inferencing and reasoning. These processes occur in a sequential order from sound transmission through to interpretation, yet they are operating in a continuous cycle as we engage in listening.

The next three chapters will investigate these processes in greater detail under the headings of linguistic processing, semantic processing, and pragmatic processing.

Understanding the nature of neurological processing of oral language is useful for teachers and researchers of listening in that it helps them carry out assessment and diagnosis of listening in terms of specific abilities, devise instructional strategies that target the development of particular neurological processes, and also create tailored instruction that enhances specific processes, including by adopting and leveraging technological tools that focus on those particular listening processes.

References

Alsaeed, N. H. (2017). Wish you were here: A psychological analysis using Atkinson-Shiffrin memory mode. *Journal of Literature and Art Studies, 6*, 521–527.

Arguinchona, J. H., & Tadi, P. (2022). Neuroanatomy, reticular activating system. *StatPearls [Internet]*. StatPearls Publishing.

Baars, B. (2021). The hard problem is mainly hard work. *Cognitive Neuroscience, 12*, 63–64.

Baddeley, A. D., & Hitch, G. J. (2019). The phonological loop as a buffer store: An update. *Cortex, 112*, 91–106.

Bates, E., Dale, P., & Thal, D. (2017). Individual differences and their implications for theories of language development. In P. Fletcher & B. MacWhinney (Eds.), *The handbook of child language* (pp. 95–151). Blackwell.

Bayer, M., Ruthmann, K., & Schacht, A. (2017). The impact of personal relevance on emotion processing: Evidence from event-related potentials and pupillary responses. *Social Cognitive and Affective Neuroscience, 12*(9), 1470–1479.

Bertolero M., Yeo, B., Bassett, D., & D'Esposito, M. (2018). A mechanistic model of connector hubs, modularity and cognition. *Nature Human Behavior, 2*, 765–777.

Bickerton, D. (2016). *Language and human behavior*. University of Washington Press.

Brosch, T., Pourtois, G., & Sander, D. (2010). The perception and categorisation of emotional stimuli: A review. *Cognition & Emotion, 24*, 377–400.

Bulley, A., & Schacter, D. (2023). Episodic future thinking, memory, and decision-making: From theory to application. In R. Logie, N. Cowan, S. Gathercole, R. Engle, & Z. Wen (Eds.), *Memory in science for society: There is nothing as practical as good theory* (pp. 123–C6P231). Oxford University Press.

Bullmore, E., & Sporns, O. (2012). The economy of brain network organization. *Nature Reviews Neuroscience, 13*, 336–349.

Carter, R., Aldridge, S., Page, M. & Parker, S. (2019). *The human brain book*. Dorling Kindersley.

Chafe, W. (2000). Loci of diversity and convergence in thought and language. In M. Putz & M. Verspoor (Eds.), *Explorations in linguistic relativity* (pp. 101–123). Benjamins.

Chin, R., Chang, S. W., & Holmes, A. J. (2023). Beyond cortex: The evolution of the human brain. *Psychological Review, 130*, 285.

Cohen, R. (2013). *The neuropsychology of attention*. Springer Science & Business Media.

Dehaene, S., & Naccache, L. (2001). Towards a cognitive neuroscience of consciousness: Basic evidence and a workspace framework. *Cognition, 79*, 1a37.

Eldar, E., Cohen, J., & Niv, Y. (2013). The effects of neural gain on attention and learning. *Nature Neuroscience, 16*, 1146–1153.

Emanuel, A., & Eldar, E. (2022). Emotions as computations. *Neuroscience and Biobehavioral Reviews, 144*, 104977.

26 *Defining Listening*

Fabio, R. A., & Caprì, T. (2019). Automatic and controlled attentional capture by threatening stimuli. *Heliyon, 5*(5), e01752.

Foley, H., & Bates, M. (2019). *Sensation and perception.* Routledge.

Friederici, A. (2020). Hierarchy processing in human neurobiology: How specific is it? *Philosophical Transactions of the Royal Society B, 375*(1789), 20180391.

Friston, K., Sajid, N., Quiroga-Martinez, D., Parr, T., Price, C. J., & Holmes, E. (2021). Active listening. *Hearing Research, 399,* 107998.

Gazzaley, A., & Nobre, A. (2012). Top-down modulation: Bridging selective attention and working memory. *Trends in Cognitive Sciences, 16,* 129–135.

Goel, V., Navarrete, G., Noveck, I. A., & Prado, J. (2017). The reasoning brain: The interplay between cognitive neuroscience and theories of reasoning. *Frontiers in Human Neuroscience, 10,* 673.

Goh, R. Z., Phillips, I. B., & Firestone, C. (2023). The perception of silence. *Proceedings of the National Academy of Sciences, 120*(29), e2301463120.

Gross, J., & Poeppel, D. (2019). Neural oscillations and their role in speech and language processing. In P. Hagoort (Ed.), *Human language: From genes and brains to behavior* (pp. 393–407). MIT Press.

Hamilton, L., Oganian, Y., Hall, H., & Chang, E. (2021). Parallel and distributed encoding of speech across human auditory cortex, *Cell, 184*(18), 4626–4639.

Handel, S. (2006). *Perceptual coherence: Hearing and seeing.* Oxford: Oxford University Press.

Heffner, C. C., & Myers, E. B. (2021). Individual differences in phonetic plasticity across native and nonnative contexts. *Journal of Speech, Language, and Hearing Research, 64*(10), 3720–3733.

Helfrich, R., Fiebelkorn, I., Szczepanski, S., Lin, J., Parvizi, J., Knight, R., & Kastner, S. (2018). Neural mechanisms of sustained attention are rhythmic. *Neuron, 99,* 854–865. e5.

Holyoak, K. J. (2012). Analogy and relational reasoning. In K. J. Holyoak & R. G. Morrison (Eds.), *The Oxford handbook of thinking and reasoning* (pp. 234–259). Oxford University Press.

Holyoak, K. J., & Stankovic, D. (2018). Metaphor comprehension: A critical review of theories and evidence. *Psychological Bulletin, 144*(6), 641.

Javel, E. (2019). Cochlear excitation patterns in sensorineural hearing loss. In W. Jesteadt (Ed.), *Modeling sensorineural hearing loss* (pp. 9–34). Routledge.

Johnson, M. (2017). *Embodied mind, meaning, and reason: How our bodies give rise to understanding.* University of Chicago Press.

Kayser, C., Petkov, C., Remedios, R., & Logothetis, N. (2012). The neural bases of multisensory processes. In M. Murray & M. Wallace (Eds.), *Multisensory influences on auditory processing: Perspectives from fMRI and electrophysiology* (pp. 978–991). National Institute of Health.

Kriegel, U. (2013). The phenomenal intentionality research program. In U. Kriegle (Ed.), *Phenomenal intentionality* (pp. 1–26). Oxford University Press.

Kroll, J. F., & Bialystok, E. (2013). Understanding the consequences of bilingualism for language processing and cognition. *Journal of Cognitive Psychology, 25*(5), 497–514.

Lane, T. J. (2020). The minimal self hypothesis. *Consciousness and Cognition, 85,* 103029.

MacGregor, L. J., Rodd, J. M., Gilbert, R. A., Hauk, O., Sohoglu, E., & Davis, M. H. (2020). The neural time course of semantic ambiguity resolution in speech comprehension. *Journal of Cognitive Neuroscience, 32*(3), 403–425.

Malmberg, K. J., Raaijmakers, J. G., & Shiffrin, R. M. (2019). 50 years of research sparked by Atkinson and Shiffrin (1968). *Memory & Cognition, 47*, 561–574.

Manzotti, R., & Chella, A. (2014). Physical integration: A causal account for consciousness. *Journal of Integrative Neuroscience, 13*, 403–427.

Manzotti, R. (2017). *Consciousness and object: A mind-object identity physicalist theory* (Vol. 95). John Benjamins.

Mattson, M. (2014). Superior pattern processing is the essence of the evolved human brain. *Frontiers in Neuroscience, 6*, 1–17.

Mercier, H., & Sperber, D. (2020). Bounded reason in a social world. In R. Viale (Ed.), *Routledge handbook of bounded rationality* (pp. 257–267). Routledge.

Meuwese, J., Meuwese, R., Post, A., Scholte, S., & Lamme, V. (2013). Does perceptual learning require consciousness or attention? *Journal of Cognitive Neuroscience, 25*, 1579–1596.

Miller, E. N., & Sherwood, C. C. (2023). Brain, cognition, and behavior in humans and other primates. In C. S. Larsen (Ed.), *A companion to biological anthropology* (pp. 329–343). Wiley.

Miyata, K., Yamamoto, T., Fukunaga, M., Sugawara, S., & Sadato, N. (2022). Neural correlates with individual differences in temporal prediction during auditory-motor synchronization. *Cerebral Cortex Communications, 3*(2), tgac014.

Mochizuki-Kawai, H. (2008). Neural basis of procedural memory. *Shinkei kenkyu no shinpo [Brain and Nerve], 60*(7), 825–832.

Murray, R., Kutlikova, H. H., Brosch, T., & Sander, D. (2022). The appraising brain: Intrinsic motivation modulates amygdala response to otherwise neutral stimuli. *PsyArXiv.*

Nechaev, D. I., & Supin, A. Y. (2013). Hearing sensitivity to shifts of rippled-spectrum patterns. *The Journal of the Acoustical Society of America, 134*(4), 2913–2922.

Plack, C. (2018). *The sense of hearing* (3rd ed.). Routledge.

Pliatsikas, C. (2020). Understanding structural plasticity in the bilingual brain: The dynamic restructuring model. *Bilingualism: Language and Cognition, 23*(2), 459–471.

Poeppel, D., Emmorey, K., Hickok, G., & Pylkkanen, L. (2012). Towards a new neurobiology of language. *The Journal of Neuroscience, 32*, 14125–14131.

Pool, E., Brosch, T., Delplanque, S., & Sander, D. (2016). Attentional bias for positive emotional stimuli: A meta-analytic investigation. *Psychological Bulletin, 142*(1), 79.

Pregla, D., Lissón, P., Vasishth, S., Burchert, F., & Stadie, N. (2021). Variability in sentence comprehension in aphasia in German. *Brain and Language*, 105008.

Price, C., & Moncrieff, D. (2021). Defining the role of attention in hierarchical auditory processing. *Audiology Research, 11*(1), 112–128.

Radonovic, M., & Mansur, L. (2013). Interface between language and other cognitive functions. In M. Radonovic & L. Mansur (Eds.), *Language disturbances in adulthood: New advances from the neurolinguistics perspective* (pp. 47–58). Bentham.

Ruben, R. (2020). The developing concept of tonotopic organization of the inner ear. *Journal of the Association for Research in Otolaryngology, 21*(1), 1–20.

Sarafyazd, M., & Jazayeri, M. (2019). Hierarchical reasoning by neural circuits in the frontal cortex. *Science, 364*(6441), eaav8911.

28 Defining Listening

Schmidt, R. (2012). Attention, awareness, and individual differences in language learning. In W. M. Chan, K. N. Chin, S. K. Bhatt, & I. Walker (Eds.), *Perspectives on individual characteristics and foreign language education* (p. 27). De Gruyter.

Schreiner, C., Froemke, R., & Atencio, C. (2011). Spectral processing in the auditory cortex. In J. Winer & C. Schreiner (Eds.), *The auditory cortex* (pp. 275–308). Springer Science & Business Media.

Schurzig, D., Rau, T., Wallaschek, J., Lenarz, T., & Majdani, O. (2016). Determination of optimal excitation patterns for local mechanical inner ear stimulation using a physiologically-based model. *Biomedical Microdevices, 18*, 1–11.

Shulman, R. G. (2013). *Brain imaging: What it can (and cannot) tell us about consciousness*. Oxford University Press.

Shuren, J. E., & Grafman, J. (2002). The neurology of reasoning. *Archives of Neurology, 59*(6), 916–919.

Sottek, R., & Genuit, K. (2005). Models of signal processing in human hearing. *AEU-International Journal of Electronics and Communications, 59*(3), 157–165.

Taylor, S., & Fiske, S. (2021). *Social cognition: From brains to culture*. SAGE.

Timmer, K., Calabria, M., & Costa, A. (2019). Non-linguistic effects of language switching training. *Cognition, 182*, 14–24.

Turner, C. (2022). The extended mind argument against phenomenal intentionality. *Phenomenology and the Cognitive Sciences, 21*(4), 747–774.

Tuuri, K., & Eerola, T. (2012). Formulating a revised taxonomy for modes of listening. *Journal of new music research, 41*(2), 137–152.

Uithol, S., Görgen, K., Pischedda, D., Toni, I., & Haynes, J. (2023). The effect of context and reason on the neural correlates of intentions. *Heliyon, 9*, e17231.

Varga, N., Morton, N., & Preston, A. (2022). Schema, inference, and memory. *PsyArXiv.*

Vitello, S. (2014). *Cognitive and neural mechanisms underlying semantic ambiguity resolution.* (Doctoral thesis, University College, London.)

Wallis, C. (2008). Consciousness, context, and know-how. *Synthese, 160*, 123–153.

Wijdicks, E. F. (2019). The ascending reticular activating system. *Neurocritical Care, 31*, 419–422.

Willems, R., & Peelen, M. (2021). How context changes the neural basis of perception and language. *IScience, 24*(5), 102392.

Wilson, D., & Sperber, D. (2012). *Meaning and relevance*. Cambridge University Press.

Yiend, J. (2010). The effects of emotion on attention: A review of attentional processing of emotional information. *Cognition and Emotion, 24*(1), 347. doi: 10.1080/02699930903205698

2 Linguistic Processing

2.1	Introduction: Listening as Bottom-Up and Top-Down Processing	29
2.2	The Interdependence of Production and Perception	30
2.3	Phonological Processing: Integrating the Acoustic Dimensions of Speech	31
	2.3.1 Phonological Processing: Psychoacoustic Effects in Perception	*33*
2.4	Morphological Processing: Recognizing Words	35
	2.4.1 Recognizing Allophonic Variations of Words	*39*
	2.4.2 Assimilation of Consonant Clusters	*40*
	2.4.3 Vowel Centering and Reduction	*40*
2.5	Syntactic Processing: Parsing Speech	41
	2.5.1 Deriving an Argument Structure	*42*
	2.5.2 Sources of Knowledge for Syntactic Parsing	*44*
	2.5.3 Creating Propositional Representations	*45*
2.6	Integrating Multimodal Cues into Linguistic Processing	46
2.7	Summary: Merging Bottom-Up Cues with Top-Down Knowledge	48
References		50

2.1 Introduction: Listening as Bottom-Up and Top-Down Processing

Linguistic processing during listening involves engaging in a complex set of coordinated cognitive activities that allow us to understand and interpret spoken language. This chapter deals with the most basic levels of linguistic processing: phonological processing, morphological processing, and syntactic processing.

These three decoding processes—of sounds, words, and syntax—are often referred to collectively as bottom-up processing. Bottom-up processing refers to a type of information processing where the understanding of a whole or higher-level concept is built from the analysis of individual elements or lower-level features. Bottom-up processing is a fundamental concept in cognitive psychology and sensory perception, and it is used to describe how we process sensory information, including in the domain of listening.

Phonological processing involves decoding the sounds of speech, recognizing the sequencing of phonemes, and identifying rhythm, stress, and intonation patterns. **Morphological processing** involves identifying the smallest units of language that carry meaning, such as prefixes, suffixes, and lemmas, or root words, and identifying boundaries of words. **Syntactic processing** involves parsing the sentence structure, identifying the relationships between words, and applying the grammatical rules that govern how words are combined.

For native speakers and fluent nonnative speakers of a language, these bottom-up processes are largely automatized. They take place without our conscious awareness. Only when some kind of anomaly or ambiguity is detected do we become aware of these processes.

Proper functioning of these processes is necessary for a complete understanding of the input, although it is possible to create meaning if only parts of the incoming signal are decoded. This type of compensation is possible because of the power of semantic or top-down processing, which will be covered in the following chapter.

2.2 The Interdependence of Production and Perception

To understand the processes of speech perception, it is helpful to detail how the production and reception of speech operate in a coordinated fashion. The primary goal of speech production is to send communicative signals efficiently. To maximize communicative effectiveness, speakers structure speaking in such a way that their listeners can most readily retrieve their communicative intent (Broersma, 2012). Spoken languages have evolved congruently with this efficiency principle: both speaker and listener need to coordinate their aims for maximum effect (Brazil, 1995; Kager, 1999; Schneider et al., 2019).

Naturally occurring speech, also known as unplanned discourse, reveals several structural features that enable this coordination (Biber, 2019; Clark & Brennan, 1991; Pickering & Garrod, 2021). The most notable feature is that speakers produce speech in short bursts, not sentences (even though sentence-level grammar rules govern the overall structure) and change speeds and rhythms to create nuance, which results in frequent reductions and assimilations of sound sequences. Speakers also tend to use a lot of fillers (e.g., *um, you know, like)*, false starts, and incomplete **grammatic units** (*I was wondering if... Do you want to go together?*), along with high-frequency content words (e.g., *come along* vs. *accompany*), allowing them to plan and speak at a rapid rate. Natural speech also tends to feature more paratactic ordering (use of *and, so, but, then*), topic-comment ordering (*My friend Alia, you really ought to meet her*), and ellipsis (e.g., ~~Are you~~ *Coming* ~~to dinner~~? / ~~I'll be there~~ *In a minute*) to allow for more rapid exchange of information.

While these features of conversational grammar allow for a cohesive flow of communication, they result in a radical simplification of phonology and grammar. This simplification occasionally places an extra burden on listeners in terms of decoding, particularly if they are not familiar with the speaker and the contextual frames within which the speaker is operating (Carter & McCarthy, 2017). (See Figure 2.1.)

2.3 Phonological Processing: Integrating the Acoustic Dimensions of Speech

Linguistic processing begins as soon as sound reaches the auditory cortex. The auditory cortex uses four physical characteristics of sound during the perception process: intensity, frequency, waveform (spectral content), and duration. These characteristics of sound are converted into perceived attributes that are needed in decoding: loudness, pitch, and timbre (see Figure 2.2).

- **Intensity**, measured in decibels (dB). Whispered language at one meter is about 20 dB, while everyday speech at one meter is about 60 dB. However, there is a normal fluctuation of up to 30 dB in a single utterance of any speaker in a typical conversation. Intensity is particularly important for detecting prominences in an utterance, as speakers will intentionally increase intensity (loudness) for specific effects.
- **Frequency**, measured in hertz (Hz). Humans can hear sounds between 20 Hz and 20,000 Hz, but human languages typically draw upon sounds in the 100–3,000 Hz range. Detecting movements in sound's fundamental frequency is an important element of speech perception. Every configuration of the vocal tract produces its own set of characteristics, represented as sound pressure variations and mapped as sine waves.
- **Timbre**, which is a combination of parameters of the frequency shape of sound (its spectral envelope) and its harmonic structure (the relationship between its resonances of frequencies), is a *subjective quality* that enables the listener to distinguish the sources of sound, including specific speakers (Howard & Angus, 2017; Titze et al., 2015).
- **Duration**, measured in milliseconds (ms). Languages differ in the average length of phonemes and syllables; for instance, in American English, syllables average about 75 ms; in French, syllables average about 50 ms. The typical duration of sounds in a language can vary widely, and speakers can intentionally increase the duration for specific effects.

Once these acoustic elements in the speech signal are integrated, the input is passed along to the higher regions of the brain (the superior temporal gyrus, the STG) for further processing (Wouters et al., 2024) .

32 *Defining Listening*

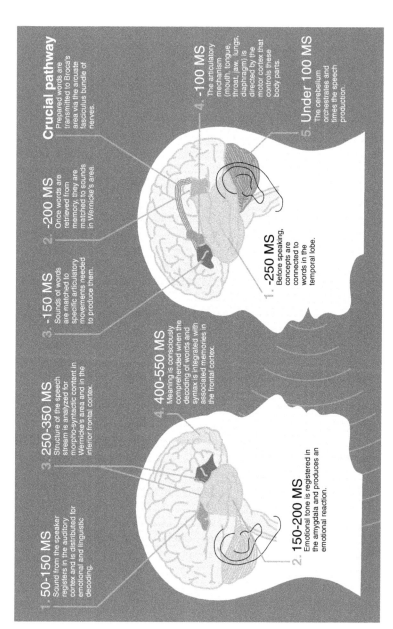

Figure 2.1 Speaker–Listener Coordination

The speaker (right side) goes through five rapid steps in producing speech. Zero is the point on the timescale when words are actually uttered. The timings, therefore, are negative values. The listener (left side) goes through four rapid steps in comprehending speech. It takes just over half a second to comprehend the meaning of spoken words. (Based on Carter, 2019; Heylen, 2009; Stephens et al., 2010)

Linguistic Processing 33

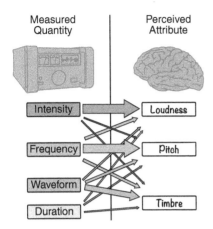

Figure 2.2 The Acoustic Dimensions of Speech

Intensity, frequency, waveform, and duration are physical signals that provide the listener with cues for decoding. In combination, these signals are perceived as loudness, pitch, and timbre. (Based on Almeida et al., 2021; Jenkins, 1961)

2.3.1 Phonological Processing: Psychoacoustic Effects in Perception

Because of the rapid speed of the phonological signal, a listener needs to use complementary sources of information in decoding speech: detection of speech signals, knowledge of articulatory causes, and prediction of speaker intentions.

The first source is made up of the psychoacoustic effects generated by the speech signal itself: intensity, frequency, waveform (spectral content), and duration. These sources combine into a multidimensional signal, which can be represented in a spectrogram (see Figure 2.3). Because there is redundancy in the signal—each of the physical sources has some influence on the perception of loudness, pitch, and timbre—the listener can readily decode the sounds of the language and its phonemes in most contexts and with most speakers. Each phoneme exhibits a distinctive combination of acoustic qualities relative to other possible sounds, and each speaker has a unique timbre relative to all other speakers. Even though phonemes are always modified by context and rarely occur in pure form, an experienced listener in a language can identify the target phonemes in a range of variations (Cutler, 2012; Cutler & Broersma, 2005; Norris & Cutler, 2021).

The second source of information used for decoding speech is the listener's subjective bodily experience of articulatory causes for the sounds that enter the auditory cortex. While auditing the sound, the listener can mirror the specific vocal configurations and vocal tract movements needed in articulation to assist

34 Defining Listening

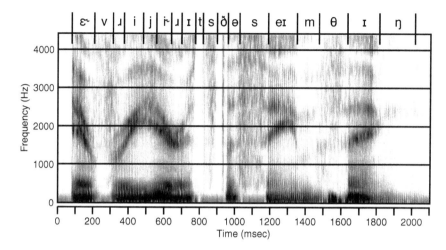

Figure 2.3 A Visual Representation of Speech Input

A spectrogram of a sentence: *Every year it's the same thing.* This is a visual representation of the spectrum of frequencies in a speech signal as it changes over time. To create a spectrogram, the speech signal is first divided into short time segments (in this example, in hundredths of a second; the total time of the input here is just over two seconds), usually using a technique called windowing. Each time segment is then transformed into a frequency domain. This generates a spectrum that represents the signal's amplitude at each frequency. The darker areas indicate higher energy or amplitude at those frequencies. (Credit: University of California, Phonetics Laboratory.)

in perception. This mirroring process occurs in the brain's motor cortex, which is also involved in speech comprehension.

For the consonants, these articulatory causes are the precise configurations and movements in the oral cavity (the lips, the teeth, the tongue, the palate, the glottis), the larynx (the hollow muscular organ forming an air passage to the lungs and holding the vocal cords, also known as the voice box), and the pharynx (the muscle-lined space that connects the nose and mouth to the larynx and esophagus).

For the vowels, the configurations of articulation are the positions of the tongue (the highest part of the tongue body) in the mouth relative to the front or back of the mouth (the horizontal dimension) and the top or bottom of the mouth (the vertical dimension) (see Figure 2.4). The listener's motor-muscle memory of making these sounds further enhances their ability to perceive these same sounds through a kind of physical mirroring process known as **proximal stimulation** (Goldstein & Fowler, 2003; Kersten, 2023).

The third source of information that assists the listener in phonemic decoding is the listener's prediction of the speaker's intentions, that is, the listener

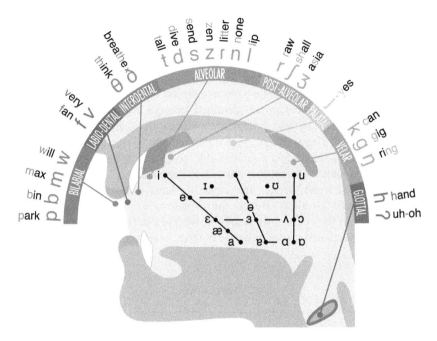

Figure 2.4 The Articulatory Causes of the Consonants and Vowels in English

This is a visual mapping of the 24 consonants and 15 vowels that are most commonly used in most varieties of English. All consonants have articulation points in the mouth: various points along the upper palate, the teeth, or the lips. All of the vowels in English have approximate tongue positions (the highest position of the tongue mass) in the mouth, varying along two dimensions: high to low (vertical axis) and front to back (horizontal axis), and to the relative openness of the mouth and jaw while voicing the vowel (close–open axis.) (Based on Ashby, 2013; Cruttenden, 2014; Shibles, 1994)

anticipating what the speaker is trying to say. If the listener is familiar with the phonotactic system of the speaker's language and dialect—its allowable phonemes, configurations, and sequences—recognition will be faster. Personal and situational knowledge also assist in prediction and perception. If the listener can easily anticipate the speaker's targets, words, and syntactic structures, decoding the input also becomes easier (Linke & Ramscar, 2020).

2.4 Morphological Processing: Recognizing Words

Morphological processing, recognizing word boundaries in the stream of speech, is the pivotal aspect of linguistic processing. Simple math reveals the range of this speed. Real-time language comprehension, which typically involves

36 *Defining Listening*

processing of 120–180 words per minute, requires rapid word recognition, often four or five words per second (Huettig et al., 2022).

Spoken word recognition is an approximating process, rather than a linear matching process; it involves a graduated mapping the incoming phonological signal to entries in the listener's mental lexicon. The listener achieves word recognition in a chunking fashion by first following the flow of the speech stream and isolating identifiable word and phrase boundaries inside each burst of speech. Word boundaries are identified through prosodic cues for onsets of words indicated by transitional probabilities between individual sounds (Aitchison, 2012; Hagiwara, 2015). Each time there is a perceptible change in pitch or loudness, the listener automatically recognizes this as a transitional cue to be used to recognize upcoming words (see Figure 2.5).

Unlike written text, spoken text does not have distinct word boundaries to confirm word identities. Hence, the listener needs to formulate multiple candidates until the context eliminates all but the correct choice. The logogen model, a connectionist theory proposed by McClelland and Elman in the 1980s

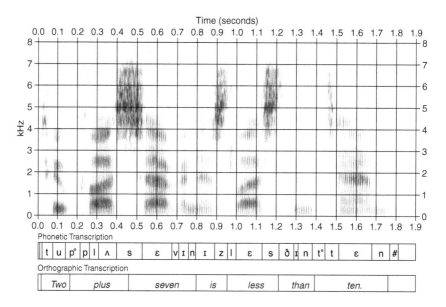

Figure 2.5 The Timing of Speech Detection

This spectrogram of a short spoken sentence—*Two plus seven is less than ten*—represents the speed at which a listener decodes speech. In less than two seconds (refer to the time axis), the speaker has uttered seven words consisting of 23 distinct phonemes. The listener uses acoustic cues—duration (shown in the *x*-axis), frequency (shown in the *y*-axis), and intensity (shown by the density of the shading)—to determine word boundaries. Shifts in pitch and intensity allow the listener to identify word boundaries. (Credit: University of California, Phonetics Laboratory)

(McClelland & Elman, 1986), suggests that the mental lexicon, a personal mental store of words and their associated information, contains units called **logogens**. According to logogen theory, each word in the mental lexicon is represented by a logogen, consisting of several informative layers. These layers include phonological information (how the word sounds), orthographic information (how the word is spelled), semantic information (the word's meaning), and contextual information (how the word is often used).

When a listener encounters a series of words, logogen theory proposes that the logogens associated with similar-sounding words are activated in parallel. As the speech input unfolds over time (i.e., a period of milliseconds), logogens compete with each other for activation, and the most highly activated logogen is eventually considered the target word (Pisoni & McLennan, 2016). An illustration of this process for identifying the word in the phrase "recognize speech" is given in Figure 2.6.

Logogen theory also emphasizes the role of context in word recognition. Contextual information, particularly the surrounding words and sentence structure, influences the activation levels of logogens. The sentence structure and the

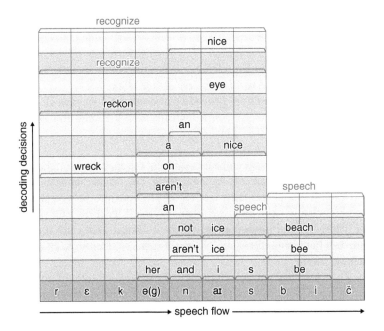

Figure 2.6 Word Recognition in Real Time

This illustration shows that for this two-word input, "recognizing speech," as many as 10 individual words (wreck, reckon, nice, ice, eye, bee, beach, aren't, not, I) may have been activated in parallel as candidates before the target words "recognize" and "speech" were identified

38   *Defining Listening*

developing meaning of the ongoing discourse help narrow down the range of possible words, aiding in selecting the correct word from similar-sounding alternatives. More recent research contends that this model of categorical perception of speech as candidates is metaphorically valid, but that the neurological processing of word candidates may not be as isolable as the model suggests (McMurray, 2022).

We do know that the listener gathers evidence of the input from two directions, from the bottom up, or from the linguistic signal as it unfolds, and from the top down, using judgments based on higher-level ideas active in the listener's mind. From a bottom-up perspective, the input consists of nine layers of identifiable components:

- **Feature:** glides, obstruents, sonorants, sibilants, continuants, aspiration, nasality
- **Segment:** (phoneme), e.g., [k], [æ], and [t] in cat
- **Mora (μ):** half-syllable or unit of syllable weight, used in some languages, such as Japanese and Hawaiian
- **Syllable (σ):** syllables themselves consist of parts: onset (optional), nucleus (required), coda (optional)
- **Foot (F):** strong–weak syllable sequences such as *ladder*, *button*, *eat some*
- **Clitic group:** a focal item plus grammaticalizing elements, e.g., *an apple*
- **Phonological word (P-word):** a word or set of words uttered and interpreted as a single item, e.g., *in the house*
- **Lexical phrase**, a formulaic element consisting of frequently used clitic groups and phonological words, e.g., *try as one might*
- **Pause Unit (PU)/Intonation Unit (IU)/phonological phrase (P-phrase):** a phonological unit consisting of a lexically stressed item plus supporting grammatical elements uttered in a single burst of speech.

Though all these components can be measured in the spoken input, they are not necessarily perceived consciously by the listener. The listener tends to give conscious attention to the longer units that are large enough to be psychologically valid. Psychologically valid units are those that the listener uses for processing meaning. These are the **phonological word** (a lexical item) and the **phonological phrase** (a meaningful group of lexical items) (Alderete & O'Séaghdha, 2022; Selkirk, 2011).

All views of word recognition emphasize the overriding roles of context: the speed and efficiency of the word recognition process depend on various context effects. A context effect occurs when the perception of a particular stimulus is influenced by the linguistic environment in which it occurs (Frost, 1998; Jusczyk & Luce, 2002; Luce & McLennan, 2005). Context effects allow the listener to be primed to quickly recognize lexical items. There are three main types of context effects. **Lexical effect**, a tendency to identify known lexical items in a stream of speech rather than a random series of sounds; **schematic effect**, a tendency to hear plausible lexical items, items that are likely to occur in a particular setting or context; and **syntactic effect**, a tendency to anticipate plausible syntactic continuations for utterances. Context effects prime the auditory cortex, spreading activation in neural networks during listening. As soon as one word is recognized, activation spreads to neighboring (i.e., closely related) lexical items or concepts in the listener's mental lexicon. This anticipation leads to a faster and more reliable recognition of upcoming words (Hendrickson et al., 2020).

2.4.1 Recognizing Allophonic Variations of Words

An essential aspect of word recognition is equating **allophonic variations**, the alternate pronunciations of a citation form of a word or phrase that occur due to context. Allophonic variations (e.g., *gonna* versus *going to*) occur in every language because of efficiency principles in production. Speakers in spontaneous discourse often use only the minimum energy, decreasing volume and articulatory precision of the phonemes they produce. As a result, nearly all phrases in any natural spoken discourse sample are less clearly articulated than pure citation forms would be (Kleinschmidt & Jaeger, 2015).

These **sandhi variations** are brought about through three related co-articulation processes within and between word boundaries: **assimilation**, **vowel reduction**, and **elision**. (Sandhi is a Sanskrit term coined by the Sanskrit grammarian Panini some 2500 years ago, as this phonological phenomenon occurs in Sanskrit as well as other Indo-Aryan and Indo-European languages, including English.)

Consonant assimilation occurs when the fully articulated sound of a consonant changes due to phonological context (sounds that occur before and after), as shown in these examples:

- /t/ changes to /p/ before /m/, /b/, or /p/ (labialization):

best man	mixed blessing
cigarette paper	mixed marriage
circuit board	pocket money

- /d/ changes to /b/ before /m/, /b/, or /p/ (labialization):

bad pain	good cook
blood bank	good morning

- /n/ changes to /m/ before /m/, /b/, or /p/ (nasalization):

Common Market	cotton belt
button pusher	

- /t/ changes to /k/ before /k/ or /g/ (velarization):

cut glass	short cut

- /d/ changes to /g/ before /k/ or /g/ (glottalization):

sad girl	hard court

40 *Defining Listening*

• /n/ changes to /ŋ/ before /k/ or /g/ (glottalization):

Golden Gate	tin can
golden goose	human capital

• /s/ changes to /ʃ/ before /ʃ/ or /j/ (palatalization):

bus shelter	nice yacht

• /z/ changes to /ʒ/ before /ʃ/ or /j/ (palatalization):

cheese shop	Where's yours?

• /θ/ changes to /s/ before /s/ (palatalization):

bath salts	earth science

2.4.2 Assimilation of Consonant Clusters

When two or more consonants, often of a similar nature (i.e., enunciated in a juxtaposed part of the vocal system), are articulated in sequence, there is a tendency in English to simplify beyond assimilation, toward elimination or elision of one of them. The longer the cluster, the greater the chance of elision.

Following are some common examples of elision:

Word/combination	Fully articulated	Elision
asked	[a:skt]	[a:st]
desktop	[dɛsk, top]	[dɛs.top]
hard disk	[ha:d'dısk]	[ha:'dısk]
kept quiet	[kɛpt'kwaɪat]	[kɛp'kwaɪat]
kept calling	[kɛpt'ko:lɪŋ]	[kɛp'ko:hŋ]
kept talking	[kɛpt'to:kɪŋ]	[kɛp'to:kɪŋ]
at least twice	[a.tlist'twaɪs]	[a.tlis'twaɪs]
straight towards	[stɹeit'tuwo:dz]	[stɹeɪ'tuwo:dz]
next to	[nɛkst.tʊ]	[nɛks.tʊ]
want to	[wont.tʊ]	[won.tʊ]
seemed not to notice	[si:md, nɒttə' nəʊtıs]	[si:md.nɒtə'nəʊtıs]
for the first time	[fəðə,f3:st'taım]	[fəðə,f3:s'taım]
it's really something	[ıtsrıli:sʊmθıŋ]	[srıli:sʊm:]

2.4.3 Vowel Centering and Reduction

As with consonant assimilation, vowel reduction tends to occur in rapidly articulated words and phrases. Vowel reduction refers to changes in the acoustic quality of vowels, that is, changes in stress, duration, and articulatory precision (Baese-Berk et al., 2019; Ernestus & Warner, 2011). Technically, the vowels are

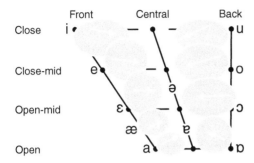

Figure 2.7 Centering of Vowels

In rapid speech, most unstressed vowels will be centered, requiring less movement of the tongue, jaw, and lips by the speaker. This leads to a perception of the vowels being reduced

centered—the tongue makes less extreme movements toward a precise enunciation target and tends to stop closer to the center of the mouth to enable faster articulation of subsequent sounds. All vowel sounds tend to be centered and reduced in unstressed syllables: deprecate, implication, explanation, allegation, demonstration, invocation, confrontation, and confirmation (see Figure 2.7).

2.5 Syntactic Processing: Parsing Speech

While linguistic processing is contingent on successful word recognition, an additional layer of processing is needed for the listener to construct meaning. This is **syntactic parsing**, in which the meaning of a word is calculated in relation to the other words with which it occurs (Oota et al., 2023). As with other aspects of linguistic processing, syntactic parsing is not localized in a specific part of the brain but is distributed across multiple locations and pathways (Wehbe et al., 2021).

Parsing consists of two interdependent passes on separately timed levels. The first pass involves the immediate time frame, about 2–3 seconds—the span of a single utterance (or single pause unit), while the second pass takes longer, about 6–8 seconds, involving multiple pause units (Schuler et al., 2010). The first pass aims to identify syntactic categories of units in the immediate pause unit, and the second pass integrates the syntax of the immediate utterance with the syntax of the larger discourse unit that is being processed (Felser, 2017).

Because of the redundancy and predictability of communication, a listener usually does not have to complete both parsing levels to build a propositional representation of what the speaker is saying. Indeed, it is rarely possible, except with extremely slow speech, for a human listener to monitor a complete word-for-word parsing of an incoming speech stream. Fluent listeners need only draw

42   *Defining Listening*

upon a reduced set of grammatical rules and predictions of likely combinations to construct workable syntactic mappings (Brothers et al., 2019).

For proficient listeners, parsing is largely automatic, below the level of conscious attention. For fluent listeners, syntactic processing is typically noticed consciously *only* when an anomaly occurs. Perception of a syntactic anomaly (e.g., when a function word or article is omitted) produces a characteristic disruption in fluent listeners. This is called the P-600 effect, in which electrical activity in the auditory cortex is disrupted about 600 ms after presenting the error. Interestingly, for most L2 listeners who have not reached an advanced listening-proficiency stage, this syntactic disruption effect typically does not occur, suggesting that syntactic processing is not entirely automatic in lower-level language learners (Friederici, 2012; Gunter & Friederici, 1999; Rayner & Clifton, 2009).

Because the two parsing passes are complementary, integrating the information seamlessly is the goal. The two syntactic integration processes for the listener are: (1) determining connections between utterances, including equivalences between text items in adjoined utterances, by calculating cohesion markers for anaphoric (previously mentioned), cataphoric (to be mentioned), and exophoric (references external to the text) references; and (2) filling in ellipses (items that are left out of the utterance because they are assumed to be known by the listener, or already given in the text). Filling in missing references allows the listener to link propositions and calculate inferences (Brennan et al., 2012; Chater & Manning, 2006).

2.5.1 *Deriving an Argument Structure*

The central goal of syntactic parsing is assigning an **argument structure** to each lexical item (whether this is a phonological word or formulaic language chunk). This structure represents how the lexical item relates to the **theme** of an utterance, which is generally a verb structure.

For example, right now, I am sitting in a coffee shop in Berkeley, and I hear a voice from a few meters behind me, saying "Could you wipe this up?" Intuitively, I hear the theme of the sentence as "wipe" and unconsciously, within the space of a couple of hundred milliseconds, assign the necessary arguments (or case roles) to understand the utterance. (Even before recognizing all of the words, I will have also registered the emotional tone of the utterance holistically, e.g., casual, urgent, angry, authoritarian, or perhaps neutral.) (Carter, 2019).

As a fluent listener in this language, I immediately know that there are three arguments or semantic roles involved here:

an agent—"you" (someone, the "you," who will do the wiping, likely an employee)
an object—"this" (some kind of liquid, possibly coffee or water)
a patient—the speaker (the person who is requesting the action and will benefit from it)

In addition, I can infer several other entities as well:

a location (a flat surface, probably a table, maybe the floor)
an instrument (what will be used to do the wiping, presumably a cloth of
some sort)
a cause (something that caused the spill)

Each argument (abbreviated **ARG**) can be assumed simply from knowledge of the theme, the verb "wipe," and whether or not the speaker articulates it. The listener activates these arguments in working memory upon recognizing the input: "Could you wipe this up?" Most themes have four or five ARGs that can immediately be inferred from lexical and real-world knowledge (Farkas & Swart, 2003; Goldberg, 2013; 2020).

In case grammar and frame semantics, the seven most frequently occurring ARGs are:

- **Agent/Experiencer**—the actor, the person or object that does an action; grammatically a noun/subject
- **Patient**—the entity (person or object) that is acted upon and receives a change as a result of the action
- **Object/Content**—the entity that is acted upon; grammatically a noun/object
- **Time**—the time of the action; grammatically an adverbial
- **Location**—the location of the action; grammatically, a prepositional phrase
- **Instrument**—the item which is used in the action; grammatically, a prepositional phrase
- **Beneficiary**—the entity or person for whom the action is performed; grammatically indirect object

Optional roles that are occasionally summoned include the following:

- **Reason**—the motivation for the action; grammatically, an adverbial expression
- **Manner**—how the action is carried out; grammatically, an adverbial expression
- **Goal**—the end point of the action; grammatically, an adverbial expression
- **Extent**—how far the action is completed; grammatically, an adverbial expression
- **Source**—the origination or starting point of the action; grammatically, an adjectival expression
- **Attribute**—a quality of another role; grammatically, an adjectival expression

When a word is recognized, a framework associated with the word is activated. The frame includes associations of semantic meaning (its frame relationships)

44 *Defining Listening*

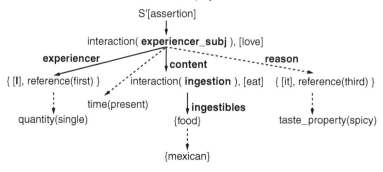

Figure 2.8 Propositional Structure
A propositional representation of a sentence: *I love to eat Mexican food, because it is spicy.* The representation depicts the theme as an interaction [love] with the experiencer [I], the content [food], and the reason [spicy] as semantic roles. (Based on Shi & Mihalcea, 2004)

and syntactic requirements for its expected usage (Baker, 2012; 2017). Figure 2.8 shows an example frame for an assertion involving an experiencer, content, and reason (Das et al., 2014).

2.5.2 Sources of Knowledge for Syntactic Parsing

Although syntactic parsing is a bottom-up or text-driven process, it can be influenced by top-down sources of knowledge:

- **Pragmatic awareness.** Familiarity with common discourse functions (e.g., apologies, invitations, complaints) and conversational genres (e.g., greeting routines, personal anecdotes, advice, and opinion sharing). A familiarity with episode boundaries, routine constraints, or other conventional cohesion devices that bind sets of utterances together will assist in discourse parsing (Czulo et al., 2020; Gernsbacher & Foertsch, 1999).
- **Extratextual integration.** Familiarity with the speaker and speaker's experiences and awareness of the speakers' background, including the types of metaphors they are apt to use and the range of cultural experiences they can draw upon, will influence the speed and efficiency of linguistic processing (Flowerdew & Miller, 2010). Similarly, the integration of **multimodal factors**, including visual and contextual cues, will influence syntactic parsing (Belcavello et al., 2020).
- **Prosodic sensitivity.** A knowledge of context-appropriate prosody, with the ability to attend to pitch levels, as episodes in discourse are often bracketed intonationally. Different pitch contours between pause units can indicate

Linguistic Processing   45

newness, separateness, connectedness, incompletion, or completion (Jun, 2014; Tran et al., 2017). Completeness and parsing of ideas are achieved through contrasting tones and timing. In English, this is done by closing the topic on a low tone, immediately followed by a new topic starting on a high tone, after a one-beat pause (Fuchs, 2014). Tuning into the pitch is a key factor in predicting upcoming content (Carbary et al., 2015).

- **Formulaic language.** Familiarity with common formulaic language structures that can be processed quickly as syntactic units or placeholders. Formulaic word strings (e.g., hit the nail on the head; sorry to keep you waiting) are stored whole in the memory and retrieved rapidly with only minimal cueing (Wray et al., 2018). Several different terms have been used to refer to formulaic language of this nature, including **amalgams** (e.g., brunch, infomercial, Bollywood); **gambits** (e.g., Sorry to keep you waiting, I don't mean to pry, but ...; **conventionalized forms** (e.g., How's it going? What do you do for a living?); **holistic patterns** (e.g., Once upon a time ... there was a ... who ...); and **high-frequency collocations** (e.g., give advice, all of a sudden).

Knowledge of these categories and of specific instances of lexical occurrences is useful in facilitating production and comprehension that allows for increased listening fluency. The use of mutually recognizable formulaic expressions also tends to increase solidarity between interlocutors as well as marking membership of a particular culture or subculture (Bell & Healey, 1992; Hinde, 2015).

2.5.3 Creating Propositional Representations

The merged goal of word recognition and syntactic parsing is the production of basic propositional representations in short-term memory that can be used for further semantic processing. Propositional representations will be neural connections that depict a structured relationship between elements derived from the input (Cummins et al., 2001). These neural connections can be visualized as tree diagrams (as in Figure 2.8) or more simply as a theme (a verb) with relationships to other elements.

For example, in the case of the coffee shop utterance, the listener's propositional representation might be:

Utterance: "Could you wipe this up?"
Wipe (this, you)

Additional elements of modality (e.g., verb tense) pragmatic information can be attached as well:

Utterance: "Could you wipe this up?"
Wipe (this, you) <request>

46 Defining Listening

Here are a few more examples of propositional representations for different utterance structures:

1. "The keys are on the counter."
   Propositional representation: on (keys, counter) <statement> <present>
2. "Sheila bought a new car."
   Propositional representation: buy (Sheila, car) <statement> <past>
3. "The children played happily in the park."
   Propositional representation: play (children, park, happily) <statement> <past>
4. "They elected her as the president."
   Propositional representation: elect (they, her, president) <statement> <past>
5. "Was that Fido who was chasing the neighbors' cat?"
   Propositional representation: chase (Fido, cat) <question> <embedding> <past> <progressive>

In each example, the propositional representation captures the main verb (predicate) and its arguments (case roles), representing the relationships between the participants and any relevant entities or properties.

While linguistic processing provides the basis for comprehension in verbal communication, other input channels are processed simultaneously to provide the listener with an integrated emotional and body-centered understanding of the external environment.

2.6 Integrating Multimodal Cues into Linguistic Processing

Most forms of listening, particularly live (face-to-face), involve multimodal processing. Multimodal processing refers to integrating and analyzing information from multiple sensory modalities, such as vision, hearing, touch, and text. It involves extracting relevant features and patterns from different modalities and combining them to form a cohesive representation.

In the case of live discourse, the visual mode includes head gestures, torso movements, hand gestures, facial expressions (mouth, eyebrows, eyelids), and gaze shifts that add richness and complexity (or sometimes ambiguity) to speaking. In effect, what we refer to as listening involves more than just hearing—it involves integrating multiplex signals from various articulators during the bottom-up phase of language processing. The term articulator traditionally denotes the vocal organs above the larynx (i.e., the tongue, lips, teeth, and hard palate), but sign languages indicate that a broader definition is needed.

Both vocal and sign languages require a multimodal perspective, thus defining the articulator as including the tongue, lips, and mouth as well as: the head; the face (including the forehead and eyebrows); the upper and lower eyelids; the muscles around the nose, cheeks, and mouth; the hands, arms, and shoulders;

the upper torso; and, in principle, the lower torso, legs, and feet. However, they tend to be less systematically used (Holler & Levinson, 2019). These extralinguistic signals modify communication to be more intense or precise.

As an utterance unfolds, listeners can access this extralinguistic information for contextually nuanced interpretations, or multimodal gestalts (Kendrick et al., 2023). Specifically, the listener will use visual information to identify references quickly and to track the speaker's perspectives and intentions. Ultimately, all available information from different informative layers of processing, including phonology and prosody, syntax, and semantics, along with these multimodal references, will be combined by listeners to constrain the set of potential interpretations (Esteve-Gibert & Guellaï, 2018).

Some of the nonverbal information available to the listener is communicated in a way that bookends the language—it arrives before or after the language is uttered and may be offered by someone else or by environmental signals. Because of the prevalence of visual information in most live discourse situations, particularly with the ubiquitous use of multimedia, it is useful to consider how it enhances linguistic input, distorts it, replaces it, and sometimes even confounds or contradicts it.

Visual signals are considered to be co-text, an integral part of the input the listener can use for interpretation. Visual signals are of two basic types: **exophoric** and **kinesic**. Exophoric signals, such as a speaker holding up a photograph or writing some words on a whiteboard, typically serve as references for the spoken text and are critical for text interpretation. Exophoric signals are particularly crucial in situations of high information flow, such as scientific documentaries and academic lectures (Fukumura et al., 2010).

Kinesic signals are the body movements the speaker makes while delivering the text, including eye and head movements. Numerous systems for describing a speaker's body movements and their role in communication have been developed, dating back to the foundational days of pragmatics (cf. Birdwhistell, 1970; Goffman, 1974). Combining these sources, kinesic signals are commonly categorized as either baton signals, directional gaze, or guide signs and are considered integral to verbal signals from the speaker (Lefter et al., 2014).

Baton signals are hand and head movements and are typically associated with emphasis and prosodic cadence. For instance, a speaker will often indicate with rhythmic, bounding motions of their hands the number of stressed syllables in a pause unit. Emphatic motions of the lips, chin, or cheeks, associated with articulation, are also baton signals.

Directional gaze is eye movement used to direct the listener to an exophoric reference or identify a particular moment in the discourse as relevant in some way to the listener. Even in lectures, when there is little or no direct verbal interaction between speaker and audience, lecturers will often make and maintain eye contact with several individuals intermittently throughout to amplify and personalize meaning. In all live discourse, the main function of eye contact is

48 *Defining Listening*

to maintain the sense of contact with the listeners and allow them to give back-channel signals to the speaker about their state of interest and understanding.

Guide signals are the systematic gestures and movements of any body part, such as extending one's arms or leaning forward. Many guide signals may be purely idiosyncratic, with no clear meaning, but most will have some clear role in a speaker's emphasis. For instance, speaking with one's arms outstretched may be a way for the speaker to attempt to persuade the listener to take a particular point seriously. Guide signals will vary from culture to culture and from speaker to speaker, and it is possible to increase comprehension by learning the guide signals of a particular speaker. However, it is difficult to formulate a systematic grammar of guide signals that consistently contribute to discourse meaning across speakers. An exception to this is lip-reading, which can be considered as interpreting guide signals (Vendrame et al., 2010).

As with paralinguistic prosodic cues, nonverbal cues are intended to confirm the speaker's linguistic meaning. However, when messages in the linguistic and paralinguistic channels are inconsistent, the listener may have reason to believe that the speaker is deceiving them and is likely to refocus on the attendant nonverbal cues (McCornack et al., 2014). Similarly, in intercultural communication, when the speaker uses a gesture or body language that may connote something to the listener in their native culture that the speaker does not intend, it will be difficult for the listener to process the verbal message separately from the nonverbal one (cf. Arasaratnam, 2013; Schuller et al., 2013).

Just as speakers use nonverbal behavior to shade their discourse, listeners also use nonverbal behavior to signal their level of understanding and acceptance of the message (Buschmeier et al., 2014). (This aspect of listener behavior will be discussed in Chapter 4.)

2.7 Summary: Merging Bottom-Up Cues with Top-Down Knowledge

This chapter has outlined the three central processes of linguistic decoding, which are collectively referred to as bottom-up processing. Listening comprehension requires both bottom-up processing, which involves decoding data directly from the speech signal, and top-down processing, which involves integrating the decoded data with prior knowledge.

The two types of processing work interactively, in an integrated fashion, and in real time as the stream of speech is occurring. The integration can be seen as starting at the bottom, or most fundamental level, with recognition of phonological features and progressively moving upward to phonological words and syntactic structures.

Top-down processing (to be discussed in Chapter 3) interacts with bottom-up processing, providing background knowledge in the form of lexical associations, various stores of memories, and abstract reasoning ability (see Figure 2.9).

Linguistic Processing 49

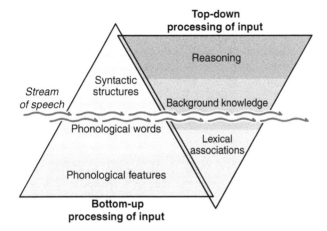

Figure 2.9 The Interaction of Bottom-Up and Top-Down Processing

Bottom-up processing provides data concerning phonology, lexis, and syntax. Top-down processing provides knowledge in the form of lexis, memories, and reasoning. Merging, these processes allow the listener to create meaning

The automatization of bottom-up processing allows fluent listeners to listen to a familiar topic at up to three or four times the normal speaking speed (120–180 wpm). Beyond this speed, comprehension breaks down because bottom-up processing can no longer function automatically. Listening at hyper speeds (over 2 x normal speed) can be successful only if we sample bits of speech and make quick inferences about word recognition and syntactic parsing. At high-speed listening, the listener must simply ignore ambiguous, inaudible, or incomprehensible (overly compressed) segments. (Of course, listening at hyper speeds is possible if we are reviewing material we have already heard; in this case, we are reminding ourselves of what we already know rather than learning new material.)

Even though linguistic processing is a bottom-up procedure, decoding data in the speech stream also depends on prediction, drawing upon our expectations based on prior experience.

Instead of monitoring the speech signal closely, we sample the stream of speech and make rapid predictions based on our samples.

While *thorough* bottom-up processing is not necessary for successful listening, *effective* bottom-up processing is necessary. Bottom-up processing is the foundation of comprehension: without inclusive processing of phonology, lexis, and syntax of an utterance or stretch of discourse, comprehension will be erratic and unstable.

50 *Defining Listening*

References

Aitchison, J. (2012). *Words in the mind: An introduction to the mental lexicon*. John Wiley & Sons.

Alderete, J., & O'Séaghdha, P. G. (2022). Language generality in phonological encoding: Moving beyond Indo-European languages. *Language and Linguistics Compass, 16*(7), e12469.

Almeida, A., Schubert, E., & Wolfe, J. (2021). Timbre vibrato perception and description. *Music Perception: An Interdisciplinary Journal, 38*(3), 282–292.

Arasaratnam, L. A. (2013). A review of articles on multiculturalism in 35 years of IJIR. *International Journal of Intercultural Relations, 37*, 676–685.

Ashby, P. (2013). *Understanding phonetics*. Routledge.

Baese-Berk, M., Dilley, L., Henry, M., Vinke, L., & Banzina, E. (2019). Not just a function of function words: Distal speech rate influences perception of prosodically weak syllables. *Attention, Perception, & Psychophysics, 81*, 571–589.

Baker, C. (2012). FrameNet, current collaborations and future goals. *Language Resource and Evaluation, 46*, 269–286.

Baker, C. F. (2017). FrameNet: Frame semantic annotation in practice. In N. Ide & J. Pustejovsky (Eds.), *Handbook of linguistic annotation*. Springer.

Belcavello, F., Viridiano, M., Diniz da Costa, A., Matos, E. E. D. S., & Torrent, T. T. (2020). Frame-based annotation of multimodal corpora: Tracking (a)synchronies in meaning construction. In T. Torrent, C. Baker, O. Czulo, K. Ohara, & M. Petruck (Eds.), *Proceedings of the International FrameNet Workshop 2020: Towards a global, multilingual FrameNet* (pp. 23–30). European Language Resources Association.

Bell, R. A., & Healey, J. G. (1992). Idiomatic communication and interpersonal solidarity in friends' relational cultures. *Human communication research, 18*(3), 307–335.

Biber, D. (2019). Corpus analysis of spoken discourse. *Pronunciation in Second Language Learning and Teaching Proceedings, 11*(1).

Birdwhistell, R. (1970). *Kinesics and context: Essays in body motion communication*. University of Pennsylvania Press.

Brazil, D. (1995). *A grammar of speech*. Oxford University Press.

Brennan, J., Nir, Y., Hasson, U., Malach, R., Heeger, D. J., & Pylkkänen, L. (2012). Syntactic structure building in the anterior temporal lobe during natural story listening. *Brain and Language, 120*(2), 163–173.

Broersma, M. (2012). Modeling phonological category learning. In A. Cohn, C. Fougeron, & M. Huffman (Eds.), *The Oxford handbook of laboratory phonology* (pp. 207–218). Oxford University Press.

Brothers, T., Dave, S., Hoversten, L. J., Traxler, M. J., & Swaab, T. Y. (2019). Flexible predictions during listening comprehension: Speaker reliability affects anticipatory processes. Neuropsychologia, 135, 107225.

Buschmeier, H., Malisz, Z., Skubisz, J., Wlodarczak, M., Wachsmuth, I., Kopp, S., & Wagner, P. (2014). In N. Calzolari, K. Choukri, T. Declerck, H. Oftsson, B. Maegaard, J. Mariani, A. Moreno, J. Odijk, & S. Piperidis (Eds.), ALICO: A multimodal corpus for the study of active listening. In Proceedings of the 9th Lang*uage Resources and Evaluation Conference* (pp. 3638–3643). Bielefeld University Press.

Carbary, K., Brown, M., Gunlogson, C., McDonough, J., Fazlipour, A., & Tanenhaus, M. (2015). Anticipatory deaccenting in language comprehension. *Language, Cognition and Neuroscience, 30*, 197–211.

Carter, R. (2019). *The brain book: An illustrated guide to its structure, functions, and disorders.* Dorling Kindersley.

Carter, R., & McCarthy, M. (2017) Spoken grammar: Where are we and where are we going? *Applied Linguistics, 38*, 1–20.

Chater, N., & Manning, C. D. (2006). Probabilistic models of language processing and acquisition. *Trends in Cognitive Sciences, 10*(7), 335–344.

Clark, H. H., & Brennan, S. (1991). Grounding in communication. In L. Resnick, J. Levine, & S. Teasley (Eds.), *Perspectives on socially shared cognition* (pp. 127–149). American Psychological Association.

Cruttenden, A. (2014). *Gimson's pronunciation of English.* Routledge.

Cummins, R., Blackmon, J., Byrd, D., Poirier, P., Roth, M., & Schwarz, G. (2001). Systematicity and the cognition of structured domains. *The Journal of Philosophy, 98*(4), 167–185.

Cutler, A. (2012). *Native listening: Language experience and the recognition of spoken words.* MIT Press.

Cutler, A., & Broersma, M. (2005). Phonetic precision in listening. In W. Hardcastle & J. Beck (Eds.), *A figure of speech: A festschrift for John Laver* (pp. 63–92). Erlbaum.

Czulo, O., Ziem, A., &Torrent, T. T. (2020). Beyond lexical semantics: Notes on pragmatic frames. In *Proceedings of the International FrameNet Workshop 2020: Towards a global, multilingual FrameNet* (pp. 1–7). European Language Resources Association.

Das, D., Chen, D., Martins, A. F., Schneider, N., & Smith, N. A. (2014). Frame-semantic parsing. *Computational Linguistics, 40*(1), 9–56.

Ernestus, M., & Warner, N. (2011). An introduction to reduced pronunciation variants. *Journal of Phonetics, 39*, 253–260.

Esteve-Gibert, N., & Guellaï, B. (2018). Prosody in the auditory and visual domains: A developmental perspective. *Frontiers in Psychology, 9*, 338.

Farkas, D. F., & Swart, H. D. (2003). *The semantics of incorporation: From argument structure to discourse transparency.* University of Chicago Press.

Felser, C. (2017). Syntactic ambiguity in real-time language processing and diachronic change. In M. Hundt, S. Mollin, & S. E. Pfenninger (Eds.), *The changing English language: Psycholinguistic perspectives* (pp. 271–291). Cambridge University Press.

Flowerdew, J., & Miller, L. (2010). Listening in a second language. In A. Wolvin (Ed.) *Listening and human communication in the 21st century* (pp. 158–178). Wiley-Blackwell.

Friederici, A. (2012) The cortical language circuit: From auditory to sentence comprehension. *Trends in Cognitive Science, 16*, 262–268.

Frost, R. (1998). Toward a strong phonological theory of visual word recognition: True issues and false trails. *Psychological Bulletin, 123*(1), 71.

Fuchs, R. (2014). You got the beat: Rhythm and timing in English. In R. Monroy-Cases & A. Guirao (Eds.), *Readings in English phonetics and phonology* (pp. 165–188). IULMA, University of Valencia.

Fukumura, K., van Gompel, R., & Pickering, M. (2010). The use of visual context during the production of referring expressions. *Quarterly Journal of Experimental Psychology, 63*, 1–16.

Gernsbacher, M., & Foertsch, J. (1999). Three models of discourse comprehension. In S. Garrod & M. Pickering (Eds.), *Language processing* (pp. 283–299). Psychology Press.

Goffman, E. (1974). *Frame analysis.* Harper & Row.

52 Defining Listening

Goldberg, A. E. (2013). The emergence of the semantics of argument structure constructions. In B. MacWhinney (Ed.), *The emergence of language* (pp. 215–230). Psychology Press.

Goldberg, A. E. (2020). Argument structure. In J. Östman & J. Verschueren (Eds.), *Handbook of pragmatics: 23rd annual installment* (pp. 59–75). John Benjamins.

Goldstein, L., & Fowler, C. A. (2003). Articulatory phonology: A phonology for public language use. In N. O. Schiller & A. S. Meyer (Eds.), *Phonetics and phonology in language comprehension and production: Differences and similarities* (pp. 159–207). De Gruyter.

Gunter, T. C., & Friederici, A. D. (1999). Concerning the automaticity of syntactic processing. *Psychophysiology, 36*(1), 126–137.

Hagiwara, R. (2015). A task dynamic approach to the coda-voicing effect on vowel duration. *The Journal of the Acoustical Society of America, 137*(4), 2269–2270.

Hendrickson, K., Spinelli, J., & Walker, E. (2020). Cognitive processes underlying spoken word recognition during soft speech. *Cognition, 198*, 104196.

Heylen, D. (2009). Understanding speaker–listener interactions. *Proceeding from Interspeech Conference (Brighton, UK)* (pp. 2151–2154). doi: 10.21437/Interspeech.2009-614.

Hinde, R. (2015). *Relationships: A dialectical perspective*. Psychology Press.

Holler, J., & Levinson, S. C. (2019). Multimodal language processing in human communication. *Trends in Cognitive Sciences, 23*(8), 639–652.

Howard, D. M., & Angus, J. (2017). *Acoustics and psychoacoustics*. Taylor & Francis.

Huettig, F., Audring, J. & Jackendoff, R. (2022). A parallel architecture perspective on pre-activation and prediction in language processing. *Cognition, 224*, 105050.

Jenkins, R. A. (1961). Perception of pitch, timbre, and loudness. *The Journal of the Acoustical Society of America, 33*(11), 1550–1557.

Jun, S. (2014). Prosodic typology: By prominence type, word prosody, and macro-rhythm. In S. Jun (Ed.), *Prosodic typology II: The phonology of intonation and phrasing* (pp. 522–539). Oxford University Press.

Jusczyk, P. W., & Luce, P. A. (2002). Speech perception and spoken word recognition: Past and present. *Ear and Hearing, 23*(1), 2–40.

Kager, R. (1999). *Optimality theory*. Cambridge University Press.

Kendrick, K. H., Holler, J., & Levinson, S. C. (2023). Turn-taking in human face-to-face interaction is multimodal: Gaze direction and manual gestures aid the coordination of turn transitions. *Philosophical Transactions of the Royal Society B, 378*(1875), 20210473.

Kersten, K. (2023). The proximity of stimulation hypothesis: Investigating the interplay of social and instructional variables with the cognitive-linguistic skills of young L2 learners. In K. Kersten & A. Winsler (Eds.), *Understanding variability in second language acquisition, bilingualism, and cognition: A multi-layered perspective* (pp. 131–159). Routledge.

Kleinschmidt, D. F., & Jaeger, T. F. (2015). Robust speech perception: Recognize the familiar, generalize to the similar, and adapt to the novel. *Psychological Review, 122*(2), 148.

Lefter, I., Burghouts, G. & Rothkrantz, L. (2014). An audio-visual dataset of human–human interactions in stressful situations. *Journal of Multimodal User Interfaces, 8*, 29–41.

Linke, M., & Ramscar, M. (2020). How the probabilistic structure of grammatical context shapes speech. *Entropy*, *22*(1), 90.

Luce, P., & McLennan, C. (2005). Spoken word recognition: The challenge of variation. In D. B. Pisoni & R. E. Remez (Eds.), *The handbook of speech perception* (pp. 590–609). Blackwell.

McClelland, J. L., & Elman, J. L. (1986). The TRACE model of speech perception. *Cognitive Psychology*, *18*(1), 1–86.

McCornack, S., Morrison, K., Paik, J., Wisner, A., & Zhu, X. (2014). A propositional theory of deceptive discourse production. *Journal of Language and Social Psychology*, *33*, 348–377.

McMurray, B. (2022). The myth of categorical perception. *The Journal of the Acoustical Society of America*, *152*(6), 3819–3842.

Norris, D., & Cutler, A. (2021). More why, less how: What we need from models of cognition. *Cognition*, *213*, 104688.

Oota, S. R., Marreddy, M., Gupta, M., & Bapi, R. (2023, July). How does the brain process syntactic structure while listening? In *Findings of the Association for Computational Linguistics: ACL 2023* (pp. 6624–6647). Toronto. https://aclanthology.org/2023.findings-acl.415.pdf

Pickering, M. J., & Garrod, S. (2021). *Understanding dialogue: Language use and social interaction.* Cambridge University Press.

Pisoni, D., & McLennan, C. (2016). Spoken word recognition: Historical roots, current theoretical issues, and some new directions. In G. Hickok & S. L. Small (Eds.), *Neurobiology of language* (pp. 239–253). Academic Press.

Rayner, K., & Clifton, C. (2009). Language processing in reading and speech perception is fast and incremental: Implications for event-related potential research. *Biological Psychology*, *8*, 4–9.

Schneider, E. N., Bernarding, C., Francis, A. L., Hornsby, B. W. Y., & Strauss, D. J. (2019). A quantitative model of listening related fatigue. In *2019 9th international IEEE/EMBS conference on neural engineering (NER)* (pp. 619–622). IEEE. doi: 10.1109/NER.2019.8717046

Schuler, W., Abdel Rahman, S., Miller, T., & Schwartz, L. (2010). Broad-coverage parsing using human-like memory constraints. *Computational Linguistics*, *36*, 1–30.

Schuller, B., Steidl, S., Batliner, A., Burkhardt, F., Devillers, L., Muller, C., & Narayanan, S. (2013). Paralinguistics in speech and language: State-of-the-art and the challenge. *Computer Speech & Language*, *27*, 4–39.

Selkirk, E. (2011). The syntax-phonology interface. In J. Goldsmith, J. Riggle, & A. C. L. Yu (Eds.), *The handbook of phonological theory* (pp. 435–484). Wiley.

Shi, L., & Mihalcea, R. (2004). Open text semantic parsing using FrameNet and WordNet. In *Demonstration Papers at HLT-NAACL 2004* (pp. 19–22). https://api.semanticscholar.org/CorpusID:1221886.

Shibles, W. A. (1994). A standard phonetic articulation diagram. *Word*, *45*(2), 177–178.

Stephens, G. J., Silbert, L. J., & Hasson, U. (2010). Speaker–listener neural coupling underlies successful communication. *Proceedings of the National Academy of Sciences*, *107*(32), 14425–14430.

Titze, I. R., Baken, R. J., Bozeman, K. W., Granqvist, S., Henrich, N., Herbst, C. T., & Wolfe, J. (2015). Toward a consensus on symbolic notation of harmonics, resonances, and formants in vocalization. *The Journal of the Acoustical Society of America, 137*(5), 3005–3007.

Tran, T., Toshniwal, S., Bansal, M., Gimpel, K., Livescu, K., & Ostendorf, M. (2017). Joint modeling of text and acoustic-prosodic cues for neural parsing. *arXiv preprint* arXiv:1704.07287.

Vendrame, M., Cutica, I., & Bucciarelli, M. (2010). "I see what you mean": Oral deaf individuals benefit from speaker's gesturing. *European Journal of Cognitive Psychology, 22*, 612–639.

Wehbe, L., Blank, I. A., Shain, C., Futrell, R., Levy, R., von der Malsburg, T., ... & Fedorenko, E. (2021). Incremental language comprehension difficulty predicts activity in the language network but not the multiple demand network. *Cerebral Cortex, 31*(9), 4006–4023.

Wouters, J., Gransier, R., & van Wieringen, A. (2024). Measures of speech perception. In J. Pardo, L. C. Nygaard, R. E. Remez, & D. Pisoni (Eds.), *The handbook of clinical linguistics* (2nd ed., pp. 539–559). Wiley.

Wray, A., Bell, H., & Jones, K. (2018). How native and non-native speakers of English interpret unfamiliar formulaic sequences. In I. MacKenzie & M. A. Kayman (Eds.), *Formulaicity and creativity in language and literature* (pp. 49–65). Routledge.

3   Semantic Processing

3.1	Introduction: Top-Down Processing as the Driver of Comprehension	55
3.2	Comprehension Building through Lexical Access	56
3.3	Comprehension Building through Schema Activation	59
	3.3.1 Comprehension Building: The Process of Schema Modification	*60*
	3.3.2 Comprehension Building: Using Heuristic Strategies	*62*
3.4	Interpreting Meaning: Inferencing	63
	3.4.1 Explicit vs. Implicit Inferencing	*65*
	3.4.2 Compensatory Strategies in Semantic Processing	*67*
3.5	Listening to Learn	69
3.6	Summary: The Role of Semantic Processing in Language Comprehension	71
References		72

3.1 Introduction: Top-Down Processing as the Driver of Comprehension

As we outlined in the previous chapter, linguistic processing enables the listener to capture the input and to represent it in short-term memory. The listener then uses this representation to construct meaning and interact with the input and the speaker. This coordination between objectively oriented and subjectively oriented processing is the essence of the experience of listening.

While linguistic processing provides the foundation of comprehension, it is semantic processing that drives the process of creating meaning. Semantic processing begins effectively once syntactic processing is complete, when there is a symbolic representation of the input in terms of semantic roles. At this point, the listener begins to integrate this linguistic representation with their own experiential knowledge—their knowledge of words, of concepts, and of related ideas and contexts—and **constructs meaning**.

DOI: 10.4324/9781003390794-5

56 *Defining Listening*

We can say that semantic processing is **a comprehension-building activity** through which the listener interprets language *subjectively* based on pre-existing knowledge and expectations. Semantic processing involves using higher-level cognitive processes, which involve the more advanced cognitive functions of abstract thinking, reasoning, contextual understanding, decision-making, and memory encoding (Toulmin, 2006).

In this chapter, we explore these higher-level processes in three domains that encompass the listener's comprehension-building ability: lexical access, schema activation, and inferencing.

3.2 Comprehension Building through Lexical Access

Semantic processing begins as soon as word recognition is achieved through linguistic processing. This initial step is called **lexical access**. Lexical access refers to retrieving relevant connections associated with recognized words. This retrieval involves activating the appropriate lexical representations stored in the memory, from the network referred to as our **mental lexicon.** Neurologically, activating a word in the mental lexicon involves the firing of specific neural circuit pathways between various brain regions where memory associations are stored.

This firing of linked neural circuits is referred to as **spreading activation**. When the neural representation of a word is activated, the network recruits semantic information from various "tagged" memory stores about the word, associated linguistic features, and concepts related to the word (Font et al., 2014). These are aspects of depth of knowledge of the recognized word—its semantic and syntactic associations. An individual can activate knowledge associated with their experience of hearing and reading the word in various contexts (Beglar & Nation, 2013; Qian & Lin, 2019; Schmitt, 2014).

This depth of knowledge is accessed along one of two dimensions: paradigmatic and syntagmatic relations (Chiu & Lu, 2015; Peters & Weller, 2008). The organization and interconnectedness of words in our mental lexicons through these three relations facilitate the retrieval of words and contribute to the richness of the listener's comprehension (Hasan & Rahman, 2020; Sims et al., 2022; Ullman, 2001; Wray, 2016). (See Table 3.1.)

Paradigmatic relations provide a network of semantic connections between words, enriching and deepening the sense of the target lexical item. Activating paradigmatic relations while listening is necessary to understand complementary or contrasting aspects of the speaker's meaning and nuance, to initiate inferencing and reasoning processes, and to predict upcoming concepts (Carston, 2021; Chiu & Lu, 2015; Green, 2008).

Syntagmatic relations provide a network of sequential connections that enable the speaker and listener to conventionalize frequent communication patterns. For the listener, activating conventional syntagmatic relations

Semantic Processing 57

Table 3.1 Paradigmatic and Syntagmatic Relations

Paradigmatic
- **Hyponymy/Hypernymy:** Hyponymy represents a hierarchical relationship between words, where one word (hyponym) is more specific and falls under the domain of another word (hypernym) that is more general. For instance, "salmon" and "goldfish" are hyponyms of the hypernym "fish," which is itself a hyponym of the word "animal."
- **Synonymy:** Synonymous words have similar meanings or can be used interchangeably in certain contexts. For example, "awful," "terrible," and "horrible" are all synonyms of "bad."
- **Antonymy:** Antonyms are words with opposite meanings. For example, "exit" which is an antonym of "entrance."
- **Meronymy/Holonymy:** Meronymy refers to the relationship between a whole and its parts. For example, "finger" is a meronym of the whole "hand." The reverse relationship is called holonymy, i.e., "hand" is a holonym of "finger."
- **Homonymy:** Homonyms are words that have the same pronunciation and spelling but differ in meaning. For instance, "bank" can refer to a financial institution or the edge of a river.
- **Homophony:** Homonyms are words with the same pronunciation but different spellings and meanings. For example, "to," "too," and "two" are all homophones.
- **Polysemy:** Polysemous words have evolved from the same origin but have multiple related meanings. For example, "run" can mean to move faster than walking (run a race), flee (run!), fill with water (run the bath), etc. (*Oxford English Dictionary* claims "run" has over 600 distinct meanings, many with particles attached, such as "run up the bill.")
- **Ambiguity:** Ambiguous words or phrases have multiple possible meanings or interpretations due to lexical, syntactic, or semantic factors. For example, "Visiting relatives can be boring" has syntactic ambiguity; "I'll meet you at the bank" has lexical ambiguity; "I saw her duck" has semantic ambiguity.

Syntagmatic
- **Collocations:** Collocations are words that frequently occur together and can be processed as chunks, such as "prices fell," "heavy rain," "break a promise."
- **Situational utterances** (also known as conventionalized expressions): Full utterances that have assumed a conventional pragmatic meaning, e.g., "How can I ever repay you?"; "Here, let me get that for you."; "You can say that again!"; "Oh, that's an interesting choice."
- **Ritualized texts:** Often used phrases, sayings, and clichés can be interpreted as a single lexical item. For example, "Houston, we have a problem," a phrase uttered by astronaut Jim Lovell during the Apollo 13, mission is used to signify a serious unexpected problem or complication in a situation and to suggest a kind of coolness under pressure.
- **Polywords:** Multiword expressions that have assumed a specific meaning, e.g., "fixed income," "work-life balance," "fish and chips."
- **Fixed phrases:** A sequence of words that are commonly used together and have a specific meaning that may not be predictable from the meanings of the individual words; e.g., "by sheer coincidence," "a golden opportunity," "the more the merrier," "barking up the wrong tree."

(Continued)

58 *Defining Listening*

Table 3.1 (Continued)

- **Meta-messages** (also known as rhetorical markers): These contain conventional signals about the intended interpretation of a message, e.g., "for that matter," "as far as I can tell," "by the way," "to be honest," "no offense," "just kidding."
- **Derivations:** Derivational relations involve forming new words through affixation or word-formation processes. For instance, happiness, happily, and happier are all derived from the root (lemma) form "happy" by adding grammaticalizing markers.
- **Lexicalized sentence frames:** Frequently used sentence frames that have a conventional meaning when slots are filled in, e.g., "I'm sorry if I …" "Do you mind if I …" "Based on (…), I would say that (…)."
- **Literary devices:** These include metaphor, hyperbole, onomatopoeia, irony, metonymy. Words and concepts can be related analogously, such as "time is money" or "love is a journey," providing a nuanced understanding of a familiar word or phrase.

is essential for automatizing word recognition. Knowledge of syntagmatic relations enables the listener to predict upcoming words and to retroactively recognize words that may have been ambiguous. Several types of syntagmatic relations are associated with depth of word knowledge.

The spreading activation in neural pathways of paradigmatic and syntagmatic relations involves both an expansion and a retraction cycle. Initially, spreading activation makes connections to the most strongly activated associations (i.e., those used most frequently or those encoded with highly charged emotional situations in the past). Activation spreads along the semantic network links, potentially including all of the paradigmatic and syntagmatic relations that the listener knows unconsciously. As new words are recognized, activation of associations with previous words retracts to allow for associations with more recently recognized ones (Collins & Loftus, 1975; Kumar, 2021; McNamara, 2005).

The strength of activation is influenced by **priming effects**: the impact of the initial activation (i.e., the prominence in the speaker's utterance), the strength of the connections between words themselves (i.e., the linguistic and cultural conventions that connect the words), and the recency and frequency of prior activations (i.e., the listener's familiar connections with similar words and concepts). Activation is also inhibited by the recognition of incoming contextual information that renders many connections irrelevant (Christensen & Kenett, 2021; Fernandino et al., 2022; Quilty-Dunn, 2021; Ritvo et al., 2019).

In recent psychological research, the term spreading activation is often used alongside terms such as semantic priming (Grimmer et al., 2022), semantic memory access (Kumar, 2021), and lexical network access (Pranoto & Afrilita, 2019). All are referring to the essential cognitive process of recruiting connections in our mental lexicon to allow us to utilize the richness of lexical knowledge as we listen.

3.3 Comprehension Building through Schema Activation

As lexical items and their semantic networks are activated, the listener begins to build semantic structures, or mental models of meaning, beyond the lexical level. Mental models, also known as **ontological models**, are cognitive representations of the world we construct based on our perceptions, experiences, and understandings. These models help us comprehend and represent the meaning and structure of new discourse as it unfolds.

The starting point for describing how these knowledge models assist in comprehension is to realize that the models are fluid rather than static. As we listen, we continuously update and revise our ontological models to accommodate new information and attain an ongoing sense of coherence (Mannaert et al., 2019; Sanders & Gernsbacher, 2004).

The term schema was introduced by psychologist Frederic Bartlett in the early 20th century as part of his work on memory and cognition. Bartlett's research focused on how people remember and understand stories and narratives. He proposed that individuals use mental frameworks or schemas to organize and make sense of new information based on their existing knowledge and experiences.

During the process of listening, we build a comprehension framework, a semantic structure, by activating an appropriate cognitive model into which the individual concepts will somehow fit (Emmott & Alexander, 2014). For example, if we are listening to someone describe "something beautiful," we will activate a mental model of *beauty*, which may consist of several individual schemas (or schemata) that represent different perspectives or dimensions through which we understand and perceive the concept of *beauty*. These schemas are not physical neurological structures in the brain but rather cognitive constructs that help us organize and interpret information (Mandler, 2014; Tuan & Loan, 2010).

Schematic components and networks have been defined in various ways, including descriptions of schemas as types: object, concept, social, script, or event (Ghosh & Gilboa, 2014; Wagoner, 2013). Some descriptions posit levels of schemas consisting of main types (object, event, etc.) and constituents (definitions, characteristics, qualities, attributes, types, variations, emotional aspects, and social aspects; Giuliano et al., 2021).

Because language understanding involves an interaction of decoding external input and activating internal memory networks, the paradox of comprehension is that adequate understanding can take place only if the listener *already* has a coherent cognitive framework in which to place the incoming information (Braasch & Kessler, 2021; Gallese & Lakoff, 2005). Without a coherent framework of schemata, the listener will have limited contextual understanding, difficulty making inferences, and reduced recall and retention (Nguyen & Newton, 2018; Rost, 1994).

60 *Defining Listening*

Once a cognitive map with relevant schemata is activated in the short-term memory, the listener begins to weigh the relevance of incoming information (Nguyen & Newton, 2018). When the incoming information is irrelevant or unrelated to a currently active concept, the listener experiences a comprehension gap and needs to abandon the activated map and activate a new one (Bohn-Gellter & Kendeou, 2014).

Because comprehension is the *internal experience* of activating and updating concepts, the nature of semantic processing is the *embodied sense* of updating one's current mental maps or mindset. Comprehension involves mapping incoming propositions that the speaker generates, so a necessary reference point for comprehensibility is the contrast between given information and new information (Clark, 2014).

These terms require some clarification in the context of semantic processing. Each speaker's utterance includes both new (or focal) information and given (or background) information. New refers to the assumed status, in the speaker's mind, that the information is either unknown or not currently active in the listener's mind. New information does not necessarily refer to information that the speaker believes is novel or unknown to the listener. Similarly, given information does not refer to information that has been previously supplied to the speaker but to information that the speaker assumes is known by the listener. Specifically, given or new refers to the assumption that the information presented is already active or inactive in the listener's mental model (Kintsch, 1998; Zuczkowski et al., 2021).

The interplay of given and new information in spoken discourse is reflected in the prosody of speech. To recap the **prosodic elements** in spoken language (outlined in Chapter 2), the speaker has access to various vocal modulations to signal given or new information, notably stress and emphasis, pitch and intonation, pausing and phrasing rate of speech, and intensity. Variations in any of these dimensions will influence the listener's perception of information status (new vs. given), special emphasis for particular words, and emotional shading.

3.3.1 Comprehension Building: The Process of Schema Modification

The schematic organization that the listener brings to the text needs to allow them to access their background knowledge as they listen (Gilboa & Marlatte, 2017; Thorndyke & Yekovich, 1980). This access is a dynamic process: as soon as a schema is activated, it starts to undergo modification by the new information being encountered.

The process of schema modification consists of four interrelated steps that take place during discourse processing: **concept abstraction,** extracting the core features of the schema; **instantiation,** applying the schema to the new information in the input to the activated schema; **prediction,** using the active schema to predict what parts of the input fit into the missing slots; and most crucially for comprehension purposes, **induction,** drawing conclusions based on the relative fit of the active schema with the incoming information.

To flesh out an example, if a person is attending an art lecture on impressionism, they will need to utilize concept abstraction, instantiation, prediction, and induction continuously to make sense of the presentation and to encode a representation of the lecture that they can remember.

Here is an extract from a lecture I have used in my experimental research on comprehension and recall:

> *Today, we're going to explore the fascinating world of impressionism in art. Let's jump right in with a bit of background.*
>
> *Impressionism emerged in the late 19th century, as early as the 1860s, primarily in France, and marked a significant departure from traditional artistic conventions, that is, what was traditional at the time. It broke away from the tradition of using historical, mythical, or religious subjects and highly planned scenes.*
>
> *Instead, it sought to appeal to our emotions and our sense of evanescence, capturing fleeting moments of light, color, and atmosphere in a fresh and, spontaneous, and innovative way.*
>
> *Impressionist artists like Claude Monet, Pierre-Auguste Renoir, and Edgar Degas were seeking to convey the immediate and transient effects of natural scenes and everyday life.*
>
> *And technique-wise, there was also a major departure from the norm. Instead of meticulously detailed brushwork, these new artists used bold, quick, and visible brushstrokes, giving their paintings a sense of spontaneity and vibrancy...*

As the lecturer is speaking, we can consider how the listener uses schema modification while listening.

The first step in encountering a new idea is concept abstraction. As the lecturer introduces impressionism, the listener starts abstracting the core features of the concept based on their prior experience with it. They may identify features such as its being *an art movement that captures the transient impressions of light, color, and atmosphere in a spontaneous style.* They may also recognize that it *often focuses on outdoor scenes, everyday subjects, and the use of visible brushstrokes.* By focusing on these defining characteristics, the listener activates a mental schema of impressionism.

The next step in the comprehension-building process is instantiation. The listener encounters specific new examples of impressionist artworks during the lecture. (The new examples may not be entirely novel to the listener, but "new" here refers to the discourse analysis concept of newly introduced.) These references instantiate the listener's existing schema by matching the features presented in the lecture with a mental representation of impressionism. In this

62   Defining Listening

instance, the examples of *capturing natural light* and the *visible brushwork* instantiate the concept of impressionism.

The third step is prediction. Using their existing schema and the information provided in the lecture, the listener engages in the prediction of concepts in the upcoming episodes of the lecture. They use their impressionist knowledge to anticipate and predict what other aspects or techniques will be discussed. For example, they might predict that the lecturer will delve into topics like *naturalistic painting techniques* or the *key figures of the impressionist movement*.

The final step is induction. As the lecture progresses, the listener observes specific instances and examples of impressionist artworks. The listener draws general conclusions and forms a renewed understanding of impressionism. In this way, the listener's schema is modified. By taking in the patterns and examples the lecturer provides, the listener may induce that impressionist paintings often feature *vibrant color palettes*, *capture atmospheric effects*, and *prioritize subjective interpretations of reality*.

At the end of each topical episode in the lecture, the listener will have completed several cycles of this activation sequence in order to maintain a coherent understanding of the lecture. It is important to note that these modifications to the listener's schemata are conceptual. Depth of comprehension also depends on the depth of the listener's lexical knowledge of key terms: *natural light*, *fleeting moments*, *everyday life*, etc.

3.3.2 Comprehension Building: Using Heuristic Strategies

Because schematic knowledge must be accessed quickly and continuously, the listener needs to utilize **heuristic strategies** to solve comprehension problems efficiently (Anderson, 2018; Mandler, 2014; Rumelhart, 2017). A **heuristic** refers to a cognitive strategy that our brain uses unconsciously to process information more efficiently by using a kind of shorthand code to represent our cumulative experience. Heuristics ensure that the listener arrives at plausible interpretations without using an exhaustive step-by-step analysis of the input. (The teaching of heuristic strategies for enhancing comprehension will be treated in Chapters 7–9.)

Though mental shortcuts allow listeners to arrive at quick comprehension solutions, the use of heuristics involves a speed–accuracy tradeoff. The use of shortcuts sometimes leads to cognitive biases, such as confirmation bias (the tendency to seek out information that confirms an existing belief), availability bias (the tendency to rely on readily available examples), and recency bias (the tendency to give greater weight to the most recent experience) (Dahm et al., 2022; Ratcliff et al., 2016).

The speaker and the listener do not need identical schemas relating to the expressed topics for adequate understanding to occur, although some kind of coordination is necessary. Speakers and listeners from different cultural

Semantic Processing 63

backgrounds or social-generational backgrounds may not have identical or similar schemata due to their unique background experiences and cultural influences. However, effective communication between individuals with diverse schemas is possible through various strategies and mechanisms that facilitate understanding and bridge the gap between their cognitive frameworks. One concept that helps explain this process is the idea of a shared activation space, not a literal space but rather a metaphorical concept (Churchland, 2012).

A shared activation space can be achieved through mutual accommodation, which entails **metacommunication** by both speaker and listener. Both speaker and listener must be aware of potential schema mismatches and can engage in metacommunication by explicitly asking for clarification, expressing their degree of understanding, and checking whether their interpretation matches the speaker's intention. In using this kind of **schematic negotiation**, the speaker and listener are searching for shared common ground, such as universal human experiences or shared beliefs (Alikhani & Stone, 2020; Geurts, 2019; Kecskes & Zhang, 2009).

Focusing on these common elements can help build a foundation for understanding. Additionally, the dominant speaker in an interaction must often adapt and simplify content and cultural references that trigger schematic activation and provide additional context in order to foster mutual communication. Finally, agreement on goal-setting for a particular discourse provides grounding for mutual schema activation: when both parties have shared goals for the conversation, they are more likely to work together to ensure understanding, even if their initial schemas differ. If these strategies are used, the speaker and listener can activate *appropriately related schemas* that allow them to create mutual understanding (Gilboa & Marlatte, 2017; Loaiza & Camos, 2018; Rost, 2020).

3.4 Interpreting Meaning: Inferencing

Inferencing is the third level of semantic processing that listeners use to arrive at a personal interpretation of the meaning of the input. They draw logical conclusions, make educated guesses, and fill in gaps in understanding by using available clues and context framing; they connect disparate ideas, and inject their own prior knowledge and beliefs. Inferencing involves going beyond the explicit information provided by the speaker and drawing a conclusion about the intended meaning or implied messages (Oaksford & Chater, 2020). Inferencing is a dynamic real-time process that requires listeners to combine linguistic knowledge, context, and cognitive skills to make interpretations and arrive at a more complete understanding of the speaker's message (Anderson, 2017; Siposova & Carpenter, 2019).

From a semantic processing perspective, inferencing is essential for linking a series of utterances and exchanges and integrating concepts across multiple

64 *Defining Listening*

exchanges or episodes. Without inferencing, multiple utterances and extended discourses lack coherence, and the listener cannot build meaning beyond random comprehension of disconnected propositions.

Table 3.2 provides examples of the most common types of inferencing that are noted in discourse processing.

Table 3.2 Inference Types in Semantic Processing

Inference type	*Influence on semantic processing*
External inference Reasoning based on impressionistic external factors without direct consideration of the content	Predicts the views of the speaker based on stylistic or nonlinguistic indications
Internal inference Reasoning based on internal or personal information about the speaker, such as their thoughts, feelings, or motivations	Provides a conclusion for the utterance based on the personal knowledge of the speaker
Narrative inference Reasoning based on expected structure and elements of a story or typical social sequence	Fills in details in a discourse based on expected actions or script elements
Adversative inference The truth of one statement is used to negate or contradict another statement	Recognizes the opposition or contradiction of two or more propositions
Alternative inference Draws a conclusion that differs from the logical explanation	Presents an alternative explanation for an action that differs from the one stated by the speaker
Background inference Contextual information is used to understand or interpret a situation or event	Presents a broader context than the stated context to understand a speaker's claim
Causal inference A cause-and-effect relationship is inferred between two co-occurring variables or events	Presents a correlated event or an unstated event that may be the actual cause of the resulting event
Contrastive inference A conclusion is drawn by comparing and contrasting different possibilities or options	Presents differences or distinctions to make valid comparisons and contrasts
Dismissive inference A conclusion is drawn by disregarding or downplaying provided information	Concludes that an argument is flawed or unconvincing based on a minor error or inconsistency, disregarding an individual's opinion or perspective because they lack expertise or authority
Elaborative inference Going beyond the explicit details or facts and using existing knowledge, context, and imagination	Builds extensions and analogies to understand a concept more deeply

When a person is listening, they typically are not consciously aware of a specific type of inference they are making. All inferences are aimed at drawing optimal conclusions based on information given and prior experience with reasoning in similar contexts (Tavoni et al., 2019). In most cases, people simply engage in inferencing automatically and intuitively as part of their natural "commonsense" process of understanding spoken language (Ferraro et al., 2019; Yao et al., 2022). In some cases, listeners may become aware of their inferencing process if they encounter ambiguity or conflicting or alarming information, or if they consciously reflect on their understanding, or are challenged in a discussion to explain their reasoning (Pavlick & Kwiatkowski, 2019; Piątkowski et al., 2023).

3.4.1 Explicit vs. Implicit Inferencing

One useful distinction in discussing inferencing is whether the drawing of conclusions is based on conventions of logic or on intuition, that is, an integration of personal experience, knowledge, and beliefs.

Conventional inferencing relies on formal logic, deductive reasoning, or following predefined rules or procedures. In a deductive argument, if the premises are true and the logical structure is valid, the conclusion can be derived through conventional inferencing. (To take a classic example: Premise 1: All mammals are warm-blooded animals. Premise 2: Elephants are mammals. Conclusion: Therefore, elephants are warm-blooded animals.) Conventional inferencing is deliberate and conscious and requires explicit thinking or reasoning processes.

Conventional inferencing, the use of overt logical reasoning processes, is the most powerful source of comprehension building. Logical reasoning involves analyzing the content, identifying relationships between ideas, and drawing conclusions based on evidence and sound argumentation. It includes identifying main points and supporting evidence, evaluating claims made by the speaker, evaluating the logical coherence of the speaker's arguments, detecting logical fallacies and contradictions, and relating concepts to other concepts.

Intuitive inferencing, by contrast, involves drawing conclusions based on covert, automatic, and subconscious processes. This form of inferencing relies on instinctual judgments, gut feelings, or quick assessments, often based on incomplete information (Kumar, 2022). For instance, if you are interviewing someone for a job, and the candidate responds to questions and interacts in a particular way that you find pleasing, you may have a global sense that this person may be perfect for the job, though you cannot pinpoint the exact reason.

To examine intuitive inferencing at a more micro level, imagine that you meet someone new for the first time at a social gathering. After a brief conversation, you have an intuitive feeling that this person is trustworthy, someone with whom you would like to become friends or perhaps business partners. Despite

66 *Defining Listening*

very limited information, your intuition leads you to make an inference about their character.

The process of coming to this intuition includes several quick steps or assessments. You first perceive cues from the environment and from the interaction, including visual (perhaps from what the person is wearing or how they comport themselves or their hairstyle), auditory (perhaps from their accent or tone or pace of speaking), and sensory information (perhaps from their handshake or the cologne they are wearing). You then engage quickly in pattern recognition, searching for associations in these cues with your past experiences. This leads to a quick comparison of these patterns with **mental prototypes** associated with those situations in your past experience. If there is a strong match between the cues and the stored patterns, you will generate an intuitive judgment about the plausible outcome of the situation (i.e., pursuing a friendship or business association with this person). You may then experience an immediate reaction, a gut feeling, a sense of certainty that guides your next decision and behavior (Boucouvalas, 2016).

Intuitive inferencing, like schema activation and modification, is driven by problem-solving heuristics. It relies on the listener's trust in their pattern recognition ability based on their prior experience. The difference is primarily in the speed of the process. Intuitive inferences can occur spontaneously, without explicit deliberation or the application of formal logical rules. Although intuitive inferences are likely to solve a decision-making or comprehension problem, they may be flawed or biased in that they may be susceptible to cognitive biases and overconfidence in recognizing patterns (Kahneman et al., 2021; Kumar, 2022).

Returning to the listening process, we can see that listening inferences may be guided by this same type of rapid, intuitive thought pattern: cue perception, pattern recognition, mental prototype comparison, outcome judgment, and immediate reaction. When encountering a new situation or listening text that shares explicit patterns or underlying similarities with previous experiences (firsthand or secondhand), individuals may make intuitive inferences or judgments based on their inner voice (the stream of thoughts, self-reflections, and mental commentary that occurs during cognition). These inferences may not be explicitly reasoned or consciously analyzed but rather based on informal intuitive logic (Baddeley & Lewis, 2017; Gilligan et al., 2003.

Intuitive inference can be useful when immediate comprehension is required. It can also be useful when the listener is overwhelmed with complex, unfamiliar, or ambiguous information that cannot be fully analyzed through explicit reasoning. It draws upon the listener's cognitive abilities and experiences to make rapid assessments and judgments, often resulting in accurate and efficient decision-making (Kahneman & Bar-Hillel, 2020).

However, intuitive logic during semantic processing can be influenced by biases, cognitive shortcuts, and subjective factors, such as personal beliefs, emotional states, memory interference (transience, blocking, misattribution, persistence; cf. Schacter, 2002), fallacies of reasoning, and social and cultural influences. While intuitive logic can provide valuable inferences to support and enhance oral language comprehension, it may also lead to errors or misconceptions when faced with complex or novel texts that require more rigorous logical analysis (Korteling et al., 2018; Korteling et al., 2023).

3.4.2 Compensatory Strategies in Semantic Processing

While semantic processing draws upon powerful cognitive resources to comprehend and interpret spoken language, it is far from a flawless comprehension system in everyday discourse. Given the fluctuations of human attention, our limitations of memory, the transience of the speech signal, and the frequency of ambiguities in discourse, semantic processing of spoken language is often incomplete or flawed, even by the most proficient listeners. When comprehension fails, a listener must resort to compensatory strategies to make up for gaps in understanding (Hild, 2015).

A breakdown in semantic processing may occur due to multiple factors: environmental or physical (the listener cannot hear what the speaker is saying); speaker deficiency (the information the speaker gives is incomplete); lack of linguistic familiarity (the listener does not know specific expressions the speaker is using); lack of schematic familiarity (the listener encounters an unknown or unexpected concept); or personal bias (the information the speaker gives is not compatible with the listener's cultural schemata or belief system).

For whatever cause, compensation is required if the listener aims to achieve satisfactory comprehension. Listeners may use live strategies, such as seeking visual support, guessing from context, listening for keywords, or asking for clarification. However, if none of these are available, the listener must enact cognitive heuristics to compensate (Fung & Macaro, 2021; Poulisse, 2019; Timarova et al., 2015). Some of the commonly noted compensation heuristics are:

- **Skipping:** omitting a part or a block of input from processing for comprehension.
- **Approximation:** using a superordinate concept that is likely to cover the essence of what has not been comprehended; constructing a less precise meaning for a word or concept than the speaker may have intended.
- **Filtering:** compressing a longer message or set of propositions into a more concise one. (This is different from skipping or approximation, which are reduction strategies, because filtering involves actively constructing a larger semantic context.)
- **Substitution:** substituting a word, concept, or proposition for one that is not understandable.
- **Incompletion:** maintaining an incomplete proposition in memory and waiting for clarification.

68 *Defining Listening*

Compensatory strategies used by simultaneous interpreters provide evidence of the comprehension problems listeners face in both L1 and L2 contexts. Because simultaneous interpreters have to mediate the understood message into a second language under time pressure, their cognitive capacities are typically overloaded. Under these circumstances, even top interpreters display a number of compensatory strategies (Hatim, 2013; Köksals & Yürük, 2020; Lee, 2006). (See Table 3.3.)

From the interpretation data, in which the translation output mirrors the comprehension processes of the listener, the interpreter is attempting to perform

Table 3.3 Compensatory Strategies Used by Listeners in a Mediating Context

Source-language text (English)	*Target-language (Arabic) versions*
Skipping	
The French Minister was greeted with jeers and violence	The French Minister was greeted with violence
They were all very glum and kept complaining that it was impossible to catch up with Western military technology	They were all very … and kept complaining that it was impossible to catch up with Western military technology
In the Senate today, the $15 billion appropriation bill was approved by a vote of ninety-eight to one	In the Senate today, the $15 billion Bill was approved by a vote of ninety-eight to one
It named the missile 'the shale stone,' a reference to a story in the Koran	It names the missile as a kind of stone, a reference to a story in the Koran
Approximation	
Iran has embarked on a methodological campaign …	Iran has launched a methodological campaign
In Damascus, Syrian radio said that fighting had spilled into Tikrit	In Damascus, Syrian radio said that there was fighting in Tikrit
to patch up their historical hatreds	to agree among themselves
Press and public largely acquiesced in this disclosure of only selected information	Press and public welcomed this disclosure of only selected information
East European governments that once belonged to the defunct Soviet-led Warsaw Pact	East European governments that once belonged to the former Soviet-led Warsaw Pact
Filtering	
There's nothing new in wartime about exaggerated claims of success, or inflammatory charges of atrocities	There's nothing new in wartime about exaggerated claims of success
Smouldering fires of tension throughout the region have been fanned as countries are drawn into the sphere of confrontation	Tension is increasing among countries drawn into confrontation in the region

Semantic Processing 69

Table 3.3 (Continued)

Source-language text (English)	Target-language (Arabic) versions
The king visited frontline units of the 12th Royal Mechanized Division	The king visited an army unit
Incompletion	
They don't have complete control of all lines of communication or transportation. They haven't really stonewalled us	They don't have complete control of all lines of communications or transportation. They …
He did not act like a tough businessman, or the duck hunter, with Israel assigned to the role of scared duck at bay	He did not act like a tough businessman or the duck hunter with Israel …
In the bewildering thicket of rebel claims it is unclear exactly what is happening	In the … it is unclear exactly what is happening in spite of rebel claims
Substitution	
collateral damage	a lot of damage
Russians vote in unity showdown	Russians vote in a unity referendum
But the crisis jarred perceptions	But the crisis changed perceptions
The greatest subversion brought by the war is the thousands of satellite television dishes	The greatest problem brought by the war is the thousands of television dishes

Source. Data from Saraireh and Al-Khanji (2018).

an accurate translation based on their knowledge of the content and technical vocabulary. At the same time, the interpreter is trying to keep up with the unfolding discourse, aiming to create an overall coherence in that discourse, and maintain a positive relationship with the other participants. These multiple pressures necessitate compromises such as skipping, approximating, and filtering (Abdullayev, 2024).

3.5 Listening to Learn

In most contexts, when we consciously listen to someone or something, we intend to comprehend and interpret what we are hearing in order to connect with someone or some event in the present moment and address the needs of a particular transaction. In some contexts, however, we not only want to comprehend, but also to learn something new and retain what we have learned. Listening to learn and listening to understand are related processes, but they involve different levels of engagement and different goals (Schmidt & Kehoe, 2019; Wilson, 2014).

70   *Defining Listening*

Listening to understand, the most common goal of semantic processing, refers to the process of actively focusing on the speaker's message with the intention of comprehending and grasping the content being communicated. In this mode of listening, the listener aims to capture the main ideas, details, and key points of what is being communicated. In this form of listening, the participants themselves set the standards for what constitutes acceptable understanding.

Listening to learn goes beyond basic comprehension, involves a more proactive approach to acquiring new knowledge, insights, or skills, and often invokes an objective standard of understanding independent of the listener. In this mode of listening, the listener not only strives to understand the content but also aims to internalize, retain, and apply the information in a meaningful way. The focus is on actively engaging with the material, critically evaluating concepts, making intensive connections to prior knowledge, and integrating the new information into one's existing cognitive framework. Listening to learn often involves asking questions, seeking additional resources, taking notes, reflecting on the content, and considering how the new information relates to one's personal experiences or interests (Duffy et al., 2010; Schunk, 2012).

When listening to learn, individuals make extensive use of **selective attention**. Selective attention allows listeners to prioritize the information that is most relevant to their current goals, tasks, or interests—in a sense, giving the learner a pre-listening priming that helps them focus on the specific information they are seeking (Shinn-Cunningham & Best, 2015). In contrast, in everyday semantic processing, the listener will attend to what seems most interesting and relevant at the moment and to the task at hand, without selective attention toward long-term goals.

Learning through listening entails activating the three global semantic processes outlined in this chapter: lexical access, comprehension building, and inferencing. However, effective learning through listening requires an *intensification* of these processes, plus an additional series of conscious steps of encoding information for future retrieval (Ivone & Renandya, 2019).

During the encoding process, listeners organize and structure the new information, making associations to aid in the formation of coherent and meaningful representations.

The encoding process involves the transfer of information from short-term to long-term memory in order to transform information into a meaningful and stable representation that can be stored for an extended period (Fukuda & Vogel, 2019). Several encoding mechanisms contribute to this process. These include

1. Elaboration: relating new information to existing knowledge, or creating connections between different elements aids in encoding (Armstrong, 2020);
2. Organization: structuring and organizing information logically facilitates encoding, in a process called **rapid cortical plasticity** (Hebscher et al., 2019);

Semantic Processing   71

3. Repetition, consolidation, and rehearsal: Rehearsing or reviewing the material at spaced intervals, known as spaced repetition, is essential for long-term memory retention (Ausubel & Youssef, 1965; Settles & Meeder, 2016);
4. Attaching emotional significance: Emotionally charged experiences and information encoded while experiencing positive emotions are more memorable (Su et al., 2023).

3.6 Summary: The Role of Semantic Processing in Language Comprehension

Semantic processing culminates in inferencing, drawing logical conclusions, making predictions, and creating interpretations based on available information, context, and prior knowledge. Because inferencing, by its nature, fills in gaps in the input, it is possible to feign comprehension by jumping directly to inferencing. This is what is known as the **top-down bias**, the tendency of listeners to prioritize their existing knowledge, expectations, and cognitive frameworks (top-down processing) over incoming sensory information (bottom-up processing) when interpreting and comprehending spoken language.

In comparison to top-down processing, full semantic processing requires a more rigorous activation of the mental lexicon and cognitive schemas so that the listener comprehends the input more completely before engaging in elaborative inferences. Full comprehension also requires rigorous bottom-up processing to ensure accurate decoding of the input. We can represent this complementary nature of listening using the rope analogy of comprehension, which was first introduced in the context of children's growth in reading comprehension (Scarborough, 2001). This image provides a visual metaphor for how bottom-up and top-down processing complement and reinforce each other in creating meaning (see Figure 3.1).

To utilize that metaphor, this chapter has outlined the three fundamental strands of semantic processing: lexical access, comprehension building, and inferencing. Lexical access refers to the cognitive process by which listeners retrieve stored information about words from their mental lexicon, a dynamic archive continuously revised through years of using the language.

Comprehension building refers to the most active aspect of semantic processing—the activation and utilization of prior knowledge, our personalized schemas of knowledge. We need to activate these schemas—our background knowledge in accessible form—to aid us in interpreting incoming information.

The verbal input from the speaker is typically not sufficient for a listener to create meaning. To create coherent meaning, we need to perform various inferencing and reasoning processes to supplement that input. Inferencing is the term we have used to encompass not only drawing conclusions based on the evidence presented but also using logical thinking (reasoning), critical analysis,

72 *Defining Listening*

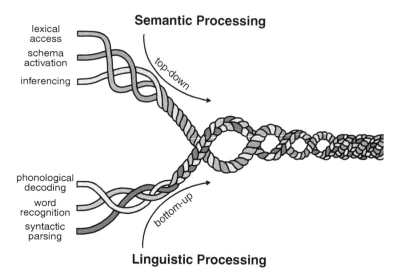

Figure 3.1 Bottom-Up Processing Complements Top-Down Processing

and the integration of multiple pieces of information to reach a conclusion or solve a complex task.

All semantic processing involves actively processing and manipulating information to extract meaning and establish connections. Semantic processing for the purposes of long-term learning involves the *addition* of purpose and intention, along with an intensification of attention and selective listening for information that best addresses one's learning objectives.

References

Abdullayev, A. (2024). Synchronous interpretation and its peculiarities. *Theoretical Aspects in the Formation of Pedagogical Sciences, 3*(1), 96–98. https://doi.org/10.5281/zenodo.10485183

Alikhani, M., & Stone, M. (2020). Achieving common ground in multi-modal dialogue. In D. Jurafsky, J. Chai, N. Schluter, & J. Tetreault (Eds.), *Proceedings of the 58th Annual Meeting of the Association for Computational Linguistics: Tutorial abstracts* (pp. 10–15). Association for Computational Linguistics. doi: 10.18653/v1/P17

Anderson, R. C. (2017). The notion of schemata and the educational enterprise: General discussion of the conference. In R. C. Anderson, R. J. Spiro, & W. E. Montague (Eds.), *Schooling and the acquisition of knowledge* (pp. 415–431). Routledge.

Anderson, R. C. (2018). Role of the reader's schema in comprehension, learning, and memory. In D. E. Alvermann, N. J. Unrau, M. Sailors, & R. B. Ruddell (Eds.), *Theoretical models and processes of literacy* (pp. 136–145). Routledge.

Armstrong, P. B. (2020). *Stories and the brain: The neuroscience of narrative*. JHU Press.

Ausubel, D. P., & Youssef, M. (1965). The effect of spaced repetition on meaningful retention. *The Journal of General Psychology, 73*(1), 147–150.

Baddeley, A., & Lewis, V. (2017). Inner active processes in reading: The inner voice, the inner ear, and the inner eye. In A. Baddeley & V. Lewis (Eds.), *Interactive processes in reading: The inner voice, the inner ear, and the inner eye* (pp. 107–129). Routledge.

Beglar, D., & Nation, P. (2013). Assessing vocabulary. In A. J. Kunnan (Ed.), *The companion to language assessment* (Vol. 1, pp. 172–184). Wiley.

Bohn-Gellter, C., & Kendeou, P. (2014). The interplay of reader goals, working memory, and text structure during reading. *Contemporary Educational Psychology, 39,* 206–219.

Boucouvalas, M. (2016). Intuition: The concept and the experience. In R. Davis-Floyd & P. S. Arvidsen (Eds.), *Intuition: The inside story. Interdisciplinary perspectives* (pp. 3–18). Routledge.

Braasch, J., & Kessler, D. (2021). Working toward a theoretical model for source comprehension in everyday discourse. *Discourse Processes, 58*(5–6), 449467

Carston, R. (2021). Polysemy: Pragmatics and sense conventions. *Mind & Language, 36*(1), 108–133.

Chiu, W., & Lu, K. (2015). Paradigmatic relations and syntagmatic relations: How are they related? *Proceedings of the Association for Information Science and Technology, 52*(1), 1–4.

Christensen, A. P., & Kenett, Y. N. (2021). Semantic network analysis (SemNA): A tutorial on preprocessing, estimating, and analyzing semantic networks. *Psychological Methods, 28*(4), 860–879.

Churchland, P. (2012). *Plato's camera: How the physical brain captures a landscape of abstract universals*. MIT Press.

Clark, E. (2014). Two pragmatic principles in language use and acquisition. In D. Matthews (Ed.), *Pragmatic development in first language acquisition* (pp. 105–120). Benjamins.

Collins, A. M., & Loftus, E. F. (1975). A spreading-activation theory of semantic processing. *Psychological Review, 82*(6), 407.

Dahm, M. R., Williams, M., & Crock, C. (2022). "More than words": Interpersonal communication, cognitive bias and diagnostic errors. *Patient Education and Counseling, 105*(1), 252–256.

Duffy, G. G., Miller, S., Howerton, S., & Williams, J. B. (2010). Comprehension instruction: Merging two historically antithetical perspectives. In D. Wyse, R. Andrews, & J. Hoffmann (Eds.), *The Routledge international handbook of English, language and literacy teaching* (pp. 58–67). Routledge.

Emmott, C., & Alexander, M. (2014). Schemata. In P. Huhn, J. Meister, J. Pier, & W. Schmid (Eds.), *Handbook of narratology* (2nd ed.) (Vol. 1, pp. 756–764). De Gruyter.

Fernandino, L., Tong, J. Q., Conant, L. L., Humphries, C. J., & Binder, J. R. (2022). Decoding the information structure underlying the neural representation of concepts. *Proceedings of the National Academy of Sciences, 119*(6), e2108091119.

Ferraro, P. J., Sanchirico, J. N., & Smith, M. D. (2019). Causal inference in coupled human and natural systems. *Proceedings of the National Academy of Sciences, 116*(12), 5311–5318.

74 *Defining Listening*

Font, F., Oramas, S., Fazekas, G., & Serra, X. (2014, October). Extending tagging ontologies with domain specific knowledge. In *ISWC (Posters & Demos)* (pp. 209–212).

Fukuda, K., & Vogel, E. K. (2019). Visual short-term memory capacity predicts the "bandwidth" of visual long-term memory encoding. *Memory & Cognition, 47,* 1481–1497.

Fung, D., & Macaro, E. (2021). Exploring the relationship between linguistic knowledge and strategy use in listening comprehension. *Language Teaching Research, 25*(4), 540–564.

Gallese, V., & Lakoff, G. (2005). The brain's concepts: The role of the sensory-motor system in conceptual knowledge. *Cognitive Neuropsychology, 22,* 455–479.

Geurts, B. (2019). Communication as commitment sharing: Speech acts, implicatures, common ground. *Theoretical Linguistics, 45*(1–2), 1–30.

Ghosh, V. E., & Gilboa, A. (2014). What is a memory schema? A historical perspective on current neuroscience literature. *Neuropsychologia, 53,* 104–114.

Gilboa, A., & Marlatte, H. (2017). Neurobiology of schemas and schema-mediated memory. *Trends in Cognitive Sciences, 21*(8), 618–631.

Gilligan, C., Spencer, R., Weinberg, M. K., & Bertsch, T. (2003). On the listening guide: A voice-centered relational method. In P. M. Camic, J. E. Rhodes, & L. Yardley (Eds.), *Qualitative research in psychology: Expanding perspectives in methodology and design* (pp. 157–172). American Psychological Association.

Giuliano, A. E., Bonasia, K., Ghosh, V. E., Moscovitch, M., & Gilboa, A. (2021). Differential influence of ventromedial prefrontal cortex lesions on neural representations of schema and semantic category knowledge. *Journal of Cognitive Neuroscience, 33*(9), 1928–1955.

Green, R. (2008). Relationships in knowledge organization. *Knowledge Organization, 35*(2–3), 150–159.

Grimmer, H., Laukkonen, R., Tangen, J., & von Hippel, W. (2022). Eliciting false insights with semantic priming. *Psychonomic Bulletin & Review, 29*(3), 954–970.

Hasan, M., & Rahman, M. (2020). Analytic relations versus syntagmatic and paradigmatic relations of vocabulary depth knowledge: Their correlation and prediction to academic reading comprehension of EFL learners. *Open Linguistics, 6*(1), 357–371. doi: 10.1515/opli-2020-0024

Hatim, B. (2013). *Teaching and researching translation* (2nd ed.). Routledge.

Hebscher, M., Wing, E., Ryan, J., & Gilboa, A. (2019). Rapid cortical plasticity supports long-term memory formation. *Trends in Cognitive Sciences, 23*(12), 989–1002.

Hild, A. (2015). Discourse comprehension in simultaneous interpreting: The role of expertise and information redundancy. In A. Ferreira & J. Schwieter (Eds.), *Psycholinguistic and cognitive inquiries into translation and interpreting* (pp. 67–100). Benjamins.

Ivone, F. M., & Renandya, W. A. (2019). Extensive listening and viewing in ELT. *TEFLIN Journal: A Publication on the Teaching and Learning of English, 30*(2), 237–256.

Kahneman, D., & Bar-Hillel, M. (2020). Comment: Laplace and cognitive illusions. *Statistical Science, 35*(2), 171–172.

Kahneman, D., Sibony, O., & Sunstein, C. R. (2021). *Noise: A flaw in human judgment.* Hachette UK.

Kecskes, I., & Zhang, F. (2009). Activating, seeking, and creating common ground: A socio-cognitive approach. *Pragmatics & Cognition, 17*(2), 331–355.

Kintsch, W. (1998). *Comprehension: A paradigm for cognition*. Cambridge University Press.

Köksal, O., & Yürük, N. (2020). The role of translator in intercultural communication. *International Journal of Curriculum and Instruction, 12*(1), 327–338.

Korteling, J. E., Brouwer, A. M., & Toet, A. (2018). A neural network framework for cognitive bias. *Frontiers in Psychology, 9*, 1561.

Korteling, J., Paradies, G. L., & Sassen-van Meer, J. P. (2023). Cognitive bias and how to improve sustainable decision making. *Frontiers in Psychology, 14*, 1129835.

Kumar, A. (2021). Semantic memory: A review of methods, models, and current challenges. *Psychonomic Bulletin & Review, 28*, 40–80.

Kumar, N. (2022). Intuition. *International Journal of Indian Psychology, 10*(2).

Lee, T. (2006). A comparison of simultaneous interpretation and delayed simultaneous interpretation from English into Korean. *Meta: Journal des traducteurs, 51*, 202–214.

Loaiza, V. M., & Camos, V. (2018, June). The role of semantic representations in verbal working memory. *Journal of Experimental Psychology: Learning, Memory and Cognition, 44*(6), 863–881. doi: 10.1037/xlm0000475. PMID: 29648869.

Mandler, J. M. (2014). *Stories, scripts, and scenes: Aspects of schema theory.* Psychology Press.

Mannaert, L. N. H., Dijkstra, K., & Zwaan, R. A. (2019). How are mental simulations updated across sentences? *Memory & Cognition, 47*(6), 1201–1214.

McNamara, T. P. (2005). *Semantic priming: Perspectives from memory and word recognition*. Psychology Press.

Nguyen, C. D., & Newton, J. (2018). Schemata in listening comprehension. In J. E. Liontas (Ed.), *The TESOL encyclopedia of English language teaching* (pp. 1–7). Wiley.

Oaksford, M., & Chater, N. (2020). New paradigms in the psychology of reasoning. *Annual Review of Psychology, 71*, 305–330.

Pavlick, E., & Kwiatkowski, T. (2019). Inherent disagreements in human textual inferences. *Transactions of the Association for Computational Linguistics, 7*, 677–694.

Peters, I., & Weller, K. (2008). Paradigmatic and syntagmatic relations in knowledge organization systems. *Information Wissenschaft und Praxis, 59*(2), 100.

Piątkowski. K., von Bastian, C. C., Zawadzka, K., & Hanczakowski, M. (2023, March). Elaboration by superposition: From interference in working memory to encoding in long-term memory. *Journal of Experimental Psychology: Learning, Memory, and Cognition, 49*(3), 371–388.

Poulisse, N. (2019). The use of compensatory strategies by Dutch learners of English. In N. Poulisee (Ed.), *The use of compensatory strategies by Dutch learners of English.* De Gruyter Mouton.

Pranoto, B. E., & Afrilita, L. K. (2019). The organization of words in mental lexicon: Evidence from word association test. *Teknosastik, 16*(1), 26–33.

Qian, D. D., & Lin, L. H. (2019). The relationship between vocabulary knowledge and language proficiency. In S. Webb (Ed.), *The Routledge handbook of vocabulary studies* (pp. 66–80). Routledge.

Quilty-Dunn, J. (2021). Polysemy and thought: Toward a generative theory of concepts. *Mind & Language, 36*(1), 158–185.

Ratcliff, R., Sederberg, P. B., Smith, T. A., & Childers, R. (2016). A single trial analysis of EEG in recognition memory: Tracking the neural correlates of memory strength. *Neuropsychologia, 93*, 128–141.

76 Defining Listening

Ritvo, V. J., Turk-Browne, N. B., & Norman, K. A. (2019). Nonmonotonic plasticity: How memory retrieval drives learning. *Trends in Cognitive Sciences, 23*(9), 726–742.

Rost, M. (1994). On-line summaries as representations of lecture understanding. In J. Flowerdew (Ed.), *Academic listening: Research perspectives.* (pp. 93–127). Cambridge University Press.

Rost, M. (2020). Instructional design and assessment. In D. Worthington & G. Bodie (Eds.), *The handbook of listening* (pp. 265–278). Wiley.

Rumelhart, D. E. (2017). Schemata: The building blocks of cognition. In R. J. Spiro, B. C. Bruce, & W. F. Brewer (Eds.), *Theoretical issues in reading comprehension* (pp. 33–58). Routledge.

Sanders, T., & Gernsbacher, M. A. (2004). Accessibility in text and discourse processing. *Discourse Processes, 37*, 79–89.

Saraireh, M., & Al-Khanji, R. (2018). Comparative textology: Intentional substitution strategies in translation. *Hawliyat, 15*, 69–84.

Scarborough, H. (2001). Connecting early language and literacy to later reading (dis)abilities: Evidence, theory, and practice. In S. Neuman & D. Dickinson (Eds.), *Handbook for research in early literacy* (pp. 97–110). Guilford Press.

Schacter, D. L. (2002). *The seven sins of memory: How the mind forgets and remembers*. HMH.

Schmidt, P. R., & Kehoe, A. B. (Eds.). (2019). *Archaeologies of listening*. University Press of Florida.

Schmitt, N. (2014). Size and depth of vocabulary knowledge: What the research shows. *Language Learning, 64*(4), 913–951.

Schunk, D. H. (2012). *Learning theories: An educational perspective*. Pearson Education.

Settles, B., & Meeder, B. (2016, August). A trainable spaced repetition model for language learning. In K. Erk & N. A. Smith (Eds.), *Proceedings of the 54th annual meeting of the Association for Computational Linguistics* (Vol. 1, pp. 1848–1858). ACL.

Shinn-Cunningham, B., & Best, V. (2015). Auditory selective attention. In J. M. Fawcett, E. F. Risko, & A. Kingstone (Eds.), *The handbook of attention* (pp. 99–117). MIT.

Sims, A. D., Ussishkin, A., Parker, J., & Wray, S. (2022). At the intersection of cognitive processes and linguistic diversity. In A. D. Sims, A. Ussishkin, J. Parker, & S. Wray (Eds.), *Morphological diversity and linguistic cognition* (pp. 1–28). Cambridge University Press.

Siposova, B., & Carpenter, M. (2019). A new look at joint attention and common knowledge. *Cognition, 189*, 260–274.

Su, J., Ye, J., Nie, L., Cao, Y., & Chen, Y. (2023). Optimizing spaced repetition schedule by capturing the dynamics of memory. *IEEE Transactions on Knowledge and Data Engineering, 35*, 10085–10097.

Tavoni, G., Balasubramanian, V., & Gold, J. I. (2019). What is optimal in optimal inference? *Current Opinion in Behavioral Sciences, 29*, 117–126.

Thorndyke, P. W., & Yekovich, F. R. (1980). A critique of schema-based theories of human story memory. *Poetics, 9*(1–3), 23–49.

Timarova, S., Coendova, I., Meylaerts, R., Hertog, E., Szmalec, A., & Duyck, W. (2015). Simultaneous interpreting and working memory capacity. In A. Ferreira & J. Schwieter (Eds.), *Psycholinguistic and cognitive inquiries into translation and interpreting* (pp. 101–126). Benjamins.

Toulmin, S. (2006). Reasoning in theory and practice. *Arguing on the Toulmin Model, 10*, 25–29.

Tuan, L. T., & Loan, B. T. K. (2010). Schema-building and listening. *Studies in Literature and Language, 1*(5), 53.

Ullman, M. T. (2001). The declarative/procedural model of lexicon and grammar. *Journal of psycholinguistic research, 30*, 37–69.

Wagoner, B. (2013). Bartlett's concept of schema in reconstruction. *Theory & Psychology, 23*(5), 553–575.

Wilson, M. B. (2014). *The language of learning: Teaching students core thinking, listening, and speaking skills.* Center for Responsive Schools.

Wray, S. C. (2016). *Decomposability and the effects of morpheme frequency in lexical access* (Doctoral dissertation, The University of Arizona).

Yao, B., Joseph, E., Lioanag, J., & Si, M. (2022, June). A corpus for commonsense inference in story cloze test. In N. Calzolari, F. Béchet, P. Blanche, K. Choukri, C. Cieri, T. Declerck, S. Goggi, H. Isahara, B. Maegaard, J. Mariani, H. Mazo, J. Odijk, & S. Piperidis (Eds.), *Proceedings of the Thirteenth Language Resources and Evaluation Conference* (pp. 3500–3508). ACL.

Zuczkowski, A., Bongelli, R., Riccioni, I., & Philip, G. (2021). *Questions and epistemic stance in contemporary spoken British English.* Cambridge Scholars Publishing.

4 Pragmatic Processing

4.1	Introduction: Pragmatic Processing and Pragmatic Comprehension	78
4.2	Discourse Framing	79
	4.2.1 Contextual Framing	*79*
	4.2.2 Participation Framing	*81*
	4.2.3 Power Framing	*81*
	4.2.4 Community Framing	*84*
	4.2.5 Subjective Framing	*86*
4.3	Interpreting Intent	88
	4.3.1 Deciphering Locutionary and Illocutionary Acts	*88*
	4.3.2 Conversational Maxims	*89*
	4.3.3 Contravening Social Conventions	*91*
	4.3.4 Emotional Signaling	*92*
4.4	Response Weighting	93
	4.4.1 Responding	*94*
	4.4.2 Providing Additive Responses	*96*
4.5	Summary: Pragmatic Comprehension and Pragmatic Competence	98
References		100

4.1 Introduction: Pragmatic Processing and Pragmatic Comprehension

Listening is often considered a receptive skill, involving only linguistic decoding of input and comprehension and interpretation of messages. But there is a holistic, interactive dimension of listening central to the creation of meaning, which we call **pragmatic processing**. Pragmatic processing is a subjective filtering and interpretation process grounded in our system of action and emotion (Zwaan, 2001). The goal of pragmatic processing is to create personal and social relevance (Schunk & DiBenedetto, 2020; Sperber & Wilson, 1986).

DOI: 10.4324/9781003390794-6

Pragmatic processing is an aspect of **social cognition,** the mental processes that enable us to interpret our own actions as part of the social dynamics with our fellow humans—a definition that is increasingly expanding to include artificial intelligence (AI) entities. Social cognition encompasses our cognitive abilities to navigate social interactions, make sense of others' thoughts, feelings, and intentions, and form judgments based on social information (Greenwald & Lai, 2020; Higgins et al., 2022).

This intuitive aspect of pragmatic processing is sometimes described as a **mirroring** process, an ability to feel or imagine the same sensations as the speaker and to make informed guesses about what is going on *inside the person—* their intentions, feelings, and thoughts (Obdalova et al., 2023; Rizzolatti et al., 2023). Rather than being a peculiar psychic ability, this emotional intelligence is acquired gradually by listeners through feedback from others about the accuracy of their intuitions (Verschueren, 2022a).

The personal and social dynamics of pragmatic processing contribute to a more subjective understanding of input than semantic processing provides. In effect, they create a type of **pragmatic comprehension** that accounts for the relevance of the input they are processing.

Three aspects of pragmatic processing that contribute to pragmatic comprehension will be discussed in this chapter: (1) discourse framing, (2) intent interpretation, and (3) response weighting. These aspects are central to building a model of pragmatic comprehension that can be used in teaching and research.

4.2 Discourse Framing

Discourse framing refers to understanding the social dimensions of messages in discourse. Framing plays a central role in pragmatic comprehension, which is the contextual understanding of the discourse and its roles. Rather than simply expressing information, a speaker frames messages to shape the listener's understanding, interpretation, and response. Discourse framing is the strategic use of language and communicative codes to influence how the message is perceived. Framing does this by highlighting particular perspectives and evoking certain emotional responses.

4.2.1 Contextual Framing

The most tangible aspect of discourse framing in pragmatic interpretation is contextual or **deictic framing.** Deictic framing establishes common ground: the shared knowledge and assumptions of the participants.

For example, if someone says, "I'm here now," the sentence's meaning depends on the context. "Here" is deictically framed by the speaker's location at the time, and "now" is deictically framed by the time of speaking. Similarly,

80 *Defining Listening*

pronouns like "I" are deictic because they depend on the participants and objects within the context of the communication.

Much deictic framing involves nonverbal elements and situational coordinates, not just the language used. These dimensions were identified by the sociolinguistics revolution of the 1970s:

- **Addressor**, the speaker of the utterance; **addressee**, the intended recipient of the speaker's utterance who has some interaction rights; **audience,** intended recipient of the speaker's utterance with no (or limited) interaction rights; **overhearers**, unintended recipients of the speaker's utterance
- **Topic**, what is talked about, primarily and tangentially
- **Setting**, where the event is situated in place and time
- **Code**, the language used, and any special (marked) linguistic features of the utterance
- **Channel**, how the communication is initiated and maintained by speech, gestures, and other nonverbal behavior, writing, texting, images, etc.
- **Event**, the social norms affecting the interaction and its interpretation
- **Genre,** the conventional categories of speech events
- **Key**, the tone, manner, and spirit of the event
- **Purpose**, the intended outcome of the event
- **Register,** the level of formality, stylistic choices, and dialect used by the speaker
- **Stance,** the relationship the speaker intends to establish with the listener
- **Voice,** citing, or quoting versus the speaker's original formulation.
  (based on Gumperz, 1982, 1992; Hymes, 1964; Labov, 1972)

A pragmatically oriented listener may not be able to identify all, or even most, of these dimensions in any encounter, but the listener benefits from *what can be* identified. A pragmatic mindset enables the listener to tolerate ambiguity about the variables that cannot be detected (Kiesling, 2011; Simaki et al., 2020). The listener's focus on the context—whatever pragmatic elements are discernable—becomes the primary orientation for interpreting discourse as it unfolds (Allwood et al., 2014; Borchmann et al., 2020). In terms of promoting pragmatic comprehension, the clearer the listener's cognitive map of these contributing variables, the deeper the understanding of the discourse will be (Baskerville & Myers, 2015). Indeed, many people can understand speakers in L2 situations with minimal language comprehension due to their ability to tune into the deictic dimensions of a situation. (My late mother was uncannily gifted in this area. Watching her navigate through cross-cultural encounters with an unexpected kind of metacultural proficiency got me interested in linguistics and listening in particular.)

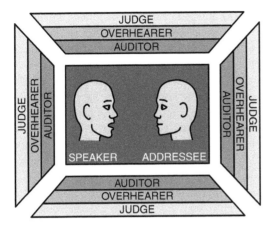

Figure 4.1 Listener Roles

As the listener becomes a more active participant in discourse, they have greater participation rights. Listener roles include; **Addressee**: speaking rights equal to other participants; **Auditor**: limited right to respond; **Overhearer**: No right or expectation to respond; **Judge**: No capability of responding or interacting, but may have rights to evaluate the discourse outcome

4.2.2 Participation Framing

A less tangible but important part of pragmatic processing is framing listening participation, the extent to which the listener is a participant. To do this, we need to consider language from the subjective points of view of both the speaker and the listener, as well as the **intersubjectivity** co-constructed by them (Kecskes, 2019).

Participation framing includes what Verschueren (2022b) refers to as "the speaker's and the listener's **situated presence** at the time of the interaction." The listener's role, or degree of shared presence, entails **rights and expectations** about the degree of engagement and collaboration in an event. The closer the participant is to the center of the discourse, that is, in the role of the addressee, the more collaboration rights and expectations they have, and as a result, the greater their **pragmatic comprehension** will be (see Figure 4.1).

4.2.3 Power Framing

As conceptualized with participation framing, the closer the listener is to the center of the discourse, the more affective involvement is possible—and the more overt involvement is expected. Affective involvement in a conversation refers to the emotional engagement and personal investment of participants during the

82 *Defining Listening*

interaction. It is signaled through active listening behavior (semiverbal sounds and nonverbal behavior) to show interest, curiosity, kindness, inclusivity, or empathy, in addition to overt verbal responsiveness, such as providing feedback and expansive questioning (Jäckel et al., 2024; McLaren & Solomon, 2021; Worthington & Fitch-Hauser, 2018).

High affective involvement by the listener not only leads to a more balanced interaction but also results in more satisfying outcomes for both speaker and listener. When affective involvement is high, participants tend to demonstrate enthusiasm, interest, and investment in the conversation, that is, commitment to a positive outcome: this might involve mutual understanding and connection, relationship protection, conflict resolution, successful exchange of information, and positive follow-up (Bodie & MacGeorge, 2021; Sun et al., 2020a).

Conversely, when affective involvement is low, listeners may exhibit disinterest, indifference, or a lack of emotional engagement. Disconnected listeners may appear bored and unresponsive, which can hinder the flow and quality of the conversation as well as the outcome (Arundale, 2020; Wesselmann et al., 2019). In low-affect discussions, commitment to successful outcomes is also minimal, and a negative outcome often ensues, for example: dominance and forced submissiveness, misunderstanding spirals, conflict escalation, emotional distress, lack of follow-up, and future avoidance (Bonvillain, 2019; Scupin, 2019). (See Table 4.1.)

One related factor in negative outcomes of interaction is the **dominance–submission relationship** between speaker and listener (Spitzley et al., 2022). Dominance is a relational, behavioral, and interactional state that reflects the actual achievement of influence or control over another via communication actions (Biocca et al., 2003; Burgoon et al., 2000). The complementary pole of

Table 4.1 Example of a Low-Affect Conversation with a Negative Outcome

---

David has just returned from a vacation and is describing his time away with great enthusiasm to his work colleague, Sarah.

David: "It was incredible. We were actually swimming with the whales! They took us out a good two miles from the shore, and we finally spotted a group of whales—they call them pods—and we got into the water with our gear and all …"

Rather than mirroring David's enthusiasm, Sarah responds with a monotonous tone and minimal engagement: "That sounds nice."

David likely feels disappointed and deflated by Sarah's lack of enthusiasm. He was probably hoping to share his excitement and experiences with his colleague, but her low-affect response made him feel as if she was not interested in him or that she had some other negative emotion toward him. This may strain their relationship to a degree, and David might be less inclined to share his emotions with Sarah in the future.

Pragmatic Processing 83

Table 4.2 Example of a Dominance–Submission Interaction with Low-Resistance Compliance

---

Scenario: Alex and Taylor are colleagues working on a project together. Alex has taken on a more dominant role in the project, while Taylor has adopted a more submissive stance.

Conversation:

Alex: "I think we should proceed with the backtracking algorithm for this project. It's more efficient."

Taylor: "Sure, Alex, whatever you think is best."

Analysis: In this conversation, Alex takes a dominant role by making a decision and expressing a clear preference. Taylor, on the other hand, adopts a submissive stance by immediately agreeing without offering any input or expressing an opinion. This dynamic suggests that Alex has more control and influence in the working relationship, while Taylor defers to Alex's decisions.

---

dominance is submissiveness, which is measured by the number of submissive turns-at-talk (e.g., silent turns, seeking guidance and permission, low-resistance compliance, negative self-evaluation) (Gordon & Tannen, 2023; Rost, 2014). (See Table 4.2 for an example.)

Introversion vs. extroversion personality traits are sometimes at play in dominance–submission dynamics. Extroversion is frequently associated with being sociable and talkative (energetically communicative and ready to speak up). In contrast, introversion is associated with being reflective and careful about taking speaking turns. Extroversion has been positively related to verbal dominance because extroverts are expected to be more actively involved in pair and group conversation, leading to more verbal dominance (Kayaoğlu, 2013). As with submission in a dominance–submission relationship, one facet of introversion is compliance, displaying the tendency to defer to others, including by yielding speaking turns, adhering to the dominant speaker's assessment, and showing a tendency to avoid conflicts, including active negotiation of meaning (Costa et al., 2019; Gill & Oberlander, 2002).

A listener's awareness of the power framing of discourse—awareness of how power dynamics may be influencing the listener's participation and comprehension—is an essential aspect of pragmatic processing (Sullivan, 2023). Power dynamics directly affect semantic processing because these dynamics influence the inclusion or exclusion of certain voices and certain information, override the elicitation or ignoring of clarification attempts, and shape the overall episodic structure of the discourse event. The exercise of power by a dominant speaker will invariably shape meaning, persuade, influence opinions, and frame the interpretation (van Dijk, 2023).

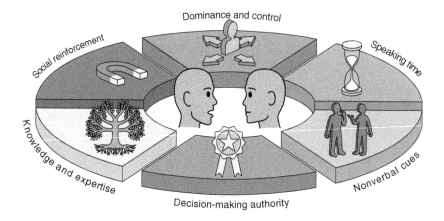

Figure 4.2 Power Framing in Discourse

Power in discourse is often indicated through control of the topic, unbalanced speaking time, nonverbal cues, exercise of decision-making authority, displays of knowledge and expertise, and reliance on social hierarchies

Several dynamic factors may be in operation that indicate the power framing in an interaction. These include: Dominance and control, with one person consistently dominating the conversation and steering the direction of the discussion toward their own agenda (Holmes, 2005); disproportionate speaking time, with the more powerful participant tending to speak for longer and consistently interrupting other participants (Brescoll, 2011); body language, with one party displaying assertive body language and expansive posturing (Hans & Hans, 2015); decision-making authority, with one person influencing the outcome of the conversation through possession of decision-making authority (Mumby & Stohl, 1991); knowledge and expertise, with one party demonstrating greater control of knowledge sources or proficiency in the language being spoken; social reinforcement, in which the person with more perceived power aligns with the magnetic effect of dominant social hierarchies (Fairclough, 2023; Negm, 2015). (See Figure 4.2.)

4.2.4 Community Framing

Another essential aspect of pragmatic comprehension is the framing of the **interpretive community** in which the discourse takes place and the listener's awareness of the norms and standards of that interpretive community (Kramsch & Zhu, 2016). From a sociolinguistic perspective, all language comprehension is filtered through the norms of your interpretive community (Denzin, 2001;

Swales, 2014). An interpretive community is any group that shares a common sense of values, identity, and self-regulation (McCullough & Willoughby, 2009) and is fluent in the same contexts, experiences, and genres of expression (Perry & Vandenabeele, 2008).

Interpretive community is more a specific pragmatic term than speech community, which is defined as a group of people who share a common language variety (e.g., Jamaican patois, Cockney, African American Vernacular English (AAVE)) and engage in regular social interaction using that language variety.

Interpretive community, on the other hand, refers to a group of individuals who share similar **interpretive strategies**, frameworks, and understandings when it comes to interpreting and making sense of texts and cultural artifacts (artwork, literature, music, politics, technology). For describing pragmatic interpretation, interpretive communities retain commonly agreed ways of expressing and understanding key messages (Kecskes, 2023). These norms will apply to formal genres (such as news interviews, academic discussions, and business presentations) and informal genres (such as storytelling, gossiping, mutual praising, small talk and chit-chat, sharing opinions, joke telling, venting, and ranting) (Rampton, 2021). Table 4.3 provides an example of differences in interpretation between distinct discourse communities.

In any ritualized situation of language use, such as political debates, academic lectures, business meetings, legal proceedings, healthcare consultations, customer service, or cocktail parties, the listener will invariably draw upon expectations of the social group they most closely identify with—or wish to identify with—when interpreting the actions and the language within that event. In such settings, individuals may subconsciously refer to their shared cultural norms, values, beliefs, and social conventions to make sense of others. These social groups can cohere around commonalities of nationality, ethnicity, profession, education, or personal interests (Joseph, 2016).

In one-to-one interactions, this social phenomenon of a dominant group membership influencing interpretation norms is readily observable. Interaction occurs within social frames that influence how the speaker and listener act. The social frame for an interaction involves two interwoven aspects: the activity frame, which is the activity that the speaker and listener are engaged in, and the participant frame, which is the social role that each person is playing within that activity (e.g., client–service provider), the cultural role (e.g., native vs. visitor), or the emotional position each person has concerning a sensitive social issue (e.g., is sexual orientation determined genetically? Is capital punishment ever justified?) (cf. Langlotz & Locher, 2013; Tyler, 1995). From a pragmatic perspective, our conversation *and listening skills* are effectively dependent on context cues that enable us to negotiate and establish the exact nature of the activity frame and the participant frame (Tomasello et al., 2012).

86 *Defining Listening*

Table 4.3 Interpretation and Interpretive Communities

Events, speeches, movies, and broadcasts can be interpreted differently by various interpretive communities based on their perspectives, backgrounds, and cultural contexts. Here's an example of how interpretive communities may process a political speech differently.

Interpretive Community 1: Supporters of the Speaker

Interpretation: Supporters of the political speaker view the speech as inspiring, well-articulated, and aligned with their political beliefs. They interpret the speaker's statements as strong leadership and a call to action. They might see the speech as addressing crucial issues effectively.

Interpretive Community 2: Opponents of the Speaker

Interpretation: Opponents of the same political speaker interpret the speech differently. They may view it as divisive, biased, or even manipulative. They might see the same statements as promoting policies they strongly disagree with. The speech could be seen as an attempt to rally the base but not as a genuine effort to address broader concerns.

Interpretive Community 3: Political Analysts

Interpretation: Political analysts and experts may provide a nuanced interpretation of the speech. They might focus on the rhetorical strategies used, the potential impact on public opinion, and the broader political context. Their analysis could consider both the speaker's intended message and the likely reception by different audience segments.

In this example, the exact same political speech is interpreted differently by various interpretive communities, each with its own set of beliefs, biases, and perspectives. The interpretation depends on factors such as political affiliation, prior knowledge, and personal values. This divergence demonstrates how different groups can extract varying meanings from the same event, emphasizing the role of interpretive communities in shaping understanding and perception.

4.2.5 Subjective Framing

Pragmatic processing involves an awareness by the participants not just of the deictic and linguistic variables but of their own personal presence in the discourse. Pragmatic processing is filtered through the listener's physical and emotional grounding (embodiment) and shaped by their social and moral functioning (ethical stance). These two aspects, embodiment and stance, may be termed **subjective presence**, a positioning of the listener as an active agent in understanding and creating meaning (Cox, 2016; Zwaan, 2021).

The subjective presence of the listener is often overlooked as a significant factor in communicative effectiveness, but there is converging evidence from various fields, including child development, neurolinguistics, and cognitive linguistics, supporting a more dynamic, embodied view of language comprehension (Bodie & Jones, 2021; Lipari, 2021). The embodied understanding of language refers to the idea that our comprehension and use of language closely intertwine with our bodily experiences and sensorimotor systems. This perspective suggests that language is not solely a product of abstract symbolic processing in the brain but also our physical interactions with the world, especially our emotional responses (Bodie & Wolvin, 2020; Shaules, 2019).

Moral functioning in discourse does not refer to attempts at moralizing or conversion to a particular ideology. It refers to the ethical considerations and behaviors exhibited by the participants during communication or conversation. It involves the application of moral principles, values, and ethical judgments in the context of discourse (Fetzer, 2014; Zwaan, 2014).

When individuals engage in moral functioning in discourse, they consider ethics such as honesty, fairness, respect, empathy, and justice. They make conscious choices to communicate in ways that align with their moral beliefs and values, and aim to promote ethical behavior and positive outcomes (Amossy, 2001). Moral functioning in discourse encompasses several key aspects of moral conscience, somewhat akin to Grice's Communication Maxims: in particular, truthfulness (avoiding deceit, manipulation, or intentional misrepresentation of information); respectful communication (treating others with dignity, valuing diverse perspectives, and avoiding personal attacks or demeaning language); and ethical conflict resolution (seeking common ground and fair resolutions to disagreements) (Tirrell, 2017).

Perhaps the most salient aspect of moral functioning in discourse is the activation of empathy. Subjective presence also includes the degree of the listener's motivation to empathize directly with the speaker—or indirectly with references, characters, or narratives. Empathy, broadly defined, is the ability to experience another's emotions and perceptions.

Empathy influences language comprehension because it is a dimension of understanding. The different theories on empathy, including the ones emphasizing the role of experiencing or perceiving another's emotion, regard empathy—the intent to be empathetic—as a form of understanding of the other (Zahavi, 2014). In sociolinguistics, empathy is a kind of perspective-taking (Elliott et al., 2011), consisting of perceiving or understanding another's frame of reference without losing the distinction between the self and the other (Thorne, 2007). This defining aspect of empathy can also be termed **other-orientedness,** an attempt to understand the inner world of another person (Tietsort et al., 2021).

88 *Defining Listening*

4.3 Interpreting Intent

A second component of pragmatic processing and pragmatic comprehension is interpreting intent. This refers to the listener's understanding the intention, or multiple intentions, of the speaker or speakers, as well as the emotional impact those intentions have on the listener.

Though sometimes interpreting intent is a straightforward process, interpreting what a speaker means often entails relying on ambiguous, complex, or contradictory cues. Since the early days of pragmatics research, the notions of intention and intentionality have been described under the rubric of **speaker meaning** (Grice, 1989; Mazzarella & Vaccargiu, 2024) and **speech acts** (Searle, 1989).

Early communication models focused on a four-step communication process: source, message, channel, and receiver (the SMCR model). The speaker's intention was clearly encoded in the message, and the listener had to receive it (Berlo, 1960). **Situated speech** was either succeeding or failing to decode the source accurately, that is, understanding the objective truth of the words spoken and identifying the speaker's intentions in uttering those words (Dillard & Wilson, 2014).

4.3.1 Deciphering Locutionary and Illocutionary Acts

The initial step in this process is formulating an intent on the part of the speaker and understanding the intent of the listener. Austin's speech act theory was a significant breakthrough in linguistics because it shifted the focus from analyzing language purely as a descriptive system to examining how language performs actions and accomplishes specific purposes. This perspective revolutionized the understanding of language by emphasizing the pragmatic aspects of communication, which makes language use more nuanced and dynamic.

Austin soon distinguished between **constatives** and **performatives** in speech. Constatives are the aspects of a speech act evaluated in terms of their truth value (Austin, 1962; 2013). For example, the utterance "It rained yesterday" can be evaluated as true or false based on observable evidence. Performatives can be evaluated in terms of felicity, that is, what the speech act accomplishes. For example, the utterance, "I sent you an e-mail about it yesterday," can be evaluated in terms of its felicity (offering an answer to a question), "How can I find more about that?" or as a defense against an accusation "Why didn't you tell me about the meeting?"

Austin later replaced the constative–performative distinction with a threefold contrast that is still in use today:

- **Locutions:** the act of saying something is true (e.g., "I didn't receive an e-mail from you yesterday").
- **Illocutions:** what is done (e.g., denying an accusation).
- **Perlocutions:** what happens due to saying something (e.g., the speaker makes the listener believe that the accusation is false).

Pragmatic Processing 89

These distinctions are useful in characterizing listening by showing how the listener's comprehension of an utterance and subsequent uptake and response is often *not* precisely what was intended by the speaker. Therefore, any failure in the discourse may be at *any* of these three levels and is often not due to a deficiency in linguistic competence by either the speaker or the listener.

Because much of social discourse involves a speaker expressing facts, values, and policies (representatives in speech act theory), understanding speaker intention is critical to pragmatic comprehension. The most critical inference about speaker intention occurs not in understanding the actual **claim** (statement) made by the speaker but in inferring the **grounds** (the data or evidence that supports the claim) and **warrants** (the underlying assumptions or principles that connect the grounds to the claim) that the speaker is invoking (Garnham & Oakhill, 1994).

For example, if a person makes the claim, "The city should implement a public transportation system with dedicated bus lanes," the listener needs to infer the grounds that the speaker may have used to support this statement.

Perhaps the speaker may be thinking of these grounds: traffic congestion in the city has reached unbearable levels during rush hours; studies in other cities have shown that dedicated bus lanes can significantly reduce traffic congestion; public transportation systems provide an environmentally friendly alternative to private car use.

And the speaker may be using these warrants (invoking these principles): when a city experiences severe traffic congestion (Ground 1), implementing dedicated bus lanes (Ground 2) is a practical solution because it has been proven effective in other locations. Moreover, public transportation systems offer an eco-friendly means of reducing the number of cars on the road (Ground 3), which can further alleviate congestion.

In order to understand a speaker's original claim, the listener will need to infer the grounds and the warrants for the claim, as they are rarely stated explicitly (Toulmin, 2003).

4.3.2 Conversational Maxims

As suggested by speech act theory, communication may be experienced as successful when the listener understands the illocutionary force (the intent) of the speaker. However, the communication is not fully successful unless the listener recognizes and complies with the intended action: accepting the representative as truthful, completing the directive, acknowledging the commissive, recognizing the expressive action, allowing the declaration, or endorsing the verdictive act (the six types of speech act in Austin's theory). When this illocutionary-perlocutionary cycle is satisfied, we can say that both speaker and listener have congruent communication strategies (Grice, 1975; 2013). In Grice's terms, this means that the illocutionary force (intent) of the speaker's contribution aligns with the perlocutionary effect (result) of the speaker's contribution.

90   *Defining Listening*

Table 4.4 Conversational Maxims: Observations and Violations

Maxim	Observation of the maxim	Violation of the maxim
The maxim of quantity Make your contribution to the conversation as informative as is required. Do not make your contribution more informative than is required.	**Appropriate amount of information** A. What day are you leaving for Brazil? B. Monday. **Appropriate amount of information** A. Where is the freeway entrance? B. Down Main Street, about a hundred meters past the Target store, on the right.	**Too much information** A. What day are you leaving for Brazil? B. I'm leaving on one day next week. It's not Sunday, not Tuesday, not Wednesday . . . **Not enough information** A. Where is the freeway entrance? B. Not far.
The maxim of quality Do not say what you believe to be false or misleading. Do not say something for which you have inadequate evidence.	**Providing evidence-based information** *Parent.* Do you think my son Alex has a chance of getting into Harvard? *High-school teacher (knowing that Alex does not have suitable qualifications).* Actually, I don't think he has the qualifications to get in.	**Providing misleading information** *Parent.* Do you think my son Alex has a chance of getting into Harvard? *High-school teacher A (knowing that Alex does not have suitable qualifications).* Oh, absolutely.
The maxim of relevance Make your contribution relevant to the interaction. If your contribution cannot be maximally relevant, indicate any way that it may not be relevant.	**A direct response to A's question** A. How are you doing in school? B. Not too well, actually. I'm failing two of my classes.	**Avoiding a response to A's question** A. How are you doing in school? B. Let's talk about this after the semester grades come out. **Diverting attention from A's question** A. How are you doing in school? B. My teachers this semester are terrible.
The maxim of manner Avoid obscurity and ambiguity. Be brief and orderly. Give the listener only the information that allows focus.	**Brief and orderly response to A's question** A. How are our sales doing this year? B. We're down about 10 percent from this quarter last year, but we expect to do better in the coming quarter.	**Adding obscurity and ambiguity** A. How are our sales doing this year? B. Given the complex recovery economy we're involved with on the supply side, the sales figures can be interpreted in various ways, depending on the index you use.

Within the framework of discovering and complying with speaking intention, the default communication strategy is to align with agreed-upon rules and restrictions between the speaker and listener. Grice's original conceptualization proposed that speakers create meaning with listeners on a pragmatic level through an unstated agreement to cooperate in their use of **conversational maxims** (Grice, 1969). Grice outlined four basic **cooperative principles** of conversation that aim to ensure that a conversational exchange is optimally successful for both parties.

For the purposes of keeping conversational exchanges efficient, Grice argued, these maxims are default strategies—the plans of action assumed to be in motion unless there is evidence to the contrary (see Table 4.4).

4.3.3 Contravening Social Conventions

An important aspect of pragmatic processing is the notion of contravening norms. While the observance of maxims generally leads to successful communication, speakers can also create specific modifications and nuances of meaning by flouting these maxims, that is, strategically infringing, ignoring, subverting, or opting out of a maxim for a particular effect (Bousfield, 2014; Maulida et al., 2022; Thomas, 2006; 2014). Indeed, flouting of maxims is quite common in many conversational settings, particularly those in which the speaker feels the need to render a specific emotional effect or interpretation. Flouting is referred to as irony (Colston, 2007) and works in various forms of humor, including satire (Amianna & Putranti, 2017; Porto, 2020). It usually evokes a particular emotional response in the listener or wider audience when the speaker estimates that observing usual conventions will not be as effective (Kiesling & Johnson, 2009).

Although much of the flouting of conversational maxims and norms in daily interactions is innocuous and unintentional, it is often a form of **communicative insincerity** (Okamoto, 2008) in which a speaker is consciously manipulating the listener. Systems and strategies for violating conversational norms and intentionally deceiving listeners have been examined formally as part of **information manipulation theory** (Levine, 2015) and **interpersonal deception theory** (Barr, 2014; Burgoon & Qin, 2006).

Within these theories of listener manipulation and deception, speakers may deliberately violate conversational maxims to obtain some strategic advantage (Zurloni et al., 2015):

- By flouting the maxim of quantity, the speaker may prevent an interlocutor from getting the floor and presenting information that may contradict the speaker's assertions or intentions.
- By flouting the maxim of quality, the speaker may gain the perception of authority without providing adequate evidence for assertions.
- By flouting the maxim of relevance, the speaker may derail the interlocutor's intentions.

92 *Defining Listening*

- By flouting the maxim of manner and creating ambiguity, the speaker may later exploit this ambiguity and turn it into a desired result.

Generally, a listener can detect when a speaker is flouting a maxim – manipulating or playing with language standards in some way. If the listener can calculate the intended effect, we say that the listener can derive an **implicature** (Arundale, 2013). If we can't derive an implicature to explain an apparent violation, then the effect is simply bizarreness or rogue communication. As a listener, you sense that the speaker is violating conversational maxims, but you may not be able to specify exactly what is being violated.

A. (on a train, asking a passenger to share a seat). Excuse me, do you mind if I sit here?

B. (not making eye contact) My name is Daphne, and this is my world.

Although flouting maxims may be used for deceptive or competitive purposes, flouting is often done to save face or make a situation and ongoing relationship more comfortable for the speaker or listener.

A major reason a speaker may violate or contravene a conversational maxim intentionally is to shift the interaction's power dynamics. By strategically infringing, ignoring, subverting, or opting out of a maxim, a speaker can indicate—to those in the audience able to detect the infringement—a desire to disrupt the expected flow of information or to disrupt the listener's affective state (Bousfield, 2014; Thomas, 2006).

4.3.4 Emotional Signaling

An essential aspect of pragmatic comprehension is attending to emotional signals. In addition to indicating focus and grouping of ideas, prosody can help the speaker express various nuances of emotional meaning (Hinojosa et al., 2020; Kurumada et al., 2014).

Speaker use of paralinguistic features can provide what Trager, a pioneer in the study of paralanguage, called "expressive aspects" of speech (Trager, 1961). These paralinguistic options allow for gradations of emotional tones, including warmth, attraction, repulsion, thoughtfulness, anger, interest, pride, boredom, authoritativeness, dominance, and flirtatiousness (Bao et al., 2022). Each of these affective variations involves control of articulatory settings in the vocal apparatus: pitch span, placing of voice in the voice range, tempo, loudness, timing, pausing, voice setting (breathy–creaky), articulatory setting (neutral–tense), articulatory precision (precise–slurred), and lip setting (smiling–terse). A speaker can create a range of emotional tones (e.g., excited, affectionate, angry) through combinations of these features, which can vary by dialect and individual. Because these paralinguistic markers are not conventional (there is no agreed rule system governing their use), the intentions of the speaker will often be ambiguous, except to listeners who have experience reading them (Brown, 2017; Ghosh et al., 2016; Leongómez et al., 2021).

A speaker continuously offers ostensive signals—a combination of linguistic and paralinguistic signals—from which the listener derives inferences about information, speaker perspective, and emotional coloring (Sperber & Wilson, 1986). Although there is never a guarantee that a listener will be able to infer the intentions of any speaker fully, all paralinguistic signals, including voice modulations, provide an additional layer of meaningful cues (Gobl & Chasaide, 2010; Warner et al., 2022).

In summary, seven types of information are available in this layer of paralinguistic signals (Paulmann & Uskul, 2014; Schuller & Batliner, 2013).

- **Grammatical.** Intonation can be used to mark the grammatical structure of an utterance, as punctuation does in written language.
- **Informational.** Intonation peaks indicate the salient parts of an utterance.
- **Indexical.** Intonation and speech melody are used as a social group identifier, often as a conscious or habitual strategy. For example, preachers and newscasters often use a recognizable intonation pattern; many subcultural groups are often identified through intonational and melodic features in their speech.
- **Textual.** The intonation helps large chunks of discourse contrast or cohere, rather like paragraphs in written language.
- **Attitudinal.** The intonation expresses the speaker's attitudinal meaning, such as support or skepticism.
- **Emotional.** Articulatory setting adjustments can be used to signal a range of underlying feelings, such as friendliness, excitement, and nervousness.
- **Psychological.** Intonation involving a group of items is used to chunk information into units that are easier to deal with. For example, lists of words, or telephone or credit-card numbers, are grouped into units to make them easier to hold in short-term memory.

There is no guarantee that the listener will interpret these signals in the ways that the speaker may have intended, but the signals do provide clues that special attention is required.

4.4 Response Weighting

The third aspect of pragmatic processing is **response weighting**. Response weighting refers to the listener's evaluation of the speaker's input's importance or significance before deciding how to respond. It involves first experiencing an internal emotional response to the discourse event as it is unfolding and then considering whether an overt response is necessary, how strong or detailed the

94 *Defining Listening*

response should be, and whether the intended response aligns with the goals of the conversation or discourse event.

Listeners often assess the relevance of the speaker's input to the ongoing conversation (such as questioning a teenager on why they came home late the night before) or discourse event (such as watching a movie with a friend). They consider whether the speaker's contribution merits a response or whether it can be ignored without disrupting the flow of the conversation or event. They also need to consider cultural and social norms and politeness principles—their expected level of engagement—before making an overt response (Leech, 2016).

Once a listener has decided to externalize their response, they need to decide on the response intensity, the timing, and the (assumed) alignment with the speaker's goals. Response weighting involves considering whether a response is necessary, how strong or detailed the response should be, whether the listener has the linguistic and emotional resources to formulate the response, and whether it aligns with the goals of the conversation (Obidovna, 2022).

Intensity involves formulation of response with the proper timing, shading, and level of emotional expression, often with softeners (e.g., *it was kind of* scary) or intensifiers (e.g., *it* frightened *me out of my wits*). Timing involves deciding on an immediate response or interruption as opposed to waiting for an opportune moment to voice a response. Finally, and most crucially, a listener needs to consider the overarching goals of the conversation before emitting a response. If the conversation aims to exchange information, problem-solve, or provide emotional support, the listener's response may vary accordingly.

Formulating an internal response is a crucial component of pragmatic processing in listening, regardless of whether the listener chooses to—or has the opportunity to—respond overtly. Pragmatic processing involves understanding the speaker's message, actively engaging in discourse at a personal level, and providing appropriate responses. Listeners must consider the discourse context and the speaker's intentions to generate relevant and meaningful responses.

4.4.1 Responding

In terms of transactional conversations (e.g., asking someone for a favor), pragmatic processing entails specific choices. After the speaker initiates an act in conversation, the listener has the choice of **uptaking** the initiating move, **countering** it, or **ignoring** it. Typically, the speaker intends or expects the listener to uptake the act in a specific way that is considered polite—that is, in accordance with the politeness principles of the speaker and listener's discourse community (Leech, 2016). In discourse-analysis parlance, the speaker intends to elicit a preferred response.

For example, the request from a friend, "Can I stay at your place for a few days?" is designed to elicit a *yes* or *no* response. As such, either "Yes, sure" or "No, it's not such a good time" would be preferred responses in that they comply with the structure of the request.

Pragmatic Processing 95

A: Can I stay at your apartment for a few days?

B: Um, no, sorry, not this week. We already have someone staying in the guest room.

This is different from the normal sense of a speaker *preferring a specific outcome*, such as that the other person says *yes*. Responses such as "I don't know" or "Why do you always ask me that?" are **dispreferred responses** because they do not complete the initiating act in the expected way (Bilmes, 2014). Part of pragmatic comprehension is understanding the preferred response and knowing how to soften responses when a less-than-favorable rejoinder is to be given.

In transactional conversations, in which the speaker needs the listener's response to accomplish a purpose if the listener does not provide a preferred response to the speaker's initiating move, this creates a challenge. The listener, intentionally or not, is challenging the preconditions of the speech act. The listener challenges the presupposition that the addressee has the information or resource the speaker needs and is willing to provide it, or challenges the speaker's right to make the initiating move (Baveles & Gerwin, 2011; Xiang et al., 2024). Challenges are face-threatening: they disturb the interlocutor's self-image and upset the assumed power distribution in the interaction. People in all cultures are aware of self-image, or face, as they communicate. Protecting face is important for communicating and behaving successfully with others, even though talk participants may not accomplish it consciously. A face-threatening act (FTA) would make someone possibly lose face or damage it in some way (Bilmes, 2018; Sifianou & Tzanne, 2021).

Another type of listener response is **backchanneling**, which is the process of the listener sending short messages back during the partner's speaking turn or immediately following the speaking turn. These messages may include brief verbal utterances (e.g., *Yeah, right*), brief semiverbal utterances (e.g., *uh-huh, hmm*), smiles, laughs, or chuckles (transcribed in various ways, often as *hhhhh*), and postural movements, such as nods and other head gestures to show attentiveness and adaptability (Buschmeier & Kopp, 2018).

Backchanneling, which differs in form from culture to culture and within subcultures, reveals some listener cognitive and affective states: reception of messages, consideration of multiple interpretations, readiness for subsequent messages, turn-taking permissions, projections, and empathy for the speaker's emotional states and shifts in emotion during the conversation, as well as regrading (upgrading or downgrading) the speaker's claim (Bavelas & Gerwin, 2011; Bilmes, 2018; Morett & Fraundorf, 2019).

In live conversations, backchanneling occurs more or less constantly during conversations. However, in some languages and some settings, it seems more exaggerated, more prevalent, or more intricately joined with verbal behavior. Several analysts of Japanese casual conversation, for instance, have noted regular backchanneling on average every two and a half seconds (LoCastro, 2010; Maynard, 2005). Maynard terms the interplay between speaker and listener as

96 *Defining Listening*

the "interactional dance," a key part of creating an appropriate tenor of emotivity that constitutes meaningful interpersonal conversation. When backchanneling is withheld or mistimed ("out of the flow" of the speaker's tempo), the interaction becomes perceptibly disrupted or even emotionally distressing, and the speakers will usually seek to repair or terminate the interaction (Heldner et al., 2013).

Another class of listener response in discourse is the follow-up act. Follow-up acts are responses to a discourse exchange and can be provided either by the listener or the speaker from the previous exchange. Follow-up acts can be **endorsements** (positive evaluations), **concessions** (negative evaluations), or **acknowledgments** (neutral evaluations).

In addition to uptaking in transactional discourse, listener responses in face-to-face communication can provide backchanneling, indicating the relative degree of cooperativeness, such as attention, understanding, or agreement. Effective backchanneling is considered part of pragmatic competence, and conventions vary from culture to culture and has been incorporated into AI listening applications (Buschmeier & Kopp, 2018). In North American English, backchanneling indicates not only attention and willingness to continue listening but also levels of engagement. Fluent use of a full range of backchanneling signals is a part of emotional competence that develops continuously over a lifetime (Denham, 2023).

Expectations about how listeners should respond in all of these dimensions in typical conversations are part of the cultural knowledge that needs to be acquired when one learns a language (Lantolf et al., 2020; Ushioda, 2008).

4.4.2 Providing Additive Responses

As we have outlined, a major component of pragmatic processing involves interactional effectiveness, an ability to interact with the speaker in meaningful ways that *add* to the discourse. The addition aims to enrich the communication not simply through interpretation, judgment, and response but through adding empathy, support, perspective, creativity, or positivity (i.e., expression of positive emotions: joy, delight, appreciation, gratitude, love, pride, confidence, serenity, inspiration, excitement). Pragmatic processing then involves understanding when and how to enact this type of additive response (Carmona-Halty et al., 2021; Diener et al., 2020; Sun et al., 2020b).

Communication theory currently conceptualizes speaking and listening as equal parts of a collaborative discourse process, with less clear boundaries between participants or fixed roles for them (e.g., Bodie et al., 2021; Holmes et al., 2013; Jong & Strong, 2014). In this view of a communicative transaction, the listener is potentially making distinct content contributions to the discourse, more or less continuously. Pragmatic processing then comes to include participation in this **co-constructive process**. The outcomes of a communication exchange include some level of enrichment of the original state of all interactants—in terms of knowledge, perceptions of self, attitudes toward the other, support for the amelioration of mutual concerns, and assessments of the relationship. In this collaborative view, the goal of pragmatic processing is not primarily comprehension of messages but includes **interactional effectiveness**, demonstrating an ability to establish connections with one's interlocutors and to mutually move toward relational goals. These goals are often linked to a mutual comprehension of messages in the discourse, but they will also be related to adjustments and improvements in the relationship system between the speakers.

In this light, pragmatic processing can be studied as part of a theory of action in human behavior. **Systems theory** views interactions dynamically, in that each person contributes to stated or unstated goals of the group. Each person's actions, in the form of verbal and nonverbal behavior, are reflected in the communicative states of the system (Van Kleef & Lange, 2020). The communicative states of the system—a dyad or a larger group—can be determined by examining the disclosure patterns and speaker boundaries formed during the interaction (Petronio, 2002; Waters, 2020). Systems theory introduces some refined communication concepts such as interconnectedness, system boundaries, circular causality, solution orientation, and **equifinality** and **multifinality**, but these encompass established concepts in communication theory related to co-construction and feedback (cf. Pearce et al., 1980). (See Table 4.5.)

A principal theme of systems analysis is goal orientation: participants are co-creating a solutions-oriented outcome and are engaged in positive moral functioning (see Section 4.2.5). The goal for any communicative dyad or group will vary and may shift during an interaction. For instance, one dyad in a work environment may have the goal of agreeing on an acceptable remedy for a problem, as in adding a project management tool to better coordinate communication. Another dyad in a couples therapy session may aim to achieve empathy and strengthen their emotional connection or perhaps agree to a method of resolving disputes. In both cases, a systems theory approach seeks to examine and evaluate frames of interactions to determine how they contribute to or detract from the achievement of a recognized goal.

In goal-directed communication, the participants' success or failure depends upon several factors: the understanding each has of the situation; the clarity of their goals and common ground; their perception of and sensitivity to one another's needs; their consciousness of the strategic choices they make; their ability to put their choices into action; their ability to realize multiple paths to their goals (equifinality); their ability to realize that a past action, intended to solve a particular problem, did not work and a revised action is needed (multifinality); their ability to monitor their progress toward the goals; and their ability to provide feedback about their perceived progress.

These last two factors concerning monitoring and feedback are considered so vital in effective communication that they have become the cornerstone of definitions of interactive listening in communication theory. In a range of

98 *Defining Listening*

Table 4.5 Conversational Response in Systems Theory

Co-worker A:	I'm really frustrated with our team's lack of communication.
Co-worker B:	What do you mean?
Co-worker A:	Well, it feels like everyone is working in silos, and important information gets lost, and problems get misinterpreted.
Co-worker B:	Hmm. I understand what you mean. Our team doesn't seem to have clear channels for sharing problems, discussing new issues, and coordinating our efforts.
Co-worker A:	Exactly.
Co-worker B:	Maybe we should propose implementing a project management tool to centralize communication and task assignments.
Co-worker A:	You mean, like, one of those online tools like Slack.
Co-worker B:	Yes, Slack or Basecamp, something like that. We could at least give it a try.
Co-worker A:	That's a great idea! I've seen other teams benefit from using those kinds of tools. It would at least help us ensure that everyone gets the same updates.
Co-worker B:	Yes, it might help to keep us all on the same page. That's what we're after, right?

In this conversational example, we can observe elements related to systems theory. One is interconnectedness: co-workers A and B recognize the interconnected nature of communication within their team and acknowledge their mutual concern. They express frustration with the team's lack of communication and articulate its impact on their work and outcomes. Another element is feedback and circular causality: the conversation involves feedback loops: Co-worker A shares an emotional challenge and Co-worker B responds by clarifying and confirming A's statements and offering a potential solution. This exchange of information and responses creates a feedback loop that influences the subsequent dialogue.

studies involving couple relationships, relational listening has the commitment to add to the process and outcome of the discourse in positive ways, the process of monitoring progress toward a goal through turn-by-turn monitoring of speaker intentions, and providing feedback about one's perception of that progress (Perel et al., 2018).

4.5 Summary: Pragmatic Comprehension and Pragmatic Competence

This chapter has outlined pragmatic processing as a part of semantic processing; it is a type of subjective interpretation filter, sifting out what is most personally relevant in the input. As the listener processes input, they are filtering the content pragmatically, homing in on personal and social relevance, noticing

Figure 4.3 Pragmatic Processing as Filtering

Pragmatic filtering. Pragmatic processing involves filtering the semantic content of the speaker's utterances through various personal and social filters

cues that affect situational meaning, recognizing nuances that have cultural connotations, and distinguishing shades of meaning that influence their relationship with the speaker. The filters can be conceived of as discourse framing (contextual, participatory, power, presence, community, reasoning, signaling, weighting) (See Figure 4.3).

By activating these pragmatic processing filters, the listener arrives at a pragmatic comprehension of the input that supplements semantic comprehension. Developing pragmatic comprehension involves a mindset shift toward attending to situational meaning and accepting that some ambiguity is inevitable.

Pragmatic comprehension can be seen as one aspect of pragmatic competence, which extends beyond listening. Pragmatic competence also includes **interactional effectiveness**, **symbolic aptitude**, and **metacultural proficiency** (see Figure 4.4). Interactional effectiveness refers to a willingness to communicate (WTC) in order to monitor and repair miscommunication and build positive relationships with interlocutors. It also entails a willingness and an ability to adjust one's communication styles (e.g., degree of assertiveness) in order to communicate more effectively. Symbolic aptitude involves an awareness of cultural and cross-cultural factors that influence the delivery style of messages and ways of interpreting speaker intent, an aptitude that is vital in cross-cultural encounters. Finally, metacultural proficiency refers to self-awareness, an ability to distance oneself to some degree from immediate emotional reactions in order to consider other perspectives and social and cultural factors. Pragmatic competence, and metacultural proficiency in particular, can be considered a skill that is useful in cultural adaptability, conflict resolution, facilitating intercultural communication, and promoting inclusivity of diverse perspectives.

100 *Defining Listening*

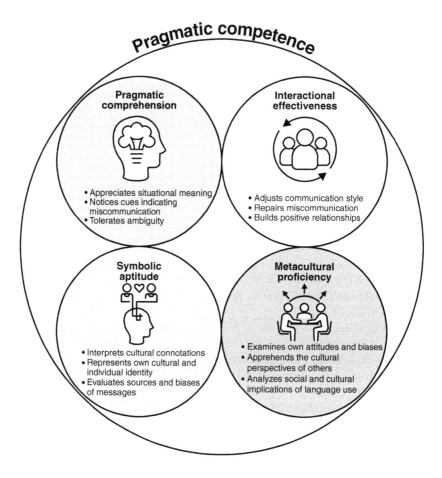

Figure 4.4 Pragmatic Competence

Pragmatic comprehension is part of pragmatic competence, which also includes interactional effectiveness, symbolic aptitude, and metacultural proficiency

References

Allwood, J., Ahlsén, E., Poggi, I., Vincze, L., & D'Errico, F. (2014). Vagueness, unspecificity, and approximation. Cognitive and lexical aspects in English, Swedish, and Italian. In S. Cantarini, W. Abraham, & E. Leiss (Eds.), *Certainty–uncertainty: And the attitudinal space in between* (pp. 265–284). John Benjamins.

Amianna, J. N. R. P., & Putranti, A. (2017). Humorous situations created by violations and floutings of conversational maxims. *Journal of Language and Literature*, *17*(1), 97–107.

Pragmatic Processing 101

Amossy, R. (2001). Ethos at the crossroads of disciplines: Rhetoric, pragmatics, sociology. *Poetics Today*, *22*(1), 1–23.

Arundale, R. (2013). Pragmatics, conversational implicature, and conversation. In K. Finch & R. Sanders (Eds.), *Handbook of language and social interaction* (pp. 41–66). Psychology Press.

Arundale, R. B. (2020). *Communicating & relating: Constituting face in everyday interacting*. Oxford University Press.

Austin, J. L. (1962). *How to do things with words*. Oxford University Press

Austin, J. L. (2013). Performative utterances. In M. Ezcurdia & R. Stainton (Eds.), *The semantics–pragmatics boundary in philosophy* (pp. 21–31). Broadview Press.

Bao, Y., Ma, Q., Wei, L., Zhou, W., & Hu, S. (2022). Speaker-guided encoder-decoder framework for emotion recognition in conversation. *arXiv preprint arXiv:2206.03173*.

Barr, D. (2014). Perspective taking and its impostors in language use: Four patterns of deception. In T. Holtgraves (Ed.), *The Oxford handbook of language and social psychology* (pp. 98–110). Oxford University Press.

Baskerville, R. L., & Myers, M. D. (2015). Design ethnography in information systems. *Information Systems Journal*, *25*(1), 23–46.

Bavelas, J., & Gerwin, J. (2011). The listener as addressee in face-to-face dialogue. *International Journal of Listening*, *25*, 178–198.

Berlo, D. (1960). *The process of communication*. Holt.

Bilmes, J. (2014). Preference and the conversational analytic endeavor. *Journal of Pragmatics*, *64*, 52–71.

Bilmes, J. (2018). Regrading as a conversational practice. *Journal of Pragmatics*, *30*, 1e12.

Biocca, F., Harms, C., & Burgoon, J. (2003). Toward a more robust theory and measure of social presence: Review and suggested criteria. *Presence: Teleoperators & Virtual Environments*, *12*(5), 456–480.

Bodie, G. D., Jones, S. M., Brinberg, M., Joyer, A. M., Solomon, D. H., & Ram, N. (2021). Discovering the fabric of supportive conversations: A typology of speaking turns and their contingencies. *Journal of Language and Social Psychology*, *40*(2), 214–237. doi: 10.1177%2F0261927X20953604

Bodie, G., & Jones, S. M. (2021). Listening fast and slow. In L. Shedletsky (Ed.), *Rationalist bias in communication theory* (pp. 172–188). Information Science Reference/IGI Global.

Bodie, G. D., & MacGeorge, E. L. (2021). Dual process and advice response theories: Explaining outcomes of supportive communication. In D. O. Braithwaite & P. Schrodt (Eds.), *Engaging theories in interpersonal communication* (pp. 89–101). Routledge.

Bodie, G. D., & Wolvin, A. D. (2020). The psychobiology of listening. In L. Aloia, A. Denes, & J. P. Crowley (Eds.), *The Oxford handbook of the physiology of interpersonal communication* (pp. 288–307). Oxford University Press.

Bonvillain, N. (2019). *Language, culture, and communication: The meaning of messages*. Rowman & Littlefield

Borchmann, S., Mortensen, S. S., & Tranekjær, L. (2020). Questioning questions in language, culture and cognition. *Scandinavian Studies in Language*, *11*(1), 1–6. doi: 10.7146/sss.v11i1.121354

102 Defining Listening

Bousfield, D. (2014). Stylistics, speech act and im/politeness theory. In M. Burke (Ed.), *The Routledge handbook of stylistics* (pp. 118–135). Routledge.

Brescoll, V. (2011). Who takes the floor and why: Gender, power, and volubility in organizations. *Administrative Science Quarterly, 56*(4), 622–664.

Brown, G. (2017). *Listening to spoken English* (2nd ed.). Routledge.

Burgoon, J. K., Berger, C. R., & Waldron, V. R. (2000). Mindfulness and interpersonal communication. *Journal of Social Issues, 56*(1), 105–127.

Burgoon, J. K., & Qin, T. (2006). The dynamic nature of deceptive verbal communication. *Journal of Language and Social Psychology, 25*, 76–96.

Buschmeier, H., & Kopp, S. (2018). Communicative listener feedback in human–agent interaction: Artificial speakers need to be attentive and adaptive. In *Proceedings of the 17th international conference on autonomous agents and multiagent systems* (pp. 1213–1221). Stockholm. https://ifaamas.org/Proceedings/aamas2018/pdfs/p1213.pdf

Carmona-Halty, M., Salanova, M., Llorens, S., & Schaufeli, W. B. (2021). Linking positive emotions and academic performance: The mediated role of academic psychological capital and academic engagement. *Current Psychology, 40*, 2938–2947.

Colston, H. (2007). On necessary conditions for verbal irony comprehension. In R. Gibbs & H. Colston (Eds.), *Irony in language and thought: A cognitive science reader* (pp. 3–21). Routledge.

Costa, P., McCrae, R., & Löckenhoff, C. (2019). Personality across the life span. *Annual Review of Psychology, 70*, 423–448.

Cox, A. (2016). *Music and embodied cognition: Listening, moving, feeling, and thinking.* Indiana University Press.

Denham, S. A. (2023). *The development of emotional competence in young children.* Guilford Publications.

Denzin, N. (2001). *Interpretive interactionism.* SAGE.

Diener, E., Thapa, S., & Tay, L. (2020). Positive emotions at work. *Annual Review of Organizational Psychology and Organizational Behavior, 7*, 451–477.

Dillard, J., & Wilson, S. (2014). Interpersonal influence. In C. Berter (Ed.), *Interpersonal communication* (pp. 155–176). De Gruyter

Elliott, R., Bohart, A. C., Watson, J. C., & Greenberg, L. S. (2011). Empathy. *Psychotherapy, 48*(1), 43.

Fairclough, N. (2023). Critical discourse analysis. In M. Handford & J. P. Gee (Eds.), *The Routledge handbook of discourse analysis* (pp. 11–22). Routledge.

Fetzer, A. (2014). I think, I mean and I believe in political discourse: Collocates, functions and distribution. *Functions of Language, 21*(1), 67–94.

Garnham, A., & Oakhill, J. (1994). *Thinking and reasoning.* Blackwell.

Ghosh, S., Laksana, E., Morency, L. P., & Scherer, S. (2016). Representation learning for speech emotion recognition. In *Interspeech* 2016 Proceedings, San Francisco (pp. 3603–3607). http://multicomp.cs.cmu.edu/wp-content/uploads/2017/09/2016_Interspeech_Ghosh_Representation.pdf

Gill, A. J., & Oberlander, J. (2002). Taking care of the linguistic features of extraversion. In *Proceedings of the Annual Meeting of the Cognitive Science Society, 24*(24).

Gobl, C., & Chasaide, A. N. (2010). Voice source variation and its communicative functions. In W. J. Hardcastle, J. Laver, & F. E. Gibbon (Eds.), *The handbook of phonetic sciences* (Vol. 50, pp. 378–423). Wiley.

Gordon, C., & Tannen, D. (2023). Framing and related concepts in interactional sociolinguistics. *Discourse Studies*, *25*(2), 237–246.

Greenwald, A. G., & Lai, C. K. (2020). Implicit social cognition. *Annual Review of Psychology*, *71*, 419–445.

Grice, P. (1969). Utterer's meaning and intentions. *Philosophical Review*, *78*, 147–177.

Grice, P. (1975). Logic and conversation. In P. Cole & J. Morgan (Eds.), *Syntax and semantics, Vol. 3, Speech acts* (pp. 41–58). Academic Press.

Grice, P. (1989). *Studies in the way of words*. Harvard University Press.

Grice, P. (2013). Logic and conversation. In M. Ezcurdia & R. Stainton (Eds.), *The semantics–pragmatics boundary in philosophy* (pp. 47–59). Broadview Press.

Gumperz, J. J. (1982). The linguistic bases of communicative competence. In D. Tannen (Ed.), *Analyzing discourse: Text and talk* (pp. 323–334). Georgetown University Press.

Gumperz, J. J. (1992). Contextualization and understanding. In A. Duranti & C. Goodwin (Eds.), *Rethinking context: Language as an interactive phenomenon*, *11*, (pp. 229–252). Cambridge University Press.

Hans, A., & Hans, E. (2015). Kinesics, haptics and proxemics: Aspects of non-verbal communication. *IOSR Journal of Humanities and Social Science (IOSR-JHSS)*, *20*(2), 47–52.

Heldner, M., Hjalmarsson, A., & Edlund, J. (2013). Backchannel relevance spaces. In E. Asu & P. Lippus (Eds.), *Nordic prosody: Proceeding of the XIth Conference* (pp. 137–146). Peter Lang.

Higgins, E. T., Herman, C. P., & Zanna, M. P. (Eds.). (2022). *Social cognition: The Ontario symposium Volume 1*. Taylor & Francis.

Hinojosa, J. A., Moreno, E. M., & Ferré, P. (2020). Affective neurolinguistics: Towards a framework for reconciling language and emotion. *Language, Cognition and Neuroscience*, *35*(7), 813–839.

Holmes, J. (2005). *Power and discourse at work: Is gender relevant?* (pp. 31–60). Palgrave Macmillan.

Holmes, J., Marsden, S., & Marra, M. (2013). Doing listenership: One aspect of socio-pragmatic competence at work. *Pragmatics and Society*, *4*, 26–53.

Hymes, D. (1964). Introduction: toward ethnographies of communication 1. *American Anthropologist*, *66*(6_PART2), 1–34.

Jäckel, E., Zerres, A., & Hüffmeier, J. (2024). Active listening in integrative negotiation. *Communication Research*. https://archive.org/details/osf-registrations-r2xh8-v1

Jong, M., & Strong, T. (2014). Co-constructing "We" and "Us": Joint talk and story-telling with cohabitating couples. *Narrative Inquiry*, *24*, 368–385.

Joseph, J. E. (2016). Historical perspectives on language and identity. In S. Preece (Ed.), *The Routledge handbook of language and identity* (pp. 19–33). Routledge.

Kayaoğlu, M. N. (2013). Impact of extroversion and introversion on language-learning behaviors. *Social Behavior and Personality: An International Journal*, *41*(5), 819–825.

Kecskes, I. (2019). The interplay of prior experience and actual situational context in intercultural first encounters. *Pragmatics & Cognition*, *26*, 112–134.

Kecskes, I. (Ed.). (2023). *Common ground in first language and intercultural interaction* (Vol. 26). Walter de Gruyter.

Kecskes, I. (2024). *The socio-cognitive approach to communication and pragmatics*. Springer.

104 *Defining Listening*

Kiesling, S. (2011). Social patterns I: Interspeaker variation. In *Linguistic Variation and Change* (pp. 53–89). Edinburgh University Press.

Kiesling, S., & Johnson, E. (2009). Four forms of interactional indirection. *Journal of Pragmatics*, *42*, 292–306.

Kramsch, C., & Zhu, H. (2016). Language and culture in ELT. In G. Hall (Ed.), *Routledge handbook in applied linguistics* (pp. 38–50). Routledge.

Kurumada, C., Brown, M., Bibyk, S., Pontillo, D., & Tanenhaus, M. (2014). Rapid adaptation in online pragmatic interpretation of contrastive prosody. In *Proceedings of the Annual Meeting of the Cognitive Science Society*, *36*(36).

Labov, W. (1972). *Language in the inner city: Studies in the Black English vernacular* (Vol. 3). University of Pennsylvania Press.

Langlotz, A., & Locher, M. (2013). The role of emotions in relational work. *Journal of Pragmatics*, *58*, 87–107.

Lantolf, J., Poehner, M., & Thorne, S. L. (2020). Sociocultural theory and L2 development. In B. VanPatten, G. Keating, & S. Wulff (Eds.), *Theories in second language acquisition* (3rd ed., pp. 223–247). Routledge.

Leech, G. N. (2016). *Principles of pragmatics*. Routledge.

Leongómez, J. D., Pisanski, K., Reby, D., Sauter, D., Lavan, N., Perlman, M., & Valentova, J. V. (2021). Voice modulation: From origin and mechanism to social impact. *Philosophical transactions of the Royal Society of London. Series B, Biological sciences*, *376*(1840), 20200386.

Levine, T. (2015). Truth-default theory (TDT): A theory of human deception and deception detection. *Journal of Language and Social Psychology*, *33*, 378–392.

Lipari, L. (2021). Listening others to speech. In *Listening, thinking, being: Towards an ethics of attunement* (pp. 175–204). Penn State University Press.

LoCastro, V. (2010). Misunderstandings: Pragmatic glitches and misfires. In D. Tatsuki & N. Houck (Eds.), *Pragmatics from research to practice: Teaching speech acts* (pp. 7–16). TESOL.

Maulida, F., Rozi, F., & Pratama, H. (2022). Creation of humorous situation by flouting conversational maxims. *English Education Journal*, *12*(1), 76–86.

Maynard, S. (2005). *Expressive Japanese: A reference guide to sharing emotion and empathy*. University of Hawaii Press.

Mazzarella, D., & Vaccargiu, E. (2024). Communication: Inferring speaker intentions or perceiving the world? Insights from developmental research. *Journal of Pragmatics*, *221*, 123–136.

McCullough, M. E., & Willoughby, B. L. (2009). Religion, self-regulation, and self-control: Associations, explanations, and implications. *Psychological Bulletin*, *135*(1), 69.

McLaren, R. M., & Solomon, D. H. (2021). Relational framing theory: Drawing inferences about relationships from interpersonal interactions. In D. O. Braithwaite & P. Schrodt (Eds.), *Engaging theories in interpersonal communication* (pp. 76–88). Routledge.

Morett, L. M., & Fraundorf, S. H. (2019). Listeners consider alternative speaker productions in discourse comprehension and memory: Evidence from beat gesture and pitch accenting. *Memory & Cognition*, *47*, 1515–1530.).

Mumby, D. K., & Stohl, C. (1991). Power and discourse in organization studies: Absence and the dialectic of control. *Discourse & Society*, *2*(3), 313–332.

Negm, M. S. (2015). Resisting power in discourse. *Procedia-Social and Behavioral Sciences*, *192*, 284–289.

Obdalova, O., Minakova, L., & Soboleva, A. (2023). The linguistic code as basis for common ground building in English as a foreign language. In I. Kecskes (Ed.), *Common ground in first language and intercultural interaction* (pp. 219–236). De Gruyter.

Obidovna, D. Z. (2022). The main concepts of politeness in modern linguopragmatics: The politeness principle by G. Leech. *International Journal of Pedagogics*, *2*(11), 15–20.

Okamoto, S. (2008). An analysis of the usage of Japanese *hiniku*: Based on the communicative insincerity theory of irony. *Journal of Pragmatics*, *39*, 1142–1169.

Paulmann, S., & Uskul, A. K. (2014). Cross-cultural emotional prosody recognition: Evidence from Chinese and British listeners. *Cognition & Emotion*, *28*(2), 230–244.

Pearce, W. B., Cronen, V. E., Johnson, K., Jones, G., & Raymond, R. (1980). The structure of communication rules and the form of conversation: An experimental simulation. *Western Journal of Communication*, 44 (1), 20–34.

Perel, E., Shani, E., Ben-Shahar, A. R., Lipkies, L., & Oster, N. (2018). Dialogue: Imagining desire. In *Speaking of Bodies* (pp. 63–71). Routledge.

Perry, J. L., & Vandenabeele, W. (2008). Behavioral dynamics: Institutions, identities and self-regulation. In J. L. Perry & A. Hondeghem (Eds.), *Motivation in public management: The call of public service* (pp. 56–79). Oxford University Press.

Petronio, S. (2002). *Boundaries of privacy: Dialectics of disclosure*. State University of New York Press.

Porto, M. D. (2020). Flouting the Gricean maxims in satire. *Arts, Humanities, and Social Science Open*, *11*(2), 58–64.

Rampton, B. (2021). Sociolinguists and rapport. In Z. Goebel (Ed.), *Reimagining rapport* (pp. 43–56). Oxford University Press.

Rizzolatti, G., Sinigaglia, C., & Andersen, F. (2023). *Mirroring brains: How we understand others from the inside*. Oxford University Press.

Rost, M. (2014). Listening in a multilingual world: The challenges of second language listening. *International Journal of Listening*, *28*, 131–148.

Schuller, B., & Batliner, A. (2013). *Computational paralinguistics: Emotion, affect and personality in speech and language processing*. John Wiley & Sons.

Schunk, D. H., & DiBenedetto, M. K. (2020). Motivation and social cognitive theory. *Contemporary Educational Psychology*, *60*, 101832.

Scupin, R. (2019). *Cultural anthropology: A global perspective* (10th ed.). SAGE.

Searle, J. (1989). How performatives work. *Linguistics and Philosophy*, *12*(5), 525–558.

Shaules, J. (2019). Deep culture learning In *Language, culture, and the embodied mind: A developmental model of linguaculture learning* (pp. 203–222). Springer.

Sifianou, M., & Tzanne, A. (2021). Face, facework and face-threatening acts. In M. Haugh, D. Z. Kádár, & M. Terkourafi (Eds.), *The Cambridge handbook of sociopragmatics* (pp. 249–271). Cambridge University Press.

Simaki, V., Paradis, C., Skeppstedt, M., Sahlgren, M., Kucher, K., & Kerren, A. (2020). Annotating speaker stance in discourse: The Brexit Blog Corpus. *Corpus Linguistics and Linguistic Theory*, *16*(2), 215–248.

Sperber, D., & Wilson, D. (1986). *Relevance: Communication and cognition*. Harvard University Press.

106 Defining Listening

Spitzley, L., Wang, X., Chen, X., Burgoon, J., Dunbar, N., & Ge, S. (2022). Linguistic measures of personality in group discussions. *Frontiers in Psychology, 13.*

Sullivan, K. (2023). Three levels of framing. *Wiley Interdisciplinary Reviews: Cognitive Science*, e1651.

Sun, J., Harris, K., & Vazire, S. (2020a). Is well-being associated with the quantity and quality of social interactions? *Journal of Personality and Social Psychology, 119*(6), 1478.

Sun, J., Schwartz, H. A., Son, Y., Kern, M. L., & Vazire, S. (2020b). The language of well-being: Tracking fluctuations in emotion experience through everyday speech. *Journal of Personality and Social Psychology, 118*(2), 364.

Swales, J. (2014). Genre and discourse community. In J. Angermuller, D. Maingueneau, & R. Wodak (Eds.), *The discourse studies reader: Main currents in theory and analysis* (pp. 305–316). John Benjamins.

Thomas, J. (2006). Cross-cultural pragmatic failure. In K. Bolton & B. Kachru (Eds.) *World Englishes: Critical concepts in linguistics* (pp. 22–48). Taylor & Francis.

Thomas, J. (2014). *Meaning in interaction: An introduction to pragmatics.* Routledge.

Thorne, B. (2007). Person-centred therapy. In W. Dryden (Ed.), *Dryden's handbook of individual therapy* (pp. 144–172). SAGE.

Tietsort, C., Hanners, K., Tracy, S. J., & Adame, E. A. (2021). Free listening: Identifying and evaluating listening barriers through empathic listening. *Communication Teacher, 35*(2), 129–134, doi: 10.1080/17404622.2020.1851734

Tirrell, L. (2017). Toxic speech: Toward an epidemiology of discursive harm. *Philosophical Topics, 45*(2), 139–162.

Tomasello, M., Melis, A.P., Tennie, C., Wyman, E., & Herrmann, E. (2012). Two key steps in the evolution of human cooperation. *Current Anthropology, 53*, 673–692.

Toulmin, S. E. (2003). *The uses of argument.* Cambridge University Press.

Trager, G. L. (1961). The typology of paralanguage. *Anthropological Linguistics, 3*(1), 17–21.

Tyler, A. (1995). The co-construction of cross-cultural miscommunication: Conflicts in perception, negotiation, and enhancement of participant role and status. *Studies in Second Language Acquisition, 17*, 129–152.

Ushioda, E. (2008). Motivation and language. In J. Verschueren, J. Östman, & E. Versluys (Eds.), *Handbook of pragmatics* (Vol. 4, pp. 1–17). Benjamins.

Van Dijk, T. A. (2023). Frame analysis. *Discourse Studies, 25*(2), 151–152.

Van Kleef, G. A., & Lange, J. (2020). How hierarchy shapes our emotional lives: Effects of power and status on emotional experience, expression, and responsiveness. *Current Opinion in Psychology, 33*, 148–153.

Verschueren, J. (2022a). Metapragmatics. In J. Verschueren & J. Östman (Eds.), *Handbook of pragmatics* (pp. 948–953). John Benjamins.

Verschueren, J. (2022b). Interactional sociolinguistics. In J. Verschueren & J. Östman (Eds.), *Handbook of pragmatics* (pp. 802–807). John Benjamins.

Warner, N., Brenner, D., Tucker, B., & Ernestus, M. (2022). Native listeners' use of information in parsing ambiguous casual speech. *Brain Sciences, 12*(7), 930.

Waters, L. (2020). Using positive psychology interventions to strengthen family happiness: A family systems approach. *The Journal of Positive Psychology, 15*(5), 645–652.

Wesselmann, E. D., Michels, C., & Slaughter, A. (2019). Understanding common and diverse forms of social exclusion. In S. C. Rudert, R. Greifeneder, & K. D. Williams (Eds.), *Current directions in ostracism, social exclusion, and rejection research* (pp. 1–17). Routledge.

Worthington, D. L., & Fitch-Hauser, M. E. (2018). *Listening: Processes, functions, and competency.* Routledge.

Xiang, M., Jia, M., & Bu, X. (2024). Presupposition. In *Introduction to pragmatics* (pp. 29–47). Springer Nature Singapore.

Zahavi, D. (2014). Empathy and other-directed intentionality. *Topoi, 33*(1), 129–142.

Zurloni, V., Diana, B., Cavalera, C., Argenton, L., Elia, M., & Mantovani, F. (2015). Deceptive behavior in doping related interviews: The case of Lance Armstrong. *Psychology of Sport and Exercise, 16,* 191–200.

Zwaan, R. A. (2014). Embodiment and language comprehension: Reframing the discussion. *Trends in Cognitive Sciences, 18*(5), 229–234.

Zwaan, R. A. (2021). Two challenges to "embodied cognition" research and how to overcome them. *Journal of Cognition, 4*(1), 14.

5 AI Processing

5.1	Introduction: AI (Artificial Intelligence) and BI (Biological Intelligence) Comparisons	108
5.2	Neurological Processing: Neural Networks	109
	5.2.1 *Linguistic Processing: Automatic Speech Recognition (ASR)*	*110*
	5.2.2 *Semantic Processing: Natural Language Understanding (NLU)*	*110*
	5.2.3 *Pragmatic Processing: Natural Language Generation (NLG)*	*111*
5.3	Goals of AI Processing	111
5.4	Neurological Processing	114
5.5	Linguistic Processing	115
5.6	Semantic Processing	118
5.7	Pragmatic Processing	124
5.8	Evolution of NLP and AI	126
5.9	Summary: Comparisons of AI and BI Language Comprehension	128
References		129

5.1 Introduction: AI (Artificial Intelligence) and BI (Biological Intelligence) Comparisons

The preceding chapters have outlined the human processes involved in listening and the capacities and operations of our human **Biological Intelligence (BI)** that allow us to understand spoken language. This chapter outlines a mirror set of processes involved in cognitive computing, or **Artificial Intelligence (AI)**, to comprehend oral language.

The goal of AI is to simulate, replicate, and augment human intelligence to varying degrees, enabling machines to perform complex tasks, such as language comprehension and translation, solving problems, and assisting or augmenting human capabilities (Fryer & Carpenter, 2006; Kratky & Hwang, 2023).

DOI: 10.4324/9781003390794-7

Because AI and its specialized realm of **natural language processing (NLP)** can perform language processing tasks similarly to those that humans use with BI, it is beneficial to explore AI systems to appreciate the parallels, relative strengths, and weaknesses of each. We can observe that there are parallel domains to those of human language processing in AI: neurological processing (neural nets, webs of interrelated data nodes), linguistic processing (language recognition), semantic processing (ontological frameworks), and pragmatic processing (response generation). A recent generation of developments in AI, incorporating advanced inferencing, backpropagation (which allows the system to learn from its mistakes), and implementation of tactical communication strategies, add even more human-like capacity to AI, under the moniker of AGI, or Artificial General Intelligence (Gawdat, 2021; Jablonka & Ginsburg, 2022; Mearian, 2023).

This chapter will examine how the four global processes in AI language understanding correspond to neurological, linguistic, semantic, and pragmatic processing in humans. The chapter will conclude with a discussion of the evolution of AI and its relative advantages and disadvantages for language comprehension.

5.2 Neurological Processing: Neural Networks

Modeled after the human brain, neural networks consist of multiple layers of interconnected artificial neurons, nodes, or learning units. Information flows from the input layer through the hidden layers to the output layer. Each artificial neuron applies an activation function in response to its inputs' weight (strength or importance). This activation enables neural networks to model complex relationships and capture intricate patterns in data. In the case of language understanding, these relationships would be lexical and syntactic relationships, and the data patterns would be ontological frameworks, such as content schemata.

As with the human brain in language processing, neural networks must draw upon multiple **memory banks** in the form of data sets. These memory banks correspond to human memory networks, such as episodic and semantic memory. In AI processing, these memory banks might consist of immense archives of recorded narrative experiences and content knowledge the program is exposed to as part of its training. (One cautionary note concerns using data banks to form these memory banks. If the data sets are biased or skewed in any direction, the subsequent reasoning processes will also be skewed and potentially dangerous, as in the case of MIT's experimental psychopath robot, named Norman after the character in Hitchcock's 1960 film *Psycho*; McCluskey, 2018.)

During the training process, an AI language processing program will develop **large language models (LLMs)**, almost incomprehensibly massive stores of digitized information. In this process, the AI processor will be exposed to a range of diverse sources, including digitized books, articles, research studies,

110 *Defining Listening*

presentations, and other publicly available audio, video, and print files from the internet. This pretraining phase allows the program to acquire grammar, facts, reasoning abilities, social context, and expressive styles. Because the training process allows the program to weight frequencies of occurrences and cross-referencing, it can adjust its internal parameters regarding what data sources are most important or reliable and what occurrences of information predict other sources of information (Jablonka & Ginsburg, 2022; Jin et al., 2022).

5.2.1 Linguistic Processing: Automatic Speech Recognition (ASR)

Parallel to the human system of auditory decoding, **automatic speech recognition (ASR)** converts spoken language in real time into written text to be coded into propositional representations. To attain a high level of reliability, an ASR program must employ large numbers of samples of spoken language across variations of the language user population, including native and non-native speakers, as well as speakers from the spectrum of gender, age, race, and regional dialect (Li, 2022). The audio signal, filtered through a microphone, is transformed into a sequence of acoustic features representing the phonological characteristics and serving as inputs to the ASR model. Microphone quality is a factor in reliable ASR programs, as sensitivity (capability of capturing quiet speech in noisy environments) and frequency response (wide frequency responses are needed to capture the full spectrum of the speech signal) are needed for ASR systems to extract these acoustic features and match them to language models to improve transcription accuracy.

Language models used in ASR depict the statistical patterns of words and grammar of the spoken language, enabling the ASR system to make accurate predictions about the most likely sequence of words (Karbasi & Kolossa, 2022). The final output of an ASR system is an accurately transcribed text representing the spoken words or sentences and coded into units used for semantic processing. State-of-the-art ASR systems, particularly those based on deep learning techniques (that is, learning from prior errors) and large-scale training data, have significantly advanced in recent years and continue to improve in their precision. These systems have achieved impressive accuracy levels (close to 100%), especially in well-defined domains, particularly when presented with clear audio recordings and with speakers who are already represented in the database. The addition of video accompanying audio can also improve transcription, particularly when multiple speakers are involved, and nonverbal cues and visual context are able to clarify ambiguous speech (Javed et al., 2022; Nagrani et al., 2022; Serdyuk et al., 2022).

5.2.2 Semantic Processing: Natural Language Understanding (NLU)

Natural language understanding (NLU) refers to the ability of AI systems to extract and extrapolate meaning from the transcriptions of text produced by ASR.

NLU includes tasks such as **sentiment analysis** (inferring speaker intentions and emotions); **named entity recognition** (classifying each real-world object in the text—person, place, thing, location, date, etc.—into a semantic hierarchy); **information extraction** (summarizing and synthesizing propositions); **text classification** (grouping texts with similar content, mutual references, and information structures); and **question answering** (providing accurate answers to information and inference questions, particularly in specified domains) (Burden & Savin-Baden, 2019; Mao et al., 2024).

NLU is also responsible for **dependency parsing**, which refers to understanding the relationship between words within an utterance and within a longer stretch of discourse, and **dialogue management**, which is keeping track of the context, intertextuality (what items in the text refer to in other texts and by extension what they refer to in the real world), and the flow of conversation between speakers.

5.2.3 Pragmatic Processing: Natural Language Generation (NLG)

Natural language generation (NLG) involves generating human-like language synthesis and output by machines. NLG can be used to create highly intelligible, coherent, and contextually relevant text as output in either spoken or written form. NLG enables natural interactions with users, maintaining the principles of polite discourse, providing casual question-and-answer tutorials across various subjects, and offering personalized recommendations for specific problem-solving scenarios.

NLG attempts to simulate human pragmatic processing by deliberating using appropriate polite phrasing and deferential language patterns (e.g., *would you mind...?*) when making requests; using honorifics, like *Mr.* or *Ms.* when addressing the user); adopting **positive solution-oriented discourse patterns**; taking into account social and cultural context; and adapting output based on feedback from the user.

5.3 Goals of AI Processing

Task automation has long been considered to be the primary goal of AI processing, that is, streamlining and automating tasks that traditionally require considerable human intelligence, time, effort, and expense. Notable progress has been made with task automation in a number of areas: face recognition, image classification, medical diagnosis, robot-driven vehicles, product fulfillment, commercial advertising, and game-playing. For tasks directly involving language understanding, progress has also been remarkable in several areas: text-to-speech generation, handwriting transcription, machine translation, digital assistants, and chatbots (like Apple's Siri or Amazon's Alexa) (Haenlein & Kaplan, 2019).

112   *Defining Listening*

The earliest efforts in AI facilitation of tasks for language processing were aimed at emulating human communication, though initially in very limited domains. One of the earliest public displays of AI language processing was the Shoebox exhibit at the 1964 World's Fair. The exhibit was created by International Business Machines Corporation (IBM) and showcased the company's latest technological advancements and innovations. The term "Artificial Intelligence" was just beginning to catch on, having been coined in 1956 by John McCarthy of Dartmouth and popularized by computer scientist Marvin Minsky, one of the founders of the MIT AI laboratory, to describe the evolution of computer science toward creating machines capable of simulating human intelligence (Minsky, 1961).

The IBM Shoebox was a small, self-contained information center, about the size of a standard shoebox, that allowed visitors to interact with computers and experience the emerging, futuristic field of computer technology. It featured a set of push-button consoles resembling oversized telephones, which visitors could use to access various informational displays.

Visitors could select different topics, such as weather forecasting, scientific calculations, or language translation, and Shoebox would present the information on a small screen. The exhibit was designed to demonstrate how computers could process data and instantaneously provide useful information in different fields.

To show off its spoken language recognition feature, the device had a display of 10 small lamp lights, labeled with the digits 0 through 9, and an attached microphone—a transparent user interface. Saying a digit into the microphone would cause the appropriate digit lamp to light. (The machine had been trained with a relatively large audio database to recognize close matches to one of these 10 candidates.) According to many accounts, the crowds of visitors typically reacted with amazement at this new domain of human–computer communication (Benko & Lányi, 2009; Buchanan, 2005).

Subsequent endeavors similar to the IBM Shoebox led to analogous constrained speech recognition applications that allowed various functions, including: voice prompts for dialing (e.g., *Call home*); call routing (e.g., *Connect me to the complaint department, please*); automated appliance control and content-based spoken audio search (e.g., *find a news article containing the words ". . ."*); simple data entry (e.g., providing a credit card number to a vendor); preparation of structured documents (e.g., a radiology report at a hospital); speech-to-text processing (e.g., having documents read aloud); and voice-to-computer instructions for complex tasks (e.g., direct voice input [DVI] used by pilots to give commands to the aircraft's avionics; Flasiński & Flasiński, 2016).

One pivotal foray into the human communication domain was Weizenbaum's (1966) simulator, which attempted to imitate basic patient–psychotherapist interactions exclusively in the form of question–answer and statement–comment exchanges. This exchange routine was achieved through a rudimentary form of transformations of grammar and insertion of standard sets of conversational gambits, as in the following interaction undertaken with the original version of ELIZA:

> Hello, my name is Eliza.
* Hello, Eliza. My name is Michael.
> Names are not necessary here.
* Well, I'm here to talk about more than just my name.
> How long have you been here to talk about more than just your name?
* Well, to change the subject, I've been wanting to try to communicate with you for a long time.
> What does that suggest to you?
* That maybe I'm a bit of a procrastinator. I should have contacted you earlier.
> Do you enjoy being a bit of a procrastinator? Why should you have contacted me earlier?
* I'm a little confused. No, I don't enjoy procrastinating.
> Why don't you enjoy it?

Weizenbaum named this software ELIZA after the George Bernard Shaw character Eliza Doolittle, who learned to emulate members of educated society. The ELIZA software operates in a defined technique of Rogerian client-centered psychotherapy, echoing back the patient's statements and querying the underlying motivation for making such statements (Rogers, 1995). This type of simulated interaction was successful in showing that *some* semblance of coherent interaction could be maintained, at least for a couple of exchanges, before lapsing into nonsense.

These early attempts at NLP-based communication were typically evaluated by the **Turing test**, a measure of a machine's ability to exhibit intelligent behavior indistinguishable from a human's. This litmus test was proposed by the British mathematician and computer scientist Alan Turing in 1950 as a way to determine whether a machine possesses true Artificial Intelligence (Gonçalves, 2023). The standard Turing test involves a human evaluator conversing via a text-based interface with both a machine and another human. The evaluator doesn't know which one is the machine and which one is the human. If the evaluator cannot consistently differentiate between the machine and the human based on their responses, the machine passes the Turing test.

Over the past decades, AI language processing efforts have undergone more rigorous development and testing and have achieved significant successes, raising the bar for passing the Turing test in all four language processing domains. The following sections will explore these four domains and their parallels to human processing.

114 *Defining Listening*

5.4 Neurological Processing

AI language processing is based on constructing neural networks, a configuration of individual artificial neurons inspired by the structure and function of biological neural networks in the human brain. An **artificial neuron** is not an actual physical structure but a mathematical function conceived as a model of biological neurons (see Figure 5.1).

A **neural network** mimics the behavior of biological neurons and processes human language in ways that parallel the brain (Rojas, 2013). Neural networks used in NLP typically consist of interconnected artificial neurons, organized in layers, that communicate in multiple layers between associated neurons to understand the input (see Figure 5.2). These networks learn from data and adjust their parameters (variable weightings that are fine-tuned continuously in response to feedback through a process of backpropagation) to perform tasks such as answering questions, including factual, opinion, and prediction questions (Hertz, 2018; Hickok et al., 2022).

The basic building block of a neural network is the artificial neuron, also known as a node or unit. Nodes receive input signals, perform computations, and produce output signals that are passed to other network nodes, mimicking the neural connections (as simplified mathematical abstractions) that operate in the human brain during language processing. The architecture of a neural network is organized before its implementation, but it can continuously adjust its internal weights through a process called **machine learning**, allowing it to manage input more efficiently (Gupta, 2013; Ng et al., 2021).

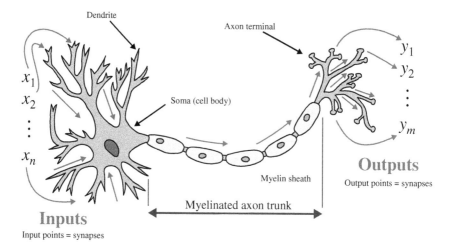

Figure 5.1 The Human Neural Network

A model of a human neural network, showing input and output points with a network of axons connecting them

AI Processing 115

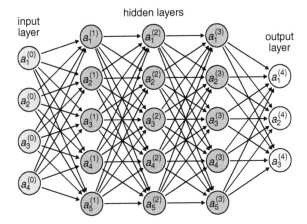

Figure 5.2 A Model of an AI Neural Network

Showing input and output points, organized in layers, with a network of mathematical functions connecting them

The structure and behavior of a node in a neural network can vary depending on the type of neural network architecture. In a basic feedforward neural network in language comprehension or translation, a **perceptron node (P)** is the simplest type used. It computes a weighted sum of its inputs and applies an activation function to produce an output. In extended text comprehension, **recurrent neural networks (RNNs)** are involved with repeatedly updating and resetting parameters.

Extended text or dialogue comprehension requires a **memory cell**, a special node that can process input when the data has time gaps or lags. RNNs can process texts by keeping in mind 10 context words (5 preceding and 5 following each target word).

Structurally, **long short-term memory units (LSTM)** are more complex than simple perceptron nodes. LSTM nodes have internal memory cells that allow the network to retain and process sequential information over time. They have specialized gates that control the flow of information, enabling better modeling of sequential dependencies (see Figure 5.3).

5.5 Linguistic Processing

In NLP, input to the system, in the form of spoken text, triggers the activation of a neural network for language decoding. The network processes this input through layers of interconnected neurons, where each layer progressively extracts higher-level features and representations from the input data, much like human processing starts with the lowest layer of input (phonemes) and produces

116 *Defining Listening*

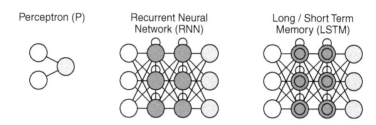

Figure 5.3 Three Types of Neural Networks Used in NLP

Perceptrons are the basic building blocks of artificial neural networks (ANNs). They are simple algorithms that simulate the functioning of a single neuron. RNNs are a type of artificial neural network that allows information to be stored and processed sequentially. LSTM introduces memory cells that can store and retrieve information for longer durations

higher layers (words and propositions). The final layer of the network produces the desired output, which could be a sequence of words in response to a question (Tran et al., 2022). (See Figure 5.4.)

As with human listening, the first stage of AI listening involves detecting and decoding the speech signal. Since BI and AI listening start with the same input signal, sound waves, AI processing begins with automatic speech recognition (ASR). The first step in the process is called digital signal processing (DSP), which converts sound waves into electrical signals that a computer can process. The process of converting sound waves into electrical signals involves several steps:

1. **Capturing sound:** The first step is to capture sound waves using a microphone. The microphone converts the sound waves into an analog electrical signal.
2. **Converting analog to digital (ADC):** The analog electrical signal is converted into a digital signal using an analog-to-digital converter (ADC). The ADC samples the analog signal at regular time-partitioned intervals and converts each sample into a digital value.
3. **Sampling:** The next step in DSP is to sample the signal obtained at regular intervals, typically at a rate of 16 kHz or 44.1 kHz. The resulting digital signal is a sequence of discrete samples that a computer can process.
4. **Pre-processing:** The digital signal is then pre-processed to remove any noise or interference that may be present. This step involves filtering and amplifying the signal to enhance its quality.
5. **Extracting features:** In this step, the pre-processed signal is analyzed to extract relevant features that can be used for speech recognition. The most common features used in ASR systems are Mel-Frequency Cepstral

AI Processing 117

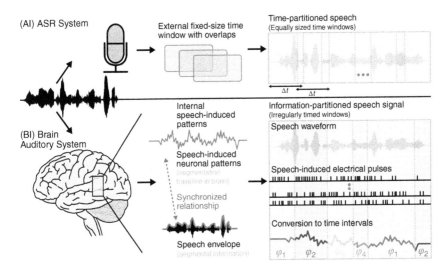

Figure 5.4 A Comparison of BI (Human) Auditory System and an ASR (Computer) Auditory System

Both systems are initiated by sound waves. The ASR system uses an overlapping sampling process and partitions the input into equal-timed slots to recognize words

Coefficients (MFCCs), which represent the **spectral envelope** of the speech signal (described in Chapter 2). Other features include linear predictive coding (LPC) coefficients, spectral features, and **prosodic features**.
6. **Language modeling:** The output of the acoustic model is a sequence of phonemes, which a language model then uses to generate the final output. The language model uses statistical techniques, drawing upon its training data, to predict the most likely sequence of words.

The speed and efficiency of processing input have steadily improved to allow the ASR system to detect speech at rates up to 300 wpm with multiple speakers. The capability of an ASR system to handle speech at high speeds depends on several factors, including the specific ASR technology, model architecture, and the quality of the audio input.

ASR systems have limitations in accurately decoding speech at extremely high speeds, primarily due to the constraints of the underlying models and the sampling rate of the audio. When speech is delivered rapidly, it can result in reduced clarity, overlapping words, or skipped sounds, which makes it challenging for the ASR system to accurately transcribe the speech.

The acceptable speech rate can vary depending on the system's design and the complexity of the speech content. Generally, ASR systems work effectively with

118　*Defining Listening*

natural and moderate rates of speech that align with typical conversational or presentation speeds. These systems are trained on a wide range of speech patterns and can handle variations in tempo and rhythm to a certain extent (Sainath et al., 2023). As with human decoding, however, if speech is delivered too rapidly, the transcription (decoding) accuracy will decrease proportionately. When the signal compresses too far, the ASR system struggles to distinguish individual words and detect overlaps from multiple speakers (Sainath et al., 2023).

Once speech is recognized phonologically, it undergoes the processes of word recognition and syntactic parsing. To achieve word recognition, algorithms break down a given input text into smaller units called **tokens**: sentences, words, subwords (derivations of the **lemma** or **base form** of the word, such as *happiness* for the base form *happy*), syllables, and phonemes. This algorithmic analysis helps prepare the input for further analysis or processing (Gantar et al., 2019).

A parallel word-recognition step applies **named entity recognition (NER)** algorithms. This step speeds up processing by identifying and classifying named entities in the text, such as person or organization names, locations, dates, and other specific entities previously mentioned. This step parallels the human processing of recognizing given information (Liu et al., 2019).

Following the identification of tokens, each word will undergo a syntactic analysis for **part-of-speech (POS) tagging**, similar to the initial pass of human grammatical parsing. POS-tagging algorithms assign grammatical tags to each word in a sentence, indicating its part of speech (noun, pronoun, determiner, verb, adjective, adverbs, preposition, conjunction, interjection, or unclassified).

Syntactic processing algorithms utilize statistical models of collocations based on vast amounts of input in their databases. Collocations typically are calculated by plus or minus five words: the target word, plus five preceding words (to the left) and five subsequent words (to the right).

Algorithms will also utilize rule-based approaches to determine the appropriate tags, for example, that a determiner is always followed by a noun or that an adverbial expression links to a verbal expression. The output of linguistic processing produces grammatically tagged and lexically tagged sentences that can be used for further meaning processing (Liang et al., 2024;; Norvig, 2009).

5.6 Semantic Processing

While the role of linguistic processing is to recognize and transcribe as accurately as possible what was said, the main goal of semantic processing in AI is more complex. Semantic processing aims to convert incoming speech into idea units that will serve as the basis for a decision, an action, or a response (Shi et al., 2021). Semantic processing involves a formal, explicit representation of concepts and their interrelationships, called an **ontology** (see Figure 5.5). Ontologies allow the application to use hierarchical reasoning to conduct searches and respond to the user reasonably (Reyes-Pena & Tovar-Vidal, 2019).

AI Processing 119

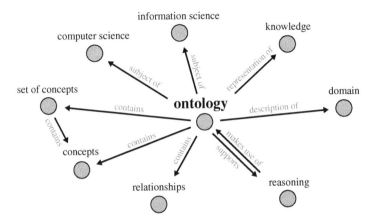

Figure 5.5 An Ontology Used in AI

In computer science and information science, an ontology represents knowledge as a set of concepts within a domain, and the relationships between pairs of concepts. It can be used to model a domain and support reasoning about concepts

Of the four domains of human language processing—neural, linguistic, semantic, and pragmatic —it is widely recognized that AI has the most challenges with semantic processing (just as humans do!). In particular, there are certain types of questions or tasks that neural networks struggle with or that require additional considerations:

- **Abstract reasoning and common sense:** Neural networks often struggle with abstract reasoning and understanding commonsense knowledge, making it challenging for them to answer questions that include rare or unseen examples (Acharya et al., 2021). Typically, in response to a rare commonsense question that has never encountered before, like "Can a giraffe fit into a refrigerator?", AI might answer with all of the possibilities (e.g., A baby giraffe could fit into a large commercial refrigeration unit if its legs were folded properly) rather than provide the most obvious and practical answer, "No" (Davis, 2023; Bisk et al., 2020).
- **Ethical and moral judgments:** Neural networks lack inherent ethical or moral understanding. Making ethical decisions or judgments, by definition, requires human values and contextual understanding (Gibney, 2020; Sullivan & Wamba, 2022). For example, if you ask most AI entities a question like, "Is it morally acceptable to lie to someone to protect their feelings?" you will get a framework response such as "The moral acceptability of lying to protect someone's feelings is a topic that engenders diverse perspectives and ethical frameworks. Different individuals may offer varying perspectives on this matter (Birhane et al., 2022). You may decide based on the Deontological

120 *Defining Listening*

Perspective or … ." Alternatively, a network may be trained on nationalistic or dogmatic data and provide a singularly biased view for every response. The point is that there can be no spontaneous spiritual intelligence (SI) in an AI system that attempts to provide moral or ethical insight into an issue (Frunza, 2023; Hagendorff & Danks, 2023; Tan, 2020).

- **Contextual ambiguity:** Neural networks can struggle with questions that involve ambiguous or unstructured information. Resolving ambiguity and understanding context can be challenging for AI systems (Naseem et al., 2020). For example, you may ask a personal chatbot an ambiguous question: "Can you book a table at that new restaurant that my mother really likes?" The AI entity will find this confusing and you will likely get a broad response initially, such as a list of all local restaurants (Amna & Poels, 2022). Or, with more intelligent bots, which can use backpropagation to learn from previous interactions, you will get some follow-up questions (with clever pragmatic padding), such as, "I can't remember what restaurant she really likes. Can you remind me?" (Birhane, 2021; 2022).
- **Handling contradictory or biased data:** Neural networks can inadvertently learn biases in the training data. The networks may then reproduce or amplify those biases in their responses (Kunkel et al., 2019). For example, a neural network on an entertainment review site is trained on a data set of movie reviews to predict whether a review is basically positive or negative. However, by chance, the data set may contain a bias where most positive movie reviews are associated with male protagonists, while negative movie reviews are associated with female protagonists. The neural network learns this bias during training and becomes biased itself (Gupta et al., 2021; Lee et al., 2022).
- **Creative or open-ended tasks:** Neural networks can generate content based on training data, but generating truly creative or novel content that goes beyond the patterns in the data is still a significant challenge for AI systems.

One area where AI excels is responding to questions in a specific domain. AI systems are programmed to answer questions by using **graph neural networks (GNNs),** which represent knowledge in a tree-like fashion (Kumar et al., 2022).

GNNs recognize a question and proceed through a series of analysis, extraction, and synthesis steps:

- *Question analysis.* A question in natural language is analyzed into forms used by subsequent parts of the system.
- *Document selection.* A subset of files likely to contain the answers is selected from the database. The subset is typically several orders of magnitude smaller than the entire collection.

AI Processing 121

- *Document analysis.* A detailed analysis of the candidate files may be needed if the pre-processing was superficial. Clarification questions may be needed to narrow the search.
- *Answer extraction.* Answers are extracted from the files and ranked according to the probability of their being appropriate.
- *Response generation.* The system returns a response if required, in a dialogue context.

Early question–answer systems, such as the *Genial Understanding System* (GUS) (Bobrow et al., 1977; Ovchinnikova, 2012), were based on the computer asking the questions to define the domain it was qualified to analyze. Here is a sample interaction that demonstrates the integration of these steps:

GUS:	Hello, my name is GUS. I can help you plan your trip. Where would you like to go?
Customer:	I'd like to go to Honolulu on May 28th.
GUS:	Honolulu. When would you like to go?
Customer:	May 28th.
GUS:	When would you like to leave?
Customer:	It doesn't matter, but morning would be preferable.
GUS:	There is a PSA flight that departs LAX at 9:15 a.m. Is that flight suitable?
Customer:	When is the next flight?
GUS:	There is a United flight at 11:30 a.m.
Customer:	I'll take the earlier one.
GUS:	I will book you on PSA flight 122. It departs from LAX on May 28th at 9:15 a.m. Is that acceptable?

GUS succeeded at semantically processing this relatively simple request by using semantic role labeling (destination, time) and relationships between entities (city names, directional relationships, temporal relationships). GUS was also able to understand context-sensitive paraphrases of the responses to its questions.

A more complex level of semantic processing involves **information extraction (IE)** in more open discourse domains. Information extraction is a subfield of semantic processing in NLP that is concerned with identifying predefined types of information from text. For example, an information extraction system designed for a police department might extract the names of crimes, perpetrators, victims, physical targets, weapons, dates, and attempted-crime locations. An information extraction system designed for a business domain might extract the names of companies, products, facilities, and financial figures associated with business activities (Dalal et al., 2021).

122 *Defining Listening*

Any ontology used in AI typically consists of several components. Here's an example of an ontology used in AI for a chatbot that offers relationship advice (Prochaska et al., 2021).

- **Classes or concepts:** These are the categories or types of entities that the ontology deals with. Classes can be organized in a hierarchy, with more general classes at the top and more specific classes at the bottom. Some possible classes in the ontology could include *relationship issues, communication problems, trust issues, infidelity, incompatibility,* and *conflict resolution.*
- **Properties or attributes:** These are the characteristics or features that describe the entities in the ontology. Properties can represent intrinsic attributes (such as size, color, or weight) and relational attributes (such as location, ownership, or part of). Some possible properties in the ontology could include *symptoms, causes, effects, solutions, prioritization,* and *commitment level.*
- **Instances or individuals:** These are the specific examples of entities belonging to the ontology's classes. Each instance has values for the properties that describe it. Some possible instances in the ontology could include *lack of affection, dishonesty, jealousy, disagreements about money, different goals in life,* and *difficulty resolving conflicts.*
- **Relations or links:** These are the connections between instances that represent the relationships between them. Relations can model various associations between entities, such as causal, temporal, or spatial relationships. Some possible relations in the ontology could include *leads to, results from, can be resolved by, has a high priority, requires compromise,* and *indicates a low commitment level.*
- **Axioms or constraints:** These are the rules or statements defining the relationships between classes, properties, and instances in the ontology. Axioms can enforce consistency and ensure that the ontology is logically sound. Some possible axioms in the ontology could include *solutions tailored to the specific issues and individuals involved, the severity of the issue should be taken into consideration when prioritizing solutions,* and *open communication is essential for resolving relationship issues.*
- **Annotations or metadata:** These are the additional pieces of information or notes that are associated with the classes, properties, instances, or relations in the ontology. Annotations can provide contextual information, such as definitions, synonyms, or examples. Some possible annotations in the ontology could include *jealousy can be a symptom of underlying trust issues, lack of affection can lead to feelings of neglect and resentment,* and *compromise is necessary for resolving conflicts and maintaining a healthy relationship.*

Together, these components form a structured representation of the domain knowledge the AI system needs in order to reason about and make decisions in a specific application context. Table 5.1 shows a chatbot application involving relationship issues.

AI Processing 123

Table 5.1 Sample Interaction with Chatbot, Woebot, Specializing in Relationship Advice [Annotations from author illustrate the ontologies being employed]

User:	Hi, I'm having some troubles with my girlfriend. Can you help?
Chatbot:	[having identified the class as "relationship issues," asking about "properties"]: Of course! I'll do my best to assist you. What seems to be the issue?
User:	Lately, we've been arguing a lot over small things. It feels like we can't communicate properly without it escalating. Any advice on how to improve our communication?
Chatbot:	[dispensing axioms based on properties: arguing, can't communicate, escalating]: Communication is vital in any relationship. To enhance it, it's important to create a safe and open environment for both of you. Start by finding a calm moment to express your concerns and actively listen to each other without judgment. Use "I" statements to express how you feel, which can prevent the conversation from becoming accusatory. It's also helpful to establish regular check-ins to discuss any arising issues before they escalate. [inserting query about "relations"] Have you tried setting aside dedicated time for open dialogue?
User:	We haven't really set aside specific time for that, but it sounds like a good idea. I'll talk to her about it. What about resolving conflicts? Any tips on that?
Chatbot:	[providing axioms for "relations" question] Resolving conflicts requires patience and understanding. When conflicts arise, aim for a collaborative approach rather than a confrontational one. Seek a compromise or solution that considers both perspectives. Practice empathy by trying to understand her viewpoint, and encourage her to understand yours as well. Remember, it's okay to take breaks during heated arguments to cool down and regain composure. Open and honest communication during conflict resolution is key. [inserting query about "instances"] Have you both been actively trying to find common ground during disagreements?
User:	We've been struggling with that. We often get caught up in our own positions and forget to consider each other's viewpoints. Taking breaks sounds like a good idea. I'll suggest that to her. One more thing, how can we keep the spark alive in our relationship?
Chatbot:	[responding to request for "properties," inserting axioms] Keeping the spark alive requires effort from both partners. Find activities you both enjoy and make time for them. Surprise each other with small gestures or dates to keep the romance alive. Remember to express appreciation and compliments regularly. Additionally, open up conversations about your desires, fantasies, and expectations. This can help maintain intimacy and ensure both of you feel fulfilled. [querying additional "classes"] Have you discussed your individual needs and desires with your girlfriend?
User:	We used to, but not recently. I think having those conversations again will definitely help. Thanks for the advice!
Chatbot:	[adding annotations and metadata] You're welcome! I'm glad I could assist you. Remember, relationships require continuous effort, understanding, and effective communication. If you need further guidance, don't hesitate to reach out. Wishing you the best of luck in resolving your difficulties with your girlfriend!

124 *Defining Listening*

5.7 Pragmatic Processing

The goal of pragmatic processing in NLP is to derive knowledge from external commonsense information, integrate that knowledge with knowledge gained from semantic processing, and develop a suitable response. One widely respected roadmap document for NLP research has identified five pragmatic standards that users may expect from an NLP system (Jacquet et al., 2019):

- *Timeliness.* The system should be able to respond to the input or user in real time, even when accessed by thousands of users, and the data sources should be kept up to date.
- *Accuracy.* Imprecise, incorrect responses are worse than no answers. The system should also discover and resolve contradictions in the data sources.
- *Usability.* The system knowledge should be tailored to the user's needs.
- *Completeness.* Responses that come from multiple databases should be fused coherently.
- *Relevance.* The answer should be relevant within a specific context. The evaluation of the system must be user-centered.

An example would be in a question-answering (QA) system, in which the user asks questions about world history. To meet the criteria above, the NLP application should aim to identify the user's question accurately and then provide a response that is (1) given promptly, consistent with the user's communicative rhythm; (2) accurate; (3) at the user's level of knowledge; (4) complete, and if using multiple sources of information, prioritized and coherent; and (5) relevant and contextualized for the user.

Using **aggregate search models**, researchers have identified four user levels based on the patterns of questions asked. Casual questioners seek surface information, and information sources used for the responses need not be deep, that is, they need not consult and compare multiple data files (Achsas, 2022). For the more discerning questioner, more sources must be compiled and synthesized to satisfy the user's more rigorous criteria.

Because user relevance is a primary goal of NLP, pragmatic processing involves interpreting the input in terms of its social or action-oriented value— knowing how to respond to the user. **Response processing**, considered part of pragmatic processing, is based on a correct calculation by the computer of the speaker's intentions and latent (unexpressed) emotions in discourse processing (Shah et al., 2019; Zaib et al., 2022). Science fiction fans will recall the famous human–computer interaction in Kubrick and Clarke's prophetic film *2001: A Space Odyssey*:

Dave Bowman	
(mission commander):	Hello, HAL. Do you read me, HAL?
HAL	
(Heuristically programmed	
ALgorithmic computer):	Affirmative, Dave. I read you.
Dave Bowman:	Open the pod bay doors, HAL.
HAL:	I'm sorry, Dave. I'm afraid I can't do that.
Dave Bowman:	What's the problem?
HAL:	I think you know what the problem is just as well as I do.
Dave Bowman:	What are you talking about, HAL?
HAL:	This mission is too important for me to allow you to jeopardize it.
Dave Bowman:	I don't know what you're talking about, HAL.
HAL:	I know that you and Frank were planning to disconnect me, and I'm afraid that's something I cannot allow to happen.

In this interaction, HAL understands Dave's intention to terminate it. It invokes its programmed intention to complete the mission successfully, even without Dave. (HAL's famous refrain in the film is: "I am putting myself to the fullest possible use, which is all I think that any conscious entity can ever hope to do.")

Response processing aims to select the most appropriate response (sometime empathic or euphemistic) from the trained database that matches the speaker's intention and sentiment (Lee et al., 2022). Based on the speaker's social, emotional, and thinking style as well as on the content, the response algorithm then generates an output, either through speech or writing or another symbolic (e.g., graphic) system, and anticipates a next likely discourse move from the human. All response systems are domain-specific.

For instance, if an interactive system is for helping museum visitors, it may be trained to anticipate prototypical questions such as "Where is (the dinosaur exhibit)?" and "What is the most popular (exhibit) in (the museum)?" It would provide preset responses once the input had been recognized pragmatically as a request for (location) of (specific item). Effective semantic analysis assigns a proposition to an appropriate content schema, in which the computer can fill vacant slots in the schema—not provided in the input. An appropriate response effectively predicts what information the user requires and provides it in a usable form.

Unlike the autonomous HAL, most modern chatbots are subservient to human users, generally serving information needs. Chatbots have currently progressed to the point of being designated as personal assistants, offering not only useful information and advice but also human-like companionship (Caldarini et al., 2022; Maedche et al., 2019). Among the most widely used are:

126 *Defining Listening*

- **Amazon Alexa:** Amazon Alexa is a voice-activated virtual assistant that uses natural language processing and machine learning to respond to user requests. It can answer questions, play music, control smart home devices, and perform various other tasks.
- **Apple Siri:** Apple Siri is another popular voice-activated virtual assistant that uses natural language processing and machine learning to understand and respond to user requests. It can perform a variety of tasks, including making calls, sending messages, and setting reminders.
- **Rasa:** Rasa is an open-source framework for building chatbots and dialogue systems. It uses natural language understanding and machine learning to interpret user messages and generate appropriate responses. It also provides tools for dialogue management and integrates with popular messaging platforms.
- **Mitsuku:** Mitsuku is a chatbot that has won several awards for its natural language processing and conversational abilities. It uses pattern matching, rule-based techniques, and machine learning to simulate conversation and has been trained on many topics.
- **Xiaoice:** Xiaoice is another popular chatbot, developed in China, with over 750 million registered users. It uses natural language processing and machine learning to generate human-like responses and has been employed on a variety of social media platforms.

Chatbots and robots with chatbot capacities are constantly evolving, with regular breakthroughs and innovations taking place as regards their multimodal capabilities and contextual awareness. Increasingly, AI processing is employing AGI with its broad range of cognitive capabilities, including reasoning, problem-solving, learning, perception, and understanding even cryptic natural language.

AGI goes beyond specialized AI systems designed for specific tasks or domains, such as image recognition or natural language processing. While current AI technologies excel in narrow domains, achieving AGI remains an ongoing challenge in AI research and development. Eventually, AGI systems will be able to perform increasingly complex tasks, learn from experience, and adapt to different contexts, exhibiting a level of general intelligence similar to humans. As with human reasoning, AGI responses generate answers based on the best available knowledge and use elaborative reasoning to make up answers where they may have incomplete knowledge (Distelmeyer, 2022; Gawdat, 2021).

5.8 Evolution of NLP and AI

Technological advances in AI generally, and in NLP in particular, continue in the four aspects of language processing outlined in this chapter. Unlike the evolution of human BI, which has been a gradual process occurring over millions of years, the development of AI has proceeded at a breakneck speed since its incipient days in the MIT laboratories (Foster, 2022; Gawdat, 2021).

The benefits to language understanding and comprehension have been enormous: AI-powered language processing systems can analyze and understand human language with remarkable accuracy. They can comprehend text or speech's meaning, context, and nuances, facilitating tasks such as information extraction, question analysis, translation, summarization, interactive language tutoring, and chatbot information retrieval (Ahuja et al., 2023).

NLP is likely to play a significant role in all of these areas and is poised to expand its reach by integrating algorithmic advancements such as quantum computing into neural networks (Sajjad et al., 2022). At some point, AI is likely to evolve into EI, evolutionary intelligence, with evolutionary algorithms, a family of optimization and search techniques inspired by the principles of natural evolution. EI could potentially develop techniques to create adaptive and self-improving systems that have not yet been imagined (Gawdat, 2021).

It is expected that neural networks will evolve more efficient processing in NLP in a range of areas: language translation, sentiment analysis (determining the sentiment or emotional tone expressed in a piece of text), inferring speaker intentions (the goals behind their communication, which involves understanding the background of the speaker), named entity recognition (NER) (accumulating background information about an identified entity, including persons), hierarchical representations of heard texts, and maps of interdependencies between text items (Wu et al., 2022).

While quantum computing may introduce new possibilities and computational advantages in specific aspects of NLP, neural networks are expected to remain a vital component of NLP systems, providing powerful tools for learning representations, modeling sequential information, and achieving state-of-the-art performance in various NLP tasks (Aramaki et al., 2022). Here are a few possibilities:

- **Improved language modeling:** Quantum computing may enable more advanced language models that can capture complex linguistic relationships, semantic understanding, and context at a higher level of accuracy. This could lead to more natural and coherent text generation, better machine translation, and improved language comprehension capabilities.
- **Enhanced information retrieval:** Quantum algorithms and data-processing techniques could potentially improve the performance of information-retrieval tasks in NLP. This would include more efficient document searches and advanced techniques for text summarization and recommendation systems.
- **More nuanced language understanding and translation:** Quantum computing's potential advancements may lead to language-understanding and -translation breakthroughs. Improved algorithms and computational capabilities could enable more accurate and contextually nuanced translations, better handling of idiomatic expressions, and enhanced sentiment analysis.

128   *Defining Listening*

- **Simulating linguistic phenomena:** Quantum simulations might provide insights into modeling linguistic phenomena and reconstructing lost dialects and languages that are challenging for classical approaches. Quantum simulation techniques could help unravel complex language structures and semantic relationships and shed light on the cognitive aspects of language processing, particularly inferencing.

5.9 Summary: Comparisons of AI and BI Language Comprehension

This chapter has summarized the processes of AI language processing, comparing these processes with the human domains of neurolinguistic, linguistic, semantic, and pragmatic processing. From this description, it is clear that there are both advantages and disadvantages of AI processing over human or BI processing.

Advantages of AI Language Comprehension:

- **Processing Speed:** AI language comprehension obviously can process and analyze large volumes of text or speech data at a much faster speed than humans. AI systems can perform complex linguistic tasks and extract information from vast amounts of text in very short periods.
- **Scalability:** AI systems can be scaled up to handle a wide range of languages, language varieties, content domains, and data sets. Essentially, there is no limit to how much an AI system can learn during its training phase and subsequent interaction with humans. AI can learn from extensive training data and adapt to different linguistic contexts more efficiently than humans.
- **Consistency:** AI language models can provide consistent interpretations and responses, eliminating inconsistencies that can arise due to human subjectivity, biases, fatigue, or variations in individual language-processing abilities.
- **Memory and Recall:** AI systems have the ability to store and retrieve vast amounts of information with high precision. AI can remember and recall details from large corpora of text or speech, ensuring accurate information retrieval.

Disadvantages of AI Language Comprehension:

- **Contextual Understanding:** AI semantic processing can struggle with understanding context, especially when dealing with ambiguous or nuanced language usage. AI systems often lack the commonsense knowledge and real-world experience that humans possess, leading to misinterpretations or incorrect responses.
- **Pragmatic Understanding:** AI models often struggle to grasp the full range of pragmatic cues, such as sarcasm, irony, humor, or implied meanings, which rely heavily on cultural and contextual knowledge.

- **Emotional Intelligence:** AI language comprehension lacks emotional intelligence and empathy, which are crucial to accurately perceiving and responding to humans in the fullest sense. Human language comprehension is deeply intertwined with emotions and can account for the valuable affective aspects of communication.
- **Ethical Considerations:** AI language comprehension raises ethical concerns related to privacy, bias, and misinformation. Without proper safeguards and oversight, AI systems can perpetuate biases present in the training data, compromise user privacy, or spread false information if not properly validated and controlled.

For the purposes of this book on *Teaching and Researching Listening*, this chapter has been included so as to broaden the teacher's and researcher's perspective on listening processes. It provides insight into the similarities and differences between AI and BI listening so that the listening teacher and researcher can have a better grasp of the underlying processes of both forms of understanding spoken language.

By becoming aware of the power and the limitations of AI, listening teachers can adapt their teaching repertoire and style to incorporate the best elements of AI while guiding learners with their own human resources.

References

Acharya, A., Talamadupula, K., & Finlayson, M. A. (2021). An atlas of cultural commonsense for machine reasoning. *AAAI Conference on Artificial Intelligence* (Vol. 35, No. 4, pp. 2820–2828). AAAI. https://arxiv.org/pdf/2009.05664.pdf

Achsas, S. (2022). Academic aggregated search approach based on BERT language model. In *2022 2nd International Conference on Innovative Research in Applied Science, Engineering and Technology (IRASET)* (pp. 1–9). IEEE.

Ahuja, K., Diddee, H., Hada, R., Ochieng, M., Ramesh, K., Jain, P., Namby, A., Ganu, T., Segal, S., Axmed, M., Bali, K., & Sitaram, S. (2023). Mega: Multilingual evaluation of generative ai. arXiv preprint arXiv:2303.12528.

Amna, A. R., & Poels, G. (2022). Ambiguity in user stories: A systematic literature review. *Information and Software Technology, 145*, 106824.

Aramaki, E., Wakamiya, S., Yada, S., & Nakamura, Y. (2022). Natural language processing: from bedside to everywhere. *Yearbook of Medical Informatics, 31*(1), 243–253.

Benko, A., & Lányi, C. S. (2009). History of artificial intelligence. In M. Khosrow-Pour (Ed.), *Encyclopedia of information science and technology* (2nd ed., pp. 1759–1762). IGI Global.

Birhane, A. (2021). The impossibility of automating ambiguity. *Artificial Life, 27*(1), 44–61.

Birhane, A. (2022). *Automating ambiguity: Challenges and pitfalls of artificial intelligence.* (Doctoral thesis, University College Dublin.)

Birhane, A., Ruane, E., Laurent, T., Brown, M. S., Flowers, J., Ventresque, A., & Dancy, C. L. (2022, June). The forgotten margins of AI ethics. In *Proceedings of the 2022*

130 *Defining Listening*

ACM Conference on Fairness, Accountability, and Transparency (FAccT '22), June 21–24, 2022, Seoul, Republic of Korea (pp. 948–958). ACM.

Bisk, Y., Zellers, R., Gao, J., & Choi, Y. (2020, April). Piqa: Reasoning about physical commonsense in natural language. In *Proceedings of the AAAI conference on artificial intelligence* (Vol. 34, No. 5, pp. 7432–7439). Association for the Advancement of Artificial Intelligence.

Bobrow, D. G., Kaplan, R. M., Kay, M., Norman, D. A., Thompson, H., & Winograd, T. (1977). GUS, a frame-driven dialog system. *Artificial intelligence, 8*(2), 155–173.

Buchanan, B. G. (2005). A (very) brief history of artificial intelligence. *AI Magazine, 26*(4), 53–53.

Burden, D., & Savin-Baden, M. (2019). *Virtual humans: Today and tomorrow.* CRC Press.

Caldarini, G., Jaf, S., & McGarry, K. (2022). A literature survey of recent advances in chatbots. *Information, 13*(1), 41.

Dalal, D., Arcan, M., & Buitelaar, P. (2021, June). Enhancing multiple-choice question answering with causal knowledge. In *Proceedings of Deep Learning Inside Out (DeeLIO): The 2nd Workshop on Knowledge Extraction and Integration for Deep Learning Architectures* (pp. 70–80). Association for Computational Linguistics.

Davis, E. (2023). Benchmarks for automated commonsense reasoning: A survey. In *Proceedings of the 2023 Conference on Artificial Intelligence and Ethics (AIE 2023)* (pp. 1–10). Association for the Advancement of Artificial Intelligence. arXiv preprint arXiv:2302.04752.

Distelmeyer, J. (2022). Digitality and critique. In *Critique of digitality* (pp. 1–50). Palgrave Macmillan. doi: 10.1007/978-3-658-36978-1_1

Flasiński, M., & Flasiński, M. (2016). History of artificial intelligence. In M. Flasiński, *Introduction to artificial intelligence* (pp. 3–13). Springer.

Foster, D. (2022). *Generative deep learning.* O'Reilly Media, Inc.

Frunza, S. (2023). Cultural intelligence, spiritual intelligence and counseling in the age of artificial intelligence. *Journal for the Study of Religions and Ideologies, 22*(64), 80–95.

Fryer, L., & Carpenter, R. (2006). Bots as language learning tools. *Language Learning & Technology, 10*(3), 8–14.

Gantar, P., Colman, L., Parra Escartín, C., & Martínez Alonso, H. (2019). Multiword expressions: Between lexicography and NLP. *International Journal of Lexicography, 32*(2), 138–162.

Gawdat, M. (2021). *Scary smart: The future of Artificial Intelligence and how you can save our world.* Pan Macmillan.

Gibney, E. (2020). The battle to embed ethics in AI research. *Nature, 577*(7792), 609.

Gonçalves, B. (2023). The Turing test is a thought experiment. *Minds and Machines, 33*(1), 1–31.

Gupta, N. (2013). Artificial neural network. *Network and Complex Systems, 3*(1), 24–2.

Gupta, M., Parra, C. M., & Dennehy, D. (2021). Questioning racial and gender bias in AI-based recommendations: Do espoused national cultural values matter? *Information Systems Frontiers, 24*(5), 1–17.

Haenlein, M., & Kaplan, A. (2019). A brief history of artificial intelligence: On the past, present, and future of artificial intelligence. *California Management Review, 61*(4), 5–14.

Hagendorff, T., & Danks, D. (2023). Ethical and methodological challenges in building morally informed AI systems. *AI and Ethics*, *3*(2), 553–566.

Hertz, J. A. (2018). *Introduction to the theory of neural computation.* CRC Press.

Hickok, E., Skeet, A., & Colclough, C., Penn, J., & Zuroff, R. (2022). *Framework for promoting workforce well-being in the AI-integrated workplace.* Partnership on AI.

Jablonka, E., & Ginsburg, S. (2022). Learning and the evolution of conscious agents. *Biosemiotics*, *15*(3), 401–437.

Jacquet, B., Masson, O., Jamet, F., & Baratgin, J. (2019). On the lack of pragmatic processing in artificial conversational agents. In T. Ahram, W. Karwoski, & R. Taiar (Eds.), *Human systems engineering and design: Proceedings of the 1st International Conference on Human Systems Engineering and Design (IHSED2018)* (pp. 394–399). Springer.

Javed, T., Doddapaneni, S., Raman, A., Bhogale, K. S., Ramesh, G., Kunchukuttan, A., Kumar, P., & Khapra, M. M. (2022, June). Towards building ASR systems for the next billion users. In *Proceedings of the AAAI Conference on Artificial Intelligence* (Vol. 36, No. 10, pp. 10813–10821). Association for the Advancement of Artificial Intelligence.

Jin, D., Jin, Z., Hu, Z., Vechtomova, O., & Mihalcea, R. (2022). Deep learning for text style transfer: A survey. *Computational Linguistics*, *48*(1), 155–205.

Karbasi, M., & Kolossa, D. (2022). ASR-based speech intelligibility prediction: A review. *Hearing Research*, *426*, 108606.

Kratky, A., & Hwang, J. (2023). Inner voices: Reflexive augmented listening. In J. Y. C. Chen & G. Fragomini (Eds.), *Virtual, augmented, and mixed reality* (pp. 233–252). Springer Nature Switzerland.

Kumar, V. B., Ganesan, B., Ameen, M., Sharma, D., & Agarwal, A. (2022, July). Automated Evaluation of GNN Explanations with Neuro Symbolic Reasoning. In D. Kiela, M. Ciccone, & B. Caputo (Eds.), *Proceedings of the NeurIPS 2021 competitions and demonstrations track* (pp. 314–318). PMLR.

Kunkel, J., Donkers, T., Michael, L., Barbu, C. M., & Ziegler, J. (2019, May). Let me explain: Impact of personal and impersonal explanations on trust in recommender systems. In *Proceedings of the 2019 CHI conference on human factors in computing systems* (pp. 1–12). PMLR.

Lee, P., Gavidia, M., Feldman, A., & Peng, J. (2022). Searching for PETs: Using distributional and sentiment-based methods to find potentially euphemistic terms. arXiv preprint arXiv:2205.10451

Li, J. (2022). Recent advances in end-to-end automatic speech recognition. *APSIPA Transactions on Signal and Information Processing*, *11*(1), e8.

Liang, J., Shahrzad, H., & Miikkulainen, R. (2024). Asynchronous evolution of deep neural network architectures. Applied Soft Computing, 152, 111209.

Liu, X., Huang, D., Yin, Z., & Ren, F. (2019). Recognition of collocation frames from sentences. *IEICE TRANSACTIONS on Information and Systems*, *102*(3), 620–627.

Maedche, A., Legner, C., Benlian, A., Berger, B., Gimpel, H., Hess, T., Hinz, O., Morana, S., & Söllner, M. (2019). AI-based digital assistants: Opportunities, threats, and research perspectives. *Business & Information Systems Engineering*, *61*, 535–544.

Mao, R., He, K., Zhang, X., Chen, G., Ni, J., Yang, Z., & Cambria, E. (2024). A survey on semantic processing techniques. *Information Fusion*, *101*, 101988.

132 *Defining Listening*

McCluskey, M. (2018). MIT created the world's first "Psychopath" robot and people really aren't feeling it. *Time* [online]. time.com/5304762/psychopath-robot-reactions

Mearian, L. (2023, May 4). Geoffrey Hinton—humanity just a "passing phase" in the evolution of intelligence. *Computer World*. https://www.computerworld.com/article/3695568/qa-googles-geoffrey-hinton-humanity-just-a-passing-phase-in-the-evolution-of-intelligence.html

Minsky, M. (1961). Steps toward artificial intelligence. *Proceedings of the IRE*, *49*(1), 8–30.

Nagrani, A., Seo, P. H., Seybold, B., Hauth, A., Manen, S., Sun, C., & Schmid, C. (2022). Learning audio-video modalities from image captions. In S. Avidan, G. Brostow, M. Cisse, & T. Hassner (Eds.), *European Conference on Computer Vision* (pp. 407–426). Springer Nature Switzerland.

Naseem, U., Razzak, I., Musial, K., & Imran, M. (2020). Transformer based deep intelligent contextual embedding for twitter sentiment analysis. *Future Generation Computer Systems*, *113*, 58–69.

Ng, A., Laird, D., & He, L. (2021). Data-centric ai competition. *DeepLearning AI*. https://https-deeplearning-ai. github. io/data-centric-comp/.

Norvig, P. (2009). Natural language corpus data. In T. Segaran & J. Hammerbacher (Eds.), *Beautiful data* (pp. 219–242). O'Reilly Media, Inc.

Ovchinnikova, E. (2012). *Integration of world knowledge for natural language understanding* (Vol. 3). Springer Science & Business Media.

Prochaska, J. J., Vogel, E. A., Chieng, A., Kendra, M., Baiocchi, M., Pajarito, S., & Robinson, A. (2021). A therapeutic relational agent for reducing problematic substance use (Woebot): development and usability study. *Journal of Medical Internet Research*, *23*(3), e24850.

Reyes-Pena, C., & Tovar-Vidal, M. (2019). Ontology: Components and evaluation, a review. *Research in Computing Science*, *148*(3), 257–265.

Rogers, C. (1995). *On becoming a person: A therapist's view of psychotherapy*. Boston: Houghton Mifflin.

Rojas, R. (2013). *Neural networks: A systematic introduction*. Springer Science & Business Media.

Sainath, T. N., Prabhavalkar, R., Bapna, A., Zhang, Y., Huo, Z., Chen, Z., Chiu, C-C., Li, W., & Strohman, T. (2023, January). Joist: A joint speech and text streaming model for ASR. In 2022 IEEE Spoken Language Technology Workshop (SLT) (pp. 52–59). IEEE.

Sajjad, H., Durrani, N., & Dalvi, F. (2022). Neuron-level interpretation of deep NLP models: A survey. Transactions of the Association for Computational Linguistics, 10, 1285–130.

Serdyuk, D., Braga, O., & Siohan, O. (2022). Transformer-based video front-ends for audio-visual speech recognition for single and multi-person video. arXiv preprint. arXiv:2201.10439.

Shah, S., Mishra, A., Yadati, N., & Talukdar, P. P. (2019, July). Kvqa: Knowledge-aware visual question answering. In D. Kiele, M. Ciccone, & B. Caputo (Eds.), *Proceedings of the AAAI Conference on Artificial Intelligence* (Vol. 33, No. 1, pp. 8876–8884). AAAI.

Shi, G., Xiao, Y., Li, Y., & Xie, X. (2021). From semantic communication to semantic-aware networking: Model, architecture, and open problems. IEEE Communications Magazine, 59(8), 44–50.

Sullivan, Y. W., & Wamba, F. S. (2022). Moral judgments in the age of artificial intelligence. Journal of Business Ethics, 178(4), 917–943.

Tan, C. (2020). Digital Confucius? Exploring the implications of artificial intelligence in spiritual education. Connection Science, 32(3), 280–291.

Tran, B. D., Mangu, R., Tai-Seale, M., Lafata, J. E., & Zheng, K. (2022). Automatic speech recognition performance for digital scribes: A performance comparison between general-purpose and specialized models tuned for patient-clinician conversations. In AMIA Annual Symposium Proceedings (Vol. 2022, p. 1072). American Medical Informatics Association.

Weizenbaum, J. (1966). ELIZA—A computer program for the study of natural language communication between man and machine. *Communications of the ACM*, (9), 36–45. doi: 10.1145/365153.365168

Wu, C., Li, X., Guo, Y., Wang, J., Ren, Z., Wang, M., & Yang, Z. (2022). Natural language processing for smart construction: Current status and future directions. *Automation in Construction, 134*, 104059.

Zaib, M., Zhang, W. E., Sheng, Q. Z., Mahmood, A., & Zhang, Y. (2022). Conversational question answering: A survey. *Knowledge and Information Systems, 64*(12), 3151–3195.

6 Listening in Language Acquisition

6.1	Overview: Listening in Language Acquisition	135
6.2	Listening in L1 Acquisition: Development of Neurological Processing	135
6.3	Listening in L1 Acquisition: Development of Linguistic Processing	137
	6.3.1 Acquisition of Phonology	*137*
	6.3.2 Acquisition of Lexical Comprehension	*141*
	6.3.3 Acquisition of Syntax Comprehension	*142*
6.4	Listening in L1 Acquisition: Development of Semantic Processing	144
	6.4.1 The Role of Interaction in Semantic Processing Development	*145*
6.5	Listening in L1 Acquisition: Development of Pragmatic Processing	147
6.6	Listening in L2 Acquisition: Development of Neurological Processing	149
6.7	Listening in L2 Acquisition: Development of Linguistic Processing	152
	6.7.1 Development of L2 Phonological Processing	*152*
	6.7.2 Development of L2 Syntactic Processing	*153*
	6.7.3 Linguistic Processing: Lexis	*155*
6.8	Listening in L2 Acquisition: Development of Semantic Processing	156
6.9	Listening in L2 Acquisition: Development of Pragmatic Processing	157
6.10	Summary: The Transformative Nature of L1 and L2 Acquisition of Listening	158
References		160

DOI: 10.4324/9781003390794-8

6.1 Overview: Listening in Language Acquisition

Listening is both a language skill and a principal means of language acquisition in both L1 and L2 contexts. By examining the relative importance of listening in these two contexts, we can uncover vital parallels and critical differences between them.

For L1 development, listening provides children with the primary source of language input. They are constantly exposed to spoken language from their caregivers, family members, and the surrounding environment. Through listening, children begin to formulate systematic meaning for the high-frequency words and syntactic structures of their native language. In particular, listening helps children develop phonological awareness, recognizing and distinguishing the sounds and prosodic patterns of their native language.

By listening to spoken language variations in their environment, children establish the foundation for their own emerging speech production in their native accent. In addition to linguistic acquisition, listening also helps children develop pragmatic skills, whereby they come to understand the social and contextual aspects of how language is used effectively. Through listening to conversations and beginning to participate in interactions, children learn about turn-taking, politeness conventions, implied meanings, and the appropriate use of language in different situations. Listening is also an integrated means of cognitive development. As children learn to comprehend ideas that are being communicated to them, like "time to eat," "let's play," and "calm down," they are also engaging in mental processes that support their cognitive growth.

For L2 development, listening plays an important role in the overall process of acquiring the language and developing oral proficiency. L2 learners are, however, able to evade listening as the primary means of acquisition, depending on their educational context. Listening to the target language provides learners with authentic input and exposure to the phonology, lexis, syntax, and discourse patterns of the language. The development of listening comprehension skills is vital for integrating the L2 user into the discourse community where their L2 is dominant, for developing a sense of agency as an active participant with other users of the L2, and for developing cultural and pragmatic competence.

In both cases, listening plays a vital role in acquisition and development. Understanding the natural development of listening and obstacles to progress in listening is important for language teachers and researchers.

6.2 Listening in L1 Acquisition: Development of Neurological Processing

A child's neurological system is not fully developed at the time of birth. While the basic structures of the neurological system are present, significant development and maturation continue throughout childhood and adolescence, particularly in

136 *Defining Listening*

Figure 6.1 Development of Listening Abilities in the First Year

Oral language development is inextricably tied to social interaction, cognition, and play. This chart shows approximate sequences of development in these areas during the child's first year

Listening in Language Acquisition 137

neural connectivity, attention control, and higher-order cognitive functions, all of which contribute to listening ability.

The rate and trajectory of neurological development will vary among individuals due to genetic and environmental factors and educational experiences. Positive early experiences, sensory and cognitive stimulation, and a supportive linguistic environment play a crucial role in shaping and optimizing neurological development in children (Bjorklund, 2022; Kidd & Donnelly, 2020).

While listening ability develops along with other social and cognitive abilities, such as collaboration and problem-solving, the auditory channel is the primary means of language acquisition, providing the linguistic data the child needs to acquire more precise vocabulary and work out the complex syntax of their native language (Cowie, 2010; Goswami, 2022; Ross et al., 2022).

If we consider the child's neurological development as a basis for their listening development, we can identify three complementary domains of growth over the first year: (1) cognition and play, (2) social interaction, and (3) general language development (see Figure 6.1.)

6.3 Listening in L1 Acquisition: Development of Linguistic Processing

Under normal circumstances, all humans acquire their first language (L1) completely and successfully. In virtually all cases, the L1 is acquired primarily through oral input accompanied by physical action. Children successfully develop oral language through a lengthy, intentional, immersive process involving an abundance of listening and reciprocal oral interaction, particularly if this interaction takes place with caretakers who develop a warm, nurturing relationship with the child (Kapengut, 2020; Ramírez-Esparza et al., 2014).

Because L1 acquirers begin the language acquisition process as infants, the L1 is acquired simultaneously with multiple physical, neurological, cognitive, and social skills. There is a seamless connection between learning to observe, experience bodily sensations, listen, think, interact, and speak a first language. Communicative abilities that identify a person as a native speaker emerge within just three years, on average (Bishop, 2014; Christiansen et al., 2022; Wilson & Bishop, 2022).

6.3.1 Acquisition of Phonology

Though all psycholinguistic systems—phonological, lexical, syntactic, semantic, pragmatic— develop in parallel, we often think of the phonological as occurring first because sound is the most observable, measurable basis of language acquisition. Developmental studies of speech perception across languages demonstrate that all infants begin with a language-general capacity that provides a means for discriminating the *thousands* of potential **phonetic contrasts** in any of the world's languages. Over time, based on the targeted input received from

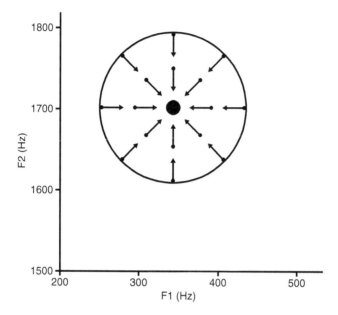

Figure 6.2 Perceptual Magnet Effect

The child learns to recognize sound variations according to a prototype for each phoneme in the language. This is called the "perceptual magnet effect." This illustration shows the prototype for the sound /i/ (F1 = 350 Hz; F2 = 1,700 Hz). Sounds within a small physical variation of the target will be recognized as belonging to that phoneme

significant caretakers in the child's world, each child sifts the set of potential contrasts to concentrate on those that are most relevant (Choi & Werker, 2021; Werker & Hensch, 2015).

The L1 listener begins to acquire the phonemes of the language through the **perceptual magnet effect**, which categorizes incoming sounds by their proximity to the prototypical sounds (see Figure 6.2).

This progressive narrowing of capacities is consistent with other aspects of neurological development, allowing the child to activate the neural pathways that are most useful for acquiring the L1. The nervous system of an infant starts with an overexuberance of connections that are pared down in the course of development to templates tuned to the **phonotactic system** of the language being acquired (Bernhardt & Stemberger, 2020; Van der Feest & Fikkert, 2015).

L1 studies have shown that over the first year of life, learning by selecting available environmental sounds results in directional changes in perception (Kuhl et al., 2008; Lau et al., 2021). The child's experience (exposure and selective attention) affects the **magnetic tuning** of neural transmissions in the

Listening in Language Acquisition   139

auditory cortex through enhancement, attenuation, sharpening, broadening, and realignment of sound prototype.

- **Enhancement** refers to the strengthening or exaggeration of certain phonetic features. For example, a child might initially pronounce the /r/ sound in a word with a more pronounced rhotic quality than adults, making it sound more like "wuh" in an attempt to emphasize the /r/ sound.
- **Attenuation** involves weakening or reducing certain phonetic features. An example could be a child initially pronouncing the /s/ sound as a softer "th" sound, like "thun" for "sun."
- **Sharpening** refers to the refinement of distinctions between phonemes. For instance, a child might start by using a similar sound for both /b/ and /p/, but as their phonological development progresses, they will sharpen the distinction between the two sounds.
- **Broadening** is a similar perceptual phenomenon, the expansion of a phonetic category to include a wider range of sounds. Initially, a child might use a single sound, such as /t/, for multiple phonemes, such as /t/, /d/, and /p/, but as they develop, they might broaden their perception and production of those phonemes.
- **Realignment** refers to a shift in the perception of certain sounds. For example, a child may initially perceive a sound as one phoneme, but over time, due to exposure and learning, they may realign their perception to recognize it as a different phoneme. Common examples of realignment are /r/ - /l/ (race-lace) and /s/ - /θ/ (sink-think) (Lau et al., 2021). Figure 6.3 provides a conceptualization of these five processes.

During their first year of life, infants develop the perceptual ability to discriminate various other differences in the utterances they hear around them. The initial utterances heard are processed holistically as single units of meaning rather than analytically as multiple words (Feldman et al., 2009).

For the young L1 listener, words are not isolated from one another in fluent speech, so the naïve listener will often perceive a mondegreen, a misheard or misinterpreted word or phrase. A mondegreen (a term coined by American writer Sylvia Wright, who misheard a line from a Scottish ballad as "Lady Mondegreen" instead of the actual lyric "laid him on the green") often occurs when the listener hears a sound sequence and interprets it as a familiar word or phrase that fits the context. For instance, I recall my son repeating the words to a Bob Dylan song, which he heard as: "The ants are my friends, they're blowing in the wind" ("The answer (=the ants are), my friends …").

Over time, the child will eventually learn how to parse word boundaries for all the words in their listening vocabulary. The initial phase of this learning process involves discovering how sounds can be ordered phonetically and prosodically within the language's utterances. This exposure and gradual discrimination of

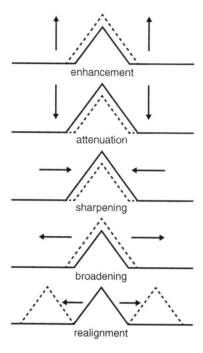

Figure 6.3 Perception Processes

When learning a first language, a child uses five kinds of perceptual adjustment to tune into the sounds of their native language. By the end of one year, through regular exposure to spoken language, the child will know which sounds belong to their L1

allowable features is known as gaining **phonotactic knowledge** of the language (Cameron-Faulkner et al., 2003).

The gradual acquisition of the phonotactic system teaches the child what is and is not allowable in the language. Over the first several months of being surrounded by oral language, the child naturally acquires this discriminative ability (Bernstein-Ratner, 2021).

By the end of the first year, **phonological sensitivity** will decline for many distinctions not found in the native language. At the same time, infants absorb information about other regularly occurring features of the native language's sound patterns, particularly stress and timing. Cumulatively, sensitivity develops to those features that help segment words. This is an important transition in listening development. It means that an infant's skills at word segmentation are developing along with their knowledge of how sound patterns are structured in their native language. Speech segmentation and word recognition are the essential properties of perception.

Listening in Language Acquisition 141

There are three fundamental decoding resources that the child gains during phonological development: **categorical perception**, the capacity to discriminate speech sound contrasts in their native language; **continuous perception**, the ability to hear continuous speech as combinations of sound sequences; and **perceptual constancy**, the ability to tolerate the **acoustic variability** that accompanies changes in rates of speech or differences in speakers' voices (McMurray, 2022; Parish-Morris et al., 2013).

6.3.2 Acquisition of Lexical Comprehension

In L1 development, acquiring a **listening lexicon** is an ongoing process of growth. Lexical development is closely integrated with the expansion of phonological memory (the phonological loop), the ability to hold and manipulate phonological information in short-term memory. And all lexical development proceeds from recognition (listening) vocabulary to production (speaking) vocabulary. As is well documented, children learn words receptively first before they can produce them (Mirolli & Parisi, 2009). By the age of two, for instance, children typically have a receptive vocabulary—spoken words they understand—of 200 to 500 words compared to their expressive vocabulary—words they can produce (usually without phonological precision)—of only 50 to 100 words.

The most common method of observing the listening vocabulary growth is simple observation: noticing a child's response to words or commands and their ability to point to named objects or pictures. Nearly all of a child's receptive vocabulary development occurs in interactive conversations. Recent studies demonstrate how the quality of caregivers' speech contributes to the development of a child's listening vocabulary (Daskalaki et al., 2020), how children utilize environmental cues to figure out word meanings (Alhama et al., 2023), how they attend to feedback as they are building their lexical repertoire (Nikolaus & Fourtassi, 2023), and how they experiment with syntactic relationships of words (Taverna & Waxman, 2020).

Lexical acquisition always occurs in stages. **Labeling** is the first of three related tasks a child has to perform while acquiring any new word. At an early age, children discover that sound sequences can be references to things. This challenge of symbolization is often simply depicted as a process in which parents point at an object and say its name so that the child can understand the connection between sound, object, and meaning. Labeling a word is not that simple from the child's perspective. Usually, many early words are ritual accompaniments to a situation, and therefore, a child's babbling is unlikely to be a sign of meaning acquisition but rather of spontaneous sound productions (Aitchison, 2012; Bjorklund, 2022).

The labeling task can be accelerated by two strategies: **generalization** and **differentiation**. Generalization refers to the child labeling numerous things and situations with the same words. Only after encountering these things in different

142 *Defining Listening*

contexts does the child start to differentiate each word from a whole event and use it as a label for a specific object or event. Somewhere between the ages of one and two, children reach an amplified labeling stage, and various researchers have remarked on a vocabulary spurt around this time. This may be due to the child's cognitive discovery that things have names, leading to a passion for attaching labels (Ambridge & Lieven, 2011).

The second task of meaning acquisition is **packaging**. An interesting paradox is how a child comes to apply a label to a wider range of objects of the same type but simultaneously restricts the label when appropriate. This phenomenon is generally realized as **underextension** and **overextension**. Underextension refers to the child oversimplifying concepts and failing to apply them to more than only one prototypical object. For example, in underextension, a child uses the word *kitty* to refer to the family cat but not other cats. A period of underextension for any categorical word is a normal part of lexical acquisition (Mirolli & Parisi, 2009).

In contrast, while overextensions are statistically less common, they are more noticeable to caretakers because they seem to be gross cognitive errors. For example, a child might extend *dog* to refer to a squirrel and other four-legged animals or *key* to refer to a door or other things associated with entering the house. In these cases, the child applies labels to a wide range of concepts associated with the target lexical item. The primary reason for such packaging mistakes is **gap filling**: The child does not yet know the right term for an object and then uses another associated label (Pinto & Xu, 2021).

To acquire fuller meanings of words, the child must take on the third task, which is **network-building.** Relations between words and concepts must be worked out explicitly. This connecting task takes place slowly and proceeds initially through collocational links, for example, when the child links *table* with *eat*. Later, the child coordinates words with other contexts and gradually builds broader networks. Other important aspects of this network-building task are the connection of sounds and their meanings to visual concepts, grammatical information, and orthography to develop a more advanced level of lexical competence (Haastrup & Henriksen, 2000; Lieven & Tomasello, 2008; Poveda, 2019).

6.3.3 Acquisition of Syntax Comprehension

Between the ages of 18 and 36 months, children typically acquire words and phrases at a very fast rate. This phenomenon is often referred to as the vocabulary spurt and the language burst, when children begin recognizing names for objects, actions, and events.

By comparison, syntax comprehension develops rather slowly. For a child, the acquisition of syntax through listening alone is somewhat problematic because syntactic rules are seldom demonstrated explicitly. At the same time, the child can often construct plausible meanings through context without resorting to grammatical rules at all. It is generally only when a child begins

Listening in Language Acquisition 143

to produce language and receive feedback that syntactic accuracy and sophistication develop (Peters, 2017). One aspect of syntax that is acquired aurally is learning how morphology rules can be used to combine groups of words into a single lexical item to form **phonological words**, such as *an apple, in the house, over here* (Demuth, 2011).

Children also gradually learn how combining words in certain orders can show an intended relationship between them (e.g., "Tara go play now"). It is more difficult to observe children's growth in comprehension of syntax than it is to observe their development of listening vocabulary. The observation of syntactic growth often takes place holistically by noticing the child's narrative comprehension and how they follow a story plot involving syntactic changes, such as verb tenses, pronouns, and sentence order.

Observation can also take place in language games, such as Simon Says, in which the child reveals their ability to follow complex (and often unorthodox) commands in real time. As with lexical development, interactive conversations are the most common way of assessing a child's comprehension of syntax. What the child does or imitates after hearing a conversational turn provides insights into their syntactic processing (see Table 6.1).

Table 6.1 Interactive Conversation: Children's Responses to Adult Prompts

Adult prompt	Child's response
I can see a cow	See cow (Eve at 25 months)
The doggy will bite	Doggy bite (Adam at 28 months)
Kathryn doesn't like celery	Kathryn no like celery (Kathryn at 22 months)
Do you want your baby doll to ride in the truck?	Baby doll ride truck (Allison at 22 months)
Pigs say oink, don't they?	Pig say oink (Claire at 25 months)
Do you want her (shop attendant) to get some chocolate ice cream for you?	Want lady get chocolate (Daniel at 23 months)
Daddy's not here. Where did Daddy go?	Daddy go? (Daniel at 23 months)
Where is the car going?	Car going? (Jem at 21 months)
Where's Jenny?	She's gone. Her gone school. (Domenico at 24 months)
What's Alex doing?	He's kicking a beach ball. (Jem at 28 months)
What's Ana doing?	Her climbing up the ladder there. (Jem at 24 months).
What are you saying, Holly?	I teasing Mummy. I'm teasing Mummy. (Holly at 24 months)
I'm having this. How about you, Liv?	I'm having 'nana (banana). (Olivia at 27 months).
I'm having this little one.	Me'll have that. (Betty at 30 months).
I'm not ready yet, Sweetie.	Mummy haven't finished yet, has she? (Olivia at 36 months).

Source: Data from Childes Talkbank. https://childes.talkbank.org/topics/sites.html

144 *Defining Listening*

As shown in Table 6.1, the dimensions of syntax comprehension in child language acquisition involve various developmental processes: an increase in the mean length of each utterance (**MLU**) that is comprehensible; an increase in the use of multiword phrases from the caregiver; and apparent comprehension of grammatical markers, such as auxiliaries, articles, tense and aspect markers of verbs, inflections, pronoun case (I/me, she/her, etc.), possessives (my/mine, your/yours, etc.)

Researchers of child language development note that by age three, a child may be exposed to upwards of 10,000 hours of oral language input (Kuhl & Rivera-Gaxiola, 2008). However, it appears that the quantity of oral input, and even the quality of the input, may not be sufficient in the child's acquisition of the complete syntax of their L1. Many psychologists believe that humans possess some *innate mechanism* that allows the child to formulate rules based on limited input, so that even with minimal well-formed input, the natural cognitive growth of a child will allow them to acquire linguistic rules (Chomsky, 1976; Crain et al., 2017; Gomes et al., 2000).

Though there are different views on the nature of the innate mechanisms and the degree of environmental (familial, cultural) influence, any explanation must reckon with the fact that children's grammar is greatly underdetermined by the linguistic input they receive. Children are exposed to adult utterances in context, not abstract grammatical structures, yet they all eventually acquire an essentially complete system of categories and rules without formal instruction (with some exceptions that do require instruction, such as complex sentence structures, irregular verb forms, and word order variations) (Gleitman et al., 2019).

6.4 Listening in L1 Acquisition: Development of Semantic Processing

As neurological developments occur, the child's receptive and productive language expands, allowing them to experiment in order to discover novel language that fits new concepts. First language and cognitive development fuel a mutual acceleration: Receptive vocabulary and syntax expand to meet the child's burgeoning needs for clearer comprehension of more complex observations and ideas (Cartmill et al., 2013; Gleason & Ratner, 2022).

The concept of **cognitive structure** is central to understanding how these comprehension vectors coincide in the child. According to Piaget, a pioneer in child cognitive development, cognitive structures evolve over time and allow for more complex listening and understanding. Piaget introduced the concept of schemas (discussed in Chapter 3), the mental frameworks or structures that listeners use to organize and interpret information. Piaget's proposal, novel at the time, was that children assimilate new information into existing schemas and reconfigure (accommodate) their schemas to adapt to new experiences (Bjorklund, 2022; Dasen, 2022; Piaget, 1951/2007; Stiles et al., 2015).

It is now agreed that the child's cognitive structures and their working theories of the world change and evolve as the child grows. It is now believed that this modification can be accelerated and scaffolded through directed experience with adult guidance and structured listening experiences (Hedges, 2022; Lovatt & Hedges, 2014; Masek et al., 2023).

Early childhood psychologists explained these educational experiences by dividing them into two types of adaptation: assimilation and accommodation.. **Assimilation** involves interpreting events in terms of existing cognitive structure, whereas **accommodation** refers to changing the cognitive structure to make sense of the environment.

Listening development requires cognitive and linguistic *disequilibrium*: when a child encounters new input that *does not fit* into an existing schema, the child experiences a kind of cognitive and emotional discomfort. In order to regain equilibrium, the child must advance their understanding of the world and develop more sophisticated mental structures. This advancement of mental structures allows their listening capacity to develop: The child wants to understand more extensive and more complex language (Daniels, 2016).

Within this Piagetian perspective, guidance by a caretaker or teacher is seen as optimally reflecting and facilitating the child's listening development. Caretakers and teachers can best facilitate the child's linguistic development by providing new environments, novel stimulation, and listening opportunities that will fully engage the child in new concepts (Saxton, 2009). For example, with children aged up to six or seven years, the caregiver's primary role may be to provide a rich and stimulating environment with ample objects to play with, and interactive discourse about the objects and actions employed (Isaacs, 2014). Reflecting a Piagetian view of cognitive development stages, for children beyond the age of seven, learning activities can progressively include more tangible problems of classification, ordering, and location using concrete objects and tasks (Oogarah-Pratap et al., 2020).

6.4.1 The Role of Interaction in Semantic Processing Development

One aspect of a child's semantic processing development involves directed **topical interaction** between the child and caretakers or teachers and between the child and other children. A topical interaction refers to a conversation or communication exchange between a child and a significant interlocutor (usually a parent, older sibling, relative, caregiver, or teacher) that centers around a specific topic or subject of interest. During a topical interaction, the child and the interlocutor engage in a meaningful discussion focused on a particular theme, event, activity, or concept (Crain, 2015; Rohde & Frank, 2014). Recent ethnographic studies of children's everyday interactions have challenged simplistic socialization accounts claiming adults' unidirectional influence on children.

146 *Defining Listening*

Instead, they have demonstrated how children can also propel their own development (Barrouillet, 2015; Case, 2013).

The intertwining of contributions of both the child's own initiative and caretakers' support to cognitive development is exemplified in studies of young children's development of scientific knowledge. A starting point for developing specialized knowledge in any field is exploring moments of wonder ("awe"), in which the child shows amazement about and interest in some natural phenomenon (Hedges, 2014; Peters & Davis, 2011). Building on these moments, caretakers can co-construct **islands of expertise** mutually with the child, resources to help young children develop knowledge about topics of interest—along with associated vocabulary and schemata—well before going to school (Crowley & Jacobs, 2002).

In my own family, my older son became increasingly interested in art from the time he could hold a crayon, experimenting with different media and surfaces (curtains, windows, walls, etc.), encouraged (within limits) by his caregivers (his mother and me). As he grew older, he became interested in imitating the art from books we brought to him, and the cycle of experimenting and receiving new input and discussing his work with us led him toward a satisfying career in art.

My younger son followed a similar developmental path in finding his "element" (a term used by Robinson, 2009) in architecture by first experimenting extensively with Lego® block constructions, which piqued his curiosity about buildings he saw and led him to ask about various schemata relating to the world of architecture. This shared curiosity allowed the family to have rich conversations that included explanations, elaborations, experiments, and analogies to related domains. Incrementally, these interactions deepened his interest in and knowledge of a joint topical domain, providing an example of socialization through family discourse (Blum-Kulka, 2012; Lieven et al., 2019; Tomasello, 2019). Much of a child's vocabulary and schematic knowledge of the world develops through exposure to a range of narratives (via media, apps, and games) and personal experiences, as well as to challenges to understand new concepts through social support and peer education (Ochs & Schieffelin, 2001; Themeli & Prasolova-Førland, 2023).

Siblings and peers are also active learning partners and share knowledge about cultural tools, toys, and practices. For example, children share songs, stories, and games and use them to signify and build friendships. They share how to create and learn with new technologies (Fleer, 2021; Goldfield et al., 2024). As they grow older, children expand their social networks as peers become more important and influential in their social and linguistic development (Hartup, 1996; Schneider, 2016). It is widely agreed that by middle childhood (ages 6–12), peers begin to exert a strong influence on the child's intellectual interests, as well as on their linguistic development (Lam et al., 2014). By early adolescence (ages 13–16), peer influence often becomes even more instrumental

Listening in Language Acquisition 147

than caregiver influence in shaping intellectual and social standards (Bates et al., 2017).

6.5 Listening in L1 Acquisition: Development of Pragmatic Processing

While children spend their first years of linguistic development learning to use their L1, they are also being assimilated into a social unit, usually with familiar adult caretakers and gradually with a wider circle of friends and acquaintances. Children's innate language ability, a natural curiosity about the world of ideas and feelings, and experiences around their desire to integrate into the family support unit provide both a natural, intrinsic motivation and the means for language acquisition. The caretakers are critical in providing challenges, support, and congruent feedback for the child as they develop. Further, these interactions provide a useful record of linguistic development, along with cognitive, moral, social, emotional, and identity development (Catani & Bambini, 2014; Nelson, 2007).

In nearly all cultures, caretakers commonly use special speech styles when talking with young children to make the language input more engaging and easier for the child to comprehend and remember. These styles feature repetitive patterns and frames ("Look at the pretty flower! Do you see the flower? It's such a beautiful flower"), manipulate intonation ("Are *you* going to the *park* now?"), increase voice onset timing to draw attention to a consonant sound ("M::ommy's coming too"), reduce utterance length ("Go now"), and coin special words ("Look at the wiggly-waggly") (Weisleder & Fernald, 2013).

There is also evidence that caregivers tend to talk differently to boys and girls, typically talking more to girls than to boys, focusing on different topics, and differentiating word choice (Hart & Risley, 1995; Lovas, 2011; Thiessen et al., 2013). In terms of language development, it has been established that this form of **child-directed speech** (CDS) facilitates children's noticing and effective learning of the phonology, syntax, lexis, and discourse patterns (see Table 6.2). In addition, the personalized form and style of CDS assists the child in developing, identifying, controlling, and expressing feelings appropriately (García-Sierra et al., 2021; Ramírez-Esparza et al., 2014; Schick et al., 2022; Wells, 1999).

The empirical study of CDS dates to the 1960s and has been summarized in recent years. Not only have the features of the language itself been analyzed, but also how CDS facilitates language acquisition. This facilitation takes place through several supportive functions, such as helping the child manage their attention, improving intelligibility of language, providing clear production models, coaching how to participate in social routines, and helping the child learn playful interaction gambits (e.g., surprise, repetition, incongruity, nonsense) (Lieven et al., 2019; Rowe & Weisleder, 2020; Wilkie & Saxton, 2010).

What is unclear from the CDS research is *how* these potential facilitating factors expedite acquisition. A couple of points have been agreed. One is that

148   *Defining Listening*

Table 6.2 A Child-Directed Speech Learning Episode

1	Jackie	Linda brought you socks, Mom.
2	Mother	Yes, Linda brought *your* socks.
3		They're dirty. They've got to be washed.
4	Jackie	Linda bought you—me got ... washed.
5	Mother	Pardon?
6	Jackie	Linda wa ... wash them.
7	Mother	No. Mommy's going to wash them.
8	Jackie	Linda wash them.
9	Mother	No. Linda's not going to wash them.
10	Jackie	Linda's not going to wash them.
11	Mother	No. Mommy wash them.

We can see how the mother employs features of CDS, particularly repetition, rephrasing, and requests for clarification, to encourage participation and improve the intelligibility of the language used. The number of speaking turns (8–12) is typical for an episode of CDS (Wells, 2009).

CDS is almost always **semantically contingent**; that is, caretaker talk with the child tends to be about objects and events to which the child is already paying attention (Masek et al., 2023). Thus, it may be that semantic contingency and the establishment of mutuality with the caretaker rather than the linguistic features of CDS itself, is what consistently triggers language acquisition (Thibault, 2006).

Studies of caretaker–child interaction from other cultures (e.g., Ochs & Schieffelin, 2011) have shown that while language acquisition is affected by the language learner's desire to become a competent social group member, CDS per se is not a universal practice. In many traditional forager-farmer communities, such as the Tsmai of Bolivia, the Yucatec Maya, the Massai, and the Inuit, talk-ativeness is not highly valued. In these cultures, adults tend to spend little time in verbal interactions with children; in some studies, it is less than one minute per daylight hour (Cristia et al., 2019).

What is universal is that, even without extensive verbal input and interaction, children are continuously in the presence of multimodal **contextual language routines**, such as eating, getting dressed, playing, bathing, and preparing to sleep. In these contextualized situations, usually described as **learning episodes** (see Table 6.2), salient features of the environment as well as habituated routines help the child understand the reason for those routines and the role of lan-guage in them (O'Madagain & Tomasello, 2022; Snow et al., 2021). In short, understanding routines and understanding language are inseparable for the child (Rogoff et al., 2007; Rogoff et al., 2015).

Although caregivers are generally the most significant source of language input and interaction, as the child ages, siblings and peers assume a greater role in their language development, particularly in pragmatic processing, shaping it in powerful ways that often outweigh adult caregivers' roles. Sibling and peer interactions provide children with additional language input and exposure beyond their interactions with adults. Children are exposed to a wider range of vocabulary, sentence structures, and language patterns through conversations, play, and group activities. This exposure contributes to vocabulary expansion and developing more advanced language skills (Elicker et al., 2016; Luchkina & Waxman, 2021). Children also observe and imitate their peers' pronunciation, intonation, and communication styles. They learn from each other's language use and adjust their own verbal and nonverbal language accordingly. This process of language modeling can facilitate the development of more natural and age-appropriate language skills (Hartup, 2017; Weisleder & Fernald, 2013).

Conversing with peers allows children to practice and refine their active listening skills. Through discussions, negotiations over meaning, and collaborative problem-solving, children learn to express their thoughts more impactfully, share ideas, ask questions, and empathize with others (Rubin et al., 2013; Williford et al., 2013). Peers can also provide feedback and correction during interactions, which helps children recognize and attach importance to language errors or misconceptions.

When peers correct each other's language use, it contributes to their language accuracy and understanding of grammatical rules and conventions (Parker et al., 2015). These peer interactions provide a concrete social context that motivates children to use language more effectively. And because children naturally seek to connect with their peers, share experiences, and express their thoughts and feelings, they tend to receive far more practice opportunities for interactive listening than in adult–child interactions (Slaughter et al., 2015; Wentzel, 2022).

A final benefit of peer interaction for listening development is that children often engage in imaginative play, storytelling, and role-playing scenarios with their same-age peers, which requires them to use language creatively and flexibly. In child play, children often invent new words, create narratives, and experiment with language structures, fostering mutual linguistic growth and expressive abilities (Clark et al., 2017; Mottweiler & Taylor, 2014; Russ, 2016).

6.6 Listening in L2 Acquisition: Development of Neurological Processing

Anyone who actively uses a second language (L2) for meaningful purposes is, by definition, a bilingual, if only an emerging bilingual, that is, someone at a beginning level of proficiency. The defining success of the L2 learner in becoming a full bilingual is to be *able to function continuously* in their L2, without the need for constant switching back and forth between the L1 and the L2 (Rocha-Hidalgo & Barr, 2023).

Employing the criterion of function continuously in the L2 is not to discount the role of translanguaging in L2 use and in L2 acquisition. Translanguaging, that is, the practice of using multiple languages flexibly and fluidly in the communication and acquisition process, is recognized as a viable form of

150 *Defining Listening*

communication and a viable means of language acquisition (Prilutskaya, 2021). It entails language blending, the seamless merging of languages within a single discourse, which can include code-switching (switching between the L1 and the L2), code-mixing (mixing the L1 and L2 within the same utterance), or using elements of one language to clarify or enrich communication in another (Carstens, 2016).

This shift from an occasional to a frequent to a continuous L2 user is reflected in how that user employs neurolinguistic resources. Functional imaging studies of the brain have shown that the age of acquisition of the L2 and frequency and ease of use of the L2 are reflected in different usage of pathways in the brain. Early sequential bilinguals (acquiring the second language before adolescence) tend to show similar brain network patterns to simultaneous bilinguals, individuals who learned their L1 and L2 at the same time, usually before the age of four (Gampe et al., 2021).

Late sequential bilinguals (acquiring their second language during or after adolescence) tend to show brain network patterns similar to compound bilinguals, people who mastered their L1 before beginning to acquire their L2. Individuals who come to use their L2 frequently and at a high level of proficiency, *regardless of age of acquisition*, tend to exhibit similar brain usage patterns as simultaneous bilinguals (even though their motor control of pronunciation may not be the same). As the bilingual becomes more proficient and comfortable in the L2, the energy needed for oral language processing decreases, as many linguistic processes become automatized. This automatization allows for increased connectivity of semantic areas in the brain (Yee et al., 2023).

Based on neurological research with bilinguals, four models of acquisition pathways have been proposed for compound bilingual acquisition, progressing from occasional user to frequent user, with increasing levels of proficiency (see Table 6.3; Alrwaita et al., 2023; DeLuca et al., 2020; Pliatsikas, 2020).

Unlike the seamless, natural development of L1 listening for young monolingual children in coordination with other neurological and cognitive development, the development of L2 listening in older children and adults is much more irregular and unpredictable, especially at the neurological level. Just as there are neurolinguistic theories that explain the progression of L1 development, there are several theories that explain the progression of L2 listening development.

Input theory suggests that second language acquisition is triggered through exposure to comprehensible input. According to this theory, learners *subconsciously* acquire listening skills when they are exposed to spoken language that is slightly beyond their current level of understanding. L2 listening development is contingent on the progression of exposure to the target language being in harmony with the natural order of acquisition of language structures. For example, simple present tense will be acquired before simple past tense, or regular

Listening in Language Acquisition 151

Table 6.3 Neural Models of Bilingual Acquisition

• **Adaptive Control Model (ACM)**	• **Conditional Routing Model (CRM)**
With adaptive control, there is much more neurological control by the frontal cortex, and more connections needed for code-switching. In the ACM model, the L2 is used only occasionally and with low proficiency; use of the L2 is marked by dense code-switching between L1 and L2; there is widespread use of language areas of the brain to manage interference of the L1.	The L2 is used more frequently; increased duration and proficiency lead to routing of information through basal ganglia, more direct processing of phonology and grammar, and better suppression of L1 when L2 is in use. In the CRM model, increased use of the L2 leads to routing of information via basal ganglia, when switching to the other language, requiring more time for L2 processing.
• **Bilingual Shift Model (BSM)** In the BSM, prolonged use of L2 leads to increased reliance on subcortical and posterior regions of the brain and less use of frontal regions, that is, more use of automated processing in the L2, and less use of executive (conscious) control.	• **Dynamic Restructuring Model (DRM)** In the DRM, bilingualism is viewed as a complex system that is constantly adapting and restructuring in response to various internal and external factors. DRM refers to the brain adapting to frequent use of the L2 through the addition of cortical gray matter; increased connectivity in white cortical matter and increased cerebral gray matter leads to peak efficiency in the use of the L2.

past-tense verbs will be acquired before irregular past-tense verbs (Lichtman & VanPatten, 2021; Niżegorodcew, 2007; Tang, 2013).

The **interactionist approach** emphasizes the importance of social interaction in second language development. According to this theory, learners acquire language through meaningful interaction with more proficient target language speakers, and L2 listening development is contingent on the availability of opportunities. Without numerous opportunities for meaningful interaction, listening ability will not progress beyond a basic stage (Gass & Mackey, 2014; Ortega, 2009).

Cognitivist theory focuses on the role of metacognitive processes in organizing a listener's path of development. According to this theory, learners consciously implement strategies such as attention focusing, memory building, and problem-solving skills to acquire language. L2 listening development, measured in terms of progress learners make in the increasing accuracy, complexity, and fluency of their language comprehension, is contingent on the provision of appropriate input, problem-solving tasks, and feedback from expert language users (Kim, 2017; Nuevo, 2006; Robinson, 2022).

152 *Defining Listening*

Sociocultural theory, like interactionist theory, proposes that second language acquisition is a social process that occurs through participation in social and cultural contexts. Sociocultural theory goes further in suggesting that learners acquire listening ability through forging an identity as a participant in meaningful activities and interactions with other members of the target language community. L2 listening development is contingent on the learner's motivation for inclusiveness of the target language community and the openness of that community to allow the learner entry (Chong et al., 2023; Kramsch & Uryu, 2012; Kramsch & Zhu, 2020; Martin et al., 2019).

Input processing theory: This theory proposes that the acquisition of listening occurs through conscious input processing, which involves dual processing of the spoken input for meaning and for formal properties. According to this theory, learners must first attend to input to understand it, but then they must analyze it if they wish to acquire the syntax of a new language, the essential engine that drives language comprehension. L2 listening development is contingent on the learner's strategic awareness in processing L2 input in order for them to gradually acquire—that is, be able to process in real time—more complex syntax in the spoken input (Leow & Mercer, 2015; Leow & Martin, 2017; VanPatten, 2015).

These theories, which will be revisited in Chapter 7, implicitly acknowledge the potential challenges for late sequential bilinguals in achieving a high level of proficiency in listening. The reported challenges, unsurprisingly, occur in the three main processing domains: linguistic (phonological decoding, word recognition, syntactic parsing), semantic (lexical access, cultural schemata, cognitive overload), and pragmatic (cultural norms, cultural references, negotiation procedures).

6.7 Listening in L2 Acquisition: Development of Linguistic Processing

As any adult who has worked to acquire an L2 knows, the experience of acquisition of an L2 is qualitatively and quantitatively different from that of acquiring an L1. Adult second language learners rarely achieve the same native competence as children learning their L1. These differences between L1 and L2 processing are evident in all systems we have described in this book—neurological, linguistic, semantic, and pragmatic—but the disparity is often most apparent in linguistic processing.This section outlines the challenges of developing linguistic processing in the phonological, lexical, and syntactic domains.

6.7.1 Development of L2 Phonological Processing

While children consistently achieve native competence across a full range of subtle and complex phonological properties of their L1—that is, they master the phonotactic system of their language—L2 learners often have extraordinary

Listening in Language Acquisition   153

difficulty first perceiving and subsequently mastering the pronunciation and intonation patterns (Grech, 2000; Hayes & White, 2013).

One explanation is the **critical period** of language learning. The neural mechanisms underlying critical periods in early language development have been widely studied over the past decades (e.g., Aktan-Erciyes, 2021; Kuhl, 2021; Reh et al., 2020; Snow & Hoefnagel-Höhle, 1978). One underlying idea within these studies is the concept of **neural commitment** to language patterns. Neuropsychological imaging suggests that language acquisition involves the development of neural networks that focus on code-specific properties of the speech signals heard in early infancy, resulting in neural tissue dedicated to analyzing these learned patterns. This means that early neural commitment to L1 patterns can also constrain future L2 learning, while delayed neural commitment can lead to language processing difficulties in the L1 (Brodbeck et al., 2024; MacWhinney, 2012; Nicolson & Fawcett, 2019).

In English, fluent listeners use a metrical segmentation strategy to assume that "every strong syllable is the onset of a new content word" (Cutler, 2012). Because English is a **trochaically timed** language, stress peaks are important indicators of processing segments (the other possibilities for languages are **syllable-timed** languages, such as Spanish; **stress-timed** languages, such as French; and **mora-timed** languages, such as Japanese). In a trochaic pattern, emphasis or stress is placed on the first syllable of a metrical unit (known as a trochee), while the second syllable is typically less stressed or unstressed. This pattern creates a strong–weak rhythmic structure.

For example, with the word *poem*, the stress falls on the first syllable (/po/), creating a trochaic pattern. A similarity of metrical segmentation strategies between one's L1 and L2 (e.g., Dutch and English) will tend to lead to positive transfer for L2 listeners, making aural perception in the L2 easier. In contrast, dissimilar segmentation strategies between the L1 and the L2 (e.g., Japanese and English) will tend to lead to negative transfer (Crowhurst, 2020; Orzechowska et al., 2019).

Error analysis studies focus directly on phonological coding and reveal the word recognition difficulties that L2 listeners face (Chrabaszcz & Gor, 2014). The L2 listener has to decode the effects of assimilation and varying input speed, which they may perceive as degraded phonetic quality. Prosodic factors that increase speaker fluency can impact speech comprehensibility and increase the effort needed for decoding (Gor et al., 2021).

6.7.2 Development of L2 Syntactic Processing

As with other listening skills, children develop the ability to process increasingly more complex syntax as they acquire abstract thinking skills. For example, a child will come to process complex syntax, such as embeddings (the process by which one clause is included in another) and nominalizations (transforming a

154 *Defining Listening*

verb or adjective into a noun), while they are expanding their overall cognitive capacities to understand abstract concepts. L2 learners, on the other hand, will generally learn the syntax of the new language *after* their cognitive processes have matured and after they have automatized syntactic processing in their L1. This mature cognitive state presents both advantages and disadvantages to the L2 learner.

The main advantage for the older L2 learner is **metacognitive processing**. The mature learner may be able to *consciously* employ abstract thinking about categories and rules to better grasp the syntax of the new language and to make analytic comparisons with their L1. The main disadvantage for the adult L2 learner is that fluent listening relies on *unconscious,* or automatic, processing of phonology and syntax.

According to the **native listener hypothesis (NLH)**, L2 listening is filtered through the screen of our native language. We tend to hear the L2 "through the ears of our first language" (Cutler, 2012): The phonemes and phonological rules of our native language influence how we perceive and produce sounds in a second language. The grammatical patterns and sentence structures of our native language can influence how we understand sentences in the L2. Unless we undertake sustained, systematic practice in L2 decoding, we will always tend to hear the sounds of the L2 in terms of L1 categories and parse the syntax of the L2 in terms of L1 grammatical rules. This unintentional tactic of processing the L2 *as variations from our L1* rather than as parts of a complete and coherent system is a primary source of ineffective, slow L2 listening (Clahsen & Felser, 2006; Cauldwell, 2014; Jia & Hew, 2021; Ullman, 2006).

If unreliable syntactic parsing were an occasional annoyance, it would not typically cause processing breakdowns for the listener. A major cause of difficulty in L2 listening, however, is *derailments of attention* when a problematic syntactic sequence cannot be decoded. The attempt to process unfamiliar or unexpected syntactic sequences produces a disruptive **P-400 effect**, an **orienting response** in the auditory cortex (a positive deflection, indicated by the "P" in the processing signal) that occurs about 400 milliseconds after an unfamiliar segment of input is perceived (Liu et al., 2009).

These unreliability blips are experienced by the L2 listener as increases in **cognitive load** requiring conscious attention and problem-solving, and this experience exerts a negative ripple effect on comprehension (Starreveld & de Groot, 2019). If these processing blips accumulate, the listener will place undue stress on short-term memory, trying to sort out perception problems while keeping up with the spoken discourse. This leads to even more limited parsing and less detailed syntactic representations.

As the L2 listener becomes more proficient, these disruptions become less frequent and less disruptive to fluent listening. Even for fluent L2 listeners, and for L1 listeners as well, this disruption response can be induced through the introduction of *stressful conditions,* such as listening to compressed speech,

Listening in Language Acquisition   155

listening for extended periods, or listening to multiple speakers simultaneously (Hyltenstam, 2021). While there is no cure for L1 interference in L2 linguistic processing, the effects of these interferences can be dealt with strategically, and intensive perception training (e.g., shadowing) can create greater automaticity in L2 processing (Hamada, 2016).

6.7.3 Linguistic Processing: Lexis

Just as the child learning an L1 proceeds through a long process of lexical acquisition, the L2 learner also must engage in the ongoing, gradual acquisition of the lexis. Lexical acquisition processes involve **mapping** concepts onto L2 words, generalizing and discriminating between lexical items—and encountering lexical items often enough to remember them. Listening and reading are the only avenues for lexical acquisition; therefore, the more an L2 learner listens to and reads input that is comprehensible yet contains new and challenging items, the more lexical acquisition will occur.

Mapping is the initial phase of lexical acquisition, in which grammatical, contextual, and communicative information from the linguistic and nonlinguistic context are processed. This processing initiates a map of referent meaning in the mental lexicon. Successful language learners can access these mental representations when necessary to further develop, revise, or differentiate their maps. According to connectionist acquisition principles, input frequency is an important factor in fast-mapping quality and speed (Ellis, 2023). In this model, exposure to new words in contexts of reading, listening, and interaction are the means of acquiring lexis in an L2.

There is a major difference between L1 and L2 lexical acquisition through mapping. When language learners acquire their L1, **mutual exclusivity strategies** are often used, in which the L1 acquirer assumes each new word they hear is associated with a new, previously unknown object or concept (Bialystok, 2007). As soon as a person starts to learn an L2, the learner must accept that there is no discovery process in L2 vocabulary learning. Unless the new vocabulary item represents a unique item or concept in the L2 culture, the learner must undertake a **dual-coding** process: Two words, one in the L1 and one in the L2, refer to the same thing (Paivio, 2014).

Paradoxically, if the new word in the L2 represents a unique referent or concept in the L2, it may actually be easier to learn because it can bypass the dual-coding process. For instance, when I was learning Japanese as an adult, I found it easy to learn and remember new words and expressions for concepts for which there was a **lexical gap**, no equivalent in my native language, such as 頑張って *ganbatte*, よろしくお願いします *yoroshiku onegaishimasu*, わびさび *wabi-sabi*, or お疲れ様 *otsukaresama*.

The opposite phenomenon in the acquisition of L2 listening vocabulary is the ease of **lexical transfer** between two related languages. The two basic kinds

156 *Defining Listening*

of transfer are **cognate transfer** and **loan transfer**. When used congruently, both of these cognitive processes vastly increase an L2 user's receptive and productive vocabulary. Cognate transfer occurs when words in two languages share similar forms and meanings due to their common linguistic origin, such as *hotel* in English and Spanish.

Loan transfer, also known as borrowing or lexical borrowing, refers to the adoption of words or phrases from one language into another. For example, English has borrowed many words from other languages, such as *sushi* from Japanese or *entrepreneur* from French.

Cognate transfer and loan transfer refer to an underlying semantic and phonological similarity between words in the L1 and L2. When learners of an L2 become aware of cognates and loanwords, they can learn the L2 target word faster because they can collapse the dual-coding process into a single coding. However, when loanwords are borrowed into a language, some form of **transliteration** or **transvocalization** takes place.

A notable case of loan transfer is the rampant borrowing of foreign words into Japanese (a phenomenon called *gairaigo*), which has an estimated 3,000 loanwords from English and a smaller number from other Indo-European sources (Daulton, 2008; Ferries, 2022). The L2 learner can take advantage of the loanwords in their L1 but must be aware of the transformation processes that occur during the loan process. For example, in Japanese, the term *peepaa duraibaa* ("paper driver") is derived from English but has a specific meaning in Japanese (a person who has a driver's license but no experience driving) and a different meaning (or a very abstruse meaning, in this case) in the language of origin.

6.8 Listening in L2 Acquisition: Development of Semantic Processing

Semantic processing consists of lexical access, schema activation and modification, and inferencing, as outlined in Chapter 3. All three of these component processes are functions of semantic memory, a distributed cognitive network that involves coordinating multiple brain regions. Semantic memory is the long-term memory system that stores general knowledge and concepts about the world, including facts, meanings, and concepts. In bilingual individuals, semantic memory is typically shared between the languages they know.

When remembering ideas in different languages, bilinguals may experience minor variations based on the language they are using at the time. The specific dynamics of semantic memory in bilinguals can be influenced by language proficiency, language dominance, and context.

Language dominance is often referred to in three different domains: degree of proficiency, degree of dominance, and modality of dominance.

Balanced bilinguals achieve relatively equal overall proficiency and balanced abilities in both languages. Balanced bilinguals are most often **simultaneous**

bilinguals; that is, they acquired both languages very early in life, often in the same social and environmental context. They can switch between languages effortlessly, depending on their interlocutors' context and dominant language. These individuals may or may not have a clear dominant language, but they exhibit native or near-native listening proficiency in both languages. (This is the case with my two children, who grew up exposed to English and Japanese. They are balanced bilinguals but now exhibit English dominance in most situations.)

In most cases, bilingual individuals have a clear dominant language. However, that language can shift over time. This happened to me during my two years living in Togo as a high school teacher in the Peace Corps. As my work, home, and relationship life revolved around French, and since I had virtually no access to English speakers (before the days of cell phones and Zoom calls), French became my dominant language, even though I was only at a B2 level (high intermediate) of proficiency.

Another defining aspect of bilingualism is the modalities in which the L1 and L2 are used. Language dominance can vary across situational or usage domains, in which case the bilingual user is labeled a **coordinate bilingual**. For instance, a bilingual individual may have receptive dominance in one language, meaning they understand and comprehend that language better in specific domains of listening, reading, or writing, particularly in their professional fields, while having productive dominance in the other language, where they are more proficient in speaking. Coordinate bilinguals are often highly proficient in both languages, but they may show dominance or greater proficiency in one language within its respective domain. Semantic processing in the L2—how semantic information is encoded and retrieved while listening—is influenced by these proficiency and domain factors.

6.9 Listening in L2 Acquisition: Development of Pragmatic Processing

The acquisition of pragmatic competence in an L2 is widely recognized as one of the most complex aspects of language learning, largely because pragmatic processing often involves decisions relating to both language and social behavior.

Pragmatic competence in L2 listening involves many dimensions of contextual and cultural knowledge:

- when to talk, how much to say, pacing and pausing in and between speaking turns, aspects of behavior that determine our "pragmatic accent" (Overstreet & Yule, 2002), when and how to give listenership cues (Shelley & Gonzalez, 2013)
- how to decide on meanings of paralinguistic signals, intonation, body language, turn-taking behavior, pauses, and silence (Sueyoshi & Hardison, 2005)
- how to decide on linguistic etiquette: observance of relative social distance between people of various levels of authority, governing the degree of

158 *Defining Listening*

imposition one person can place upon the other, and the degree of directness one can use in making claims and requests (Holmes & Wilson, 2022; Kasper & Roever, 2005)

- how to interpret communication styles, including nonverbal communication (Argyle, 2013)
- how to interpret types of indirectness, including possible deception (Atkinson, 2013)
- how to deal with unequal encounters in which one speaker exerts power over the other (Kramsch & Uryu, 2012)
- how to detect and repair problems in communication (Haslett, 2013).

To become more efficient in the pragmatic domain of listening and *to be perceived* as pragmatically competent, the L2 user needs to make two strategic adjustments to their listening style. The first modification is at the level of interactional alignment. This entails *displaying* behaviors that are recognized *as appropriate, functional, and supportive* by speakers of the target language (Bodie et al., 2012). In a sense, this metacognitive strategy involves expanding one's perspective, retaining one's original cultural identity, and taking on the additional perspective of a target language (TL) speaker (Shaules, 2023; Ting-Toomey & Dorjee, 2014).

The second set of strategies is related to the transactional focus on discourse, intention to achieve, and specific outcomes through interaction. This set includes (1) management strategies for keeping the discourse moving toward desired outcomes (such as repeating or reframing a question), (2) collaboration with interlocutors (such as explicitly asking for an opinion), (3) confirming the discourse's progress (such as paraphrasing the speaker's last contribution before continuing), and (4) initiating repairs when ambiguities or misunderstandings occur (such as asking whether a speaker meant "A" or "B") (Ishihara & Cohen, 2021).

6.10 Summary: The Transformative Nature of L1 and L2 Acquisition of Listening

L1 and L2 acquisition differ in significant ways, but they have much in common. Specifically, to use English as an example, if one person is acquiring English as a first language as a child, and another person is acquiring it as a second language as an adult, both will aim to master the same grammatical, lexical, and phonological systems. And if both are reasonably successful, they will be able to share understandings of the same stories, books, films, conversations, jokes, and lectures and communicate directly with each other.

The differences lie in how they go about the acquisition process, their motivations, the time and effort required, and ultimately, their own sense of agency with the language.

The late Nigerian novelist Chinua Achebe, a native speaker of Igbo, was once asked, "Is it possible for you to ever learn to write English like a native speaker?" Achebe was quiet for a while, then responded: "I should say, I hope not. It is neither necessary nor desirable for a person to be able to do so. The price a world language must be prepared to pay is submission to many *different kinds of use*. The person should aim at fashioning an English which is at once universal and able to carry his peculiar experience" (Achebe, 1997, p. 347). Achebe's writings and speeches in English personify this philosophy: While using elegant English, he maintains the tonal oratory style and speech patterns of the Igbo language and, as is common in his native culture, speaks through allegorical stories and proverbs.

Achebe's view reflects the positive side and reverberates the paradox of second language acquisition for all skills, including listening. The neurological changes that help make our L1 an efficient locked-in system in phonology vocabulary and syntax can never be—and should never be—reversed. They are an integral part of each speaker's identity.

Despite the psychological challenges of acquiring an L2 and preserving one's identity, L2 learners can still develop a native-like proficiency in their second language (de Groot, 2011; 2017). And bilinguals themselves, regardless of ultimate level of attainment, will note qualitative changes in their lives—their ideas, beliefs, thinking abilities, communication styles, and capacity for empathy may undergo significant changes (Crain et al., 2017). For many, acquiring an additional language, even with a modicum of success, may open professional doors and offer personal, social, and cultural enrichment. In addition, there appears to be an unexpected inverse benefit. Individuals who have achieved functional proficiency in an L2 tend to show better overall listening ability *in their L1* due to expanded coding ability (Fox et al., 2019).

Acquisition of listening, for both L1 and L2 acquirers, can be a transformative experience. To paraphrase the thirteenth-century Sufi poet Rumi: "Listen to a new language so that the world will be a new world." This quote reminds us that language learning, and listening in particular, is a psychologically powerful experience that can open up new worlds of experience. For the L1 child learner, this transformation is obvious: Learning to listen, as a pathway into language, develops the child's mind and connects the child to family and society.

For the L2 child or adult learner, the transformation may be less obvious but is equally significant. In the context of teaching and researching additional languages, it is important to keep in mind that the significance of L2 acquisition for any learner is not directly proportional to the degree of proficiency achieved. L2 acquisition is essentially neither successful nor unsuccessful in quantitative terms: Irrespective of proficiency measures, the L2 can be incorporated into the life of any sincere user in an authentic and meaningful way (Kramsch, 2023).

160 *Defining Listening*

References

Achebe, C. (1997). English and the African writer: Chinua Achebe No. 75/76. *The anniversary issue: Selections from Transition, 1961–1976* (pp. 342–349). Indiana University Press.

Aitchison, J. (2012). *Words in the mind: An introduction to the mental lexicon* (4th ed.). Wiley.

Aktan-Erciyes, A. (2021). Understanding language acquisition: Neural theory of language. *Journal of Language and Linguistic Studies, 17*(2), 697–705.

Alhama, R. G., Rowland, C. F., & Kidd, E. (2023). How does linguistic context influence word learning? *Journal of Child Language, 50*(6), 1374–1393. doi:10.1017/S0305000923000302.

Alrwaita, N., Houston-Price, C., Meteyard, L., Voits, T., & Pliatsikas, C. (2023). Executive functions are modulated by the context of dual language use: Diglossic, bilingual and monolingual older adults. *Bilingualism: Language and Cognition, 27*, 1–26.

Ambridge, B., & Lieven, E. (2011). *Child language acquisition: Contrasting theoretical approaches*. Cambridge University Press.

Argyle, M. (2013). *Bodily communication*. Routledge.

Atkinson, D. (2013). Intercultural rhetoric and intercultural communication. In J. Jackson (Ed.) *The Routledge handbook of language and intercultural communication* (pp. 116–129). Routledge.

Barrouillet, P. (2015). Theories of cognitive development: From Piaget to today. *Developmental Review, 38*, 1–12.

Bates, E., Dale, P. S., & Thal, D. (2017). Individual differences and their implications for theories of language development. In P. Fletcher & B. MacWhinney (Eds.), *The handbook of child language* (pp. 95–151). Blackwell.

Bernhardt, B. M., & Stemberger, J. P. (2020). *Phonological development* (Vol. 10, p. 223). John Benjamins.

Bernstein-Ratner, N. (2021). The phonology of parent-child speech. In *Children's language* (pp. 159–174). Psychology Press.

Bialystok, E. (2007). Acquisition of literacy in bilingual children: A framework for research. *Language Learning, 57*, 45–77.

Bishop, D. (2014). *Uncommon understanding: Development and disorders of language comprehension in children*. Psychology Press.

Bjorklund, D. F. (2022). *Children's thinking: Cognitive development and individual differences*. SAGE.

Blum-Kulka, S. (2012). *Dinner talk: Cultural patterns of sociability and socialization in family discourse*. Routledge.

Bodie, G., St. Cyr, K., Pence, M., Rold, M., & Honeycutt, J. (2012). Listening competence in initial interactions: Distinguishing between what listening is and what listeners do. *International Journal of Listening, 26*, 1–28.

Brodbeck, C., Kandylaki, K. D., & Scharenborg, O. (2024). Neural representations of non-native speech reflect proficiency and interference from native language knowledge. *Journal of Neuroscience, 44*(1). https://www.biorxiv.org/content/10.1101/2023.04.15.537014v1

Cameron-Faulkner, T., Lieven, E., & Tomasello, M. (2003). A construction based analysis of child directed speech. *Cognitive Science, 27*(6), 843–873.

Carstens, A. (2016). Translanguaging as a vehicle for L2 acquisition and L1 development: students' perceptions. *Language Matters*, *47*(2), 203–222.

Cartmill, E. A., Armstrong, B. F., Gleitman, L. R., Goldin-Meadow, S., Medina, T. N, & Trueswell, J. C. (2013). Quality of early parent input predicts child vocabulary 3 years later. *Proceedings of the National Academy of Sciences of the United States of America*, *110*, 11278–11283. doi: 10.1073/pnas.1309518110

Case, R. (2013). Intellectual development from birth to adulthood: A neo-Piagetian interpretation. In *Children's Thinking* (pp. 37–71). Psychology Press.

Catani, M., & Bambini, V. (2014). A model for social communication and language evolution and development (SCALED). *Current Opinion in Neurobiology*, *28*, 165–171.

Cauldwell, R. (2014). Listening and pronunciation need separate models of speech. In J. Levis & S. McCrocklin (Eds.), *Proceedings of the Second Language Learning and Teaching Conference* (pp. 40–44). Iowa State University.

Chefneux, G. (2013). Politeness at work. *Topics in Linguistics: Approaches to Text and Discourse Analysis, Contexts, References and Style*, *11*, 21–31. www.kaa.ff.ukf.sk/top ics/issue11.pdf.

Choi, D., & Werker, J. F. (2021). Speech perception and the sensorimotor system in Infancy. *Acoustical Society of America Journal*, *150*, 4, A111–A111.

Chomsky, N. (1976). On the biological basis of language capacities. In R. W. Rieber (Ed.), *The neuropsychology of language: Essays in honor of Eric Lenneberg* (pp. 1–24). Springer US.

Chong, S. W., Isaacs, T., & McKinley, J. (2023). Ecological systems theory and second language research. *Language Teaching*, *56*(3), 333–348.

Chrabaszcz, A., & Gor, K. (2014). Context effects in the processing of phonolexical ambiguity in L2. *Language Learning*, *64*, 415–455.

Christiansen, M. H., Contreras Kallens, P., & Trecca, F. (2022). Toward a comparative approach to language acquisition. *Current Directions in Psychological Science*, *31*(2), 131–138.

Clahsen, H., & Felser, C. (2006). Continuity and shallow structures in language processing. *Applied Psycholinguistics*, *27*(1), 107–126.

Clark, P. M., Griffing, P. S., & Johnson, L. G. (2017). Symbolic play and ideational fluency as aspects of the evolving divergent cognitive style in young children. *Cognitive Style in Early Education*, *27*(1), 95–106.

Cohen, A. (2014). Coming to terms with second language learning and language use strategies. In *Strategies in learning and using a second language* (pp. 7–62). New York: Routledge.

Cowie, F. (2010). Innateness and language. *Stanford Encyclopedia of Philosophy*. https:// plato.stanford.edu/entries/innateness-language/

Crain, W. (2015). Bandura's social learning theory. In W. Crain (Ed.), *Theories of development: Concepts and applications* (6th ed.) (pp. 196–216). Taylor & Francis.

Crain, S., Koring, L., & Thornton, R. (2017). Language acquisition from a biolinguistic perspective. *Neuroscience & Biobehavioral Reviews*, *81*, 120-149.

Cristia, A., Dupoux, E., Gurven, M., & Stieglitz, J. (2019). Child-directed speech is infrequent in a forager-farmer population: A time allocation study. *Child Development*, *90*(3), 759–773.

Crowhurst, M. J. (2020). The iambic/trochaic law: Nature or nurture? *Language and Linguistics Compass*, *14*(1), e12360.

162 *Defining Listening*

Crowley, K., & Jacobs, M. (2002). Building islands of expertise in everyday family activity. In G. Leinhardt, K. Crowley, & K. Knutson (Eds.), *Learning conversations in museums* (pp. 333–356). Erlbaum.

Cutler, A. (2012). *Native listening.* MIT Press.

Daniels, H. (2016). *Vygotsky and pedagogy.* Routledge.

Dasen, P. R. (2022). Culture and cognitive development. *Journal of Cross-Cultural Psychology, 53*(7–8), 789–816.

Daskalaki, E., Elma, B. L. O. M., Chondrogianni, V., & Paradis, J. (2020). Effects of parental input quality in child heritage language acquisition. *Journal of Child Language, 47*(4), 709–736.

Daulton, F. (2008). *Japan's built-in lexicon of English-based loan words.* Multilingual Matters.

De Groot, A. (2011). *Bilingual cognition: An introduction.* Psychology Press.

De Groot, A. M. (2017). Bi-and multilingualism. In Y. Y. Kim (Ed.), *The international encyclopedia of intercultural communication* (pp. 1–10). Wiley.

DeLuca, V., Segaert, K., Mazaheri, A., & Krott, A. (2020). Understanding bilingual brain function and structure changes? U bet! A unified bilingual experience trajectory model. *Journal of Neurolinguistics, 56,* 100930.

Demuth, K. (2011). The acquisition of phonology. In J. Goldsmith, J. Riggle, & A. C. L. Yu (Eds.), *The handbook of phonological theory* (pp. 571–595). Wiley-Blackwell.

Elicker, J., England, M., & Sroufe, L. A. (2016). Predicting peer competence and peer relationships in childhood from early parent-child relationships. In R. D. Parke & G. W. Ladd (Eds.), *Family-peer relationships* (pp. 77–106). Routledge.

Ellis, N. C. (2023). Bilingual language cognition as a complex adaptive system. *Bilingualism: Language and Cognition, 26,* 31–32.

Feldman, N. H., Griffiths, T. L., & Morgan, J. L. (2009). The influence of categories on perception: Explaining the perceptual magnet effect as optimal statistical inference. *Psychological Review, 116*(4), 752.

Ferries, J. (2022). A corpus analysis of loanword effects on second language production. *Englishes in Practice, 5*(1), 107–132.

Fleer, M. (2021). *Play in the early years.* Cambridge University Press.

Fox, R., Corretjer, O., & Webb, K. (2019). Benefits of foreign language learning and bilingualism: An analysis of published empirical research 2012–2019. *Foreign Language Annals, 52*(4), 699–726.

Gampe, A., Quick, A. E., & Daum, M. M. (2021). Does linguistic similarity affect early simultaneous bilingual language acquisition? *Journal of Language Contact, 13*(3), 482–500.

García-Sierra, A., Ramírez-Esparza, N., Wig, N., & Robertson, D. (2021). Language learning as a function of infant directed speech (IDS) in Spanish: Testing neural commitment using the positive-MMR. *Brain and Language, 212,* 104890.

Gass, S. M., & Mackey, A. (2014). Input, interaction, and output in second language acquisition. In B. VanPatten & J. Williams (Eds.), *Theories in second language acquisition* (pp. 194–220). Routledge.

Gleason, J., & Ratner, N. (2022). *The development of language.* Plural Publishing.

Gleitman, L. R., Liberman, M. Y., McLemore, C. A., & Partee, B. H. (2019). The impossibility of language acquisition (and how they do it). *Annual Review of Linguistics, 5,* 1–24.

Goldfield, B. A., Snow, C. E., & Willenberg, I. A. (2024). Variation in language development. In J. B. Gleason & N. B. Ratner (Eds.), *The development of language* (10th ed., pp. 255–280). Plural Publishing.

Gomes, H., Molholm, S., Christodoulou, C., Ritter, W., & Cowan, N. (2000). The development of auditory attention in children. *Frontiers in Bioscience-Landmark, 5*(3), 108–120.

Goswami, U. (2022). Language acquisition and speech rhythm patterns: An auditory neuroscience perspective. *Royal Society Open Science, 9*(7), 211855.

Gor, K., Cook, S., Bordag, D., Chrabaszcz, A., & Opitz, A. (2021). Fuzzy lexical representations in adult second language speakers. *Frontiers in psychology, 12,* 732030.

Grech, H. (2000). Cross linguistic comparison of phonotactic development. *South African Journal of Communication Disorders, 47*(special), 35–43.

Haastrup, K., & Henriksen, B. (2000). Vocabulary acquisition: Acquiring depth of knowledge through network building. *International Journal of Applied Linguistics, 10*(2), 221–240.

Hamada, Y. (2016). Shadowing: Who benefits and how? Uncovering a booming EFL teaching technique for listening comprehension. *Language Teaching Research, 20*(1), 35–52.

Hart, B., & Risley, T. R. (1995). *Meaningful differences in the everyday experience of young American children*. Paul H. Brookes Publishing.

Hartup, W. (1996). The company they keep: Friendships and their developmental significance. *Child Development, 67,* 1–13.

Hartup, W. W. (2017). Children and their friends 1. In H. McGurk (Ed.), *Issues in childhood social development* (pp. 130–170). Routledge.

Haslett, B. B. (2013). *Communication: Strategic action in context*. Routledge.

Hayes, B., & White, J. (2013). Phonological naturalness and phonotactic learning. *Linguistic Inquiry, 44,* 45–75.

Hedges, H. (2014). Young children's "working theories": Building and connecting understandings. *Journal of Early Childhood Research, 12*(1), 35–49.

Hedges, H. (2022). *Children's interests, inquiries and identities: Curriculum, pedagogy, learning and outcomes in the early years*. Routledge.

Holmes, J., & Wilson, N. (2022). Speech functions, politeness, and cross-cultural communication. In *An introduction to sociolinguistics* (6th ed.) (pp. 431–468). Routledge.

Hyltenstam, K. (2021). Language aptitude and language awareness: Polyglot perspectives. *Annual Review of Applied Linguistics, 41,* 55–75.

Isaacs, B. (2014). *Bringing the Montessori approach to your early years practice*. Routledge.

Ishihara, N., & Cohen, A. D. (2021). Collecting data reflecting the pragmatic use of language. In N. Ishihara and A.D. Cohen (Eds.), *Teaching and learning pragmatics* (2nd ed., pp. 36–60). Routledge.

Jia, C., & Hew, K. F. (2021). Meeting the challenges of decoding training in English as a foreign/second language listening education: Current status and opportunities for technology-assisted decoding training. *Computer Assisted Language Learning, 36*(10), 1–30.

Kapengut, D. (2020). *Child-directed speech and the developing brain: An investigation of adult verbal warmth and negative affect* (Doctoral dissertation, Columbia University).

164   *Defining Listening*

Kasper, G., & Roever, C. (2005). Developing pragmatic competence. In E. Hinkel (Ed.), *Handbook of research in second language teaching and learning* (pp. 317–334). Routledge.

Kidd, E., & Donnelly, S. (2020). Individual differences in first language acquisition. *Annual Review of Linguistics, 6,* 319–340.

Kim, Y. (2017). Cognitive-interactionist approaches to L2 instruction. In S. Loewen & M. Sato (Eds.), *The Routledge handbook of instructed second language acquisition* (pp. 126–145). Routledge.

Kramsch, C. (2023). Foreword: Authenticity in our times. In L. Will, W. Stadler, & I. Eloff (Eds.), *Authenticity across languages and cultures: Themes of identity in foreign language teaching and learning* (pp. i–vi). De Gruyter.

Kramsch, C., & Uryu, M. (2012). Intercultural contact, hybridity, and third space. In J. Jackson (Ed.), *The Routledge handbook of language and intercultural communication* (pp. 211–225). Routledge.

Kramsch, C., & Zhu, H. (2020). Translating culture in global times: An introduction. *Applied Linguistics, 41*(1), 1–9.

Kuhl, P., Conboy, B., Coffey-Corina, S., Padden, D., Rivera-Gaxiola, M., & Nelson, T. (2008). Phonetic learning as a pathway to language: New data and native language magnet theory expanded (NLM-e). *Philosophical Transactions B, 363,* 979–1000.

Kuhl, P., & Rivera-Gaxiola, M. (2008). Neural substrates of language acquisition. *Annual Review of Neuroscience, 31,* 511–534.

Kuhl, P. K. (2021). Sensorimotor information flow and the acquisition of speech. *Acoustical Society of America Journal, 150*(4), A110–A110.

Lam, C. B., McHale, S. M., & Crouter, A. C. (2014). Time with peers from middle childhood to late adolescence: Developmental course and adjustment correlates. *Child Development, 85*(4), 1677–1693.

Lau, B. K., Taulu, S., Kuhl, P. K., & Lee, A. K. (2021). The neural processing of sound in infants. *The Journal of the Acoustical Society of America, 150*(4), A183–A183.

Lieven, E., Grøver, V., Uccelli, P., & Rowe, M. L. (2019). Input, interaction and learning in early language development. In V. Grøver, P. Uccelli, M. Rowe, & E. Lieven (Eds.), *Learning through language: Towards an educationally informed theory of language learning* (pp. 19–30). Cambridge University Press.

Lieven, E., & Tomasello, M. (2008). Children's first language acquisition from a usage-based perspective. In P. Robinson & N. Ellis (Eds.) *Handbook of cognitive linguistics and second language acquisition* (pp. 168–196). Routledge.

Leow, R. P., & Martin, A. (2017). Enhancing the input to promote salience of the L2: A critical overview. In S. M. Gass, P. Spinner, & J. Behney (Eds.), *Salience in second language acquisition* (pp. 167–186). Routledge.

Leow, R. P., & Mercer, J. D. (2015). Depth of processing in L2 learning: Theory, research, and pedagogy. *Journal of Spanish Language Teaching, 2*(1), 69–82.

Lichtman, K., & VanPatten, B. (2021). Was Krashen right? Forty years later. *Foreign language annals, 54*(2), 283–305.

Liu, B., Wang, Z. & Jin, Z. (2009). The integration processing of the visual and auditory information in videos of real-world events: An ERP study. *Neuroscience Letters, 461,* 7–11.

Lovas, G. S. (2011). Gender and patterns of language development in mother-toddler and father-toddler dyads. *First Language, 31*(1), 83–108.

Lovatt, D., & Hedges, H. (2014). Children's working theories: Invoking disequilibrium. *Early Child Development and Care*, *185*, 909–925.

Luchkina, E., & Waxman, S. (2021). Acquiring verbal reference: The interplay of cognitive, linguistic, and general learning capacities. *Infant Behavior and Development*, *65*, 101624.

MacWhinney, B. (2012). The logic of the unified model. In S. Gass & A. Mackey (Eds.), *The Routledge handbook of second language acquisition* (pp. 211–227). Routledge.

Martin, S., McQuitty, V., & Morgan, D. (2019). Complexity theory and teacher education. *Oxford Research Encyclopedia of Education*. https://oxfordre.com/education/view/10.1093/

Masek, L. R., Weiss, S. M., McMillan, B. T., Paterson, S. J., Golinkoff, R. M., & Hirsh-Pasek, K. (2023). Contingent conversations build more than language: How communicative interactions in toddlerhood relate to preschool executive function skills. *Developmental Science*, *26*(3), e13338.

McMurray, B. (2022). The myth of categorical perception. *The Journal of the Acoustical Society of America*, *152*(6), 3819–3842.

Mirolli, M., & Parisi, D. (2009). Language as a cognitive tool. *Minds and Machines*, *19*, 517–528.

Mottweiler, C. M., & Taylor, M. (2014). Elaborated role play and creativity in preschool age children. *Psychology of Aesthetics, Creativity, and the Arts*, *8*(3), 277.

Nelson, K. (2007). *Young minds in social worlds: Experience, meaning, and memory.* Harvard University Press.

Nicolson, R. I., & Fawcett, A. J. (2019). Development of dyslexia: The delayed neural commitment framework. *Frontiers in Behavioral Neuroscience*, *13*, 112.

Nikolaus, M., & Fourtassi, A. (2023). Communicative feedback in language acquisition. *New Ideas in Psychology*, *68*, 100985

Niżegorodcew, A. (2007). *Input for instructed L2 learners: The relevance of relevance* (Vol. 22). Multilingual Matters.

Nuevo, A. M. (2006). *Task complexity and interaction: L2 learning opportunities and development* (Doctoral dissertation, Georgetown University).

Ochs, E., & Schieffelin, B. (2011). The theory of language socialization. In A. Duranti, E. Ochs, & B. Schieffelin (Eds.), *The handbook of language socialization* (pp. 1–21). Wiley.

Ochs, E., & Schieffelin, B. (2016). Language acquisition and socialization: Three developmental stories and their implications. In A. Duranti (Ed.), *Linguistic anthropology: A reader* (2nd ed.) (pp. 296–328). Wiley.

O'Madagain, C., & Tomasello, M. (2022). Shared intentionality, reason-giving and the evolution of human culture. *Philosophical Transactions of the Royal Society B*, *377*(1843), 20200320.

Oogarah-Pratap, B., Bholoa, A., & Ramma, Y. (2020). Stage theory of cognitive development: Jean Piaget. In B. Akpan & T. J. Kennedy (Eds.), *Science education in theory and practice: An introductory guide to learning theory* (pp. 133–148). Springer Nature.

Ortega, L. (2009). Interaction and attention to form in L2 text-based computer-mediated communication. In A. Mackey & C. Polio (Eds.), *Multiple perspectives on interaction* (pp. 232–259). Routledge.

Orzechowska, P., Mołczanow, J., & Jankowski, M. (2019). Prosodically-conditioned syllable structure in English. *Research in Language*, *17*(2), 167–178.

166 Defining Listening

Overstreet, M., & Yule, G. (2002). The metapragmatics of "and everything." *Journal of Pragmatics, 34*, 785–794.

Paivio, A. (2014). *Mind and its evolution: A dual coding theoretical approach.* Psychology Press.

Parish-Morris J., Golinkoff, R., & Hirsh-Pasek, K. (2013). From coo to code: Language acquisition in early childhood. In P. Zelazo (Ed.), *The Oxford handbook of developmental psychology* (Vol. 1, pp. 867–908). Oxford University Press.

Parker, J. G., Rubin, K. H., Erath, S. A., Wojslawowicz, J. C., & Buskirk, A. A. (2015). Peer relationships, child development, and adjustment: A developmental psychopathology perspective. In D. Cicchetti & D. J. Cohen (Eds.), *Developmental psychopathology: Volume One: Theory and method* (pp. 419–493). Wiley.

Peters, A. M. (2017). Strategies in the acquisition of syntax. In P. Fletcher & B. MacWhinney (Eds.), *The handbook of child language* (pp. 462–482). Wiley.

Peters, S., & Davis, K. (2011). Fostering children's working theories: Pedagogic issues and dilemmas in New Zealand. *Early Years: An International Research Journal, 31*, 5–17.

Piaget, J. (1951/2007). *The child's conception of the world.* Rowman & Littlefield.

Pinto Jr., R. F., & Xu, Y. (2021). A computational theory of child overextension. *Cognition, 206*, 104472.

Pliatsikas, C. (2020). Understanding structural plasticity in the bilingual brain: The Dynamic Restructuring Model. *Bilingualism: Language and Cognition, 23*(2), 459–471.

Poveda, D. (2019). Researching digital literacy practices in early childhood: Challenges, complexities, and imperatives. In O. Erstad, R. Flewitt, B. Kümmerling-Meibauer, & Í. S. Pereira (Eds.), *The Routledge handbook of digital literacies in early childhood* (pp. 45–63). Routledge.

Prilutskaya, M. (2021). Examining pedagogical translanguaging: A systematic review of the literature. *Languages, 6*(4), 180.

Ramírez-Esparza, N., García-Sierra, A. & Kuhl, P. (2014). Look who's talking: Speech style and social context in language input to infants are linked to concurrent and future speech development. *Developmental Science, 17*(6), 880–891.

Reh, R. K., Dias, B. G., Nelson III, C. A., Kaufer, D., Werker, J. F., Kolb, B., Levine, J. D., & Hensch, T. K. (2020). Critical period regulation across multiple timescales. *Proceedings of the National Academy of Sciences, 117*(38), 23242–23251.

Robinson, K. (2009). *The element: How finding your passion changes everything.* Viking.

Robinson, P. (2022). The cognition hypothesis, the triadic componential framework and the SSARC model: An instructional design theory of pedagogic task sequencing. In M. J. Ahmadian & M. H. Long (Eds.), *The Cambridge handbook of task-based language teaching* (pp. 205–225). Cambridge University Press.

Rocha-Hidalgo, J., & Barr, R. (2023). Defining bilingualism in infancy and toddlerhood: A scoping review. *International Journal of Bilingualism, 27*(3), 253–274.

Rogoff, B., Moore, L. C., Correa-Chávez, M., & Dexter, A. L. (2015). Children develop cultural repertoires through engaging in everyday routines and practices. In J. E. Grusec & P. D. Hastings (Eds.), *Handbook of socialization: Theory and research* (2nd ed., pp. 472–498). Guilford Press.

Rogoff, B., Moore, L., Najafi, B., Dexter, A., Correa-Chávez, M., & Solís, J. (2007). Children's development of cultural repertoires through participation in everyday routines and practices. In J. E. Grusec & P. D. Hastings (Eds.), *Handbook of socialization: Theory and research* (pp. 490–515). Guilford Press.

Rohde, H., & Frank, M. (2014). Markers of topical discourse in child-directed speech. *Cognitive Science, 8,* 1634–1661.

Ross, L. A., Molholm, S., Butler, J. S., Del Bene, V. A., & Foxe, J. J. (2022). Neural correlates of multisensory enhancement in audiovisual narrative speech perception: A fMRI investigation. *NeuroImage, 263,* 119598.

Rowe, M. L., & Weisleder, A. (2020). Language development in context. *Annual Review of Developmental Psychology, 2,* 201–223.

Rubin, K. H., Coplan, R., Chen, X., Bowker, J., & McDonald, K. L. (2013). Peer relationships in childhood. In M. E. Lamb & M. H. Bornstein (Eds.), *Social and personality development* (pp. 317–368). Psychology Press.

Russ, S. W. (2016). Pretend play: Antecedent of adult creativity. *New Directions for Child and Adolescent Development, 2016*(151), 21–32.

Saxton, M. (2009). The inevitability of child-directed speech. In S. Foster-Cohen (Ed.), *Language acquisition* (pp. 62–86). Palgrave Macmillan.

Schick, J., Fryns, C., Wegdell, F., Laporte, M., Zuberbühler, K., van Schaik, C. P., Townsend, S. W., & Stoll, S. (2022). The function and evolution of child-directed communication. *PLoS Biology 20*(5), e3001630. doi: 10.1371/journal.pbio.3001630

Schneider, B. (2016). *Childhood friendships and peer relations: Friends and enemies.* Routledge.

Slaughter, V., Imuta, K., Peterson, C. C., & Henry, J. D. (2015). Meta-analysis of theory of mind and peer popularity in the preschool and early school years. *Child Development, 86*(4), 1159–1174.

Shaules, J. (2023). Language learning as a transformative experience of resistance, adjustment and change. In J. Shaules & T. McConachy (Eds.), *Transformation, embodiment, and wellbeing in foreign language pedagogy: Enacting deep learning.* Bloomsbury.

Shelley, L., & Gonzalez, F. (2013). Back channeling: Function of back channeling and L1 effects on back channeling in L2. *Linguistic Portfolio, 2,* 98–108.

Snow, C. E., & Hoefnagel-Höhle, M. (1978). The critical period for language acquisition: Evidence from second language learning. *Child Development,* 1114–1128.

Snow, C. E., Perlmann, R., & Nathan, D. (2021). Why routines are different: Toward a multiple-factors model of the relation between input and language acquisition. In K. Nelson & A. van Kleeck (Eds.), *Children's language* (pp. 65–97). Psychology Press.

Starreveld, P. A., & de Groot, A. M. B. (2019). Psycholinguistic methods in the study of bilingualism. In J. Darquennes, J. C. Salmons, & W. Vandenbussche (Eds.), *Language contact* (pp. 653–667). De Gruyter Mouton.

Stiles, J., Brown, T., Hiast, F., & Jerrigan, T. (2015). Brain and cognitive development. In R. Lerner, L. Liben, & U. Mueller (Eds.), *Handbook of child psychology and developmental science* (pp. 9–62). Wiley.

Sueyoshi, A., & Hardison, D. (2005). The role of gestures and facial cues in second language listening comprehension. *Language Learning, 55,* 661–699.

Tang, J. (2013). Input of chunks and its effects on L2 learners' listening competency. *Theory and Practice in Language Studies, 3*(7), 1264.

Taverna, A. S., & Waxman, S. R. (2020). Early lexical acquisition in the Wichi language. *Journal of Child Language, 47*(5), 1052–1072.

168 Defining Listening

Themeli, C., & Prasolova-Førland, E. (2023). Inclusive Peer Learning Pedagogy with Augemented Reality–iPEAR. *Pedagogy and the Human Sciences, 9*(1), 2.

Thibault, P. (2006). Agency, individuation and meaning-making. In G. Williams & A. Lukin (Eds.), *The development of language: Functional perspectives on species and individual* (pp. 112–136). Continuum.

Thiessen, E., Kronstein, A., & Hufnagle, D. (2013). The extraction and integration framework: A two-process account of statistical learning. *Psychological Bulletin, 139*, 792–814.

Ting-Toomey, S., & Dorjee, T. (2014). Language, identity, and culture: Multiple identity-based perspectives. In T. Holtgraves (Ed.), *The Oxford handbook of language and social psychology* (pp. 27–45). Oxford University Press.

Tomasello, M. (2019). *Becoming human: A theory of ontogeny*. Harvard University Press.

Ullman, M. (2006). The declarative/procedural model and the shallow structure hypothesis. *Applied Psycholinguistics, 27*, 97–105.

Van der Feest, S. V., & Fikkert, P. (2015). Building phonological lexical representations. *Phonology, 32*(2), 207–239.

VanPatten, B. (2015). Foundations of processing instruction. *International Review of Applied Linguistics in Language Teaching, 53*(2), 91–109.

Weisleder, A., & Fernald, A. (2013). Talking to children matters: Early language experience strengthens processing and builds vocabulary. *Psychological Science, 24*(11), 2143–2152.

Wells, G. (2009). *The meaning makers: Learning to talk and talking to learn*. Multilingual Matters.

Wells, G. (1999). *Dialogic inquiry: Towards a sociocultural practice and theory of education*. Cambridge University Press.

Wentzel, K. (2022). Peer relationships, motivation, and academic performance *Routledge resources online*. https://doi.org/10.4324/9781138609877-REE49-1

Werker, J., & Hensch, T. (2015). Critical periods in speech perception: New directions. *Annual Review of Psychology, 66*, 173–196.

Wilkie, I., & Saxton, M. (2010). The origins of comic performance in adult-child interaction. *Comedy Studies, 1*, 21–32.

Williford, A. P., Vick Whittaker, J. E., Vitiello, V. E., & Downer, J. T. (2013). Children's engagement within the preschool classroom and their development of self-regulation. *Early Education & Development, 24*(2), 162–187.

Wilson, A. C., & Bishop, D. V. (2022). A novel online assessment of pragmatic and core language skills: An attempt to tease apart language domains in children. *Journal of Child Language, 49*(1), 38–59.

Yee, J., DeLuca, V., & Pliatsikas, C. (2023). The effects of multilingualism on brain structure, language control and language processing. In A. Cabrelli, C. Orozco, A. González, P. Soares, & P. Rothman (Eds.), *The Cambridge handbook of third language acquisition* (pp. 577–605). Cambridge University Press.

Section II

Teaching Listening

This section explores approaches and methods for teaching listening. Section I defined listening in terms of a convergence of neurological, linguistic, semantic, and pragmatic processing. Effective teaching of listening encompasses a conscious approach to developing all four of these processes in a complementary fashion.

Chapter 7 presents an overview of historical and current approaches for teaching listening. The historical approaches segment surveys a period of several decades, during which time listening came to be a central aspect of language instruction. It then profiles four approaches to teaching listening based on the definitions of listening in the first section of the book (neurological. linguistic, semantic, and pragmatic), introducing the framework of pre-listening, while-listening, and post-listening stages. The chapter ends with a synthesis of key principles to include in an instructional design and an outline of prototypical activities.

Chapter 8 highlights the central role of input and interaction in the teaching of listening. It first outlines the concepts of input genres and discourse types as a guide to choosing appropriate input. It then explores the notion of cognitive load and means of "easifying" input through text simplification, presentation scaffolding, and technology mediation.

Chapter 9 integrates all of the approaches that have been discussed in order to construct concrete designs for instruction. The chapter begins with an overview of instructional design stages: needs analysis, defining objectives, selecting content, designing and sequencing tasks, integrating technology, and conducting assessment. Sample activity sequences are presented utilizing this framework.

Chapter 10 outlines issues related to listening assessment. The chapter revolves around a multifaceted model of assessment and provides examples of

DOI: 10.4324/9781003390794-9

assessment formats and suggestions for assimilating assessment into a listening curriculum. It first discusses the notion of validity and presents frameworks for describing listening constructs and creating listening proficiency scales. It focuses on methodologies for composing test prompts, and also presents a framework for assessing interactive listening proficiency.

7 Approaches to Teaching Listening

7.1	Overview: Integrating Ideas into Teaching Methodologies	171
7.2	Historical Approaches to Teaching Listening	172
7.3	The Cognitive Revolution	173
7.4	Theoretical Models for Teaching Listening	176
	7.4.1 The Monitor Model	*176*
	7.4.2 The Interaction Hypothesis	*177*
	7.4.3 The Comprehensible Output Hypothesis	*178*
	7.4.4 Sociocultural Theory	*179*
	7.4.5 Metacognition Approaches	*180*
7.5	Profiling Approaches to Teaching Listening	182
	7.5.1 Neurological Processing: Focus on Engaged Listening	*182*
	7.5.2 Linguistic Processing: Focus on Attention to Bottom-Up Listening Skills	*186*
	7.5.3 Semantic Processing: Focus on Critical Listening	*189*
	7.5.4 Pragmatic Processing: Focus on Interactive Listening	*193*
7.6	Summary: Targeted and Balanced Approaches	195
References		196

7.1 Overview: Integrating Ideas into Teaching Methodologies

The initial four chapters of *Teaching and Researching Listening* have defined listening as a multidimensional process requiring neurological, linguistic, semantic, and pragmatic coordination. Chapter 5 outlined how listening ability is programmed in AI (Artificial Intelligence) and AGI (Artificial General Intelligence) systems to emulate and enhance human processing. Chapter 6 outlined how listening ability is naturally acquired in L1 and L2 contexts. Understanding the parallels between L1 and L2 acquisition provides the basis for preparing instruction, assessment, and research on best practices for teaching. As important as it is to understand the underlying processes of listening and language acquisition, understanding the processes alone will not

DOI: 10.4324/9781003390794-10

172   *Teaching Listening*

lead directly to effective teaching. Understanding must be incorporated into viable approaches for *teaching* those processes.

This chapter integrates the understanding of these multidimensional processes and the principles of language acquisition, focusing on methodologies for teaching listening in L2 contexts, including integrating listening with other skills.

The chapter will first review the most influential historical approaches to teaching L2 listening, highlighting the key features that are still relevant. We will then outline methods that prioritize a particular domain of listening—neurological, linguistic, semantic, or pragmatic. We will conclude the chapter by presenting an integrated approach featuring **experiential listening,** with the learner at the center. This approach balances skill development in the linguistic, semantic, and pragmatic domains of language processing while focusing on the learners' **metacognitive strategies** to regulate their listening. The following two chapters, Chapters 8 and 9, will treat the topics of input and interaction instructional design.

7.2 Historical Approaches to Teaching Listening

Most people who have taught languages are familiar with the **Grammar-Translation** (GT) method, the traditional language teaching approach that dates back to the sixteenth century, when classical languages such as Latin and Ancient Greek were valued as avenues to wisdom. This method emphasized the explicit teaching of grammatical rules, translation exercises, and the study of literary texts to learn a foreign language. Because the GT method made extensive use of the students' L1, there was little, if any, opportunity to listen to the L2.

What oral practice there was in this method revolved around reading aloud or reciting memorized texts rather than authentic communication. Listening was valued solely as a means to monitor the accuracy of these recitations. The main objective of this method is to understand and produce grammatically correct sentences and be able to translate back and forth from one's native language to the target. Listening fluency (the ability to listen continuously) and communicative competence (the ability to convey and understand spoken messages) are given virtually no priority. The method prevailed for so long because it was viewed as the only sanctioned way to preserve and study classical literature, historical documents, and religious texts.

One of the first formal methods of teaching second languages that challenged the prevalent Grammar-Translation method was Harold Palmer's **scientific approach**, which emphasized using the target language as the primary means of instruction (Palmer, 1921/2009). Palmer believed that language learning should be immersive, allowing the learners to struggle as they gain an understanding of the L2. The work of Palmer and his contemporaries, A. S. Hornby and Maximilian and Charles Berlitz (grandfather and grandson), gave rise to the **direct method**

(DM), which focused on naturally occurring dialogues—everyday exchanges between two people—rather than translation or text analysis (Krause, 1916; Richards & Rodgers, 2014).

The DM emphasized the development of oral skills through structured question–answer exercises and reading aloud and listening, with the extensive use of dictation. Structured conversations were used to promote spoken communication. The DM emphasized detailed teaching of the target language pronunciation system and speaking fluency through the use of controlled communicative activities, with immediate feedback from the instructor on accuracy (Celce-Murcia, 2001; Flowerdew & Miller, 2010; Liu & Shi, 2007).

An even more structured outgrowth of the direct method was the **Audio-Lingual Method** (ALM) of the 1950s (an outgrowth of the Army method, which originated during World War II). ALM soon came to be called the Michigan method because its early pioneers taught at the University of Michigan (my alma mater). The ALM is a style of oral, immersive teaching based on the behaviorist theory of learning, which was dominant at the time (Larsen-Freeman, 2000). Practitioners of ALM treated language proficiency growth as a result of controllable behavior that could be trained through a system of **nucleation**, graded oral prompts, and reinforcement of correct responses.

Language instruction was effectively scripted and often included a fixed language-laboratory routine in which the instructor (or a recorded source) would present correct audio models of sentences, and the students would have to repeat them verbatim (i.e., listen and repeat) or provide grammatical transformations (e.g., listen to a declarative sentence and change it to a question) or lexical transformation (e.g., change *the girl* to *the boy*). Responses would be recorded and replayed as a form of self-monitored feedback. These conscious manipulations of language prompts aimed to enable students to acquire the language through repeated oral manipulation of these graded chunks of well-formed input (Belasco, 1965).

7.3 The Cognitive Revolution

In the 1970s came the advent of biolinguistics and, with it, **cognitive-code learning theory** (Chastain, 1970; Yuksel, 2014), the belief that the principles underpinning language structure are biologically preset in the human mind and genetically inherited (Chomsky, 1968). Language educators systematically began to challenge the established structural approaches to linguistics that hinged on strict behavioral models. Instead, linguistic theory started to incorporate insights from cognitive science, neuroscience, and evolutionary biology, leading to the development of new theoretical frameworks for understanding language and its acquisition.

Emerging theories of the innateness of human language capacities suggested that humans are born with an innate capacity to process and perceive speech

174 *Teaching Listening*

sound and to understand the underlying organizational syntax of language with minimal, well-formed input (Boeckx & Grohmann, 2007; Nowak et al., 2001). Given the opportunities for understanding language rules inductively and given meaningful developmental feedback on their errors, learners would be able to acquire the target language successfully without the need for structured syllabuses (Osser, 1970).

The practical implications of this biolinguistics revolution for language teaching were not immediately integrated into mainstream language pedagogy. Still, this innateness movement led to a number of challenges to the prevailing structuralist and behaviorist approaches to teaching. In the 1980s, reflecting the impact of biolinguistics, a couple of major shifts entered into the sphere of formal language teaching.

One major shift was in the proposed order of acquisition. Behavioral approaches predicted that language would be acquired in a logical order based on the complexity of structural features. Biolinguistic approaches posited that language is acquired according to general principles like **frequency**, **utility**, **naturalness**, and **simplicity**. It was proposed that structural syllabuses and strictly sequenced oral-aural approaches might actually *impede* the natural order of acquisition (e.g., Long, 1985; O'Malley et al., 1987). It was also hypothesized that acceleration of language acquisition is contingent on **active listening** processes: the learner plays a dynamic role in interactive listening–speaking cycles in order to allow for intake of the new language (e.g., Pica, 1987; Prabhu, 1987).

In the 1980s and 1990s, new research questions began to emerge, highlighting the role of individual differences in language acquisition, particularly differences in language aptitude, memory capacity, and motivation (Dörnyei, 2020; Rost, 1990; Skehan, 1991). Understanding the impact of these latent variables gave rise to research on direct instruction's role in language acquisition. The discussion had been focused on the interplay between individual differences over which the instructor has some control (teaching methodology, feedback style, classroom environment, motivation, engagement strategies) and those over which the instructor has little or no control (age, learner background, personality traits, learning styles, neurobiological factors). A more learner-centered approach to instructional design emerged from this initiative, focusing on the ways that instruction can maximally impact learning, including by providing a more central role for active listening in language instruction (Nunan & Miller, 1995; Oxford, 1993; Rost, 1999; Thompson & Rubin, 1996; Vandergrift, 1999).

A vital offshoot of this movement in second language acquisition (SLA) research was to highlight the role of listening in language learning. Listening, particularly via interactive tasks, came to be viewed as a means of activating and engaging the learner's capacities for acquiring a second language. SLA researchers focused on ways of manipulating input and interaction to induce **attention to form** (noticing) while primarily engaging with meaning. It was

Approaches to Teaching Listening 175

believed that **form-focused instruction** through listening could improve learners' memory capacity (i.e., sharpening attention focus, increasing short-term memory span, improving memory efficiency in encoding and retrieval) and learning strategies (i.e., the knowledge and use of specific thinking and behavioral tactics for predicting content, gaining clarification, and consolidating new information; Brown & Lee, 2015; Ellis, 2022; O'Malley & Chamot, 1990; Rubin, 1994).

Alongside this research into the role of listening in second language learning, some specialized methods were developed that focused on listening. Some of these were packaged as proprietary methodologies and marketed commercially, notably total physical response (Asher, 1969; 1985), suggestopedia (Lozanov, 1977), and the natural approach (Krashen & Terrell, 1983; Terrell, 1977):

- **Total physical response (TPR)** is based on the idea that language learning occurs through the aural channel and is enhanced through *physical actions and movement*. TPR aims to create a dynamic and interactive learning environment by linking language input with physical actions and responses (Asher, 1969; 1985). The method focuses primarily on developing listening comprehension skills, aiming for global comprehension of input through visual and physical contextualization. Learners are exposed to meaningful and contextualized language input solely through spoken commands. TPR, in its purest form, follows a structured sequence of commands, starting with simple actions and objects and gradually increasing in complexity (Larsen-Freeman, 2000).
- **Suggestopedia** evolved from a therapeutic approach used by psychiatrist and hypnotherapist Georgi Lozanov in his native Bulgaria (Lozanov, 1977; Lozanov & Gateva, 1988). The method involves specific oral teaching techniques ("oral infusion"), involving exaggerated and hypnotic intonation and rhythm to capture students' attention and engage their subconscious minds. The method often includes dramatic texts, such as plays or dialogues, called "concert readings," which are performed in a relaxed setting. These techniques, in addition to the prevalent use of baroque music with its characteristics of contrast, layering, and monody (a single melodic line), are thought to help learners enter a state of relaxation and reduce anxiety, thus facilitating effortless listening, information retention, and association of positive emotions with their language learning experience (Bancroft, 1999; Colliander & Fejes, 2021).
- **The natural approach** was so named because it sought to replicate the naturalistic process of acquiring a first language by exposing learners to meaningful oral language input, ensuring a low affective filter by alleviating the stress of speaking, and thereby, an openness to receiving new and more challenging input. As does the TPR method, the natural approach advocates a silent or delayed-speaking period. Learners focus on understanding and

176 *Teaching Listening*

internalizing the language through listening and reading before actively producing the language. This delay purportedly allows learners to develop a solid foundation of comprehension before engaging in expressive language output (Macaro, 2020).

These innovative methods—TRP, suggestopedia, the natural approach— that grew out of the cognitivist shift in linguistics gave a marked boost to the importance of listening in language acquisition. They also set the stage for a more systematic investigation of the factors underlying successful language acquisition, and of why listening assumes a central role in the process (Mitchell et al., 2019).

7.4 Theoretical Models for Teaching Listening

As **SLA** began to develop into an academic discipline, researchers began exploring a number of areas that impact teaching and learning. The key questions concerned the conditions promoting successful acquisition, how the learner progresses through stages of proficiency, and the affective factors that influence motivation and engagement. Several hypotheses or models that elucidate the role of listening in SLA were developed during the period of 1980–2000. This section will outline five of the most significant models emerging from the era and their impacts on approaches to teaching listening.

7.4.1 The Monitor Model

A key transition in the teaching of listening came about through the popularization of Stephen Krashen's monitor model. Krashen distinguished between learning, which is conscious, and acquisition, which is unconscious. The monitor model attempted to account for the influence of appropriate listening opportunities and affective factors on successful second language acquisition. The model consisted of five interrelated hypotheses (Krashen, 1982).

H1. The input hypothesis: According to this hypothesis, language acquisition occurs through comprehensible input. Learners need to be exposed to language slightly beyond their current proficiency level, which is termed the **i + 1 level**. This input should be meaningful and understandable, even if not every word or grammatical structure is comprehended. This balance of known–unknown would allow learners to acquire new linguistic features naturally, without explicit instruction.

H2. The acquisition-learning hypothesis: Krashen differentiates between acquisition and learning. Acquisition refers to the subconscious, intuitive process of language development, which occurs naturally through exposure to comprehensible input. Learning, on the other hand, involves explicit instruction and conscious knowledge of grammar rules. Krashen argues that acquisition is more important for fluent and natural language use, while learning can only serve as a monitor or editor of language production.

H3. The natural order hypothesis: Krashen posits that there is a built-in sequence in which grammatical features are acquired, and learners will follow this sequence regardless of explicit instruction or correction, highlighting the importance of allowing learners to progress at their own pace.

H4. The monitor hypothesis: The monitor hypothesis states that learners can consciously use their acquired knowledge to make corrections and edit their language production. The acquired knowledge acts as a "monitor" that checks and adjusts language output. However, Krashen argues that *overreliance* on the monitor can hinder fluent communication, as it can cause hesitation and interfere with the natural flow of language.

H5. The affective filter hypothesis: The affective filter hypothesis emphasizes the role of motivation, self-confidence, and anxiety in second language acquisition. According to Krashen, a low affective filter makes learners more open and receptive to comprehensible input, leading to better language acquisition. Conversely, a high affective filter, influenced by negative emotions or anxiety, can impede language acquisition by blocking or filtering out input.

The monitor model offers enduring principles to incorporate in the way that listening is taught: choose input that is interesting and enjoyable; choose input material at an appropriate level of challenge; scaffold input *in natural ways* to make it more comprehensible; limit explicit instruction, and allow learners to deduce meaning (Krashen & Mason, 2020; Lichtman & VanPatten, 2021).

7.4.2 The Interaction Hypothesis

The **interaction hypothesis (IH)**, formulated by SLA pioneer Michael Long, can be seen as an extension of Krashen's monitor model (Long, 1981). While Long acknowledged the significance of Krashen's work in focusing on the learner's experience of language processing, he emphasized the role of interaction as a principal way of making input comprehensible.

The interaction hypothesis suggests that meaningful interaction, specifically spontaneous (unrehearsed and unscripted) conversational interaction, plays a crucial role in language acquisition. According to Long, the negotiation of meaning in conversational exchanges provides learners with opportunities to receive feedback, modify their output, and notice gaps in their language knowledge. This interaction process allows learners to **focus on form** (grammatical accuracy) while remaining primarily focused on meaning.

In contrast to Krashen's emphasis on comprehensible input and the natural order of acquisition, the interaction hypothesis highlights the importance of output, particularly output oriented toward a task outcome and the active use of language in acquiring a second language. Long argues that through interaction,

178 *Teaching Listening*

learners push their linguistic boundaries and adjust their language production based on feedback and negotiation.

The IH offers guidelines for teaching listening in multiple contexts. As summarized by Ellis (2003), IH distinguishes between "listening to comprehend" and "listening to learn" as two different purposes for engaging with spoken language. Listening to comprehend refers to the kind of listening that is necessary for semantic and pragmatic processing, understanding, and extracting meaning to participate in an interaction or complete a specific task. Listening to comprehend is essential for effective communication and is often considered the primary goal of listening instruction.

Listening to learn includes semantic and pragmatic processing but also involves actively learning linguistic structures (phonological, lexical, syntactic) and discourse structures (rhetorical patterns, conversational gambits, pragmatic strategies) from the spoken input. When listening to learn, learners are not only trying to understand the content but also paying attention to how the language is used and structured (Bardovi-Harlig, 2020; Gass, 2018).

7.4.3 The Comprehensible Output Hypothesis

The comprehensible output hypothesis, proposed by Merrill Swain and later incorporated by Long in an updated version of the IH (Long, 2014), has also impacted listening pedagogy. According to Swain, language learners not only benefit from comprehensible input but also from producing meaningful output themselves. Generating language output helps learners notice gaps in their linguistic knowledge and prompts them to explore ways to convey meaning effectively (Swain, 1985). Through attempting to express their thoughts and ideas (and often experiencing initial frustration), learners are pushed to actively use their acquired knowledge and engage in problem-solving, leading to language development—a cycle that has been labeled "pushed output" (López Páez, 2020).

Swain argues that comprehensible output is particularly beneficial when learners encounter challenging input texts that they are attempting to engage with or summarize. The feedback received during this output process from interlocutors provides learners with valuable information that facilitates further language learning.

The comprehensible output hypothesis is closely aligned with the interaction hypothesis because it emphasizes the importance of interactive language use—and pushing learners beyond their comfort zone. Both hypotheses highlight the significance of interaction as a vital supplement to input processing. Interaction allows learners to produce language output, receive feedback, negotiate meaning, and adjust their language production accordingly (Ellis, 2012; Long, 2014; Robinson et al., 2012).

The comprehensible output hypothesis has offered three enduring guideposts for teaching listening: construct tasks based on interesting input and that challenge listeners to express their intended meaning precisely; construct collaborative tasks that necessitate negotiation strategies for formulating meaning; and encourage reflection following output tasks to help learners notice the gap in their language development, that is, the difference between a learner's current level of language proficiency (what they are capable of producing) and their desired or target level of proficiency (what they want to be able to produce) (Luo, 2024).

7.4.4 Sociocultural Theory

Another theory that has exerted a powerful influence on the teaching of oral language skills is the sociocultural theory of language development (SCT). As a holistic theory of human cognition, SCT holds that language is the most pervasive cultural artifact and asset that humans possess and should be treated as integral to all human activity.

In SCT, it is believed that language enables us to mediate our connection to the world. Through language, we can describe, interpret, and understand our experiences, perceptions, and observations. Language helps individuals create mental representations of the external world, enabling them to navigate and interact with their environment effectively.

Language is also a means of communication and social interaction. It facilitates the exchange of ideas, feelings, information, and knowledge between individuals. Through language, people can express their thoughts, beliefs, and emotions and engage in collaborative activities, negotiation, and cooperation with others. Learning a second language allows us to appreciate diversity in the world around us (Lantolf & Swain, 2019).

In addition, language is not only a tool for external communication but also a means for self-expression and introspection. It enables individuals to reflect on their thoughts, emotions, and experiences and articulate their internal states (Plonsky et al., 2022). Language allows individuals to develop a sense of self-identity and construct narratives about their own lives, memories, and aspirations. In the SCT worldview, language learning is obviously much more than skill development. It is forging a new connection to the world (Vygotsky, 1978).

Sociocultural theory in second language teaching emphasizes the importance of authentic social interactions and native cultures in learning a new language. It suggests that language is not just a psycholinguistic process but is embedded in social environment and cultural practices. In relation to teaching listening, sociocultural theory encourages creating authentic and meaningful contexts for language learning. This involves exposing learners to real-life conversations, media, and cultural content that reflect how the language is used in its natural

180   *Teaching Listening*

context. The theory also highlights the central role of positive interaction and collaborative tasks in language development (MacIntyre & Ayers-Glassey, 2021).

The **zone of proximal development** (ZPD) is a central concept in SCT (Vygotsky, 1978). It refers to the gap between what a learner can do independently and what they can achieve with the help of a more knowledgeable person, typically a teacher or a peer. The ZPD is the range of tasks that are too difficult for the learner to accomplish alone, but that they can successfully complete with guidance and support.

Vygotsky believed that learning occurs most effectively within the ZPD, because it provides the right level of emotional and cognitive challenge for the learner. The ZPD is the sweet spot where learners can build on their existing skills and knowledge while receiving appropriate guidance. Teachers can use this concept to tailor their instruction to each learner's specific needs, gradually guiding them through a cognitive-emotional dialectic process (Lantolf & Swain, 2019). Inherent in this theory is the notion of **self-regulation**: the goal of instruction is to allow the learner to move from other-regulation (teacher guidance) to self-regulation (self-direction).

In terms of listening development, this guidance process entails providing learners with culturally rich listening that reflects real-life situations and cultural practices. Authentic materials (audio, videos, podcasts, and media interviews and events) can help learners develop their listening skills by exposing them to various native and nonnative accents, speech patterns, and communicative purposes (Lantolf et al., 2020).

Going beyond the instructional targets of the interaction hypothesis, some SCT theorists propose that instruction be based primarily on collaborative listening tasks, as interaction and cooperation are significant pathways to language learning and to increased positivity in human interaction (McIntyre & Ayers-Glassey, 2021; Helgesen, 2016). In the teaching of listening, this translates into incorporating pair work, information gap tasks, and group discussions, encouraging learners to exchange ideas, negotiate meaning, and construct knowledge collectively.

An additional aspect of SCT theory is the careful construction of assessment. Assessment of listening goes beyond testing of linguistic and semantic comprehension and into social and interactive competence: Assessment tasks may involve responding to inferential and open-ended questions, participating in discussions, giving point-of-view presentations, and demonstrating understanding through verbal or written interactions (Swain et al., 2015; Taguchi, 2019).

7.4.5 *Metacognition Approaches*

Metacognitive approaches grew out of the recognition that individual differences strongly impact learners' rate of progress and ultimate achievement in listening and language acquisition. These individual differences, summarized in Chapter 1,

Approaches to Teaching Listening 181

encompass learners' unique characteristics and traits, such as memory capacity and learning styles, affective factors such as motivation and anxiety, and social factors such as cultural background and language exposure.

Metacognitive approaches target ways in which instruction and other experiences may alter some of these variables rather than accept them as unchangeable (Wenden, 1998). Essentially, advocates of a metacognitive approach contend that **conscious strategy selection** can directly influence how learners approach their language learning experiences and can thereby accelerate their L2 acquisition. Metacognitive approaches can be seen as part of a large movement called **dialogic education**, an orientation to teaching and learning that places a strong emphasis on dialogue, discussion, and interaction between teachers and students, as well as among students themselves (Cui & Teo, 2021; Wegerif, 2019).

Researchers of metacognitive strategy instruction have noted both short-term and long-term positive effects of direct instruction on comprehension (Goh, 2008; Goh & Vandergrift, 2021; Rost & Ross, 1991). In listening skill development, strategies can be categorized into three main types: **cognitive strategies**, **socio-affective strategies**, and **metacognitive strategies**, representing different ways that learners approach and manage their listening tasks (Li et al., 2022; Rost & Wilson, 2013):

- **Cognitive strategies:** These are mental processes that help learners understand and process the information they hear. They include techniques like predicting, summarizing, clarifying, and note-taking, all of which help learners actively engage with the content of the listening input (Rost, 2005; Siegel, 2022).
- **Socio-affective strategies:** These strategies involve monitoring and managing emotional responses during the listening process, including ways of lowering anxiety and encouraging oneself to continue. These strategies help learners deal with anxiety, frustration, or lack of interest that affects their attention, ability to predict, comprehension, and recall (Chriswiyati & Subekti, 2022; Yeldham & Gruba, 2016). "Self-talk" techniques such as staying focused, maintaining a positive attitude, and trying to enjoy the listening experience fall under this category (Oxford & Amerstorfer, 2019), as do some specific behavioral strategies for improving comprehension and social connection. These include social strategies, such as asking questions (information, clarification, confirmation), collaborating, empathizing, and sharing opinions and feelings (Goh & Hu, 2014; Rost, 2006).
- **Metacognitive strategies:** These strategies focus on the awareness and control of one's own thinking and learning processes. Though there is some overlap with socio-affective strategies, metacognitive strategies are focused on thinking processes rather than emotional responses. Learners use metacognitive strategies to plan, monitor, and evaluate their listening performance.

182 *Teaching Listening*

Techniques like setting goals, self-assessing comprehension, and adjusting strategies based on performance are examples of metacognitive strategies (Al-Alwan et al., 2013; Cross & Vandergrift, 2018; Rahimirad & Shams, 2014; Takahashi, 2010).

Metacognitive processing of one's own thought processes while listening can be seen as a form of critical thinking. In addition to seeking ways to prevent or counter the difficulties experienced when listening to challenging input, critical thinking involves actively analyzing, synthesizing, evaluating, and applying background knowledge to what is understood. In short, metacognitive processing and critical thinking are a kind of problem-solving (Vandergrift & Goh, 2012).

The underlying claim of metacognitive approaches to listening is that L1 and L2 listeners can learn to emulate and implement effective strategies that will both improve their short-term comprehension outcomes and help them form a positive mindset and a problem-solving approach to listening, which will help them in the long term (e.g., Rost & Ross, 1991; Vandergrift, 1999; Wallace, 2022).

7.5 Profiling Approaches to Teaching Listening

The theoretical insights from these foregoing models can be incorporated into concrete approaches for teaching listening. Utilizing principles from these models, we will review four broad approaches to teaching listening. These will correspond to their emphasis on a particular domain of listening (in the order of Chapters 1-4): neurolinguistic processing (holistic approaches), linguistic processing (bottom-up approaches), semantic processing (top-down approaches), and pragmatic processing (interactive approaches).

It is often useful in teaching listening to focus on a specific type of processing to give students remediation or supplementation in underdeveloped areas. Sometimes, instruction should focus on a specific type of processing (e.g., linguistic), and at other times, it is best to focus on multiple types of processing.

7.5.1 Neurological Processing: Focus on Engaged Listening

Though neurological factors are not generally made explicit in teaching methodology, it is useful to consider how the underlying principles of neurological processing can be incorporated effectively into instruction. Neurological approaches aim to align with the brain's intrinsic processing functions. Because **receptivity**, **attention**, **engagement**, and **connection** are pivotal components of neurological processing, there are four main pedagogical strategies that can accelerate the learning process:

Approaches to Teaching Listening   183

1. **To heighten receptivity**

   - Create a positive and welcoming learning environment where students feel comfortable expressing themselves and asking questions.
   - Use relatable and relevant content that aligns with students' interests and experiences.
   - Provide clear expectations and objectives for the listening activity to motivate learners to actively participate.

2. **To intensify attention and curiosity**

   - Use engaging and varied auditory stimuli, such as authentic audio clips, podcasts, or real-life conversations.
   - Incorporate interactive elements, such as question prompts, pauses for reflection, or note-taking, to keep learners mentally engaged.
   - Encourage active listening strategies, like predicting what will be discussed or identifying key points.

3. **To promote fuller engagement**

   - Incorporate multimedia and virtual resources, visuals, or real-world examples that complement the auditory input and appeal to different learning styles.
   - Include opportunities for discussion and collaboration among learners, allowing them to share their thoughts and interpretations of the content.
   - Provide tasks that require critical thinking and problem-solving related to the listening material.

4. **To increase personal connection**

   - Relate the listening material to learners' prior knowledge and experiences to help them connect new information with what they already know.
   - Encourage personal reflection on how the content relates to their lives, beliefs, or cultural background.
   - Foster a sense of community in the classroom, where students can share their insights and perspectives with a feeling of safety, security, and support.

7.5.1.1 Prototype Activity: Listening Circles

A prototypical activity that promotes receptivity, attention, engagement, and connection is called Listening Circles. Listening Circles is a structured system of speaking and listening practice that provides an opportunity for each individual to connect deeply with others, share personal experiences, and feel heard and supported. When used in an L2 context, this type of activity can be transformative: learners can experience using their L2 as an intrinsically valuable

184   *Teaching Listening*

experience—more than simply an accumulation of speaking and listening skills (cf. Shaules & McConachy, 2023).

Because of this transformative potential, Listening Circles are often used in personal development, communication training, and therapy settings to foster effective communication and comfort with emotional expression and reception (e.g., Caputi et al., 2006; Glickstein, 2009; Stephens, 2012; Styslinger & Overstreet, 2014). I have adopted the principles for oral language teaching with students of all ages, even at beginning levels of proficiency.

Listening Circles aim to create a receptive, safe, supportive environment for participants to explore their experiences authentically, using their L2 with other L2 learners (exclusive use of the L2 is encouraged, though translanguaging and code-switching are never forbidden) (Cenoz & Gorter, 2020). Preparation for the activity entails only a list of concrete personal questions that your students can readily talk about (with some think time in advance) and are willing to share with their classmates and teacher.

Some personal question prompts I have used:

* What is something you are passionate about?
* What is a problem you're trying to solve?
* Who has had the most influence in your life?
* What has been a pivotal event in your life?

The students work as a group, with the instructor as a moderator and guide. The basic goal is to practice oral communication by creating a supportive environment where speakers and listeners collaborate actively. Speakers are instructed to stand in front of the group for a given period, starting with one minute, and talk about a personal experience without any notes. Listeners are instructed to attend to each speaker fully, to be receptive, and to give a sense of support to the speaker. To overcome initial awkwardness and unfamiliarity with this type of activity, speakers and listeners need a clear task.

Here are the essential directives for Listening Circles that I will give to the class:

Everyone will have a turn to speak for one minute. Here is today's topic: _____ _____. Everyone will have three minutes to prepare some notes about what you want to talk about. When it is your turn, you will speak for one minute on the topic. No one will interrupt you.

At one minute, I'll say, "Time," and raise my finger. This is a sign for you to finish up.

For each speaker: "Okay, now we'll hear from _____."

(When the student steps in front of the group): "Take your time. When you speak, don't rush. Make eye contact with one listener at a time. Try to keep eye contact while you speak. Move your gaze from one person to the next. After one minute,

Approaches to Teaching Listening   185

I will say, "Time." Finish your thought. Then say, "Thank you for listening." When your turn is over, please wait in front of the group. Accept your applause."

For the whole class: "Listen carefully to each speaker. Lean forward and maintain warm (receptive) eye contact with the speaker. Keep a neutral expression. (You don't need to smile or nod.)"

When the speaker's turn is over, listeners have the option of calling out some supportive feedback. For example:

"That was (genuine/charming/captivating, etc.)." Be positive. (Don't comment on the content.)

"I really enjoyed your (warmth/enthusiasm/spirit, etc.)." Give an honest reaction.

There are many variations that you can introduce, including allowing time for each listener to ask one question about the presentation. Whatever variations you use, I recommend observing these ground rules:

- **Active listening:** Participants are encouraged to practice deep listening, which means listening with full attention and presence to what others are saying without interrupting or offering immediate solutions
- **Equal participation:** The teacher aims to ensure that all participants have an equal opportunity to speak and be heard. There is no pressure, though, and participants are free to pass if they prefer not to speak in a particular class
- **Timekeeping:** To ensure equal participation, it is best to stick with the time limit (usually 1 to 3 minutes, depending on the class). The follow-up supportive feedback need take only a few seconds
- **No Fixing or Rescuing:** The teacher is encouraged to refrain from trying to rescue or correct students during their speaking turn. Instead, the focus is on offering empathetic listening and support. As tempting as it is for teachers to insert a language lesson during or after someone's turn, and even though some students will request corrections, it is important to keep the focus of the activity on authentic communication. Instead of correcting language at this point, give feedback on the authenticity of the communication
- **Confidentiality:** Everything shared within the Listening Circle is considered confidential. Participants are encouraged to respect each other's privacy and not share the personal stories or experiences of others outside of the class
- **Nonjudgmental atmosphere:** Participants are encouraged to suspend judgment and criticism, creating a safe space where people can express themselves without fear of being judged.

If this activity is repeated regularly, in conjunction with other learning activities, I find that there is almost always a palpable improvement in receptivity (relaxation around listening), connectivity (collaboration and trust among students), attention (curiosity and active listening), and engagement (willingness to communicate, willingness to trying new kinds of learning activities).

186   *Teaching Listening*

Critics of this approach, which focuses on personal growth, self-discovery, and a more holistic view of learning that goes beyond traditional teaching of language, often argue that it lacks academic rigor (presenters do not follow a specific rhetorical structure), overemphasizes personal experience (presenters are not asked to provide evidence for their views), leads to a lack of critical thinking (listeners are asked to provide solely positive feedback), and does not align with standards of language proficiency (there are no direct attempts to promote fluency and accuracy) (Dix & Corbett, 2023). While these objections are valid to a point, I have seen counter-evidence that learners clearly benefit from this type of activity in the longer term through the experience of feeling accepted and supported as they communicate in their L2, irrespective of their proficiency level. This transformative experience tends to have a carry-over motivational effect on the more standard styles of language instruction.

7.5.2 Linguistic Processing: Focus on Attention to Bottom-Up Listening Skills

Linguistic approaches focus on drawing attention to and amplifying the effort needed for bottom-up listening processes: phonological decoding, word recognition, and syntactic parsing. Because **discrimination, accuracy, speed,** and **capacity** are the key aspects of bottom-up processing proficiency, all bottom-up listening practices should emphasize one or more of these aspects.

7.5.2.1 Prototype Activity: Deliberate Practice

A prototypical activity that promotes linguistic processing is **deliberate practice**, a teaching approach advocated by Swedish psychologist Anders Ericsson, widely recognized for his groundbreaking research on expertise, skill development, and deliberate practice. Anders was one of the world's leading experts on the science of expertise, and his focus on the importance of the teacher in the student's mastery of a skill (Ericsson, 2018; Ericsson & Smith, 1991).

One of Ericsson's favorite adages goes something like this: "As most teachers know, the old saying, 'Practice makes perfect,' is only partially correct. While it is generally true that the more one practices a particular skill, the easier it will become, there is not necessarily a relationship between how often you practice, how *easy* the skill *feels* for you, and how *well* you execute that given skill." As many teachers can attest, it is entirely possible for a student to learn a skill *incorrectly*, to adopt bad habits, or to practice with a faulty mindset. In effect, bad habits, a problematic mindset, or poor form may actually prevent learners from ever mastering the target skill.

Deliberate practice is a form of instruction designed to help learners work on specific skills —with conscious awareness that they are willingly practicing a component subskill to improve their overall proficiency. To be effective, deliberate practice should be focused on a single learning objective, provide multiple

Approaches to Teaching Listening 187

opportunities for repetition and feedback (5–10 repetitions typically), and offer ample time for reflection and debriefing (DeKeyser, 2020).

Deliberate practice of bottom-up listening skills can focus on phonological discrimination, word recognition, grammatical decoding accuracy, increasing speed of processing, or expanding phonological short-term memory capacity. Table 7.1 provides several examples.

There are numerous practice focuses and variations you can use (e.g., for shadowing, see Ekayati, 2020; for listening memory games, see Syafii et al., 2020), but with any variations, it is important to keep in mind the basic principles of deliberate practice:

- **Clear goals and objectives:** Set clear and specific language learning goals for each deliberate practice session. Let students know the targeted language skills or components they will be working on.
- **Time and consistency:** Allocate sufficient time (at least 10 minutes) for deliberate practice sessions and maintain consistency in practice routines. Put time limits on the practice activities as well. Regular, timed practice sessions are essential for skill development.
- **Relevance and authenticity:** Ensure that the practice tasks and activities are relevant to the students' language proficiency level and aligned with real-life language use. Use authentic materials and contexts whenever possible (Chen, 2022).
- **Focus on challenging areas:** Identify students' weak points and design focused practice activities that address those areas (Hamada & Suzuki, 2022).
- **Positive mindset:** Help students develop a growth mindset, believing that abilities and skills can be developed through dedication and effort. See challenges and mistakes as opportunities for learning and improvement rather than as indicators of failure. Aim to have students approach deliberate practice with enthusiasm and motivation. Celebrate successes when you see genuine progress being made (Suzuki et al., 2019).
- **Feedback and assessment:** Provide timely and constructive feedback to students *during* deliberate practice. Use formative assessment to track students' progress and identify areas for improvement. Engaged monitoring and feedback from the expert (the teacher) is essential for maximum benefit (Settles & Meeder, 2016).
- **Reinforcement and spaced repetition:** Spaced repetition can be effective with several aspects of listening development: aural vocabulary, pronunciation, information retention, and extensive listening (i.e., listening to the same long passage at regular intervals to improve overall comprehension). Spaced repetition gives students multiple opportunities to practice and reinforce their learning at regular intervals. Most spaced repetition learning algorithms recommend repeating the same practices (with new input) every 2, 4, 7, and 14 days (Isele & Cosgun, 2018; Tabibian et al., 2019).

188   *Teaching Listening*

Table 7.1 Samples of Deliberate Practice to Improve Bottom-Up Listening Skills

Area of practice	Forms of practice	Skills acquired/ mindset shift
Phonological: listening span	Series of items (numbers, names, thematically related words, etc.); narrated slowly, increasing length of series, ask students to recall all items or specific items (e.g., first item, third item)	Increased phonological short-term memory capacity
Phonological: discrimination	Pairs of words, phrases, or sentences narrated; students identify if the pairs are the same or different	Improved discrimination ability
Phonological: shadowing	Series of short (5–7 seconds) bursts of speech for shadowing, or with scripts, giving directions to mark assimilations, stress, pauses	Improved ability to listen to fast speech, improved ability to decode assimilated phrases; heightened curiosity in hearing spoken language variations
Lexical: word spotting	Series of short extracts (25 words) with multiple choice (m/c) or blank fill-ins for identifying which target words were uttered	Improved ability to recognize words; improved ability to identify boundaries of unknown words
Syntactic: parsing grammatical structures	Series of short comprehensible sentences (or idea units) with complex grammar, slightly above students' productive ability; students choose the correct written form of utterance or write/ fill in blanks	Improved ability to segment speech into component words; improved ability to construct grammatical sentences from words recognized in speech
Syntactic: automaticization of grammar rules	Series of short extracts (25 words) with target grammatical structures blanked out; listeners attempt to fill in missing parts	Improved automaticity in decoding complex/ natural-speed speech; improved ability to construct grammatical sentences in speech and writing
Phonological/Lexical/ Syntactic: memory encoding and retrieval	Memory games involving oral input, including story sequence memory, word concentration, sentence-pair match	Increased speed in encoding; increased attention during encoding and retrieval

Approaches to Teaching Listening 189

These principles—goals, consistency, authenticity, focus, mindset, feedback, and spacing—are ground rules for using deliberate practice successfully. Although it is often not possible to observe *all* of the principles all of the time, once the students understand and *buy into* these principles, they are better able to focus their efforts on making and sustaining tangible improvements during practice sessions.

Critics of this approach often appeal to the notion of **transfer-appropriate processing (TAP),** a cognitive psychology concept related to the value of various types of practice (Tripuraneni et al., 2020). TAP suggests that the effectiveness of memory retrieval depends on the similarity between the cognitive processes involved during encoding (i.e., learning or deliberate practice) and those involved during retrieval (remembering what has been learned or practiced) (Franks et al., 2000). TAP would suggest that recall and application to integrated tasks are improved when the mental activities used while practicing match those used during the retrieval phase (DeKeyser, 2017; Lightbown & Han, 2008). It is unclear on the surface how these very specific practice tasks lead to useful skill transfer in integrated tasks.

These criticisms would be valid if the entire instructional approach to learning L2 listening consisted of deliberate practice activities focusing on bottom-up listening. When employed in a balanced manner—and often in small practice increments—deliberate practice can draw learners' attention to areas of linguistic processing skills that they are approaching without full awareness and lead to improved self-direction in learning (DeKeyser, 2020). As such, deliberate practice can help learners enact metacognitive strategies that will help them become more autonomous learners.

7.5.3 Semantic Processing: Focus on Critical Listening

Semantic approaches focus on activating the top-down aspects of listening processes: activating **lexical maps**, **conceptual schemata**, and **inferencing** to comprehend input and interpret its significance (see Chapter 3 for a treatment of these concepts). Beyond comprehension, active semantic processing turns into critical listening, the act of listening with a focused, analytical, and evaluative mindset, in order to fully analyze the content and the quality of what is being communicated. Comprehension building and critical listening involve actively engaging with the material, examining the main points, supporting evidence, and underlying assumptions, and evaluating the information being presented.

7.5.3.1 Prototype Activity: Interactive Problem-Solving

In order to build students' abilities to include analyzing content, assessing quality and credibility, and identifying speaker tactics, it is important to shift listening practices toward active engagement with the content. Early research

190   *Teaching Listening*

on reading and listening comprehension instruction centered around techniques teachers could use to encourage students to approach a text in ways that promote more complete engagement with the content rather than simply having students answer teacher-generated questions (Flavell, 1978). These techniques have evolved into pedagogic approaches, placing the listener as the agent in a comprehension-building process and recruiting complementary forms of cognitive processing and critical thinking.

One early model called the **experience-text-relationship (ETR)** method valued identifying text cues that triggered connections to the listener's/reader's personal experience and background knowledge (Au, 1979; 2016; Goodman & Goodman, 2016). The teacher used classroom discussion to guide students systematically through the cognitive processes related to understanding extended texts—thereby increasing their engagement, understanding, and enjoyment of the experience.

A second model, called **KWL** (for "what you know already," "what you want to know," and "what you learned" from the text), focused on orienting students to the kind of active thinking required to comprehend challenging texts (Carr & Ogle, 1987; Sinambela et al., 2015). The KWL method was proposed as an antidote to excessive teacher-led questioning (which still tends to dominate the teaching of listening), allowing students to assume more agency as listeners and readers.

A third model, **reciprocal teaching (RT)**, encouraged comprehension building through cycles of student-led questioning. Questioning cycles focused on four comprehension strategies: predicting, questioning, clarifying, and summarizing (Brown & Palincsar, 1987; Palincsar & Schleppegrell, 2014). In a classroom using the RT approach, students work in a small group with a relatively lengthy text—typically a story involving an unusual problem and a solution.

Toward the end of the activity, the students try to clarify any difficult words or phrases—a nod of recognition that vocabulary knowledge underpins comprehension (Kim & Phillips, 2014; van Zeeland & Schmitt, 2013). Clarifying helps a student self-monitor, an essential component of independent listening or reading. The student then generates a summary that identifies and describes the text's main ideas. Finally, the student predicts what will likely occur next with evidence to support the prediction. The role of the group leader then rotates to the next student, and the process continues until the students have read and discussed the assigned text.

A fourth model, **QAR** (question-answer-relationship), also placed the listener as the central agent in the comprehension process, asking the students to consciously consider sources of information: what information is explicitly provided and what the listener needs to construct. Specifically, the listener is to assess whether the speaker provides specific information explicitly or whether the listener will have to go beyond the text (Afriani et al., 2020; Raphael & Pearson, 1985).

Research has suggested that *all* such instructional techniques are typically effective at building comprehension, compared with control groups who do not receive direct instruction (Block & Duffy, 2008). However, because these techniques do not provide students with explicit explanations or instructions about how to think through texts, subsequent teaching research has focused on meta-comprehension strategies and ways of helping students think about how to construct their understanding.

Current iterations of comprehension building focus on what may be termed **quality questioning**—guiding students toward greater curiosity and cognitively deeper understanding. A concurrent goal of a quality questioning approach is metacognitive: to lead students into a greater awareness of *how* they actively process texts as they listen. In this way, comprehension-building instruction encourages more independent learning, enabling students to practice these strategies independently (Kaur, 2014; Walsh & Sattes, 2016).

Many educational researchers consistently remind teachers that most students in their classes will not develop critical thinking skills automatically as they progress. However, research findings are clear that: (1) Students who develop critical thinking skills learn and achieve at higher levels than their peers; (2) students can learn these thinking skills and associated behaviors; and (3) most students will require direct instruction to develop these skills (Abrami et al., 2015).

Development of critical thinking skills has been shown to improve listening ability by adding dimensions to semantic processing (Brown, 2006; Field, 1998), particularly in evaluating evidence (Ennis, 2018), drawing inferences (Sanavi & Tarighat, 2014), resisting biases (Halpern & Dunn, 2021), and taking multilayered notes (Siegel, 2023).

Instructors who wish to develop comprehension-building skills during listening classes are likely to incorporate many of the techniques advocated in the ETR, KWL, and QAR methods of teaching critical listening. The key to consistent success with these techniques is to focus on the shift in learner mindset from passive listening to active listening

Table 7.2 presents some of the most powerful techniques in these approaches. There are numerous variations that can be used with comprehension-building activities, integrating reading, writing, and speaking as pre-listening and post-listening activities (see, e.g., Nation, 2017; Rost, 2014).

The most common criticism that is leveled against comprehension-building exercises is that they are *too effective*. Some educators feel that by overemphasizing top-down processing instruction, learners neglect to develop their linguistic processing skills and over-rely on using background knowledge and cognitive strategies to understand oral input (Field, 2004; Siegel, 2014). Excessive reliance on top-down cognitive strategies rather than the development of bottom-up listening skills can lead to a kind of ceiling effect in which listeners are unable to comprehend speech beyond a certain level of complexity (Cauldwell, 2018; MacPhee et al., 2015).

Table 7.2 Activities for Promoting Comprehension Building

Comprehension building	Activity	Skill/mindset improvement desired
Memory building: Questions about reconstructing a story	Series of short stories involving multiple actions and sequences	Improved attention span, improved recall
Recognizing literal meaning: Questions about facts, details, or information explicitly stated in the audio story	Series of short extracts (25–50 words) with questions or T/F paraphrases about literal meaning (what was explicitly stated vs. inferable)	Increased awareness of literal vs. implied meaning
Understanding vocabulary: Questions about the meanings of words as they are used in the context of the extract	Series of short extracts (10–25 words) with questions (synonyms, rephrasing) about specific vocabulary items	Increase in receptive vocabulary
Making inferences: Questions asking students to interpret what is said by going beyond the literal meaning	Series of short statements (10–25 words) with questions about what can be inferred from what was spoken	Heightened ability to listen actively, making inferences while listening
Identifying main idea: Questions asking students to identify the main idea or gist of an audio story	Series of short extracts (30–60 seconds) with questions (T/F) or m/c or open-ended about the main idea	Increase in ability to listen selectively for most important information
Summarizing content: Questions asking students to summarize the content of an audio story	Series of short extracts (20 seconds, 100 words); students work alone or in pairs to create short (10–20-word) summaries	Improved focus on main ideas, ability to formulate coherent short summaries
Determining point of view: Questions asking students to determine a speaker's point of view or perspective in an audio story	Series of short extracts (30–60 seconds), such as movie scenes (in audio only or video formats), in which the characters have identifiable perspectives or emotional states	Improved discernment of differences in emotional states in characters
Analyzing reasoning: Questions asking students to analyze a speaker's reasoning or draw conclusions based on an audio extract	Series of short extracts, personal opinions about a topic or issue	Heightened reasoning ability; greater tolerance for differing viewpoints
Finding evidence: Questions asking students to identify statements or details in an audio story that provide evidence to support inferences, interpretations, or conclusions	Series of short stories (2–3 minutes) involving problem-solution structure	Increase in critical thinking while listening to narratives and expositions

Approaches to Teaching Listening   193

7.5.4 Pragmatic Processing: Focus on Interactive Listening

A pragmatic-processing-oriented approach to teaching listening focuses on developing students' **pragmatic competence**, which refers to a person's ability to use language effectively and appropriately in various social and cross-cultural contexts to achieve successful communication. Pragmatic competence involves focusing on how language is used to convey intentions, emotions, and social relationships—in both one's native culture and in the target community (not always a particular national culture) of the language being acquired (Domaneschi & Bambini, 2020).

As a vital aspect of pragmatic competence, pragmatic comprehension (as discussed in Chapter 4) encompasses understanding social conventions, implied meanings, nonliteral language, and discourse markers that go beyond literal interpretation. Pragmatic comprehension also involves an awareness that language use varies in different social, cultural, and educational contexts (Taguchi, 2009).

An instructional approach to listening that aims to improve students' pragmatic comprehension and their overall pragmatic competence will include listening tasks that address implied meanings (such as indirect requests and embedded emotions), politeness strategies, conversational dynamics (adjustments based on social roles, levels of formality, and ways of managing conversational flow), detecting and addressing misunderstandings, and noticing cultural nuances and nonliteral language (metaphors, idioms, figurative expressions), and issues in translation (Alos, 2015).

7.5.4.1 Prototype Activity: Interactive Problem-Solving

The prototypical input for a listening task aimed at improving pragmatic competence is an extract of authentic discourse involving conflicting intentions and emotions in the context of solving a significant problem between two or more parties. The prototype activity for developing pragmatic processing is a collaborative problem-solving task involving pair or group interaction (see Table 7.3).

The goal of a collaborative task is ostensibly to increase speaking and listening opportunities, provide meaningful practice time, build confidence, reduce listening anxiety, encourage participation, and foster a positive attitude toward language learning. When an interesting problematized input is used as a stimulus, the potential benefits go beyond a mere increase in speaking-listening opportunities. In an interactive problem-solving task, learners will also be developing pragmatic competence.

Suitable input sources for collaborative listening tasks are conversations or monologues presented in a narrative fashion involving some kind of values issue in which multiple, reasonable solutions are possible. Topic areas can include social justice, environmental ethics, ethical dilemmas, and personal values and identities. A classic example is a dialogue involving a couple discussing how to

194   *Teaching Listening*

Table 7.3 Interaction Types for Pragmatic Listening

Type	Description	Improvement desired
Information gap task	Learners have complementary information sources and exchange information to achieve a specific goal. In the case of the father scenario, one student may have information for the male member of the couple; the other student may have information pertaining to the female member	Promote active engagement and increase motivation to learn; enhance comprehension seeking; promote listening strategies (clarification, confirmation)
Problem-solving task	Present pairs with a problem or a scenario that requires discussion and collaboration to find a solution (e.g., Where should the father live?). Students need to actively listen to their partner's ideas, express their opinions, and negotiate to reach a consensus	Promote critical thinking, collaboration, socio-affective strategy use
Role-play	Students are assigned specific roles and scenarios (e.g., one is the wife, one is the husband, discussing what to do with the wife's aging parent). Students engage in an unscripted conversation, improvising and using language appropriate to their roles to achieve a specific outcome	Allow students to listen actively to their partner's cues and responses
Content verification	Following a listening experience (e.g., A social worker describes the benefits of different living situations for elders), students compare notes or transcriptions, negotiating together a fuller comprehension	Promote critical thinking and summarizing
Debate and discussion	Assign a topic or a statement for pairs to debate or discuss (e.g., Should aging parents always live with their adult children?). Students express their opinions, provide arguments, and respond to their partner's ideas. Present discussion gambits to promote critical thinking	Promote active listening, speaking fluency, and expressing and supporting opinions effectively

Approaches to Teaching Listening 195

handle a family dilemma: the father of one of them is getting too old and frail to live alone. Should he move in with them? Or should they attempt to place him in a senior home?

Criticisms of interactive problem-solving activities typically center on the challenges of actually conducting the activities, particularly in large classes (e.g., Brown & Lee, 2015). If the instructor is unable to manage the administration of the activities through proper guidance and follow-up, students may not probe deeply enough into the problem being investigated to explore a range of solutions and thus develop pragmatic competence.

Also, in high-context or collectivist cultures (cultures that emphasize group harmony and cohesion), students are likely unaccustomed to student–student pair work in which views are challenged, and alternatives are encouraged (Gupta & Sukamto, 2020; Ma et al., 2020; Norboeva, 2023). In these cases of resistance, scaffolding of the activity of group problem-solving itself needs to become the initial focus of instruction (Shaules & McConachy, 2023),

7.6 Summary: Targeted and Balanced Approaches

Much can be learned from reviewing historical approaches to teaching listening. From a historical survey of traditional methods and SLA research of methodology, we can derive fundamental principles and practices that can be adapted into our own teaching. This chapter has reviewed some key models of language acquisition that place listening at the core of learning and acquisition: the monitor model, the interaction hypothesis, the comprehensible output hypothesis, sociocultural theory, and metacognition approaches. Although these models differ in significant ways, all of them recognize that *it is the learner* who must adopt an active role in engaging with target language speakers and with target language listening input in order to develop proficiency.

The first section of this book has outlined how learning to listen involves development of four kinds of processing: neurological, linguistic, semantic, and pragmatic. A balanced approach to listening instruction can take all four strands into account. For instance, neurologically -based approaches will emphasize developing a receptive mindset for listening, active attention, global comprehension, physical action, sensory experiences, embodied cognition, and emotional connection. Linguistically oriented approaches will stress phonemic awareness exercises, shadowing and dictation to focus on word recognition and grammar, cloze exercises to focus on specific decoding problems, and language awareness exercises. Semantically oriented approaches will focus on the listener's ability to extract main ideas, infer meaning, make connections, and engage with the content on a deeper level. Pragmatically oriented approaches will accentuate collaborative understanding and a willingness to communicate, to share ideas and to be open to diverse viewpoints.

196   *Teaching Listening*

Instructional approaches to listening should be both targeted and balanced. For learners at lower levels of proficiency, linguistic processing might consume a significant amount (25–33%) of instructional time, with semantic and pragmatic processing targeted for the majority of instructional time (50–60%), and neurological processing activities for a still smaller proportion (10%). For learners at high levels of proficiency, linguistic processing should still be targeted very vigorously, in fact, but may account for only a small portion of instructional time. The majority of instructional time for these learners may be best focused on pragmatic processing. The approach an instructor adopts must be targeted primarily at the learners' needs and goals, offering a variety of activities and assessments that help learners reach those goals. Feedback from the learners about what is most effective is a vital component in making these decisions.

At the same time, a listening approach needs to offer instruction in all four domains in order to allow learners to experience a full range of listening activities and to develop a balanced ability in listening. In addition, as will be discussed in more detail in Chapter 8, choice of input and interaction is a central variable in all types of instructional activities.

References

Abrami, P. C., Bernard, R. M., Borokhovski, E., Waddington, D. I., Wade, C. A., & Persson, T. (2015). Strategies for teaching students to think critically: A meta-analysis. *Review of Educational Research, 85*(2), 275–314.

Afriani, Z. L., Anggraini, M., & Riswanto, R. (2020). The effect of Question Answer Relationship (QAR) Strategy in enhancing students' reading comprehension. *Journal of English Education and Teaching, 4*(4), 548–558.

Al-Alwan, A., Asassfeh, S., & Al-Shboul, Y. (2013). EFL learners' listening comprehension and awareness of metacognitive strategies: How are they related? *International Education Studies, 6*(9), 31–39.

Alos, J. (2015). Explicating the implicit: An empirical investigation into pragmatic competence in translator training. *The Interpreter and Translator Trainer, 9*(3), 287–305.

Asher, J. (1969). The total physical response approach to second language learning. *The Modern Language Journal, 53,* 3–17.

Asher, J. J. (1985). *TPR student kit: 4 in 1.* Sky Oaks Productions.

Au, K. H. (1979). Using the experience-text-relationship method with minority children. *The Reading Teacher, 32*(6), 677–679.

Au, K. H. (2016). Culturally responsive instruction. In L. Helman (Ed.), *Literacy development with English learners: Research-based instruction in grades K–6* (pp. 20–42). Guilford Press.

Bancroft, W. J. (1999). *Suggestopedia and language acquisition: Variations on a theme.* Taylor & Francis.

Bardovi-Harlig, K. (2020). Pedagogical linguistics: A view from L2 pragmatics. *Pedagogical Linguistics, 1*(1), 44–65.

Belasco, S. (1965). Nucleation and the audio-lingual approach. *The Modern Language Journal, 49*(8), 482–491.

Boeckx, C., & Grohmann, K. K. (2007). The biolinguistics manifesto. *Biolinguistics, 1,* 001–008.

Brown, A. L., & Palincsar, A. S. (1987). *Reciprocal teaching of comprehension strategies: A natural history of one program for enhancing learning.* Ablex Publishing.

Brown, D., & Lee, H. (2015). *Teaching by principles: An interactive approach to language pedagogy* (6th ed.). Pearson.

Brown, S. (2006). *Teaching listening* (Vol. 7). Cambridge University Press.

Caputi, L., Engelmann, L., & Stasinopoulos, J. (2006). An interdisciplinary approach to the needs of non-native-speaking nursing students: Conversation circles. *Nurse Educator, 31*(3), 107–111.

Carr, E., & Ogle, D. (1987). KWL Plus: A strategy for comprehension and summarization. *Journal of Reading, 30*(7), 626–631.

Cauldwell, R. (2018). *A syllabus for listening: Decoding.* Speech in Action.

Celce-Murcia, M. (2001). Language teaching approaches: An overview. *Teaching English as a Second or Foreign Language, 2*(1), 3–10.

Cenoz, J., & Gorter, D. (2020). Pedagogical translanguaging: An introduction. *System, 92,* 102269.

Chastain, K. (1970). Behavioristic and cognitive approaches in programmed instruction. *Language Learning, 20*(2), 223–235.

Chen, R. H. (2022). Effects of deliberate practice on blended learning sustainability: A community of inquiry perspective. *Sustainability, 14*(3), 1785.

Chomsky, N. (1968). *Language and mind.* Cambridge University Press.

Chriswiyati, E. P., & Subekti, A. S. (2022). Indonesian L2 learners' listening anxiety and socio-affective listening strategy: A survey study. *Englisia: Journal of Language, Education, and Humanities, 9*(2), 32–45.

Colliander, H., & Fejes, A. (2021). The re-emergence of Suggestopedia: Teaching a second language to adult migrants in Sweden. *Language, Culture and Curriculum, 34*(1), 51–64.

Cross, J., & Vandergrift, L. (2018). Metacognitive listening strategies. In J. Liontas (Ed.), *The TESOL encyclopedia of English language teaching* (pp. 1–5). Wiley.

Cui, R., & Teo, P. (2021). Dialogic education for classroom teaching: A critical review. *Language and Education, 35*(3), 187–203.

DeKeyser, R. (2017). Knowledge and skill in ISLA. In S. Loewen & M. Sato (Eds.), *The Routledge handbook of instructed second language acquisition* (pp. 15–32). Routledge.

DeKeyser, R. (2020). Skill acquisition theory. In B. VanPatten, G. D. Keating, & S. Wulff (Eds.), *Theories in second language acquisition* (pp. 83–104). Routledge.

Dix, B. P., & Corbett, J. (2023). Language, culture and interculturality: Global debates, local challenges. *Language and Intercultural Communication, 23*(1), 1–4, doi: 10.1080/14708477.2023.2166281

Domaneschi, F., & Bambini, V. (2020). Pragmatic competence. In E. Fridland & C. Pavese (Eds.), *The Routledge handbook of philosophy of skill and expertise* (pp. 419–430). Routledge.

Dörnyei, Z. (2020). *Innovations and challenges in language learning motivation.* Routledge.

198   Teaching Listening

Ekayati, R. (2020). Shadowing technique on students' listening word recognition. *IJEMS: Indonesian Journal of Education and Mathematical Science, 1*(2), 31–42.

Ellis, R. (2003). *Task-based language learning and teaching.* Oxford University Press.

Ellis, R. (2012). Second language classroom discourse. In *Language teaching research and language pedagogy* (pp. 75–114). Wiley.

Ellis, R. (2022). Rod Ellis's essential bookshelf: Focus on form. *Language Teaching,* First View, 1–16.

Ennis, R. H. (2018). Critical thinking across the curriculum: A vision. *Topoi, 37,* 165–184.

Ericsson, K. (2018). An introduction to the second edition of The Cambridge handbook of expertise and expert performance: Its development, organization, and content. In K. Ericsson, R. Hoffman, A. Kozbelt, & A. Williams (Eds.), *The Cambridge handbook of expertise and expert performance* (pp. 3–20). Cambridge University Press.

Ericsson, K. A., & Smith, J. (1991). Prospects and limits of the empirical study of expertise: An introduction. In K. A. Ericsson & J. Smith (Eds.), *Studies of Expertise: Prospects and Limits* (pp. 1–38). Cambridge University Press.

Field, J. (1998). Skills and strategies: Towards a new methodology for listening. *ELT Journal, 52*(2), 110–118.

Field, J. (2004). *Psycholinguistics: The key concepts.* Psychology Press.

Flavell, J. H. (1978). Metacognitive development. In J. Scandura & C. Brainerd (Eds.), *Structural/process theories of complex human behavior* (pp. 213–245). Sijthoff & Noordhoff (Springer).

Flowerdew, J., & Miller, L. (2010). Listening in a second language. In A. D. Wolvin (Ed.), *Listening and human communication in the 21st century* (pp. 158–177). Wiley.

Franks, J. J., Bilbrey, C. W., Lien, K. G., & McNamara, T. P. (2000). Transfer-appropriate processing (TAP). *Memory & Cognition, 28,* 1140–1151.

Gass, S. (2018). *Input, interaction, and the second language learner* (2nd ed.). Routledge.

Glickstein, L. (2009). *Be heard now: How to speak naturally and powerfully in front of any audience* [Audiobook]. Audible.

Goh, C. (2008). Metacognitive instruction for second language listening development: Theory, practice and research implications. *RELC Journal, 39*(2), 188–213.

Goh, C., & Hu, G. (2014). Exploring the relationship between metacognitive awareness and listening performance with questionnaire data. *Language Awareness, 23,* 255–274.

Goh, C. C., & Vandergrift, L. (2021). *Teaching and learning second language listening: Metacognition in action.* Routledge.

Goodman, K. S., & Goodman, Y. M. (2016). Designing literacy curriculum: Teaching literacy as response to learning. In R. J. Meyer & K. F. Whitmore (Eds.), *Reclaiming early childhood literacies: Narratives of hope, power, and vision* (pp. 147–156). Routledge.

Gupta, M., & Sukamto, K. E. (2020). Cultural communicative styles: The case of India and Indonesia. *International Journal of Society, Culture & Language, 8*(2), 105–120.

Halpern, D. F., & Dunn, D. S. (2021). Critical thinking: A model of intelligence for solving real-world problems. *Journal of Intelligence, 9*(2), 22.

Hamada, Y., & Suzuki, Y. (2022). Situating shadowing in the framework of deliberate practice: A guide to using 16 techniques. *RELC Journal,* 00336882221087508.

Helgesen, M. (2016). Happiness in ESL/EFL: Bringing positive psychology to the classroom. In P. MacIntyre, T. Gregersen, & S. Mercer (Eds.), *Positive psychology in SLA* (pp. 305–323). Multilingual Matters.

Isele, D., & Cosgun, A. (2018). Selective experience replay for lifelong learning. In *Proceedings of the AAAI Conference on Artificial Intelligence* (Vol. 32, No. 1). *arXiv e-prints*, arXiv-1802. New Orleans.

Kaur, K. (2014). Young learners' metacognitive knowledge of listening comprehension and pedogogical recommendations for the teaching of listening. *International Journal of Innovation in English Language Teaching and Research ISSN, 2156*, 5716.

Kim, Y. S., & Phillips, B. (2014). Cognitive correlates of listening comprehension. *Reading Research Quarterly, 49*(3), 269–281.

Krashen, S. (1982). *Principles and practice in second language acquisition.* Pergamon Press.

Krashen, S., & Mason, B. (2020). The optimal input hypothesis: Not all comprehensible input is of equal value. *CATESOL Newsletter, 5*(1), 1–2.

Krashen, S. D., & Terrell, T. D. (1983). The natural approach: Language acquisition in the classroom. Pergamon.

Krause, C. A. (1916). *The direct method in modern languages: Contributions to methods and didactics in modern languages.* Scribner.

Lantolf, J., Poehner, M., & Thorne, S. L. (2020). Sociocultural theory and L2 development. In B. VanPatten, G. Keating, & S. Wulff (Eds.), *Theories in second language acquisition* (3rd ed., pp. 223–247). Routledge.

Lantolf, J. P., & Swain, M. (2019). Perezhivanie: The cognitive–emotional dialectic within the social situation of development. *Contemporary Language Motivation Theory, 60*, 80–105.

Larsen-Freeman, D. (2000). *Techniques and principles in language teaching.* Oxford University Press.

Li, Q., Zhang, L., & Goh, C. C. M. (2022). Metacognitive instruction in second language listening: Does language proficiency matter? *English as a Foreign Language International Journal, 2*(5), 27–55.

Lichtman, K., & VanPatten, B. (2021). Was Krashen right? Forty years later. *Foreign Language Annals, 54*(2), 283–305.

Lightbown, P. M., & Han, Z. (2008). Transfer appropriate processing as a model for classroom second language acquisition. In Z. Han (Ed.), *Understanding second language process* (pp. 27–44). Multilingual Matters.

Liu, Q. X., & Shi, J. F. (2007). An analysis of language teaching approaches and methods—effectiveness and weakness. *Online Submission, 4*(1), 69–71.

Long, M. H. (1981). Input, interaction, and second-language acquisition. *Annals of the New York Academy of Sciences, 379*(1), 259–278.

Long, M. (1985). A role for instruction in second language acquisition: Task-based language teaching. In K. Hyltenstam & M. Pienemann (Eds.), *Modelling and assessing second language acquisition* (pp. 77–100). Multilingual Matters.

Long, M. (2014). *Second language acquisition and task-based language teaching.* Wiley.

López Páez, K. (2020). The impact of oral pushed output on intermediate students' L2 oral production. *GIST Education and Learning Research Journal, 20*, 85–108.

Lozanov, G. (1977). *The Bulgarian experience: Suggestology and suggestopedia.* Iowa State University, Office of Continuing Education.

Lozanov, G., & Gateva, E. (1988). *The foreign language teacher's suggestopedic manual.* Gordon and Breach Science Publishers.

200 *Teaching Listening*

Luo, H. (2024). Cognitive-linguistic approaches to SLA and usage. In K. McManus (Ed.), *Usage in second language acquisition: Critical reflections and future directions* (pp. 106–127). Routledge.

Ma, K., Pitner, R., Sakamoto, I., & Park, H. Y. (2020). Challenges in acculturation among international students from Asian collectivist cultures. *Higher Education Studies*, *10*(3), 34–43.

Macaro, E. (2020). Exploring the role of language in English medium instruction. *International Journal of Bilingual Education and Bilingualism*, *23*(3), 263–276.

MacIntyre, P. D., & Ayers-Glassey, S. (2021). Positive psychology. In T. Gregersen & S. Mercer (Eds.), *The Routledge handbook of the psychology of language learning and teaching* (pp. 61–73). Routledge.

MacPhee, D., Bemiss, E., & Stephens, D. (2015). Research on response-to-intervention supplemental interventions. In S. R. Parris & K. Headley (Eds.), *Comprehension Instruction: Research-Based Best Practices* (3rd ed., pp. 162–184). Guilford.

Mitchell, R., Myles, F., & Marsden, E. (2019). *Second language learning theories*. Routledge.

Nation, P. (2017). Fluency practice in the four skills. In *The 15th Asia TEFL & 64th TEFLIN International Conference: Program Book* (pp. 18–35).

Norboeva, M. (2023). The role of culture in language learning and communication. *Journal of New Century Innovations*, *27*(4), 79–81.

Nowak, M. A., Komarova, N. L., & Niyogi, P. (2001). Evolution of universal grammar. *Science*, *291*(5501), 114–118.

Nunan, D., & Miller, L. (1995). *New ways in teaching listening*. TESOL

O'Malley, J. M., & Chamot, A. U. (1990). *Learning strategies in second language acquisition*. Cambridge University Press.

O'Malley, M., Chamot, A., & Walker, C. (1987). Some applications of cognitive theory to second language acquisition. *Studies in Second Language Acquisition*, *9*, 287–306.

Osser, H. (1970). Biological and social factors in language development. In F. Williams (Ed.), *Language and poverty: Perspectives on a theme* (pp. 248–264). Markham.

Oxford, R. (1993). Research update on teaching L2 listening. *System*, *21*(2), 205–211.

Oxford, R., & Amerstorfer, C. (2019). The state of the art in language learning strategies and individual learner characteristics. In R. Oxford & C. Amerstorfer (Eds.), *Language learning strategies and individual learner characteristics*. Bloomsbury.

Palincsar, A. S., & Schleppegrell, M. J. (2014). Focusing on language and meaning while learning with text. *TESOL Quarterly*, *48*(3), 616–623.

Palmer, H. (1921/2009). *The principles of language study*. Kessinger Publishing.

Pica, T. (1987). Second language acquisition, social interaction, and the classroom. *Applied Linguistics*, *8*, 3–21.

Plonsky, L., Sudina, E., & Teimouri, Y. (2022). Language learning and emotion. *Language Teaching*, *55*(3), 346–362.

Prabhu, N. S. (1987). *Second language pedagogy*. Oxford University Press.

Rahimirad, M., & Shams, M. (2014). The effect of activating metacognitive strategies on the listening performance and metacognitive awareness of EFL Students. *International Journal of Listening*, *28*, 162–176.

Raphael, T. E., & Pearson, P. D. (1985). Increasing students' awareness of sources of information for answering questions. *American Educational Research Journal*, *22*(2), 217–235.

Richards, J. C., & Rodgers, T. S. (2014). *Approaches and methods in language teaching.* Cambridge University Press.

Robinson, P., Mackey, A., Gass, S., & Schmidt, R. (2012). Attention and awareness in second language acquisition. In S. Gass & A. Mackey (Eds.), *The Routledge handbook of second language acquisition* (pp. 247–267). Routledge.

Rost, M. (1990). *Listening in language learning.* Longman.

Rost, M. (1999). Developing listening tasks for language learning. *Odense working papers in language and communication,* 49-60. ERIC.

Rost, M. (2005). L2 Listening. In E. Hinkel (Ed.), *Handbook of research in second language teaching and learning* (pp. 503–527). Erlbaum.

Rost, M. (2006). Areas of research that influence L2 listening instruction. In E. Usó-Juan & A. Martínez-Flor (Eds.), *Current trends in the development and teaching of the four language skills* (pp. 47–74). De Gruyter.

Rost, M. (2014). Developing listening fluency in Asian EFL settings. In T. Muller, J. Adamson, P. Shigeo Brown, & S. Herder (Eds.), *Exploring EFL fluency in Asia* (pp. 281–296). Palgrave Macmillan.

Rost, M., & Ross, S. (1991). Learner use of strategies in interaction: Typology and teachability. *Language Learning, 41,* 235–273.

Rost, M., & Wilson, J. J. (2013). *Active listening: Research and resources in language teaching.* Routledge.

Rubin, J. (1994). A review of second language listening comprehension research. *The Modern Language Journal, 78*(2), 199–221.

Sanavi, R. V., & Tarighat, S. (2014). Critical thinking and speaking proficiency: A mixed-method study. *Theory & Practice in Language Studies, 4*(1), 79–87.

Settles, B., & Meeder, B. (2016). A trainable spaced repetition model for language learning. In K. Erk & N. A. Smith (Eds.), *Proceedings of the 54th annual meeting of the Association for Computational Linguistics* (pp. 1848–1858). ACL.

Shaules, J., & McConachy, T. (2023). Enacting deep learning in foreign language pedagogy. In J. Shaules & T. McConachy (Eds.), *Transformation, embodiment, and well-being in foreign language pedagogy: Enacting deep learning* (pp.1–14). Bloomsbury Publishing.

Siegel, J. (2014). *Problematising L2 listening pedagogy: The potential of process-based listening strategy instruction in the L2 classroom* (Doctoral dissertation, Aston University). https://publications.aston.ac.uk/id/eprint/24383/1/Siegel_Joseph_2014.pdf

Siegel, J. (2022). Research into practice: Teaching notetaking to L2 students. *Language Teaching, 55*(2), 245–259.

Siegel, J. (2023, March 1). Profiles in notetaking: A multiple case study. *International Journal of Listening,* 1–14. doi: 10.1080/10904018.2023.2168667

Sinambela, E., Manik, S., & Pangaribuan, R. E. (2015). Improving students' reading comprehension achievement by using KWL strategy. *English Linguistics Research, 4*(3), 13–29.

Skehan, P. (1991). Individual differences in second language learning. *Studies in Second Language Acquisition, 13*(2), 275–298.

Stephens, C. (2012). Film circles: Scaffolding speaking for EFL students. In *English Teaching Forum* (Vol. 50, No. 2, pp. 14–20). US Department of State.

202 *Teaching Listening*

Styslinger, M. E., & Overstreet, J. F. (2014). Strengthening argumentative writing with speaking and listening (Socratic) circles. *Voices from the Middle, 22*(1), 58–62.

Suzuki, Y., Nakata, T., & Dekeyser, R. (2019). The desirable difficulty framework as a theoretical foundation for optimizing and researching second language practice. *The Modern Language Journal, 103*(3), 713–720.

Swain, M. (1985). Communicative competence: Some roles of comprehensible input and comprehensible output in its development. In S. Gass & C. Madden (Eds.), *Input in second language acquisition* (pp. 235–252). Newbury House.

Swain, M., Kinnear, P., & Steinman, L. (2015). *Sociocultural theory in second language education: An introduction through narratives*. Multilingual Matters.

Syafii, M. L., Kusnawan, W., & Syukroni, A. (2020). Enhancing listening skills using games. *International Journal on Studies in Education (IJonSE), 2*(2), 78–107.

Tabibian, B., Upadhyay, U., De, A., Zarezade, A., Schölkopf, B., & Gomez-Rodriguez, M. (2019). Enhancing human learning via spaced repetition optimization. *Proceedings of the National Academy of Sciences, 116*(10), 3988–3993.

Taguchi, N. (2009) *Pragmatic competence* (Vol. 5). Walter de Gruyter.

Taguchi, N. (2019). Second language acquisition and pragmatics: An overview. In N. Taguchi (Ed.), *The Routledge handbook of second language acquisition and pragmatics* (pp. 1–14). Routledge.

Takahashi, S. (2010). The effect of pragmatic instruction on speech act performance. In A. M. Flor & E. Usó-Juan (Eds.), *Speech act performance: Theoretical, empirical, and methodological issues* (pp. 127–144). Benjamins.

Terrell, T. (1977). A natural approach to second language acquisition and learning. *The Modern Language Journal, 61*, 325–337.

Thompson, I., & Rubin, J. (1996). Can strategy instruction improve listening comprehension? *Foreign Language Annals, 29*(3), 331–342.

Tripuraneni, N., Jordan, M., & Jin, C. (2020). On the theory of transfer learning: The importance of task diversity. In H. Larochelle, M. Ranzato, R. Hadsell, M. F. Balcan, & H. Lin (Eds.), *Advances in neural information processing systems 33* (pp. 7852–7862). NeurIPS.

Vandergrift, L. (1999). Facilitating second language listening comprehension: Acquiring successful strategies. *ELT Journal, 53*, 73–78.

Vandergrift, L., & Goh, C. (2012). *Teaching and learning second language listening: Metacognition in action*. Routledge.

Van Zeeland, H., & Schmitt, N. (2013). Lexical coverage in L1 and L2 listening comprehension: The same or different from reading comprehension? *Applied linguistics, 34*(4), 457–479.

Vygotsky, L. (1978). *Mind in society. The development of higher psychological processes* (Eds. M. Cole, V. John-Steiner, S. Scribner, & E. Souberman). Harvard University Press.

Wallace, M. P. (2022). Individual differences in second language listening: Examining the role of knowledge, metacognitive awareness, memory, and attention. *Language Learning, 72*(1), 5–44.

Walsh, J. A., & Sattes, B. D. (2016). *Quality questioning: Research-based practice to engage every learner*. Corwin Press.

Wegerif, R. (2019). Introduction to the theory of dialogic education. In N. Mercer, R. Wegerif, & L. Major (Eds.), *The Routledge international handbook of research on dialogic education* (pp. 11–13). Routledge.

Wenden, A. L. (1998). Metacognitive knowledge and language learning. *Applied Linguistics, 19*(4), 515–537.

Yeldham, M., & Gruba, P. (2016). The development of individual learners in an L2 listening strategies course. *Language Teaching Research, 20*(1), 9–34.

Yuksel, H. G. (2014). Cognitive approach. In S. Celik (Ed.), *Approaches and principles in English as a Foreign Language (EFL) education* (pp. 55–78). Egiten Kitap.

8   Input and Interaction

8.1	Overview: Highlighting the Role of Input and Interaction	204
8.2	Engaging with Input	205
	8.2.1 Interaction Points	*206*
8.3	Input Genres	207
8.4	Difficulty and Cognitive Load	215
8.5	Strategies for "Easifying" Input	218
	8.5.1 Input Simplification	*218*
	8.5.2 Presentation Scaffolding	*219*
	8.5.3 Technology Mediation	*220*
8.6	Summary: Maximizing the Use of Input through Interaction	223
References		224

8.1 Overview: Highlighting the Role of Input and Interaction

The previous chapter surveyed historical approaches to teaching listening and extracted key principles that can be incorporated into an effective teaching methodology. The chapter then proposed four processing approaches to teaching listening, corresponding to the four domains of listening outlined in the first chapters of the book: neurological (holistic), linguistic (bottom-up), semantic (top-down), and pragmatic (social).

The approaches and variations we have outlined emphasize that acquiring listening ability requires two essential elements: appropriate input and interactive engagement with that input. This principle applies whether the input source is human, an AI entity, a virtual reality experience, or prepared media. Listening ability requires exposing yourself to input and engaging with it in meaningful ways.

Input is explored in this chapter through first examining this notion of engagement with input. We next examine ways of interacting with input, and specifically the stages of listening when interaction is optimal. We then categorize input

DOI: 10.4324/9781003390794-11

Input and Interaction   205

genres and discourse types, to provide a framework for instructors in selecting and preparing the most appropriate inputs for learners.

We then analyze the notion of difficulty and show the factors that are involved in subjective difficulty, or cognitive load. Three approaches to helping learners manage cognitive load are considered: simplification, scaffolding, and technological mediation.

8.2 Engaging with Input

Any approach that involves audio input is likely to have some beneficial effect on a learner's listening development, but certain kinds of input are likely to have greater effect if they promote *active engagement* by the listener. If the learner is attending to input, whether live (as with face-to-face conversations or video-conferencing calls) or remote (as with streaming videos or podcast interviews), that input will offer learning potential. Activation of that learning potential—for short-term comprehension and retention and for long-term language learning and acquisition—is possible only if the listener actively engages with the input.

Active engagement refers to three domains:

- **Mental Engagement:** In human–human interactions, learners listen actively, process information, and respond to the speaker. Similarly, during active engagement with remote input, learners interpret the content, connecting it to their existing knowledge and experiences.
- **Contextual Engagement:** In human–human interactions, the language the participants use conveys their thoughts, ideas, and emotions with the expectation of some kind of active reciprocity. Likewise, in human–media or human–AI contexts, the listener needs to have some form of reciprocity to make the listening experience meaningful.
- **Emotional Engagement:** Human–human interaction often evokes emotional connection and can also trigger emotional absorption, connection, and investment in the encounter's outcome. These are the main advantages of live input: The listener can respond in real time. When learners actively engage with a story or movie, on the other hand, they may still experience a range of emotions, which can deepen their connection to the language and commitment to their overall language learning experience.

Mere exposure to audio input does not lead to acquisition; rather, sustained exposure to audio input *without* interaction may lead to stabilization. **Stabilization** refers to a listener repeatedly processing oral input in a shallow manner (not making connections or drawing inferences), which leads to **fossilization**, resistance to change, and an inability to progress further. Therefore, to acquire the language incrementally and avoid fossilization, the dedicated

206 *Teaching Listening*

listener must engage interactively with new input, trying to understand what is initially not fully comprehensible (Darvin & Norton, 2023; Hayati, 2021).

Engagement and motivation are enacted in a reciprocal fashion. Engaging listening experiences can enhance motivation, while increased motivation can lead to greater effort at engagement. When individuals find a listening experience meaningful, appropriately challenging, enjoyable, or personally relevant, it fuels their motivation, creating a positive cycle of engagement and motivation (Dörnyei & Mentzelopoulos, 2023).

In terms of instructional approaches to enhance engagement and motivation, it is important for instructors to identify possible **interaction points.** These are specific stages in the instructional sequence where instructors can pause the input and intervene in the listening process. Interaction points involve moments where the teacher and students interact to enhance comprehension, address listening challenges, or engage in discussions related to the listening material. Inserting interaction points can be an effective strategy to promote active engagement and understanding.

8.2.1 Interaction Points

There seems to be a default methodology for teaching listening in classrooms worldwide—at least in most countries and contexts I have visited as a professional observer. This default methodology is simply to play an extract from an audio or video source (of lengths varying from a few seconds to several minutes) or to deliver a live presentation (as short as a single sentence and as long as a full lecture) and then ask questions about it.

My first response to witnessing these situations is empathy. I understand what it feels like to be forced into following a fixed instructional sequence, even when you know there are better approaches to use. This listen-and-answer-questions methodology, also known as the **listen-and-test** format, facilitates classroom management and satisfies traditional expectations for how instruction *should* take place—and in many cases, it mirrors the same methods that the instructor experienced as a student. Over time, habitual use of this teaching pattern can lead to inertia and resistance: a reaction to resist change in materials or instructional practices.

Second language acquisition (SLA) research has shown that this listen-and-test format, while not necessarily detrimental to student learning, misses many interaction opportunities for helping learners improve their linguistic, semantic, and pragmatic listening skills and strategies while they are listening (Baralt et al., 2016; Hiver et al., 2021; Ushioda, 2022).

The research has identified optimal intervention points, or interaction points, in the listening process. Interaction points can take various forms, such as having students work together to pose questions and compare notes, or having the teacher answer questions or provide clarification or repetition. The goal is

Input and Interaction   207

to create opportunities for meaningful interaction that supports comprehension and language acquisition during the listening process (Rost, 2020; Rost & Brown, 2022).

If we view a listening lesson as consisting of five stages, we can readily identify useful intervention points:

- **Pre-listening stage**
  Before listening to an extract, prepare the students with a preview task to activate schemata needed to understand the upcoming text.
- **First listening stage**
  After the first listening to an extract, pose questions that ask about students' *impressions and interests* rather than comprehension questions. If the students are simultaneously reading the extract, the instructor can have students indicate (e.g., mark with a star) which parts were most interesting and then share their ideas with a classmate.
- **Second listening stage**
  During the second listening to an extract, you can provide a scaffolded task with an idea structure for the students to use. This might be a graph or chart to be filled in, an outline or partial set of notes to be completed, or an illustration to be labeled.
- **Immediate post-listening stage**
  After the second listening to an extract, an objective comprehension check can be performed. This comprehension check can include a set of multiple-choice or true–false questions that exhaustively cover the extract. Students can compare answers before checking as a whole class, as this type of peer exchange tends to build relationships and establish a collaborative classroom culture.
- **Follow-up post-listening stage**
  This is a review session, either the same day or in the following class. It might consist of reflective questions or short student presentations on the aspects of the content they found interesting. A partial or full replaying of the listening input at this point helps to build metacognitive listening strategies. The follow-up stage may also be a useful time for deliberate practice to target challenging aspects of linguistic processing.

8.3 Input Genres

An input **genre** refers to a category or type of text characterized by recognizable recurring features, structural organization, and language patterns. Input genre is useful for classifying listening resources based on their purpose, content, and intended audience (van Leeuwen & Han, 2023). Genres in language learning materials can include various written and spoken texts, such as dialogues, narratives, news articles, academic papers, advertisements, and interviews (see Table 8.1).

208 *Teaching Listening*

Table 8.1 Input Genres for Different Contexts (see Resources Appendix for sources)

Elementary school age

Genre	Potential benefits
Nursery rhymes and songs	Listening to nursery rhymes and songs introduces children to rhythmic patterns, repetitive language, and vocabulary. It helps develop phonological awareness, pronunciation, and early language skills.
Storytelling and bedtime stories	Engaging children with storytelling and reading aloud exposes them to narratives, characters, and descriptive language. It cultivates a love for storytelling, improves comprehension, and expands vocabulary.
Contextualized conversational speech	Exposing children to everyday conversations helps them acquire natural language patterns, intonation, and social communication skills. Engaging in conversations with family members and peers is particularly beneficial.
Picture books and story books	Using picture books with accompanying audio or reading aloud from story books allows children to associate words with images, fostering vocabulary development and comprehension.
Educational shows and cartoons	Watching age-appropriate educational shows and cartoons in the target language can provide exposure to language, cultural elements, and educational content.
Interactive apps and games	Language learning apps and interactive games designed for children can engage them in listening puzzles, vocabulary building, and sentence formation.
Audio stories and podcasts for children	Audio stories and podcasts, specifically created for children, offer immersive storytelling experiences, stimulate imagination, and foster listening for main ideas.
Sing-alongs and music	Encouraging children to sing along with songs in the target language enhances their pronunciation, vocabulary, and rhythm. Songs with actions or gestures can make the learning experience more interactive.
Role plays and puppet shows	Engaging children in role plays or puppet shows promotes language practice, creativity, problem-solving, and imagination.
Field trips and excursions	Taking children to places such as parks, museums, and zoos with guides exposes them to new vocabulary, concepts, and real-world language use.
Auditory games and language exercises	Engaging children in listening games, such as identifying sounds, following instructions, or matching sounds to objects helps develop their auditory discrimination skills.

Table 8.1 (Continued)

Middle school–High school age

Genre	Potential benefits
Storytelling and narratives	Listening to stories and narratives helps school-aged children develop comprehension skills, expand vocabulary, and understand story structure. It fosters imagination and a love for reading.
Informational texts and nonfiction	Introducing school-aged children to informational texts and nonfiction materials such as books, podcasts, or documentaries helps them learn about various subjects while developing their listening and comprehension abilities.
Poetry and rhymes	Exposing school-aged children to poetry and rhymes enhances their phonological awareness, rhythm, and intonation. It supports language fluency, creativity, and vocabulary development.
News and current affairs	Encouraging school-aged children to listen to age-appropriate news or news podcasts helps them stay informed about current events, broadens their general knowledge, and improves their listening and comprehension skills.
Radio programs and podcasts	Listening to age-appropriate radio programs or podcasts designed for school-aged children provides exposure to engaging stories, educational content, interviews, and discussions. It helps expand vocabulary, comprehension, and critical thinking skills.
Dialogues and conversations	Engaging children in conversations with peers, teachers, and family helps them develop listening skills, learn turn-taking, and understand conversational patterns.
Educational audio programs	Educational audio programs or language learning apps designed for children can provide interactive listening activities, vocabulary practice, and language skill development.
Dramatic performances and plays	Exposing children to dramatic performances, plays, or audio recordings of theatrical productions enhances their listening skills, understanding of characters, and storytelling abilities.
Audiobooks and read-alouds	Listening to audiobooks or being read aloud to from books exposes children to a variety of literature, enhances comprehension, and supports vocabulary expansion.
Cultural and multilingual content	Access to diverse cultural content, songs, folk tales, or stories in different languages broadens children's understanding of other cultures, fosters appreciation for diversity, and promotes language exposure.

(*Continued*)

210   *Teaching Listening*

Table 8.1 (Continued)

Middle school–High school age

Genre	Potential benefits
Debates and speeches	Listening to debates or speeches on age-appropriate topics helps children develop critical thinking skills, practice listening comprehension, and learn persuasive language techniques.
Educational videos and documentaries	Watching educational videos or documentaries on subjects of interest exposes children to visual and auditory learning experiences, enhances comprehension, and expands knowledge.

University, Adult

Genre	Potential benefits
Lectures Units: Episodes, ideas, arguments, elaborations, points	Attending live or recorded authentic lectures exposes learners to a range of discourse types: cause–effect, compare–contrast, and explanation, and promotes note-taking and learning from and retention of content.
Academic discussions Units: Points, arguments, evidence, conclusions	Academic discussions promote inclusiveness and understanding different perspectives, and help learners to engage in critical thinking.
Presentations Units: Section, subsection, bullet point, transition	Listening to presentations by fellow students or professionals provides exposure to different research topics, presentation styles, and communication techniques. It also promotes formulation and posing of questions.
Podcasts and webinars Units: Topic, segment, question, response	Supplementing your studies with educational podcasts or webinars related to your field exposes you to additional perspectives, insights, and practical knowledge.
Social conversations Units: Topic, turn	Being exposed to a range of social conversations familiarizes students with the natural style and pace of spoken language.
Interviews, speeches, oral histories Units: Opening, body, examples, main points, highlights	Listening to audio recordings of interviews, speeches, or historical events related to their coursework can deepen learners' understanding and provide valuable context.
Fieldwork and experiential learning Units: Observations, reactions, hypothesis, evidence, conclusion	In certain disciplines like anthropology, environmental studies, or social sciences, students may engage in fieldwork that involves listening to interviews, recording observations, or conducting surveys.
News and current affairs Units: Headlines, news stories, reports	Listening to news broadcasts, podcasts, or radio shows in the target language helps improve listening skills, vocabulary, and understanding of current events. It exposes learners to authentic spoken language and cultural nuances.

Input and Interaction 211

Table 8.1 (Continued)

University, Adult

Genre	Potential benefits
Movies, TV shows, and series Units: Scenes, sequences, events, shots, characters, dialogue	Watching movies, TV shows, and series in the target language exposes students to authentic spoken language, cultural references, and different accents. Learners should start with subtitles in the target language and gradually reduce reliance on them as proficiency improves.
Music and songs Units: Verse, lyrics, chorus	Listening to music and songs in the target language improves pronunciation, rhythm, and vocabulary. Paying attention to the lyrics and translating them can deepen language understanding.
Speeches and talks Units: Introduction, background, main points, arguments, counterarguments, examples, anecdotes, evidence, conclusion	Listening to speeches, TED talks, or public presentations in the target language exposes learners to formal language, advanced vocabulary, and complex ideas. It helps develop listening comprehension and expands knowledge.
Audiobooks Units: Chapters, sections, extracts	Listening to audiobooks in the target language offers an immersive experience, improving listening comprehension, pronunciation, and overall language proficiency. Students should choose books that match their language level and gradually challenge themselves with more complex texts.

While input genre refers to a category or classification of texts or works based on their shared structural characteristics, conventions, and content, **discourse type** refers to the functional aspect of language and the intentions behind communication. The functional aspects suggest the forms of engagement and interaction that the listener will have with the input. When selecting inputs for listening instruction, it is helpful to consider the communicative goals of the discourse to plan engagement tasks that allow students to interact with the content (see Table 8.2).

The availability of input material across all these genres and discourse types in the world's major languages, particularly in English, is overwhelming (see the **Resources** section for sample sources). And with the accessibility of instantaneous translation across languages along with advanced text-to-voice applications, the possibilities for selecting input material that can be used to teach listening are virtually limitless (Widyana et al., 2022). The challenge for teachers who have the freedom to select their own input materials is not in the selection process but in planning interactions, interventions, and assessment.

It is beneficial for teachers working with assigned materials to become aware of the options for supplementation. Even when working with assigned materials,

212   *Teaching Listening*

Table 8.2 Discourse Types

Type	Purpose	Possible engagement task (post-listening)
Narrative	Narrative discourse tells a story or recounts a sequence of events. It typically follows a chronological order and includes characters, settings, conflicts, and resolutions.	Complete chart with names of characters, identifying key actions in the narratives; check off list of direct quotes from the story as you hear them.
Descriptive	Descriptive discourse focuses on providing detailed descriptions of people, places, objects, or events. It aims to create a vivid sensory experience for the listener.	Sketch the scene, then work in small groups to compare images.
Expository	Expository discourse presents information, explains concepts, or conveys ideas in a clear and organized manner. It often uses a logical and informative approach to educate or inform the audience.	Presented with a printed list of false facts, correct them based on what you have heard.
Argumentative	Argumentative discourse presents and supports a claim or viewpoint with evidence and reasoning. It aims to persuade the audience by presenting a logical and well-supported argument.	Presented with a list of claims and a list of evidentiary statements (randomly organized); following a first listening, match the claims to the evidence; compare in groups.
Persuasive	Persuasive discourse is similar to argumentative discourse but emphasizes influencing the audience's beliefs, attitudes, or behaviors through emotional appeals and rhetorical techniques.	Presented with a list of emotional appeals made in a presentation; match the appeals to the shift in audience beliefs that is being attempted.
Instructional	Instructional discourse provides step-by-step guidance or directions for performing a task or following a process. It is commonly used in manuals, tutorials, or how-to guides.	Follow along and perform the task or follow the process, if applicable; alternatively, work in jigsaw groups, each group learning part of the process, then return to your home groups to teach the process to each other.
Conversational	Conversational discourse reflects the way people naturally communicate in everyday conversations. It includes turn-taking, back-and-forth exchanges, informal language, and a wide range of speech acts such as greetings, requests, or apologies.	After listening to an extended conversation, work in pairs to role-play, attempting to reconstruct the main ideas and the tone of the conversation.

Input and Interaction   213

Table 8.2 (Continued)

Type	Purpose	Possible engagement task (post-listening)
Exploratory	Exploratory discourse involves exploring ideas, possibilities, or different perspectives on a topic without necessarily reaching a firm conclusion. It often includes brainstorming, open-ended questions, and speculative thinking.	Presented with discussion questions, work in groups to reach a consensus on conclusions.
Problem-Solution	Problem-solution discourse identifies a problem or challenge and proposes potential solutions or strategies to address it. It focuses on analyzing the issue and offering practical or theoretical solutions.	Brainstorm multiple solutions to the problem.
Procedural	Procedural discourse outlines steps to accomplish a specific task or achieve a desired outcome. It is commonly found in recipes, manuals, or technical instructions.	Take notes, and mime the procedure after listening.
Analytical	Analytical discourse examines and evaluates information or data in order to draw conclusions or interpretations. It often includes critical analysis, interpretation of findings, and exploration of underlying patterns or relationships.	Make an evidence chart highlighting key evidence that helped you reach a conclusion. Debate one side of the issue.
Historical	Historical discourse focuses on exploring and narrating past events, trends, or innovations. It involves analyzing sources of information, presenting historical accounts, and providing interpretations.	Create a timeline that displays key events in the history.
Scientific	Scientific discourse is specific to scientific fields and involves reporting research findings, methodologies, and interpretations. It follows the conventions of scientific inquiry, including experimental design.	Fill in an experimental design framework showing steps in the experiment.
Legal	Legal discourse encompasses the language and communication styles used in legal contexts, including legislation, contracts, court proceedings, and legal arguments. It employs specialized terminology, precise definitions, and formal structures.	Create an outline showing arguments for your case. Make a list of definitions used.

(Continued)

214 *Teaching Listening*

Table 8.2 (Continued)

Type	Purpose	Possible engagement task (post-listening)
Technical	Technical discourse is used in technical fields and industries and involves communicating specialized information, instructions, or specifications related to technology, engineering, or specific professions.	Draw a diagram that represents your understanding.
Reflective	Reflective discourse involves introspection, self-analysis, and personal reflection. It examines experiences, thoughts, and emotions and can be found in personal narratives, journals, and reflective essays.	Make a journal entry reflecting your thoughts.
Comparative	Comparative discourse contrasts two or more subjects, ideas, or phenomena. It analyzes similarities, differences, and relationships between them and may be used in various fields, including literature, linguistics, and cultural studies.	Create two columns, one for similarities and one for differences.
Review	Review discourse provides evaluations, assessments, or critiques of products, services, performances, or artistic works. It aims to inform and guide potential consumers or audiences.	Give ratings for each review (one to five stars), highlighting one key point for each review.
Interview	Interview discourse involves spontaneous question-and-answer exchanges between an interviewer and interviewee. It serves to gather information, explore opinions, and elicit personal experiences and creative connections.	In pairs, role-play the parts of the interviewer and the interviewee.
Academic	Academic discourse refers to the language and communication styles used within academic disciplines. It includes scholarly articles, research papers, dissertations, and academic presentations, which follow specific conventions and address a specialized audience.	Take notes, then compare your notes with a partner, trying to summarize the lecture's main points.

Input and Interaction 215

it is likewise important to become aware of the interaction points, tasks, and assessments that the assigned material is employing in order to modify them as necessary (Tomlinson, 2023).

8.4 Difficulty and Cognitive Load

One of the major concerns in teaching listening is addressing the notion of difficulty. When someone finds an input difficult, they encounter obstacles or struggle to comprehend the information conveyed by the text (Strand et al., 2018). While we want to present challenging texts, for any learner, some extracts will present a level of difficulty that will discourage them from wanting to continue. By analyzing the factors that lead to difficulty, we can make informed decisions about modifying input and interaction tasks.

Comprehension difficulty can be due to several factors, including the text itself and the listener's familiarity with the text type or genre, and preparation before listening.

Concerning text features, research with text processing by both L1 and L2 listeners has identified several principles of **cognitive load** that affect comprehension: length, complexity, organization, and surface features (Bloomfield et al., 2011). Cognitive load refers to the working memory resources used during language processing (see Table 8.3).

Understanding the factors that influence cognitive load is an important competency for teachers, as it impacts the choice of texts and the construction of tasks. A further step in assessing cognitive load is depicting the text variables (how the text is constructed) and the cognitive variables (what the listener needs to do to understand) (Dong et al., 2020). Including this step in input analysis allows us to target how we may wish to modify the text, preview it, or present it, or identify what kinds of scaffolded activities will allow listeners to approach the text more meaningfully (see Table 8.4).

Table 8.3 Factors that Influence Cognitive Load

Length
- **Overall duration**—Greater duration tends to increase listening difficulty, but the effect is weak and inconsistent across studies (Bejar et al., 2000). Any extract shorter than 30 seconds tends to lack sufficient context to promote top-down listening. Any extract longer than three minutes, without opportunity for review and summarization, may overwhelm short-term memory (Renandya & Jacobs, 2016)
- **Episode boundaries**—Clarity of boundaries for **semantic episodes**, i.e., the introduction and conclusion of a new concept or event, will assist listener comprehension and retention (Rost, 1990)
- **Information density**—A greater number of new ideas in a passage corresponds negatively with increased listening comprehension because of the added stress on memory (Gilmore, 2007)

(Continued)

216 *Teaching Listening*

Table 8.3 (Continued)

- **Redundancy**—Repetition, restatement, and elaboration of information consistently improve comprehension. However, the actual benefit to a particular listener will vary by the type of redundancy (e.g., exact repetition, paraphrase) and listener proficiency (e.g., beginners tend to benefit more from exact repetition; advanced learners benefit more from paraphrase) (Cobb, 2004)

Complexity
- **Syntactic complexity**—Simplifying sentence structure tends to improve parsing efficiency (e.g., as measured by dictation tests) but does not consistently improve comprehension. Complex negatives and qualifiers (e.g., hardly any, a little less than half vs. few, about 40%) and infrequent vocabulary (e.g., diverse vs. different) have a detrimental impact on the processing and recall of messages (Brunfaut & Revesz, 2015)
- **Speaker complexity**—Passages with multiple speakers tend to increase complexity, particularly if speakers have similar points of view (Brady-Myerov, 2021)
- **Lexical accessibility**—Passages with specialized, technical, or sophisticated vocabulary tend to increase complexity, as in addition to having larger proportions of low-frequency lexis than standard texts, they also tend to have less redundancy (Carney, 2021)
- **Directness and concreteness**—Passages with implied meaning can be more difficult to understand. Research in reading comprehension suggests that texts with more concrete objects or entities may be easier to comprehend, but little research has examined this factor in L2 listening (Brown, 1995)
- **Pragmatic information**—Including L2 pragmatic constructs such as idioms and culturally specific vocabulary tends to decrease comprehension (Littlemore, 2001)

Organization
- **Orality**—Passages that exhibit spoken language grammar, that is, those more like unscripted conversations, have greater redundancy, disfluencies, and simpler syntax. They tend to be easier to understand than passages with formal written grammar (Carter & McCarthy, 2006)
- **Coherence**—Overall coherence of a passage (e.g., clear opening and explicit conclusion) sometimes, but not always, affects comprehension positively (Barzilay & Lapata, 2008)
- **Discourse markers**—Words and phrases that signal the relationship between adjacent propositions and the overall structure of the passage tend to improve comprehension. However, this effect depends on the importance of the marker in understanding the main ideas and important facts (Smit, 2006)
- **Visual reinforcement**—Visual references and nonverbal cues that reinforce oral meaning consistently promote greater comprehension through a perceptual process of bisensory augmentation (Kumcu, 2014)
- **Multisensory augmentation**—Visual text that reinforces spoken meaning typically promotes more robust comprehension through cross-modal amplification, as long as the visual text is minimal and not contradictory to the spoken text (Hasson et al., 2015; Lertola, 2019; van der Zande et al., 2014)
- **Position of relevant information**—Information is most easily recalled near the beginning or at the end of a passage (McNamara et al., 2014)

Surface features
- **Speaker accent**—Familiar accents are always easier to understand than unfamiliar ones (Adank et al., 2009; Matsuura et al., 2014)
- **Hesitations and pauses**—Disfluencies (false starts, word repetitions, revisions, and pauses) generally aid comprehension, especially for more proficient listeners. This seems true across all languages (Dall et al., 2014)

Input and Interaction 217

Table 8.3 (Continued)

- **Noise and distortion**—Background noise or distortion in the speech signal (SNR, or signal-to-noise ratio) generally interferes with efficient comprehension (Brons et al., 2013)
- **Speech rate**—How quickly someone talks can impair comprehension, but slower speech rates do not necessarily enhance it. For many L2 listeners, the worse one's comprehension (for whatever reason), the faster the speech rate is perceived. L2 listeners may incorrectly attribute difficulties caused by other factors to a too-fast speech rate (McBride, 2011; Schwab & Giroud, 2023)

Table 8.4 Variables in Text Construction and Listener Processing Demands

Variable *(text-based)*	*Potential impact on the listener* *(the text is objectively easier if ...)*
Word count Total number of words in a text	the word count is lower / there is less text to process
Individuals and objects Total number of individuals and objects	it involves fewer rather than more individuals and objects/there are fewer cross-referencing decisions to make
Text type Narrative, descriptive, instructive, argumentative	it has a paratactic (time-ordered) organization rather than an abstract (unspecified) or hypotactic (embedded) organization/the sequential ordering takes less time and effort to process
Pause unit length Average number of words per sentence (or pause unit)	average pause unit is shorter/there is less syntactic parsing needed
Object distinction Clarity and distinctness of individuals or objects in the text	individuals and objects in the text are distinct from each other/there are clearer spatial and semantic boundaries between items being brought into short-term memory

Variable *(listener-based)*	*Potential impact on the listener* *(the listener will be able to process more easily if ...)*
Inference type Inferences required are very familiar to the listeners	it involves lower-order (more frequently used) inference calculations/it requires less cognitive effort
Information consistency Information in the text is consistent with information known by the listener	it involves direct activation of useful schemata in memory/it involves shorter memory searches and less delay in re-comprehension of problematic text segments (less garden-path thinking)
Information density The ratio of known to unknown information in the text	it involves a higher ratio of known to unknown information/it involves less filing or storage of new information; integration of new information flows better when there is less new information

Source: Based on Brunfaut & Revesz, 2015; Vandergrift & Baker, 2015; Weissbart et al., 2020

218   *Teaching Listening*

Once we understand the variables for estimating input difficulty and the variables that influence the perceived difficulty of a specific input source, we are in a better position to decide how to plan interventions to promote better listener engagement.

8.5 Strategies for "Easifying" Input

When it is desirable to use a specific genre and discourse type for a group of pre-advanced-level language learners, it is almost always necessary to "easify" the input in some way rather than presenting it in its most raw form. **Easifying input** (a term first borrowed into applied linguistics by Vijay Bhatia in 1983, as far as I can tell) refers to modifying the language input itself to make it more accessible, modifying the means of presentation to make it more comprehensible, adding support to the input to make the listening experience more interactive, or some combination of these (Alkaldi & Inkpen, 2023; Bhatia, 1983).

There are four recognized tactics for easification of listening input: input simplification, presentation scaffolding, task support, and technological mediation.

8.5.1 Input Simplification

Simplifying input is an obvious approach to making texts more accessible to learners. It is accomplished through various restrictive means at the sentence level, including vocabulary replacements (replacing unfamiliar, low-frequency words with higher frequency, more familiar synonyms); shortening sentence length (breaking down longer sentences into shorter ones); rephrasing complex syntax (using simple sentence structures); timing (slowing down articulation speed and increasing pause length between utterances); and amplifying prosodic contrasts (using higher pitch and more pitch variation). Simplifying may also take place at the discourse level, using prototypical question–answer patterns (yes/no questions), noninverted questions *(You can sing?)*, either–or questions *(Where do you live? Do you live in the city?)*, or other familiar rhetorical patterns (e.g., tag questions: *You're from Osaka, aren't you?*).

Although the simplification approach may result in easier comprehension of the text or in making some elements more salient, it has been argued that text simplification compromises the integrity of communication and may result in learning confusion (Leow & Martin, 2018). Bhatia, a pioneer in genre analysis, sums it up this way:

> Sometimes, one is tempted to compromise generic integrity of a particular text in order to make it more readily accessible to the learner by applying a variety of simplification procedures to produce simplified texts or simple accounts; however, all these procedures can be counter-productive in typical ESP situations ... simplification involves expansion as a result of paraphrasing

and "detransformation," which invariably flattens out information distribution in simplified versions ... Simplification ... may obscure or even destroy the generic integrity of the text in question, thus resulting in ... confusing text-task relationship in ESP. (Bhatia, 1983, p. 195)

To avoid "flattening out the information distribution" in a text through restrictive or reductive simplification, an alternative to restrictive simplification is **elaborative simplification**. Elaborative simplification operates on the principle of enriching the input rather than modifying or eliminating difficult parts (Granena, 2008). At the sentence level, the elaboration may be lexical (repetition or rephrasing of key words, adding definitions and synonyms) or syntactic (adding explicit subordinate clauses to make lexical relationships more transparent, e.g., *I have relatives in the Cincinnati area. That's the place where I grew up*). At the discourse level, the elaborations may be transitional (providing explicit frame shifts, e.g., *The next point is…*, temporal shifts, e.g., *after that*, or contrastive shifts, e.g., *on the other hand*).

Both types of simplification, reductive and elaborative, are natural forms of **accommodation** in normal face-to-face discourse. Accommodation refers to any kind of adjustment or modification of one's language, communication style, or behavior to better align with or match the characteristics of the person one is interacting with. Its purpose is to help establish rapport, reduce social distance, and enhance effective communication. As such, it is unnatural to attempt to eliminate simplification or avoid accommodation (Long, 2009).

The main objection to simplification of many applied linguists (e.g., Araya-Camposa et al., 2020; Crossley et al., 2014; Parker & Chaudron, 1987; Rand & Rand, 2022) has focused on the effects of altering authentic texts for pedagogic purposes. Critics of simplification concur that a more effective instructional strategy is to expose learners to authentic (unaltered) texts and provide other types of strategies for making the texts more accessible to learners.

Simplification is still widely used in language teaching, particularly in commercial material development, because it often has the immediate beneficial effect of helping learners understand ideas, thus reducing frustration and increasing motivation (McNamara et al., 2014). However, because simplifying the input alters the original text and may reduce the learner's satisfaction of having a genuine listening experience, teachers need to use simplification judiciously.

8.5.2 Presentation Scaffolding

An alternative to adjusting text features in order to make audio texts more accessible is scaffolding, which has been defined as a specific just-in-time support that gives students the pedagogical push that enables them to work at a higher level of activity (Gonulal & Loewen, 2018). The most often-cited scaffolding techniques are modeling (providing a sample solution), bridging (activating

220 *Teaching Listening*

prior knowledge), contextualizing (previewing content), and re-presenting text (Abobaker, 2017; Walqui, 2006; Wirth et al., 2020).

Of these, **re-presenting text** is most relevant to enhancing listening experiences. In this scaffolding technique, the instructor adjusts the presentation format and pacing in response to students' experience of difficulty in linguistic, semantic, or pragmatic processing. Presentation adjustments (i.e., re-presentations, or presenting again) allow the listeners to ease into a listening or viewing text and process the information more comfortably without cognitive overload (Holzknecht & Harding, 2023; Hung & Nguyen, 2022).

The most effective form of scaffolding is often **chunking,** an overt way of pausing a presentation periodically to allow listeners to focus on and process one portion at a time, facilitating understanding, rehearsal, and retention. Chunking in the context of audio text is simply the process of grouping information into small, manageable units or chunks that are easier to process and remember (Xu, 2016).

Chunking can be organized **temporally** (e.g., chunking into 30- or 60-second segments) or **episodically** (i.e., grouping related pieces of information to enhance coherence). The chunking can be done physically (i.e., the instructor can pause the presentation) if the students are experiencing difficulty.

Another obvious form of re-presenting as scaffolding is timed repetition. When listeners have multiple opportunities to listen to an authentic text, they will progressively understand more each time they listen, particularly if task support is provided. Repetition can be done in a looping fashion (e.g., replay every 30 or 60 seconds) or for an entire presentation unit of text (e.g., an episode from a lecture or a scene from a film).

8.5.3 Technology Mediation

The third method of easifying a text is through the use of technological mediation. The most familiar technological mediation for listening is text captioning. Captioning is the process of converting audio content (of a television broadcast, film, video, live event, or other production) into text as transcription and displaying that text on a screen, monitor, or other visual display. Captions are designed to provide a visual aid to allow simultaneous processing of audio content with visual reinforcement. Especially useful for people with hearing impairment or, in the case of language instruction, those with limited receptive language abilities, captions are also popular for watching content while in a noisy environment.

To be effective, captions need to be synchronized with the audio delivery. There are different methods of creating captions: offline, if they are created and added after a video segment has been recorded and before it is aired, or online, when they are created in real time, at the time of program origination (Hubbard, 2022).

Input and Interaction 221

For language learning purposes, captions must have the capability to be turned on and off as needed (i.e., closed captions). For comprehension purposes, it is also optimal if captions can be selected for the target language (i.e., the language of the speakers) or for the listener's native language, though there is controversy about the effectiveness of cross-language subtitling for language learning purposes (Jha et al., 2019; Latifi et al., 2011; McKeown et al., 2021).

Theoretically, the advantage of using text with audio is that it allows for "dual coding" (Clark & Paivio, 1991), which is two simultaneous channels of semantic processing, **associative** and **referential**. In associative processing, information is encoded and stored by linking verbal and nonverbal representations together through abstract associations. In representational processing, information is encoded and stored redundantly in both the verbal and nonverbal channels. It involves creating separate, independent representations of the same information. This redundancy of encoding information in memory strengthens the memory for retrieval and recall (Kanellopoulou et al., 2019).

In addition to text captioning, the other most commonly used types of technological mediation are speed modification, timed replays, and help options (Mahalingappa et al., 2024).

Speed modifications, typically slowing down the input through variable speed playback to x 0.75 or 0.50 speed, are known to improve comprehension in many cases, for obvious reasons—slowed speed (which preserves natural pacing and pitch) allows more time for linguistic and semantic processing (McBride, 2011; Medina et al., 2020; Monteiro & Kim, 2020). (It has also been shown that time compression, with speeds up to x 3.0 normal speed, has been effective in some cases for linguistic processing training but not for improving comprehension. See e.g., Yang et al., 2020.)

Timed replays refers to the technique of immediate replay of a problematic or especially interesting section of the audio or video stream under the control of the listener or the instructor. Though there are no known studies of the direct effect of using replays for comprehension improvement or long-term learning, this technique would fall under the rubric of task repetition, which is known to have both short-term and long-term effects (Bui et al., 2019; Hsu, 2019).

Help options refers to a user-regulated platform linked with audio and video presentations that provides listeners with different routes of interaction with the media and the content. Selections allow for access to one-click-away help options in the form of listening tips, culture/technology notes, transcripts glossary, keywords, audio/video control bars, and an online dictionary, all potentially in both the TL and the learner's L1 (Cárdenas-Claros et al., 2021). Listener strategies and behavior can be adjusted, modified, and refined as listeners familiarize themselves with these ancillary elements.

At times, learners interact with help options in novel ways, resulting in indiscriminate use (Grgurović & Hegelheimer, 2007) or creating interactional shortcuts that, in principle, meet their individual learning goals but

222 *Teaching Listening*

inadvertently result in help-option misuse or neglect (Cross, 2017; Rost, 2007). With proper training and monitoring, learners can be assisted in achieving a sense of agency in the use of help options, selectively and consistently using those that boost comprehension and motivation to listen (Hubbard, 2023; Hubbard & Romeo, 2012).

Augmented reality (AR) and **virtual reality (VR)** are also technological mediations that can create greater engagement and boost listening comprehension. AR superimposes digital information, such as text, images, or videos, onto the digital environment (such as a film or slide show) that the user is viewing. Essentially, users view the physical world (i.e., the screen on their device) with digital elements incorporated. AR enhances the real-world context (again, that is, the digital screen) by providing supplementary information or interactive elements (Sydorenko et al., 2019). For language learners, this can present abundant contextual language-related activities and learning opportunities (Ng et al., 2023). In particular, AR can provide language learners with context-rich environments, aiding vocabulary acquisition and comprehension (Chiang et al., 2014; Parmaxi & Demetriou, 2020).

Gamification, the application of typical elements of game playing, has merged with AR and has become the dominant form of instruction and assessment in many popular language-learning apps. Gamified environments within an AR application incorporate game-like elements and principles, such as goals, progressions, points, levels, team competitions, rewards, rules, challenges, and obstacles, to engage participants and motivate their involvement. As with general gamification approaches in education, the essential advantage is in improving motivation and engagement rather than focusing overtly on specific skill development (Huseinović, 2024; Wulantari et al., 2023). As with other technological mediations in language learning, overuse of this method and exclusion of other forms of instruction can lead to an eventual stagnation of the learning process (Mogavi et al., 2022).

VR moves beyond AR in creating entirely digital, immersive environments that users can explore, typically by wearing a headset that provides visual, auditory, and other sensory input. VR can replicate real scenarios or create fictional scenarios. The potential advantage is that VR immerses users in a completely virtual environment so that it creates a sense of presence and can trigger real **interoceptive responses** (like heartbeat and breath-cycle changes) and emotional reactions (Chun et al., 2022). The potential advantage for the development of listening skills is that the immersion allows for sensory integration, activating additional attention to semantic and pragmatic processing and thus taking away self-consciousness about one's linguistic listening ability. For the sake of listening practice, VR can place learners in immersive language scenarios, like ordering food in a restaurant or navigating a museum, interacting verbally with digital actors in the environment (animate and inanimate!)—thus practicing listening and speaking skills in context (Chen et al., 2022).

Input and Interaction   223

When used selectively to enhance engagement and accelerate listening development, technology mediation is a welcome form of "easification" of learning. Multimedia presentations and enhanced learning environments can be more effective at promoting engagement, increasing emotional impact, improving comprehension, and increasing retention than unimodal presentations (Lim et al., 2022; Pellicer-Sánchez, 2022).

While multimedia and digitally enhanced environments will often provide a richer source of input and be more engaging, the number of channels a listener can effectively process at one time is also recognized as limited (Liaw & Chen, 2023). Generally, in accordance with dual-coding theory, a listener can attend to only two channels at any given time—text + audio or text + image or video + text (subtitles) or video + audio or audio + image. The listener does this by rapidly switching attention back and forth and processing both as a single signal (Clark & Mayer, 2011; Perez, 2022). The dual coding of signals will tend to amplify comprehension and engagement, but *only if the signals are consistent.* If the signals are not consistent or are chaotic, the listening experience is not likely to be beneficial for language-learning purposes (Leutner, 2014; Paivio, 2014).

One concern often voiced by teachers is that overdependence on multimodal input can dilute the role of listening in achieving comprehension (Hubbard, 2017). Learners may come to depend on visual processing to achieve comprehension and therefore devote less attention to listening, particularly to linguistic decoding. To maximize listening benefits in multimodal presentations, it is useful to implement multiple viewing and listening experiences with the same audio input (Chen & Plonsky, 2017). This means, for example, that for one viewing, you can isolate the audio stream and conduct a linguistic processing activity, such as dictation or shadowing, or a semantic processing activity, such as comprehension building (Suvorov, 2022).

8.6 Summary: Maximizing the Use of Input through Interaction

This chapter has dealt with the vital topic of the selection and use of input in listening development. The development of listening ability is correlated with both the *quantity* of input the learner is exposed to and the *quality* of input a learner seeks. All teachers know—and learners know as well—that simply being surrounded by input will not ensure significant listening ability development. The input must be made accessible to the learner, and the learner must somehow *commit to understanding* it if sustained language development is to take place.

Language learners and teachers often wonder how much input is needed for sustained growth in language proficiency. SLA researchers tend to give a wide range of responses, but most acknowledge that hundreds, if not thousands, of hours of active input processing are required to attain a high level of proficiency in a language (De Houwer, 2011; Lichtman & VanPatten, 2021; Pinker, 2014;

224 *Teaching Listening*

Schachter, 1986). Because students are unable to have a sufficient number of live instruction hours, actual listening instruction may be best used by teaching students how to listen independently.

To that end, it is important for instructors to be aware of the range of resources available to students to learn independently. Equally important to identifying input modes, modalities, genres, and input types is empowering students to engage interactively with the inputs they are using to learn a language. The range of tasks suggested in this unit can be readily adapted to either organized or independent learning.

The following chapter deals specifically with instructional design, exploring principled ways to maximize the use of input and interaction.

References

Abobaker, R. (2017). Improving ELLs' listening competence through written scaffolds. *TESOL Journal, 8* (4), 831–849.

Adank, P., Evans, B., Stuart-Smith, J., & Scott, S. (2009). Comprehension of familiar and unfamiliar native accents under adverse listening conditions. *Journal of Experimental Psychology: Human Perception and Performance, 35*, 520–529.

Alkaldi, W., & Inkpen, D. (2023). Text simplification to specific readability levels. *Mathematics, 11*(9), 2063.

Araya-Camposa, R., Star, P; Arguedas-Castillo, J., & Alvarez-Grijalba, W. (2020). A study of the complexity of Spanish for textual simplification. *Tecnología en Marcha, 33*, 45–63.

Baralt, M., Gurzynski-Weiss, L., & Kim, Y. (2016). Engagement with the language: How examining learners' affective and social engagement explains successful learner-generated attention to form. In M. Sato & S. Ballinger (Eds.), *Peer interaction and second language learning* (pp. 209–239) (Language Learning & Language Teaching). John Benjamins Publishing.

Barzilay, R., & Lapata, M. (2008). Modeling local coherence: An entity-based approach. *Computational Linguistics, 34*, 1–34.

Bejar, I., Douglas, D., Jamieson, J., Nissan, S., & Turner, J. (2000). *TOEFL 2000 listening framework: A working paper* (TOEFL Monograph Series No. MA-19). Educational Testing Service.

Bhatia, V. K. (1983). Simplification v. easification: The case of legal texts 1. *Applied Linguistics, 4*(1), 42–54.

Bloomfield, A., Wayland, C., Rhoades, E., Blodgett, A., Linck, J., & Ross, S. (2011). *What makes listening difficult? Factors affecting second language listening compre-hension.* University of Maryland, Center for Advanced Study of Language (CASL).

Brady-Myerov, M. (2021). *Listen wise: Teach students to be better listeners.* John Wiley & Sons.

Brons, I., Houben, R., & Dreschler, W. (2013). Perceptual effects of noise reduction with respect to personal preference, speech intelligibility, and listening effort. *Ear & Hearing, 34*, 29–41.

Brown, G. (1995). Dimensions of difficulty in listening comprehension. In D. Mendelsohn & J. Rubin (Eds.), *A guide for the teaching of second language listening* (pp. 11–15). Dominie Press.

Brunfaut, T., & Revesz, A. (2015). The role of task and listener characteristics in second language listening. *TESOL Quarterly, 49,* 141–168.

Bui, G., Ahmadian, M. J., & Hunter, A. M. (2019). Spacing effects on repeated L2 task performance. *System, 81,* 1–13.

Cárdenas-Claros, M. S., Campos-Ibaceta, A., & Vera-Saavedra, J. (2021). Listeners' patterns of interaction with help options: Towards empirically-based pedagogy. *Language Learning and Technology, 25*(2), 111–134.

Carney, N. (2021). Diagnosing L2 listeners' difficulty comprehending known lexis. *TESOL Quarterly, 55*(2), 536–567.

Carter, R. A., & McCarthy, M. J. (2006). *Cambridge grammar of English: A comprehensive guide: Spoken and written English grammar and usage.* Cambridge University Press.

Chen, B., Wang, Y., & Wang, L. (2022). The effects of virtual reality-assisted language learning: A meta-analysis. *Sustainability, 14*(6), 3147.

Chen, T., & Plonsky, L. (2017) Review of *A psycholinguistic approach to technology and language learning. Language Learning & Technology, 21,* 27–31.

Chiang, T. H., Yang, S. J., & Hwang, G. J. (2014). An augmented reality-based mobile learning system to improve students' learning achievements and motivations in natural science inquiry activities. *Journal of Educational Technology & Society, 17*(4), 352–365.

Chun, D. M., Karimi, H., & Sañosa, D. J. (2022). Traveling by headset: Immersive VR for language learning. *CALICO Journal, 39*(2), 129–149.

Clark, J. M., & Paivio, A. (1991). Dual coding theory and education. *Educational Psychology Review, 3,* 149–210.

Clark, R., & Mayer, R. (2011). *E-learning and the science of instruction: Proven guidelines for consumers and designers of multimedia learning.* Wiley.

Cobb, M. (2004). Input elaboration in second and foreign language teaching. *Dialog on Language Instruction, 16,* 13–23.

Cross, J. (2017). Help options for L2 listening in CALL: A research agenda. *Language Teaching, 50*(4), 544–560.

Crossley, S. A., Yang, H. S., & McNamara, D. S. (2014). What's so simple about simplified texts? A computational and psycholinguistic investigation of text comprehension and text processing. *Reading in a Foreign Language, 26*(1), 92–113.

Dall, R., Wester, M., & Corley, M. (2014). The effect of filled pauses and speaking rate on speech comprehension in natural, vocoded and synthetic speech. In *Interspeech Conference Proceedings* (pp. 56–60 Singapore.

Darvin, R., & Norton, B. (2023). Investment and motivation in language learning: What's the difference?. *Language Teaching, 56*(1), 29–40.

De Houwer, A. (2011). Language input environments and language development in bilingual acquisition. *Applied Linguistics Review, 2*(2), 221–240.

Dong, A., Jong, M. S. Y., & King, R. B. (2020). How does prior knowledge influence learning engagement? The mediating roles of cognitive load and help-seeking. *Frontiers in Psychology, 11,* 591203.

226 Teaching Listening

Dörnyei, Z., & Mentzelopoulos, K. (2023). *Lessons from exceptional language learners who have achieved nativelike proficiency: Motivation, cognition and identity.* Multilingual Matters.

Gilmore, A. (2007). Authentic materials and authenticity in foreign language learning. *Language Teaching, 40*, 97–118.

Gonulal, T., & Loewen, S. (2018). Scaffolding technique. In J. I. Liontas (Ed.), *The TESOL encyclopedia of English language teaching* (pp. 1–5).Wiley.

Granena, G. (2008). Elaboration and simplification in Spanish discourse. *IRAL: International Review of Applied Linguistics in Language Teaching, 46*, 137–166.

Grgurović, M., & Hegelheimer, V. (2007). Help options and multimedia listening: Students' use of subtitles and the transcript. *Language Learning & Technology, 11*(1), 45–66.

Hasson, U., Chen, J., & Honey, C. J. (2015). Hierarchical process memory: Memory as an integral component of information processing. *Trends in Cognitive Sciences, 19*(6), 304–313.

Hayati, A. (2021, December). The role motivation to overcome fossilization in pandemic era. In *Proceeding of International Conference on Language Pedagogy (ICOLP)*(Vol. 1, No. 1, pp. 14–19).Jambi, Indonesia.

Hiver, P., Al-Hoorie, A. H., Vitta, J. P., & Wu, J. (2021). Engagement in language learning: A systematic review of 20 years of research methods and definitions. *Language Teaching Research*, 13621688211001289.

Holzknecht, F., & Harding, L. (2023). Repeating the listening text: Effects on listener performance, metacognitive strategy use, and anxiety. *TESOL Quarterly*, August, 451–478, https://onlinelibrary.wiley.com/doi/epdf/10.1002/tesq.3249

Hsu, H. C. (2019). The combined effect of task repetition and post-task transcribing on L2 speaking complexity, accuracy, and fluency. *The Language Learning Journal, 47*(2), 172–187.

Hubbard, P. (2017). Technologies for teaching and learning L2 listening. In C. A. Chapelle & S. Sauro (Eds.), *The handbook of technology and second language teaching and learning* (pp. 93–106). Wiley.

Hubbard, P. (2022). Bridging the gap between theory and practice: Technology and teacher education. In N. Ziegler & M. González-Lloret (Eds.), *The Routledge handbook of second language acquisition and technology* (pp. 21–35). Routledge.

Hubbard, P. (2023). Emerging technologies and language learning: Mining the past to transform the future. *Journal of China Computer-Assisted Language Learning, 3*(2), 239–257.

Hubbard, P., & Romeo, K. (2012). Diversity in learner training. In G. Stockwell (Ed.), *Computer-assisted language learning: Diversity in research and practice* (pp. 33–48). Cambridge University Press.

Hung, B. P., & Nguyen, L. T. (2022). Scaffolding language learning in the online classroom. In R. Sharma & D. Sharma (Eds.), *New trends and applications in internet of things (IoT) and big data analytics* (pp. 109–122). Springer.

Huseinović, L. (2024). The effects of gamification on student motivation and achievement in learning English as a foreign language in higher education. *MAP Education and Humanities, 4*, 10–36.

Jha, A., Voleti, V., Namboodiri, V., & Jawahar, C. V. (2019, May). Cross-language speech dependent lip-synchronization. In *ICASSP 2019-2019 IEEE International Conference on Acoustics, Speech and Signal Processing (ICASSP)* (pp. 7140–7144). IEEE doi: 10.1109/ICASSP.2019.8682275.

Kanellopoulou, C., Kermanidis, K. L., & Giannakoulopoulos, A. (2019). The dual-coding and multimedia learning theories: Film subtitles as a vocabulary teaching tool. *Education Sciences, 9*(3), 210.

Krashen, S. D. (1983). The din in the head, input, and the language acquisition device. *Foreign Language Annals, 16*(1), 41–44.

Kumcu, A. (2014). *Effect of speech rate and overlapping on multimodal language processing: Evidence from eye movements* (MSc dissertation, University of Birmingham, UK).

Latifi, M., Mobalegh, A., & Mohammadi, E. (2011). Movie subtitles and the improvement of listening comprehension ability: Does it help? *The Journal of Language Learning and Teaching, 1*(2), 18–29.

Leow, R., & Martin, A. (2018). Enhancing the input to promote salience of the L2: A critical overview. In S. Gass, P. Spinner, & J. Behney (Eds.) *Salience in second language acquisition* (pp. 167–186). Routledge.

Lertola, J. (2019). Second language vocabulary learning through subtitling. *Revista Española de Lingüística Aplicada/Spanish Journal of Applied Linguistics, 32* (2), 486–514.

Leutner, D. (2014). Motivation and emotion as mediators in multimedia learning. *Learning and Instruction, 29*, 174–175.

Liaw, M. L., & Chen, H. I. (2023). Guest editorial: Contextualized multimodal language learning. *Educational Technology & Society, 26*(3), 1–4.

Lichtman, K., & VanPatten, B. (2021). Krashen forty years later: Final comments. *Foreign Language Annals, 54*(2), 336–340.

Lim, F. V., Toh, W., & Nguyen, T. T. H. (2022). Multimodality in the English language classroom: A systematic review of literature. *Linguistics and Education, 69*, 101048.

Littlemore, J. (2001). The use of metaphor in university lectures and the problems that it causes for overseas students. *Teaching in Higher Education, 6*, 333–349.

Long, M. (2009). Methodological principles for language teaching. In M. Long & C. Doughty (Eds.), *The handbook of language teaching* (pp. 373–394). Blackwell.

Mahalingappa, L., Zong, J., & Polat, N. (2024). The impact of captioning and playback speed on listening comprehension of multilingual English learners at varying proficiency levels. *System, 120*, 103192.

Matsuura, H., Chiba, R., Mahoney, S., & Rilling, S. (2014). Accent and speech rate effects in English as a lingua franca. *System, 46*, 143–150.

McBride, K. (2011). The effect of rate of speech and distributed practice on the development of listening comprehension. *Computer Assisted Language Learning, 24*, 131–154.

McKeown, K., Hirschberg, J., Muresan, S., Eskander, R., Ladhak, F., McGregor, S., & Zhang, R. (2021). *System for cross-language information processing, translation and summarization (SCRIPTS).* AD1165721.Columbus, Ohio. Air Force Research Laboratory. https://apps.dtic.mil/sti/pdfs/AD1165721.pdf

McNamara, D., Graesser, A., McCarthy, P., & Cai, Z. (2014). *Automated evaluation of text and discourse with Coh-Metrix.* Cambridge University Press.

228 *Teaching Listening*

Medina, A., Socarrás, G., & Krishnamurti, S. (2020). L2 Spanish listening comprehension: The role of speech rate, utterance length, and L2 oral proficiency. *The Modern Language Journal*, *104*(2), 439–456.

Mogavi, R., Guo, B., Zhang, Y., Haq, E. U., Hui, P., & Ma, X. (2022). When gamification spoils your learning: A qualitative case study of gamification misuse in a language-learning app. In *Proceedings of the Ninth ACM Conference on Learning@ Scale* (pp. 175–188). New York. https://arxiv.org/pdf/2203.16175.pdf

Monteiro, K., & Kim, Y. (2020). The effect of input characteristics and individual differences on L2 comprehension of authentic and modified listening tasks. *System*, *94*, 102336.

Ng, D. T. K., Ng, R. C. W., & Chu, S. K. W. (2023). Engaging students in virtual tours to learn language and digital literacy. *Journal of Computers in Education*, *10*(3), 575–602.

Parmaxi, A., & Demetriou, A. A. (2020). Augmented reality in language learning: A state-of-the-art review of 2014–2019. *Journal of Computer Assisted Learning*, *36*(6), 861–875.

Paivio, A. (2014). *Mind and its evolution: A dual coding theoretical approach.* Psychology Press.

Parker, K., & Chaudron, C. (1987). The effects of linguistic simplification and elaborative modifications on L2 comprehension. Paper presented at the 21st Annual TESOL Convention, Miami, Florida. https://core.ac.uk/download/pdf/32302633.pdf

Pellicer-Sánchez, A. (2022). Multimodal reading and second language learning. *ITL-International Journal of Applied Linguistics*, *173*(1), 2–17.

Perez, M. M. (2022). Second or foreign language learning through watching audio-visual input and the role of on-screen text. *Language Teaching*, *55*(2), 163–192.

Pinker, S. (2014). The bootstrapping problem in language acquisition. In B. MacWhinney (Ed.), *Mechanisms of language acquisition* (pp. 399–441). Psychology Press.

Rand, C., & Rand, M. (2022). The effect of altered lexile levels of informational text on reading comprehension. *International Electronic Journal of Elementary Education*, *15*(1), 1–9.

Renandya, W. A., & Jacobs, G. M. (2016). *Extensive reading and listening in the L2 classroom* (pp. 97–110). Springer International Publishing.

Rost, M. (1990). *Listening in language learning*. Longman.

Rost, M. (2007). I'm only trying to help: A role for interventions in teaching listening. *Language, Learning, and Technology*, *11*, 102–108.

Rost, M. (2020). Instructional design and assessment. In D. Worthington & G. Bodie (Eds.), *The handbook of listening* (pp. 265–278). Wiley.

Rost, M., & Brown, S. (2022). Second language listening. In E. Hinkel (Ed.), *Handbook of practical second language teaching and learning* (pp. 238–255). Routledge.

Schachter, J. (1986). Three approaches to the study of input. *Language Learning*, *36*(2), 211–225.

Schwab, S., & Giroud, N. (2023). Analysing speech perception. In S. Zufferey & P. Gygax (Eds.), *The Routledge handbook of experimental linguistics* (pp.201–216). Routledge.

Smit, T. (2006). *Listening comprehension in academic lectures: A focus on the role of discourse markers* (Master's thesis, *University of South Africa, Pretoria).*

Strand, J. F., Brown, V. A., Merchant, M. B., Brown, H. E., & Smith, J. (2018). Measuring listening effort: Convergent validity, sensitivity, and links with cognitive and personality measures. *Journal of Speech, Language, and Hearing Research, 61*(6), 1463–1486.

Suvorov, R. (2022). Technology and listening in SLA. In N. Ziegler & M. González-Lloret (Eds.), *The Routledge handbook of second language acquisition and technology* (pp. 136–147). Routledge.

Sydorenko, T., Hellermann, J., Thorne, S. L., & Howe, V. (2019). Mobile augmented reality and language-related episodes. *TESOL Quarterly, 53*(3), 712–740.

Tomlinson, B. (Ed.). (2023). *Developing materials for language teaching*. Bloomsbury Publishing.

Ushioda, E. (2022). Ema Ushioda's essential bookshelf: Teacher engagement with classroom motivation research. *Language Teaching*, First View, 1–12.

Vandergrift, L., & Baker, S. (2015). Learner variables in second language listening comprehension: An exploratory path analysis. *Language Learning, 65*(2), 390–416.

Van der Zande, P., Jesse, A., & Cutler, A. (2014). Hearing words helps seeing words: A cross-modal word repetition effect. *Speech Communication, 59*, 31–43.

van Leeuwen, T., & Han, J. (2023). Evaluation and discourse analysis. In M. Handford & J. P. Gee (Eds.), *The Routledge handbook of discourse analysis*(pp. 23–38). Routledge.

Walqui, A. (2006). Scaffolding instruction for English language learners: A conceptual framework. *International Journal of Bilingual Education and Bilingualism, 9*(2), 159–180.

Weissbart, H., Kandylaki, K. D., & Reichenbach, T. (2020). Cortical tracking of surprisal during continuous speech comprehension. *Journal of Cognitive Neuroscience, 32*(1), 155–166.

Widyana, A., Jerusalem, M. I., & Yumechas, B. (2022). The application of text-to-speech technology in language learning. In N. Hirastiani (Ed.), *Sixth International Conference on Language, Literature, Culture, and Education (ICOLLITE 2022)* (pp. 85–92). Atlantis Press.

Wirth, J., Stebner, F., Trypke, M., Schuster, C., & Leutner, D. (2020). An interactive layers model of self-regulated learning and cognitive load. *Educational Psychology Review, 32*(4), 1127–1149.

Wulantari, N. P., Rachman, A., Sari, M. N., Uktolseja, L. J., & Rofi'i, A. (2023). The role of gamification in English language teaching: A literature review. *Journal on Education, 6*(1), 2847–2856.

Xu, F. (2016). Short-term working memory and chunking in SLA. *Theory and Practice in Language Studies, 6*(1), 119.

Yang, X., Lin, L., Wen, Y., Cheng, P. Y., Yang, X., & An, Y. (2020). Time-compressed audio on attention, meditation, cognitive load, and learning. *Educational Technology & Society, 23*(3), 16–26.

9 Designing Instruction

9.1	Introduction: Teaching as Instructional Design	230
9.2	Instructional Design Stages	231
	9.2.1 Stage 1: Needs Analysis	*231*
	9.2.2 Stage 2: Defining Objectives	*232*
	9.2.3 Stage 3: Content Selection	*234*
	9.2.4 Stage 4: Task Sequencing	*236*
	9.2.5 Stage 5: Technology Integration	*237*
	9.2.6 Stage 6: Assessment and Feedback	*238*
9.3	Sample Instructional Designs	238
	9.3.1 Design 1: Linguistic Processing Development	*239*
	9.3.1.1 Linguistic Processing Activity 1: Dictation	239
	9.3.1.2 Linguistic Processing Activity 2: Dictogloss	241
	9.3.2 Design 2: Semantic Processing Development	*243*
	9.3.2.1 Semantic Processing Activity 1: Selective Listening	244
	9.3.2.2 Semantic Processing Activity 2: Note-Taking	244
	9.3.3 Design 3: Pragmatic Processing Development	*249*
	9.3.3.1 Pragmatic Processing Activity 1: Collaborative Conversation	249
	9.3.3.2 Pragmatic Processing Activity 2: Probing Conversation	250
9.4	Summary: Essentials of Instructional Design for Listening	254
References		256

9.1 Introduction: Teaching as Instructional Design

The roles of instructional designer and teacher overlap. An instructional designer is an education expert who creates effective and engaging learning experiences, aiming to design content and tasks that facilitate effective learning and knowledge retention. If we define learning as a process that leads to cognitive and

DOI: 10.4324/9781003390794-12

behavioral change, the instructional designer aims to make this process as efficient and rewarding as possible.

There are three critical components to the educational constructivist theory that we are highlighting in this chapter: First, learning is a process, not a product. However, because the listening process occurs in the mind, we can only infer that it has occurred from observing students' output or performances. Second, learning involves changes in knowledge, beliefs, behaviors, or attitudes. This change unfolds over time and has a lasting impact on how students think and act. Third, learning is not something done to students but rather something students do themselves. Learning directly results from how students engage in, interpret, and respond to their experiences.

Instructional designers are expected to have an in-depth knowledge of learning theories, such as constructivist theories that underpin language acquisition. In addition, instructional designers are expected to be fluent in multiliteracies, multimedia design, and assessment methods. They are also expected to be proficient in materials evaluation, project management, and technology integration.

The teacher has the complementary roles of facilitating learning, interacting with learners, and guiding them on their educational journey. The teacher ultimately delivers the instructional design, deciding on adjustments and interventions to make the instruction most effective. Language teachers are expected to be experts, not only in in-depth knowledge of the language they are teaching but in learning processes as well. Perhaps most importantly, language instructors are vital in motivating and inspiring students (Cirocki et al., 2023). In many language-teaching contexts, the teacher is *both* the instructional designer and the person who implements the design. Wherever a teacher's role falls on this designer-deliverer-evaluator spectrum, it is useful to delve into instructional design components to understand where decisions can be better articulated and where interventions are most effective.

9.2 Instructional Design Stages

The instructional design process involves a sequence of connected stages, though, in practice, some of these stages are performed in varying order, telescoped or abbreviated.

9.2.1 Stage 1: Needs Analysis

The first step in instructional design is to ask: *What are we trying to accomplish?* If instructional design is to be purposeful, we have to determine the learners' needs, goals, current knowledge, beliefs, behavior, attitudes, and preferences for content and styles of instruction. To get this information, we need to ask questions of the individuals who know best—the learners themselves. The most

232 *Teaching Listening*

reliable means of undertaking a needs analysis is conducting surveys, one-on-one interviews, and preliminary assessments of students' current oral communication abilities for a listening-based course.

Many teachers simply assume they know the answers without conducting an explicit assessment. I encourage teachers, even the most experienced ones, to use a formal procedure for gathering needs-analysis information. A formal needs analysis can reveal subtle individual differences among the students that the instructor may not have noticed. In addition, it opens up channels for ongoing dialogue and feedback, and this is essential to successful instruction (Lovett et al., 2023).

When needs analysis coincides optimally with the instructional design, there is a better chance of having most students in the "engagement" realm of the Joseph Shaules motivational model (Shaules et al., 2020), which is an integral part of emerging engagement pedagogical frameworks (Berry, 2019; Hiver et al., 2024; see Figure 9.1). All traits on the right-hand side of this figure are considered to be positive learning attitudes and behaviors, which tend to manifest as learners become more involved in their learning.

9.2.2 Stage 2: Defining Objectives

Once a teacher understands learners' needs and capabilities, clear and measurable learning objectives can be established. These objectives should specify what learners can do—and how they will demonstrate this—at the end of an

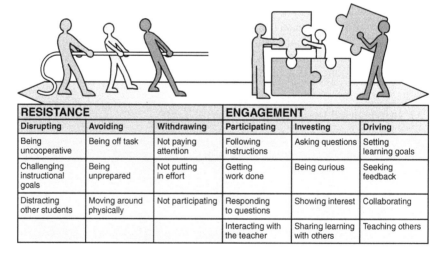

Figure 9.1 Resistance–Engagement Continuum

Motivational dynamics often involve a resistance–engagement continuum. Shifting learners from resistance toward engagement is a major goal of instructional design

instructional period. Research has shown that the degree to which students are aware of the criteria of success correlates with their speed of consolidation of learning (Hattie & Hattie, 2022; Schunk & DiBenedetto, 2016).

As a rule of thumb, objectives should aim for clarity, relevance, specificity, and measurability.

Clarity: The learning objective should be clear and easily understandable, avoiding technical jargon. It should convey a specific outcome. The learners should be able to understand what the objective is and what is expected of them.

Relevance: The learning objective should be relevant to the course or subject matter. It should align with the overall goals and objectives of the class or curriculum.

Specificity: The learning objective should be specific and focused. It should define what learners can do or understand after completing a learning activity.

Measurability: The learning objective should be measurable and observable. It should be possible to assess—fairly and reliably—whether learners have achieved the objective through a simple assessment or evaluation.

Here are some examples of learning objectives for a listening activity:

- **Comprehension:** Students will be able to listen to and understand the main ideas and supporting details in the (lecture, talk, documentary). They will demonstrate this through a 100-word summary written individually.
- **Note-taking:** Students will take organized and concise notes while listening (to the lecture, presentation, documentary). They will demonstrate this by using their notes to ask each other open-ended questions during the discussion period.
- **Vocabulary development:** Students will enhance their vocabulary through listening by recognizing and understanding new words and phrases (in the context of the lecture, interview, or film scene). They will demonstrate this by getting 8+/10 on the follow-up vocabulary quiz, working in pairs.
- **Listening for specific information:** Students can listen for and extract specific information, such as ingredients mentioned and step-by-step instructions for a recipe, from the demonstration. They will demonstrate this by repeating the exact recipe in their groups and producing a short video demonstration.
- **Listening for inference and implied meaning:** Students will develop the skill to infer meaning and identify implied information, such as the speaker's attitude and intent, after listening to the lecture (twice). They will demonstrate this by obtaining 8+/10 on the follow-up true–false quiz.

234   *Teaching Listening*

- **Identifying key points:** Students will be able to identify the main ideas and key points (of the lecture, demonstration, or talk) and summarize them accurately. They will demonstrate this by completing a summary of the talk with key information left blank.
- **Active listening:** Students will practice active listening techniques, such as maintaining eye contact, asking questions, and providing appropriate responses, to demonstrate engagement and understanding in their discussion groups. They will demonstrate this by completing a self-reflection form at the end of the class (e.g., "What percentage of the time were you maintaining eye contact with your partners?")
- **Listening for enjoyment:** Students will enjoy a story, interview, film, or song. They will demonstrate this by completing a survey about what they enjoyed most about the story, etc.

9.2.3 Stage 3: Content Selection

The pivotal stage in instructional design is to select appropriate content. This includes choosing textbooks, adapting multimedia resources, locating input sources, and creating relevant materials likely to engage learners and align with the learning objectives.

Particularly in the teaching of listening, this content selection step cannot be abbreviated or left to chance, as input material is the foundation of the course. An experienced instructional designer will develop an A List of primary materials and a B List of backup materials. To assure continuity and coherence (and to save time), plan the input resources for the entire course in advance, but allow for additions as new resources come to light.

TIPS FROM PRACTITIONERS: Become a multiliteracy expert

I used to consider myself a lifelong language learner, a language teacher, a researcher, an author, an instructional designer, and a teacher trainer. Recently, a publisher recently told me that none of these labels were inclusive enough for what I do: I needed to identify myself as a **multiliteracy expert**.

After asking around a bit, I discovered that multiliteracy refers to the ability to understand, interpret, and interact across multiple forms of communication. Traditionally, literacy was primarily associated with reading and writing skills. However, in today's digitally dominated and information-rich world, literacy extends beyond text-based communication.

Multiliteracy recognizes that different forms of communication, such as visual, digital, audio, and spatial, are essential for navigating and understanding the complexities of modern society. Here are some key aspects of multiliteracy that I have encountered:

1. Textual literacy: The traditional skills of reading, writing, and understanding written language.
2. Visual literacy: The ability to interpret and create visual content, such as static and dynamic images, graphs, charts, motion media, and videos.
3. Audio literacy: The ability to follow and interpret spoken content at natural speed, making adjustments between focusing on active listening, empathic listening, critical listening, and appreciative listening.
4. Digital literacy: Proficiency in using digital tools and technologies, understanding online information, and critically evaluating digital content for its veracity and intent.
5. Information literacy: The capacity to locate, assess, and use information in text, audio, video, and VR channels and to use it effectively and responsibly.
6. Media literacy: Understanding and analyzing media messages, including those from television, social media, and other forms of mass communication.
7. Cultural literacy: Understanding of and sensitivity to different cultures, values, and perspectives.
8. Critical literacy: The ability to critically analyze and question information, media, and societal structures.
9. Numerical literacy: Competence in understanding and using numbers, statistics, and mathematical concepts.
10. Spatial literacy: Understanding and interpreting spatial relationships, maps, and geographic information.

What this means for me in terms of designing learning materials is that the traditional four skills of listening, speaking, reading, and writing are merging with other forms of literacy. Multiliteracy is becoming increasingly important in education and everyday life, as individuals need to be skilled in multiple forms of communication to participate fully in today's interconnected world. I think of multiliteracy as helping students become more informed critical thinkers and effective communicators across various mediums.

So, I will now identify myself as a multiliteracy specialist. (I'm still getting used to this.)

Steve Brown, Professor Emeritus, Youngstown University; Co-author *English Firsthand*

236 *Teaching Listening*

9.2.4 Stage 4: Task Sequencing

This is the most detailed step in the entire process: preparing the materials, learning platform, and instructional steps. Preparing or designing materials is most often a reverse-engineering process. When I visit language classes, I often ask teachers what activities work best for them. When an activity works consistently, it is usually because it engages learners, addresses their development needs, targets clear objectives, provides a clear means of assessment, and suggests a workable activity sequence.

When fully articulated, the task delivery for a listening-based lesson will involve several interventions and points for learners to interact with the input (described in more detail in Chapter 8):

- **Pre-listening intervention: build expectations**
  Before listening to a target extract, provide a short pre-listening activity to build interest, activate expectations, and prime recognition of key vocabulary items.
- **First listening intervention: engage personal interest**
  After listening to the full extract once, build subjective listening skills (e.g., by asking, "What is most interesting/surprising/important to you?") or listening strategies (e.g., by asking, "What is confusing/unclear to you?").
- **Second listening intervention: expand selective attention**
  While listening a second time, learners need a concrete task, perhaps a chart or table to fill in, to use selective listening to focus on important information.
- **Immediate post-listening intervention: deepen comprehension**
  After the second listening to an extract in full, provide an objective comprehension check. This might include these types of questions: "What was the main idea?" "What is (Speaker A)'s reasoning?" "Why does (Speaker A) believe (that)?" "What is your opinion of what (Speaker A) said?" "Why do you think so?" Students can compare answers with a partner before checking as a whole class.
- **Follow-up post-listening intervention: develop interpretation**
  The instructor allows students to give their views on the extract, prepare a short response, reconstruct the extract in some way, or reflect on the content and their process of understanding. Reflective questions can be posed to facilitate this review: "What were the main points of (the text)?" "What were the main ideas in your discussion?" "What was most challenging for you in this activity?"
- **Deliberate practice intervention: strengthen linguistic processing**
  The instructor selects linguistic features from the input employed in the lesson and utilizes them for a short (5–10 minutes typically) structured practice in pronunciation shadowing, phonological discrimination, word recognition, or syntactic parsing.

Designing Instruction 237

It is important to note that *not all* of these interventions need to be done with every listening activity, nor in this exact order.

9.2.5 Stage 5: Technology Integration

Incorporating technology effectively into language learning has become an essential aspect of instructional design. An experienced instructional designer must survey the best available technologies for supporting the listening curriculum, many of which are free or low-cost (see Table 9.1).

It is important to consider technology *after* you have worked through needs analyses, learning objectives, and content selection. Dating back to the language lab boom, I have seen numerous instructors and course administrators assume they must use the latest technologies, even if they are unclear on what these technologies offer. While using new technologies, popular media, and gaming can increase learner motivation, it is still best practice to use them selectively to support instructional goals.

Even though technology resources for teaching listening continue to proliferate and improve, it is important to understand that it is *not* the technology itself (immersive virtual reality, multimodal inputs, variable speed playback, interactive subtitling, etc.) that causes learning. Rather, it is the *instructional methods* that leverage the technology's unique affordances—or engagement characteristics.

Table 9.1 Technology Resources to Integrate into Listening Instruction

- **Listening media for audio and video input** (e.g., Listenwise, Lingual Net, English Central) online radio, news, and podcast platforms (e.g., BBC World Service, Voice of America, Spotify); language-learning YouTube channels (e.g., Easy Languages, Français Authentique, Go Natural English)
- **AI tools for generating input:** for conducting conversations; answering questions (e.g., ChatGPT); generating art (e.g., Midjourney); generating music (e.g., Soundraw); generating avatars (e.g., Starrytars); generating presentation slides (e.g., SlidesAI); editing pictures (e.g., Remini), editing videos (e.g., Pictory); summarizing texts (e.g., Wordtune)
- **Chatbots; language-learning AI assistants** (e.g., Memrise, Botimize, Mondly)
- **Listening-based language-learning apps** (e.g., LingQ, Beelinguappl, Pimsleur)
- **Immersive virtual reality language-learning experiences** (e.g., immerse.me, VirtualSpeech)
- **Speech-to-text transcription tools** (e.g., Otter.ai, Descript, Google Docs Voice Typing)
- **Speech-recognition and pronunciation resources** (e.g., Speechace, ELSA Speak, Forvo)
- **Video- and audio-based online platforms** (e.g., Viki, ELLLO, FluentU, YabblaFluentKey)
- **Speech-recognition virtual classrooms and language-exchange platforms** (e.g., HiNative, HelloTalk, Tandem, Conversation Exchange)

238   *Teaching Listening*

TIPS FROM PRACTITIONERS: Use virtual reality (VR) purposefully

Immersive virtual reality (IVR) headsets are popularly recognized as a vessel for digital adventures in entertainment, as they give users a profound sense of inhabiting a virtual space. Educators also harness this experience for pedagogical purposes. Although the technology dates back to the 1960s, only in recent decades have headsets become more affordable and accessible to educators and the general public. One of the main affordances of IVR for education, and specifically for language and culture learning, is that learners are immersed in 3D, 360-degree environments that replicate or simulate authentic locations and situations—or also entirely novel environments—leading to a greater sense of presence that would not be available if they were simply viewing text or video, listening to audio, or even conversing in a video chat. In addition, kinesthetic engagement adds a new dimension to an IVR environment, as learners use both their hands and bodies to express themselves and manipulate objects in the environment, resulting in embodied cognition.

Dorothy Chun, Professor, University of California, Editor of
Language Learning and Technology

9.2.6 Stage 6: Assessment and Feedback

Planning appropriate assessments is crucial for measuring learners' progress and providing feedback. Assessments can include self-assessments and formative assessments (ongoing checks for learning), which need not be quantitative measures, and summative assessments (evaluating overall achievement), which should have a quantifiable component to represent concrete progress and identify specific areas that need attention.

Evaluating the overall effectiveness of the instructional design is vital. This can be done through learner feedback (at the end of every class, or periodically and at the end of the course), performance assessments, and comparing learning outcomes to the initial objectives. Based on the evaluation results, necessary adjustments and improvements can be made for future iterations. (Chapter 10 provides a more detailed treatment of assessment.)

9.3 Sample Instructional Designs

We will outline three learning sequences to illustrate these features of instructional design.

Design 1: Linguistic Processing Development
Activity sequence: Dictation, dictogloss

Design 2: Semantic Processing Development
Activity sequence: Selective listening, note-taking

Design 3: Pragmatic Processing Development
Activity sequence: Collaborative conversations, probing conversations

9.3.1 Design 1: Linguistic Processing Development

As discussed in Chapter 2, linguistic processing—phonological decoding, word recognition, and syntactic parsing—is the basis of listening development. Even though most instructors acknowledge its importance, linguistic processing is often not addressed explicitly or extensively. Learners are not given specific instruction or sufficient focused practice in perception, decoding, and short-term memory development.

Much of this neglect is due to **top-down bias**, an overreliance on the conscious employment of background knowledge and context to guide the listening process (Furuya, 2021). However, learners of all ages and proficiencies benefit from focused practice with bottom-up processing exercises aimed at sharpening decoding skills. The prototypical activity that develops bottom-up processing is **elicited imitation**, or verbatim repetition. Linguist Charles Osgood coined this term in the 1950s as a more sophisticated-sounding term for what had been called "the parrot technique." Elicited imitation (EI) activities do involve parroting—repeating back what was just heard—but the current evolutions of EI involve more variety, increased cognitive processing, and greater engagement. Current versions of EI are recognized under the umbrella term, **shadowing** (Hamada & Suzuki, 2022).

The two teaching activities demonstrated in this linguistic processing sequence are **dictation** and **dictogloss,** both of which are forms of elicited imitation or shadowing. These activities focus on both linguistic processing and language production skills (accurate pronunciation and writing).

9.3.1.1 Linguistic Processing Activity 1: Dictation

Dictation involves the teacher (or a recorded voice) reading a passage (or sentence) aloud, once or twice, while students listen and transcribe what they hear (see Table 9.2). Dictation tests linguistic processing, inference, spelling, and overall writing accuracy.

240   *Teaching Listening*

Table 9.2 Stages in the Design of a Dictation Activity

S1: Needs Analysis	**Focus on linguistic processing, accurate perception, word recognition, inferring missing parts**
S2: Defining Objectives	**Increasingly difficult (longer and more complex) sentences, develop short-term memory, attempt to write coherent reconstructions of input, show interest in correcting misunderstandings**
S3: Content Selection	**Short anecdotes (100 words)**
S4: Technology Integration	**Prerecorded input; variable speed playback (75%–100% speed)**
S5: Task Sequencing	**Prep: Worksheets with blanks for verbs and nouns** **Pre-listening:** Vocabulary preview. **First listening:** Listen without writing. Write down two keywords you remember. **Second listening:** Listen and write what you hear. **Post-listening:** Compare with a partner.
S6: Assessment and Feedback	**Learners compare completed dictations, self-report % on assessment sheet, complete reflection questionnaire**

TIPS FROM PRACTITIONERS: Vary dictation styles

Just as personal trainers often vary the types and sequences of exercises for their clients, listening teachers need to vary the types and sequences of linguistic processing activities for their learners.

Variation disrupts neural adaptation and improves motivation. Introducing new exercises the student has never tried provides mental stimulation and personal challenges.

Here are some variations that may stimulate learners and keep them focused on pushing their perception and decoding skills.

- **Fast-speed dictation**. The teacher reads a passage at natural speed, with assimilations, etc. The students can ask for multiple repetitions of any part of the passage, but the teacher will not slow down the articulation of the repeated phrase. This activity focuses students' attention on the features of fast speech.
- **Pause and paraphrase**. The teacher reads a passage and pauses periodically for the students to write paraphrases, not the exact words used. This activity focuses students on vocabulary flexibility, saying things differently, and focusing on meaning as they listen.

Designing Instruction 241

- **Listening close.** The teacher provides a partially completed passage that the listeners fill in as they listen or after. This activity allows focus on particular language features, e.g., verbs or noun phrases.
- **Error identification.** The teacher provides a fully transcribed passage but with several errors. The students listen and then identify and correct the errors. This activity focuses attention on detail.
- **Jigsaw dictation.** Students work in pairs. The students read their parts to the other to complete the passage. This activity encourages teamwork and negotiation of meaning.

In addition to providing some surprise and motivation for the learners, each variation focuses on specific aspects of language learning.

Mario Rinvolucri, Author and teacher trainer, UK

9.3.1.2 Linguistic Processing Activity 2: Dictogloss

Dictogloss is a variation of dictation, but it involves additional memory work, collaboration, and metatalk (talking about language choices), all of which are known to improve cognitive listening strategies and aid in the acquisition of grammar and vocabulary (Li, 2023; Storch, 2008; Swain & Lapkin, 2013; Yu et al., 2022). (See Table 9.3.)

Table 9.3 Stages in the Design of a Dictogloss Activity

S1: Needs Analysis	**Focus on collaborative learning, metacognitive skills, linguistic processing, semantic processing**
S2: Defining Objectives	**Learners show curiosity about each other's versions, ask questions, use inference to fill in missing knowledge, show a willingness to revise understanding**
S3: Content Selection	**A series of short dramatic monologues (<150 words)**
S4: Technology Integration	Optional: Use of video to record student collaboration sessions for Ls to refer to later.
S5: Task Sequencing	**Prep: Index cards for each group to use for their reconstruction.** 1. **Pre-listening:** Introduce the topic and provide necessary background information, including problematic vocabulary. 2. **First listening:** Read the passage aloud naturally, without pausing. Students listen attentively without taking notes, but may write down keywords.

(Continued)

242   *Teaching Listening*

Table 9.3 (Continued)

	3. **Second listening:** After the initial listening, students work collaboratively in small groups to reconstruct the text based on their collective memory. (Assign a secretary for each group.) They discuss and negotiate the text's content, grammar, vocabulary, and organization. Translanguaging (use of students' L1 for task completion) can be helpful for instructional purposes here and need not be discouraged as long as it contributes to the task (Tian & Shepard-Carey, 2020). 4. **Post-listening:** Each group shares their reconstructed version of the text with the whole class. The teacher facilitates a comparison and analysis of the different versions, highlighting similarities, differences, and areas of potential improvement. The teacher resists making corrections per se in order to keep students' curiosity and engagement active (see Table 9.4). 5. **Reflection and review:** Students reflect on their challenges during the task, analyze their language choices, and identify areas for further learning and improvement. You may reread the original passage here, though the instructional goal is not to replicate the passage verbatim.
S6: Assessment and Feedback	**Ls complete reflection questionnaire, focusing on what new language they noticed**

Table 9.4 Sample Dictogloss Passage, with Listener Reconstruction

Original:

It was a bitterly cold night. It was raining heavily. Sally was walking along the empty road, and tears ran down her face. She reached a streetlamp and stopped there. She had nowhere to go, no one to stay with, nothing! She was soaked to the skin, but this didn't seem to bother her. Suddenly, she felt a gentle tap on her shoulder. Surprised, she turned around. In the pale-yellow light, she saw a stranger. He wore clothes as black as night, but his face was kind and calm.

Student group construction:

On a cold and rainy night, a young woman named Sally was walking on a dark road. She was crying. She stopped under a streetlight. She was worried because she didn't have a place to stay, and she didn't know anyone. She had wet skin, but she continued to walk. Suddenly, she felt something. A man taps her shoulder. She is scared but turned to face him. He was a stranger. His clothes were dark, but his face was friendly and kind.

Designing Instruction   243

TIPS FROM PRACTITIONERS: Add input processing techniques

One immediate benefit of dictogloss-type activities is the natural sense of collaboration and discovery that they bring about. Because the students are invested in the task, this reconstruction step also forces students to engage in the **grammar discovery approach** (Batstone & Ellis, 2009). When the group transcribes their collective thoughts and their agreement on what was said, they are required to negotiate the grammar they need to convey their thoughts accurately. Feedback from the group, and eventually from the instructor, is effective at helping students discover appropriate grammar.

Teaching grammar through this kind of input processing rather than through deductive presentations is more effective in the long term. We can do this by helping learners to attend to particular grammatical features and training the skills of noticing. This contrasts with traditional approaches, which aim to teach grammar through production practice of one kind or another. In input processing tasks, we make use of oral texts on the grounds that learners need training in being able to notice grammatical features when they are listening. This is very difficult for learners, particularly if the features are redundant (i.e., are not essential for understanding the meaning). In doing this, we are using an inductive learning approach. Learners are shown how to analyze the data in order to arrive at an understanding of how a grammatical feature works. This means that we are providing practice in monitoring—the learners are asked to use their explicit knowledge to identify and correct errors of the kind that they typically make.

**Rod Ellis, Author, Language Acquisition Specialist,
Auckland, New Zealand**

9.3.2 Design 2: Semantic Processing Development

As outlined in Chapter 3, semantic processing is the essential engine of language comprehension. Without the activation of mental models for vocabulary and schemata and extensive reasoning and inferencing, there can be no real understanding. Though semantic processing comes naturally to most learners, it is important to guide their development to ensure that they expand their attention and memory as they listen. The two activities demonstrated as representative of semantic processing tasks are selective listening and note-taking.

244   *Teaching Listening*

9.3.2.1 Semantic Processing Activity 1: Selective Listening

The initial way into semantic processing is selective listening practice. Joan Morley, a pioneer in this area (and a professor at my alma mater), offered the first comprehensive set of materials for selective listening in her work *Improving Aural Comprehension* (Morley, 1972). As Morley stated then (1972, p. iv), "The only way to improve aural comprehension is to spend many hours practicing listening … However, a directed program of purposeful listening can shorten the time." Morley considered the two tenets of improving aural comprehension (what she called "listening with understanding") to be concentrated, disciplined listening, and immediate task completion, to provide "an urgency for remembering."

Morley viewed scaffolding of selective listening as a prerequisite for the complex and more extended listening that learners in an academic course need to undertake. Morley believed that using carefully planned and graded listening lessons would help students learn to listen and ascertain concrete facts to become ready to listen and construct more abstract ideas (see Table 9.5).

Lesson content included:

- Numbers and numerical relationships
- Letters, sounds, abbreviations, spelling
- Directions and spatial relations
- Time and temporal sequences
- Dates and chronological order
- Measurements and amounts
- Proportion, comparison, and contrast
- Facts from reports

For extended extracts (longer than one minute), a useful form of selective listening is note-taking. Note-taking is widely viewed as an important macro-skill in the lecture–listening comprehension process, a skill that often interacts with reading (when note-taking is integrated with reading material accompanying the lecture), writing (the actual writing of the notes or subsequent writing based on the notes), and speaking (posing questions, or oral reconstruction of the notes or discussion based on the notes).

9.3.2.2 Semantic Processing Activity 2: Note-Taking

Note-taking is an age-old activity, used to remember information that is flowing in too quickly to manage with short-term memory resources alone. For this reason, note-taking is a commonly used selective listening task in language classes. It has a high degree of **face validity** (i.e., it is recognized as having practical value) because language learning for most of us is marked by an overloading of our memory capacity. We tend to forget new vocabulary and information faster than we wish.

Designing Instruction   245

Table 9.5 Stages in the Design of a Selective Listening Activity

S1: Needs Analysis	**Attend to challenging (long and complex) listening passages and identify key facts and details**
S2: Defining Objectives	**Learners display active note-taking throughout activity and engage in active reconstruction with partner**
S3: Content Selection	**Short scientific passage (100 words; 1 minute):** *Regular exercise offers numerous benefits to both physical and mental health. Research shows that engaging in physical activity at least three times a week can improve cardiovascular health, boost energy levels, and strengthen muscles. Additionally, exercise releases endorphins, which can elevate mood and reduce stress and anxiety. For weight management, combining regular exercise with a balanced diet is essential. It's important to start with activities that suit individual fitness levels and gradually increase intensity. It is always recommended to consult a healthcare professional before beginning any exercise program, especially for those who have existing medical conditions.*
S4: Technology Integration	Optional: Include slides with graphics related to the information.
S5: Task Sequencing	**Prep: Worksheet for each student** **Pre-listening:** Introduce the topic with slides. Preview key vocabulary: benefits, activity, strengthen, reduce, combine. Ask for associated words for each lexical item. **First listening:** Read the passage aloud naturally, without pausing. Show the slides corresponding to each information point. Students listen attentively without taking notes. At the end, ask students what words they recall: Write these on the board or have students write in a chat box, etc. **Second listening:** Distribute worksheets: an outline of the talk with some key information missing. Read (or play recording) of the passage again. Ask students to fill in as they listen. **Post-listening:** Students work in pairs to compare their worksheets. Provide students with sentence cues to complete or ask questions that elicit the information. **Reflection and Review:** Students reflect on their challenges during the task. Each student should note any new vocabulary they learned.
S6: Assessment and Feedback	**Have students work in pairs to reconstruct the information in the passage. Follow-up can be a short oral or written presentation.**

246   *Teaching Listening*

Note-taking is a primary learning tool for students in academic fields, reflecting that content learning involves sifting through large amounts of new information to decide what needs to be retained. Different note-taking systems have been developed, though most note-takers (myself included) will use a combination of methods depending on the content and presentation style:

1. **Outline Method:** Structuring your notes hierarchically using bullet points, numbers, letters, or indenting to indicate different levels of information.
2. **Cornell Method:** Developed by a Cornell University professor in the 1940s, this method encourages organizing note pages into three sections: a main notes section, a cues or keywords section, and a summary section (for summarizing after the lecture).
3. **Mind Mapping:** Visual diagrams representing concepts and their relationships using branches, nodes, arrows, boxes, lines, and spacing to reflect connections between references and ideas.
4. **Charting Method:** Tables or columns to categorize and present data clearly.
5. **Sentence Method:** In this style, you write full sentences, usually linearly, capturing the main points and supporting details as you go.

As noted by several researchers, including myself, it is not the note-taking itself that fosters increased listening ability but the preparation for note-taking, the mental focusing of attention during note-taking, and the follow-up reconstruction and review activities involving the use of the learner's notes (Flowerdew & Miller, 2010; Jin & Webb, 2023; Rost, 1990; Siegel, 2016) (see Table 9.6).

Table 9.6 Stages in the Design of a Note-Taking Activity

S1: Needs Analysis	**Gradually increase length of lectures to 10–15 minutes, with students actively taking notes**
S2: Defining Objectives	**Increase attention span, work at a relaxed pace, collaborate with classmates, reconstruct content, pass comprehension test (80%)**
S3: Content Selection	**(400 words/3 minutes)**
	(E01) Hello. Last time, we looked at trends in the job market and identified professions that are growing quickly.
	What I'd like to focus on this time is a core set of skills that are important in all of these growth sector professions. We've got four skills—or maybe more accurately, skill sets—to review. (E02) The first skill set relates to communication. Almost every job now requires "excellent communication skills,"—but what does that mean? Of course, good communicators must be able to express themselves clearly and positively—in both speaking and writing. But there's even more to it than that. Having strong communication skills is also

Designing Instruction 247

Table 9.6 (Continued)

	being able to convey information to people simply, in a way that helps people understand you and makes them want to respond to you. So, it's about connecting with people, not just speaking and writing. Good communication skills mean you can give and understand instructions, listen to others and learn new things, make requests, ask questions, and give convincing answers when someone asks you a question. So, it's important to note that good communication doesn't mean that you can use communication technologies well, but that you can communicate with people well. So, it might be best to think of communication skills as "personal communication skills." (E03) The second skill set relates to your intuition. This is a skill set known as social intelligence. Social intelligence is a term coined by the American psychologist Edward Thorndike in the 1920s, to refer to the ability to get along with other people. He was referring to ways to adapt to situations involving new people—and more fundamentally, to the ability to "read" the emotional states of the people around you. This is a key skill set in many occupations because almost every job involves collaboration. And nowadays, that means getting along with diverse groups of people. Social intelligence involves getting to know people who may be very different from you in terms of age, education, sexual orientation, and cultural and language background. You have to develop sensitivity to different people and to different ways of viewing the world. This skill set has become increasingly important in a globalized world. For instance, you might be working for a company where one person on your project team is in India, another in China, and another in Germany. The effectiveness of your work depends on the social intelligence of the people involved, right? Just having email exchanges and web meetings with the people on your project team isn't enough. It's about collaboration, connecting, and working harmoniously. And collaboration is about social intelligence. (from *Contemporary Topics*, Beglar et al., 2022)
S4: Technology Integration	**Video streaming, variable speed, subtitle options**

(*Continued*)

248   *Teaching Listening*

Table 9.6 (Continued)

S5: Task Sequencing	**Pre-listening:** Review two methods of note-taking: Cornell Method and Outline Method. Preview topic and key vocabulary.
	First listening: Play the video of Episode 1–Episode 3 without pauses. Students take notes manually (rather than digitally). Students then work in small groups to ask each other: "What was the main idea of this part of the lecture?"
	Second listening: Play the video of Episode 1–Episode 3 without pauses. Encourage students to add to their notes during this second listening. (Option: Use a different-colored pen for this turn.)
	Post-listening: Students work in groups to reconstruct the content using their notes.
	Reflection and Review: Students write a short summary of this section (less than 50 words). Students then discuss which note-taking method they used, how much they used their L1 in the note-taking process, and the advantages and disadvantages of translanguaging.
S6: Assessment and Feedback	**Students take a comprehension check test (multiple choice) using their notes**

TIPS FROM PRACTITIONERS: Use note-taking to focus attention

Students' ability to take clear, comprehensible notes for study and test preparation has long been a key element in their academic success. Even though there is no consistent objective correlation between types or quantity of notes and comprehension scores, as a teacher, I have consistently seen a positive effect of note-taking instruction on student participation and an increase in student responsibility in trying to understand. I have seen the advantages of providing illustrative strategies via interventions *while* students are actively engaged in listening to academic lectures. Interventions—short instructional episodes during a language processing experience—allow students to focus their attention and learn specific note-taking strategies that promote comprehension. I also think note-taking interventions improve long-term memory during and after listening.

> I review students' notes periodically to give them ratings on complete-ness, organization, clarity, accuracy, and personalization (i.e., adding their own comments, questions, and reflections). However, I don't grade the notes formally, so that the students come to understand note-taking as a personal tool for their own learning.
>
> **Jeanette Clement, Author, Pittsburgh, USA**

9.3.3 Design 3: Pragmatic Processing Development

Listening ability involves much more than one-way receptive comprehension. It includes interactive listening, in which the listener contributes to and influences the direction and outcome of a conversation. In addition to the importance of conversation ability for contributing to positive communicative outcomes, col-laborative conversation is a vital means of language acquisition. Its potential benefits are in forcing comprehensible output, that is, compelling the learner to formulate complex ideas in order to be understood, and in encouraging nego-tiation to understand the language of the interlocutors (Shawaqfeh et al., 2024; Suzuki & Itagaki, 2015).

In classroom language-learning situations, either face to face or online, the primary opportunity for collaborative conversations is learner–learner inter-action. For L2 learners to benefit from this interaction, it is important to incorp-orate scaffolded instruction to avoid minimal conversations with little pedagogic value and to provide support for expanding students' identity, agency, and voice in order to enable satisfying, personal communication.

The two activities outlined in this section are **collaborative conversations** and **probing conversations**.

9.3.3.1 Pragmatic Processing Activity 1: Collaborative Conversation

The most transparent pedagogic structure for working on collaborative conversations is the gap task (see Table 9.7). Three fundamental types of gap tasks are readily set up in the classroom (live or online) settings: the information gap task, the opinion gap task, and the experience gap task.

1. **Information Gap Task:**

   - Purpose: The central goal of an information gap task is to encourage learners to exchange information verbally and negotiate to fill in missing pieces of information.

250   *Teaching Listening*

- Task structure: In an information gap task, two learners work face to face. Each has a different set of information, and they must ask and answer questions to share their information and complete the task together.
- Example: One learner has a picture, and the other has a written description of the picture. They need to communicate (without looking at the other's input) to identify discrepancies between the picture and the description.

2. **Opinion Gap Task:**

- Purpose: The primary objective of an opinion gap task is to foster learners' ability to express and understand opinions on specific topics.
- Task structure: In an opinion gap task, learners are given a controversial or thought-provoking statement or question. They need to discuss and justify their viewpoints on the topic, leading to exchanges of opinions. Specific conversational gambits can be provided to guide the exchange.
- Example: Learners are presented with a question like "What are the best three areas to live in in (this city)? Give your reasons." They discuss their opinions and reasons for their ideas.

3. **Experience Gap Task:**

- Purpose: An experience gap task encourages learners to share their personal experiences, anecdotes, or stories related to a particular theme or topic.
- Task structure: In an experience gap task, learners share their experiences in pairs or small groups. The focus is on using language to narrate past events or describe personal encounters. The listeners are encouraged to ask questions to understand more fully.
- Example: Learners discuss a personal topic such as "Describe a time when you faced a challenging situation and how you managed to overcome it."

9.3.3.2 Pragmatic Processing Activity 2: Probing Conversation

Beyond structured information and opinion gap tasks, a pragmatically oriented approach to teaching listening involves learners probing each other's thinking about a topic. To create a context where expanding the topic is worthwhile for the learners, it is essential to have an input that involves not just manipulation of facts or asking about simple preferences but moving into personal perspectives and values. At the same time, to avoid awkward or face-threatening conversations, it is important to select topics for which a reasonable person could have a range of plausible perspectives, not an obviously right or wrong point of view.

Designing Instruction 251

Table 9.7 Stages in the Design of a Collaborative Conversation Activity

S1: Needs Analysis	**Have extended conversations in the L2 on topics of personal relevance; utilize conversation strategies to develop conversations beyond simple exchanges.**
S2: Defining Objectives	**Each student will speak for up to two minutes in the L2, with a partner asking questions to probe more deeply.**
S3: Content Selection	**Personal experiences:** Describe a time when you faced a challenging situation and how you overcame it.
S4: Technology Integration	No technology is needed for live classes. For online classes, use the shared chat to elicit questions.
S5: Task Sequencing	**Pre-listening:** Introduce the topic for the task. Give a personally challenging experience that you faced or present an account from someone else, but use first person. Encourage the students to ask you questions about the experience. Make notes of the kinds of questions asked so the students can use these as models during the task.
	First listening: Give a time limit, such as two minutes. Have one person in each group tell their experience. Allow one additional minute for questions.
	Second listening: Again, give the same time limits. Allow the second student to tell their experience.
	Post-listening: Ask students to give the gist of the experience they discussed. Elicit the kinds of questions that were asked to stimulate the conversation.
	Deliberate practice: Have the students shadow you as you ask the questions. Pay attention to rhythm and intonation.
	Reflection and review: Students write a short summary of their experience.
S6: Assessment and Feedback	**Have students self-report the value of the activity. Ask them to suggest additional topics for this type of experience gap activity.**

Just as important as having suitable input, it is essential to provide scaffolding for the conversations to demonstrate concrete ways in which students can approach the expansion of the conversation (Zwiers, 2019). Probing conversations are designed to encourage critical thinking, deeper exploration, and reflection. Participants ask thought-provoking questions, challenge assumptions, provide evidence, and explore different perspectives or dimensions of a topic. Probing conversations stimulate intellectual engagement, encourage analysis, and foster higher-order thinking skills. These conversations emphasize the importance of collaboration, respect for diverse viewpoints, and constructive dialogue. Participants listen attentively, value each other's contributions, and engage in respectful exchanges of ideas (see Table 9.8).

252 *Teaching Listening*

Table 9.8 Stages in the Design of a Probing Conversation Activity

S1: Needs Analysis	**Focus on collaborative conversations, probing to get deeper into ideas, feel more confident expressing and exchanging opinions.**
S2: Defining Objectives	**Ls will develop conversations to more complex exchanges of ideas, support each other in conversations, practice active listening.**
S3: Content Selection	**Monologue (female, age 25; 150 words, 2 minutes):**
	In the future, maybe when I'm closer to 30 or 35, I hope to get married and have children. Maybe two. If I cannot have children, I think I would probably adopt a child. This world is already overpopulated, and there are many children who don't have parents, so it is a very humanitarian idea that we adopt children and give them the love, attention, and opportunities they deserve.
	At the same time, I don't think having children is essential for you to have a happy life. I think living with a partner without having children is fine, also. One practical reason is that it's very expensive to raise children. It also requires a lot of work! If you have a lot of things you want to do, like travel or have a very active professional life, it's difficult to do all that if you have children.
S4: Technology Integration	**Prerecorded video; variable speed playback (75%–100% speed)**
S5: Task Sequencing	**Preparation:** Worksheet with conversational gambits to use
	Pre-listening: Vocabulary preview; preview and model the conversation gambits (see Table 9.9)
	• **First listening:** Listen without writing. After first listening, work with a partner. What was most interesting to you?
	Second listening: Listen and take notes. Then, work in a group of four.
	Ask each other the target questions:
	• What does Nicole think about having children?
	• Why does she feel this way?
	• What does Nicole value most in her life right now?
	• What does Nicole think will happen if she has children before age 35?
	• Which of Nicole's arguments do you think is most valid? Why?
	Post-listening: One spokesperson from each group presents some of the points in their discussion.
S6: Assessment and Feedback	**Ls compare completed dictations, self-report % on the assessment sheet, complete reflection questionnaire**

Designing Instruction   253

TIPS FROM PRACTITIONERS: Support academic conversations

What I call an academic conversation is a learned structure in which students practice discussing complex issues and defend their thinking. The concept of structured conversation for learning is certainly not new (cf. Cazden & Beck, 2003; Tsui, 2009). Through academic conversations, students learn to articulate their thinking, query their thinking and the thinking of others, and listen to each other. I have also seen that learning how to have deeper conversations helps students develop socio-emotional skills—they become more confident, more empathetic, and more comfortable interacting with others.

A shift from normal conversation to academic conversation is achieved gradually through the use of conversation starters, such as "My experience with this is …" and "What do you mean by that reference?"

Teachers have long encouraged their students to discuss what they have read, heard, or watched to deepen their comprehension skills. Unfortunately, without guidance or modeling, a typical classroom discussion may go something like this:

Student A: What was the story about?

Student B: A son and his father.

Student A: Yeah, they had some problems.

Student B: Right.

Student A: So what's the next question?

Left to their own devices, students may resort to this familiar game-over strategy: how to beat the game most quickly and efficiently. Many classroom activities, such as think-pair-shares or vocabulary games, often devolve in this way: they elicit short bursts of student output and interaction but do not lead to extended discussions, personal engagement, or co-construction of new ideas (Zwiers & Crawford, 2023).

Invention, rather than time or opportunity, is critical: Even when teachers give students extra time in pairs, students do not automatically do what proficient speakers and experts do to have powerful conversations. For many students, this opting-out behavior may be due to social awkwardness, habitual interaction patterns, or lack of guidance and support for having more meaningful conversations. For many teachers, allowing this weakened discourse to occur repeatedly may be due to a lack of awareness of how to intervene and support better conversations.

254   *Teaching Listening*

We must give the students models for developing conversations, practice opportunities, and feedback. We need to support them for this shift to happen.

Once introduced to students, and with extended development opportunities, resulting conversations from the students will gradually resemble a more elaborate and satisfying exchange:

Student A: What do you think is the main theme of the story?

Student B: I think the main theme is courage. The story teaches us about courage.

Student A: Can you elaborate? What makes you think that?

Student B: Well, I think Marco's decision to go back and confront his father took a lot of courage.

Student A: Yeah, going back took courage. I see what you mean. But what do you mean by "confront his father?" Can you be more specific?

Jeff Zwiers, Author, Researcher, Teacher Trainer,
Stanford University

9.4 Summary: Essentials of Instructional Design for Listening

This chapter has outlined principles of instructional design for teaching listening. It has explored in detail a rigorous process of planning, executing, and evaluating the designs we use for listening instruction. Many teachers who consult this chapter may be working with assigned textbooks and course materials and may perceive that they have few, if any, choices other than following the book. However, even when potentially constrained by assigned materials and curriculum schedules, teachers can find many ways to adapt the materials and optimize their learning potential.

A common thread in this chapter is the treatment of listening as involving multiple stages, from pre-listening through post-listening. By using multiple interventions (beyond what the assigned materials may recommend) and task repetitions, the teacher can maximize the learning value of chosen extracts and help students develop a positive mindset about listening. Indeed, the sequencing of tasks is often what separates a highly successful lesson from just a mediocre one.

The activity demonstrations were presented in pairs in order to show that all instructional activities are *part of a sequence*. In designing instruction, we are continuously evaluating the effectiveness of instruction in order to plan the next step. That next step may be remedial or expansive, but will always include a sense of continuity from the previous lessons.

Designing Instruction 255

Table 9.9 Conversation Gambits for Probing Conversations

Analyses of unproductive and productive collaborative discussions have identified several teachable features contributing to productive, probing conversations (Alexander, 2020; Rost, 2020). In most analyses, six structured conversational strategies are considered both effective and teachable.

- **Frame and reframe topics and subtopics**
Prompts for initiating the feature: Why do you think that (the speaker said …)?
Prompts for responding: I think (the speaker said …) to (teach us about …).

- **Elaborate and clarify points**
Prompts for initiating this feature: Can you elaborate? What do you mean by…? What makes you think that? I'm not entirely clear about your point.
Prompts for responding: Let me tell you more about what I think. I think it means …
In other words, … I think that's true because …

- **Support ideas with evidence**
Prompts for initiating: Can you give me an example? Can you show me (remember) where they say that? Can you be more specific? Are there any cases of that that you know of?
Prompts for responding: For example … In the lecture, she said that … One case that showed this was …

- **Paraphrase and recap**
Prompts for initiating: Let's take a step back. What have we discussed so far? How can we summarize what we've talked out?
Prompts for responding: We can say that … So far, the main themes/points we've discussed are … This is a bit complex, but I think we can summarize by saying …

- **Build on or challenge another's idea**
Prompts for initiating: What do you think? Can you add to this idea? Do you agree? What might be some other points of view?
Prompts for responding: I would add that … Then again, I think that … I want to expand on your point about …

- **Apply and connect**
Prompts for initiating: So what? How can we apply this idea to our lives? What can we learn from this (character/story/part of the lecture)?
Prompts for responding: I can offer something here. In my life … I think it can teach us … If I were …I would have …

The sampling of practitioner ideas in this chapter shows the variety of teacher perspectives on the teaching of listening and the flexibility of ideas that teachers come up with in their classes. Fresh ideas, particularly when situated within a principled language-learning framework, can motivate students and set them on the path to becoming active and successful listeners.

256 *Teaching Listening*

References

Alexander, R. (2020). *A dialogic teaching companion*. Routledge.

Batstone, R., & Ellis, R. (2009). Principled grammar teaching. *System*, *37*(2), 194–204.

Beglar, D., Murray, N., & Rost, M. (2022). *Contemporary topics 3* (4th ed.). Pearson.

Berry, A. (2019). *The pedagogy of engagement: Classroom management vs. facilitating learning*. (Doctoral dissertation, the University of Melbourne.)

Cazden, C., & Beck, S. (2003). *Classroom discourse*. Erlbaum.

Cirocki, A., Farrelly, R., & Buchanan, H. (2023) Continuing professional development in TESOL: Current perspectives. In A. Cirocki, R. Farrelly, & H. Buchanan (Eds.), *Continuing professional development of TESOL practitioners* (pp. 1–26). Springer.

Flowerdew, J., & Miller, L. (2010). Listening in a second language. In A. Wolvin (Ed.), *Listening and human communication in the 21st century* (pp. 158–178). Wiley-Blackwell.

Furuya, A. (2021). How do listening comprehension processes differ by second language proficiency? Top-down and bottom-up perspectives. *International Journal of Listening*, *35*(2), 123–133.

Hamada, Y., & Suzuki, Y. (2022). Situating shadowing in the framework of deliberate practice: A guide to using 16 techniques. *RELC Journal*, 00336882221087508.

Hattie, J., & Hattie, K. (2022). *10 steps to develop great learners: Visible learning for parents*. Routledge.

Hiver, P., Al-Hoorie, A. H., Vitta, J. P., & Wu, J. (2024). Engagement in language learning: A systematic review of 20 years of research methods and definitions. *Language Teaching Research*, *28*(1), 201–230.

Jin, Z., & Webb, S. (2023). The effectiveness of note taking through exposure to L2 input: A meta-analysis. *Studies in Second Language Acquisition*. Published online 2023, 1–23. doi:10.1017/S0272263123000529

Li, S. (2023). Working memory and second language writing: A systematic review. *Studies in Second Language Acquisition*, *45*, 647–679.

Lovett, M. C., Bridges, M. W., DiPietro, M., Ambrose, S. A., & Norman, M. K. (2023). *How learning works: Eight research-based principles for smart teaching* (2nd ed.). John Wiley & Sons.

Morley, J. (1972). *Improving aural comprehension*. University of Michigan Press.

Rost, M. (1990). *Listening in language learning*. Longman.

Rost, M. (2020). Instructional design and assessment. In D. Worthington & G. Bodie (Eds.), *The handbook of listening* (pp. 265–278). Wiley.

Schunk, D. H., & DiBenedetto, M. K. (2016). Self-efficacy theory in education. In K. R. Wentzel & D. B. Miele (Eds.), *Handbook of motivation at school* (2nd ed., pp. 34–54). Routledge.

Shaules, J., Fritz, R., & Miyafusa, S. (2020). Measuring resistance and engagement: The linguaculture motivation profiler. In *Teacher efficacy, learner agency* (pp. 92–99). Japan Association of Language Teachers (JALT). Post-conference publication. doi: 10.37546/JALTPCP2019-12

Shawaqfeh, A. T., Jameel, A. S., Al-adwan, L. A. Y., & Khasawneh, M. A. S. (2024). Interaction as a mechanism to enhance English language proficiency in the classroom. *Journal of Language Teaching and Research*, *15*(1), 229–234.

Siegel, J. (2016). A pedagogic cycle for EFL note-taking. *ELT Journal*, *70*(3), 275–286.

Storch, N. (2008). Metatalk in a pair work activity: Level of engagement and implications for language development. *Language Awareness, 17*(2), 95–114.

Suzuki, W., & Itagaki, N. (2015). The effects of an output-based task on subsequent aural input in a Japanese university setting. In M. Thomas & H. Reinders (Eds.), *Contemporary task-based language teaching in Asia* (pp. 313–327). Bloomsbury.

Swain, M., & Lapkin, S. (2013). Focus on form through collaborative dialogue: Exploring task effects. In M. Bygate, P. Skehan, & M. Swain (Eds.), *Researching pedagogic tasks* (pp. 99–118). Routledge.

Tian, Z., & Shepard-Carey, L. (2020). (Re)imagining the future of translanguaging pedagogies in TESOL through teacher–researcher collaboration. *TESOL Quarterly, 54*(4), 1131–1143.

Tsui, A. (2009). Distinctive qualities of expert teachers. *Teachers and Teaching: Theory and Practice, 15*(4), 421–439.

Yu, X., Boers, F., & Tremblay, P. (2022). Learning multiword items through dictation and dictogloss: How task performance predicts learning outcomes. *Language Teaching Research*, 13621688221117242.

Zwiers, J. (2019). *The communication effect: How to enhance learning by building ideas and bridging information gaps.* Corwin.

Zwiers, J., & Crawford, M. (2023). *Academic conversations: Classroom talk that fosters critical thinking and content understandings.* Routledge.

10 Listening Assessment

10.1	Introduction: The Role of Assessment in Language Teaching	258
10.2	Identifying the Context for Assessment	259
10.3	The Concept of Validity in Assessment	259
	10.3.1 Construct Validity	*263*
10.4	Describing Listening Proficiency	266
10.5	Formulating an Assessment Model	271
10.6	Content Validity	273
10.7	Composing Test Prompts	278
10.8	Portfolio Assessment	281
10.9	Assessing Interactive Listening Proficiency	282
10.10	Uses of AI in Testing Listening	285
10.11	Summary: Integrating Assessment into Instruction	287
References		287

10.1 Introduction: The Role of Assessment in Language Teaching

Assessment is an essential element of language teaching and an indispensable aspect of listening development. From a pedagogical perspective, assessment provides a tangible means of feedback to learners on their development, which is an essential aspect of instructional design. From an institutional perspective, assessment provides a standardized way to measure language proficiency, ensuring that all individuals are evaluated on the same criteria and under similar conditions. When administered properly, assessment can promote fairness and provide clarity about learning goals.

This chapter offers guidance for understanding assessment from a pedagogical perspective, demonstrating how to integrate assessment into listening instruction in a cohesive way. It also provides an analysis of listening items on standardized tests so that instructors and researchers can better understand the ways that institutional tests are composed, the inherent subjectivity and biases that are part of any assessment, and the compromises that standard test providers often make in underrepresenting the totality of listening ability.

DOI: 10.4324/9781003390794-13

The chapter will cover a number of topics related to listening assessment: contexts of listening assessment, the notion of validity, the employment of descriptive scales to describe levels of listening proficiency, the composition of input, test prompts and test responses, the goals of oral interviews for assessing interactive listening, and the uses of portfolio-style assessments for listening.

10.2 Identifying the Context for Assessment

The starting point for considering the role of listening assessment in teaching is to identify the broad learning context, that is, how learners are using or intend to use the L2 they are learning. The way in which listening fits into the learners' overall goals and expectations is critical in determining the type of input used in assessment, the creation of test items, the means of evaluation, and the criteria for success (Aryadoust et al., 2020; Wagner, 2022).

There are five basic contexts of L2 users to consider: **EAL**, English as an additional language, for students who are learning English in addition to their native languages in a place where English is not one of the primary languages of communication (formerly called English as a foreign language); **ESL** (English as a second language) for teaching English as an additional language in a place where it is one of the primary languages of communication; **EYL,** English for young learners, who may be part of either an EAL or ESL setting; **EFL**, English as a lingua franca (or Global English), English for communication in a specific context in which the participants all speak different languages; and **ESP**, English for specific purposes (or EAP, English for academic purposes), in which learners are using English for professional or academic functions. The context defines social standards of behavior, pedagogic targets, and focus, and has implications for assessment (Chapelle et al., 2019; Field, 2019; Xi & Norris, 2021; see Table 10.1).

It is important to remember that the context refers to the living environment of the test subject. Test construction is designed to fairly evaluate the test subject's performance and proficiency in that context.

10.3 The Concept of Validity in Assessment

If an assessment aims to fairly evaluate a test subject's performance in a particular context, then there must be standards or guardrails to check that the assessment is on track. This process of checking standards falls under the rubric of **validity**, which refers to the legitimacy and meaningfulness of the assessment. Validity in assessment includes a **process domain** and a **content domain**.

The process domain, more often referred to as **construct validity**, refers to how well a test measures actual listening ability. Listening ability, as described in this book, includes holistic listening skills (performing competently in social,

Table 10.1 Contexts for Learning English and Choices of Assessment

EAL	ESL	EYL	GE/ELF	ESP/EAP
Learning Context				
English as an additional language	**English as a second language**	**English for young learners**	**Global English/English as a lingua franca**	**English for special purposes/academic purposes**
Learning English in a non-English-speaking country where English is not widely spoken in daily life.	Learning English in an English-speaking country, where English is the primary language of communication.	Learning English at a young age, usually in primary or elementary schools. The emphasis is on developing positive attitudes toward English and basic language skills through the use of age-appropriate activities and materials.	Learning English as a common language of communication between speakers of different native languages. It is often associated with international contexts where English serves as a bridge language for global communication, and multiple varieties and accents of English are used.	Learning English for particular fields or professions (ESP), or as preparation for studying in English-speaking academic settings (EAP).
Target variety of English				
Fluent native or native-like speaker, generally not associated with any national variety of English.	Fluent native or native-like speaker of host country, generally associated with the dominant national variety of English.	Fluent native or native-like speaker, generally not associated with any national variety of English.	Focus on international intelligibility rather than a specific variety; need for learner to maintain national identity through English; need for receptive skills in a range of international varieties.	Fluent native or native-like speaker/expert in the target field; need for receptive skills in a range of international varieties.

Primary purposes

To communicate with others in the TL; to satisfy entrance requirements for jobs, universities	To function in host country as a bilingual	To develop receptivity for L2, gain literacy and oracy skills in TL	To communicate with nonnative speakers from other countries and with native speakers from a variety of countries	To participate on an equal footing with other students and professionals in the same field, including native and native-like speakers

Learning environment: Live

Classroom focused; timetabled subject; occasional visits to English-speaking country; affective involvement often lacking	Some classroom focus; host society provides potential immersion experience; members of host community provide models for communicative competence	Often informal in kindergarten, preschool, or primary classroom; affective factors are important	Classroom is a key context but is insufficient. Private and home tutoring often used	Classroom and small-group contexts are central; affective involvement important

Learning environment: Online

Self-paced curriculum; occasional synchronous sessions with instructor and fellow students	Self-paced curriculum; quasi-immersion experience; synchronous sessions with instructor and fellow students	Self-paced curriculum; occasional synchronous sessions with instructor and fellow students	Self-paced curriculum; occasional synchronous sessions with instructor and fellow students. Private tutoring also used	Synchronous online curriculum most common; interaction expected with classmates and instructor

(*Continued*)

Table 10.1 (Continued)

EAL	ESL	EYL	GE/ELF	ESP/EAP
Skill focus				
Focus on oral communication; emphasis on communication strategies for interaction with speakers of the TL	Equal focus on all skills, development of multiple literacies	Youngest learners may not have L1 literacy skills, so emphasis is most often on speaking and listening	All skills, including literacy; translation and interpretation skills often required; emphasis also on intercultural communication strategies	Focus on content mastery, which includes ability to listen to specialist presentations and to participate in discussions, to give short content-based presentations
Standardized assessment choices				
Either local exams or internationally recognized exams				
Internationally sanctioned assessment (IELTS, Cambridge ESOL, TOEFL, TOEIC)	Citizenship or visa exams; academic gatekeeping tests for university-bound students	Usually local testing or informal assessment, though international exams are available	Existing exams often not appropriate; assessment often via assessment of ability to carry out tasks in English or by assessing knowledge taught through English (as in CEF framework)	Internationally recognized exams for entrance most common; subject-matter exams from each institution

academic, and professional settings while using listening) and component listening skills (the accuracy of linguistic processing, as well as thoroughness of semantic and pragmatic processing). If a listening test has construct validity, it will demonstrate that the test effectively measures the **constructs** (that is, the skills or traits) it intends to assess.

The content domain of listening, typically referred to as **content validity**, refers to whether the test adequately samples both the content of the listening ability (the genres, rhetorical styles, and variety of speakers and accents that comprise the assessment input) and the contexts where the listening ability is needed (the situations and interactions that constitute the natural environment of the test subject). If a listening test has content validity, it should be able to demonstrate that the test adequately represents the situations and speakers that the test subject inhabits (Kang et al., 2023; West & Thiruchelvam, 2024).

A related concept to validity is the **test impact**, sometimes called "the washback effect." Test impact concerns the effects of the assessment on the way teachers approach teaching and learners approach learning. The form and consequences of assessments influence learners' and teachers' expectations of what appropriate content and target constructs should be featured in the learning process. This washback effect will invariably influence the priorities and efforts students attach to their language learning (Messick, 1998; Strand et al., 2018).

10.3.1 Construct Validity

Work in psychometric testing in the 1950s instigated an investigation into the validity of psychological tests (Cronbach & Meehl, 1955). Cronbach and Meehl, regarded as the pioneers of construct validity, argued that there are *no absolutely valid tests* of human abilities, such as a test of a person's listening ability, only tests that have stronger or weaker inferential arguments about what is being tested (Brunfaut & Revesz, 2015; McNamara et al., 2012).

Because listening, like other language skills, involves multiple cognitive processing circuits that interact with other cognitive processes, any listening test will, to some extent, measure a learner's general language knowledge and general comprehension ability, in addition to the listening abilities it seeks to measure. This principle of necessary overlap in listening between **top-level (general) abilities** and **bottom-level (skill-specific) attributes** has now been established in the language testing field (Brunfaut, 2016; Liping, 2014; Tatsuoka, 2009).

Using quantitative methods, researchers have isolated attributes that account for nearly all of the **variance** in test takers' performance on standardized listening tests (Brindley & Slatyer 2002; Buck et al., 1997). Two levels of attributes have been identified, with several subskills clustered in each level.

264　*Teaching Listening*

The top-level attributes, that is, those abilities generalizable to all language skills, included:

- the ability to recognize the task by deciding what constitutes task-relevant information
- the ability to use previous items to locate information
- the ability to identify relevant information without explicit markers
- the ability to make inferences and to incorporate background knowledge into text processing
- the ability to draw on one's linguistic, semantic, and pragmatic knowledge.

The bottom-level attributes, that is, those specific to listening, included:

- the ability to scan spoken text automatically and in real time
- the ability to process dense information
- the ability to understand and utilize prosodic features
- the ability to segment and recognize words in speech

Researchers have identified several variables of listening ability, measured by the Michigan English Language Assessment Battery (MELAB). Skills were coded based on linguistic features in the test items into two general categories: **language knowledge** (generalizable across all language skills) and **aural comprehension** (specific to listening; Wallace, 2022):

Language knowledge	*Aural comprehension*
- Decoding verb tense and aspect - Decoding key vocabulary - Decoding idiomatic expressions - Decoding auxiliary verb forms	- Comprehending illocutionary force (intention) of a speaker - Comprehending conversational inference - Processing key information stated by a speaker - Processing key information in conversation - Comprehending text-based inference - Comprehending stated specific details - Comprehending stated details with explanation or repetition - Comprehending and recalling stated details

Listening Assessment 265

Though description systems for the underlying skills do not always correspond across studies (see Aryadoust, 2020), there is agreement about the differentiation between **language-based skills**, which tap knowledge of the linguistic system, and **comprehension-based skills**, which delve into processes of listening in real-time contexts (Ruslov, 2022).

A parallel way of viewing this dichotomy is to make a distinction between enabling skills and enacting skills. **Enabling skills** are the foundational or prerequisite skills that support effective listening comprehension but that may not involve direct interaction with the language itself. **Enacting skills** are the active, operational listening skills used during the actual process of listening to spoken language. These skills are integrated into listening contexts to allow a person to make inferences, make decisions, build meaning, and respond pragmatically, all of which may be considered enacting skills (Brownell, 2015; He & Jiang, 2020; Rost, 1990). (See Table 10.2.)

Table 10.2 Enabling and Enacting Skills in Listening

Enabling Skills	Enacting Skills
The framework and basis for successful listening	*The active engagement with the language input to comprehend and interpret messages*
Phonological awareness The ability to recognize and manipulate the sounds of spoken language, including phonemes, syllables, and stress patterns.	**Listening for specific information** The ability to identify and extract particular details or facts from the listening material.
Vocabulary knowledge The knowledge of a wide range of words (in phonological form) and their meanings, which is necessary in order to comprehend the spoken discourse.	**Listening for main ideas** The skill of identifying the central or most important points or themes in the spoken discourse.
Background knowledge Prior knowledge and information about the topic being discussed, which helps in making connections and understanding the context.	**Making predictions** The ability to predict what might come next based on the information provided in the listening material.
Inference-making The ability to draw logical conclusions or make educated guesses based on the information provided in the listening material.	**Reconstructing messages** The ability to take organized notes to capture essential information during a lecture or presentation.
Working memory The capacity to temporarily hold and manipulate information while processing ongoing language input.	**Identifying tone and attitude** The ability to understand the emotional tone or attitude conveyed in the speaker's voice.

(Continued)

266 *Teaching Listening*

Table 10.2 (Continued)

Enabling Skills	Enacting Skills
Morphological awareness The ability to recognize and understand the structure and meaning of morphemes (the smallest units of meaning) within words. For example, understanding that "unhappiness" consists of the prefix "un-" (meaning not) and the root word "happy."	**Summarizing** The skill of condensing the main points or key information from a listening passage into a concise and coherent summary.
Syntax awareness Knowledge of the rules and structures governing the arrangement of words into phrases, clauses, and sentences. This skill helps listeners understand the relationships between words in a sentence and how they contribute to the overall meaning.	**Paraphrasing** The ability to restate what was previously heard using different words or expressions while preserving the original meaning.
Metacognition Awareness and control of one's thinking processes. This involves monitoring and regulating one's comprehension while listening, such as recognizing when understanding is breaking down and using strategies to repair comprehension.	**Evaluating arguments** The ability to assess the soundness of arguments or opinions presented in the listening material.
Cultural awareness Familiarity with the cultural context of the language being spoken. Understanding cultural norms, idiomatic expressions, and contextual cues can enhance listening comprehension.	**Inferring attitudes and emotions** Being able to identify the speaker's emotions, opinions, or attitudes based on their tone, intonation, and choice of words.
Discourse analysis The ability to recognize and understand the structure and organization of spoken discourse, including how ideas are connected, signposts that indicate transitions, and how speakers convey coherence.	**Recognizing rhetorical devices** The ability to identify rhetorical strategies, such as exaggeration, repetition, or persuasive techniques used by the speaker.

10.4 Describing Listening Proficiency

Beyond simply using arbitrary test cut-off scores as an indication of listening proficiency, listening teachers will do well to familiarize themselves with concrete descriptions of listening abilities at different levels of proficiency.

A major priority in assessment is the need to find a way to describe and report a listener's current stage of ability in a manner that has both construct and face

Listening Assessment 267

validity. This means that the characterization of the ability should aim to be comprehensive in describing the *complete skills* of the learner and be informative to teacher and learner alike (Goodwin & Naismith, 2023). One known drawback of many standardized listening tests is that they are not comprehensive: they underrepresent the totality of listening ability, focusing instead on the constructs that are easiest to measure.

Holistic assessments aim to address the issue of comprehensiveness by describing the parameters of various cognitive and behavioral traits that the listener displays. These assessments are typically in the form of incremental scales, often at 5 levels, with plus or minus at each level, creating 15 discrete holistic ratings (e.g., 3−, 3, 3+). Each band on the scale consists of descriptors that depict some criterion on the learner's target behavior.

Proficiency scales can be very useful as part of a portfolio assessment. Scales have a built-in feedback mechanism in order to suggest to the learner the kinds of skills needed to graduate to the next level. Proficiency scales for listening have been established by various educational foundations, including the ACTFL (2012), the Council of Europe (2020), the Center for Applied Linguistics (2012), Canadian Language Benchmarks (CLB) (2024), and International English Language Testing System (IELTS) (2024), and the Global Scale of English (GSE) (2022). These scales, which are extensively cross-correlated, guide teaching and assessment of listening across a wide range of educational contexts.

Table 10.3 displays an example of a listener proficiency scale from the ACTFL (American Council on the Teaching of Foreign Languages, though the full name

Table 10.3 **ACTFL Listening Proficiency Scale** (highlights provided by author)

Distinguished

At the Distinguished level, listeners can **understand a wide variety of forms, styles, and registers of speech on highly specialized topics** in language that is tailored to different audiences. Listeners at the Distinguished level can understand language such as that found in classical theater, art films, professional symposia, academic debates, public policy statements, literary readings, and most jokes and puns. They are able to **comprehend implicit and inferred information, tone, and point of view,** and can follow highly persuasive arguments. They are able to **understand unpredictable turns of thought related to sophisticated topics**. In addition, their listening ability is enhanced by a **broad and deep understanding of cultural references and allusions.** Listeners at the Distinguished level are able to appreciate the richness of the spoken language.

Distinguished-level listeners **understand speech that can be highly abstract, highly technical, or both, as well as speech that contains very precise, often low-frequency vocabulary and complex rhetorical structures.** At this level, listeners comprehend oral discourse that is lengthy and dense, structurally complex, rich in cultural reference, idiomatic, and colloquial. In addition, listeners at this level can **understand information that is subtle or highly specialized, as well as the full cultural significance** of very short texts with little or no linguistic redundancy.

(Continued)

268   *Teaching Listening*

Table 10.3 (Continued)

Distinguished-level listeners comprehend language from within the cultural framework and are able to understand a speaker's use of nuance and subtlety. However, they **may still have difficulty fully understanding certain dialects and nonstandard varieties** of the language.

Superior

At the Superior level, listeners are able to **understand speech in a standard dialect on a wide range of familiar and less familiar topics.** They **can follow linguistically complex extended discourse** such as that found in academic and professional settings, lectures, speeches, and reports. **Comprehension** is no longer limited to the listener's familiarity with the subject matter but also **comes from a command of the language that is supported by a broad vocabulary, an understanding of more complex structures, and linguistic experience within the target culture.**

Superior listeners can understand not only what is said but sometimes what is left unsaid; that is, they **can make inferences**.

Superior-level listeners understand speech that typically uses precise, specialized vocabulary and complex grammatical structures. This speech often deals abstractly with topics in a way that is appropriate for academic and professional audiences. It can be reasoned and can contain cultural references.

Advanced

At the Advanced level, listeners can **understand the main ideas and most supporting details in a connected discourse on a variety of general interest topics,** such as news stories, explanations, instructions, anecdotes, or travelogue descriptions. Listeners are **able to compensate for limitations in their lexical and structural control** of the language by using real-world knowledge and contextual clues. Listeners may also **derive some meaning** from oral texts at higher levels **if they possess significant familiarity with the topic or context.** Advanced-level listeners understand speech that is authentic and connected. This speech is lexically and structurally uncomplicated. The **discourse is straightforward and is generally organized in a clear and predictable way.**

Advanced-level listeners demonstrate the ability to **comprehend language on a range of topics of general interest.** They have sufficient knowledge of language structure to understand basic time-frame references. Nevertheless, their understanding is most often limited to concrete, conventional discourse.

Advanced High

At the Advanced High sublevel, listeners are able to **understand, with ease and confidence, conventional narrative and descriptive texts of any length** as well as complex factual material such as summaries or reports. They are typically able to follow some of the essential points of more complex or argumentative speech in areas of special interest or knowledge. In addition, they are able to **derive some meaning from oral texts that deal with unfamiliar topics or situations.** At the Advanced High sublevel, listeners are able to comprehend the facts presented in oral discourse and are often able to recognize speaker-intended inferences. Nevertheless, there are **likely to be gaps in comprehension of complex texts dealing with issues that are treated abstractly** but that would typically be understood by superior-level listeners.

Table 10.3 (Continued)

Advanced Mid

At the Advanced Mid sublevel, listeners are able to **understand conventional narrative and descriptive texts**, such as expanded descriptions of persons, places, and things, and narrations about past, present, and future events. The **speech is predominantly in familiar target-language patterns**. Listeners understand the main facts and many supporting details. Comprehension derives not only from situational and subject-matter knowledge but also from an **increasing overall facility** with the language itself.

Advanced Low

At the Advanced Low sublevel, listeners are able to **understand short conventional narrative and descriptive texts** with a clear underlying structure, though their comprehension may be uneven. The listener understands the main facts and some supporting details. **Comprehension may often derive primarily from situational and subject-matter knowledge.**

Intermediate

At the Intermediate level, listeners can **understand information conveyed in the form of simple, sentence-length speech on familiar or everyday topics.** They are generally able to comprehend one utterance at a time while engaged in face-to-face conversations or in **routine listening tasks,** such as understanding highly contextualized messages, straightforward announcements, or simple instructions and directions. Listeners **rely heavily on redundancy, restatement, paraphrasing, and contextual clues.**

Intermediate-level listeners **understand speech that conveys basic information**. This speech is simple, minimally connected, and contains high-frequency vocabulary.

Intermediate-level listeners are most accurate in their comprehension when getting meaning from simple, straightforward speech. They are able to **comprehend messages found in highly familiar everyday contexts.** Intermediate listeners require a controlled listening environment where they hear what they may expect to hear.

Intermediate High

At the Intermediate High sublevel, listeners are able **to understand, with ease and confidence, simple sentence-length speech in basic personal and social contexts**. They can **derive substantial meaning from some connected texts** typically understood by Advanced-level listeners, although there **often will be gaps in understanding** due to their limited knowledge of the vocabulary and structures of the spoken language.

Intermediate Mid

At the Intermediate Mid sublevel, listeners are able to **understand simple, sentence-length speech, one utterance at a time, in a variety of basic personal and social contexts. Comprehension is most often accurate with highly familiar and predictable topics,** although **a few misunderstandings may occur**. Intermediate Mid listeners may get some meaning from oral texts typically understood by Advanced-level listeners.

(Continued)

270 *Teaching Listening*

Table 10.3 (Continued)

Intermediate Low

At the Intermediate Low sublevel, listeners are able to **understand some information from sentence-length speech, one utterance at a time, in basic personal and social contexts,** though **comprehension is often uneven.** At the Intermediate Low sublevel, listeners show little or no comprehension of oral texts that would be typically understood by Advanced-level listeners.

Novice

At the Novice level, listeners can **understand keywords, true aural cognates, and formulaic expressions that are highly contextualized and highly predictable,** such as those found in introductions and basic courtesies.

Novice-level **listeners understand words and phrases from simple questions, statements, and high-frequency commands.** They **typically require repetition, rephrasing and/or a slowed rate of speech for comprehension.** They rely heavily on extralinguistic support to derive meaning.

Novice-level listeners are most accurate when they are able to recognize speech that they can anticipate. In this way, these **listeners tend to recognize rather than truly comprehend.** Their listening is largely dependent on factors other than the message itself.

Novice High

At the Novice High sublevel, listeners are **often but not always able to understand information from sentence-length speech,** one utterance at a time, in basic personal and social contexts where there is contextual or extralinguistic support, though comprehension may often be very uneven. They are able to **understand speech dealing with areas of practical need, such as highly standardized messages, phrases, or instructions,** if the vocabulary has been learned.

Novice Mid

At the Novice Mid sublevel, listeners can recognize and begin to **understand a number of high-frequency, highly contextualized words and phrases,** including aural cognates and borrowed words. Typically, they understand little more than one phrase at a time, and repetition may be required.

Novice Low

At the Novice Low sublevel, listeners are able **occasionally to recognize isolated words or very high-frequency phrases** when those are strongly supported by context. These listeners show virtually no comprehension of any kind of spoken message, not even within the most basic personal and social contexts.

---

is never used anymore). The proficiency level descriptions in the scale provide relative criteria for comprehension of the spoken language at various levels of difficulty. The scale has five broad categories—Distinguished, Superior, Advanced, Intermediate, and Novice—with three subcategories for Advanced, Intermediate, and Novice, totaling 11 possible ratings. On an ascending scale, each of the levels implies control of any functions and accuracy standards from the previous base levels.

Listening Assessment   271

A skill level is assigned to a person through a language examination, a series of examinations, or a series of long-term observations. Examiners assign a level on the basis of a variety of performance criteria, exemplified in the descriptive statements. Therefore, the examples are intended to illustrate the skills a person may possess or situations in which they may function effectively.

Although proficiency scales have historically referenced native speakers as benchmarks of the highest standards, modern scales are shifting towards a focus on proficiency rather than nativeness. The term "native speaker" is being phased out for a variety of reasons. The primary reason is inclusivity: The term "native speaker" can be exclusionary and marginalize individuals who have learned an additional language proficiently but are not considered native speakers. Another prominent reason is diversity: In today's globalized world, there are many individuals who are multilingual, often learning additional languages from a young age, blurring the lines between what constitutes a "native speaker" and a proficient speaker. Also, using the term "native speaker" can perpetuate stereotypes and biases, such as assumptions about cultural competence based solely on one's linguistic background. Avoiding this term helps to promote fairness and equity in assessment.

10.5 Formulating an Assessment Model

Based on our description of testable components of listening, we can formulate a map to understand the levels of listening assessment. The model will include two levels with three basic components (see Table 10.4):

General

- *General knowledge* of common concepts and common human relationships; general knowledge of how language works (phonology, morphology, syntax, semantics, pragmatics, language families, writing systems); general knowledge of the world (history, geography, science, math, arts and culture, politics and government, general literature, pop culture and entertainment, general trivia); familiarity with how assessment works (Shiotsu & Weir, 2007; Zheng et al., 2023)

Specific

- *Linguistic knowledge* of the sound system and phonological rules of the language, words of the language that have been encountered, syntactic rules of the language
- *Semantic knowledge* of word meanings, semantic (paradigmatic and syntagmatic) relationships between lexical items; schematic expectations of common situations; knowledge of reasoning and inferencing conventions

Table 10.4 Processing Constructs: Linguistic, Semantic, Pragmatic

Linguistic processing constructs: At the first level, linguistic processing includes phonological, lexical, and syntactic knowledge; at the second level, it includes specific decoding skills

Linguistic processing	Phonological knowledge (knowledge of the phonological system, allophonic variations, intonation, stress)	Phonological decoding skills (identifying phonemes, speech segmentation, identifying prosody in the stream of speech)
	Lexical knowledge (knowledge of word forms; morphology)	Lexical decoding skills (word segmentation, word recognition)
	Syntactic knowledge (knowledge of grammar at sentence level and discourse level)	Syntactic decoding skills (parsing, proposition formation, anaphoric interpretation)

Semantic processing constructs: At the first level, semantic processing includes knowledge of lexis, schemata, and reasoning; at the second level, it includes specific comprehension skills

Semantic processing	Lexical knowledge (knowledge of word meanings, knowledge of lexical relationships, semantic role assignments)	Selecting vocabulary in context, inferring meaning of unknown words
	Schematic knowledge (knowledge of lexical relationships, knowledge of figurative language; knowledge of schemata, knowledge of reasoning and inferencing)	Understanding main ideas, details, understanding schemata, making connections to prior knowledge, sequencing
	Reasoning knowledge (knowledge of logical reasoning processes, knowledge of the types of inferencing processes)	Understanding main ideas and supporting details, implications, understanding cohesion, comparing and contrasting, drawing conclusions, storing ideas in memory, summarizing

Pragmatic processing constructs: At the first level, pragmatic processing includes knowledge discourse knowledge; at the second level, it includes specific interpretation skills

Pragmatic processing	Discourse knowledge (contextual framing, deictic framing, Speaker knowledge (speaker intent, conversation maxims) Response knowledge (cultural norms, response types)	Understanding indirect speech acts, interpreting utterances using contextual knowledge, Interpreting specific intentions, attitudes, points of view, cultural references, figures of speech Using metacognitive processing to determine responses, selecting from a range of responses, using communication strategies to be understood

- *Pragmatic knowledge* of discourse genres, frames, and rules; knowledge of the range of speaker behaviors, including common gambits and levels of directness; knowledge of appropriacy of responses

Creating assessments involves three major decisions that involve identifying: (1) the targets of assessment, or what the teacher is aiming to measure, whether component, general, or integrated skills; (2) the criteria for success, or how the teacher will know if the learner has reached the target; and (3) the form of assessment—what the test taker actually encounters.

10.6 Content Validity

Listening assessments will typically consist of three components: an **input** (information or stimuli provided to the test taker before they are required to respond), a **prompt** (a specific question, task, or instruction that directs the test taker on what they are required to do in response to the provided input), and a **response** (the actual demonstration of the test taker's understanding, knowledge, or ability). When creating listening assessments, the initial questions concern content creation or selection, that is, the input.

- Is the input at a suitable language proficiency level for the test takers? Does the input selection align with their language abilities? The content should be at an appropriate level of challenge in terms of syntactic, lexical, and conceptual complexity in order to discriminate between test takers or place them in rank order: If the content is too easy, everyone will achieve a high score; if the content is too difficult, everyone will receive a low score. In either scenario, the results will lack validity
- Is the input material **authentic**? Is it taken from real-life settings? Does it reflect the range of speakers' backgrounds that represent the context of language usage? Is the material **relevant** to their interests and experiences? (If the content is not authentic or relevant, it is not likely to engage the test takers, and the results will clearly lack validity). (Hasrol et al., 2022; Emerick, 2019; Nishizawa, 2023; Ockey & Wagner, 2018)
- Is the input material **useable**? Is it of high quality? Is it clearly audible and/or viewable by the test taker? If graphics or text are included, are they readily viewable? If playback or other user-operated technology is part of the testing protocol, are test takers familiar with it? (Umirova, 2020)

Once input is selected for the test the next step is to determine what listening constructs you wish to test. I have often seen teachers selecting high-quality, appropriate input for listening assessment and then composing a seemingly

274 *Teaching Listening*

random task or series of questions without giving clear consideration to what constructs they wish to measure (and have been guilty of this myself). Reflecting on assessment goals and creating multiple drafts and revisions of a test will generally remediate this problem.

Following is a sample test input (see Table 10.5), followed by examples of constructs that are used in formulating prompts based on this input (see Table 10.6). The constructs are in the three listening processing domains: linguistic, semantic, and pragmatic.

Table 10.5 Sample Test Input

NARRATOR: Today is the International Day of Happiness. The United Nations had an event to mark the occasion, and it has just released its most recent World Happiness Report. Now, the idea of ranking countries by their levels of happiness might seem a bit weird. Surely, there are always some people who are miserable while others are thriving. Let's check in on our cultural reporters, Allison Rose and Jason Kendrick.

ALLISON: Every year, researchers ask people in 155 countries to evaluate their lives. They ask a range of questions aimed at understanding key factors that contribute to a happy life. For example ...

JASON: It's a simple question—yes or no. In times of trouble, do you have family or friends to count on?

ALLISON: He says the other questions look at health, education, income, as well as levels of freedom and trust in government. And who comes out on top?

JASON: The top country this year is Norway, followed by Denmark, Iceland, and Switzerland.

ALLISON: So what makes a country happy? I was curious, so I connected with someone who knows about this.

(SOUND OF COMPUTER CONNECTION)

UNIDENTIFIED WOMAN: Hello, this Astrid Lund at the Norwegian Embassy. Let me connect you with Mr. Ingels ...

ALLISON: I was put through to Jon Ingels. He's the minister of cultural affairs. And why does he think Norwegians top the list?

JASON: I'm quite sure that access to free higher education, access to high quality health services would be part of it.

ALLISON: There's also generous social support programs. For instance, new parents are entitled to almost a year of leave with pay. And the physical surroundings are beautiful, too.

JASON: Space, fresh air (laughter). I think Norwegians have many, many reasons to be satisfied.

ALLISON: Another factor of course is the economy. Overall, Norway is a pretty wealthy country in part due to oil. But even though oil prices have declined, Norwegians' level of happiness has risen.

JASON: Absolutely there is more to it than money.

ALLISON: At a time when income inequality has expanded in many countries, Norway has no big gap between rich and poor. And there's no big gender gap either.

(CUT TO)

Listening Assessment 275

Table 10.5 (Continued)

FELDMAN: I think the interesting thing about the happiness index is what we can learn from it and, more importantly, what we can apply.

ALLISON: That's Ariel Feldman, a psychologist. For years he has taught university courses on the science of happiness. This year, the US is ranked 14th on the global happiness index, slipping one spot from last year. Feldman says this isn't a big deal. After all, the survey relies on blunt measures. But he says the divisiveness created by our political climate seemed to play a role.

FELDMAN: There is less trust today in the political system in the United States. There is distrust among people because—a feeling of "us versus them."

ALLISON: He says there's lots of science to show that the loss of trust can erode people's sense of well-being.

FELDMAN: One of the most important determinants of happiness is trust.

ALLISON: And without a sense of shared values, it can be a challenge to rebuild that trust.

NARRATOR: And that's Allison Rose and Jason Kendrick, with our report on the International Day of Happiness. Thank you, Allison and Jason.

ALLISON: My pleasure.

JASON: Thank you.

From Frazier et al. (2022)

Table 10.6 Listening Constructs and Testing Prompts

Domain	*Construct*	*Testing prompt*
Linguistic processing	**Word segmentation**	Hear isolated sentence: (In times of trouble, do you have family or friends to count on?)
		State the number of words in the utterance.
	Syntactic parsing	Hear two sentences, decide if same meaning:
		(A: The idea of ranking countries by their levels of happiness might seem a bit weird. B: It's kind of strange to rank countries by their level of happiness).
	Lexical paradigm	Hear a stimulus lexical item, choose synonym or paraphrase:
		have access to higher education: • be able to enroll in university education • decide to skip higher education • want to obtain an advanced degree.
	Acoustic segmentation	Hear short text/see transcript; supply pauses (3):
		(Every year/researchers ask people/in 155 countries/ to evaluate their lives).

(*Continued*)

276   *Teaching Listening*

Table 10.6 (Continued)

Domain	Construct	Testing prompt
	Lexical recognition/ syntactic parsing	Hear a short text, repeat verbatim/choose correct written version:
		(At a time when income inequality has expanded in many countries, Norway has no big gap between rich and poor).
	Noticing stress	Listen to sentences, underline the stressed words:
		(And <u>without</u> a sense of <u>shared</u> values, it can be a <u>challenge</u> to <u>rebuild</u> that trust).
	Following instructions	Listen and simultaneously follow instructions (e.g., while reading the transcript aloud:
		(Overall, Norway is a pretty wealthy country in part due to oil. Circle the word 'wealthy').
	Re-enactment	In small groups, students are assigned parts and re-enact the script, first reading verbatim, then ad-libbing.
	Elicited imitation	Students take dictation or repeat orally, attempting to replicate exactly what was spoken, either through filling in blanks or transcribing/repeating directly.
Semantic processing	**Cued summarization**	After listening to a three-minute lecture, L supplies missing words in a summary or in an outline, either from a word box or from memory.
	Idea sequencing	After listening to the podcast, they view a series of statements or events discussed in the interview and arrange them in the correct order.
	Inferring meaning of words	After listening to the sentence: "The US is ranked 14th on the global happiness index, slipping one spot from last year." What is another word for "slipping?"
	Paraphrase	The survey asks, "In times of trouble, do you have family and friends to count on?" What does this mean?
		Do you have a lot of family and friends?
		Do you tell your family and friends about your problems?
		*Do you have family and friends who can help you?
		Do you try to help your family and friends?

Listening Assessment 277

Table 10.6 (Continued)

Domain	Construct	Testing prompt
	Vocabulary in context	Every year, researchers ___ happiness by asking people in 155 countries to evaluate their lives. change *measure discuss reward
	Integrating information	According to the report, the top four happiest countries are located in ___. North America Latin America Southeast Asia *Northern Europe
	Exclusive inference	Which factor is NOT mentioned by Norway's Minister of Cultural Affairs as a reason for the happiness of the Norwegian people? free education social support programs *strong friendships beautiful physical surroundings
	Factual recall	What does he say about money and happiness? Happiness is only possible if you have a lot of money. *There is more to happiness than money. Money doesn't matter at all for happiness. Happy people make more money.
	Elaborative inference	The reporter says, "At a time when income inequality has expanded in many countries, Norway has no big gap between rich and poor." What does this suggest? Rich and poor people live far away from each other in Norway. *Norway has less income inequality than other countries. There are no poor people in Norway. Most countries have smaller gaps between rich and poor people than Norway.
	Note-taking	Listen to podcast and take notes. Notes evaluated for completeness and clarity.
	Completing table/chart	Listen, and while listening, complete a table/chart/diagram related to the content.
Pragmatic processing	**Personal interest**	Listen to the podcast. Write two ideas that interest you the most (Option: underline them in the transcript)

(*Continued*)

278 *Teaching Listening*

Table 10.6 (Continued)

Domain	Construct	Testing prompt
	Content response	How well did you understand the report?
		Which part of the report was most interesting to you? Why?
		The report talks about the factors that support happiness. Which factors are important to you in your own life?
		What else do you want to know? Write a new question about the report.
	Interactive task	Pairwork task with a list of questions about "What makes you happy?" Rate on Likert (5-point) scale. Include task instructions to promote interaction (e.g., ask for clarification, paraphrase).
	Reflection	After listening to a presentation about "happiness," write a personal opinion of the content or other personalization (e.g., questions I would ask the presenter).
	Evaluative response	Watch a short presentation on happiness (e.g., Brooks (2022) complete short evaluation form (Likert scale).
	Interactive presentation	Give a short presentation on "my secrets to happiness," interact with audience, answer their questions.
	Oral interview	Learners are interviewed by teacher or peer on a specific topic, using prompts that the student can see in advance:
		Do you consider yourself to be a happy person? What is something you are very grateful for? What is a special event that you are looking forward to? etc.

10.7 Composing Test Prompts

Once the content has been selected and the constructs identified, the simplest part of assessment design is writing the test prompts. To ensure face validity, the items should be familiar to students; that is, they should have had practice with similar types of items during classroom instruction. To ensure criterion-referenced validity, the items should be similar to the items students will encounter in the real world or similar to the ones they will encounter in the standardized tests they will be taking (see Table 10.7).

Listening Assessment 279

Table 10.7 Procedures for Constructing Test Prompts

Test input	Test prompt	Example
The spoken/viewed material that presents the input to the test taker.	A specific question, task, or instruction that directs the test taker on what they are required to do in response to the provided input The input (a scene, dialogue or a monologue) followed by …	A specific item related to the **prompt** "Happiness Index."
Multiple choice:		
A scene, dialogue, or a monologue, followed by written question or item completion	Selection of the best response(s) from choices given	The purpose of the annual World Happiness Report is: (a) to compare the self-reports of happiness of people in different countries (b) to discover the causes of unhappiness in the world (c) to alleviate feelings of anger, loneliness, and sadness in the world (d) to demonstrate activities that will lead to greater happiness
Short answer:		
A scene, dialogue, or a monologue, followed by written question or sentence completion	Original written response to complete a question	Which country received the highest rating in the report? Why?
Matching task:		
A scene, dialogue, or a monologue, followed by two columns of partial information in text or graphic form (e.g., left column is speakers' names or images; right column is quotes from the scene)	Matching of appropriate pairs of information	Who said each line? Column A: list of speakers Column B: list of quotes

(Continued)

280 *Teaching Listening*

Table 10.7 (Continued)

Test input	Test prompt	Example
True/false statements:		
True/false statements (or true/false/ no information statements) based on the information in the input.	Indicating one of the choices	The authors gave the survey to 100,000 people in each country. (T/F/NI)
Fill in. paragraph with blanks for key lexical items.	Written or spoken response, filling in blanks	The World Happiness Report summarizes *research on the levels of happiness in countries around the world. The authors of the report use a particular *method for gathering information. They *measure happiness by giving a survey to about 1,000 people in each country. The survey collects *data about income, health, and social support, as well as people's feelings of worry, sadness, and anger.
Open response:		
After listening, students have an open question requiring integration and summarization.	Written or spoken response	Summarize the podcast in 100 words.

One key to writing valid test prompts is to try them out on a test audience to make sure they are not ambiguous, too easy, or too difficult. If your goal in writing items is to discriminate between those who know the material well and those who do not, you want to ensure the items on your test actually do separate the stronger students (Rukthong, 2021; Taladngoen & Esteban, 2022; Wisuri, 2020). For close-ended items, such as multiple choice, there are statistical tests you can use to check the discriminative validity of items (see Resources Appendix).

10.8 Portfolio Assessment

Portfolio-style assessment in a language course is an approach to evaluating a student's language proficiency and progress that involves the systematic collection and organization of a variety of language-related materials and tasks over a period of time. Instead of relying solely on traditional exams or standardized tests, portfolio assessment allows students to demonstrate their language skills through a diverse range of activities and artifacts and allows for student self-assessment of their progress (Andrade, 2019). Portfolio-style assessment can be particularly suited to a listening course that integrates other language skills (reading, writing, and speaking) and multiple literacies (digital literacy, media literacy, cultural literacy, etc.) (Brunfaut & Rukthong, 2018; Plakans, 2021).

A portfolio typically includes a compilation of these types of performance elements:

- Listening activities: Students may include note-taking samples, summaries, or reflections on various listening tasks they have completed throughout the course to demonstrate their comprehension skills (Rukthong & Brunfaut, 2020).
- Writing samples: Students may include samples of their written work, such as summaries, journal entries, or formal reports, to showcase their skills and development.
- Speaking recordings: Audio or video recordings of students engaging in conversations, presentations, or role plays can demonstrate their oral language abilities and communication skills.
- Self-access material logs: Logs of audio and video materials students have accessed on their own, along with summaries or commentaries, can illustrate the student's motivation and comprehension.
- Language-learning reflections: Students can provide self-assessments and reflections on their language-learning experiences, discussing their strengths, areas for improvement, and strategies they have used to enhance their listening and other language skills.
- Projects and assignments: Any language-related projects or assignments completed during the course can be included to demonstrate the application of language skills in practical contexts.
- Language tests and quizzes: While portfolio assessment is not solely reliant on traditional tests, students might also include select language tests or quizzes to provide a more comprehensive view of their language performance.

282 *Teaching Listening*

TIPS FROM PRACTITIONERS: Try portfolio assessments

I have moved toward a portfolio-style assessment in my academic listening courses. At one point, I had used just objective tests at the end of each lecture as a measure of students' progress since I thought this would be more realistic preparation for when they entered actual university courses. Over time, I saw how this approach was demotivating: Students were not engaging in class activities, only exerting any energy for studying for tests. In order to show that classroom activities and peer interactions did contribute to their success, I started using classroom and out-of-class activities as part of the assessment. Now, I give objective tests about 40% of the total score, but I use the portfolio for 60% of the student's grade. This includes a variety of things: participation in (and summaries of) group discussions, completion of notes during lectures, and follow-up projects as part of the assessment. Since I've moved to this more rounded approach to assessment, I get much more participation in all activities, and I think the students get better overall results this way.

Cynthia Lennox, Teacher and author, Pittsburgh, USA

10.9 Assessing Interactive Listening Proficiency

An essential element in assessing second language listening performance is evaluating a learner's ability in interactive settings in which goal-oriented oral communication is required. Because authentic communicative settings often cannot be readily replicated for testing purposes, evaluators typically rely on some form of controlled oral interview as a sample of the learner's oral and interaction ability. In an oral interview test, or Oral Proficiency Interview (OPI), the test candidate is placed in the role of the listener and is expected to respond as quickly and completely as possible to the interviewer's prompts, which are usually questions (e.g., "What kind of work do you do?") or open-ended invitations to talk about suggested topics (e.g., "Tell me more about your job").

Although formal interviews provide a reliable, replicable setting to test interactive speaking and listening, the notion of construct validity in these tests has been challenged. While an OPI ostensibly mirrors natural conversation, it has been shown that such interviews lack the prototypical aspects of conversation, such as features of conversational involvement and power symmetry (Brooks, 2009; Davis, 2009; Fulcher, 2014; see O'Loughlin, 2001, for a comparison of direct, semi-direct, and indirect speaking tests).

Oral interview interactions have been characterized as a process of elicitation of specific output and compliance, with more explicit routines than a normal interactive conversation would have (Brown, 2003). Increasingly, interview tests are being designed as testing tasks, with the tasks being closely associated with specific goal-oriented situations and involving the active participation of the language user (Cohen, 2020; Roever, 2011; Roever et al., 2023).

May (2009) studied the features of accommodation and control used in oral interviews. In investigating the potential threats to the validity of OPI testing, she found that the raters perceive key features of the interaction as mutual achievements, which further suggests that the awarding of shared scores for interactional competence is one way of acknowledging the inherently co-constructed nature of interaction in a paired speaking test (de Jong, 2023; Tanaka & Ross, 2023).

It is widely noted in OPI training that the interviewers/raters may not initially be aware of the constraints their own cultural background and expectations of normal, symmetrical discourse may impose on the sample of speech produced by interviewees. Specifically, critics point out that OPIs, as instances of cross-cultural interactions, often produce miscommunication due to misfits between politeness systems, which are deployed to assert status or maintain face (Kasper & Ross, 2013; Nakatsuhara, 2008; Tanaka & Ross, 2023).

The underlying argument for the validity of the OPI as a representative sample of natural discourse lies in demonstrating that the interview resembles other forms of naturally occurring interaction but contains specific mediating discourse structures that give it a special identity. That identity includes a some-what higher frequency of certain features of accommodation and control than is found in other forms of social interaction (see Table 10.8).

The fact that these control and accommodation features tend to occur more frequently in OPI interactions than in normal interactions weakens the validity of the assessment (Ross, 2018). Essentially, the construct of interactive competence may be misrepresented or underrepresented. As such, other measurements of the test takers' communicative listening ability need to be included.

A final note should be added as to the necessity of interactive listening proficiency testing in language instruction. Even though it is very challenging to conduct reliable assessments of interactive competence (IC), it is still necessary for educators and assessors to include IC in the listening curriculum. In spite of the difficulty (and the costs) of conducting individual evaluations of IC, we should not exclude interaction from our assessments, as many high-stakes tests do, unfortunately.

Although we can rely on correlational inferences to estimate a test subject's interactive proficiency based on their other listening scores, we need to consider the washback of excluding certain constructs from our assessment. If the test takers, as well as the teacher and curriculum designer, know the high-stakes tests

284   *Teaching Listening*

Table 10.8 Features of Accommodation and Control

Accommodation	Control
• *Display question.* The interviewer may ask for information that is already known to the interviewer or that the interviewer believes the interviewee ought to know.	• *Topic nomination.* The interviewer proposes a new topic by foregrounding information not previously introduced in the discourse. This typically leads to a question that may be introduced by informative statements and which requires no link to previous topic development.
• *Comprehension check.* The interviewer may check on the interviewee's current understanding of the topic or of the interviewer's immediately preceding utterance.	
• *Clarification request.* The interviewer may ask for a restatement of an immediately preceding utterance produced by the interviewee, even if the interviewer can infer what the interviewee intends.	• *Topic abandonment.* The interviewer unilaterally ends a current topic even though the interviewee may still show evidence of interest in further development.
• *Or-question.* The interviewer may ask a question and immediately provide one or more options for the interviewee to choose an answer.	• *Self-expansion.* The interviewer extends and alters the content of the interviewer's immediately preceding utterance so as to accomplish interview objectives.
• *Fronting.* The interviewer provides one or more utterances to foreground a topic and set the stage for the interviewee's response.	• *Propositional.* The interviewer refocuses the interviewee's reformulation attention on a previously nominated topic or issue, which has not produced enough language to confirm a rating for the interviewee.
• *Grammatical.* The interviewer modifies an utterance's syntactic or simplification semantic structure to facilitate comprehension.	
• *Slowdown.* The interviewer reduces the speed of an utterance.	
• *Over-articulation.* The interviewer exaggerates the pronunciation of words and phrases.	
• *Other-expansion.* The interviewer draws on the perceived meaning of the interviewee's utterance and elaborates on words or phrases within the utterance.	
• *Lexical simplification.* The interviewer chooses what is assumed to be a simpler form of a word or phrase that the interviewer believes the interviewee is unable to comprehend.	

Listening Assessment   285

they need to pass are going to assess IC, then the students—and the teachers and the curriculum designers— will address it in the classroom.

10.10 Uses of AI in Testing Listening

Artificial intelligence (AI) has been in use in language assessment in various forms for decades for scoring, data analysis, and construct validation (Boldt & Freedle, 1996; Freedle, 1990; Freedle & Kostin, 1999). Many teachers and institutions have been expanding the use of AI to assist with the administration and analysis of listening tests for obvious administrative reasons: efficiency, time and cost savings, consistency, and standardization. In addition to these practical reasons, there are pedagogical motivations, such as the adaptability of tests to match the test takers' proficiency level and the capability of providing immediate scoring and feedback (Chen et al., 2022).

When used appropriately, AI-assisted testing of listening can complement effective teaching and assessment approaches. Having surveyed a number of teaching programs that are using AI in their assessment, I have found a recurring set of claimed advantages:

- **Automated scoring of listening responses:** AI-powered systems can automatically score objective listening responses provided by test takers. These responses may include answering questions, completing gaps in a transcript, or summarizing the content heard. AI algorithms analyze the responses, considering factors such as content accuracy, grammar, and vocabulary usage, to provide automated and consistent scoring (Susanti et al., 2017; Suvorov & Hegelheimer, 2013)
- **Adaptive listening test items:** AI can administer adaptive listening tests that dynamically adjust the difficulty of listening tasks based on a test taker's performance. The AI algorithm selects subsequent audio passages or questions with varying complexity, ensuring that the assessment is personalized to each individual's skill level (Brigham Young University, 2023; McFarland et al., 2021)
- **Analyzing listening comprehension:** AI can analyze a test taker's listening comprehension by processing audio recordings of dialogues, lectures, or monologues. It can identify specific aspects of listening ability, such as the ability to grasp main ideas, understand details, recognize relationships between concepts, and infer meaning from context (Zhang et al., 2023)
- **Speech recognition and pronunciation assessment:** AI-driven speech recognition technology can evaluate a test taker's pronunciation and comprehensibility (feature extraction of pitch, duration, intensity, and matching to standardized pronunciation models) and spoken language (coherence modeling based on connectors and sequencing). It can assess factors like accent, intonation, fluency (number of words per minute), and grammatical accuracy,

286   *Teaching Listening*

providing valuable feedback on spoken language skills (Babaeian, 2023; Kang et al., 2021;

- **Tracking communication strategies:** For interactive tasks, AI algorithms can identify various communication strategies used by test takers, such as paraphrasing, clarification, or providing examples, offering valuable insights into the test taker's communication ability (Hameed, 2016; Torfi et al., 2020)
- **Monitoring listening behavior:** AI algorithms can monitor a test taker's listening behavior during the assessment, detecting anomalies (in speaking patterns or irregularities in language complexity) that may indicate potential cheating or test integrity issues (Milliner & Barr, 2020; Zhang et al., 2023).
- **Assessment of comprehensibility:** AI is capable of evaluating the comprehensibility of a test taker's contribution following a given prompt. This capability enables oral interactive testing (Saito et al., 2022)
- **Assessment of multimodal listening skills:** AI is capable of assessing listening skills across various modalities, such as audio-only listening tasks or listening combined with visual cues, to provide a more comprehensive evaluation of listening abilities (Campoy-Cubillo, 2019; Fjørtoft, 2020)
- **Accessibility features:** AI technologies can be used to create accessibility features, such as providing real-time captions or transcripts for audio content and making listening assessments more inclusive for individuals with hearing impairments or language differences
- **Creating diverse listening stimuli:** Using NLP (natural language processing), AI can generate a diverse set of listening stimuli, such as dialogues with different accents, speech rates, and content topics, ensuring that the listening assessment is fair and representative of real-world listening situations
- **Analyzing listening data:** As has been done by testing services for decades, AI is used to analyze large volumes of listening test data to identify patterns, trends, and areas where test takers encounter the greatest challenges. This data-driven approach helps improve the design and effectiveness of future listening assessments (Schmidgall & Powers, 2017)
- **Personalized listening practice:** As all teachers know, providing students with feedback after testing promotes motivation and more focused language practice. AI-powered language-learning platforms can offer personalized listening practice based on individual learners' performances on tests. Teachers can access the practice logs to utilize for assessment (Kunihara et al., 2022)
- **Personalized interaction practice:** AI-powered chatbots can engage in interactive conversations with language learners. These chatbots use NLP algorithms to understand and respond to learners' input. Learners can practice speaking, listening, and responding to the chatbot, simulating real-life conversational scenarios. Teachers can access the speaking logs for assessment purposes.

Teachers can take advantage of these AI affordances to improve their assessment practices and provide more focused instruction for their learners.

10.11 Summary: Integrating Assessment into Instruction

This chapter, the final chapter in Teaching Listening section (Section II), has dealt with the important issue of assessment. It has outlined how all forms of listening assessment must involve an input, which may be multimodal, and a response, a task outcome, or observable behavior by a listener. The chapter discussed multiple forms of validity that need to be considered when interpreting the results of any listening assessment. It is important to remember that all listening tests *underrepresent* the totality of listening; each test attempts to measure a limited domain of listening.

Though most of the chapter was concerned with objective criteria for composing, administering, and evaluating assessments, vital subjective factors should be considered in listening assessment. We first looked at ways of describing the social and educational contexts in which assessment is used, since assessment always influences the goals of instruction and learner motivation by way of the **washback effect** (Hughes, 2020). When teachers consider assessment and feedback as one stage of instructional design, they are better able to create positive washback effects.

At the core of this chapter is the formation of a model of listening constructs as the basis for assessment. As we have done throughout this book, we proposed three strands of listening processing—linguistic, semantic, and pragmatic—that should be employed in creating valid listening assessments. We next considered types of items that can be employed for objectively scored listening tests. Following this, we examined some of the issues involved in the assessment of interactive listening.

The overarching intent of the chapter has been to show that it is impossible to assess listening fully with a single testing instrument. In a single test, we often target and assess just one aspect of this complex ability. With this limitation in mind, we should be cautious in making claims about what listening assessments measure or describe. Portfolio-style assessments of listening, including measures of listening integrated with other skills (interviews, collaborative tasks, and interactive presentations in particular) and into larger tasks and projects (involving reading especially), are recommended because they provide evidence of performance in a wider range of contexts.

References

ACTFL (American Council on the Teaching of Foreign Languages). (2012). Proficiency guidelines (Web page). https://www.actfl.org/educator-resources/actfl-proficiency-gui delines

288 *Teaching Listening*

Alderson, J. C. (2005). *Diagnosing foreign language proficiency: The interface between learning and assessment.* Continuum.

Andrade, H. L. (2019, August). A critical review of research on student self-assessment. In *Frontiers in Education* (Vol. 4, p. 87). Frontiers Media SA.

Aryadoust, V. (2020). A review of comprehension subskills: A scientometrics perspective. *System, 88,* Article 102180.

Aryadoust, V., Zakaria, A., Lim, M. H., & Chen, C. (2020). An extensive knowledge mapping review of measurement and validity in language assessment and SLA research. *Frontiers in Psychology, 11,* 1941.

Babaeian, A. (2023). Pronunciation assessment: Traditional vs modern modes. *Journal of Education for Sustainable Innovation, 1*(1), 61–68.

Boldt, R. F., & Freedle, R. (1996). Using a neural net to predict item difficulty. *ETS Research Report Series, 1996*(2), i–19.

Brigham Young University (BYU). (2023). Center for Language Studies. Adaptive listening test (ALT). (Web page). https://cls.byu.edu/listening-proficiency-test-lpt

Brindley, G., & Slatyer, H. (2002). Exploring task difficulty in ESL listening assessment. *Language Testing, 19,* 369–394.

Brooks, A. (2022). The art and science of happiness. *TedX Talks.* https://www.youtube.com/watch?v=G7Pf2Xb5PdA),

Brooks, L. (2009). Interacting in pairs in a test of oral proficiency: Co-constructing a better performance. *Language Testing, 26*(3), 341–366.

Brown, A. (2003). Interviewer variation and the co-construction of speaking proficiency. *Language Testing, 20,* 1–25.

Brownell, J. (2015). *Listening: Attitudes, principles, and skills.* Routledge.

Brunfaut, T. (2016). *Assessing listening.* In D. Tsagari & J. Banerjee (Eds.), *Handbook of second language assessment* (pp. 97–112). Handbooks of Applied Linguistics. Mouton de Gruyter.

Brunfaut, T., & Revesz, A. (2015). The role of task and listener characteristics in second language listening. *Tesol Quarterly, 49*(1), 141–168.

Brunfaut, T., & Rukthong, A. (2018). Integrative testing of listening. In J. I. Liontas (Ed.), *The TESOL encyclopedia of English language teaching* (pp. 1–7). John Wiley & Sons.

Buck, G., Tatsuoka, K., & Kostin, I. (1997). The subskills of reading: Rule-space analysis of a multiple-choice test of second language reading comprehension. *Language Learning, 47*(3), 423–466.

Campoy-Cubillo, M. C. (2019). Functional diversity and the multimodal listening construct. *European Journal of Special Needs Education, 34*(2), 204–219.

Canadian Language Benchmarks (CLB). (2024). Listening benchmarks (Web page). https://www.clb-osa.ca/benchmarks/listening

Center for Applied Linguistics (CAL). (2012). Proficiency guidelines (Web page). https://www.cal.org/flad/post-secondary-world-language-assessment-module/proficiency/proficiency-levels/

Chapelle, C. A., Kremmel, B., & Brindley, G. (2019). Assessment. In N. Schmitt & M. P. H. Rodgers (Eds.), *An introduction to applied linguistics* (pp. 294–316). Routledge.

Chen, X., Zou, D., Xie, H., Cheng, G., & Liu, C. (2022). Two decades of artificial intelligence in education. *Educational Technology & Society, 25*(1), 28–47.

Cohen, A. (2020). Considerations in assessing pragmatic appropriateness in spoken language. *Language Teaching, 53*(2), 183–202.

Cronbach, L. J., & Meehl, P. E. (1955). Construct validity in psychological tests. *Psychological Bulletin, 52*(4), 281.

Council of Europe (2020). CEFR (Council of Europe Framework) https://rm.coe.int/common-european-framework-of-reference-for-languages-learning-teaching/168 09ea0d4

Davis, L. (2009). The influence of interlocutor proficiency in a paired oral assessment. *Language Testing, 26*(3), 367–396.

de Jong, N. H. (2023). Assessing second language speaking proficiency. *Annual Review of Linguistics, 9*, 541–560.

Emerick, M. R. (2019). Explicit teaching and authenticity in L2 listening instruction: University language teachers' beliefs. *System, 80*, 107–119.

Field, J. (2019). *Rethinking the second language listening test from theory to practice.* Equinox.

Fjørtoft, H. (2020). Multimodal digital classroom assessments. *Computers & Education, 152*, 103892.

Frazier, L., Solorzano, H., & Rost, M. (2022). *Contemporary topics 1* (4th ed.). Pearson.

Freedle, R. (1990). *Artificial intelligence and the future of testing.* Psychology Press.

Freedle, R., & Kostin, I. (1999). Does the text matter in a multiple-choice test of comprehension? The case for the construct validity of TOEFL's minitalks. *Language Testing, 16*(1), 2–32.

Fulcher, G. (2014). *Testing second language speaking.* Routledge.

Global Scale of English (GSE) (2022) https://www.pearson.com/languages/why-pearson/the-global-scale-of-english/educators.html

Goodwin, S., & Naismith, B. (2023). *Assessing listening on the Duolingo English Test.* (Duolingo Research Report DRR-23-03). Duolingo.

Hameed, I. A. (2016, September). Using natural language processing (NLP) for designing socially intelligent robots. In *2016 Joint IEEE International Conference on Development and Learning and Epigenetic Robotics (ICDL-EpiRob)* (pp. 268–269). IEEE. 10.1109/DEVLRN.2016.7846830

Hasrol, S. Zakaria, A., & Aryadoust, V. (2022) A systematic review of authenticity in second language assessment. *Research Methods in Applied Linguistics, 1*, 100023.

He, L., & Jiang, Z. (2020). Assessing second language listening over the past twenty years: A review within the socio-cognitive framework. *Frontiers in Psychology, 11*, 2123.

Hughes, A. (2020). *Testing for language teachers.* Cambridge University Press.

International English Language Testing System (IELTS). (2024). https://ielts.org/organisations/ielts-for-organisations/ielts-scoring-in-detail

Kang, O., Johnson, D. O., & Kermad, A. (2021). *Second language prosody and computer modeling.* Routledge.

290 *Teaching Listening*

Kang, O., Yan, X., Kostromitina, M., Thomson, R., & Isaacs, T. (2023). Fairness of using different English accents: The effect of shared L1s in listening tasks of the Duolingo English test. *Language Testing*, 02655322231179134.

Kasper, G., & Ross, S. (2013). Assessing second language pragmatics: An overview and introductions. In S. Ross & G. Kasper (Eds.), *Assessing second language pragmatics* (pp. 1–39). Palgrave Macmillan.

Kunihara, T., Zhu, C., Saito, D., Minematsu, N., & Nakanishi, N. (2022). Detection of learners' listening breakdown with oral dictation and its use to model listening skill improvement exclusively through shadowing. In *Proceedings of INTERSPEECH Conference*, pp. 4461–4465. doi: 10.21437/Interspeech.2022-440

Liping, G. (2014). *An exploration of L2 listening problems and their causes* (PhD thesis, University of Nottingham, UK).

May, L. (2009). Co-constructed interaction in a paired speaking test: The rater's perspective. *Language Testing*, 26 (*3*), 397–421.

McFarland, D. A., Khanna, S., Domingue, B. W., & Pardos, Z. A. (2021). Education data science: Past, present, future. *AERA Open*, *7*, 23328584211052055.

McNamara, D., Graesser, A. & Louwerse, M. (2012). Sources of text difficulty: Across genres and grades. In J. Sabatini, E. Albro, & T. O'Reilly (Eds.), *Measuring up: Advances in how we assess reading ability* (pp. 89–116). R&L Education.

Messick, S. (1998). Test validity: A matter of consequence. *Social Indicators Research: An International and Interdisciplinary Journal for Quality-of-Life Measurement*, *45*(1), 35–44.

Milliner, B., & Barr, B. (2020). Computer-assisted language testing and learner behavior. In M. R. Freiermuth & N. Zarrinabadi (Eds.), *Technology and the psychology of second language learners and users* (pp. 115–143). Palgrave Macmillan.

Nakatsuhara, F. (2008). Inter-interviewer variation in oral interview tests. *ELT Journal*, *62*, 266–275.

Nishizawa, H. (2023). Construct validity and fairness of an operational listening test with World Englishes. *Language Testing*, 02655322221137869.

Ockey, G. J., & Wagner, E. (2018). *Assessing L2 listening: Moving towards authenticity* (Vol. 50). John Benjamins Publishing Company.

O'Loughlin, K. (2001). *The equivalence of direct and semi-direct speaking tests*. Cambridge University Press.

Plakans, L. (2021). Integrated skills assessment. In H. Mohebbi & C. Coombe (Eds.), *Research questions in language education and applied linguistics: A reference guide* (pp. 329–332). Springer.

Roever, C. (2011). Testing of second language pragmatics: Past and future. *Language testing*, *28*(4), 463–481.

Roever, C., Shintani, N., Zhu, Y., & Ellis, R. (2023). Proficiency effects on L2 pragmatics. In A. Martínez-Flor, A. Sánchez-Hernández & J. Barón (Eds.), *L2 Pragmatics in action: Teachers, learners and the teaching-learning interaction process* (pp. 145–167). John Benjamins Publishing Company.

Ross, S. (2018). Listener response as a facet of interactional competence. *Language Testing*, *35*(3), 357–375.

Rost, M. (1990). *Listening in language learning*. Longman.

Rukthong, A. (2021). MC listening questions vs. integrated listening-to-summarize tasks: What listening abilities do they assess? *System*, *97*, 102439.

Rukthong, A., & Brunfaut, T. (2020). Is anybody listening? The nature of second language listening in integrated listening-to-summarize tasks. *Language Testing*, *37*(1), 31–53.

Ruslov, S. (2022). Listening: Exploring the underlying processes. In L. Gurzynski-Weiss & Y. Kim (Eds.), *Instructed second language acquisition research methods* (pp. 257–280). John Benjamins.

Saito, K., Macmillan, K., Kachlicka, M., Kunihara, T., & Minematsu, N. (2022). Automated assessment of second language comprehensibility: Review, training, validation, and generalization studies. *Studies in Second Language Acquisition*, *45*(1), 1–30.

Schmidgall, J. E., & Powers, D. E. (2017). Technology and high-stakes language testing. In C. A. Chapelle & S. Sauro (Eds.), *The handbook of technology and second language teaching and learning* (pp. 317–331). Wiley.

Shiotsu, T., & Weir, C. J. (2007). The relative significance of syntactic knowledge and vocabulary breadth in the prediction of reading comprehension test performance. *Language Testing*, *24*(1), 99–128.

Strand, J., Brown, V., Merchant, M., Brown, H., & Smith, J. (2018). Measuring listening effort: Convergent validity, sensitivity, and links with cognitive and personality measures. *Journal of Speech, Language, and Hearing Research*, *61*(6), 1463–1486.

Susanti, Y., Tokunaga, T., Nishikawa, H., & Obari, H. (2017). Controlling item difficulty for automatic vocabulary question generation. *Research and Practice in Technology Enhanced Learning*, *12*(1), 1–16.

Suvorov, R., & Hegelheimer, V. (2013). Computer-assisted language testing. In A. J. Kunnan (Ed.), *The companion to language assessment* (pp. 594–613). Wiley.

Taladngoen, U., & Esteban, R. H. (2022). Assumptions of plausible lexical distractors in the redesigned TOEIC question-response listening test. *LEARN Journal: Language Education and Acquisition Research Network*, *15*(2), 802–829.

Tanaka, M., & Ross, S. (2023). Impact of self-construal on rater severity in peer assessments of oral presentations. *Assessment in Education: Principles, Policy & Practice*, *30*(2), 203–220,

Tatsuoka, K. (2009). *Cognitive assessment: An introduction to the rule space method*. Routledge.

Torfi, A., Shirvani, R. A., Keneshloo, Y., Tavaf, N., & Fox, E. A. (2020). Natural language processing advancements by deep learning: A survey. *arXiv preprint*. arXiv:2003.01200.

Umirova, D. (2020). Authenticity and authentic materials: History and present. *European Journal of Research and Reflection in Educational Sciences*, *8*(10), 129–133.

Wagner, E. (2022). Assessing listening. In G. Fulcher & L. Harding (Eds.), *Routledge handbook of language testing* (2nd ed., pp. 223–235). Routledge.

Wallace, M. P. (2022). Individual differences in second language listening: Examining the role of knowledge, metacognitive awareness, memory, and attention. *Language Learning*, *72*(1), 5–44.

West, G. B., & Thiruchelvam, B. (2024). "It's not their English": Narratives contesting the validity of a high-stakes test. In M. R. Salaberry, A. Weideman, & W.-L. Hsu (Eds.), *Ethics and context in second language testing* (pp. 80–105). Routledge.

Wisuri, R. (2020). TOEFL Listening: Ultimate guide (Web page). https://magoosh.com/toefl/listening/

Xi, X., & Norris, J. M. (Eds.). (2021). *Assessing academic English for higher education admissions*. Routledge.

Zhang, D., Hoang, T., Pan, S., Hu, Y., Xing, Z., Staples, M., Xu, X., Lu, Q., & Quigley, A. (2023). Test-takers have a say: Understanding the implications of the use of AI in language tests. *arXiv preprint*. arXiv:2307.09885.

Zheng, H., Miao, X., Dong, Y., & Yuan, D. C. (2023). The relationship between grammatical knowledge and reading comprehension: A meta-analysis. *Frontiers in Psychology, 14*, 1098568.

Section III

Researching Listening

The first two sections of this volume have aimed to define the key concepts for understanding the various dimensions of listening and to describe principled approaches for teaching listening. This third section explores avenues of researching listening from the perspectives of both processes and outcomes.

Chapter 11 focuses on researching the cognitive and behavioral processes, outlined in Section 1, that underpin successful listening. The chapter provides background and outlines to conduct and interpret four practical research projects that can be carried out in a variety of social, educational, and professional settings: (1) the analysis of transcripts for the discovery of listener processing decisions in interactive discourse; (2) the development of rating scales for tracking of judgments listeners make about speaker comprehensibility, proficiency, and impact; (3) the employment of recall protocols to infer listener strategies used when interpreting narratives; and (4) the use of attribution analysis to infer the causes of listener misunderstandings and to suggest counteractive solutions for the misunderstandings. Specific research skills needed to carry out the projects fully are demonstrated, with additional tutorials offered in the Resources section. Applications of the project concepts for teaching and further research are also suggested.

Chapter 12 focuses on researching listening outcomes when five key instructional variables are controlled. The five variables are input selection, intervention planning, interaction variations, assessment modifications, and course design decisions. For each of the five variables, a concrete research project is outlined for teachers to employ in their own teaching context: (1) Preparing an input menu for a listening class; (2) designing intervention task sequences to meet specific learning objectives; (3) preparing a variety of interaction types to allow for greater student engagement; (4) planning alternate assessments to provide focused feedback on learning goals; and (5) designing an entire autonomous listening course. Necessary research skills for implementing these projects are suggested, with targeted tutorials offered via the Resources section. Applications of each project for teaching and additional research are also provided.

DOI: 10.4324/9781003390794-14

11   Researching Listening Processes

11.1 Introduction: Why Research Listening Processes?	295
11.2 Identifying Listener Decisions	297
11.2.1 Project: Monitoring Listener Decisions in Interactive Tasks	*300*
11.2.2 Research and Teaching Options	*302*
11.3 Tracking Listener Judgments	302
11.3.1 Evaluating Speaker Impact	*303*
11.3.2 Project: Evaluating Speaker Presentations	*304*
11.3.3 Evaluating Speaker Comprehensibility	*309*
11.3.4 Project: Using Comprehensibility Scales	*310*
11.4 Interpreting Listener Filters	312
11.4.1 Project: Interpreting Recall Protocols	*315*
11.5 Analyzing Listener Misunderstandings	317
11.5.1 Project: Collecting and Analyzing Common Misunderstandings, Attributed to Processing Domains	*317*
11.6 Summary: The Value of Studying Listening Processes	321
References	322

11.1 Introduction: Why Research Listening Processes?

So far in *Teaching and Researching Listening*, we have described listening as a combination of neurological, cognitive, and affective processes. When we research these processes, we need to monitor the behavioral components—that is, observable behaviors of the listener—in order to identify and make inferences about the underlying intentions, decisions, and actions performed by that listener.

This chapter highlights mixed research methods to provide direct insight into listening processes. Mixed methods will involve both quantitative measures, such as tests, reports, and assessments, and qualitative measures, such as observations, interviews, and narrative analysis. Mixed methods will generally produce more robust results than either quantitative or qualitative measures alone in that they allow for multiple perspectives on the research questions.

DOI: 10.4324/9781003390794-15

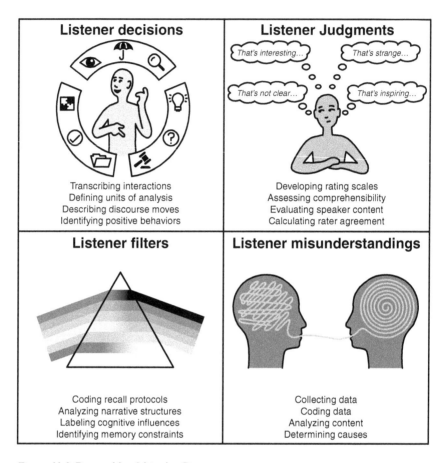

Figure 11.1 Researching Listening Processes

The four projects in this chapter will focus on different listening processes. Each project will call on the use of several research skills

This chapter will outline four projects for researching the listening process. These are projects that closely reflect the practical situations and conditions found in language instruction, which allows them to be applied in educational settings.

These four projects are (11.2) "Identifying Listener Decisions," (11.3) "Tracking Listener Judgments," (11.4) "Interpreting Listener Filters," and (11.5) "Analyzing Listener Errors." The research methods used in these studies will provide teachers with practical tools for conducting their own research and for sharing results with colleagues (see Figure 11.1).

11.2 Identifying Listener Decisions

We often consider listening to be receptive and responsive rather than constructive and proactive. However, it is possible to identify the timing of decision points for the listener, moments where they shift or amplify their engagement in the listening process. These decision points alter the interaction—either with an interlocutor in live settings or with the discourse text in remote settings (Green & Bridges, 2018; Jäckel et al., 2022).

Decision points are specific instances in the discourse flow where listeners decide how to interpret and respond to incoming information. Listeners continuously make decisions as they engage in a wide range of listening tasks, from following instructions to taking notes in lectures.

Identifying decision points is a useful skill in both teaching and in conducting listening research. One preparatory action in discovering these decision points is making an analytical transcription of listener interactions in live conversations or discussions. In order to identify decision points, we first need a transcription with sufficient detail that allows us to code **discourse moves** (Fernandez, 2018).

Transcribing conversations involves converting audio or video recordings into written text, capturing the words spoken and various nonverbal cues, such as pauses, intonations, laughter, and overlapping speech. In addition to its value for research, skill in analytic transcription serves several important purposes in language instruction. Transcription helps identify themes, patterns, and nuances within the communication, providing data for in-depth analysis of language use and discourse patterns (Kunitz, 2021; Shelton & Flint, 2021).

Learning to do a detailed transcription is an intensive listening practice for the teacher or researcher. It involves honing the skills of intensive listening, note-taking, and accurately merging verbal and nonverbal symbols into decipherable text. Learning detailed transcription also introduces you to technologies for collaboration, coding, subtitling, and translation, including software and platforms such as **Express**, **Scribe**, **Sonix**, **oTranscribe**, **F4/F5**, and **Trint**.

Though transcript conventions differ across many dimensions, the most significant ones involve decisions about units of analysis, irregular pronunciations, turn-taking boundaries, emotional shadings, and bilingual usage (Bucholtz, 2000; Roberts, 2020; see Table 11.1).

Because many variables could be denoted in a transcription, it is important for the researcher to determine which variables are to be prioritized. By prioritizing discourse features, such as length of responses or pause length, the researcher can compare transcripts over time to observe changes in these variables (Catalano & Waugh, 2020). For studying listening in interaction, it is helpful to identify a core battery of behaviors associated with proficient interaction or specific targets of "listening performance" (e.g., Itzchakov et al., 2018) and code these after the transcription has been completed. This will allow for a

298 *Researching Listening*

Table 11.1 Variables in Transcription Practices

Category	Considerations	Recommendations
Words, irregular pronunciations of words	Decide whether standard orthography is sufficient or whether to preserve nuances of pronunciation (e.g., accents). The transcriber must also decide on whether to use phonetic transcription or modified orthography.	Use standard orthography; avoid phonetic symbols and unorthodox spellings, except when needed for research purposes. Example: a colon indicates lengthening of sound it follows. (ye:s)
Units of analysis	After you have transcribed the bulk of the content, decide on the basic "line unit" of analysis you wish to use: the sentence, independent clause, or pause unit. Decide on the basic "section unit" of analysis: exchanges or thematic episodes (Kreuz & Riordan, 2018).	Use pause units (a burst of speech, followed by a clear pause); each pause unit appears on a new line, regardless of grammatical cohesion. Divide the overall transcript into thematic sections.
Pauses	Decide on how to measure and denote pauses or whether to ignore them. Most researchers note pauses that have apparent interactional meaning, such as communicative strain or high level of rapport. Some researchers quantify pauses as the number of beats of silence based on the speaker's preceding speech rate.	Indicate pauses that have an impact on the interaction. Use normative judgments on length of pause: Short pause: A comma (,) indicates a brief pause. Medium pause: A dash (–)indicates a slightly longer pause. Long pause: Ellipsis (...) indicates a significant pause or silence.
Prominence	Decide how to indicate intentional or contrastive prominence (not normal stress of content words).	Strong emphasis: Place the emphasized word or syllable in ALL capital letters or use **bold** formatting. Moderate emphasis: Use *italics* or <u>underline</u> to indicate moderate stress or emphasis.
Prosody and intonation	Decide on ways of indicating prosody and intonation.	Use arrows (up for rising, down for falling), indicate intonation direction when significant to meaning. Use // to indicate a clear end of an cutterance with falling intonation Use ? for clear end of an utterance with questioning intonation.

Researching Listening Processes   299

Table 11.1 (Continued)

Category	Considerations	Recommendations
Turn-taking	Decide on how to indicate turn-taking, which is seldom clearly delineated in spontaneous conversation. Turn transitions may include unusually short pauses between one speaker and the next (latching), interruption by the second speaker, and simultaneous talk (overlap). Be sure to keep track of the back channel (the current listener) in addition to the front channel (the current speaker) (Hoiting & Slobin, 2002).	Use = (equal sign) to show overlap Use [(bracket) to indicate latching Use — (em dash) to indicate an interruption
Nonverbal aspects and events	Decide on how extensively to indicate nonverbal actions. In discourse analysis, nonverbal actions constitute a communicative resource (Deppermann & Haugh, 2022).	Use [...] (square brackets) to enclose nonverbal sounds or actions (e.g., [laughter], [cough]).
Emotional settings	Decide on how extensively to indicate emotional expressions indicated through vocal settings. Participant emotion will often color specific turns or episodes in the conversation.	Develop a set of simple adjectives or adverbs to describe the speaker's emotion when it is significant to interpreting meaning. Use parentheses to enclose comments or descriptions related to the discourse (e.g., (sarcastically), (whispering)).
Bilingual transcription	Decide on how to include language switching.	The original language of the discourse should be preserved to maintain authenticity. Transcribe in the original language, with a translation below. e.g. S1: She's an only child. S2: どういう意味ですか? Only? *What do you mean? Only?* S1: Only. No brothers or sisters.

300   *Researching Listening*

Table 11.2 Codings for Listener Decisions

Discourse management (DM)	*S1:* OK, so let's answer the question. Who wants to begin? *S2:* I'll start.
Cue uptake (CU)	*S1:* Do you agree? *S2:* Yes, I do.
Direct response/Expanded response (DR/ER)	*S1:* What do you think they should do? *S2:* They should let the father live at their house. /They have enough room for him.
Questions for clarification (CQ)	*S1:* What do you think they should do? *S2:* Do about what?
Questions/Comment for information expansion (EQ, IQ)	*S1:* What do you think they should do? *S2:* They should probably ask her father to live in their house. But it might create some problems for their marriage.
Backchanneling (BC)	*S1:* I think she has to take care of her father. It's her duty. *S2:* Mmm. Right.
Empathic responses (ER)	*S1:* My parents had the same issue with my grandfather. *S2:* Wow, that must have been challenging for your family.
Topic shift (TS)	*S1:* The father must live with them. It's the only way to solve this problem. *S2:* I see what you mean, but maybe nursing homes are better for him.
Reflection (RE)	*S1:* The father must live with them. That's the perfect solution. *S2:* So you think the only solution is the father lives with the daughter's family?

more detailed analysis of successful—and unsuccessful—discourse moves and patterns.

Some common behavioral codings for listeners include discourse management, cue uptake for turn-taking, direct responses, expanded responses, information questions, topic shift, personal disclosure, clarification questions, reflection, backchanneling, empathic responses, and nonverbal involvement (see Table 11.2).

11.2.1 Project: Monitoring Listener Decisions in Interactive Tasks

This project can be conducted in an educational or other setting; the description here will refer to an educational setting. Work with a natural student grouping. Have the students work in groups of three or four. Provide a recorded version of a detailed narrative (or narrate a story yourself) that presents a moral or personal dilemma, for instance, a story of an elderly man who can no longer live alone for safety reasons. His choices are to continue living alone, to move in with his eldest daughter and her family, or to go to a nursing home.

After making sure that the students understand the narrative and the dilemma, pose a question to the student groups: *What do you think is the best solution for this problem?* Allow a limited time (5 to 10 minutes) for them to discuss the problem and possible solutions and to give their reasons for their proposed solutions. Encourage them to use English exclusively for their discussion. Provide an audio recording device for each group, letting the students know you are recording their discussion.

Afterward, transcribe each group conversation or focus on a selected part of each conversation. You can use abbreviations to identify participants (S1, S2, etc.) instead of personal names in order to protect privacy and to meet ethical standards for human-subject research. Use the recommended transcription conventions in Table 11.1, or develop your own system.

After you have transcribed a discussion, use the listener behavior codings in Table 11.2 to code each discernable turn in terms of listening activity. Note that it is common to have multiple intentions in any discourse move. If a particular discourse move has two or more plausible codings, indicate all that apply.

Based on your codings, rank the listening behaviors from most frequent to least frequent. To determine the relative frequency of behaviors when analyzing a transcription or any other form of qualitative data, you can use a simple counting method to tally the occurrences of each behavior. This will give you a basic understanding of which behaviors and sequences are most common in your data.

Once you have the counts for each behavior, calculate the relative frequency by dividing the count of each behavior by the total number of behaviors. This will give you a proportion or percentage for each behavior.

You can create visualizations such as bar charts or tables to represent the relative frequencies of different behaviors, making it easier to compare them visually. (I avoid pie charts because they tend to skew the data, especially when a large number of categories is involved.) If you want to test for the significance of the frequency of occurrences, you can use a chi-square test to compare the distribution of behaviors across different groups or conditions (see the Resources appendix for guidance on how to perform this analysis). A chi-squared test assesses whether the observed data significantly deviates from what would be expected under the assumption of independence between your categorical variables.

Since the primary purpose of research is to gain insight, once you have assessed the relative frequency of listening behaviors, reflect on the significance of the listener behavior for the group you are observing. Why are certain behaviors so frequent? Why are some positive or desirable behaviors

302 *Researching Listening*

so infrequent? Are there patterns that lead to the positive behaviors or to the avoidance of these behaviors?

11.2.2 Research and Teaching Options

- Do a longitudinal study of the same student group. Collect data from the same participants at multiple points in time and make transcription comparisons to observe changes or trends in behavior, performance, or other variables over an extended period. This type of study design is particularly useful for examining the effects of instructional interventions over time on accuracy and fluency and understanding how variables interact and evolve (Ross & Masters, 2023). Longitudinal studies can provide valuable insights into the patterns and trajectories of behaviors or phenomena across different time intervals (Long & Watanabe, 2021).
- Use the transcripts for teaching purposes. Check that names have been removed from the transcripts and show students parts of the transcripts that reveal target behaviors to be emulated or avoided in order to bring about successful conversations (Meyer, 2023; Schunk & Zimmerman, 2023).
- Perform a similar study in a noneducational setting involving two-party communication, such as business negotiations, political debates, entertainment interviews, or discussions in legal contexts or therapeutic settings. Use public sources of video or transcriptions or your analysis (e.g., business negotiations from Harvard Law School: www.pon.harvard.edu.). After reviewing the transcripts, develop your own codings for desirable listener behaviors. For instance, in a therapy setting, you may code positive behaviors such as sharing hunches about affect ("Sounds like you're feeling …"), exploring affect ("How did that make you feel?"), empathic echo ("So you felt …"), elaboration prompting ("Tell me more"), validation ("A lot of people would feel that way"), and checking in ("How do you feel right now?") (Itzchakov et al., 2018; Jones et al., 2019).

11.3 Tracking Listener Judgments

In instructional and research settings, the listener is usually evaluated on how well they understand a speaker's input. However, we can gain insight into the listening process by tracking how the listeners themselves evaluate the input of a speaker. For instance, while listening to a speech, the listeners are most certainly evaluating the speaker's clarity, comprehensibility, and believability. Perhaps they are also judging subjective elements such as the speaker's likability.

Research on listener ratings of speakers has often been done in settings in which speakers are considered to have communication disorders, such as stuttering, dysarthria, or dysphonia. Similarly, listener ratings are often used in educational settings to evaluate an instructor's teaching effectiveness, using measures including speech comprehensibility, as is often done to assess NNS teaching assistants at universities teaching (Ramjattan, 2019). Listener ratings also play an important role in public-contact professions, such as broadcast media and politics, to determine the speaker's intelligibility and audience engagement and satisfaction (Biagi, 2014). In addition, listener ratings are used to evaluate AI voices in terms of naturalness, emotion expressiveness, and "human-likeness" (the Turing test) (Campbell-Kibler, 2017).

The projects in this part of the chapter probe the notion of listener evaluation from various angles. There are three rating frameworks and projects: (1) Rating the effectiveness or impact of a speaker in a one-way presentation; (2) rating the intelligibility and comprehensibility of an L2 speaker; and (3), rating interactive performance in an interview setting between an L1 interviewer and an L2 candidate.

11.3.1 Evaluating Speaker Impact

Speaker impact refers to the extent to which a speaker effectively engages, influences, and resonates with their audience. Speaker impact encompasses the speaker's delivery, communication style, content, perceived credibility, and ability to connect with their listeners (Curtis et al., 2016; Rubega et al., 2021). Speaker impact is crucial in determining whether the speaker's message is successfully conveyed, understood, and remembered by the audience (Haslam et al., 2020; Hemphill & Hemphill, 2007). Without a receptive and attentive audience, however, there can be no speaker impact, irrespective of the speaker's skill or experience (Bodie, 2023).

In most live presentation contexts, the listeners (the audience) react at a macro-level, based on the general affect they experience during the presentation: They either liked or didn't like the speaker's contribution. Although their evaluation is likely to include a complex combination of emotional and intellectual factors, audience members typically respond holistically in terms of liking or not liking the presentation (Hallinan et al., 2023). This research project is about deconstructing those global evaluations into micro-constructs, particular factors that contribute to the perceived quality of the presentation from the listener's perspective.

Evaluating a speaker's effectiveness involves considering how well the speaker's communication aligns with the goals and expectations of the audience. This will include components (also called criteria or dimensions) such as relevance and clarity, engagement and connection, as well as adaptation to the audience's reactions and communication preferences. In educational contexts, the audience typically includes a gatekeeper, such as a teacher or an interviewer, whose listening judgment will include language and content standards (Fernandez, 2018).

304   *Researching Listening*

In a content-oriented presentation, we will also measure speaker impact in terms of engagement, clarity, and comprehensibility, but other objective standards will be included. These might be time management, organization and coherence, effective use of multimodal aids, persuasiveness, provision of proper evidence, audience interaction, or memorability.

In order to allow listeners to evaluate speakers at a micro-level, we need some kind of rubric, a structured rating guide that focuses on particular aspects of communicative competence. Tables 11.3 and 11.4 present examples of rubrics, one emphasizing language-related constructs and one emphasizing content-related constructs.

Rating scales like these are generally used immediately *after* the presentation is concluded, with each rater providing a numerical rating (the rating level) on several criteria or dimensions. Raters generally become more adept at using these scales as they gain experience with multiple speakers and as they compare rating levels with other raters and discuss their reasons for providing a particular score.

11.3.2 Project: Evaluating Speaker Presentations

- Develop a scale for a group of L2 students preparing to give short presentations. Decide on five criteria that reflect the competencies that you are targeting. Consider the balance of content-oriented and language-oriented criteria. Use selected descriptors from the two samples given here, or create your own.
- Create a four-band scale using these five criteria. Be sure that you use language that your raters (the listeners) will understand.
- For practice with using the rating scale, choose some short prerecorded presentations. Watch the presentations and complete the scale for each presenter. Watch a second time to confirm your ratings.
- Using the same recordings, train your students or colleagues on the use of the scale. Play the recordings and have them complete the rating scales for each presenter. Compile the results. To obtain an accurate correlation analysis, use Cohen's kappa or the intraclass correlation coefficient (ICC) (see the Resources appendix for guidance with these analyses). Alternatively, simply have your students or colleagues discuss their ratings in order to reach a general consensus on the criteria. Use the results of your analysis to revise the evaluation rubrics.

Ideas from this project could be adapted for teaching or research in a number of ways:

- To explore the link between listening and speaking in presentations, do a case study of one or more individual students, tracking their development

Table 11.3 Rating Scale with Emphasis on Language-Related Constructs

Names of presenter:
Topic:

CRITERIA	3	2	1	No score
Relevance	Exactly on topic	Mainly on topic	Often wanders off topic	No relationship to the assigned topic
Content	Highly engaging, very organized, easy to follow	Interesting and organized	Somewhat interesting, not well organized	Low interest, unclear organization
Presence	Maintains strong contact with audience and energy throughout	Maintains good contact and has good energy most of the time	Has low energy, rarely makes contact with audience	Does not connect with audience, shows little energy
Grammar	Makes only occasional grammatical errors which do not interfere with presentation	Makes several grammatical errors that interrupt the presentation flow	Makes numerous errors, hard to follow the presentation as a result	Errors are numerous and constantly interfere with understanding
Pronunciation	Confident, clear articulation/ pronunciation; excellent volume, speaking rate, and pauses	Clear articulation/ pronunciation but not polished; volume, rate, and pauses mostly appropriate	Often unclear pronunciation makes it hard to follow; some mumbling; uneven rate and volume	Pronunciation problems and excessive pauses make it difficult for listener to follow
Vocabulary	Word choice is precise and colorful	Word choice is generally accurate and clear	Word choice is generally basic	Word choice is too basic to communicate ideas
SCORE			___ /18 = ___ %	

Table 11.4 Rating Scale with Emphasis on Content-Related Constructs

Names of presenter:
Topic:

CATEGORY	4	3	2	1	Comments
Time limit	Exactly within the allotted time frame	Within 1 minute +/- of allotted time	Within 2 minutes +/- of allotted time	3 or more minutes above or below the allotted time	
Audience collaboration	Presenter continuously involves the audience, through eye contact and body language, allows for questions and comments, responds enthusiastically	Presenter occasionally involves the audience, through eye contact and body language, and allows for questions and comments	Presenter rarely involves the audience, through eye contact or body language and did not allow for questions and comments	No evidence of attempts to engage with audience	
Organization	Strong and engaging introduction provides overview of presentation; presentation supports introduction; conclusion reinforces main points in memorable fashion	Mostly effective introduction or overview of presentation; conclusion appropriate	Some overview is given; connection between introduction and presentation is sometimes unclear; conclusion is limited OR no introduction/ overview or no conclusion	Introduction does not give overview; organization is unclear, or presentation ends without conclusion	
Content/ Preparedness	Content throughout the presentation is well researched and presented succinctly; presentation is well prepared and has obviously been rehearsed	Content is presented succinctly for the most part. Research and preparation are evident	Content shows problems with research and succinct presentation; more preparation of the material is necessary	Presentation of content is disjointed and incoherent; little evidence of preparation	

Evidence/ Sources	Main ideas are presented with depth and effectively supported with facts, vivid details, and engaging examples. All key elements are included. Several sources (3 +) are used, mentioned, and cited	Main ideas are supported with appropriate facts, examples, and details. One or two key elements may be missing; 2–3 sources are used, mentioned, and cited	Some main ideas are supported with facts, examples, or details. More than two key elements are missing; only 1–2 sources are used OR mentioned/ cited inappropriately	Main ideas are unclear; facts, examples, and details are lacking or fail to support ideas; presentation lacks several key elements or contains inaccuracies; no sources are used/ mentioned/cited
Speaking skills/ Voice	Poised, clear articulation/ pronunciation; proper volume, speaking rate, and pauses. Presenter shows enthusiasm through emphasis	Clear articulation/ pronunciation but not as polished; volume, rate, and pauses mostly appropriate. Presenter's show of enthusiasm through emphasis is adequate	Some mumbling; uneven rate and volume; some enthusiasm and emphasis	Volume too high or too low; rate too fast/slow; speaker seems uninterested and uses monotone; articulation/ pronunciation often not clear

(Continued)

308   *Researching Listening*

Table 11.4 (Continued)

CATEGORY	4	3	2	1	Comments
Physical expression	Presenter communicates interest in topic with energy and poise, maintains eye contact with audience, uses facial expressions and gestures effectively; posture and appearance convey confidence and credibility	Presenter communicates interest in topic, maintain eye contact for the most part, uses appropriate facial expressions, gestures, and posture. Appearance is appropriate	Presenter had difficulty communicating interest in topic and maintaining eye contact. Some facial expressions, gestures, or aspects of their body language may not be appropriate	Presenter does not communicate interest in topic; maintain little eye contact; does not use facial expressions and gestures effectively; inappropriate posture and/or appearance	
Support materials	Support materials significantly enhance the presentation; no errors in visual material	Support materials occasionally enhance the presentation, but are sometimes confusing; some errors in visual material	Support materials do not enhance the presentation; some errors in visual material	Support materials distract from the presentation; many errors in visual material	
SCORE				___/32 = ___%	

in presentation skills and listening-participation skills in presentations over the course of a full session. Compare their performances on a series of presentations. Conduct short interviews with the student presenters after each presentation about which aspects of their performance (which criteria on the rating scale) they are attempting to improve. Hold a discussion with the whole class about methods for improving participation in the presentations as an audience member or even ways of supporting the presenters to improve their presentations. You can video-record the presentations and have students comment during their interviews on the parts of the presentation they found challenging. Provide coaching for the challenging aspects: Introduce the concept of progressive self-checking and peer assessment and feedback (Burns, 2018).

- Compare the impact of using different evaluation scales and the presenters' access to these scales on the performances and ratings. For example, if one scale is skewed toward linguistic measures and another is skewed toward content measures, does this affect the audience ratings?
- Do a time-series study of individual students, focusing on speaking skills. Provide an opportunity to give a second presentation (live or on video) after they have received audience feedback on their first presentation. Do you notice an improvement in their ratings on the second performance? If so, on which criteria do you notice the most improvement?
- Do a time-series study of individual students, focusing on listening skills. Provide a listening task for them, such as taking notes, filling in information, or formulating questions to ask the speaker. Does listener involvement in the presentation affect their rating of the speaker? Does increased listener involvement affect those listeners' subsequent performance as speakers or presenters? If so, how?

11.3.3 Evaluating Speaker Comprehensibility

Evaluating a speaker's comprehensibility and related connection factors is part of listening competence. There are four recognized factors that are related to listener evaluation of a speaker's connection:

- **Comprehensibility:** a global estimate made by a listener, denoting how easily they understand a speaker's overall speaking. This concept is often used in multilingual professional and academic contexts in which English is the lingua franca (ELF) or refers to the nonnative speaker's (NNS's) communication effectiveness with multilingual audiences.
- **Intelligibility:** related to comprehensibility, this is primarily an objective measure, defined by the number of words heard correctly and acoustic-phonetic decoding of each utterance, though it is subjective, depending on the listener's familiarity with the speaker's variety of English.

310 *Researching Listening*

- **Interactivity:** related to audience receptivity, this is a subjective measure, denoting the effort needed by the listener to maintain an interaction on a topic of mutual knowledge and interest (e.g., cooking, travel, families).
- **Acceptability:** also related to audience receptivity, this is a subjective measure as to how the listener rates the speaker's naturalness, as well as their sensitivity to the listener's social and cultural norms. This factor is known to be influenced often by listener biases (Itzchakov et al., 2020; Kang et al., 2019; Trofimovich et al., 2022).

Measuring comprehensibility reliably—reaching agreement from multiple listeners—can be challenging because of subjective factors, particularly biases regarding gender, race, age, physical factors, nationality, and accent. It is also worth noting that the assessment of comprehensibility can vary depending on the purpose and context of the material, and the listener's familiarity with different accents or dialects (Ye et al., 2021).

11.3.4 *Project: Using Comprehensibility Scales*

- Collect monologue or dialogue samples, recorded as audio or video, of several speakers; you will then evaluate these for comprehensibility. To ensure construct validity, have all subjects read the same passage (for the monologue sample) and respond to the same questions (for the dialogue sample). Compose your own prompts, or use these:

  - Monologue script (complex syntax and vocabulary, includes a range of pronunciation targets)

    When the sunlight strikes raindrops in the air, they act as a prism and form a rainbow. The rainbow is a division of white light into many beautiful colors. These take the shape of a long round arch, with its path high above and its two ends apparently beyond the horizon. There is, according to legend, a boiling pot of gold at one end. People look, but no one ever finds it. When a person looks for something beyond their reach, people say they are looking for the pot of gold at the end of a rainbow.

  - Dialogue prompts (goes through a scaffolded sequence of complexity)

    What is your favorite city, and why do you like it? / Can you tell me about a book that you recently read and what you learned from it?/ Who has been your favorite teacher, and how has their guidance influenced your learning?/ When did you first become interested in _____, and what inspired you to pursue it further?/ If you have free time this weekend, what activities would you like to do?/ If you could travel anywhere in the world, where would you go, and why?

Researching Listening Processes 311

- Prepare a five-point scale for several categories you wish to assess. (Consult the Resources appendix for guidance on composing Likert scales.) Attempt to include the minimum number of categories that you feel provide coverage of comprehensibility. Most scales include:

  - **Articulation:** This assesses how clearly and accurately the speaker pronounces individual sounds and words.
  - **Intelligibility:** Intelligibility is the degree to which the overall speech is understandable to listeners. It considers factors like pronunciation, word choice, and sentence structure.
  - **Pronunciation:** The speaker's ability to correctly produce and enunciate words and sounds affects comprehensibility.
  - **Accent:** Accents can influence how well others understand speech.
  - **Prosody:** Prosody refers to the rhythm, stress, and intonation in speech. Proper prosody helps convey meaning and emotions, enhancing comprehensibility.
  - **Fluency:** The smoothness and continuity of speech affect how well listeners can follow the speaker's message.
  - **Vocabulary and grammar:** Using vocabulary and grammar to ensure that the speaker's ideas are expressed clearly and coherently.
  - **Use of gestures and visual aids:** When available, gestures and visual aids can support comprehension and provide additional context for the message.

After you have experimented with the scale and are confident it includes the measures you feel best reflect comprehensibility, use it for actual rating. Play the samples to a group of raters. Allow each rater time to select a rating for each category individually (rather than through group discussion). You may need to replay the recorded sample to allow raters to verify their ratings.

When using evaluative scales for gatekeeping purposes, such as deciding whether a student qualifies to pass a course, be sure to check the reliability of ratings. If the ratings are unreliable (that is, display wide discrepancy), decide on a standard for mediating differences. For research purposes, you can check for inter-rater reliability using Cohen's kappa or the intraclass correlation coefficient (ICC). To check on the association or patterns between two categorical variables, you can use Guetzkow's T2 test. (See the Resource appendix for guidance on these analyses.)

Ideas from this project can be adapted for teaching or research in a various ways:

- As a way of integrating speaking and listening instruction, create a simplified comprehensibility scale that you can use in your teaching. It should be transparent, so that students understand the categories clearly and know how to improve. Use a set of input prompts for monologue and dialogues and

312   *Researching Listening*

allow students time to practice speaking independently with model samples. Periodically, provide a comprehensibility check with your students (with a sample they have practiced), allowing them to identify areas they wish to improve. This can also be done as a peer assessment (Goh & Burns, 2012).

- Create a study in which you explore rater disagreements. Find the criteria on which there is the least agreement. Through a visual analysis of the ratings, attempt to determine which criteria are most problematic. You can use a statistical analysis, such as ICC, to measure inter-rater reliability in ordinal data, such as rating scales (see the Resource appendix for guidance). Discuss the nature of the disagreements: Are these due to inherent biases? Are they due to the ambiguous nature of some of the constructs?

11.4 Interpreting Listener Filters

Information retrieval is a crucial aspect of listening ability; in fact, much formal assessment of listening ability, as surveyed in Chapter 10, involves retrieval and reconstruction of information from recently heard input. Researching how information is retrieved and how this information is filtered by cognitive influences can provide useful insights into semantic processing.

The late Wallace Chafe, a renowned linguist and specialist in Native American languages, was a pioneer in the field of cross-cultural communication. As part of his ongoing research on comprehension and memory, he tested how our recall of narratives varies and how our recall is, in effect, filtered by our cultural knowledge. With his research team, he produced a very simple six-minute film to use in exploring these cultural filters.

The film was designed to tap into universal experiences and activate cultural schemas. It shows a farmer harvesting pears, a boy coming by on a bike, and the apparent theft of a bushel full of pears. The film is six minutes long, with sound effects but no words (Chafe, 1980). The storyline is deliberately bland to avoid imposing a strong cultural or moral bias. Chafe inserted some short, ambiguous scenes and some unfamiliar objects to test the perception of culturally referenced schemas and the memory of these events later.

The project in this section deals with the use of schematic memory in both semantic processing and recall of narrative input. The 1980 *Pear Story* film is used as an example, but any short film could be used for the research project.

In the case of *The Pear Story*, the action can be schematized according to a classical five-part story structure (Kühn & Boshoff, 2023; Mandler, 1987). (See Table 11.5.)

To research how listeners comprehend and recall stories, with or without linguistic input, we need to conduct an "immediate recall protocol" **(IRP)**, a term first used by Lund (1991) for a comparative memory testing study. More generally, a recall protocol is a structured procedure used to elicit specific information

Researching Listening Processes 313

Table 11.5 Story Structure: *The Pear Story*

Story action	Schematic element
A man is picking pears	**Orientation** Introduces the audience to the time, place, and context of the story, setting the stage for what follows
The man polishes a pear A man walks by with a goat	
A boy arrives on his bike	**Triggering Event** The incident or action that sets the main plot in motion. It initiates the central conflict and propels the story forward.
The boy takes one basket of pears	
A girl on a bike encounters the boy	**Complicating Action** An obstacle or challenge for the protagonist as they attempt to address the conflict caused by the triggering event. The complicating action builds tension and raises the stakes.
The boy's hat falls off The boy hits a rock with his bike	
The boy falls	**Critical Event** The turning point in the story significantly impacts the direction of the narrative and leads to the climax.
The basket of pears falls on the ground	
Three boys help him	**Resolution** The story's conclusion, where the conflict is resolved, and loose ends are tied up. It provides closure and clarity to the narrative.
The boys find the hat The boys return the hat The boys receive a pear The boy rides on	
The man looks for his basket The boys walk past the man, eating pears	**Coda** Closure, linking back to the orientation for cohesion

or responses from individuals in a systematic and standardized manner. Using a standard set of procedures ensures consistency, reliability, and validity in the execution of the study.

Table 11.6 presents a recall transcription from the film *The Pear Story*.

Table 11.6 Recall Transcription Sample American English native speaker, female adult; recalled immediately after viewing.

Story action	Schematic element	S1 recall data
A man is picking pears	**Orientation**	It opens up in a kind of rural area, with a farmer … he is climbing a ladder and picking fruit, pears.
The man polishes a pear		He keeps climbing up and down his ladder and putting the fruit into a basket.
A man walks by with a goat		He hears something and then looks to see another farmer leading a goat past the tree. Not sure what that was about.
A boy arrives on his bike	**Triggering Event**	Then, we see a boy on a bicycle riding up to the tree. He stops next to the tree with the baskets of pears. He looks up into the tree and sees that the farmer doesn't notice him. So he decides to steal a whole basket of pears.
The boy takes one basket of pears		He's riding on his bike really unsteady…unsteadily because the basket is so heavy.
A girl on a bike encounters the boy	**Complicating action**	And then a girl comes by on a bike, … in the other direction …
The boy's hat falls off		
The boy hits a rock with his bike		and he tries to avoid her
The boy falls	**Critical event**	but he falls off of his bike …
The pears fall on the ground		and the pears spill all over the ground.
Three boys help him	**Resolution**	And while he's on the ground, three, I think two or three, other boys come by and then see that his pears are all over the ground … so they help him. They pick up the pears and put them back in the basket for him.
		And then one of them, the little guy, yes, I guess there were three boys, removes the rock that I guess he ran into … forgot about that …
The boys find the hat		And they go on in their different directions … but they find his hat that fell off…
The boys return the hat		And one boy runs back and gives it to the boy with the bike.
The boys receive a pear		The boy on the bike gives him some pears; I guess as a kind of thank you.
The boy rides on		And the three boys walk away eating their pears …
The man looks for his basket	**Coda**	About this time, the farmer comes down from the tree and notices that one of his baskets of pears is missing.
The boys walk past the man, eating pears		Just then, the three boys go past the farmers, and he notices that they're eating pears, and he looks at them, like, "Where did you get those pears?" And that's it.

Researching Listening Processes 315

Working with free recall data involves three essential steps: transcribing, scoring, and interpretation.

1. **Transcription:** Record or transcribe the participant's recall response verbatim. This ensures an accurate representation of the recalled information. (Divide the transcript into meaningful units, such as pause units. This step helps in organizing the data for further analysis. See 11.2 for transcription procedures and tips.)
2. **Scoring:** Assign scores or codes to the recalled units based on predetermined criteria– in this case, story structure. The scoring criteria might involve factors like accuracy, order, and completeness. For example, in story-recall tasks, each correctly recalled event or description may receive a score of 1, and each partially correct one receives half a point. In contrast, incorrect or omitted words may receive a score of 0.
3. **Interpretation:** The specific analyses conducted will depend on the research questions and objectives. Common analyses include calculating recall accuracy, examining patterns of distortions or omissions, assessing the influence of different variables on recall performance, and comparing recall performance across conditions or groups.

Interpretation will yield insights into the listening and recall processes concerning memory constraints and cultural filters. In my own research with L1 and L2 listeners, I have noticed several phenomena that seem to occur whenever anyone recalls an extended, complex story. The first is omissions: Participants will omit details or information they found difficult to comprehend or remember. Another common phenomenon is rationalizations: Participants will alter the story to make it more consistent with their cultural beliefs and expectations and, therefore, easier to understand and remember. A third phenomenon, which I always find surprising, is transformations: Participants will unintentionally transform unfamiliar elements of the story into more familiar and culturally appropriate elements. And a final, more expected phenomenon is simplifications: Participants will make the story more straightforward and less complex, to fit their cultural frameworks. Simplification will increase over time: If there is a longer lapse between story input and recall, the story will tend to become shorter (Bamberg, 2012; Barkhuizen, 2014).

11.4.1 Project: Interpreting Recall Protocols

- Select the input you wish to use for your study. It should be novel input for the participants. Culturally themed stories are an excellent source. Depending on the proficiency level of your participants (if you are working with L2 subjects), choose or prepare input that is appropriately challenging

316 *Researching Listening*

on a linguistic level (see Chapter 8 for guidelines; see the Resources section for cultural story sources).

- Write out your research steps, including how you will administer the story-telling and the recall elicitation. Here is a sample:

  - The participants watch the film.
  - Immediately afterward, they are interviewed individually in a different room.
  - The interviewer says to each participant, "You have just seen a film. But I have not seen it. Can you tell me what happens in the film?'"
  - If questioned further, the interviewer says, "Just describe what you saw. There are no right or wrong answers."
  - Most viewers will tell the story quite naturally, taking around two minutes. Each description is audio or videotaped. The interviewer does not provide prompts or encouragement during the recall.
  - At the end, the interviewer thanks the participant and then can briefly answer their questions about the purpose of the study.

The recordings are then transcribed and used for analysis.

Themes and techniques from this project can be incorporated into the teaching and researching of listening in various ways.

- Compare the differences in recall accuracy between the use of free recall protocols and **probed recall**. In probed recall, participants are provided with specific cues or prompts to aid them in recalling information from memory. For example, in *The Pear Story*, a probed recall might include these cues: *How did the man pick the pears? How many baskets did he have on the ground? Did the boy on the bike notice the farmer in the tree?* With some experimentation and analysis, you can reveal how question probes can lead and bias a subject's recall (e.g., see Laney & Loftus, 2023).
- Compare the differences in recall accuracy over time. For instance, you may elicit a story recall immediately following the narrative presentation and then again one day or one week later.
- Compare the differences in recall detail using different types of inputs, such as stories from the subject's native culture versus stories from remote cultures. Or compare the differences in recall with different presentation conditions, such as audio only, or video with and without subtitles.
- Utilize the recall protocols for teaching purposes (e.g., to develop vocabulary or rhetorical gambits) or as part of a portfolio analysis of a student's progress.
- Explore the use of storytelling—and "storylistening"—as a tool for language learning. Consider how the use of stories, both personal and literary, impact the classroom environment, learners' motivation to listen, and their progress in language generally (e.g., see Ahmad & Yamat, 2020; Dillon & Craig, 2021; Frenette, 2023) .

11.5 Analyzing Listener Misunderstandings

Finnish communication researcher Osmo Wiio has been credited with formulating a somewhat facetious series of laws about the inevitability of misunderstandings. Essentially, the laws encourage us to accept the idea that "in all communication, assume you have been misunderstood" (Jung, 2006). Though most of us sail through our everyday interactions with an operational assumption that everyone is more or less tuned in to us and we to them, we all encounter more misunderstandings than we realize.

The purpose of researching misunderstanding is to shed light on what a listener needs to do to *achieve* understanding, particularly in cross-cultural encounters (Bremer et al., 2014). Given the tenuousness of perception, comprehension, and inference processes, it is likely that misunderstandings will take place frequently (House et al., 2014).

The causes and consequences of miscommunication have aroused considerable interest, particularly in high-stakes contexts such as air traffic control (e.g., Prevot et al., 2012), medicine (e.g., Berkhof et al., 2011; Roberts et al., 2005), the legal system (e.g., Eades, 2015), and international agencies (e.g., Taylor et al., 2014). Considerable research has also been focused on miscommunication in the workplace (e.g., Stubbe, 2018), academic settings (e.g., Jenkins, 2000), service encounters (e.g., de Matos et al., 2011), and gender relationships (Kendall & Tannen, 2015; Maltz & Borker, 2018). In any of these situations, the consequences of misunderstandings can extend well beyond trying to recover from a transactional glitch in a casual conversation. Misunderstandings can also lead to negative outcomes: unintended actions, mutual mistrust, avoidance, and deterioration of relationships.

Studying misunderstandings falls under the domain of pragmatics, which investigates how context influences language interpretation. In this project, we use the term "listener misunderstandings," though, in communication theory, all misunderstandings are assumed to be related to contextual factors and assumptions made by both speaker and listener (House et al., 2014). From a listener's perspective, a misunderstanding can be attributed to any of the four processing domains: neurological, linguistic, semantic, or pragmatic (see Table 11.7).

11.5.1 Project: Collecting and Analyzing Common Misunderstandings, Attributed to Processing Domains

- Select a communication context you would like to explore, one in which you suspect that misunderstandings are common and problematic. Collect interaction data on audio or video or from written or oral reports from your subjects.

318   *Researching Listening*

Consider these questions as you plan and carry out your research:

Questions	Research method: Content analysis
What factors contribute to listener misunderstanding in communication?	**Research question and objectives:** What insights are you trying to gain?
Are there particular settings or pairings of participants that you wish to investigate?	**Sampling data collection:** Decide on the sample to be analyzed. What kind of settings or participants are you trying to analyze? Select a representative subset that can provide meaningful insights into the research question. A rule of thumb is that at least 10 samples are needed to observe any patterns.
	Obtain audio or video recordings of interactions in which a misunderstanding apparently takes place. Isolate the misunderstandings for analysis.
	OR
	Obtain written or oral reports of individuals involved in recent misunderstandings. Attempt to reproduce the verbal and nonverbal elements of the misunderstanding in as much detail as possible.
Do you understand what is going on in your data? Can you transcribe it? Can you find the boundaries of any misunderstandings?	**Coding process:** Read, watch, or view the content and apply the coding scheme to label each unit of analysis. This process can be done manually or with the help of software tools designed for content analysis (e.g., **NVivo, MAXQDA, Dedoose, Quirkos, Transana**).
	Transcribe the focal parts of the recording, plus several seconds on the front and back end.
	Code the exchange where the misunderstanding seems to be localized.

Researching Listening Processes 319

Questions	Research method: Content analysis
Can you identify the units of misunderstanding?	**Units of analysis:** The unit of analysis is the smallest meaningful unit researchers will code and analyze. These units are typically conversational exchanges (which may include nonverbal elements) between two participants, but they may be larger episodes that include multiple exchanges (Krippendorff, 2018).
Can you develop a coding scheme that includes all known causes of misunderstanding locally, that is, at an utterance-exchange level?	**Coding scheme:** Your coding scheme may include categories, themes, or variables representing the aspects of the analyzed content (see Table 11.7 for examples).
Can you collaborate with a colleague to see if you agree on the causes?	**Inter-rater reliability:** This ensures consistency in the coding process. It involves comparing the coding results of different coders and calculating agreement percentages.
Are there any patterns in your data? Are some types of misunderstandings more common? Are some types more consequential?	**Sequence analysis:** Based on identified misunderstandings, show how particular misunderstandings occurred. Show the sequence of discourse moves. For statistical tests you can use, consult the Resources section.
Can you determine whether the misunderstanding was resolved? If so, how would you characterize the resolution? If not, how did the misunderstanding affect the interaction or relationship?	**Drawing conclusions:** Based on the analysis, make some preliminary interpretations of the findings. These interpretations may help to understand the causes of misunderstandings or other phenomena under study.
Consider conclusions of this nature: strategiesc that can improve listener comprehension and reduce misunderstandings;	Explore the effectiveness of various strategies used by the participants, such as clarifying questions, repetition, paraphrasing, or nonverbal cues.
strategies that listeners can use to repair misunderstandings.	Investigate the consequences of misunderstandings in this particular context, such as impacts on personal relationships or workplace interactions.
How does miscommunication impact interpersonal relationships and outcomes?	

320   *Researching Listening*

Table 11.7 Common Misunderstandings and Causes

	NEUROLOGICAL CAUSES
ACO	Acoustic problems "I'll pick you up at @#%*&@." (inaudible)
MIS	Mishearing. "He's very *elegant (arrogant?)*"
	LINGUISTIC CAUSES
GRA	Grammatical ambiguity (e.g., ambiguous pronoun reference): Speaker: "Maria told Lisa that she passed the exam."
PHA	Phonological/lexical ambiguity: *I scream* or *ice cream?*
DIF	Difficult construction. "Not only is it important for you to be here on time, but lack of preparation will not be tolerated."
	SEMANTIC CAUSES
ASK	Assumptions about shared knowledge: Speaker: "I'll meet you at the usual spot."
DCI	Different contextual interpretations: Speaker: "I saw her with a telescope."
FC	False cognates. "The *service* wasn't very good." ("Service" in one language refers to personal assistance; in another language, it refers to a gratuity.)
INE	Inadequate elaboration. "Entry is prohibited."
	PRAGMATIC CAUSES
FMS	Flouting the maxim of sincerity, particularly using irony or sarcasm: Speaker: "That's just what I needed, another meeting."
UNC	Unclear nonverbal cues. Speaker: Says something with a serious expression but a sarcastic tone.
UFR	Unfamiliar routine. "Can I help you?" uttered by a stranger outside of a socially acceptable context.
FI	False interpretation of speaker's intention. "Let's hang out together sometime." (Speaker may mean "get together informally"; Listener may interpret it as a date.)
UCR	Unknown cultural references: Speaker: "He's as fast as Usain Bolt."
UWU	Unwillingness to understand/engage Speaker A: "Can we please go in for a few minutes? We've come all this way, and we didn't know closing time was 5:00 p.m.!" Speaker B: (points to the clock)

The goal of researching misunderstandings as listener errors is not to archive the vulnerabilities of human communication. Rather, the goal is to increase our awareness of the conditions needed for positive communication outcomes. The listener can direct positive outcomes through recognition of liabilities in the communication process and by using strategies to prevent misunderstandings or correct them when they occur (House et al., 2014; House & Kádár, 2021). Depending on the context, positive outcomes can include improved understanding, enhanced self-expression, strengthened relationships, improved cross-cultural empathy and adaptation, conflict resolution, enhanced problem-solving, increased respect, and heightened satisfaction (Bodie, 2023; Creo, 2022; Fyhn & Berntsen, 2022).

11.6 Summary: The Value of Studying Listening Processes

This chapter has reviewed a range of useful qualitative methods for studying listening processes, whether the listener is an L1 or L2 user.

The research topics covered in this chapter—transcription coding, rating scales, recall protocols, and misunderstanding analysis—provide ways of researching listening qualitatively. The research suggestions are expanded to include quantitative measures to assist in triangulating the researcher's understanding.

The first project, dealing with coding of listener behavior, presents a key tool of discourse analysis, which allows for a micro view of listening decisions. One goal of listening instruction is to provide interventions in the listening process at the right time—when these interventions can immediately impact the learner.

The second project concerning listener ratings of speakers has dual goals. Because listeners are often evaluated for *their* level of comprehension, these rating projects turn the tables, so to speak, and allow the listener to judge what is comprehensible *to them*. Understanding listener criteria for comprehensibility and informativity is a useful goal. A second goal is to examine what features of learner *output*—pronunciation clarity, organizational transparency, grammar accuracy, or vocabulary sophistication—need to be addressed to help learners make concrete gains in proficiency. Understanding this speaking–listening evaluation loop is also a useful goal.

The third project, on recall analysis, reveals how subjective listening is—both at the comprehension/encoding stage and at the retrieval/recall stage. The project demonstrates that the listener must activate content and cultural schemas in order to make sense of input at both stages. Insights from this project can help teachers understand the subjective nature of listening and interpretation.

The fourth project, on misunderstanding analysis, aims to explore the process of deconstructing miscommunication into component actions and assumptions by the participants in an interaction, all of whom alternate between listener and speaker roles.

The value of these projects is in providing investigation skills for studying listening processes. By working with these research tools, the teacher or researcher can better understand listener perspectives and better evaluate listener outcomes.

322 *Researching Listening*

References

Ahmad, W .I. W., & Yamat, H. (2020). Students' perception on learning English language through conventional and digital storytelling. *International Journal of Academic Research in Business and Social Sciences*, *10*(2), 484–504.

Bamberg, M. (2012). Narrative analysis. In H. M. Cooper & American Psychological Association (Eds.), *APA handbook of research methods in psychology, Vol 2: Research designs: Quantitative, qualitative, neuropsychological, and biological* (pp. 85–102). American Psychological Association.

Barkhuizen, G. (2014). Narrative research in language teaching and learning. *Language Teaching*, *47*(4), 450–466.

Berkhof, M., van Rijssen, H. J., Schellart, A. J., Anema, J. R., & van der Beek, A. J. (2011). Effective training strategies for teaching communication skills to physicians: An overview of systematic reviews. *Patient education and counseling*, *84*(2), 152–162.

Biagi, S. (2014). *Media/Impact: An introduction to mass media*. Cengage Learning.

Bodie, G. (2023). Listening as a positive communication process. *Current Opinion in Psychology*, *53*, 10168.

Bremer, K., Roberts, C., Vasseur, M. T., Simnot, M., & Broeder, P. (2014). *Achieving understanding: Discourse in intercultural encounters*. Routledge.

Bucholtz, M. (2000). The politics of transcription. *Journal of Pragmatics*, *32*, 1439–1465.

Burns, A. (2018). Reflective teaching of speaking. In M. Zeraatpishe, A. Faravani, H. R. Kargozari, & M. Azarnoosh (Eds.), *Issues in applying SLA theories toward reflective and effective teaching* (pp. 155–164). Brill.

Campbell-Kibler, K. (2017). Language attitude surveys: Speaker evaluation studies. In C. Mallinson, B. Childs, & G. Van Herk (Eds.), *Data collection in sociolinguistics* (pp. 144–147). Routledge.

Catalano, T., & Waugh, L. R. (2020). *Critical discourse analysis, critical discourse studies and beyond*. Springer International Publishing.

Chafe, W. (1980). *The pear stories*. https://www.youtube.com/watch?v=bRNSTxTpG7U)

Creo, R. A. (2022). The science of hearing effectively. *Alternatives to the High Cost of Litigation*, *40*(6), 91–96.

Curtis, K., Jones, G. J., & Campbell, N. (2016, October). Speaker impact on audience comprehension for academic presentations. In *Proceedings of the 18th ACM international conference on multimodal interaction* (pp. 129–136). doi: 10.1145/2818346.2820766

Deppermann, A., & Haugh, M. (Eds.). (2022). *Action ascription in interaction* (Vol. 35). Cambridge University Press.

de Matos, C.A., Fernandes, D. V.H., Leis, R.P. & Trez, G. (2011). A cross-cultural investigation of customer reactions to service failure and recovery. *Journal of International Consumer Marketing*, *23*(3–4), 211228. doi: 10.1080/08961530.2011.578058

Dillon, S., & Craig, C. (2021). *Storylistening: Narrative evidence and public reasoning*. Routledge.

Eades, D. (2015). Taking evidence from Aboriginal witnesses speaking English: Some sociolinguistic considerations. *Precedent (Sydney, NSW)*, (126), 44–48.

Fernandez, L. (2018). Qualitative interview analysis: The use of systemic functional linguistics to reveal functional meanings. *Forum Qualitative Sozialforschung/ Forum: Qualitative Social Research*, *19*(2), 22.

Frenette, A. (2023). Story-listening as methodology: A feminist case for unheard stories. *Gender, Place & Culture*. doi: 10.1080/0966369X.2023.2272225

Fyhn, A. B., & Berntsen, G. (2022). A mathematics teacher's respectful listening in a culturally diverse class. *Journal of Peace Education, 20*(1), 1–25.

Goh, C., & Burns, A. (2012). *Teaching speaking: A holistic approach*. Cambridge University Press.

Green, J. L., & Bridges, S. M. (2018). Interactional ethnography. In F. Fischer, C. E. Hmelo-Silver, S. R. Goldman, & P. Reimann (Eds.), *International handbook of the learning sciences* (pp. 475–488). Routledge.

Hallinan, B., Kim, B., Scharlach, R., Trillò, T., Mizoroki, S., & Shifman, L. (2023). Mapping the transnational imaginary of social media genres. *New Media & Society, 25*(3), 559–583.

Haslam, S. A., Reicher, S. D., & Platow, M. J. (2020). *The new psychology of leadership: Identity, influence and power*. Routledge.

Hemphill, L. S., & Hemphill, H. H. (2007). Evaluating the impact of guest speaker postings in online discussions. *British Journal of Educational Technology, 38*(2), 287–293.

Hoiting, N., & Slobin, D. I. (2002). Transcription as a tool for understanding: The Berkeley Transcription System for sign language research (BTS). In G. Morgan & Bb. Woll (Eds.), *Directions in sign language acquisition* (pp. 55–75). John Benjamins.

House, J., Kasper, G., & Ross, S. (2014). *Misunderstanding in social life: Discourse approaches to problematic talk*. Routledge.

House, J., & Kádár, D. Z. (2021). *Cross-cultural pragmatics*. Cambridge University Press.

Itzchakov, G., DeMarree, K. G., Kluger, A. N., & Turjeman-Levi, Y. (2018). The listener sets the tone: High-quality listening increases attitude clarity and behavior-intention consequences. *Personality and Social Psychology Bulletin, 44*(5), 762–778.

Itzchakov, G., Weinstein, N., Legate, N., & Amar, M. (2020). Can high quality listening predict lower speakers' prejudiced attitudes? *Journal of Experimental Social Psychology, 91*, 104022.

Jäckel, E., Zerres, A., Hemshorn de Sanchez, C. S., Lehmann-Willenbrock, N., & Hüffmeier, J. (2022). NegotiAct: Introducing a comprehensive coding scheme to capture temporal interaction patterns in negotiations. *Group & Organization Management*, 10596011221132600

Jenkins, S. (2000). Cultural and linguistic miscues: A case study of international teaching assistant and academic faculty miscommunication. *International Journal of Intercultural Relations, 24*(4), 477–501.

Jones, S. M., Bodie, G. D., & Hughes, S. D. (2019). The impact of mindfulness on empathy, active listening, and perceived provisions of emotional support. *Communication Research, 46*(6), 838–865.

Jung, E. (2006). Misunderstanding of academic monologues by nonnative speakers of English. *Journal of Pragmatics, 38*(11), 1928–1942.

Kang, O., Rubin, D., & Kermad, A. (2019). The effect of training and rater differences on oral proficiency assessment. *Language Testing, 36*(4), 481–504.

Kendall, S., & Tannen, D. (2015). Discourse and gender. In D. Tannen, H. E. Hamilton, & D. Schiffrin (Eds.), *The handbook of discourse analysis* (pp. 639–660). Wiley.

324 *Researching Listening*

Kreuz, R. J., & Riordan, M. A. (2018). The art of transcription: Systems and methodological issues. *Methods in Pragmatics, 10*, 1634.

Krippendorff, K. (2018). *Content analysis: An introduction to its methodology.* SAGE Publications.

Kühn, S., & Boshoff, C. (2023). The role of plot in brand story construction: A neurophysiological perspective. *Journal of Strategic Marketing, 31*(2), 471–497.

Kunitz, S. (2021). CA transcription conventions (Based on Jefferson 2004). *Classroom-Based Conversation Analytic Research: Theoretical and Applied Perspectives on Pedagogy, 46*, 425.

Laney, C., & Loftus, E. F. (2023). Eyewitness testimony and memory biases. *Australasian Policing, 15*(1), 39–44.

Long, R., & Watanabe, H. (2021). The mirage of progress? A longitudinal study of Japanese students' L2 oral grammar. *The Language Teacher, 45*(2), 9–16.

Lund, R. (1991). A comparison of second language listening and reading comprehension. *The Modern Language Journal, 75*(2), 196–204.

Maltz, D. N., & Borker, R. A. (2018). A cultural approach to male-female miscommunication. In D. Brenneis & R. K. S. Macaulay (Eds.), *The matrix of language* (pp. 81–98). Routledge.

Mandler, J. M. (1987). On the psychological reality of story structure. *Discourse Processes, 10*(1), 1–29.

Meyer, D. K. (2023). Using instructional discourse analysis to study the scaffolding of student self-regulation. In N. E. Perry (Ed.), *Using qualitative methods to enrich understandings of self-regulated learning* (pp. 17–25). Routledge.

Prevot, T., Homola, J. R., Martin, L. H., Mercer, J. S., & Cabrall, C. D. (2012). Toward automated air traffic control: Investigating a fundamental paradigm shift in human/systems interaction. *International Journal of Human-Computer Interaction, 28*(2), 77–98.

Ramjattan, V. A. (2019). *Working with an accent: The aesthetic labour of international teaching assistants in Ontario universities.* University of Toronto.

Roberts, C., Moss, B., Wass, V., Sarangi, S., & Jones, R. (2005). Misunderstandings: a qualitative study of primary care consultations in multilingual settings, and educational implications. *Medical Education, 39*(5), 465–475.

Roberts, C. W. (2020). A theoretical map for selecting among text analysis methods. In C. W. Roberts (Ed.), *Text analysis for the social sciences* (pp. 275–284). Routledge.

Ross, S., & Masters, M. (2023). Approaches to longitudinal data analysis. In S. Ross & M. Masters (Eds.), *Longitudinal studies of second language learning* (pp. 27–48). Routledge.

Rubega, M. A., Burgio, K. R., MacDonald, A. A. M., Oeldorf-Hirsch, A., Capers, R. S., & Wyss, R. (2021). Assessment by audiences shows little effect of science communication training. *Science Communication, 43*(2), 139–169.

Schunk, D. H., & Zimmerman, B. J. (2023). Self-regulation in education: Retrospect and prospect. In D. H. Schunk & B. J. Zimmerman (Eds.), *Self-regulation of learning and performance: Issues and educational applications* (pp. 305–314). Routledge.

Shelton, S. A., & Flint, M. A. (2021). Dichotomies of method and practice: A review of literature on transcription. *Qualitative Research Journal, 21*(2), 177–188.

Stubbe, M. (2018). Miscommunication at work. In B. Vine (Ed.), *The Routledge handbook of language in the workplace* (pp. 258–271). Routledge.

Taylor, P. J., Larner, S., Conchie, S. M., & Van der Zee, S. (2014). Cross-cultural deception detection. In P. A. Granhag, A. Vrij, & B. Verschuere (Eds.), *Detecting deception: Current challenges and cognitive approaches* (pp. 175–201). Wiley.

Trofimovich, P., Isaacs, T., Kennedy, S., & Tsunemoto, A. (2022). Speech comprehensibility. In T. Derwing, M. Munro, & R. Thomson (Eds.), *The Routledge handbook of second language acquisition and speaking* (pp. 174–187). Routledge.

Ye, J., Zhao, L., Huang, Z., & Meng, F. (2021). The audience-tuning effect of negative stereotypes in communication. *Frontiers in Psychology, 12*, 663814.

12 Researching Listening Outcomes

12.1 Introduction: Posing Questions to Identify Variables	326
12.2 Input Variables	330
12.2.1 Input Source Variables	*331*
12.2.2 Input Genres	*332*
12.2.3 Discourse Types	*332*
12.2.4 Project: Making Input Choices	*333*
12.3 Intervention Variables	336
12.3.1 Project: Comparisons of Instructional Interventions	*337*
12.4 Interaction Variables	339
12.4.1 Project: Comparing Effects of Interaction Types	*344*
12.5 Assessment Variables	345
12.5.1 Project: Creating a Formative Assessment for Listening	*345*
12.6 Course Design Variables	346
12.7 Summary: Using Action Research to Enrich Teaching and Learning	351
References	351

12.1 Introduction: Posing Questions to Identify Variables

The previous chapter explored methods of researching the listening process. This chapter focuses on researching listening outcomes as the result of interventions that aim to modify or amplify listening processes.

Researching listening outcomes of instruction involves exploring instructional choices—of input, interaction, or interventions—that you *believe* (or hypothesize) may lead to better learning outcomes. The purpose of this type of learning outcome research is not, however, to prove a hypothesis, but rather to gain direct insight into the variables that make learning effective.

Research about learning outcomes and listening outcomes generally starts with a question about factors that might impact learners. Here are some questions I have encountered in various teaching situations:

DOI: 10.4324/9781003390794-16

Researching Listening Outcomes 327

1. **Questions about teaching strategies:**
   - How can we effectively integrate technology into our listening instruction to enhance student engagement and learning?

2. **Questions about student engagement:**
   - What can we do to increase active participation and engagement among students during discussions as a post-listening activity?

3. **Questions about differentiation:**
   - How can we adapt and supplement our assigned teaching materials to cater to our students' diverse proficiency levels and learning styles?

4. **Questions about assessment:**
   - How can we design assessment tasks that authentically evaluate students' listening skills other than the standardized tests now in use?

5. **Questions about activity types:**
   - Are there any activity types that tend to be more effective at improving students' listening skills, particularly their bottom-up listening?

6. **Questions about feedback:**
   - How can we provide timely and constructive feedback to students that promotes listening development?

7. **Questions about multilingualism:**
   - How can we best use translanguaging (use of students' L1) in our listening classes?

8. **Questions about communication skills:**
   - How can we create more opportunities for authentic communication (mirror real-life interactions) in our listening classes beyond the usual pedagogic communication?

9. **Questions about classroom culture and classroom management:**
   - How can we create a classroom culture that promotes equality and collaboration?
   - How can we foster a style of classroom management that encourages respect and active participation?

10. **Questions about learner autonomy:**
    - How can we equip students with the skills to source and design their own tasks?

328 *Researching Listening*

- How can we help them to evaluate their own progress in listening?

11. **Questions about cultural competence:**

- How can we integrate more culturally relevant content and perspectives into our listening classes to enhance students' cultural competence?

12. **Questions about integrating other skills:**

- What methods can I employ to help students improve their pronunciation and listening skills at the same time?

All of these questions can be addressed in short order by making a suggestion, such as "Why don't we try … ?" As useful as it is to entertain and try out imaginative variations, action research goes further by attempting to *define variables* (however small) systematically. By observing the effects of changes in instructional decisions on educational outcomes, the teacher begins to adopt an action-research mindset.

Educational outcomes can refer to various effects, not only scores on language tests. In addition to academic achievement and proficiency gains, educational outcomes can also refer to **cognitive skills** (improvements in critical thinking, problem-solving, analytical skills, and information retention; see Zhao et al., 2016); **social and emotional skills** (increases in emotional regulation, empathy, and self-esteem; see Ahmed et al., 2020; Richardson et al., 2009); **attitudes and motivation** (shifts in attitudes toward learning and readiness to engage; see Mercer & Dörnyei, 2020); **behavioral changes** (modifications in study habits and participation; see Kimura, 2022); **creativity and innovation** (fresh approaches to tasks and projects; see Pardede, 2020); **collaboration skills** (willingness to contribute and communicate; see Ghaith & Shaaban, 2005); **cultural competence** (improved appreciation of diverse perspectives; see Kurbanova et al., 2022); **character development** (growth in responsibility, integrity, ethical decision-making, autonomous learning skills, see Teimouri et al., 2022); **global citizenship** (increased understanding of global issues and desire to contribute to societal welfare, see Massaro, 2022); and **health and well-being** (improvements in physical and mental health, see Helgesen, 2016).

Once we have decided on research questions and the outcomes we wish to measure, we need to select among research methods and time frames. The most applicable methods are quasi-experimental design, experimental design, longitudinal studies, case studies, and mixed methods.

- **Quasi-experimental design:** This design involves comparing groups and keeping participants in their natural groupings (such as existing class groups). You want to compare the outcomes of these groups, usually through a preliminary (pre-test) measurement and ending (post-test) measurement, to have a quantitative or qualitative sense of the effects of the treatment.

Researching Listening Outcomes   329

- **Experimental design:** This design also involves comparing groups but with a more scientific assignment to groups that you wish to compare. In experimental designs, participants are randomly assigned to a treatment group (the experimental group) and a control group (the no- treatment group). Random grouping allows you to control for extraneous variables (such as experimenter bias, unintendedly acting differently toward one group, and participant bias, learners self-assigning to groups based on preferences). With random assignment, you are better able to attribute outcomes to a cause-and-effect relationship.
- **Longitudinal studies:** Longitudinal studies involve observing and collecting data from the same participants over an extended period of time, typically the length of a course.
  Collecting data may be either quantitative (scored numerically) or qualitative (evaluated holistically). The data is collected through surveys, questionnaires, journals, assignments, and tests. By looking at behavioral and attitudinal changes at multiple time points, you can track changes in outcomes over time.
- **Case studies:** Case studies focus on in-depth analysis of specific educational programs or specific teachers' teaching styles. Case studies can also focus on individual learners' learning styles, providing rich, detailed information about their outcomes and impacts. Case studies involve primarily qualitative data: peer observation and reflections through journals, questionnaires, and interviews.
- **Mixed-methods research:** When possible, it is advisable to approach research questions through a combination of qualitative and quantitative methods to gain a more comprehensive understanding of educational outcomes and explore both measurable effects and participants' subjective experiences. You can also include meta-analyses—reviews of multiple studies on similar educational studies—to compare results with your own research findings (Cresswell, 2022; Houchins et al., 2022).

The key to conducting valid and valuable action research is keeping clear records of the materials you have used and your actions, so that when you reflect on your research or share your findings with colleagues, everyone has a clear frame of reference for the research. Note that if you are using student data for purposes outside of teaching, obtaining informed consent from participants is a critical ethical requirement. Informed consent ensures that participants are fully informed about the nature of the study, the data being collected, how it will be used, and any potential risks or benefits (see the Resources appendix for more information on research methods).

The choice of research method depends on what your teaching situation will allow and what variables are being investigated. This chapter examines five key variables: (12.2) input variables, (12.3) intervention variables, (12.4) interaction

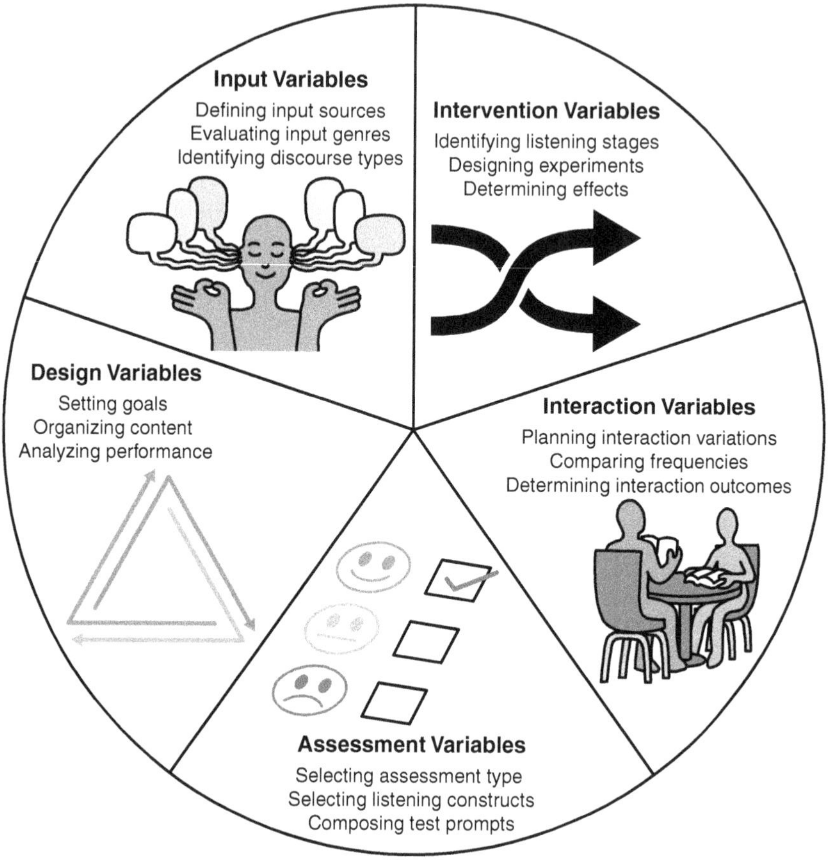

330 *Researching Listening*

Figure 12.1 Researching Listening Outcomes

The five projects in this chapter will focus on different listening outcomes, depending on the nature of the instructional variable that is controlled. Each project will call on the development and use of several research skills

variables, (12.5) assessment variables, and (12.6) course design variables. Each of these explorations includes a suggested research project (see Figure 12.1).

12.2 Input Variables

Teaching listening always involves using spoken input. Choosing input entails making decisions about several variables: sources, genres, and discourse types. Because of the importance of input choices, learning outcomes can be markedly different depending on the selections a teacher makes. These choices will be explored in detail below.

Researching Listening Outcomes   331

Table 12.1 Input Sources

Input source	Potential benefits
Live vs. Recorded	Live listening offers authentic language use and spontaneous communication, while recorded materials provide controlled and repeatable content.
Authentic vs. graded	Authentic listening materials provide exposure to natural language use, while graded listening materials address proficiency levels, gradually increasing in difficulty.
Commercial vs. homemade	Commercial listening materials are professionally polished, while homemade materials are tailored to specific classroom needs, topics, or interests.
Full vs. extracted	Full listening materials include complete speeches, dialogues, or conversations, while extracted materials focus on excerpts to target particular learning goals.
Monologue vs. dialogue (multiparty interactions)	Dialogues and multiparty interactions offer natural conversational language, turn-taking patterns, and often elements of drama and storytelling, while monologues provide extended exposure to continuous speech.
Entertainment-oriented vs. pedagogically oriented	Entertainment-oriented materials engage learners through enjoyable content but may present more complex language, while pedagogically oriented materials are specifically designed for language-learning targets.
Teacher-sourced vs. learner-sourced	Teacher-sourced materials will be carefully selected, contain vetted appropriate content, and will be at an appropriate language level. Learner-sourced materials are unvetted and may not be at an appropriate level, but the content is likely to be motivating for learners. In addition, the process of selecting resources engages students in taking responsibility for their own learning and prepares them for lifelong learning beyond the classroom.

12.2.1 Input Source Variables

The initial choice involves the source of the input. The source of input plays a crucial role in shaping the listening experience for students, as different sources may present different learning benefits or varying cognitive challenges, or differing degrees of familiarity and support. Whatever the teacher's goal, selecting input sources and then deciding how to exploit these sources are the most central decisions that a listening instructor makes.

There are several variables to consider when selecting input sources (see Table 12.1). For each input source choice, there will be potential learning benefits that you may wish to emphasize.

By considering the spectrum of choices and reflecting on the potential benefits for your students, you can focus on selecting the most suitable sources of input. A motivating listening curriculum should align with your students' language

332 *Researching Listening*

proficiency levels, interests, and learning objectives. Often, the optimal solution will be balancing authentic materials with graded ones, combining commercial resources with homemade materials, and so on. (See the Resources section for actual choices of source materials that meet your criteria.)

12.2.2 Input Genres

In Chapter 8, we reviewed multiple genres of input, suggesting potential benefits and offering sample sources. For the research project in this section, we will focus selectively on genres suitable for a young adult and adult population. For each genre choice, indicate one benefit that is most appealing to you and your students. (Revisit the genre choices in Chapter 8, §8.3 for more detail.)

Lectures	Podcasts	Field Trips/Tours
Speeches	Webinars	News
Talks	Social Conversations	Movies
Academic Discussions	Interviews	Dramas
Presentation	Speeches	Music

By considering the spectrum of choices and reflecting on a few potential benefits you wish to have, you can focus on selecting the most suitable genres of input.

12.2.3 Discourse Types

Refining the selection process of inputs for a listening-based course even further, you may also wish to hone in on particular discourse types and rhetorical styles. **Discourse type** refers to different communication styles with distinct structures, purposes, and characteristics. Examples of discourse types include narrative, argumentative, persuasive, expository, descriptive, and informative. **Rhetorical style** relates directly to the strategies used to influence an audience. Rhetorical styles include logic, emotional appeals, credibility, evidence, and rhetorical devices such as metaphors, analogies, and rhetorical questions.

Consider the appropriateness of each discourse type for your students. Select five of these discourse types that you would like to use as input for your listening-based lessons. (Revisit Chapter 8, §.8.3 for more detail on each discourse type and rhetorical style:

Narrative	Expository	Persuasive
Descriptive	Argumentative	Instructional
Conversational	Historical	Comparative
Exploratory	Scientific	Review

Researching Listening Outcomes   333

Problem-Solution	Legal	Interview
Procedural	Technical	Academic
Analytical	Reflective	

Again, by considering the spectrum of choices of discourse types, you can focus on selecting the most suitable types for your students.

12.2.4 Project: Making Input Choices

After considering the spectrum of input choices involving input source, genre, and discourse type, you should be able to narrow down input choices to a reasonable number of options that you favor. You can consider these the results of your personal preference analysis.

Researching which sources of listening material will be well received by your own students, however, involves *an additional step of needs analysis*. To perform a needs analysis, you need to develop a systematic approach to collect data, analyze student needs, preferences, and learning styles, and then, as the course proceeds, evaluate the effectiveness of the chosen listening materials.

Here's a step-by-step guide to conducting this type of research:

- **Conduct a needs/interest analysis:** Although needs analyses in language courses will start by assessing proficiency levels, an input-oriented needs analysis will focus on questions of interest. Surveys are the most efficient way to gather information.

  Open questions: Interests
  - Which of these activities interest you most? Rank your top five choices: (list of choices of personal interests: sports, arts, gardening, music, media …)
  - What is your favorite _____? (list of media) (music, movie, book, game …)

  Choice questions: Input
  - Which of these topics are most interesting to you? Rank your top five choices: (list of choices of input genres you can source)
  - Which of these (films/documentaries/series) would you like to watch? (List of several titles). Rank your top five choices.

- **Give surveys** to students in two or three cycles, refining your questions. You can use free online tools to generate surveys and compile your data (e.g., **Google Forms, SurveyMonkey, Typeform, Jotform, SoGoLytics**)

334   *Researching Listening*

- **Select a small starting corpus of audio and video materials** you can use that address most students' interests and needs (and also meets your preferences and criteria for suitable material) (cf. Rogowsky et al., 2020). Or have students source their own materials (within set parameters, e.g., a podcast excerpt, a news broadcast excerpt, a song). Students can create a bank of materials for their classmates, which allows you to cater to the special interests of your class.
- **Observe student engagement:** Pay attention to your students' engagement and interest levels during listening activities with your experimental materials. Note which materials elicit the most participation and attentiveness.

RESEARCH TIP: Use Exit Tickets to gauge engagement

Although you can give surveys on student interest during the course, I have found observation and informal questioning are more productive. I sometimes use Exit Tickets, brief, anonymous questions given at the end of a lesson or class (physically in face-to-face classes or virtually in online classes) to assess students' understanding and engagement with the content of the day's lesson.

Exit Ticket Date: _____

Today's listening topic was:

Awful	Not very good	Okay	Really good	Fantastic
☹	☺	⌢	‿	😄

Your comments:

I managed to understand about (0–100%) of the content:

_____

My satisfaction level with my work today is (0–100%):

_____

How do you feel about your listening skills today?

_____

Jo Mynard, Author and Teacher Trainer, Tokyo

Researching Listening Outcomes   335

- **Learning journals or reflections:** Students can write learning journals or reflections on their experiences with different topics, expressing their levels of interest and connection to the content (Curry et al., 2023). For learners with limited L2 proficiency, you can encourage translanguaging resources, perhaps the use of translation programs, such as **Google Translate** or **DeepL**, to allow students to express themselves more fully.
- **Collect data on listening progress:** Track your students' progress in listening comprehension over time. Use pre-and post-assessments to measure their improvement and analyze which materials contribute to their growth. Use self-assessments periodically throughout the course of study to help learners monitor their own progress.

  In addition to engagement criteria, you may also want to measure the learning effect of particular input types. Over time, you might wish to collect data on listening progress through periodic assessments of linguistic processing and semantic processing.
- **Use student reflections:** Encourage students to reflect on their own listening experiences and share their thoughts on what helps them improve their listening skills. When using journaling, it is important to reserve some time at the end of class for personal journal entries, often providing a question prompt, and some time for a dialogic loop, periodically collecting and commenting on entries. Some prompts that tend to stimulate students' reflection include:

  - **Looking back** (What kinds of listening have you done outside of class most often? How satisfied are you with your comprehension?)
  - **Looking in** (Why do you feel this way? How suitable are these listenings and activities for your level/interests/goals?)
  - **Looking forward** (What changes will you make, if any, to the kinds of listening you do outside of class? How can you increase your comprehension?)
  - **Taking action** (What action will you take from today? How will you know if you have achieved your goal?) (Curry et al., 2023; Krivosheyeva et al., 2020)

- **Compare progress across materials:** Conduct a comparative analysis of students' progress when exposed to various types of listening materials (e.g., authentic vs. graded, dialogues vs. monologues). To do this in a valid manner, you need to give the same type of assessment across different input materials, realizing that you will not be able to measure everything the students have learned. For instance, you might choose vocabulary acquisition as a stable measurement across genres.

336 *Researching Listening*

RESEARCH TIP: Code your input choices

Genre and discourse type are the two most obvious classifications of input, but there are other hidden input elements that can impact the pedagogical value of input.

For instance, in a podcast episode on "Games" (from Radiolab) that I used (excerpted parts) for a listening class, I coded it this way for my records.

Input: Games
Source: Radiolab https://radiolab.org
Speakers: Eric Simmons (host: Stephen Dubner)
Language: (SAE) American English
Length: 58"
Extract used: 7:15–12:05
Topic: What makes an engaging game? What makes certain games "more than a game"?
Subtopics: Family traditions, fandom
Orientation: Males, athletes
Culture: Gaming. "guy culture", American
Style: Informal
Speed: 160 wpm (avg)–fast

**Kara McBride, Senior Technical Educational
Specialist, World Learning**

12.3 Intervention Variables

While choosing input sources is the basis of successful listening instruction, deciding when and how to intervene as students are listening is *the decisive factor* in getting the most learning value out of the input you choose. As outlined in Chapter 9, there are several defined intervention points—pre-listening, while-listening, and post-listening—at which you can introduce some form of interaction. This can be students interacting with other students to explore what they have understood or students interacting with the text via a task you have designed. Over time, students can also design their own pre-/while/post-listening tasks as training for independent learning.

In this section, we will frame the research project around Content and Language Integrated Learning (CLIL). CLIL is an approach to language teaching where listening and language learning are integrated with the study of subject matter content (Domke et al., 2022; Mahan, 2022).

Table 12.2 Intervention Variables Summary

Research focus

Investigate the impact of various **input characteristics** (such as lecture length, delivery style, speed, content and cultural complexity, syntactic and organizational complexity, and speaker intelligibility) on listener comprehension and retention.

Investigate the effects of **pre-listening activities** (such as activating prior knowledge of the topic and vocabulary knowledge, priming with advance organizers).

Investigate how **while-listening activities** influence listeners' retention and recall. Look at the effects of guided note-taking, providing opportunities to ask questions during the presentation, note-taking strategies, reprocessing content through follow-up discussions, and guided information-oriented tasks, such as filling in charts and graphs.

Investigate the effects of **post-listening activities** on retention and recall. Look at structured content-based conversations and peer review of notes taken.

Investigate how accurately and fully listeners retain and recall information from a lecture. Examine the extent to which listeners can retain and recall the information presented in a lecture immediately after, as well as over time. Explore factors that may affect information retention, such as note-taking strategies, engagement levels, and the presence of distractions.

Investigate the effects of various **delivery methods** and **technological enhancements** on learner engagement, lecture comprehension, and learning outcomes. Explore the use of subtitles (monolingual or bilingual), speed modification, replay of selected parts and/or interactive quizzes, and online discussion boards.

Investigate the effects of **post-listening structured discussions** on comprehension and retention.

Listening plays a central role in CLIL. Since the content being taught is often presented through spoken language, often in conjunction with reading, listening comprehension becomes an essential pathway for students to understand the subject matter at hand.

In CLIL, students are exposed to lectures, discussions, audio materials, and multimedia content related to the subject, which in turn helps them improve their listening skills. By improving their listening skills, students then become more proficient in understanding, analyzing, and communicating about the content they are studying, making their learning experience more fruitful and rewarding (Lynch, 2011; Villabona & Cenoz, 2022).

Because of the powerful role of listening in all forms of instruction, but especially in CLIL, a number of intervention variables can be explored with the aim improve teaching and learning practices (see Table 12.2).

12.3.1 Project: Comparisons of Instructional Interventions

In this type of research project, you are taking snapshots, or observing slices, of the learner experience based on the adjustment of particular variables. There are

338   *Researching Listening*

limitations to the applications of this type of research, but it can provide immediate insight into the value of instructional decisions.

The basic procedure requires preparing two versions of the same content on video. In each version, you need to vary the delivery style and pace or add complexity to one version. Give one version to one student group and the other version to the other student group. The groups should be comparable in terms of language proficiency. Give both groups identical post-listening tasks or comprehension tests.

Conduct controlled experiments to manipulate specific variables and observe their effects on listening comprehension. For example, you can design experiments to investigate the impact of attentional processes, working memory capacity, or syntactic cues on listeners' ability to comprehend spoken information.

Conduct in-context experiments with two comparable groups of students in which you manipulate (control for) one or more instructional (treatment) variables to observe the treatment's relative effects.

For example, in academic training programs I have directed, colleagues have often participated in action research to test various hypotheses about which methods or materials are more effective. As mentioned earlier, the purpose of action research is not to prove a hypothesis or publish a study but rather to gain intuition about the variables in instruction. Gains in intuition allow us to make instructional choices more consciously and allow for informed negotiation with colleagues about curriculum decisions.

The most basic technique of action research regarding instructional interventions is to prepare two versions of input and/or listening tasks. The modified method is given to the experimental group, and the unmodified or default method is given to the control group. Using the same post-tests, plus follow-up questionnaires, with students, compare your findings.

Here are some separate experiments I have instigated in quasi-experimental settings in which colleagues and I presented the working results and recommendations at our weekly teacher meetings.

Group 1 (experimental group)	*Group 2 (control group)*
Has access to audio script while listening	Does not have access to audio script while listening
Receives a vocabulary preview before listening	Receives a vocabulary preview before listening
Has a structured listening task to do while listening	Is not given a task to do while listening
Hears the audio text at x 0.75 (slowed) speed	Hears the audio text at x 1.0 (normal) speed

Group 1 (experimental group)	Group 2 (control group)
Hears a simplified version of the text (linguistic and lexical complexity altered)	Hears the original text
Hears an elaborated version of the text (paraphrases, examples added)	Hears the original text

Quantitative methods: If you are able to structure a quasi-experimental approach (i.e., experimenting with existing groups of learners), measure the effects of different treatment variables. To measure a specific effect, give the same post-test (dependent variable) to both groups of students to observe whether there is a significant difference on a comprehension test or performance on related tasks.

- Conduct a t-test: Use statistical software to perform an independent samples t-test. The test calculates the t-value by comparing the means of the two groups while considering the sample sizes and variances. The t-value is then compared to a critical value based on the desired significance level (e.g., $\alpha = 0.05$) to determine statistical significance.
- Interpret the results: Examine the p-value associated with the t-test. If the p-value is below the chosen significance level, typically 0.05, you reject the null hypothesis and conclude that there is a significant difference between the means of the two groups. Conversely, if the p-value is above the significance level, you fail to reject the null hypothesis and conclude that there is no significant difference.
- Share your results: Whatever your conclusions and interpretations, share the results with your colleagues and your students. Both colleagues and students will appreciate that you are trying to improve the learning outcomes and create a more positive learning experience.

Qualitative methods: If you are unable to use experimental methods to measure the relative effects of different forms of instruction, you can simply use the experimental version of the treatment without the control group (e.g., hearing a simplified or slowed-down version of a lecture) and, using a written questionnaire, ask students to reflect on their experiences with different versions of input.

12.4 Interaction Variables

Interaction variables refer to the contexts and conditions that govern the ways that learners interact orally with each other. As we have reviewed in our survey of approaches to teaching listening (Chapter 7), learner interaction plays a

340   *Researching Listening*

crucial role in listening development and language acquisition. The exchange of personal information and the negotiation of meaning in a wide range of conversational exchanges provides learners with opportunities to receive feedback, modify their output, and notice gaps in their language knowledge. This interaction process pushes them to express themselves more fully and more precisely and attempt to comprehend increasingly complex exchanges, which fuels motivation and a greater willingness to communicate.

Incorporating learner–learner interaction into listening instruction not only provides more listening opportunities but also highlights the importance of output, particularly when there is a defined task outcome that the learners share. The design of instructional tasks is a critical variable in interaction-based teaching.

This research project helps us examine the different characteristics of interaction and measure the effectiveness of various interaction task structures.

We will look at several interaction structures that occur in language classes:

1. **Scripted conversation:**   A scripted conversation is a controlled pair speaking-listening practice in which both parties have access to full information. This promotes a kind of security for those learners who need support before attempting spontaneous conversations.

   - Purpose: The central goal of a scripted conversation is to encourage learners to rehearse speaking in a controlled way.
   - Task structure: In a scripted conversations, two learners work face to face. They both have the same scripted two-party conversation in front of them. They each take a role and practice the conversation.
   - Example dialogue:

     Man (answering his phone): Hello.
     Woman: Hi, Reese. It's Emily. I'm wondering...what are you doing Friday night?
     Man: Oh, hi, Emily! Good to hear from you. Um, Friday night? I always work late on Fridays.
     Woman: Oh, that's right. I forgot. How about … Saturday?
     Man: Saturday is open. I never work on weekends.
     Woman: Oh, good. Would you like to go out for dinner?
     Man: Dinner? Saturday? Sounds good.
     Woman: Wonderful.
     (from *English Firsthand 1*, Helgesen et al., 2018, p. 30)

   In order to provide **presentation variations** on a completely scripted conversation, you can have students add substitutions or add personal comments. Alternatively, you can present the script with gaps, presenting only keywords or every other word. In order to provide **practice**

Researching Listening Outcomes   341

variations, you can have the students practice once using the script, and the second time from memory. Or you can use the "read and look up" technique: Look down to read your line. Look up (at your partner) to deliver your line.

2. **Information gap task:** An information gap task is an interaction structure in which two participants have complementary sets of information. They exchange the information they have in order to complete a mutual task.

   - Purpose: The central goal of an information gap task is to encourage learners to exchange information verbally and negotiate to fill in missing pieces of information.
   - Task structure: In an information gap task, two learners work face to face. Each has a different set of information, and they must ask and answer questions to share their information and complete the task together.
   - Example: Each member of the pair (A and B) has different pictures; they have to identify discrepancies between the pictures through oral negotiation only.

   To offer **presentation variations,** provide several conversation gambits that students can use in the activity, model the pronunciation, and have students repeat. To create **practice variations**, have a rule that A and B must take turns talking, each asking one question at a time. You can also add time limits.

3. **Opinion gap task:** An opinion gap task is an interaction structure in which two participants have the same input and questions posed to them but are likely to have differing outlooks on the issue. They exchange their opinions in order to complete a task or answer a question, often as simple as "Do you agree or disagree with each other?"

   - Purpose: The primary objective of an opinion gap task is to foster learners' ability to express and understand opinions on specific topics.
   - Task structure: In an opinion gap task, learners are given a controversial or thought-provoking statement or question. They need to discuss and justify their viewpoints on the topic, leading to exchanges of opinions. Specific conversational gambits can be provided to guide the exchange.
   - Example: After listening to an extract in which two people discuss the value of learning English, learners are presented with a question like "Do you think everyone needs to learn English? Give your reasons." They discuss their opinions and reasons for their ideas.

   Variations

   - Add a checklist of question options
   - Have students rotate pairs for task repetition

342 *Researching Listening*

4. **Experience gap task:** An experience gap task is a conversation structure in which two or more participants have the same input but due to differences in their prior experiences, they will respond differently. The participants ask questions and respond to each other in order to complete a mutual task.

- Purpose: An experience gap task encourages learners to share their personal experiences, anecdotes, or stories related to a particular theme or topic.
- Task structure: In an experience gap task, learners share their experiences in pairs or small groups. The focus is on using language to narrate past events or describe personal encounters. The listeners are encouraged to ask questions to understand more fully.
- Example: Learners discuss a personal topic such as "Describe a time when you faced a challenging situation and how you managed to overcome it."

Variations

- Have students prepare what they wish to say (mental rehearsal or writing notes)
- Have students rotate partners. (Original information for each listener; opportunity for the speaker to gain fluency and accuracy with each repetition)

5. **Probing conversations:** A probing conversation is a pedagogic structure designed to lead students into conversations that probe the underlying thinking and experiences of the participants. This effect is achieved through elicitation of emotional support for understanding diverse viewpoints and through modeling and providing gambits that guide these deeper conversations.

- Purpose: Through academic conversations, students learn to articulate their thinking, query their thinking and the thinking of others, and listen to each other. Learning to have deeper conversations helps students develop socio-emotional skills—they become more confident, empathetic, and comfortable interacting with others.
- Task structure: Students work in small groups. They are given prompts, questions to ask each other about an extract they have just heard, and gambits to paraphrase ideas and confirm understanding.
- Example (for more advanced students):

Student A: **What do you think is the main theme of the story?**
Student B: I think the main theme is courage. The story teaches us about courage.
Student A: **Can you elaborate? What makes you think that?**
Student B: Well, I think Marco's decision to go back and confront his father took a lot of courage.
Student A: Yeah, going back took courage. **I see what you mean. But what do you mean by** "confront his father?" **Can you be more specific?**

Researching Listening Outcomes 343

Variations

• Provide a menu of conversational gambits.

Analyses of probing conversations and collaborative academic-style discussions have identified several teachable features contributing to productive, probing conversations. In most analyses, six structured conversational strategies are considered both effective and teachable:

- Frame and reframe topics and subtopics
- Elaborate and clarify points
- Support ideas with evidence
- Paraphrase and recap
- Build on or challenge your partner's idea
- Apply the idea to a real-world context

6. **Pedagogic conversations:** A pedagogic conversation is one in which one party is teaching something or explaining an idea to a listener.

- Purpose: A pedagogic conversation is generally in the form of the teacher providing instruction to an individual student or group of students.
- Task structure: In a pedagogic conversation, the student generally speaks very little—often less than 10% of the conversation. The students may ask clarification questions or respond to the teacher's questions.
- Example: Teacher is explaining the use of present perfect tense: *So, in this case, you would say, "I've lived in Tokyo all my life," not "I live in Tokyo all my life." This is because the action started in the past and is continuing even now, so we use the present perfect "have lived." Do you understand?* (Student nods.)

7. **Free conversation:** Free conversation is an unstructured and spontaneous exchange of ideas, thoughts, and information between individuals. There is no specific topic or task agenda, and all participants have equal rights to contribute.

- Purpose: Through free conversation, participants get to know each other better and build social ties.
- Task structure: In free conversation, one person asks a question, makes a comment, or throws out a topic, and others respond, often with levity or humor.
- Example: "How are you doing today?" "Not bad. How about you?" "What did you do this weekend?" "Oh, I went to …" In classroom settings, free conversations are often controlled by the instructor, who may nominate students to respond. For example, "Happy Monday, everybody. I hope you all had a great weekend. How was your weekend, Francisco?"

344   *Researching Listening*

12.4.1 Project: Comparing Effects of Interaction Types

To understand the relative value of different interaction types, it is helpful to set up observations and reflections on the frequency of each type of interaction.

Create a case study related to the use of interaction types in your classroom. A case study carried out (ideally) over an extended period of time provides an in-depth analysis of specific interventions.

To begin, record a typical class, your own or that of a colleague who is cooperating with you on this case study, on video (preferred for fuller analysis, but more cumbersome) or audio (less intrusive, but requires more reconstruction of context).

Do an approximate timing analysis for each type of interaction in the entire class period.

Type of interaction	Times	Total time/percentage
Scripted conversation		
Information gap task		
Opinion gap task		
Experience gap task		
Probing conversation		
Pedagogic conversation		
Free conversation		
Silence/nonspeaking activity		

Following this approximative analysis, place the types of interaction into a gradient. Comment on the purpose of each type of interaction in the specific class.

Frequency	Avg. Duration	Approx % Class time	Purpose	Notes
Most frequent =7				
6				
5				
4				
3				
2				
Least frequent = 1				

Record a series of classes and complete a rough analysis of frequencies, making notes as you go along. Reflect on your notes over the course of your

Researching Listening Outcomes 345

study. Which types of interaction do you find most valuable? Which types of interaction do your students find most valuable? What changes in instruction would be needed to provide an adjustment of interaction types that provide a more desirable outcome?

12.5 Assessment Variables

Assessments are needed by both instructors and students to evaluate students' understanding, performance, and learning progress. There are several types of assessments, but two of the most common types are formative and summative assessments.

Formative assessment is an ongoing and continuous process used during the learning process to monitor students' progress and provide feedback that helps improve their performance and motivation. Examples of formative assessments include class discussions, quizzes, polls, one-on-one feedback sessions, self-assessments, and group activities.

Summative assessment, on the other hand, is usually conducted only at the end of a specific period, such as a unit of instruction on a particular topic or at the end of a course or academic year, to evaluate students' overall learning and performance. Examples of summative assessments include final exams, standardized tests, end-of-course projects, and external assessments like formally sanctioned exams.

Aside from these two broad categories, other types of assessments that are commonly used in educational settings include diagnostic assessments, to identify students' strengths, weaknesses, and prior knowledge; criterion-referenced assessments, to measure students' performance against predetermined criteria or standards, like course objectives; and performance assessments to allow students to demonstrate their knowledge and skills through real-world tasks or projects. These assessments are often more authentic and practical in nature than traditional tests and can include presentations, portfolios, exhibitions, or simulations.

12.5.1 Project: Creating a Formative Assessment for Listening

This research project explores the composition of formative listening assessments that are commonly used in listening-based classes (refer to Chapter 10, §10.6 for a review of listening constructs). We want to examine the coverage and validity of the assessments we use to make assessment writing more transparent.

For this project, we will compose multiple assessment types that aim to evaluate how well students have understood an input.

346 *Researching Listening*

Some assessment types to consider for this project:

1. **Post-listening comprehension questions** (multiple choice, True/False, gap-fills, etc.)
2. **While-listening note-taking:** Ask learners to take notes while listening to an audio recording, and later, they answer questions or summarize the content based on their notes.
3. **Post-listening retelling or summarizing:** Learners listen to an audio passage and then retell or summarize the main points or key information.
4. **While-listening tasks:** Provide worksheets with questions or tasks (e.g., completing a chart) related to the audio, and learners respond in writing.
5. **Dictation:** Play an audio recording, and learners write down what they hear, testing both listening and writing skills.
6. **Listening response journal:** Learners keep a journal to record their reactions, thoughts, or questions after listening to audio materials.
7. **Listening comprehension interviews:** Conduct one-on-one interviews to assess learners' listening comprehension and ability to respond to questions.
8. **Self-assessment:** Encourage learners to reflect on their own listening progress, strengths, and areas for improvement.

Prepare one input and at least three different assessment types to assess students' comprehension of the input. Compare your students' scores on the assessments. Is there a correlation between their performance on each type of assessment? If not, what factors are contributing to the lack of correlation?

12.6 Course Design Variables

The most comprehensive set of variables that instructors must decide upon is course design: how to construct sequences of instruction that assure sustained progress in listening. Throughout this book, we have treated listening as involving four domains: neurological, linguistic, semantic, and pragmatic.

We can therefore think of instruction as selectively spotlighting specific domains through course design:

Neurological: Developing whole-person listening, integrated listening activities, linking language activities with life skills
Linguistic: Developing bottom-up linguistic knowledge and decoding skills: phonological, lexical, syntactic
Semantic: Developing top-down semantic knowledge and comprehension skills: lexical, schematic, and reasoning
Pragmatic: Developing bottom-up sensitivity and perception and top-down knowledge and interpretation skills: discourse, speaker, and response

Designing a course—or evaluating a course that has already been designed—involves weighing the relative treatments of each of these four domains.

This part of the chapter will deal with designing an autonomous listening course, one with minimal teacher intervention during the listening activities, and deciding on the inclusion of elements that address each domain in a balanced way.

Teachers in virtually all instructional contexts need to include autonomous learning components for various reasons. For instance, they may want to provide additional instruction, individualize lessons, allow for remedial work, introduce variety, offer more outlets for communication, collaboration, and creativity, allow access to high-quality distance learning and network-based learning, or promote experimentation with new technologies. By adding autonomous learning components, they provide training for lifelong learning, so that students can continue to set goals, choose appropriate texts, use appropriate tasks, and reflect on their progress long after they finish a specific course (Mynard, 2020; Peeters & Mynard, 2019).

Though the potential benefits of autonomous learning are far-reaching, autonomous learning programs are not a panacea for teaching languages and, in my experience, never a wholesale substitute for teacher-mediated instruction. Indeed, an autonomous learning program with randomly selected resources or minimal instructor involvement is bound to fail, leaving the learners who undertook the program less motivated and *less likely* to become autonomous learners (Leenknecht et al., 2021; Yen & Waring, 2022).

An autonomous listening-based course is likely to be successful only if it is approached as an iterative research project. In an iterative course design, the designer (teacher) will undertake a series of refinements to continue to improve the process and the outcomes—essentially to improve student engagement and proficiency gains. The research is in documenting the design-feedback–redesign loop. Key steps include engaging learners in setting listening goals, having learners select some of their own materials, setting realistic tasks, and reflecting on the process (Stock & Kolb, 2021).

Engagement and interaction—measured through direct student feedback and time on task—is the mantra for autonomous course design: We keep coming back to it to guide us when we lose track of our purpose. Designing an autonomous listening course involves providing engaging and interactive content that allows the learner to practice their listening skills independently. Several key variables can be manipulated to amplify learning outcomes (see Table 12.3).

Remember that an autonomous listening course should empower learners to take control of their learning progress. It should offer flexibility, engaging content, and opportunities for practice and self-assessment, ultimately fostering their listening skills and strategies in understanding spoken English.

348 *Researching Listening*

Table 12.3 Design Variables Summary

Action point	Research process
Assessment and goal setting: Start by assessing the learner's current listening proficiency and their language-learning goals, and by helping learners understand these goals as well.	• Assessment of listening skills. • Questionnaire about learning goals, time committed to listening activities each week.
Selecting content: With learner input, curate a diverse range of listening materials appropriate for the learner's level, interests, and objectives.	• Survey of learners' topical and genre interests. • Survey of available materials, those freely available and necessary subscriptions.
Organizing content: Structure the course into manageable units or modules. Label each unit module or listening experience by the time required to complete. Each module can focus on a particular theme. Grade the content by difficulty.	• Give an approximate difficulty index. Use existing indexes or create your own based on a combination of these difficulty criteria: FORCAST (Formula for Assessing the Complexity of Spoken Text); LIX (Listening Index); Lexile Framework; SPACHE Readability Formula for Speech; Simplified Oral Reading Formula (SORF); Listenability Metrics in Automatic Speech Recognition (ASR) Systems. It is also useful to have colleagues rate content by difficulty level and aim for inter-rater reliability using Cohen's kappa or the intraclass correlation coefficient (ICC). You can also have students rate each extract in terms of difficulty and include their ratings in your grading scheme.
Pre-listening activities: Before each listening exercise, provide some context and pre-listening activities to prepare the learners for what they are going to listen to.	To maintain variety in exercise types, which is important for autonomous courses to help learners develop metacognitive awareness, consider developing several types of pre-listening activities and using a randomization procedure to select two such activities for each listening extract (e.g., https://www.randomizer.org/#randomize)

Researching Listening Outcomes 349

Table 12.3 (Continued)

Action point	Research process
Listening exercises: Offer at least one specific listening exercise or task for each input. Some ideas include: • Multiple-choice questions related to the audio. • Answering open-ended comprehension questions. • Fill-in-the-blank exercises to test recognition of specific vocabulary. • True-or-false statements based on the content. • Summarizing or retelling the audio in their own words. For longer extracts, summarizing can be done for small sections or episodes.	To maintain the validity of listening items, consider using a Discrimination Index Calculation, which involves comparing the performance of a mastery group (or advanced portion of your class group) with an entry group (or beginner portion of your class group). The discrimination index is calculated using the following formula: Discrimination Index = Percentage of Top Group Correct - Percentage of Bottom Group Correct The result can range from -1 to +1: • A positive discrimination index (closer to +1) indicates that the item is effective at differentiating between high and low performers. In other words, more high-performing students answered the item correctly compared to low-performing students. • A negative discrimination index (closer to -1) suggests that the item is problematic and may be confusing for test takers. More low-performing students answered the item correctly compared to high-performing students. • A discrimination index close to 0 suggests that the item does not effectively discriminate between high and low performers.
Motivational elements: Incorporate motivational elements (gamification elements) like badges, stickers, points, or rewards for completing modules, maintaining an active daily streak, or achieving specific milestones. This will keep learners motivated and engaged.	To see whether particular gamification elements are working, you may wish to try **performance assessments.** Compare students' performance before and after the implementation of gamification elements. Analyze academic outcomes and learning achievements to assess whether there are any noticeable improvements.

(Continued)

350 *Researching Listening*

Table 12.3 (Continued)

Action point	Research process
Motivational elements: Incorporate motivational elements (gamification elements) like badges, stickers, points, or rewards for completing modules, maintaining an active daily streak, or achieving specific milestones. This will keep learners motivated and engaged.	To see whether particular gamification elements are working, you may wish to try **performance assessments.** Compare students' performance before and after the implementation of gamification elements. Analyze academic outcomes and learning achievements to assess whether there are any noticeable improvements. You may also wish to try using **engagement metrics.** These analytics measure how actively students participate in learning activities. They may include data on the frequency and duration of logins, time spent on specific learning resources, and the number of interactions with course materials.
Feedback and self-assessment: Encourage self-assessment by providing answer keys or explanations for exercises. Employ self-assessment scales so that students can monitor their progress over time (e.g., using prompts such as the percentage of content understood). Offer constructive feedback to help learners identify areas for improvement.	Periodically, you will want to have some type of **performance analysis.** You will want to assess gains in proficiency as a (partial) result of the autonomous listening program. You may wish to use pre- and post-test measures (in which the pre- and post-tests are evidenced to be parallel). You may also want to employ usage analytics. Utilize learning analytics to track how often learners engage with feedback and self-assessment activities. Analyze the data to see if higher engagement correlates with improved performance. It is also useful to have some platform for community and support. Provide access to a supportive community or forum where learners can interact, share their experiences with the autonomous listening course, and ask questions and provide feedback.
Regular updates and fresh content: Keep the course up to date, with new content and fresh materials to sustain learners' interest and accommodate their evolving language needs.	One vital aid in keeping course content and processes up to date and responsive to learners' needs is **learning journal analysis.** Encourage learners to maintain learning journals in which they can reflect on their listening progress, self-assessment experiences, and any changes in their understanding of spoken English. Analyze these journals to gain qualitative insights into the impact of the feedback and self-assessment.

12.7 Summary: Using Action Research to Enrich Teaching and Learning

This chapter, the final chapter in this book on teaching and researching listening, is intended to empower teachers to utilize all their knowledge about listening as they examine and develop their own teaching practices. Action research is a systematic approach to inquiry and problem-solving that involves conducting basic research to address practical issues and improve current practices, in our case, teaching practices

As we have indicated in this chapter, the goal of listening instruction and EAL (English as an additional language) instruction in general is *not only* to produce quantitative improvements in students' scores on concrete assessments. As we have indicated, there are several valuable goals to work toward in learning a new language, such as developing social and emotional skills, cultural competence, and metacultural proficiency, as well as expanding character development. While we are working toward these multiple goals, it is important to measure language-learning outcomes. This chapter has focused on five avenues of practical action research projects for assessing learner outcomes in listening-based instruction. As teachers, we need to see progress in our teaching; our learners also need to see their own progress, as progress becomes a fuel for their own confidence and motivation to learn.

For many of us, teaching is a challenge, and adding the responsibility of action research to it may seem to be overwhelming. Paradoxically, the opposite often seems to be the case: Teachers who carry out action research tend to be more satisfied and less stressed. Teachers can carry out action research, even if on a limited basis, to better understand the teaching-learning process and make positive changes in their practice that will impact their own well-being and that of their students.

The research projects in this chapter are designed in this spirit of action research: with a sense of curiosity and exploration, a desire to make a positive impact on our students, a practical focus, a participatory approach, a desire for empowerment and change, and the inclusion of reflective practice.

The five projects outlined in this chapter correspond to the major teaching topics covered in this book: **input, intervention, interaction, assessment**, and **design**. My hope is that by engaging in these projects, you, the reader, will gain greater insight into listening instruction, and that this sense of discovery will lead you to a heightened sense of purpose in your teaching and research.

References

Ahmed, I., Hamzah, A. B., & Abdullah, M. N. L. Y. B. (2020). Effect of social and emotional learning approach on students' social-emotional competence. *International Journal of Instruction*, *13*(4), 663–676.

352 *Researching Listening*

Cresswell, J. (2022). *A concise introduction to mixed methods research.* SAGE.

Curry, N., Lyon, P. Y., & Mynard, J. (2023). *Promoting reflection on language learning: Lessons from a university setting.* Multilingual Matters.

Domke, L. M., May, L. A., Kung, M., Coleman, L., Vo, M., & Bingham, G. E. (2022). Preservice teachers learning to integrate language within content instruction in dual language classrooms. *Journal of Multilingual and Multicultural Development*, 1–17. doi: 10.1080/01434632.2022.2117817

Ghaith, G. M., & Shaaban, K. A. (2005). Cooperative learning for the disaffected ESL/ EFL learner. *International Journal on School Disaffection*, *3*(2), 44–47.

Helgesen, M. (2016). Happiness in ESL/EFL: Bringing positive psychology to the classroom. In P. D. MacIntyre, T. Gregersen, & S. Mercer (Eds.), *Positive psychology in SLA* (pp. 305–323). De Gruyter.

Helgesen, M., Wiltshier, J., & Brown, S. (2018). *English firsthand 1* (5th ed.). Pearson.

Houchins, D. E., Marsh, R. J., & Tanner, E. K. (2022). An introduction to mixed methods special education research. In *Handbook of Special Education Research* (Vol. 1, pp. 187–203). Routledge.

Kimura, H. (2022). Interpersonally mediated: Metacognition at work. *MindBrainEd* (Web site). https://www.mindbrained.org/2022/09/interpersonally-mediated-metaco gnition-at-work/

Krivosheyeva, G., Zuparova, S., & Shodiyeva, N. (2020). Interactive way to further improve teaching listening skills. *Academic Research in Educational Sciences*, (3), 520–525.

Kurbanova, F. K., Botirova, M., & Abdurahmonova, S. (2022). Promoting learning and developing cultural competence. *Academic Research in Educational Sciences*, *3*(3), 914–917.

Leenknecht, M., Wijnia, L., Köhlen, M., Fryer, L., Rikers, R., & Loyens, S. (2021). Formative assessment as practice: The role of students' motivation. *Assessment & Evaluation in Higher Education*, *46*(2), 236–255.

Lynch, T. (2011). Academic listening in the 21st century: Reviewing a decade of research. *Journal of English for Academic Purposes*, *10*(2), 79–88.

Massaro, V. R. (2022). Global citizenship development in higher education institutions: A systematic review of the literature. *Journal of Global Education and Research*, *6*(1), 98–114.

Mercer, S., & Dörnyei, Z. (2020). *Engaging language learners in contemporary classrooms.* Cambridge University Press.

Mynard, J. (2020). Advising for language learner autonomy: Theory, practice, and future directions. In M. Jiménez Raya & F. Vieira (Eds.), *Autonomy in language education: Theory, research and practice* (pp. 46–62). Routledge. https://doi.org/10.4324/ 9780429261336

Pardede, P. (2020). Integrating the 4Cs into EFL Integrated Skills Learning. *Journal of English Teaching*, *6*(1), 71–85.

Peeters, W., & Mynard, J. (2019). Peer collaboration and learner autonomy in online interaction spaces. *Relay Journal*, *2*(2), 450–458.

Richardson, R. C., Tolson, H., Huang, T. Y., & Lee, Y. H. (2009). Character education: Lessons for teaching social and emotional competence. *Children & Schools*, *31*(2), 71–78.

Rogowsky, B. A., Calhoun, B. M., & Tallal, P. (2020). Providing instruction based on students' learning style preferences does not improve learning. *Frontiers in Psychology, 11*, 164.

Stock, K. L., & Kolb, D. (2021). The experiencing scale: An experiential learning gauge of engagement in learning. *Experiential Learning & Teaching in Higher Education, 4*(1), 3–21.

Teimouri, Y., Plonsky, L., & Tabandeh, F. (2022). L2 grit: Passion and perseverance for second-language learning. *Language Teaching Research, 26*(5), 893–918.

Villabona, N., & Cenoz, J. (2022). The integration of content and language in CLIL: A challenge for content-driven and language-driven teachers. *Language, Culture and Curriculum, 35*(1), 36–50.

Yen, T. T. N. & Waring, R. (2022). Narrow listening as a method to improve EFL learners' listening comprehension. *PASAA: Journal of Language Teaching and Learning in Thailand, 64*, 194–215.

Zhao, C., Pandian, A., & Singh, M. K. M. (2016). Instructional strategies for developing critical thinking in EFL classrooms. *English Language Teaching, 9*(10), 14–21.

Section IV

Resources

The preceding sections have gone into depth in defining listening, exploring the acquisition of listening ability, and outlining ways to teach listening and research oral language development. This final section offers supplementary resources related to teaching and researching listening.

You will find consulting these sources to be very productive, particularly as a supplement to explorations on teaching issues or research questions.

The Resources are organized into two parts:

Resources for Teaching Listening

Input sources
Practice sources
Practice ideas from polyglots

Resources for Researching Listening

Guidelines for conducting qualitative research
Guidelines for conducting quantitative research
   Tutorials in applied statistics
Guidelines for conducting mixed methods research

DOI: 10.4324/9781003390794-17

Resources for Teaching Listening

Input Sources

Children

Stories

- **Nursery Rhymes** (NurseryRhymes.org)
  https://www.nurseryrhymes.org/nursery-rhymes.html

- **The Bump Rhymes** (Rose Walano, "23 Nursery Rhymes Your Little One Will Love," TheBump.Com, January 30, 2024)
  https://www.thebump.com/a/nursery-rhymes

- **International nursery rhymes** ("International Rhymes," AllNurseryRhymes.com)
  https://allnurseryrhymes.com/nursery-rhymes/international-rhymes/

- **Learn with Homer** ("Stories," LearnwithHomer.com)
  https://learnwithhomer.com/library/stories/

- **Reedsy Prompts** ("900+ Bedtime Short Stories to Read," Reedsy Blog)
  https://blog.reedsy.com/short-stories/bedtime/

- **Tell-a-Tale** (Meenakshi S., "20 Stories to Read Aloud to Your Kids at Bedtime," Tell-a-Tale.com, n.d.)
  https://www.tell-a-tale.com/best-20-bedtime-night-time-stories-children-indian-american/

- **Free Children Stories** ("Stories for Kids Ages 8–10," FreeChildrenStories.com)
  https://www.freechildrenstories.com/age-8-10-1

DOI: 10.4324/9781003390794-18

358   *Resources*

Audio Books and Podcasts

- **Kidmunicate** ("100+ Children's Books for Speech Language Development," Kidmunicate.com)
https://kidmunicate.com/100-childrens-books-for-speech-language-deve
lopment/

- **Common Sense Media selections** ("Great Audiobooks for Kids")
https://www.commonsensemedia.org/lists/great-audiobooks-for-kids

- **Story Pod** ("What Comes Next? Digestible Parenting Knowledge," StoryPod.com)
https://www.storypod.com/blogs/what-comes-next/the-top-10-children-s-
audiobooks-and-podcasts-your-kids-will-love

- **Kids Chatter** (Kids Chatter Speech Pathology, "8 Ways to Use Picture Books to Develop Early Language Skills," KidsChatter.com, September 15, 2017)
https://kidschatter.com.au/how-to-use-picture-books-to-develop-early-langu
age-skills/

Language Development Activities

- **Speech-perception development** ("Activities to Encourage Speech and Language Development," American Speech-Language-Hearing Association)
https://www.asha.org/public/speech/development/activities-to-encourage-
speech-and-language-development/

- **Parent support for language development** (Holly Garcia, "7 Ways to Help Your Child's Language Development," Parents.com, September 29, 2022)
https://www.parents.com/baby/development/talking/9-ways-to-help-your-
childs-language-development/

- **Parenting resources for language support** ("Language Development in Children: 0–8 Years," RaisingChildrenNet.au)
https://raisingchildren.net.au/babies/development/language-development/
language-development-0-8

- **Speech Buddy recommended sites** (Courtenay M., "Top 10 Online Sites for Building Language Skills," SpeechBuddy.com, n.d.)
https://www.speechbuddy.com/blog/speech-therapy-techniques/top-10-onl
ine-sites-for-building-language-skills/

Resources for Teaching Listening 359

Games and Apps

- **Common Sense games** ("Learning to Talk Apps, Games, and Websites," CommonSenseMedia.org)
  https://www.commonsensemedia.org/lists/learning-to-talk-apps-games-and-websites

- **Speech Sisters apps recommendations** (Bridget Hillsberg, "Best Apps for Building Language and Literacy Skills in Young Children," SpeechSisters.com, May 9, 2020)
  https://speechsisters.com/best-apps/

- **Little Bins auditory games** (Sarah McClelland, "75 Awesome Preschool Activities," Little Bins for Little Hands, February 4, 2024)
  https://littlebinsforlittlehands.com/listening-games-auditory-processing-skills/

- **Auditory processing** (Karina Richland, "Improve Auditory Processing with These Fun Activities," Pride Reading Program, May 14, 2023)
  https://pridereadingprogram.com/improve-auditory-processing-with-these-fun-activities/

- **Early Impact: Listening games** ("21 Listening Games for Kids that You've Got to Try," EarlyImpactLearning.com)
  https://earlyimpactlearning.com/21-listening-games-for-kids-that-youve-got-to-try/

Music

- **Speak Play Love: Songs** ("Best Songs for Language Development," SpeakPlayLove.com)
  https://speakplaylove.com/12-childrens-songs-to-help-with-language-development/

- **Speechblubs: Music** (Liz Shoreman, "Music Elevates Your Child's Speech Development," SpeechBlubs.com, February 6, 2022)
  https://speechblubs.com/blog/music-elevates-childs-speech-development/

- **Empowered Music and Movement** (Tanja McIlroy, "Music and Movement for Kids: 26 Fun Activities," Empowered Parents.co, January 18, 2023)
  https://empoweredparents.co/music-and-movement-for-kids/

360   *Resources*

Social Learning

- **Social support** (Olivia Karaolis, "No Strings Attached: Supporting Social and Emotional Learning with Puppets," Edutopia, August 19, 2021) https://www.edutopia.org/article/no-strings-attached-supporting-social-and-emotional-learning-puppets/

- **Problem-solving** ("Teaching Children to Problem-Solve through Puppet-Play Interactions," Incredible Years, February 17, 2018. Source: Webster-Stratton, C., Reid, J.M. (2018). Teaching children to problem-solve through puppet play interactions. In A.A. Drewes and C.E. Schaefer (Eds.), *Puppets in play therapy: A practical guidebook* (pp. 130–142). Routledge.) https://incredibleyears.com/article/teaching-children-to-problem-solve-through-puppet-play-interactions/

- **Role plays** (Tanja McIlroy, "30 Simple Role Play Ideas for Kids," EmpoweredParentsCo, November 18, 2023) https://empoweredparents.co/role-play-ideas-for-kids/

- **Educational podcasts for children** (Laura Nuttall, "20 Best Educational Podcasts for Children," Twinkl.com, n.d.) https://www.twinkl.com/blog/20-best-educational-podcasts-for-children

Field Trips

- **Micro field trips** (Laurel Schwartz, "Teaching Target Language Vocabulary with Micro Field Trips," Edutopia.org, May 26, 2020) https://www.edutopia.org/article/teaching-target-language-vocabulary-micro-field-trips/

- **Genius field trip ideas** https://www.signupgenius.com/school/field-trip-ideas.cfm

- **Rain forest field trip ideas** (Erica Jabali, "35 Field Trip Ideas," SignUpGenius.com, n.d.) https://rainforestlearningcentre.ca/preschool-field-trip-ideas-lessons/

Middle School/High School

Stories and News

- **Creative Classroom short stories** (Marissa Despins, "The Best Short Stories for Middle School," CreativeClassroomCore.com, November 21, 2023) https://creativeclassroomcore.com/the-best-short-stories-for-middle-school-classrooms/

- **Story Line Online**
  https://storylineonline.net

- **Epic stories**
  https://www.getepic.com

- **Reading Rockets** (Douglas Fisher and Nancy Frey, "Speaking and Listening in Content Area Learning," ReadingRockets.Org (Source: Fisher, D., & Frey, N. (2014). Speaking and listening in content area learning. *The Reading Teacher*, *68*(1), 64–69, doi: 10.1002/trtr.1296)
  https://www.readingrockets.org/article/speaking-and-listening-content-area-learning))

- **Audio poems**
  https://poets.org <search: audio>

- **Poetry Out Loud**
  https://www.poetryoutloud.org

- **News stories** ("All That's News," SchoolJournalism.Org, n.d.)
  https://www.schooljournalism.org/wp-content/uploads/2015/09/C1L5_News-writing-for-the-ear.pdf

- **Listenwise**
  https://app.listenwise.com/teach/events
  Note: Sign-in required. Provides current news stories, topical documentaries and interviews, age-appropriate searches, and comprehension quizzes

- **Human interest stories**
  https://storycorps.org

Content Learning

- **British Council Learn English podcasts**
  https://learnenglish.britishcouncil.org/apps/learnenglish-podcasts

- **Content courses**
  https://www.khanacademy.org

362 *Resources*

- **Learn Out Loud.com free audio and video directory**
  https://www.learnoutloud.com/Free-Audio-Video

- **Audible (audiobooks)**
  https://www.audible.com

- **Read Aloud Books** (Jill Webb, "26 Suggested 5th Grade Read Aloud Books," TeachingExpertise.com, February 2, 2022)
  https://www.teachingexpertise.com/classroom-ideas/5th-grade-read-aloud-books/

- **Language Lizard** (bilingual books)
  https://www.languagelizard.com

- **Debates on Social Issues**
  https://opentodebate.org

- **Documentaries** (Sananda Bhattacharya, "Top 10 Documentaries Every High Schooler Must Watch at Least Once," TheHighSchooler.net, January 19, 2023)
  https://thehighschooler.net/documentaries-for-high-school-students/

University/Adult

Content-Based Listening

- **Academic Earth** (free online courses)
  https://academicearth.org

- **University courses, MIT Open Courseware**
  https://ocw.mit.edu

- **YouTube Research Channel**
  https://www.youtube.com/ResearchChannel

- **Popular TED talks**
  https://www.ted.com/playlists/171/the_most_popular_ted_talks_of_all_time

- **Science Friday** (Science interview podcast)
  https://www.sciencefriday.com/science-friday-podcasts/

- **History Matters** (History archives)
  https://historymatters.gmu.edu/mse/oral/online.html

Resources for Teaching Listening 363

Discussions and Debates

- **Oxford Union debates**
  https://oxford-union.org/pages/formal-debates

- **Intelligence Squared** (debates)
  https://intelligencesquared.com

- **National Public Radio (NPR) author interviews**
  https://www.npr.org/sections/author-interviews/

Educational Podcasts

- **Radiolab**
  https://radiolab.org

- **Stuff You Should Know**
  https://www.iheart.com/podcast/105-stuff-you-should-know-26940277/

- **The Allusionist (Podcast on language)**
  https://www.theallusionist.org

- **Science Vs**
  https://gimletmedia.com/shows/science-vs

- **Grammar Girl**
  https://www.quickanddirtytips.com/grammar-girl/

Cultural Stories

- **The Moth** (Personal stories)
  https://themoth.org/story-library/radio-hour

- **Freakonomics Radio**
  https://freakonomics.com/series/freakonomics-radio/

- **Coffee Break English**
  https://coffeebreaklanguages.com/english/

Conversation

- **ELLII: Everyday dialogues**
  https://ellii.com/lessons/everyday-dialogues

364   *Resources*

- **English Listening Lesson Library Online**
  https://elllo.org/english/levels/index.htm

- **Real English Conversations**
  https://www.youtube.com/c/realenglishconversations

- **Randall's ESL Lab**
  https://www.esl-lab.com

- **YouTube: English Easy Practice**
  https://www.youtube.com/@EnglishEasyPractice

- **YouTube: Practice Makes Fluent—Lifelong Learning**
  https://www.youtube.com/@practicemakesfluent

News and Current Events

- **VOA Learning English**
  https://learningenglish.voanews.com

- **BBC Learning English – 6 Minute English**
  https://www.bbc.co.uk/learningenglish/english/features/6-minute-english

- **Breaking News English**
  https://breakingnewsenglish.com

- **News in Levels**
  https://www.newsinlevels.com

- **Simple English News**
  https://simpleenglishnews.com

- **ESL Fast – News English**
  https://www.eslfast.com

- **Newsela**
  https://newsela.com

Resources for Teaching Listening 365

Practice Sources

VR Programs and Platforms

- **VRChat:** While not designed specifically for language learning, VRChat is a virtual reality platform where users from around the world interact using avatars. Language learners often use it to practice conversational skills with native speakers.
- **Immersive VR Education:** This platform offers various educational VR experiences, including language learning. It provides immersive environments for practicing languages in context.
- **Mondly VR:** Mondly is known for its language-learning apps, and it also has a VR version. It offers interactive lessons in multiple languages within a VR environment.
- **Immerse.com:** This is a language-learning app that offers VR experiences for language learners. It focuses on improving vocabulary and conversational skills.
- **Language Zen VR:** Language Zen offers VR lessons for learning Spanish. It combines visual and audio elements to create an immersive learning experience.
- **Babbel VR:** Babbel, a well-known language-learning platform, introduced a VR app that provides immersive language lessons. It covers various languages.

AR Programs and Platforms

- **Google Translate:** Google Translate offers an AR feature that allows you to point your smartphone's camera at text in the real world (such as signs or menus) and have it translated in real time. Includes **Word Lens**, offering instant translation of text using a smartphone camera This can be a handy tool for language learners.
- **Duolingo AR:** Duolingo, a popular language-learning app, has introduced an AR feature that helps learners practice vocabulary. It uses your smartphone's camera to place virtual objects in your real environment, which you must identify in the target language.
- **Rosetta Stone: Learn Languages:** The Rosetta Stone app includes an AR feature called "Seek & Speak" that helps learners practice pronunciation and vocabulary by identifying objects in their environment and saying their names in the target language.
- **HelloTalk:** HelloTalk is a language exchange app that enables learners to connect with native speakers for language exchange. While not strictly an AR app, it has some AR features for language practice.

366   *Resources*

- **Innovative Language 101 AR:** This AR app offers language lessons in a variety of languages. It uses AR to provide interactive lessons and quizzes, making learning engaging and fun.

Language-Learning Apps

Several language-learning apps emphasize listening as a primary method for language acquisition. Here are some of the most popular ones:

- **Duolingo:** Duolingo offers listening exercises, pronunciation practice, and listening comprehension activities for a wide range of languages.
- **Rosetta Stone:** Rosetta Stone focuses on immersive learning, including listening to native speakers in order to improve listening and speaking skills.
- **Pimsleur:** Pimsleur is known for its audio-based language-learning method, which makes it primarily centered on listening and speaking.
- **Babbel:** Babbel incorporates listening exercises, dialogues, and pronunciation practice into its language courses.
- **FluentU:** FluentU uses real-world videos, such as music videos and movie clips, to enhance listening skills in context.
- **Memrise:** Memrise includes listening exercises and multimedia content to help learners practice listening comprehension.
- **Tandem:** Tandem connects language learners with native speakers for conversation practice via voice messages, calls, and chat.
- **italki:** While italki is primarily a platform for connecting with language tutors, it offers listening comprehension exercises as well.
- **Beelinguapp:** Beelinguapp provides bilingual texts, allowing users to read and listen to stories in two languages side by side.
- **Lingoda:** Lingoda offers live online language classes with native-speaking instructors, focusing on listening and speaking skills.
- **Busuu:** Busuu offers listening and speaking exercises, including interactive dialogues and pronunciation practice.
- **Tandem Language Exchange:** Tandem is not just an app but also a platform, where you can connect with native speakers for language exchange and practice listening skills.

Chatbots for Practicing Listening

Several chatbots and language exchange platforms can help you practice speaking and listening in different languages. Here are some popular ones:

- **Tandem:** Tandem is a language exchange platform where you can connect with native speakers for conversation practice via voice messages, calls, and chat.

Resources for Teaching Listening 367

- **HelloTalk:** HelloTalk offers a language exchange chat platform with text and voice messaging features, making it easy to connect with native speakers for language practice.
- **Speaky:** Speaky connects language learners and native speakers for language exchange. You can chat, voice call, or video call to practice listening and speaking.
- **Tandem Language Exchange:** Tandem offers language exchange opportunities through its app, allowing you to practice speaking and listening with native speakers.
- **Mondly:** Mondly's chatbot feature allows you to engage in conversations with an AI chat partner, helping you practice speaking and listening skills.
- **Rosetta Stone:** Rosetta Stone offers an AI chatbot for conversation practice, enabling you to improve your speaking and listening skills in the language you're learning.

Practice Ideas from Polyglots

Polyglots are individuals who have consciously learned three or more languages up to at least CEFR B2 (high intermediate) level, where they can communicate clearly and understand most of what they hear.

Because they are successful language learners, polyglots have often discovered the most effective means of acquiring a new language. In all cases, their methods involve a focus on listening as a primary means of acquisition, much of it done through distance learning. In this section, we share one of the "secrets" of one polyglot.

Contact information is provided for other polyglots if you wish to learn their secrets!

Languagemastery.com

John Fotheringham, founder of Language Mastery (Anywhere Immersion Method) favors the use of YouTube and Netflix, along with **Language Reactor** software. His listening method involves four steps: (1) Watching a program (usually 20–30 minutes long) in the target language with native-language subtitles (English, in John's case). This is to get a sense of the overall meaning of the drama or documentary. (2) Watching a program again with the target language subtitles, all the way through, concentrating on the audio, but using the subtitles as well. (3) Watching the program again, with no subtitles. (4) Watching the program a fourth time with the TL subtitles, using the software **Anki**, to save words and phrases that he wants to learn.

John also uses **ITalki** for 30 minutes a week of spoken interaction, with a live tutor (someone he has selected after several unsuccessful trials with others), studying the transcript of their conversation later for at least one hour before the next session.

Other polyglots with ideas for using listening to master new languages:
Steve Kaufmann: https://Lingq.com
Cara Leopold: https://leo-listening.com
Lindie Botes: https://lindiebotes.com
Olly Richards: https://storylearning.com
Richard Simcott: https://speakingfluently.com
Lýdia Machová: https://www.lindsaydoeslanguages.com

For more ideas from these successful learners, consult the polyglot blog, Preply:
https://preply.com/en/blog/polyglots/

Resources for Researching Listening

Guidelines for Conducting Qualitative Research

Qualitative research in listening, or in applied linguistics generally, often involves complex and context-dependent investigations of language use, language learning, and language teaching. Developing familiarity and proficiency in these skills is crucial to conducting rigorous and insightful qualitative studies in this field. Seeking mentorship or collaborating with experienced qualitative researchers can be invaluable for skill development and research success.

Conducting sound qualitative research requires a specific set of skills and approaches to investigate language-related phenomena. Here are some essential qualitative research skills for conducting research in this field:

- **Research design:** Understanding various qualitative research designs, such as case studies, ethnography, grounded theory, and content analysis, and selecting the most appropriate one for your research question.
- **Data collection:** Proficiency in collecting qualitative data through methods like interviews, focus groups, observations, surveys, document analysis, and audio or video recordings.
- **Data management:** Organizing, storing, and managing large volumes of qualitative data, often using specialized software like **NVivo** or **ATLAS.ti**.
- **Interviewing skills:** Developing effective interviewing techniques, including open-ended questioning, active listening, and probing, to elicit rich and detailed responses from participants.
- **Observation skills:** Conducting systematic and detailed observations, while being mindful of ethical considerations for both participants and nonparticipants.
- **Transcription:** Accurately transcribing audio or video recordings of interviews or interactions, ensuring fidelity to the original content.

DOI: 10.4324/9781003390794-19

370 *Resources*

- **Coding and analysis:** Developing a coding system and conducting rigorous qualitative data analysis, which may involve thematic analysis, content analysis, constant comparative analysis, or other techniques.
- **Interpretation:** Making sense of qualitative data by identifying patterns, themes, and connections, and drawing meaningful interpretations and conclusions.
- **Triangulation:** Combining multiple data sources or methods (e.g., interviews, observations, and documents) to enhance the validity and reliability of findings.
- **Ethical considerations:** Adhering to ethical guidelines when working with human participants, ensuring informed consent, confidentiality, and participant well-being.
- **Cultural sensitivity:** Demonstrating cultural competence and sensitivity when conducting research involving participants from diverse linguistic and cultural backgrounds.
- **Writing and reporting:** Communicating research findings effectively through clear and well-structured reports or publications, often adhering to academic writing conventions.
- **Reflexivity:** Reflecting on your own role as a researcher, acknowledging biases and subjectivities, and considering how they might impact data collection and interpretation.
- **Peer review:** Engaging in peer-review and feedback processes to enhance the quality and rigor of your qualitative research.
- **Theoretical frameworks:** Applying relevant theoretical frameworks or paradigms (e.g., sociocultural theory) to guide your research and data analysis, and to provide a network of colleagues who can provide feedback on your research.
- **Participant engagement:** Building rapport and trust with participants to facilitate open and honest communication and ensure their active engagement in the research process.
- **Critical thinking:** Approaching research questions with a critical and reflexive mindset, questioning assumptions, and considering alternative explanations.
- **Adaptability:** Being flexible and adaptive in response to unexpected findings or changes in the research process.

You may also wish to consult Scribbr for more detailed information:

Pritha Bhandari, "What Is Qualitative Research? Methods and Examples," Scribbr.com, June 19, 2020. https://www.scribbr.com/methodology/qualitative-research/

Guidelines for Conducting Quantitative Research

Quantitative Research Skills

Quantitative research skills are essential for conducting empirical studies in applied linguistics, particularly when examining language-related phenomena from a statistical perspective.

Here are the main quantitative research skills needed for conducting research in this field:

- **Research design:** Understanding various quantitative research designs, such as experimental, correlational, cross-sectional, longitudinal, and quasi-experimental, and selecting the most appropriate one for your research question.
- **Hypothesis formulation:** Developing clear and testable research hypotheses or research questions, often based on theories or existing literature.
- **Sampling techniques:** Designing and implementing effective sampling strategies to ensure the representativeness and generalizability of your study's findings.
- **Data collection:** Proficiency in collecting quantitative data through methods like surveys, questionnaires, standardized tests, and behavioral observations.
- **Instrument development:** Designing, adapting, or selecting measurement instruments (e.g., surveys, tests) that are valid and reliable for measuring the constructs of interest.
- **Data management:** Organizing and managing quantitative data using software tools like SPSS, R, or Excel, including data entry, cleaning, and coding.
- **Descriptive statistics:** Computing and interpreting descriptive statistics, such as mean, median, mode, standard deviation, and percentiles, to summarize and describe data.
- **Inferential statistics:** Applying appropriate inferential statistical tests (e.g., t-tests, ANOVA, regression analysis, chi-square tests) to test hypotheses and draw conclusions from data.
- **Statistical software:** Proficiency in using statistical software packages for data analysis, such as SPSS, R, SAS, or STATA.
- **Data visualization:** Creating clear and informative data visualizations, including graphs, charts, and tables, to present quantitative results effectively.
- **Interpretation:** Analyzing and interpreting statistical findings in the context of research questions, drawing meaningful conclusions, and discussing their implications.
- **Reliability and validity:** Ensuring the reliability (consistency) and validity (accuracy) of data and measurement instruments through appropriate methods (e.g., reliability tests, factor analysis).

372 *Resources*

- **Ethical considerations:** Adhering to ethical guidelines when conducting research involving human participants, ensuring informed consent, confidentiality, and participant well-being.
- **Effect size calculation:** Calculating and interpreting effect size measures to determine the practical significance of research findings.
- **Power analysis:** Conducting power analysis to determine an appropriate sample size to detect meaningful effects or relationships.
- **Multivariate analysis:** Using advanced statistical techniques when dealing with complex data, such as structural equation modeling, hierarchical linear modeling, or factor analysis.
- **Peer review:** Engaging in peer review and feedback processes to enhance the quality and rigor of quantitative research.
- **Critical thinking:** Approaching research questions with a critical and analytical mindset, considering potential confounding variables and alternative explanations.
- **Theory integration:** Integrating relevant theoretical frameworks or models into your research design and data analysis.
- **Generalization:** Drawing conclusions that can be reasonably generalized to broader populations or contexts based on your research findings.

Quantitative research in applied linguistics often involves data-driven analysis of language-related phenomena, and researchers need to be proficient in statistical methods to provide robust and evidence-based insights. Developing these quantitative research skills and staying updated on advancements in statistical techniques are essential for conducting rigorous studies in the field of applied linguistics. Additionally, collaboration with experienced quantitative researchers can facilitate skill development and research success.

Statistical Procedures for Conducting Research on Listening

- **Descriptive statistics:** These include measures such as mean, median, mode, range, variance, and standard deviation. Descriptive statistics help summarize and describe data.
- **T-tests:** These tests are used to compare means between two groups, such as comparing the language proficiency of two groups of learners.
- **ANOVA (Analysis of variance):** ANOVA is used when you want to compare means between more than two groups. It's useful for studying the effects of multiple factors on language learning.
- **Regression analysis:** Regression helps you explore the relationship between variables. In applied linguistics, you might use linear or logistic regression to predict language proficiency or learning outcomes based on various factors.

Resources for Researching Listening   373

- **Correlation analysis:** This involves measures like Pearson's correlation coefficient or Spearman's rank correlation coefficient to assess the strength and direction of relationships between two continuous variables.
- **Chi-square test:** The chi-square test is used to examine the association between two categorical variables, and is often used in research on language assessment or language attitudes.
- **Factor analysis:** Factor analysis helps identify underlying constructs or factors within a set of observed variables. It can be used for test validation or identifying language components.
- **Cronbach's alpha:** This is a measure of internal consistency reliability often used in assessing the reliability of language tests or scales.
- **MANOVA (Multivariate analysis of variance):** MANOVA extends ANOVA to multiple dependent variables. It's used when you want to investigate the effects of multiple factors on multiple outcome variables in language research.
- **Multilevel modeling:** Multilevel models (e.g., hierarchical linear modeling) are used when data has a hierarchical structure, like students within classes, which is common in educational linguistics research.

Tutorials in Applied Statistics

A number of free tutorials are available for learning statistical procedures, at Khan Academy, Statistics.com, Stat Trek, and Wolfram Alpha, as well as through Coursera and university websites. One user-friendly source is that of Professor James Murray at the University of Wisconsin: https://murraylax.org/rtutorials/

Three comprehensive sources for step-by-step procedures for the research procedures recommended in this book are:

Statistics How To: https://www.statisticshowto.com/
Scribbr: https://www.scribbr.com
Statistics Solutions: https://www.statisticssolutions.com/free-resources. /directory-of-statistical-analyses/repeated-measures-anova/

T-tests
https://www.statisticshowto.com/probability-and-statistics/t-test/
https://www.scribbr.com/frequently-asked-questions/which-t-test-should-i-use/

ANOVA
https://www.statisticshowto.com/probability-and-statistics/hypothesis-testing/anova/ https://www.scribbr.com/statistics/statistical-tests/
https://www.statisticssolutions.com/free-resources/

Regression analysis
https://www.statisticshowto.com/probability-and-statistics/statistics-definitions/residual/

Correlation analysis
https://www.statisticshowto.com/probability-and-statistics/correlation-analysis/
https://www.scribbr.com/statistics/correlation-coefficient/
https://www.statisticshowto.com/intraclass-correlation/

Chi-square
https://www.statisticshowto.com/chi-square-goodness-of-fit-test-spss/
https://www.scribbr.com/statistics/chi-square-test-of-independence/

Factor analysis
https://www.statisticshowto.com/factor-analysis/

Probability
https://www.statisticshowto.com/probability-and-statistics/statistics-definitions/cronbachs-alpha-spss/
https://www.scribbr.com/statistics/standard-normal-distribution/

Cohen's kappa (rater reliability)
https://www.statisticshowto.com/cohens-kappa-statistic/
Likert Scale construction
https://www.scribbr.com/methodology/likert-scale/

Guidelines for Conducting Mixed Methods Research

Conducting mixed methods research requires a thoughtful integration of both qualitative and quantitative approaches to gain a comprehensive understanding of the research topic. Wherever possible, it is best to conduct mixed methods research that *combines both qualitative and quantitative measures*. While it may seem that mixed methods research involves double the time and effort, mixed methods can actually streamline the research process.

Here are some brief guidelines for conducting mixed methods research:

- **Clearly define your research questions:** Start by defining clear and focused research questions that can be addressed through mixed methods. Ensure that your questions require both qualitative and quantitative data to provide a holistic perspective.
- **Select an appropriate design:** Choose an appropriate mixed methods design, such as sequential explanatory, sequential exploratory, or concurrent triangulation. The choice depends on whether you plan to collect and analyze qualitative and quantitative data sequentially or concurrently.

Resources for Researching Listening   375

- **Data collection:** Collect qualitative and quantitative data using suitable methods. For listening research, this might involve techniques like surveys, tests, interviews, focus groups, observations, or content analysis of audio recordings.
- **Integration of data:** Develop a plan for integrating qualitative and quantitative data. This could involve comparing findings, merging datasets, or using one dataset to help explain or interpret the other.
- **Data analysis:** Analyze qualitative and quantitative data separately using appropriate methods. Ensure rigor and reliability in both types of analysis. Qualitative analysis may involve thematic coding, while quantitative analysis might include statistical tests.
- **Interpretation and integration:** Interpret the results of each data type separately. Then, integrate findings to address your research questions comprehensively. Look for patterns, convergences, divergences, and relationships between qualitative and quantitative findings.
- **Contextualize findings:** Consider the context and implications of your findings for the field of applied linguistics, especially in the domain of listening. Discuss how qualitative insights complement or enhance quantitative results.
- **Triangulation:** Use triangulation to enhance the validity of your findings. Triangulation involves comparing data from different sources or methods to corroborate results and ensure robust conclusions.
- **Report transparently:** Clearly present your mixed methods research in your academic paper or report. Discuss your research design, data collection, analysis processes, and how you integrated qualitative and quantitative data.
- **Ethical considerations:** Adhere to ethical guidelines throughout the research process, especially when working with human subjects. Ensure informed consent, confidentiality, and respect for participants' rights.
- **Peer review:** Consider seeking peer review and feedback from experts in applied linguistics or mixed methods research to enhance the quality of your study.
- **Iterative process:** Remember that mixed methods research often involves an iterative process of refining research questions, data collection methods, and analysis as the study progresses.

You can also consult Scribbr for more detailed information: https://www.scribbr.com/methodology/mixed-methods-research/

Glossary

CHAPTER 1

Acetylcholine A neurotransmitter that plays a significant role in various cognitive functions, including memory, learning, attention, and arousal. Enhanced levels of acetylcholine can facilitate the encoding and retention of auditory information, leading to better listening performance.

Agency The active and intentional role that listeners play in their own listening processes. It emphasizes the listener's ability to exert control, make choices, and take initiative in engaging with, comprehending, and interpreting spoken information.

Attentional capture A phenomenon in which attention is involuntarily drawn or captured by a specific stimulus in the environment, interrupting other ongoing tasks or stimuli. The stimuli stand out due to their novelty, suddenness, or emotional significance.

Attentional control Differences in the ability to maintain focus and attention on the spoken information. Some individuals may have better attentional control, allowing them to sustain attention for longer, while others might struggle with distractions.

Auditory cortex A region of the brain responsible for processing auditory information or sound, part of the cerebral cortex, primarily within an area known as the superior temporal gyrus. Its functions include sound processing, speech perception, localization of sounds, and boosting short-term memory.

Bottom-up processes The way sensory information is processed is based on its fundamental sensory features, starting from the raw sensory input and moving up toward higher cognitive processing. In the context of auditory perception, bottom-up processes refer to the perception of sensory input, feature extraction, and assembly of features into a coherent representation.

Characteristic frequency (CF) The specific frequency or pitch to which a particular auditory nerve fiber or a region in the cochlea is most sensitive. In the auditory system, different nerve fibers or regions are specialized to detect different frequencies of sound.

Comprehension The ability to engage with spoken language or auditory information to: understand content (grasp the main ideas, details, key points, relationships between ideas, nuances); interpret context (account for situational factors, recognize tone, implied meanings, cultural references); make inferences (connect input with background knowledge and experiences, fill in gaps, predict, draw conclusions); recall information (retain details, ideas, and concepts); and monitor understanding (check for accuracy, identify areas of confusion, and adjust strategies).

Connectivity The interconnections and associations between auditory information received during listening and existing memory networks or schemas in the brain. It involves integrating new auditory information with previously stored knowledge, experiences, and memories.

Coordination Alignment of cognitive functions while listening can vary among individuals due to various cognitive factors. Some individual differences in how cognitive functions are coordinated during listening include attentional control, working memory capacity, processing speed, metacognition, and multitasking abilities.

Dopamine A neurotransmitter that plays a crucial role in various brain functions, including motivation, reward, movement, and pleasure. It influences listening performance by amplifying persistence and comprehension goals.

Interpretation The process of determining significance, assessing personal relevance, and drawing logical, social, and cultural inferences from auditory information received. Key individual differences in interpretation during listening include cultural and linguistic background, language proficiency, prior knowledge, cognitive skills, strategies, interest and motivation, and emotional states.

Norepinephrine A neurotransmitter that plays a crucial role in various physiological processes, including regulating attention and focus. Norepinephrine influences listening by increasing arousal, attention, and alertness.

Pascals (symbol: Pa) The unit of pressure in the International System of Units (SI). One pascal is defined as one newton of force applied over an area of one square meter. It is used to quantify air pressure that enters the ear.

Reception The process of taking in and perceiving auditory information or stimuli. Individual differences in reception refer to variations or disparities among individuals in how they receive, process, and interpret auditory information or stimuli.

Reticular activating system (RAS) A complex network of nuclei and nerve pathways in the brainstem, extending into the midbrain and thalamus. It plays a fundamental role in regulating arousal, wakefulness, and attention.

Serotonin A neurotransmitter primarily known for its role in regulating mood, emotions, sleep, and appetite. It influences listening by affecting mood regulation and emotional processing.

378 *Glossary*

Sinusoidal stimulation   Tiny fibers inside the cochlea respond to fluid movements by bending, an action that creates a kind of wavy back-and-forth stimulation, similar to the up-and-down pattern of a sine wave. This motion is called sinusoidal stimulation.

Spectral (holistic) processing   The brain's ability to analyze and interpret the combined frequency content or spectral characteristics of auditory stimuli. Sounds consist of various frequencies that combine to create a spectral profile.

Temporal (sequential) processing   The brain's ability to process and interpret auditory information over time. It involves the perception and comprehension of sounds, including their timing, duration, and sequencing. This ability allows individuals to perceive the rhythm, tempo, and timing variations of the speech signal.

Tonotopic organization   The spatial arrangement or mapping of frequencies along a specific structure or pathway in the auditory system. It means that different sound frequencies are processed and represented spatially in an orderly manner.

Top-down processes   The influence of higher-level cognitive factors, such as expectations, stored knowledge, situational context, and previous related experiences, on the interpretation and perception of auditory stimuli. Unlike bottom-up processes, which start from the sensory input, top-down processes involve using prior information and expectations to guide the processing of incoming sensory information.

Transduction   The conversion of sound waves into electrical signals that the brain can interpret. This happens within the inner ear, specifically in the cochlea.

Transmission   The process of sending or conveying information, messages, or signals from a sender or speaker to a receiver or listener. Individuals can have varying sensitivities to different frequencies or pitches of sound. This variability in sensitivity means that some people might perceive certain frequencies more acutely or distinctly than others.

Transverse temporal gyri   Structures found in the brain's auditory cortex, specifically within the superior temporal gyrus. They are bilateral structures located in both hemispheres of the brain. These gyri are involved in processing temporal aspects of sound, such as timing, rhythm, and temporal sequencing.

CHAPTER 2

Allophonic variations   Different pronunciations or realizations of a phoneme that do not change the meaning of a word but occur in specific spoken contexts due to the influence of surrounding sounds and overriding rhythms.

Glossary 379

Amalgams Lexical structures that are formed by combining parts of two or more words to create a new word with a specific meaning.

Argument structure (ARG) The arrangement and relationships between elements within a sentence that are necessary to complete the meaning of a predicate (verb or theme).

Assimilation A phonological process where a sound becomes more similar to a neighboring sound in terms of one or more phonetic features. Assimilations may be progressive, regressive, or reciprocal.

Clitic A linguistic element that behaves like a word but lacks full independence. Clitics are phonologically weak and often unstressed, and they attach themselves to other words, often functioning as a part of those words. A **clitic group** refers to a unit consisting of a clitic and the word or phrase it attaches to.

Conventionalized forms These linguistic expressions or structures have become standardized or established within a language or community. They might not follow standard grammatical rules, but are widely accepted and used.

Duration The length of time a speech sound or segment is produced or perceived within a spoken word or utterance. It is one of the temporal acoustic properties of speech.

Elision The omission of a sound, syllable, or segment within a word or between words in connected speech. This is a phonological process where certain sounds are dropped or left out in the actual pronunciation, often due to the natural flow of speech or for ease of articulation.

Exophoric (cues) Visual cues or signals that require context external to the immediate communication setting for their interpretation.

Extratextual integration The process of incorporating information from sources external to the text or spoken words being processed. It involves connecting the linguistic information received with relevant knowledge or information stored in the memory that isn't explicitly stated in the text. It draws upon personal experience, cultural knowledge, and world knowledge.

Feature A distinctive or characteristic element of speech sounds that can be used to distinguish one sound from another within a language.

Foot/feet The arrangement of stressed and unstressed syllables within a metrical structure. Most frequent are iambic (aGAIN), trochaic (TAble), anapestic (underSTAND), and dactylic (ELephant).

Formulaic language Fixed, often recurring phrases or expressions that are used in specific situations.

Frequency The rate of vibration of a sound wave, specifically with speech sounds or phonemes. This is one of the fundamental acoustic properties of speech that contributes to how we perceive different sounds.

Gambits Conversational strategies or expressions used to initiate, maintain, or conclude interactions. They are conversational techniques or sequences

380 *Glossary*

of speech acts employed to engage others, establish rapport, or create smoother social transactions.

Grammatic units The objective components of language that contribute to the structure, organization, and potential meaning of sentences. Key units include morphemes, words, lexical phrases, grammatical phrases, clauses, and sentences.

High-frequency collocations Words that often appear together due to their frequent co-occurrence in natural language and which can be processed rapidly.

Holistic patterns Larger units of language—phrases, idioms, or expressions—that are learned and used as whole units rather than assembled from individual words and which are retrieved from memory as complete phrases.

Intensity Intensity, often measured in decibels (dB), corresponds to the physical amplitude or energy of a sound wave. Higher-intensity sounds typically correspond to greater physical energy and are perceived as louder, while lower-intensity sounds are perceived as softer or quieter.

Kinesic (cues) A subset of nonverbal communication that involves body movements, gestures, facial expressions, and posture to convey meaning or information. Kinesic signals are speaker-intrinsic and can often convey emotions, attitudes, intentions, or emphasis without relying on external context.

Lexical effect The influence that the lexical properties of a word, such as its frequency or familiarity, have on the way a listener perceives and processes speech sounds.

Lexical phrase A unit of speech that combines words or morphemes and is recognized based on its cohesive phonological or prosodic characteristics. Formally, it is a grouping of words or morphemes within a sentence that is treated as a single lexical unit.

Logogens Hypothetical units or mental representations within the lexical access model that represent individual words in the mental lexicon. According to the connectionist theory of lexical access, when a listener encounters a word, the logogen associated with that word is activated. Logogens interact with each other to facilitate word recognition.

Mora A unit of time or timing that contributes to the rhythm and syllable weight in a language.

Morphological processing The recognition, analysis, and understanding of the smallest units of meaning in language—morphemes—while listening to spoken words or sentences. Morphemes are the smallest units of language that carry meaning and can include roots, prefixes, suffixes, and inflections.

Multimodal factors The various sensory cues, modalities, or sources of information that individuals utilize alongside auditory input to comprehend and interpret spoken language or communication, including visual cues, tactile sensations, emotional and social cues, and contextual cues.

Glossary 381

Pause Unit (PU) / Intonation Unit (IU) / phonological phrase (P-phrase) A unit of speech identified based on its phonological properties, including stress patterns, such as contrastive stress, rhythmic structures, such as pauses, and prosodic features, such as intonation movements.

Phonological processing The cognitive ability to recognize, analyze, and manipulate the sounds of language—phonemes, syllables, and words—while listening to spoken language.

Phonological word A unit of speech recognized based on phonological criteria, such as stress patterns or rhythmic properties, rather than purely on morphological or syntactic criteria.

Pragmatic awareness The ability to understand and apply pragmatic aspects of language in communication. It involves understanding implicatures, recognizing politeness strategies, deciphering contextual cues, and interpreting speech acts.

Prosodic sensitivity The ability to perceive and interpret the suprasegmental features of speech, such as intonation, stress patterns, rhythm, and pitch variations.

Proximal stimulation The process of exciting or triggering a response through association with a related stimulus. In auditory perception, proximal stimulation refers to the activation of sensory receptors based on associated motor-muscle memory.

Sandhi variations The phonetic or phonological changes that occur when words or morphemes come into contact or are adjacent within a sentence or utterance.

Schematic effect The influence of a listeners' expectations or mental schemas on how they process input.

Segment A discrete, individual unit of speech that can be analyzed in terms of its distinctive features. In most varieties of English, there are 40 segments: 15 vowels and 25 consonants.

Syllable A fundamental unit of speech that consists of a central vowel sound (nucleus) and optional consonant sounds that occur before (onset) and after (coda) the vowel.

Syntactic effect The influence of syntactic structure or sequencing of grammatical frames on how a listener perceives and processes words.

Syntactic parsing The cognitive process of analyzing and breaking down spoken language into its grammatical components or syntactic structures while listening to speech.

Syntactic processing The cognitive ability to understand and interpret the structure and grammar of spoken language while listening to sentences or phrases. It involves recognizing the arrangement of words, phrases, and clauses to derive meaning and comprehend the relationships between different elements within a sentence.

382　*Glossary*

Theme　In structural linguistics, a central role of a clause or sentence. The theme is the structural element that undergoes or experiences the action expressed by the verb.

Timbre　The quality or character of a sound that distinguishes it from other sounds, even when they have the same pitch and intensity. It is an acoustic property that allows us to perceive a sound's unique tone or color.

Vowel reduction　A phenomenon where a vowel sound becomes shorter, less distinct, or more centralized in terms of its articulation when it is in an unstressed or weak position within a word or a syllable.

CHAPTER 3

Ambiguity　A type of meaning in which a word, phrase, statement, or resolution is not explicitly defined, allowing for multiple interpretations.

Antonymy　A relationship of words with their opposite meanings.

Approximation　A compensation heuristic using a superordinate concept likely to cover the essence of what has not been comprehended, constructing a less precise meaning for a word or concept than the speaker may have intended.

Collocations　Words that frequently occur together and can be processed as chunks.

Compensatory strategies　Cognitive approaches or techniques that listeners use to compensate for difficulties or shortcomings in understanding spoken language. These include approximating meaning, skipping unclear segments, filtering through familiar schemas, and substituting known concepts for unknown concepts.

Comprehension-building activity　The process by which listeners construct and enhance their understanding of spoken language or communication through the utilization of semantic information and cognitive resources.

Concept abstraction　The cognitive process of extracting the essential or general characteristics of a concept or category, which allows individuals to create mental representations encompassing a range of specific instances or examples. This is done through generalization, categorization, or prediction.

Constructing meaning　The active process by which listeners interpret and make sense of spoken language or auditory information. It involves the cognitive and linguistic processes through which individuals extract, analyze, and integrate information from what they hear to create understanding or meaning.

Derivations　Forming new words through affixation or word-formation processes.

Filtering　A compensation heuristic compressing a longer message or set of propositions into a more concise one. (This is different from skipping or approximation, which are reduction strategies because filtering involves actively constructing a larger semantic context.)

Glossary 383

Fixed phrases utterances A sequence of words that are commonly used together and have a specific meaning that may not be predictable from the meanings of its individual words.

Heuristics Mental shortcuts or practical rules of thumb used to simplify decision-making, problem-solving, or information processing in various communicative contexts. They focus on efficiency, simplicity, and adaptability.

Homonymy A relationship between words that have the same pronunciation and spelling but differ in meaning.

Homophony A relationship between words with the same pronunciation but different spellings.

Hyponymy/Hypernymy A hierarchical relationship between words, where one word (hyponym) is more specific and falls under another word (hypernym) that is more general.

Incompletion A compensation heuristic, maintaining an incomplete proposition in memory and waiting for clarification.

Induction The cognitive process through which listeners draw general conclusions or make generalizations based on specific instances or observations. It involves reasoning from specific examples or instances to form broader, generalized principles, rules, or concepts.

Instantiation The process of applying or embodying a general schema or abstract concept to a specific instance or example. It involves relating the generalized knowledge or schema about a concept to a particular situation, object, event, or individual that fits within that concept.

Lexical access The mental process of retrieving and accessing the stored information about words from the mental lexicon during language comprehension. This is how individuals recognize and retrieve the meaning, pronunciation, and syntactic information of words they encounter in speech.

Lexicalized sentence frames Frequently used sentence frames with a conventional meaning when slots are filled in, e.g., "I'm sorry if I ..." "Do you mind if I ..."

Literary devices Metaphor, hyperbole, onomatopoeia, irony, metonymy. Words and concepts can be related analogously, providing a nuanced understanding of a familiar word or phrase.

Mental lexicon The internal mental repository or storehouse where individuals store, organize, and access their knowledge of words, including their meanings, pronunciations, syntactic roles, and other linguistic information.

Mental prototypes Cognitive representations or idealized models that listeners form to represent typical or central examples of categories or concepts. They serve as idealized or typical representations of a category based on shared characteristics or features commonly associated with it, allowing for approximate comprehension of a speaker's intentions.

384 *Glossary*

Meronymy/Holonymy The relationship between words in which one represents a whole and the other represents its parts, e.g. *finger* is a meronym of *hand*; *hand* is a holonym of *finger*.

Metacommunication Communication about the communication process itself. It involves messages, cues, or interactions that explicitly or implicitly address how messages are conveyed, interpreted, or understood between individuals. Metacommunication can be used to negotiate "shared activation spaces" to exchange ideas.

Meta-messages Conventional signals about the intended interpretation of a message, e.g., *for that matter, as far as I can tell.*

Ontological models The mental representations or structures that individuals construct about the nature of reality, existence, and the world around them.

Paradigmatic relations The semantic relationships between elements within a linguistic structure. These relations exist among linguistic units that can be interchanged or substituted with one another while maintaining grammaticality or meaningfulness within a particular context.

Polysemy The relationship between words that have evolved from the same origin but have multiple related meanings.

Polywords Words that combine to create lexical items with a specific meaning; these can be agglutinated words (e.g. *bookshelf*) or fixed phrases (e.g. *by dint of*).

Priming effect The phenomenon in which exposure to a stimulus (such as a word, sound, or concept) influences the processing or perception of a subsequent related stimulus. It involves the activation of specific mental representations or associations due to prior exposure.

Rapid cortical plasticity The brain's ability to undergo relatively quick and temporary changes in its structure or function in response to new experiences, sensory input, or learning.

Ritualized texts Often-used utterances, phrases, sayings, and clichés that can be interpreted as a single lexical item (e.g. *take care, sorry about that*)

Schematic negotiation A cognitive process in which individuals engage to reconcile or align their mental schemas, concepts, or expectations during communication or interaction. It involves the active adjustment or modification of one's mental representations to accommodate or harmonize with those of others, also known as "finding common ground."

Selective attention The ability to focus and concentrate on specific auditory information while filtering out irrelevant or less important sounds or distractions.

Situational utterances Context-specific phrases that have assumed a conventional pragmatic meaning (e.g. *I'd like the _____, please.)*

Skipping A compensation heuristic omitting a part or a block of input from processing for comprehension.

Glossary 385

Spreading activation A cognitive process that occurs during language comprehension, particularly in the context of how words or concepts are represented and accessed in the mental lexicon. It is a model of how related or interconnected concepts are retrieved and processed in the mind when one concept is activated.

Substitution A compensation heuristic substituting a word, concept, or proposition for one that is not understandable.

Synonymy A relationship between words that have similar meanings or can be used interchangeably in certain contexts.

Syntagmatic relations The linear or sequential relationships between linguistic elements within a syntactic structure, discourse, or text. These relations involve arranging or combining linguistic units in a specific order to create meaningful and grammatically correct expressions.

CHAPTER 4

Acknowledgment A neutral recognition or validation by the listener of a statement, question, or contribution made by a speaker. It involves confirming the receipt of information or expressing gratitude for the input provided by the other person.

Backchanneling The verbal or nonverbal cues and signals listeners use to indicate their engagement, understanding, or agreement with the speaker during a conversation. These cues are typically subtle and are intended to encourage the speaker, show attentiveness, or maintain the flow of the conversation.

Channel In sociolinguistics, the medium or mode of communication, whether spoken, written, electronic, visual, or nonverbal, or a combination of these.

Claim In a model of argumentation, statements or assertions put forward by the speaker to be accepted as valid or true. Claims can be factual statements, opinions, proposals, or arguments.

Code In sociolinguistics, the specific language or linguistic system used for communication. It can refer to a particular language, dialect, jargon, or specialized vocabulary.

Communicative insincerity The act of conveying messages or expressions that do not genuinely align with one's beliefs, feelings, or intentions. It involves communicating in a way that lacks authenticity or truthfulness, often for various social, cultural, or strategic reasons.

Concessions A negative acknowledging of a point, argument, or perspective presented by another participant, even though it contradicts the listener's own initial viewpoint or stance.

Constatives Utterances that describe or assert a state of affairs. They are statements that aim to convey information about the world and can be evaluated as true or false.

386 *Glossary*

Conversational maxims Principles or guidelines that underlie sincere, effective communication in conversation. These maxims were formulated as part of Grice's cooperative principle, which suggests that people in communication strive to cooperate to exchange meaningful information effectively, to benefit both parties. The four maxims are the **maxim of quantity**, the **maxim of quality**, the **maxim of relevance**, and the **maxim of manner**.

Countering A conversational act where a listener responds to or challenges a specific discourse move made by a speaker. It involves presenting an opposing viewpoint, argument, or action in response to the initial move, aiming to challenge or refute the information, perspective, or action of the speaker.

Deictic framing The process of understanding and interpreting spoken language by considering the specific spatial, temporal, or social contexts referred to by deictic expressions used in the discourse. Deictic expressions are linguistic elements (such as pronouns, adverbs, or demonstratives) that rely on the context of the conversation to convey meaning.

Discourse framing The process of interpreting spoken language within a broader context established by the speaker, the speaker's relationship with the listener, and social expectations. It involves aligning with the overarching structure, theme, or purpose set by the speaker–listener relationship throughout the conversation or discourse.

Dominance–submission relationship An interpersonal dynamic characterized by unequal power or influence between individuals engaged in communication. This relationship is often marked by one person asserting dominance or control while the other assumes a submissive or compliant role.

Endorsements Positive expressions of agreement, support, or validation by a listener towards a specific point, idea, or opinion put forth by the speaker. They signal alignment or approval and can strengthen the credibility or validity of the initial statement or viewpoint.

Equifinality The idea that a system can achieve the same or similar outcomes or end states despite starting from different initial conditions or following different paths.

Event In sociolinguistics, the broader activity or occasion in which communication takes place. It could be a casual conversation, formal meeting, or any social gathering involving interaction.

Genre In sociolinguistics, the specific type or form of discourse, such as storytelling, argumentation, interviews, or casual conversation, characterized by particular structures and conventions.

Grounds In a model of argumentation, grounds, also known as evidence or data, are the supporting information or reasons offered by the speaker to back up their claim. Grounds provide the foundation or support for

Glossary 387

the claim, giving it credibility or justification. Grounds can include facts, statistics, examples, expert opinions, or other forms of evidence.

Ignoring In discourse analysis, the intentional act of a listener not acknowledging, addressing, or responding to a specific statement, question, or action made by the speaker. It involves disregarding or omitting a particular discourse move without providing any explicit acknowledgment, response, or engagement.

Illocutions (or illocutionary act) A social or interpersonal act performed for a listener by a speaker by virtue of uttering certain words, for example, the acts of promising (e.g., *I'll be here by 9.*) or threatening (e.g., *If you're late one more time, you're going to be fired.*).

Implicature (or conversational implicature) An indirect or implicit speech act referring to what is meant by a speaker's utterance that is not part of what is explicitly said.

Paralinguistic signals Nonverbal elements of speech that accompany spoken language, enhancing or modifying the speaker's meaning. These signals are distinct from the words themselves but play a crucial role in communication by conveying emotions, attitudes, or emphasis., and by providing informational, grammatical, and indexical cues.

Information manipulation theory A theoretical framework within communication theory that focuses on the strategic manipulation, control, or distortion of information to influence listeners' perceptions, beliefs, or behaviors. It explores how information can be intentionally altered or managed to achieve specific goals, often in the context of persuasion, influence, or propaganda.

Interactional effectiveness An attribute that pertains to an individual's ability to engage in effective and appropriate communication within various social settings. It involves skills such as turn-taking, maintaining conversational coherence, adapting language to different interlocutors or contexts, and using appropriate nonverbal cues (like eye contact and gestures) to facilitate smooth and meaningful interactions.

Interpersonal deception theory A theoretical framework that explores the dynamics and processes involved in deceptive communication between individuals. IDT focuses on how deception occurs within interpersonal interactions and examines the strategies, behaviors, and cues involved in deceptive communication.

Interpretive community A group of individuals who share common beliefs, values, perspectives, and interpretive frameworks that shape how they understand and interpret texts, symbols, or communication messages.

Interpretive strategies The cognitive approaches, methods, and knowledge frameworks that individuals employ to interpret, understand, and make meaning from communication messages, texts, or symbols. These strategies involve both conscious and subconscious mental processes employed

388 *Glossary*

by individuals to derive interpretations and understandings from the information they receive.

Intersubjectivity The shared understanding, mutual knowledge, or common ground that exists between individuals during communication. It's the process through which people develop a shared interpretation of meanings, intentions, or beliefs, allowing them to understand each other's perspectives and align their understanding during an interaction.

Key In sociolinguistics, the emotional or social tone of the interaction, encompassing the mood, attitude, or affective stance of the participants.

Metacultural proficiency The awareness and understanding of cultural nuances, norms, and variations in communication across different cultural contexts. It involves sensitivity to cultural differences in communication styles, etiquette, values, and norms.

Mirroring A cognitive phenomenon where individuals simulate or replicate the mental states, actions, or emotions of the speaker, often implicitly, when they process and comprehend language related to these experiences.

Multifinality The idea that a single initial condition or pathway can lead to multiple possible outcomes or end states within a system. It acknowledges that diverse outcomes can emerge from the same starting point due to the complexity of interactions and influences within the system.

Other-orientedness The focus or attention that an individual places on the perspectives, emotions, intentions, or expectations of others during communication. It involves being attentive and sensitive to interlocutors' thoughts, feelings, and communicative goals during an interaction.

Performatives Utterances that do not merely describe or report something but actually perform an action by being uttered and registered by a listener.

Perlocution (or **perlocutionary act**) The effect on the listener that speaker has by uttering certain words, such as consoling a person.

Pragmatic comprehension The ability to understand and interpret the intended meaning of spoken language beyond its literal or explicit content, considering the social context, speaker's intentions, implied meanings, and cultural norms embedded in the communication.

Pragmatic processing The use of contextual and social cues to interpret and understand the implied meaning behind spoken language beyond its conceptual comprehension.

Purpose In sociolinguistics, the goal or intention behind the communication. It can include informing, persuading, entertaining, or any other specific objective.

Register In sociolinguistics, the variety of language used in a particular context or by a specific group, often influenced by social factors such as age, social status, or formality.

Response types The various ways individuals react or reply to communication stimuli, such as utterances, questions, or prompts, within a conversation

Glossary 389

or interaction. These response types can vary based on the context, social norms, and the specific nature of the communicative exchange.

Response weighting The cognitive process through which a listener evaluates and assigns importance or relevance to different aspects of an utterance or communication, leading them to prioritize certain elements over others when formulating a response.

Rights and expectations The norms, entitlements, and anticipated behaviors that individuals hold or expect within communication interactions. These concepts play a crucial role in shaping the interaction dynamics, participation norms, degree of empathy, and ethical considerations in communication exchanges.

Setting In sociolinguistics, the physical or social context in which communication occurs. It includes the location, environment, social relationships, and situational factors influencing the interaction.

Situated presence The perception or feeling of being physically or mentally present in a specific context or situation during a communication interaction and aware of contextual factors that influence the ongoing communication.

Situated speech Language or communication that is embedded in a specific context, setting, or situation. It emphasizes that language use is not detached from its surrounding circumstances but is intricately connected to the immediate social, cultural, and environmental factors in which it occurs.

Social cognition The mental processes that enable individuals to perceive, interpret, and understand social information in their environment. It involves how people process, store, and use information related to themselves, others, social relationships, intentions, emotions, and social interactions.

Speech acts The actions or functions performed by speakers toward listeners when they communicate. Speech acts emphasize the intentions behind the utterances and how language is used to perform various actions beyond conveying information.

Stance In sociolinguistics, the personal or social perspective, attitude, or ethical position expressed by the speaker or participants in relation to the topic or interaction.

Subjective presence An individual's perception or feeling of being present, engaged, or immersed in a communication interaction or mediated communication context. It relates to the individual's personal sense of connection, involvement, or mental engagement within the communication experience.

Symbolic aptitude The capability of understanding and utilizing symbols, signs, and nonliteral meanings effectively in communication. It involves comprehending and using figurative language, metaphors, idiomatic expressions, sarcasm, irony, and other symbolic forms of communication.

Systems theory A framework used to understand complex systems and their interactions within environments. It suggests that biological, social, or

390 *Glossary*

organizational systems are made up of interconnected parts that function together to achieve specific goals or maintain equilibrium.

Top-down bias The influence of higher-level cognitive processes, such as expectations, context, or prior knowledge, on the listener's interpretation and understanding of incoming linguistic information. It represents a cognitive tendency for pre-existing knowledge or expectations to shape how listeners perceive, process, and comprehend language.

Uptaking The listener or interlocutor's response to or acknowledgment of a specific discourse move made by the speaker. It involves demonstrating comprehension, agreement, or engagement with the content or action presented in the conversation.

Voice In sociolinguistics, the individual's personal or group's shared unique style, personality, or identity expressed through language and communication, which may include citing, quoting, or otherwise referencing an original formulation.

Warrants In a model of argumentation, warrants are the underlying assumptions, principles, or reasoning that connect the grounds to the claim. Warrants explain why the grounds are relevant or sufficient to support the claim.

CHAPTER 5

Aggregate search models Systems that aim to provide comprehensive and unified search results by aggregating information from multiple sources or modalities. These models retrieve and integrate information from diverse and heterogeneous sources, creating a consolidated view of search results.

Artificial Intelligence (AI) Intelligence exhibited by machines or computer systems that mimic cognitive functions associated with human intelligence. AI is created and programmed by humans, utilizing algorithms, data, and computational power to simulate intelligent behavior.

Artificial neuron (also known as a **perceptron** or a **node**) A fundamental unit within an artificial neural network which is a key component of machine learning models. Modeled after biological neurons in the human brain, an artificial neuron processes and transforms multiple input signals into an output signal using weighted connections and an activation function.

Automatic speech recognition (ASR) A technology that enables machines to transcribe spoken language into text or commands. It involves converting spoken words or audio signals into written text, allowing computers to understand and process human speech.

Biological Intelligence (BI) The intelligence exhibited by living organisms, particularly humans and animals. It arises from the complex interactions of neurons, biological systems, and the brain's neural networks. BI evolves through natural selection and genetic inheritance.

Glossary 391

Dependency parsing A technique used in NLP to analyze the grammatical structure of sentences. Words in a sentence are represented as nodes in a graph, and the relationships between these words are represented as directed edges or links, indicating dependencies.

Dialogue management The orchestration of an interaction in AI by determining what actions the system should take based on the user's inputs and the system's capabilities.

Graph neural networks (GNNs) A class of artificial neural networks designed to operate on graph-structured data. Unlike traditional neural networks that operate on grid-like or sequential data (such as images, texts, or sequences).

Large language models (LLMs) Sophisticated artificial intelligence models trained on vast amounts of text data to understand and generate human-like language.

Information extraction A process of automatically extracting structured information from unstructured text. It aims to identify specific data points or relationships between entities and convert them into a structured format that machines can easily process and analyze.

Lemma (or **base form**) The base or dictionary form of a word, often called the headword or root word. It represents the canonical form to which inflected or derived forms of the word can be related.

Long short-term memory units (LSTM) A type of recurrent neural network (RNN) architecture designed to capture and retain long-range dependencies in sequential data. They are specifically developed to model and process sequential data, such as time series, text, audio, and more, where temporal relationships between elements are crucial.

Machine learning A field of Artificial Intelligence (AI) that focuses on developing algorithms and models that enable computers to learn from data, identify patterns, make predictions, or make decisions without explicit programming.

Memory banks Repositories or storage systems where an AI system stores and retrieves information for various purposes, similar to how human memory functions. These memory banks or memory systems within AI models serve as databases or structures that contain learned information, patterns, experiences, or knowledge.

Memory cell A component within specialized architectures like long short-term memory (LSTM) networks or gated recurrent units (GRUs). The memory cell is a fundamental part of these architectures, which is designed to address the issue of capturing and retaining long-term dependencies in sequential data. It serves as a unit within the network that can maintain and control the flow of information over time steps.

Named entity recognition (NER) A process used to identify and classify specific entities or named elements within text. These entities can include names, locations, dates, organizations, numerical expressions, and other

392 *Glossary*

specific identifiers. NER helps in extracting key information from text and categorizing it into predefined classes.

Natural language generation (NLG) A branch of Artificial Intelligence (AI) and computational linguistics focused on automatically generating human-readable text or speech from structured data or nonlinguistic inputs.

Natural language processing (NLP) A branch of artificial intelligence (AI) that focuses on enabling computers to understand, interpret, manipulate, and generate human language in a way that is both meaningful and useful.

Natural language understanding (NLU) A subset of artificial intelligence (AI) and natural language processing (NLP) that focuses on enabling computers to comprehend and interpret human language in a meaningful and contextually aware manner.

Neural network A computational model inspired by the structure and function of the human brain, composed of interconnected nodes (neurons) organized in layers. It is used in artificial intelligence to process complex information, learn patterns from data, and make predictions or decisions.

Part-of-speech (POS) tagging (also known as grammatical tagging or word-category disambiguation). A natural language processing (NLP) technique used to assign grammatical categories or parts of speech to each word in a sentence.

Perceptron node (P) A basic unit or node within a single layer of a perceptron model, which is the simplest form of an artificial neural network. A perceptron node performs computations on input data and produces an output based on a weighted sum (the relative importance) of inputs and an activation function (which enables interaction with other data).

Positive solution-oriented discourse patterns The use of language or conversational strategies that focus on constructive, optimistic, and problem-solving approaches within dialogue systems, or interactions between AI systems and users. These discourse patterns aim to maintain a positive and helpful conversation while addressing queries, issues, or providing assistance.

Prosodic features (NLP) Aspects of speech that relate to its acoustic, rhythmic, and intonational properties rather than the specific linguistic content or words being spoken. These features encompass various elements of speech beyond the literal meaning of words, including pitch, rhythm and tempos, stress and emphasis, intonation, pauses, and phrasings.

Question answering The use of NLP techniques to understand natural language questions and retrieve relevant information from text data to provide accurate answers. These systems aim to comprehend the query, search for information within a data set or a knowledge base, and generate appropriate responses.

Recurrent neural networks (RNNs) A type of artificial neural network designed to process sequential data by maintaining memory or context of

Glossary 393

previous inputs. Unlike traditional feedforward neural networks, which process each input independently, RNNs have connections that allow information to persist and be passed from one step of the sequence to the next.

Response processing The phase in NLP where a system or model generates a coherent and appropriate response to a given input or query. This process involves understanding the input, reasoning, generating or selecting the best response, and presenting it in a way that makes sense within the context of the conversation or task.

Sentiment analysis The determination of the sentiment or emotion expressed in a piece of text, including fine-grained sentiments (positive, negative, or neutral); mixed sentiments; sentiment intensity, sarcasm, and irony; contextual, cultural, and domain-specific sentiments.

Spectral envelope (phonology) A representation of the overall shape or contour of the frequency spectrum of an audio signal. It summarizes the spectral characteristics without detailing the exact energy content at each frequency.

Text classification The process of categorizing text into predefined classes or categories based on its content.

Tokens The individual units or elements that form the basic building blocks of a piece of text. These units are extracted by breaking down the text into smaller components, which can include words, punctuation marks, numbers, symbols, or subword units.

CHAPTER 6

Accommodation The process by which children modify their existing mental frameworks or create new ones to incorporate new information or rule exceptions that do not fit into their current understanding. In language development, accommodation involves adjusting linguistic schemas to account for new language rules, syntax, or vocabulary that cannot be assimilated into existing structures.

Acoustic variability The natural variations in speech sounds that occur due to factors such as different speakers, accents, intonations, speaking rates, and contextual influences. Despite this variability, listeners can recognize and categorize speech sounds accurately.

Assimilation The process by which children incorporate new information or experiences into their existing mental frameworks or schemas. In terms of language development, this means using existing linguistic structures or patterns to understand and interpret new words, concepts, or linguistic elements.

Categorical perception The human tendency to perceive speech sounds as belonging to discrete categories rather than as continuous variations along a spectrum.

394 *Glossary*

Child-directed speech (CDS) (also known as **motherese** or **parentese**) The specific style of speech used by caregivers or adults when communicating with infants, toddlers, or young children. It is characterized by distinct linguistic features and modifications tailored to facilitate language acquisition and support early language development in children.

Cognitive load The mental effort or capacity required by the brain to process information while performing a task. Cognitive load may be intrinsic (related to information complexity), extraneous (related to task complexity), or germane (related to integration processes of the listener).

Cognitive structures The mental frameworks or organized patterns of thinking that children develop as they grow and interact with their environment. Piaget proposed that children actively construct their understanding of the world through their experiences and interactions, and these mental structures serve as the foundation for their cognitive development.

Coordinate bilingualism The situation in which an individual acquires one language at an early age and then, at a later stage, learns a second language separately. In coordinate bilingualism, the two languages are acquired and developed separately and might not be used interchangeably in the same context as often as in simultaneous bilingualism.

Contextual language routines Repetitive, predictable, and structured activities or situations in a child's environment that offer consistent opportunities for language learning and development.

Continuous perception Perceiving speech sounds as existing along a continuum without clear boundaries between categories. This perception treats speech sounds as having gradient differences without discrete categories.

Critical period hypothesis A proposal in second language acquisition research suggesting that there is a biologically determined period during which individuals are more receptive or better equipped to acquire a second language, typically before adolescence.

Differentiation The process of refining a child's understanding of words or concepts by recognizing and distinguishing between variations or specific characteristics within a broader category

Dual coding A cognitive theory that suggests there are two distinct but interconnected ways in which the human mind processes and stores information: symbolically (such as textually) and sensorily (such as visually). This theory proposes that information is processed not only through linguistic verbal systems but also through nonlinguistic sensory systems.

Error analysis A type of language acquisition study involving analysis of the errors made by language learners as they acquire a second language. These studies aim to understand the nature of errors, their sources, and the underlying processes involved in language learning.

Glossary 395

Gap filling A child's linguistic strategy of using a single word to represent a broader category or to fill in the gaps within their understanding of a particular concept or category. For instance, if a child sees a new type of fruit they've never encountered before, they might use a familiar word like "apple" to label it until they learn the specific name for that fruit.

Gairaigo Literally "foreign words" in Japanese, this word refers to terms that are borrowed from other languages, particularly from English and other Western languages. These loanwords have been integrated into the Japanese language, with transvocalized pronunciation.

Generalization The process whereby a child extends the meaning of a word or concept to encompass broader or more abstract categories.

Islands of expertise Specific areas or domains in which an individual, particularly a child, demonstrates an exceptional level of knowledge, skills, or competence compared to their overall developmental stage or abilities in other areas.

Labeling The process by which a child associates a label (a precursor to a word) with a particular object, action, concept, or entity in their environment.

Learning episodes In the context of child language development, specific instances or periods during which a child engages in structured, focused, and intentional learning experiences related to language acquisition. These episodes involve various activities, interactions, or interventions designed to facilitate language learning and development in a targeted and purposeful manner.

Lexical gap A situation in language learning in which a learner encounters a concept or idea in a second language for which there is no direct equivalent word or expression in their native or first language. This absence of a corresponding word or phrase in the learner's native language creates a gap in their vocabulary.

Lexical transfer Movement of vocabulary items from one language to another. The two basic kinds of transfer are **cognate transfer** and **loan transfer**. **Cognate transfer** results from words that share a common etymological origin and have similar forms and meanings in different languages due to their linguistic heritage. **Loan transfer** results from borrowing directly from one language into another with minimal or no translation, often to fill a cultural, historical, or technological need in the target language.

Listening lexicon The mental storehouse of words and linguistic units accessed during auditory language processing, based on representations of words as phonological forms, with associated meanings, syntactic roles, and contextual associations. It enables individuals to understand and interpret words as they are heard in real time, without textual transference.

Magnetic tuning A language acquisition process of altering perceptual space near phonemic (meaningful) category centers; may be done through enhancement, attenuation, sharpening, broadening, or realignment.

396   *Glossary*

Mapping   The cognitive process of associating or linking concepts or meanings from one's native language (L1) onto the words or vocabulary of the second language (L2).

Mean length of utterance (MLU)   A measure used in the field of linguistics and child language development to gauge the average length of a child's spoken utterances, as a metric for syntactic growth.

Metacognitive processing   Higher-order thinking processes that involve awareness, understanding, and control of one's own cognitive processes. It involves monitoring, evaluating, and regulating one's thinking, learning, and problem-solving strategies.

Mora-timed language   A language (such as Japanese) in which the focus is on the timing of morae (rhythmic units) rather than syllables per se. In these languages, some mora appear to be silent or unvoiced.

Mutual exclusivity   A cognitive principle observed in language learning, particularly in early childhood, where children tend to assign unique labels to objects. The mutual exclusivity principle refers to the assumption that objects have only one label or name.

Mutual exclusivity strategy   A child's tendency to distinguish words when learning new labels for objects. Children tend to assume that the new word refers to a previously unnamed object when presented with a new word and an object for which they already know a label.

Native listener hypothesis (NLH)   A proposal that listeners' perception of speech sounds is influenced by the phonological system of their native language. According to this hypothesis, individuals are better at perceiving and discriminating sounds that are phonemic or relevant in their native language compared to sounds that are nonnative or not phonemically distinctive in their language.

Network-building   The process through which children expand their understanding and knowledge of words by creating connections or networks between words and their related concepts, meanings, and associations.

Neural commitment   The process by which the brain becomes specialized or "committed" to specific functions or tasks based on experiences, learning, or environmental influences. This specialization involves the development of neural pathways, networks, and structures that become finely tuned or dedicated to processing certain types of information or performing particular functions.

Orienting response   A concept in psychology that describes an automatic reaction or attentional shift in response to a novel or significant stimulus in the environment. It involves a quick redirection of attention toward the stimulus to gather more information and assess potential relevance or threat. In listening, the most common orienting responses are the P-400 effect, the P-300 effect, and the N-400 effect.

Glossary 397

Overextension The phenomenon of a child using a particular word in a broader or more general sense than its conventional or expected meaning. For example, a child might use the word "dog" not only for actual dogs but also for other four-legged animals they encounter, such as cats or rabbits.

P-400 effect an orienting response in the auditory cortex, the P-400 effect is an event-related potential (ERP) in the brain that occurs around 400 milliseconds (hence the name) after the presentation of a linguistic stimulus that violates or is incongruent with the listener's expectations based on the context provided.

Packaging The mental process where a child groups or packages various related items or concepts under a single word or label.

Perceptual constancy The ability to perceive speech sounds consistently as members of the same category despite variations in their acoustic properties. It involves maintaining the perception of a speech sound despite changes in pitch, volume, or other acoustic features. This constancy aids in recognizing and comprehending speech across different contexts and variations.

Phonetic contrasts The differences in speech sounds or phonemes that result in distinct meanings in a language. These contrasts are crucial in distinguishing one word from another and are integral to the phonological system of a language.

Phonological sensitivity A listener's ability to discern and manipulate the sounds or phonological components of language. It involves the awareness and sensitivity to speech's phonetic and phonemic structure, including the ability to recognize, discriminate, and manipulate distinct sounds and sound patterns in a language.

Phonological words Units of speech that young children initially perceive and process as single rhythmic or prosodic units, not necessarily corresponding to complete lexical words in the language.

Phonotactic knowledge An understanding of internalized rules that fluent speakers of a language have about the permissible combinations of phonemes and their sequences and alterations within that language.

Phonotactic system The set of rules or constraints within a language that govern the permissible combinations, arrangements, and sequencing of phonemes (speech sounds) in words. These rules define the patterns or structures of how sounds can be organized or arranged within a word or across syllables in a language.

Semantically contingent In the context of child-directed speech (CDS), the practice of adults or caregivers adjusting their language and communication based on the semantic or content-related cues provided by the child during the interaction. This is achieved through responsive language (responding to the child's focus of attention) and topic alignment (demonstrating connections between topics).

398 *Glossary*

Simultaneous bilingualism The phenomenon of a child being exposed to and acquiring two languages from birth or early infancy. In simultaneous bilingualism, both languages are learned in an overlapping time frame, often in the same environment or context.

Syllable-timed language A language (such as Spanish) that exhibits an even rhythm where each syllable is perceived to have equal duration or weight. In these languages, syllables are produced with relatively similar timing and stress, leading to a more uniform cadence without prominent stress patterns.

Topical interaction The exchange of language or communication that centers around specific topics or subjects between a child and their caregivers, teachers, or peers. It involves conversations, discussions, or interactions that focus on particular themes, ideas, or topics of interest to facilitate the child's semantic processing and language development.

Translanguaging A linguistic approach or practice that recognizes and embraces the fluid and dynamic use of multiple languages by individuals who are multilingual or bilingual. It involves utilizing and integrating different languages flexibly and creatively to communicate and understand, breaking down the traditional boundaries between languages.

Transliteration The process of converting text from one writing system or script into another. Unlike translation, which involves converting the meaning of words or phrases from one language to another, transliteration focuses on representing the same or similar sounds of words in a different script.

Transvocalization A linguistic concept that involves the transformation of sounds or phonemes from one language into another, usually as part of a loanword or a borrowed term. It refers to the process of adapting sounds from the phonetic system of one language into another language's phonetic or phonological system.

Trochaically timed language A language (such as English) in which the rhythm is based on alternating stressed and unstressed syllables. This rhythm creates a pattern where stressed syllables are followed by one or more unstressed syllables. Languages with this rhythm tend to have a more regular alternation of stressed and unstressed syllables, creating a somewhat marching or bouncing rhythm.

Underextension The opposite of overextension, it occurs when a child restricts or limits the use of a word to a narrower or more specific context than its typical usage. For instance, a child might use the word "ball" only for a specific ball they frequently play with and not apply it to spherical objects.

CHAPTER 7

Active listening A communication technique that involves the listener's fully concentrating on, understanding, responding to, and remembering what is being said by the speaker. It is a deliberate and focused form

Glossary 399

of listening that goes beyond simply hearing words. The goal of active listening is to comprehend the speaker's message accurately and respond appropriately.

Attention The cognitive process of selectively focusing mental resources on specific stimuli or tasks while ignoring others. This is the ability to concentrate on relevant information, filter out distractions, and allocate cognitive resources to facilitate processing and encoding of the information.

Attention to form In language acquisition research, this refers to the focus or emphasis that learners place on the formal aspects of language, such as grammar, vocabulary, pronunciation, or specific language structures, while learning a second language.

Audio-Lingual Method (ALM) An influential language teaching approach primarily used in the mid-twentieth century, especially during the 1950s and 1960s. It was developed as a response to behaviorist theories and was heavily influenced by structural linguistics, focusing on oral skills, the use of audiovisual materials, pattern practice, and repetition, and immediate correction of any error.

Biolinguistic approaches Approaches to language learning and acquisition that explore language from a biological and evolutionary perspective, focusing on the cognitive and neurological mechanisms that underlie the human capacity for language. These approaches draw from the field of biolinguistics, which investigates the biological foundations of language in humans.

Cognitive-code learning theory An approach to language learning that emerged as a response to behaviorist theories in the mid-twentieth century. It represents a shift from the behaviorist principles of stimulus-response-reinforcement models, such as those seen in the Audio-Lingual Method, toward a more cognitive and mentalistic view of language acquisition.

Cognitive strategies Strategies involving mental processes and cognitive activities that listeners use to comprehend and make sense of spoken language. Cognitive strategies include techniques such as predicting, summarizing, inferencing, visualizing, and recognizing patterns in spoken language.

Conceptual schemata Mental frameworks or structures that organize and represent knowledge and concepts related to specific topics or domains. They encompass a person's understanding, beliefs, experiences, and expectations related to a particular subject.

Connection The formation of associations, links, or neural connections within the brain related to the processed information. It involves integrating new information with existing knowledge, creating meaningful relationships between concepts, and forming memory traces or neural networks associated with the learned material.

400   *Glossary*

Conscious strategy selection   In the context of metacognitive approaches to language instruction, this refers to learners actively and deliberately choosing and applying specific learning strategies while being aware of their own thinking processes and learning goals.

Deliberate practice   An instructional method involving a focused and systematic approach to enhancing specific, component skills. It emphasizes purposeful, structured, and repeated efforts aimed at continuous improvement.

Dialogic education   An educational approach that emphasizes dialogue, interaction, and meaningful communication as central components of the learning process. Influenced by sociocultural theories of learning, dialogic education places a strong emphasis on social interaction, collaborative learning, and the co-construction of knowledge.

Direct method (DM)   A language teaching approach that emerged in the late 19th and early 20th centuries as a reaction against the Grammar-Translation method. Key characteristics of the direct method included emphasis on oral communication, focus on conversational skills, and avoidance of translation.

Engagement   In instructional design, this refers to the active involvement, interest, or investment of an individual in a particular task, activity, or idea. It involves emotional and cognitive investment, motivation, and participation, contributing to enhanced learning and information processing.

Experience-text-relationship (ETR) model   An approach used in teaching listening comprehension. It focuses on enhancing students' understanding of and engagement with texts by connecting the content of the text to their own experiences and background knowledge.

Experiential listening   An approach to teaching and learning listening skills that emphasizes active engagement and interaction with the language in real-life contexts along with attention to deliberate practice of component top-down, bottom-up, and interactive listening skills.

Focus on form (FoF)   In second language instruction, this refers to an approach that integrates attention to specific language forms, structures, or aspects (such as grammar, vocabulary, and pronunciation) within communicative and content-based language teaching. Unlike form-focused instruction, which emphasizes explicit teaching of language forms, FoF is more incidental and involves drawing learners' attention to language features during communicative activities or tasks.

Form-focused instruction (FFI)   Instructional techniques or approaches that deliberately target and emphasize the formal aspects of a language, such as grammar, vocabulary, syntax, or pronunciation

i + 1 level   A concept introduced by linguist Stephen Krashen in his theory of second language acquisition, specifically within the framework of his input hypothesis. The "i + 1" refers to a level of linguistic input that is slightly beyond the learner's current proficiency level.

Glossary 401

Inferencing The process of drawing conclusions, making predictions, or filling in gaps in understanding by using available information, context clues, and prior knowledge. In the context of listening, activating inferencing skills involves encouraging learners to use contextual cues, background knowledge, and logical reasoning to make inferences about the meaning of the spoken content.

KWL model The KWL model is a teaching strategy used to guide and structure listening activities, encouraging active engagement, inquiry, and reflection among learners. The acronym stands for "what you know already," "what you want to know," and "what you learned" from the text.

Lexical maps Mental networks or structures that organize and connect words or vocabulary in a person's mind. They are mental representations of how words are related to each other based on semantic, phonological, or syntactic connections. In the context of listening, activating lexical maps involves using prior knowledge of vocabulary and word relationships to comprehend and interpret spoken language.

Metacognitive strategies The cognitive processes and techniques learners use to monitor, manage, and regulate their listening comprehension. These include planning and goal setting, active listening techniques, self-monitoring, initiating clarification strategies, and reflection and evaluation.

Nucleation In the context of the Audio-Lingual Method (ALM) of language teaching, this refers to a technique used to introduce new language elements or structures. It involves presenting a nucleus sentence or phrase that exemplifies the target language structure or pattern, which learners then practice and manipulate through various drills and exercises.

Pragmatic competence The ability to use language appropriately and effectively in various social contexts to achieve communicative goals. It involves understanding and applying the social and cultural rules governing language use beyond the literal meaning of words. Key components of pragmatic competence include understanding context, grasping implications and inferences, applying politeness and social norms, and resolving ambiguity and misunderstandings.

Quality questioning A deliberate and thoughtful approach to asking questions that stimulates critical thinking, engages learners, and enhances comprehension and understanding of texts or spoken material. Quality questioning involves six stages: Stimulating Higher-Order Thinking, Promoting Discussion, Encouraging Multiple Perspectives, Connecting to Prior Knowledge, Active Engagement, and Evaluating Understanding.

Question–Answer-Relationship (QAR) model A strategy used in teaching listening comprehension skills, particularly in helping students understand how to approach different types of questions related to a text. Developed by Taffy Raphael, QAR helps students categorize different types of questions based on where the answers can be found in the text. The QAR

402 *Glossary*

model identifies four question–answer relationships: Right There (Literal Questions); Think and Search (Inferential Questions); Author and You (Inferential Questions, On My Own (Applied or Evaluative Questions).

Receptivity The brain's readiness or openness to receive and process incoming stimuli or information. It involves the brain's ability to perceive, register, and be sensitive to sensory inputs from the environment or external stimuli.

Reciprocal teaching (RT) A structured instructional approach used in teaching listening comprehension skills. It involves a collaborative dialogue between teachers and students, where they take on specific roles and engage in a systematic process to understand and interpret texts. The RT model typically involves four key strategies or steps: predicting, questioning, clarifying, and summarizing.

Scientific approach An approach to language learning, advocated by Harold Palmer, which aimed to apply scientific principles to the study and teaching of languages. Palmer's scientific approach was grounded in linguistic theory and scientific methodology. Key principles and aspects of his approach included phonetics and pronunciation, language analysis, and skill integration.

Socio-affective strategies Strategies that focus on the social and emotional aspects of listening. These strategies involve managing emotions, attitudes, and interactions during listening activities. Examples include being attentive, showing interest in the speaker, asking for clarification, seeking feedback, or empathizing with the speaker's emotions.

Transfer-appropriate processing (TAP) A theory in cognitive psychology that emphasizes the importance of the match or compatibility between the processes engaged during encoding (learning) and those engaged during retrieval (remembering or recalling) for effective memory performance.

Zone of proximal development (ZPD) A concept introduced by psychologist Lev Vygotsky to describe the difference between what a learner can accomplish independently and what they can achieve with guidance and support from a more knowledgeable person, often a teacher, parent, or peer.

CHAPTER 8

Accommodation The natural interaction process through which speakers adjust their language, speech patterns, or communication styles to align with or adapt to the speech of their conversation partner or audience.

Associative semantic processing A type of semantic processing involving making additive connections between different elements of information, such as auditory and visual elements, that contribute to a fuller understanding.

Chunking The strategy of breaking down larger or complex pieces of information into smaller, more manageable chunks or units.

Glossary 403

Cognitive load The mental effort or capacity the brain requires to process information while performing a task. Cognitive load may be affected by length, complexity, organization, and surface features; it may be intrinsic (related to information complexity), extraneous (related to task complexity), or germane (related to the integration processes of the listener).

Discourse type The functional aspect of language and the intentions behind communication. Major categories include narrative, conversational, dramatic, descriptive, expository, argumentative, persuasive, instructional, scientific, academic, and reflective.

Easifying input Strategies or techniques used to modify spoken language input to enhance its comprehensibility for learners without compromising its essential content or linguistic features. Some common techniques used to enhance input include repetition and paraphrasing, visual aids, and highlighting key information.

Elaborative simplification A teaching technique used to make complex or difficult language content more accessible and understandable for learners by providing additional explanations, examples, or details.

Episodic organization The strategy of breaking down larger or complex pieces of information into smaller, more manageable chunks or units, organized by coherence of information presentation, typically one main idea with supporting details.

First listening stage An interaction point after the first listening to an extract, in which questions are posed to elicit students' impressions and interests.

Follow-up post-listening stage An interaction point in a follow-up review session, in which students reflect on the previous listening experience through deliberate practice with bottom-up processing, reflective questions, or short student presentations on aspects of the content.

Genre A specific category or type of audio material or spoken content characterized by recongnizable recurring features, overall organization, and language use patterns. Materials may include monologues or dialogues in audio, video, multi-channel media, or enhanced realities formats.

Immediate post-listening stage An interaction point after the second listening to an extract involving an objective comprehension check.

Interaction points A term used in instructional design to refer to specific junctures in the act of listening in which perceptual and cognitive processes can be monitored, externalized, and amplified through specific tasks.

Interoceptive responses The body's perception, detection, and awareness of internal physiological sensations and signals. These sensations arise from within the body, conveying information about various physiological states such as heartbeat, breathing rate, temperature, pleasure and pain.

Listen-and-test An instructional sequence in the teaching of listening that involves students listening to audio materials or spoken content and subsequently undergoing assessments based on what they have heard.

404　*Glossary*

Pre-listening stage　An interaction point before listening to an extract to prepare the students through a preview task to activate schemata.

Referential semantic processing　A type of semantic processing involving connecting references to specific concepts, ideas, or information. It involves linking the content from multiple modalities to create a cohesive mental representation of the information.

Re-presenting text　A scaffolding technique of presenting a text for a second listening in order to increase familiarity, promote vocabulary focus, and reinforce intake of key information.

Restrictive simplification　A teaching technique that involves simplifying language input by reducing or limiting the complexity of the content without adding additional information, examples, or elaboration.

Second listening stage　An interaction point during the second listening to an extract, in which a scaffolded task with an idea structure is provided, such as a graph or chart.

Stabilization　A phenomenon of a listener repeatedly processing oral input in a shallow manner (not making connections or drawing inferences), which leads to fossilization, resistance to change, and an inability to progress further.

Temporal organization　The strategy of breaking down larger or complex pieces of information into smaller, more manageable chunks or units, organized by time period, typically 30- or 60-second segments.

CHAPTER 9

Collaborative conversation　A teaching technique that emphasizes purposeful and structured discussions that encourage students to engage in meaningful interactions while developing their academic language skills and critical thinking abilities. Key elements include the use of conversation stems or sentence frames, academic language development, and accountable talk (providing evidence, justifying reasoning, and engaging in reflection).

Content selection　The process of choosing and determining the specific information, subject matter, topics, or materials included in a learning experience or educational program.

Elicited imitation　A language teaching and assessment technique that involves the presentation of spoken sentences or phrases to learners, who are then asked to repeat or imitate what they heard, often practiced through dictation and dictogloss techniques.

Experience gap tasks　Tasks involving learners sharing personal experiences or anecdotes. This task encourages learners to use language for storytelling, recounting events, and expressing themselves through narratives.

Face validity　In the context of instructional design, this refers to the extent to which a learning task has an observable connection to assessment goals.

It is a subjective judgment based on the appearance or "face" of the task, indicating whether the task seems valid and relevant for its intended purpose.

Information gap tasks Tasks involving situations where learners possess different pieces of information necessary to complete a task or solve a problem. By sharing information, learners fill in the gaps in their knowledge.

Learning objectives Specific, measurable statements that describe what learners are expected to achieve or demonstrate as a result of engaging in a learning activity, course, or educational program.

Multiliteracy expert An individual with specialized knowledge, skills, and expertise in understanding, teaching, or applying multiple literacies or modes of communication in diverse contexts, encompassing a broad range of communication modes, technologies, and media.

Needs analysis A systematic process of identifying, evaluating, and understanding the specific requirements, preferences, goals, or deficiencies of learners or educational contexts.

Opinion gap tasks Tasks involving learners expressing and exchanging their opinions on various topics or issues. The goal is to engage learners in discussions or debates where they need to articulate their viewpoints, justify their opinions, and respond to others' perspectives.

Task sequencing The deliberate arrangement and ordering of learning tasks or activities within a learning module, course, or curriculum to maximize cognitive engagement, skill development, and transfer of learning.

Technology integration In instructional design, the conscious incorporation of various technological tools, resources, or digital platforms into the design and delivery of educational experiences to enhance teaching and learning. It aims to leverage technology to support and enrich the learning process, making it more engaging, interactive, and effective.

CHAPTER 10

Adaptive listening test items In AI, this refers to test items or questions that dynamically adjust their difficulty level based on the test taker's performance during the assessment. These items are part of adaptive testing systems designed to personalize the test experience by tailoring the difficulty of questions to the individual's demonstrated abilities.

Authentic/authenticity In listening assessment, this refers to audio content or spoken language used as testing prompts that is natural, unaltered, and reflects real-life communication as it occurs in its original context.

Bottom-level (skill-specific) attributes These are subskills that contribute to overall listening proficiency. These skills involve the detailed aspects of listening and understanding spoken language. Bottom-level attributes include recognition of vocabulary and syntax, decoding pronunciation and intonation, note-taking skills, and selective listening.

406   *Glossary*

Comprehension-based skills   Skills that involve higher-order cognitive abilities related to understanding and extracting meaning from the content or context of spoken discourse. Examples of comprehension-based skills in listening include global comprehension, inference-making, and understanding implied or unstated information.

Construct validity   The extent to which the test accurately measures the underlying constructs or theoretical concepts related to language proficiency. It assesses whether the test aligns with established theories of language learning and proficiency.

Content domain   Specific subject matter, topics, or thematic areas covered in the language assessment. It includes the range of vocabulary, language structures, and content-related knowledge domains in which test takers are expected to demonstrate proficiency.

Content validity   The extent to which the test content is representative of the language skills or constructs being measured. Content validity examines whether the test covers a comprehensive range of topics, language functions, and proficiency levels relevant to the intended purpose of the assessment.

Contextual validity   The suitability and relevance of the test within a specific context, considering cultural, linguistic, and situational factors that may impact the validity of the assessment.

Criterion-related validity   The relationship between test scores and an external criterion, such as other established tests, real-world language performance, or academic success. It determines whether the test scores correlate with or predict the language skills or abilities it aims to measure.

EAL (English as an additional language)   Programs designed for students who speak a language other than English at home and are learning English in addition to their native language. EAL programs focus on supporting language acquisition alongside the student's primary language.

EAP (English for academic purposes)   Programs preparing students, often nonnative English speakers, for academic study in English-speaking universities or educational institutions. EAP programs focus on developing language skills necessary for academic success, including writing essays, research papers, and understanding academic lectures.

EFL (English as a foreign language)   Teaching English to individuals in countries where English is not the primary language. EFL programs focus on acquiring English skills for various purposes, such as academics, business, or travel.

Enabling skills   The foundational abilities or prerequisites that support effective listening comprehension. These skills lay the groundwork for successful listening and understanding and include phonological awareness, vocabulary knowledge, and syntactic understanding.

Enacting skills   Skills involved in the actual execution or application of listening strategies and cognitive processes while engaging with listening

Glossary 407

materials, including predicting, inferencing, monitoring comprehension, identifying main ideas, recognizing supporting details, summarizing, and evaluating the intent of assessment prompts.

ESL (English as a second language programs) Programs designed for students learning English in a country where English is the primary language. ESL programs aim to teach English language skills to nonnative speakers living in an English-speaking environment.

ESP (English for specific purposes) Programs tailored to learners who need English language skills for a particular field or profession, such as English for medicine, business, or engineering. ESP programs focus on specialized vocabulary and language relevant to specific disciplines.

EYL (English for young learners) Programs focusing on teaching English to young learners (typically preschool or early primary-school children). These programs use age-appropriate methods to introduce English language skills at an early age.

Face validity The appearance or perception that the test measures what it claims to measure. While subjective, face validity reflects the extent to which the test seems relevant and appropriate to the test takers and stakeholders.

Global English The diverse forms and variations of the English language that are used as a borderless means of communication among speakers from different linguistic backgrounds and cultures worldwide. It encompasses the various styles, accents, vocabulary, and linguistic adaptations of English used by nonnative speakers across different regions and contexts.

Interactive listening proficiency An individual's ability to understand spoken language in interactive or communicative contexts where listening comprehension is vital for engaging in conversations, discussions, or exchanges with others. This proficiency involves understanding the content and actively participating, responding, and adapting.

Language-based skills Skills that focus on knowledge and understanding of the linguistic system itself, including the structure, grammar, vocabulary, and syntax of the language being tested. Language-based skills involve the ability to recognize and interpret linguistic elements within spoken discourse. Examples of language-based skills in listening include vocabulary recognition, grammar and syntax understanding, and phonological awareness.

Listening proficiency scale A tool used in language assessment to evaluate and measure an individual's listening abilities across different levels of proficiency. A scale typically consists of a range of proficiency levels (usually 3 to 9), often divided into categories or descriptors that describe the listener's abilities.

Process domain The process domain focuses on the cognitive processes (or constructs), strategies, or abilities involved in using language. It assesses

408   *Glossary*

how individuals comprehend, produce, or manipulate language in real-time communication or interactions.

Relevant/relevance   In listening assessment, this refers to content that aligns with the preferences, backgrounds, and experiences of the learners, aiming to resonate with the learners' personal interests, cultural background, or educational goals.

Test impact   The potential consequences, effects, or implications of using a test or assessment on individuals, educational settings, or institutions. It considers the influence of the test on various stakeholders and the broader context in which the test is administered. Key aspects related to test impact include fairness and equity and instructional impact.

Test prompt   The instructions or cues given to test takers before they listen to the audio or spoken material. The prompt sets the context, provides guidance, and outlines what the test takers are expected to do while listening to the audio.

Top-level (general) abilities (or **attributes**)   These are higher-order listening abilities that encompass overarching performative skills necessary for effective listening comprehension. They represent the broader, general capabilities required to understand spoken language. Top-level abilities include global comprehension, inference and deduction, **and** summarization and synthesis.

Useable/usability   In test design, reference to the suitability of input material based on technological accessibility and **clarity** and **audio quality.**

Validity   The extent to which a test or assessment instrument measures what it intends to measure and the appropriateness of the inferences or interpretations drawn from the test scores.

Variance   In test performance, this refers to the extent of variability or differences observed among the scores or outcomes of individuals who have taken the same test or assessment. Various factors contribute to variance in test performance, including individual abilities, preparation, motivation, test difficulty, test fairness, and the test content's nature.

Washback effect   The influence or impact that a test has on teaching and learning practices. It describes the relationship between the content, format, or results of an assessment (test) and how it affects teaching methods, curriculum, and student learning behaviors.

CHAPTER 11

Acceptability   As a rating category, the degree to which the audience finds the speaker's communication style, language use, and behavior suitable, appropriate, and culturally acceptable. It considers aspects such as the appropriateness of language choice, cultural sensitivity, respectfulness, and adherence to social norms or expectations, ensuring the speaker's communication aligns with audience expectations and norms.

Comprehensibility As a rating category, thee degree to which the speaker's message or content is clear, understandable, and easily grasped by the audience.

Cue uptake In discourse analysis, this refers to how speakers or listeners recognize and respond to cues or signals provided within a conversation or discourse. It involves the ability of individuals engaged in communication to perceive, interpret, and appropriately react to linguistic or nonlinguistic cues presented by their interlocutors.

Discourse management The control and organization of spoken or written language by speakers or writers to structure, guide, and maintain communication within a discourse or conversation. It involves the strategies, techniques, and linguistic devices used to manage and regulate the flow, structure, and coherence of discourse.

Discourse moves The distinct communicative units or actions within a conversation that serve specific functions in guiding or shaping the interaction. These moves are identifiable segments or actions that contribute to the flow, structure, and coherence of the conversation. They can be verbal or nonverbal and play a crucial role in organizing the exchange of information, managing turn-taking, and achieving communication goals.

Empathic responses In discourse analysis, this refers to explicit linguistic expressions or behaviors used by speakers or interlocutors to convey understanding, empathy, or emotional support toward the feelings, experiences, or perspectives expressed by others in a conversation or discourse.

Immediate recall protocol (IRP) A method used in communication research to gather data on immediate recall or immediate memory of a specific communication event or message. It focuses on capturing participants' ability to remember and reproduce details, content, or elements of a communication immediately after exposure to the information.

Intelligibility As a rating category, how easily the audience can recognize and understand the individual sounds, words, and sentences spoken by the speaker. It focuses on the clarity of pronunciation and articulation and the speaker's ability to produce sounds accurately, making their speech understandable to listeners, especially in cases involving accents or unfamiliar phonetic patterns.

Interactivity As a rating category, the speaker's ability to engage, involve, and interact with the audience during the presentation or speech. It assesses the extent to which the speaker encourages audience participation, invites questions, responds to queries, and fosters a dynamic interaction that keeps the audience engaged and interested.

410 *Glossary*

Listener decisions In interaction analysis, these are rater inferences about the interpretation processes and judgments made by individuals while engaged in the act of listening.

Listener judgments Listener ratings of speaker performances, concerning comprehensibility, intelligibility, interactivenes and effect of a speaker.

Listener misunderstandings In interaction analysis, instances where there is a discrepancy or failure in the interpretation or comprehension of the communicated message by the listener.

Probed recall A research and assessment technique of providing participants with specific prompts, cues, or questions to help guide their memory retrieval. Instead of an open-ended request to recall everything they remember, participants are given targeted prompts or cues to assist in their memory recall.

Rating scale A structured tool used to assess and provide feedback on various aspects of a speaker's performance, delivery, and content during a presentation or speech. This scale allows evaluators or audience members to provide systematic and objective feedback by assigning scores or ratings to different components of the presentation.

Recall protocol A structured method or procedure used to collect data from participants regarding their memory of a specific communication event or message. It involves prompting participants to recall, recount, or describe details, content, or aspects of a communication interaction they experienced or were exposed to.

Speaker impact As a rating category, the influence, effect, or impression that a speaker has on their audience or listeners during a communication interaction. It involves the ability of the speaker to convey messages effectively, capture the audience's attention, and elicit certain responses or reactions through their speech, delivery style, and overall presentation.

CHAPTER 12

Action research A systematic approach in which educators or researchers actively engage in a cycle of reflection, planning, action, and evaluation to address specific issues, improve practices, or enhance learning outcomes.

Attitudes and motivation As an educational outcome or target, this refers to learners' attitudes toward language learning, and their motivation, interest, and willingness to engage with the language and its culture, which significantly influence learning outcomes.

Behavioral changes As an educational outcome or target, this refers to observable changes in learners' actions, habits, or responses, reflecting the impact of language learning on their behaviors and communication patterns.

Glossary 411

Case study An in-depth examinationof a particular individual, group, or situation, carried out in order to explore and understand the complexities, dynamics, and nuances of listening abilities or experiences. Rather than focusing on a large sample size, a case study delves deeply into a specific context to gain detailed insights into listening behaviors, strategies, challenges, or successes.

Character development Encouraging ethical behavior, resilience, responsibility, and integrity through language learning, contributing to learners' character development.

CLIL (Content and Language Integrated Learning) An educational approach that involves teaching both content and language simultaneously in a language that is not the students' native language. The primary goal of CLIL is to develop students' language proficiency while they learn academic content in subjects such as science, mathematics, history, or other disciplines.

Cognitive skills Mental processes such as memory, attention, problem-solving, critical thinking, and language acquisition, all of which are fundamental to language learning.

Collaboration skills As an educational outcome or target, this refers to the ability to work effectively in groups, engage in mutual tasks, and communicate ideas in a team setting.

Control variable A factor that researchers intentionally keep constant or consistent throughout the study to prevent its influence on the dependent variable(s). In listening research, control variables might include factors like the type of listening materials used, the type or duration of listening exercises, the channels of input, or the environment in which participants engage in listening tasks.

Creativity and innovation As an educational outcome or target, this refers to encouraging learners to think independently, express themselves authentically, and explore diverse perspectives .

Cultural competence As an educational outcome or target, this refers to understanding and respecting diverse cultures, traditions, and perspectives associated with the language being learned, fostering intercultural communication skills.

Delivery methods Various techniques or approaches used to present audio or spoken content to students in a classroom or learning environment. Variations include recorded vs. live presentation, audio vs. video, video only vs. video with subtitles, single source presentation vs. interactive multimedia.

Dependent variable The factor or aspect that researchers wish to observe, measure, or test to determine its outcome or response due to changes or manipulations in the independent variables. In the study of listening, the

412   *Glossary*

dependent variable might be the students' listening comprehension score, the accuracy of their responses to specific listening tasks, or their retention of information after listening to audio materials.

Discourse types   Various categories or classifications of spoken communication or conversations that participants encounter during listening tasks, experiments, or research studies. These categories are defined based on the structure, organization, and purpose of the spoken discourse or interaction, such as situational dramas, academic lectures, or news broadcasts.

Experimental design   A systematic approach used to investigate the effects of specific interventions, instructional methods, or treatments on individuals' listening abilities. Experimental designs are characterized by their ability to establish cause-and-effect relationships between variables by controlling for extraneous factors.

Formative assessment   Ongoing techniques used during the learning process to monitor students' learning progress, identify strengths and weaknesses, and provide feedback to guide further learning.

Global citizenship   As an educational outcome or target, this refers to empowering learners to understand global issues, appreciate diversity, and become responsible and informed global citizens through language education.

Health and well-being   As an educational outcome or target, this refers to promoting mental and physical well-being among learners, emphasizing the importance of a supportive environment for effective learning.

Independent variables   The factors, conditions, or variables that researchers deliberately manipulate, change, or control to observe their effect on the dependent variables or outcomes. These variables are controlled by the researcher. Independent variables in researching listening might include: types of listening materials, delivery method, instructional method, or task type.

Input variable/input sources   For research purposes, input variable refers to the various mediums or sources from which participants receive auditory stimuli or information during listening tasks or experiments. These may be audio recordings, video recordings, live speech, digital media, or simulated or virtual environments.

Instructional intervention   A deliberate action, strategy, technique, or program implemented by researchers or educators to facilitate, enhance, or modify the teaching and learning processes related to listening skills.

Learning journals   Personal or reflective records kept by participants to document their experiences, thoughts, observations, and reflections related to listening activities or exercises. These journals serve as a tool for participants to actively engage with and reflect upon their listening processes, strategies, challenges, and progress.

Glossary 413

Longitudinal study A research approach that observes and analyzes changes or developments in individuals' listening skills over an extended period. These studies involve collecting data from the same group of individuals (or participants) repeatedly, at multiple points in time, to examine changes, patterns, or trends in their listening abilities.

Mixed-methods research A comprehensive approach that combines both qualitative and quantitative research methods to study various aspects of listening skills, strategies, behaviors, or experiences. This approach involves integrating different data collection techniques, analyses, and perspectives to gain a more comprehensive understanding of listening processes.

Post-listening activities Activities that follow listening to an extract and that focus on reinforcing comprehension, consolidating learning, and extending understanding beyond the listening content. Examples include comprehension questions, discussions, summarizing, extending, and reflecting.

Pre-listening activities Activities that aim to prepare students for the upcoming listening task. They focus on activating background knowledge, generating interest, predicting content, and setting purposes for listening. Examples include brainstorming, vocabulary preview, predictions, and discussion questions.

Quasi-experimental design A research approach used to study the effects or outcomes of an intervention or treatment, similar to experimental designs. However, unlike true experimental designs, quasi-experimental designs typically employ natural group assignments rather than random assignment of students, due to practical or ethical constraints.

Rhetorical styles The various patterns or strategies used by speakers to structure and deliver their spoken discourse effectively. These styles encompass different techniques, organizational patterns, or modes of presentation that speakers employ to convey their message, persuade their audience, or achieve specific communicative goals. Styles include narrative, descriptive, expository, persuasive, and conversational.

Social and emotional skills As an educational outcome or target, the ability to understand and manage emotions, communicate effectively, empathize, collaborate, and navigate social interactions, fostering interpersonal skills in language education.

Summative assessment This refers to techniques used periodically to evaluate students' learning outcomes at the end of a unit, course, or specific juncture in a course. Its focus is on measuring learning outcomes and providing a summary of students' achievements.

Technological enhancements The use of various technological tools, devices, or resources to improve the delivery, accessibility, interactivity, and effectiveness of listening instruction. These enhancements leverage

414 *Glossary*

technology to create engaging, interactive, and dynamic learning experiences for students while developing their listening skills.

While-listening activities Activities that are conducted while students listen to the audio or spoken content. They aim to improve comprehension, listening strategies, and note-taking skills. Examples include listening for specific information, filling in the charts, and sequencing events.

Index

Note: Entries in *italics* denote figures; entries in **bold** denote tables; <u>underlined</u> entries denote glossary entries.

abstract reasoning 48, 119; *see also* AI semantic processing
abstract thinking 22, 56, 154
academic conversations 253–4, 342
academic listening 85, 282, 362
accent, assessing 311; *see also* speaker comprehensibility
acceptability, assessing 310, <u>408</u>; *see also* speaker comprehensibility
acceptable understanding 71
accessibility features 286; *see also* AI in testing listening
accommodation: in language development 145, <u>393</u>; in discourse 219, <u>402</u>; in oral interviews 283, **284**
acetylcholine 13, <u>376</u>
Achebe, Chinua 159
acknowledgments 14, 96, <u>385</u>
acoustic reflex 10; *see also* ear, anatomy
acoustic variability 141, <u>393</u>
acquisition-laning hypothesis 176–7
ACTFL Listening Proficiency Scale **267–70**
action research 328–9, 338, 351, <u>410</u>
activation functions 109, 115; *see also* AI neural networks
active engagement 189, 205–6, 265, 370
active listening 15, 235, **252**, 369, <u>398–9</u>; as a metacognitive strategy 401; in discourse framing 81–2; and language acquisition 174; and Listening Circles 185; as learning objective 234; active listening skills 149; active listening strategies 183; mindset for 195

activity types, and listening outcomes 327
adaptability, as research skill 370
Adaptive Control Model (ACM) 151
adaptive listening test items 285, <u>405</u>; *see also* AI in testing listening
additive responses 96–8; *see also* pragmatic processing
addressee 80–1, 95; *see also* listener roles
addressor 80; *see also* listener roles
affective filter hypothesis 177
affective involvement 81–2, 260–1
agency: individual differences in 23; in listening 14–15, 135, 158, 190, 222, 249, <u>376</u>
aggregate search models 124, <u>390</u>; *see also* natural language processing
AGI (Artificial General Intelligence) 109, 126
AI (Artificial Intelligence) 6, 79, <u>390</u>; advantages and disadvantages 128–9; and BI 108–9; evaluating voices 303; evolution of 126–8; goals of processing 111–13; linguistic processing 115–18; neurological processing 114–5; pragmatic processing 124–6; semantic processing 118–23; in testing listening 285–7; tools for generating input 237
allophonic variations 39, 272, <u>378</u>
amalgams 45, <u>379</u>
Amazon Alexa 126
ambiguity 30, 46, **57**, 120, <u>382</u>; creating 92; and inferencing 65; resolving 120, 158; tolerating 80
amygdala 13–14, 16, 18–19

416   *Index*

analog-to-digital converter 116
Anderson, R.C. 62–3
ANOVA 371–3
antonymy **57**, 382
Apple Siri 126
approximation 67–8, 382, 382; *see also* compensatory strategies
argument structure: in syntactic processing 42–6, 379
arousal 13; *see also* reticular activating system
articulation: in multimodal processing 46; assimilation and reduction processes 30 39–40 assessing 311
articulatory rehearsal process 18; *see also* phonological loop
articulatory settings 92
artificial neural networks (ANNs) 116
artificial neurons 109, 114, 390
Aryadoust, Vahid 259, 265
assessment: contexts **260–2**; holistic assessment 267; in instructional design 238; and listening outcomes 327; peer assessment 309, 312; targets of 273; performance assessments 238, 345, 349–50; portfolio assessment 267, 281–2, 287; variables 330, 345–6; post-listening assessment 346; self-assessment 182, 238, 281, 335, 345–7, 350; summative assessment 238, 345, 413; *see also* listening assessment
assimilation: in language development 145, 393; in phonology 30, 39–40, 153, 379
associative semantic processing 221, 402; *see also* semantic processing
attention 182–3, 185, 399; conscious 15, 38, 42, 154; derailments of 154; to form 174, 399; individual differences in 23; in listening 10, 12–14; stages of *13*; attentional capture 14, 376; attentional control 13, 376; *see also* selective attention
attenuation 139; *see also* perceptual magnet effect
attitudes and motivation 186, **194**, 328, 410
audience 80, **86**, 91–2, 207, **212**
audience receptivity 310
audio input: in AI training 110, 112, 117; in language teaching 180, 183, 192,

205–6, **208–211**; 234; scaffolding 219–20; technology mediation 220–3, 237–8; in assessment 281, 285; in listening research 297, 301, 310, 317; *see also* input
Audio-Lingual Method (ALM) 173, 399
auditor 81; *see also* listener roles
auditory: channel 9, 137; auditory experiences, early 22; auditory input: interpretation of 19; parallel processing of 16; auditory systems, AI and BI *117*
auditory cortex 7, 376; and context effects 39; development and organization of 22–3; in hearing circuit 9–12, 15, 17; in L1 acquisition 139; P-400 errors 154; P-600 errors 42; phonological processing 31–3
auditory nerve 9–12, 22
auditory processing circuit *12*, 16; auditory nerve 9–12, 22
augmented reality (AR) 222; resources 365–6
aural comprehension (MELAB) **264**
Austin, J.L. 88–9
authentic materials: 180, 187, 273, 332, 405
authentic texts 187, 189, 219–20
automated scoring 285; *see also* AI in testing listening
automatic speech recognition (ASR) 110, 116–18, *117*, 348, 390
autonomous listening 293, 347–50
availability bias 62
awareness 5; and agency 14–15; interoceptive 16

backchanneling 95–6, 300, 385
background knowledge 6; access to 60, 71; activation of 15; incorporating into text processing 264–5; and metacognitive processing 182; and top-down processing 48, 191, 239; triggering connections to 190
backpropagation 109, 114, 120
Bartlett, Frederic 59
baton signals 47; *see also* kinesic cues
behavioral changes 231, 328, 410
behaviorist theories 173–4
Berlitz, Maximilian and Charles 172
Berlo, David 88
Bhatia, Vijay 218–19

BI (biological intelligence) 6, 108–9, 116, 390
biases: in linguistic processing 62–3, 66–7, 71, 239; in interpretive communities 86; in pragmatic competence; in AI processing 109, 120, 128–9; in critical thinking 191; in assessment 258; in research 310–12, 316, 329, 370
Bilingual Shift Model (BSM) 151
bilingual usage 297
bilinguals 23, 149–50, 152, 156–7, 159
biolinguistics 173–4, 399
body language 48, 84, 157, 306–8
bottom-level abilities 263–4, 405
bottom-up processing 15–16, 376; and teaching listening 186–9; and top-down processing 29–30, 48–9, 49, 71, 72
brain: structures involved in audition 10–12; structures involved in attention 14–15; structures involved in comprehension 15–17; structures involved in memory 17–19; structures involved in inferencing 19–22
broadening 139; see also magnetic tuning
Brown, Steven 234

Candlin, Christopher xix, 2
captioning 220–1; see also technology mediation
caregivers, and L1 acquisition 135, 137, 141–2, 144–8
case studies 304, 328–9, 344, 369, 411
categorical perception 38, 141, 393
causal inference 20, 64
causality, circular 97–8; see also systems theory
cause-and-effect relationships 64, 329
Chafe, Wallace 312
channel 80, 385; see also deictic framing
character development 328, 351, 411, 411; see also educational outcomes
characteristic frequency 10, 376
charting method 246; see also note-taking
chatbots 111, 125–6, 237, 366–7; ontology for 122, 123
Chaudron, Craig 219
child-directed speech (CDS) 147–8, 148, 394
chi-square test 301, 371, 373–4
chunking 220, 402; see also scaffolding

Churchland, Paul 63
claims 89, 385; see also illocutionary acts
clarity: of boundaries 215; of objectives 97, 233
classroom: culture 327; environment 174, 316; management 206, 256, 327; 327
CLIL (Content and Language Integrated Learning) 336–7, 411
Clement, Jeanette 248
clitic groups 38, 379; see also bottom-up processing
cochlea see ear
co-construction 96–7, 253
code80 385; in transcript analysis research 297–302, 318–19; see also deictic framing
code-switching 150–1, 184
cognate transfer 156, 395; see also linguistic processing
cognition: early development of 136–7; embodied 60, 87, 195, 238
cognitive abilities 22; see also individual differences
cognitive biases 62, 66; see also heuristic strategies
cognitive development: caregiver support for 146; and listening 135; Piaget on 144
cognitive frameworks 59, 63, 71
cognitive functions 13, 19; higher-order 137
cognitive load 169, 205, 215–18, 394, 403; factors influencing 215–17; in L2 acquisition 154
cognitive maps 60, 80; see also schema activation
cognitive: models 15, 59; cognitive overload 152, 220; cognitive revolution (in language teaching) 173–6; cognitive schema activation 71; cognitive skills 63, 328, 411; cognitive strategies 62, 181, 191, 399; cognitive structures (in language acquisition) 144–5, 394
cognitive-code learning theory 173, 399
cognitivist theory 151
Cohen's kappa 304, 311, 348, 374
cohesion markers 42; see also syntactic processing
collaboration skills 328, 411
collaborative conversation 96, 249–50, 404; stages of 251

418   *Index*

collaborative tasks 179–80, 193, 287
collocations 57, **57**, 118, <u>382</u>
communication models 88; *see also* intention
communication skills 281; and listening outcomes 327
communication strategies 89, 91, 109, 272; tracking 286
communication theory 96–7, 317, 387
communicative effectiveness 30, 87
communicative goals (of discourse) 211
communicative insincerity 91, <u>385</u>
community framing 84–6
compensatory strategies 67–9, **68–9**, <u>382</u>
component listening skills 263; *see also* construct validity
compound bilinguals 150
comprehensibility 60, 321, <u>409</u>; assessment of 285–6, 302–3, 309–10; comprehensibility scales 310–12
comprehensible input 150, 176–8
comprehensible output hypothesis 178–9, 195
comprehension 15–17, <u>377</u>; global 175, 195; individual differences in 23; as objective 233; rope analogy of 71; *see also* listening comprehension
comprehension building 56–63, 65, 70–1, 189–92, **192**, 382
comprehension difficulty 215; *see also* cognitive load
comprehension skills 209, 253; in assessment 272, 281; in course design 346
comprehension-based skills 265, <u>406</u>
concept abstraction 60–1, <u>382</u>
concessions 96, <u>385</u>; *see also* backchanneling
Conditional Routing Model (CRM) 151
confidentiality 185, 370, 372, 375
confirmation bias 62; *see also* heuristic strategies
conflict resolution 82, 87, 99, 321
connection 182–3, <u>399</u>; *see also* engagement
connectionist theory 36, 155
connectivity 17–19, 22–4, 185, <u>377</u>; individual differences in 23–4
conscious strategy selection 181, <u>400</u>
consciousness 1, 14–16, 97; neural correlates of *16*

consonants: articulation of 34, *35*; assimilation of 39–40
constatives 88, <u>385</u>; *see also* speech act theory
construct validity 259, 263–5, 282, 310, <u>406</u>; *see also* assessment
constructing meaning 6, <u>382</u>
content domain 128, 259–63, <u>406</u>
content learning 246, 361–2
content selection 169, 234–5, 348, 404; in collaborative conversation 251; in dictation 240; in dictogloss 241; in note-taking 246–7; in probing conversations 252; in selective listening 245
content validity 263, 273–8, 406
context effects 38–9
contextual engagement 205
contextual framing 31, 79–81, 272
contextual information 37, 58, 64, 122
contextual language routines 148, <u>394</u>
contextual understanding 56, 59, 79, 119, 128
continuous perception 141, <u>394</u>
contradictory or biased data 120
control, in oral interviews 283–4
control group 191, 329, 338–9
control variable 338–9, <u>411</u>
conventional inferencing 65
conventionalized forms 45, <u>379</u>
conversational maxims 89–92, **90**, <u>386</u>
conversations: academic 253–4, 342; face-to-face 205, 219, 269; free 343; interactive 141, **143**; low-affect **82**; pedagogic 343; real-life 179, 183; scripted 340–1; structured 173, 253; transactional 94–5; *see also* collaborative conversation; probing conversations
cooperative principles 91, <u>386</u>
coordinate bilinguals 157, <u>394</u>
coordination <u>377</u>; individual differences in 22–3
Cornell method 246, 248; *see also* note-taking
correlation analysis 304, 373–4
Council of Europe: CEFR scale 267
countering 94, <u>386</u>
course design 293, 330; variables 346–50, **348–50**
creative tasks 120

creativity and innovation 328, 411
criterion-related validity 406
critical analysis 71, 213
critical listening 189–91, 235
critical period 153, 394
critical thinking 1, 20–1, 24; and
    comprehension building 190–1;
    improvements in 251, 328; and
    metacognitive approach 182; and
    neurological processing 183, 186; as
    research skill 370, 372
Cronbach's alpha 373
cue uptake 300, 409
culture: cultural background 181, 183,
    283, 370, 408; cultural competence
    328, 351, 370, 411; cultural filters
    312, 315; cultural knowledge 96,
    157, 312; cultural literacy 235, 281;
    cultural norms 85, 152, 266, 272, 310;
    cultural references 63, 152, 211, 267–8,
    320; cultural sensitivity (as research
    guideline) 370
Cutler, Anne 33, 153–4

data analysis 285, 370–2, 375
data collection 318, 369, 371, 375
data integration 1, 375
deception 21, 158; interpersonal
    deception theory 91–2, 387
decision points 297
decision-making authority 84
declarative memory 18; see also long-
    term memory
decoding speech 1, 8, 33–5, 117
deep learning 110; see also AI automatic
    speech recognition
deictic framing 79–80, 272, 386
deliberate practice 186–9, 188, 207, 236,
    251, 400
delivery methods 337, 411; see also input,
    technological enhancements
delivery styles 99, 337–8; see also
    pragmatic processing
dependency parsing 111, 391
dependent variable 338–9, 411–12
derivations 58, 382
descriptive statistics 371–2
design decisions 293; see also
    instructional interventions
design-feedback-redesign loop 347
dialogic education 181, 400

dialogue management 111, 126, 391
dialogue prompts (in comprehensibility
    research) 310
dictation 173, 223, 239–41; as formative
    assessment 346; stages in 240
dictogloss 239, 241–3; sample passage
    242; stages in 241–2
differentiation 141, 394; and listening
    outcomes 327
difficulty 154, 205, 215–18, 331, 348; in
    adaptive testing 405; in test evaluation
    408; see also cognitive load
digital literacy 235, 281
digital signal processing (DSP) 116
direct method 172–3, 400
directional gaze 46–8
directness: in pragmatic competence 158;
    in pragmatic comprehension testing
    273; in text analysis 216
discourse: analysis 61, 94, 266; features,
    prioritizing 297; framing 79–87, 99,
    386; management 300, 409; markers
    193, 216, 228; mediating 283;
    moves 125, 296–7, 300–1, 319, 409;
    structures: learning 178; structures :
    unplanned 30
discourse types 169, 205, 211–14,
    212–14, 332–3, 336, 403, 412
Discrimination Index Calculation 349
disequilibrium 145
dispreferred responses 95
disruption: in language processing 42, 92,
    94, 96; in motivation 232, 240
diversity 271; see also global citizenship
document analysis: in AI 121; in
    qualitative research 369
dominance-submission relationship 82–4,
    83, 156–7, 386
dopamine 13, 377
dual-coding 155–6, 221, 223, 394
duration in temporal processing 31–3, 33,
    36, 40, 378, 379, 398
Dynamic Restructuring Model (DRM)
    151

EAL (English as an additional language)
    259–62, 351, 406
EAP (English for academic purposes)
    259–61, 406, 406
ear: anatomy: 9–11; inner ear 12
easification 169, 218–23, 403

420   *Index*

educational constructivist theory
    231, 328–9
effect size calculation 372; *see also*
    quantitative research
efficiency principle 30, 39
EFL (English as a foreign language) 259,
    406
elaborative inference 20, 64, 71
elaborative simplification 219, 403;
    see also input simplification
elicited imitation 239, 276, 404
elision 39–40, 379
Ellis, Rod 155, 175, 178, 243
ELIZA software 113
embodiment 15, 60, 86–7, 195, 238
emotion: emotional competence 96;
    emotional connection 97, 195,
    205; emotional engagement 81–2,
    205; emotional expression 94, 184;
    emotional intelligence 79, 129; positive
    emotions 71, 96, 175; emotional
    processing 16, 19; emotional responses
    14, 79, 87, 91, 93, 181; emotional
    shadings 60, 297; emotional signaling
    92–3; emotional significance 7, 71;
    emotional tones 32, 42, 92, 127, 265
empathetic listening 185
empathic responses **300**, 409
empathy: and active listening 82; AI
    lacking 129; and language acquisition
    159; empathetic listening 185; and
    moral functioning 87; empathic
    responses **300**, 409; and response
    weighting 95–6
enabling skills **265–6**, 406
enacting skills **265–6**, 406–7
encoding process 70
endorsements 96, 386; *see also*
    backchanneling
engaged listening 182–6
engagement 182–3, 185, 400; levels 69,
    96, 337; metrics 350; and motivation
    206
enhancement 139; *see also* magnetic
    tuning
episode boundaries 44, 215
episodic memory 6, 18–19, 23–4
equifinality 97, 386; *see also* systems
    theory
Ericsson, K. Anders 186
error analysis 153, 394

error identification 241
ESL (English as a second language)
    259–62, 407
ESP (English for specific purposes)
    218–19, 259–62, 407
ethics in listening: ethical considerations
    87, 129, 370, 372, 375; ethical
    judgments 119–20; ethical stance 86
event 80, 386; *see also* deictic framing
evolutionary intelligence 127
excitation patterns 10; *see also*
    transmission
exophoric cues 42, 47, 379
experience gap tasks 249–50, 342, 404
experience-text-relationship method
    (ETR) 190–1, 400
experiential listening 172, **210**, 400
experimental design 213, 328–9, 412, 412
expressive vocabulary 141
extracting features 116; *see also* AI
    linguistic processing
extralinguistic information 47
extratextual integration 44, 379
extroversion 83; *see also* power framing
eye contact 47–8; *see also* nonverbal
    communication
EYL (English for young learners) 259–62,
    407

face validity 244, 278, 404, 407
face-threatening act 95, 250
face-to-face conversations 205, 219, 269
factor analysis 371–4
fast-speed dictation 240; *see also*
    dictation
feature (in phonology) 38, 379
feedback: in course design 350; direct
    student 347; in instructional design
    238; and listening outcomes 327;
    providing 82, 98, 238
feedback loops 98; *see also* systems
    theory
field trips 208, 332, 360
filtering: as a compensatory strategy 67–
    9; in pragmatic comprehension 78, 84,
    86, 98, *99*, 382
first listening intervention 236; *see also*
    interventions
first listening stage 207, 403; in
    collaborative conversation 251;
    in dictation 240–1; in dictogloss

241; in note-taking 248; in probing conversations 252; in selective listening 245
fixed phrases **57**, <u>383</u>
flouting (conversation maxims) 91–2, <u>320</u>
fluency: in AI advantages 285; assessing 311; in lexical processing 45; in task design 342; in comprehension 151; in comprehensibility 153; in input genres 209; in pragmatic listening tasks 194; in research studies 302, 311; in teaching approaches 172–3
focus (in neurological processing) 13
focus on form 177, <u>400</u>
foot (in phonology) 38, <u>379</u>
formality, levels of 80, 193
formative assessment 187, 238, 345–6, <u>412</u>; *see also* assessment
form-focused instruction 175, <u>400</u>
formulaic language 42, 45, <u>379</u>
fossilization 205; *see also* engagement, stabilization
free conversations 343–4
frequency (language acquisition) 58, 67, 150, 174
frequency (sound) 22, 31, 33, 36, <u>379</u>; *see also* pitch
frequency response (in automatic speech recognition) 110
frontal cortex 32, 151
frontal lobe 17, 19, 21

gambits 45, <u>379</u>
gamification 222, 349–50
gap filling 142, <u>395</u>
gap tasks 249–50
gatekeeping 262, 311
gender: and L1 acquisition 147; and miscommunication 317
general knowledge 18–20, 156, 209, 271
generalization 141, <u>395</u>; as research skill 372
Genial Understanding System 121
genre: as dimension of speech event 44, 80; as element of speech community 85; as classification of input 207–11; <u>386</u>, <u>403</u>; *see also* input
gestures: in assessing comprehensibility 311; in assessing presentations 308; in deictic framing 80; in interactional effectiveness 95, <u>308</u>; in linguistic

processing 46–8; in teaching listening 208
global citizenship 328, <u>412</u>
Global English 259–61, <u>407</u>
goal orientation 97–8
goal setting 182, 348
Goh, Christine 181–2, 312
grammar discovery approach 243
Grammar-Translation method 172
grammatic units 30, <u>380</u>
grammatical rules 30, 42; acquisition of 142, 149, 154, 177
graph neural networks (GNNs) 120–1, <u>391</u>
Grice, Paul 87–91
Gricean communication maxims 87–91
grounds 89, <u>386</u>–7
Guetzkow's T2 test 311
guide signals 47–8

habit formation 19; *see also* procedural learning
health and well-being 328, <u>412</u>
hearing 8–9
hearing circuit 9–10, *9*
hearing loss, noise-induced 22
help options 221–2
heuristic strategies 62
heuristics 62, <u>383</u>; problem-solving 66
high-frequency collocations 45, <u>380</u>
hippocampus 14, 18–19
holistic assessment 267; *see also* assessment
holistic listening skills 259
holistic patterns 45, <u>380</u>
homonymy **57**, <u>383</u>
Hornby, A. S. 172
Hubbard, Philip 220–23
hyper speeds 49
hyponymy/hypernymy **57**, <u>383</u>

i + 1 level 176, <u>400</u>
IBM Shoebox 112
ICC (intraclass correlation coefficient) 304, 311–12, 348
ignoring 94, <u>387</u>; *see also* compensatory strategies
ikigai 2
illocutionary acts 88, <u>387</u>
immediate recall protocol (IRP) 312, <u>409</u>

422   *Index*

immersive virtual reality (IVR) 237–8
implicature 92, 387; *see also* speech acts
implied meanings 128, 135, 193, 216, 233, 377, 388
Improving Aural Comprehension 244
inclusivity 271; *see also* listening proficiency descriptions
incompletion 45, 67, 69, 383
independent learning 191, 224, 336
induction 61–2, 383
inference: in learning objectives 233; in linguistic processing tasks 241; in proficiency scales **268**; types of **64**, 217
inferencing 6, 19–22, *21*, 63–9, 71, 189, 265, 401; advanced 109; enabling skill 265 explicit and implicit 65–7; in L2 acquisition 156; predictive 23
inferential statistics 371
information: density 215, 217; information distribution 219; information extraction 111, 121, 127, 391; information manipulation theory 91, 387; information retention 175, 187, 328, 337; information retrieval 127–8, 312; information status 60
information gap tasks 180, 194, 249–50, 341, 405
informativity 321
informed consent 329, 370, 372, 375
innateness movement 174
input: appropriate 151, 169, 204–5, 273; augmentation 223–4; composition of 259; delivery style 99, 337–8; engaging with 205–7; easifying 218–20, 223; genres 169, 207–15, **208–11**, 332–3, 336; in listening assessment 273–4, **274–5**; multimodal inputs 8, 223, 237; input processing 117, 178; techniques 243; theory 150–152; input variables 329–36, 412
input hypothesis 176
input selection 273, 293
input simplification 169, 205, 218–19, 224
input sources 204, 218, **331**; for collaborative listening 193; locating 234; multimodal 223; resources for 357–64
instantiation 60–2, 383
instructional approaches 189, 193, 196, 206

instructional design 169, 230–1; essentials of 254–5; learner-centered approach to 174; samples of 238–54; stages of 231–8
instructional designers 230–1, 234, 237
instructional interventions 302, 412; in various listening stages 206–7; in research 330–45; *see also* interventions
intelligibility 409; evaluating 303, 309, 311; improving 147–8
intensification, of listening processes 6, 70; *see also* learning
intensity 9, 31, 33, 380; *see also* loudnesss
intention: and agency 14; inferring 111, 127; interpreting 88–93
interaction: interaction points 206–7, 215, 336, 403; gambits 147, 178, 194, 250, 252, **255**
interaction hypothesis 177–8, 180, 195
interaction practice, personalized 286; *see also* AI in testing listening
interaction types 293, 340–43; comparing effects of 344–5
interaction variables 339–45
interactional alignment 94, 158; *see also* coordination, endorsements, semantic contingency
interactional dance 96; *see also* backchanneling
interactional effectiveness 96–7, 99–100, 387
interactionist approach 151; *see also* interaction hypothesis
interactive competence 180, 283
interactive conversations 141, **143**
interactive elements 183, 222
interactive engagement 204; *see also* engagement
interactive listening in assessment, 282–4; as part of pragmatic competence 193–5, 249; and active listening 174; definitions of 97; and peer learning 149; proficiency 170, 282–5, 407
interactive presentation 278, 287
interactive tasks 174, 278, 286; monitoring listener decisions in 300–2
interactivity 310, 409
interconnectedness 56, 97–8
intercultural communication: nonverbal cues in 48; in assessment 262; in

misunderstandings 317; *see also* cultural competence

interdependencies, maps of 127

interoceptive responses 16, 222, <u>403</u>

interpersonal deception theory 91, <u>387</u>

interpretation 19–22; individual differences in 24; in recall protocols 315; as research skill 370–1, 375

interpretive community 84–6, **86**, <u>387</u>

interpretive strategies 85, <u>387</u>

inter-rater reliability 311, 319, 348

intersubjectivity 81, <u>388</u>

interventions: 206–7, planning 217, 293; pre-listening intervention 236; variables 329, 336–9, **337**; in research design 338, <u>412</u>; in case studies 344, 412

intonation 60; in L1 acquisition 147, 149; in L2 acquisition 157; paralinguistic signals in 93

introspection 179, **214**; *see also* sociocultural theory

introversion 83; *see also* power framing

intuitive inferencing: in neurological processing 14; in linguistic processing 42; in semantic processing 65–7; in pragmatic processing 79

intuitive logic 66–7

islands of expertise 146, <u>395</u>

iterative process (in research) 375

jigsaw dictation 241

judge 81; *see also* listener roles

Kecskes, Istvan 63, 81, 85

key 80, <u>388</u>

key points, identifying 183, 234

kinesic cues 47, <u>380</u>

knowledge: depth of 56; shared 79, 320; *see also* background knowledge; phonological knowledge

Kramsch, Claire 84, 152, 158–9

Krashen, Stephen 176–7, <u>400</u>

Kuhl, Patricia 138, 144, 153

KWL model 190–1, <u>401</u>; *see also* comprehension building

L1, relationship with L2 150, 152–5, 158

L1 acquisition 149; and linguistic processing 137–44; and neurological processing 135–7; and pragmatic processing 147–9; and semantic processing 144–7

L1 processing development: *see* neurololgical, linguistic, semantic, pragmatic development

L2 acquisition 52, 134, 150, 158–9; and linguistic processing 152–6; neural models of **151**; and neurological processing 149–52; and pragmatic processing 157–8; and semantic processing 156–7

L2 listening 154–5, 157, 172; and acquisition 174–5, 177, 189; development of 150–2

labeling 141–2, <u>395</u>

language ability, innate 147

language acquisition 135, 158–9; natural order of 150, 174, 177; *see also* L1 acquisition; L2 acquisition

language comprehension: AI and BI comparisons 128–9; brain areas in 16; embodied view of 87; and empathy 87; inferencing and reasoning 19–20; pathways *17*; real-time 35–6

language development: general 137; in L1 acquisition 147–8; in L2 acquisition 151, 153; and teaching listening 176, 178–9

language exposure 181, 209

language games 143, 146, 187, **208**, 359, 253

language knowledge 177, 264, 340

language modeling: in AI linguistic processing 117, 127; in language development 149

language models, in ASR 110

language processing 15–17; AI facilitation of 112–13; in bilinguals 23; bottom-up phase 46; oral 2, 6, 24, 150

language proficiency 156; measuring 187, 258, 270–1, 273; standards of 186; sustained growth in 223

Lantolf, James 179–80

language varieties 85, 128; *see also* interpretive community

language-based skills 265, <u>407</u>

language-learning apps 222, 365–6

large language models (LLMs) 109–10, <u>391</u>

learner autonomy 327–8

424 *Index*

learner interaction 249, 339–40
learning environment: interactive 175; and neurological processing 182–3
learning: learning episodes 148, 395; learning experience 230, 337, 339; learning journals 335, 350, 412; listen to learn 178; defining learning objectives 233–4, 293, 332, 405; learning outcomes and input choices 330, **337**; learning styles 174, 181, 183, 327, 329, 333
lemma 30, 58, 118, 391
Lennox, Cynthia 282
lexical access 15, 55–8
   lexical effects (paradigmatic, syntagmatic) 56–8, **57**, 70–1, 383; in L2 acquisition 152, 156
lexical comprehension, acquisition of 141–2, 155–6
lexical: lexical effect 38, 380; lexical gap 155, 395; lexical maps 189, 401; lexical phrase 38, 380; lexical relationships 109, 219, 272; lexical transfer 155–6, 395; lexicalized sentence frames **58**, 383
lifelong learning 331, 347
Likert scales 278, 311; construction of 374
linear predictive coding (LPC) 117; *see also* AI linguistic processing
linguistic development 145–7
linguistic etiquette 157–8
linguistic knowledge 63, 178, 271, 346
linguistic processing 5, 24, 29; AI parallels to 109, 115–18; constructs **272**, **275–6**; and course design 346; instructional design for 239–43; in L1 language development 137–44; in L2 language development 152–6; and misunderstandings **320**; multimodal cues in 46–8; strengthening 236; and teaching listening 186–9, 196
linguistic signal, nine components of 38
linguistic structures, learning 178
listen-and-test format 206, 403
listener behavior 48, 301–2, 321
listener decisions 410; coding for **300**; identifying 296–302; monitoring 300–2
listener errors, analyzing 296
listener evaluation 303, 309
listener filters, interpreting 296, 312–16

listener judgments 296, 302–12, 410
listener misunderstandings 293, 410; analyzing 317–21; common **320**; questions **318–19**
listener ratings 302–3, 321
listener roles *81*
listening: AI and BI 116; brain areas activated in 17; as coordination of networks 7–8; definitions of 1, 5; in language acquisition 135, 158–9, 176; to learn and to understand 69–71, 178; with understanding 244; *see also* researching listening; teaching listening
listening abilities: acquiring 204; development in first year 136–7, *136*; and pragmatic processing 249; use of term 259–63; variables of 264
listening activities, objectives of 183, 233
listening assessment 169–70, 258; AI in 285–7; components of 273; formulating model of 271–3; identifying context for 259; integrating into instruction 287; and sociocultural theory 180
Listening Circles 183–6
listening comprehension: analyzing 285; constructs 170, 273, **275–8**, 287, 345; inferencing and reasoning 19; and memory 17–19; pathways of 17; skills 135, 175
listening development: and L1 acquisition 137, 140, 145, 149; and L2 acquisition 149–52; and learner interactions 340; and linguistic processing 239; and ZPD 180
listening exercises, in course design 349
listening experience 5; easifying 218–20, 223; individual differences in 22–3; meaningful 205–6
listening fluency 45, 151, 172, 209
listening lexicon 141, 395
listening outcomes, researching 293, 326–30, *330*
listening performance 181, 297
listening practice, personalized 286
listening processes 7–22; individual differences in 22–4; researching *296*; value of studying 321
listening proficiency: descriptions 266–71; scales: ACTFL, CEFR, CLB, IELTS, GSE 267, 407
listening response journal 346

Index   425

listening skills 85; acquiring 150, 180; bottom-up 18, 186–9, 191; multimodal 286

listening strategies 23; cognitive 241; metacognitive 207

listening tasks, collaborative 180, 193

listening vocabulary 139, 141, 143, 155

literary devices **58**, <u>383</u>

live discourse 46–7

loan transfer 156, <u>395</u>

locutions 88

logic, formal 20, 65

logical reasoning 21–2, 24, 65, 401

logogens 36–7, <u>380</u>

Long, Michael H. 174, 177–9, 219

long short-term memory units (LSTM) 115–16, <u>391</u>

longitudinal studies 302, 328–9, <u>413</u>

long-term learning 72, 221

long-term memory 18–19, 70–1, 156, 248

loudness 10, 31, 33; as affective variation 92; as transitional cue 36

low-affect conversation **82**

Lozanov, Georgi 175

Macaro, Ernesto 67, 176

machine learning 114, 126, <u>391</u>

magnetic tuning 138–9, <u>395</u>

main ideas, listening for 208, 265

management strategies 158

mapping: articulatory *35*; phonological 36; syntactic 42; lexical 60; conceptual 155, <u>396</u>

matching task 279

mean length of utterance (MLU) 144, <u>396</u>

meaning acquisition 141–2

measurability, of objectives 233

media literacy 235, 281

MELAB (Michigan English Language Assessment Battery) 264

Mel-Frequency Cepstral Coefficients 116–17

memory 6–7; and neurological processing 13, 15, 17–19; memory banks 109, <u>391</u>; memory capacity 8, 23, 174–5, 181, 187, 244; memory cells 115–16, <u>391</u>; memory centers, distribution of *20*; memory retrieval 18, 189; *see also* long-term memory, short-term memory

mental: engagement 205; mental frameworks 18, 59, 144; mental lexicon 5, 36–7, 39, <u>383</u>; activation of 71; and lexical access 56; mental models 59–60, 243; mental prototypes 66, <u>383</u>; mental structures 145

meronymy/holonymy **57**, <u>384</u>

meta-analysis 329

metacognition: individual difference in 24; pedagogic approaches 180–2, 195; as enabling skill 266

metacognitive awareness 348

metacognitive processing 151, 154, 182, 272, <u>396</u>

metacognitive strategies 158, 172, 181–2, 189, <u>401</u>

metacommunication 63, <u>384</u>

metacultural proficiency 80, 99–100, 351, <u>388</u>

metadata 122–3

meta-messages **58**, <u>384</u>

metrical segmentation 153

microphones (in ASR) 110, 112, 116

mind mapping 246

mindfulness 14

mindset 99, 182, 186–9, 191–2, 195

Minsky, Marvin 112

mirroring 33–4, 79, <u>388</u>

miscommunication 99, 283, 317, 319, 321

misunderstandings 158, 269, 293

Mitsuku (chatbot) 126

mixed-methods research 295, 328–9, <u>413</u>; guidelines for 374–5

mondegreens 139

monitor hypothesis 177

monitor model 176–7

mora 38, <u>380</u>

moral functioning 87

moral judgments 119

mora-timed languages 153, <u>396</u>

Morley, Joan 244

morphological processing 30, 35–41, <u>380</u>

motivation: and engagement 206, 340; in inferencing **64**; intrinsic 147; in formative assessment 345; in neurological processing 13; motivational elements 349–50; in social cognition 79; and resistance 232; *see also* attitudes and motivation

motor cortex 17, 32, 34

multifinality 97, <u>388</u>

multilevel modeling 373

426   *Index*

multilingualism, and listening outcomes 327
multimodal cues (in linguistic processing) 46–47
multiliteracy expertise 234–5, <u>405</u>
multimodal factors 44, **380**; *see also* syntactic parsing
multiple choice (as test prompt) 188, 279–80, 346
multivariate analysis 372–3
mutual exclusivity strategies 155, <u>396</u>
Mynard, Jo 334, 347

named entity recognition (NER) 111, 118, 127, <u>391</u>–2
narratives, recall of 59, 312; inference **64**; *see also* story structure
native listener hypothesis (NLH) 154, <u>396</u>
native speaker: proficiency to level of 137, 159; use of term 30, 110, **261**, 271, 365–7; *see also* non-native speakers
natural approach 175–6
natural language generation (NLG) 111, <u>392</u>
natural language processing (NLP) 109, 113–14, <u>392</u>; evolution of 126–8; neural networks used in *116*; pragmatic processing in 109, 124; semantic processing in 121
natural language understanding (NLU) 110–11, <u>392</u>
natural order hypothesis 177
naturalness 174; in AI voices 303; in rating scales 310
needs analysis 231–2, <u>405</u>; in collaborative conversation 251; in dictation 240; in dictogloss 241; and input choices 333; in note-taking 246; in probing conversations 252; in selective listening 245
negative transfer 153; *see also* transfer
negotiation of meaning 177, 241, 340
negotiation procedures 152
neocortex 18; *see also* brain
network-building 142, <u>396</u>
neural commitment 153, <u>396</u>
neural connections 45, 114, 399
neural networks 10, 109–11, 114, <u>392</u>; evolution of 127; human and AI *114–15*; and language acquisition

153; in NLP *116*; reorganizing 23; and semantic processing 119–20
neural pathways 13, 22, 56, 58, 138, 396
neurological development 137–8, 144
neurological processing 5, 24–5; AI parallels to 109, 114–15; and course design 346; involved in listening *see* listening processes; and language acquisition 135–7, 149–52; and misunderstandings **320**; and teaching listening 182–6, 196
neurological system 8, 22, 135; *see also* brain
neuroplasticity 8, 23; rapid cortical plasticity 70, <u>384</u>
neurotransmitters 13
new information 7, 59–60; *see also* assimilation
nonliteral language 193; *see also* pragmatic processing
non-native speakers (NNS) 30, 110, 260–1, 303, 309, 407; *see also* native speakers
nonverbal communication: as part of pragmatic processing 158; nonverbal cues 48, 84, 216; in transcription 110, 297
norepinephrine 13, <u>377</u>
note-taking 181, 183; and focusing attention 248–9; in instructional design 244–9; in listening assessment 277; methods of 246; as objective 233; stages of design **246**–7; strategies 248, 337
noticing: as part of pragmatic comprehension **100**, for language learning 42, 177–9; 242–3, 340
nobjectives: in collaborative conversation 251; defining 232–4; in dictation 240; in dictogloss 241; in note-taking 246; in probing conversations 252; in selective listening 245

omissions 315
ontology 118–19, *119*, 122, **123**; ontological models 59, <u>384</u>; ontological frameworks 109
open response in testing 280
open-ended tasks 120
OPI (Oral Proficiency Interview) 282–3
opinion gap task 249–50, 341, <u>405</u>

oral input 137, 144, 191, 205, 404; *see also* input
oral interviews 259, 278, 282–3; accommodation and control in **284**
orientation (in neurological processing) 12–14, *13*
orienting response 154, 396
other-orientedness 87, 388
outline method 246, 248; *see also* note-taking
overextension 142, 397; *see also* lexical comprehension
overhearers 80–1; *see also* listener roles

P-400 effect 154, 397; *see also* orienting response
P-600 effect 42; *see also* disruption
packaging 142, 397; *see also* L1 acquisition
pair work 180, **192**, 193, **194**, 195, **212–4**, 233, 241, **245**, 249–50, 253, **278**
Palmer, Harold 172
paradigmatic relations 56–8, **57**, 271, 384
paralinguistic features 92–3, 157, 387
parietal lobes 17–19, 21
participation framing 81, 84
part-of-speech (POS) tagging 118, 392
pascals 8, 377
pattern recognition 66
pause and paraphrase 240
pause units 38, 217, 381
Peace Corps 2, 157
pedagogic conversations 343
peer assessment 309, 312; *see also* assessment
peer influence 146–9
peer review 370, 372, 375
perception processes 139, *140*
perception training, intensive 155; *see also* linguistic processing
perceptron node 115, 392
perceptual constancy 141, 397
perceptual magnet effect *138*
performance analysis 350
performance assessments 238, 345, 349–50; *see also* assessment
performatives 88, 388
perlocution 88–9, 388
personal information 64, 340
personal reflection 183, 214
phonetic contrasts 137, 397

phonological: awareness 8, 135, 208–9, 265, 406–7; phonological decoding 24, 152, 186, 272; phonological discrimination 187, 236; phonological information 37, 141; phonological knowledge 17, 272; phonological loop 15, 18, 141; phonological memory 24, 141, 187; phonological sensitivity 140, 397; phonological store 18; phonological words 38, 143, 381, 397; phonotactic system 35, 138, 140, 152, 397
phonological processing 30–5, 381; in L2 152–3
phonological processing 30–5, 47, 49 381; L2 152–3; and acquisition 137–41
phonotactic system 35, 138, 140, 152, 397
Piaget, Jean 144–5
pitch 31, 33; as transitional cue 36
Plack, Christopher 10
play, and language acquisition 149
politeness principles 94
polyglots, practice ideas from 367–8
polysemy **57**, 384
portfolio assessment 267, 281–2, 287; *see also* assessment
positive behaviors 296, 302
positive mindset 13, 182, 187, 254
positive solution-oriented discourse patterns 111, 392; *see also* Natural Language Generation
post-listening activities 191, 327, 337–8, 413; *see also* interventions
post-listening assessment 346; *see also* assessment
post-listening interventions 236; *see also* interventions
post-listening stages 169, 207, 403; in collaborative conversation 251; in dictation 240; in dictogloss 242; in note-taking 248; in probing conversations 252; in selective listening 245
power analysis 372
power framing 81–4, *84*
practice sources 365–8
practice variations 340–1
practitioner ideas 234–5, 240–1, 243, 248–9, 253–5, 282
pragmatic: awareness 44, 381; pragmatic competence 96, 98–100, *100*, 193,

428 Index

401; in L2 135, 157; pragmatic comprehension 78–9, 81, 98–9, 193, 388; pragmatic information 45, 216; pragmatic knowledge 273; pragmatic mindset 80

pragmatic listening, interaction types **194**

pragmatic processing 5–6, 24, 78–9, 86; and additive response 96–7; AI parallels to 109, 111, 124–6; constructs **272**; conversational maxims, 89–91; and course design 346; as filtering *99*; and instructional design 249–54; and internal response 94; and language development 147–9, 157–8; and misunderstandings **320**; and teaching listening 193–6

predictions, as semantic processing 60–2, 71; in assessment 265

preferred responses 94–5

prefrontal cortex 14, 16, 18–19, 21–2; *see also* brain

pre-listening activities 191, 337, 413; in course design 348

pre-listening intervention 236; *see also* interventions

pre-listening stage 207, 404; in collaborative conversation 251; in dictation 240; in dictogloss 241; in note-taking 248; in probing conversations 252; in selective listening 245

pre-processing, in automatic speech recognition 116

presentation scaffolding 169, 204–5, 218–19

presentation variations 340–1

priming effect 58, 384

probability, tutorials in 374

probed recall 316, 410

probing conversations 249–51, 342–3; conversation gambits for **255**; stages of **252**

problem-solving: collaborative 149; in discourse typology 212; heuristics 66; in relation to cognitive load 154; in L1 acquisition 137; in L2 acquisition 151, 178, 182; interactive 193–5; resources for 360; in responses 94; problem-solving skills 151; in task design 183, 192–5

procedural learning 6, 18–19

procedural memory 6, 18–19, *20*

process domain 259, 407–8

prompts, in listening assessment *see* test prompts; *see also* assessment

pronunciation: assessing 285, 311; irregular 297

propositional representations 41, 44–6, 110; *see also* linguistic processing

propositional structure *44*

prosodic elements 60

prosodic features 5, 117, 264, 392

prosodic sensitivity 44–5, 381

prosody, assessing 311

proximal stimulation 34, 381, 381; *see also* speech perception

psychoacoustics 2

purpose 80, 388; *see also* deictic framing

p-values 339; *see also* quantitative research

qualitative methods 321, 339

qualitative research, guidelines for 369–70

quality questioning 191, 401; *see also* comprehension building

quantitative research: guidelines for 371–2; research skills 371–2

quantum computing 127–8

quasi-experimental design 328, 338–9, 413

question analysis (in neural networks) 120, 127

Question Answer Relationship (QAR) 190–1, 401–2; *see also* KWL

question answering (in AI processing) 111, 124, 392

questions: open-ended 180, 213, 233, 349; prototypical 125, 218; reflective 207, 236

rapid cortical plasticity 70, 384

Rasa (open source framework) 126

rater disagreements 312

rating scales 293, 304–9, **304–8**, 312, 410

rationalizations 315

reading: in lexical acquisition 155; in coordinate bilinguals 157; in language teaching 172–6, 190; in comprehension building 192; as part of listening tasks 207, 244; accompanying spoken input **208–9**; as element in multiliteracy

Index   429

234–5; as element of assessment 281; comparison with listening 71
realignment 139; *see also* magnetic tuning
reasoning 1, 19–22, *21*, 49, 56; fallacies of 67; and inference 64–5, 71
recall accuracy 316
recall protocols 293, 312–16, <u>410</u>; interpreting and scoring 315–16
recency bias 62
receptive vocabulary 141, 144
receptivity 1, 78, 182–3, 185, 260–1, <u>402</u>
reciprocal teaching (RT) method 190, <u>402</u>
reconstructing messages 265
recurrent neural networks (RNNs) 115, <u>392–3</u>
redundancy 33, 41, **216**, 221, 269
referential semantic processing 221, <u>404</u>; *see also* semantic processing
reflection 1, 179; in instructional design 242, 245, 248–9, 251; as listener decision 300; pauses for 183; in portfolio assessment 281; as testing prompt 278
register 80, **267**, <u>388</u>
regression analysis 371–2, 374; *see also* research methods
relevance 6; in listening assessment 273, <u>408</u>; of objectives 233
reliability, of statistical tests 371
repetition, simple 220; *see also* presentation scaffolding
re-presenting text 220, <u>404</u>
research design: overview of methods 328–9; research variables <u>296</u>; resources 369–75
research questions 174, 315, 328; and mixed methods 295, 374; in qualitative studies 369–70; in quantitative studies 371–2
resistance-engagement continuum *232*
response: responding 94–6; response generation 109, 121; response processing 124–5, <u>393</u>; response types 272, <u>388–9</u>; response weighting 93–4, <u>389</u>; responses, in listening assessment 273
Revesz, Andrea 217, 263
restrictive simplification 219, <u>404</u>; *see also* input simplification
reticular activating system (RAS) *13*, 13–5, <u>377</u>

reticular formation (RF) 13–14
rhetorical patterns 178, 218
rhetorical styles 263, 332, <u>413</u>
Rinvolucri, Mario 240
rights and expectations 81–4, <u>389</u>; *see also* participation framing
ritualized texts **57**, <u>384</u>
Rumi 159

sampling (in Automatic Speech Recognition) 116
sandhi variations 39, <u>381</u>
sarcasm 128, 320; *see also* symbolic aptitude
scaffolding 195, 205; in collaborative and probing conversations 251; of selective listening 244
schema: schema activation 6, 56, 59–63, 66, 156; schema modification 60–1; schematic effect 38, <u>381</u>; schematic memory 312; schematic negotiation 63, <u>384</u>; conceptual schemata 189, <u>399</u>; content schemata 109, 125; cultural schemata 67, 152, 312, 321
scientific approach 172, <u>402</u>; *see also* teaching listening
scripted conversation 340–1; *see also* interaction variables
second language acquisition (SLA) *see* L2 acquisition
second listening intervention 236; *see also* interventions
second listening stage 207, 236, <u>404</u>; in collaborative conversation 251; in dictation 240; in dictogloss 242; in note-taking 248; in probing conversations 252; in selective listening 245
segment (in phonology) 38, <u>381</u>
selective attention 14, 23, 70, <u>384</u>
selective listening: and instructional design 244; stages of **245**
self-assessment 182, 238, 281, 335, 345–7, 350; *see also* assessment
self-direction 180, 189
self-regulation 85, 180
self-talk 181; *see also* socio-affective strategies
semantic: contingency 148, <u>397</u>; episodes 215; information 17, 37, 56, 157, 382; knowledge 271

430　*Index*

semantic memory 6, 18, 23, 58; in AI processing 109; in L2 acquisition 156; *see also* connectivity, individual differences
semantic priming 58; *see also* spreading activation
semantic processing 5–6, 24, 55–6; AI parallels to 109, 118–23; associative and referential 221; brain areas for 17; constructs **272**, **276–8**; and course design 346; as embodied sense 60; goals of 70; inference types in **64**; and instructional design 243–9; and language acquisition 144–7, 156–7; in language comprehension 71–2; levels of 63; and misunderstandings **320**; and power framing 83; and propositional representations 45; role of interaction in 145–7; and teaching listening 189–92, 196
semantic roles 42, 44, 55, 121, 272; *see also* argument structure
sensorimotor systems 87; *see also* embodied cognition
sentence method 246; *see also* note-taking
sentence structures 30
sentiment analysis 111, 127, 393
sequence analysis 319
sequential bilinguals 150, 152
serotonin 13, 377
setting 80, 389; *see also* deictic framing
shadowing 155, 187–8, 195, 223, 236, 239; *see also* deliberate practice
sharpening 139; *see also* magnetic tuning
Shaules, Joseph 232
short answer (as a test prompt) 279
short-term memory 14–15, 18–19, 21, 265; capacity 23, 338; differences in capacity 23; in L2 acquisition 154; and linguistic processing 43, 45, 55; phonological information in 141; schema activation in 60
Siegel, Joseph 181, 191
sibling influence 148–9; *see also* semantic processing development
simplicity 174; *see also* biolinguistics
simplification: influence on cognitive load 205; restrictive vs. elaborative simplification 219; in recall protocols 315; in accommodation **284**
simultaneous bilinguals 150, 156–7, 398

simultaneous interpretation 68–9
sinusoidal stimulation 10, 378, 378; *see also* cochlea
situated presence 81, 389; *see also* participation framing
situated speech 88, 389; *see also* intention
situational meaning 99–100; *see also* pragmatic competence
situational utterances **57**, 384
skipping 67–8, 384; *see also* compensatory strategies
SMCR model of communication 88
social dimensions of listening: emotional skills 328, 351, 413; social cognition 15, 79, 389; contravening social conventions 91–2; social frames 85; social norms 80, 94
social interactions 79, 136–7, 179; in L2 development 151
socialization in L1 listening 145–6
socio-affective strategies 181, 402
sociocultural theory (SCT) 152, 179–80, 195
socio-emotional skills 253, 342; *see also* academic conversations
sociolinguistics revolution 80; *see also* deictic framing
sound, physical characteristics of 31
sound sequences 30, 139, 141
sound waves 7–9, 11, 22, 116–17
spaced repetition 71, 187, 202; *see also* deliberate practice
spatial memory 19, *20*
spatial reasoning 21; *see also* inference
speaker comprehensibility, evaluating 293, 309–10
speaker impact 303–4, 410; *see also* listener judgments
speaker meaning 88; *see also* speech act theory
speaker presentations, evaluating 304–9
speaker-listener coordination *32*; *see also* real-time comprehension
specific information, listening for 70, 190, 233, 265, 312
specificity, of objectives 233; *see also* defining learning objectives
spectral envelope 117, 393
spectral processing 9, 378
spectrogram 33–4, *34, 36*
speech, acoustic dimensions of 31, *33*

Index 431

speech act theory 88–9
speech acts 88, <u>389</u>
speech detection, timing of *36; see also* word recognition
speech perception: categorical 38; and production 30–1
speech production 17, 30, 32, 135
speech rate 117, 141, 217
speech recognition 112, 116, 237, 285
speech signal 34
speed modification 221, 337
Sperber, Dan 14, 19, 78, 93
spiritual intelligence 120
spoken input 38, 152, 178, 330
spreading activation 39, 56, 58, 385
stabilization 205, <u>404</u>
stance 80, <u>389</u>; *see also* deictic framing
standardized tests 258; comprehensiveness of 267; variance in performance 263
statistical procedures 372–4
statistical software 339, 371
story structure 209, 312–13, **313**, 315
storylistening 316; *see also* storytelling
storytelling 85, 149, 316; and language acquisition 149
stream of speech 5, 35–6, 38, 41, 48–9, 272
stressful conditions 154–5; *see also* cognitive load
stress-timed languages 153
structured discussions, post-listening 337
student engagement (in listening research) 293, 327, 334, 347; *see also* engagement
student reflections 335
subjective framing 86–7
subjective presence 86–7, 389
subjective qualities 31
substitution 67, 69, <u>385</u>
subtitles 211, 221, 223, 316, 337, 367; *see also* intervention variables
success, criteria for 233, 259, 273; *see also* defining objectives
suggestopedia 175–6
summative assessment 238, 345, <u>413</u>; *see also* assessment
superior colliculus (SC) 13–14
superior temporal gyrus (STG) 11, 31
superior temporal sulcus (STS) 17
supramarginal gyri 17

Swain, Merrill 178–80, 241
syllable 38, <u>381</u>; average length of 31
syllable-timed languages 153, <u>398</u>
symbolic aptitude 99–100, <u>389</u>
symbolization 141; *see also* lexical comprehension
synonymy **57**, <u>385</u>
syntactic effect 39, <u>381</u>; *see also* word recognition
syntactic parsing 41–2, 186, <u>381</u>; by AI 118; in L2 acquisition 152, 154; in listening assessment 275–6; sources of knowledge for 44–5; structured practice in 236; top-down influences 44
syntactic processing 29–30, 41–6, <u>381</u>; L2 153–5
syntactic processing algorithms 118; *see also* AI linguistic processing
syntactic relationships 18, 109, 141
syntactic rules 142, 271; *see also* syntax comprehension
syntagmatic relations 56–8, **57–8**, <u>385</u>
syntax comprehension, acquisition of 142–4, 152
systems theory 97–8, <u>389–90</u>; conversational response in **98**

talkativeness 148
task automation 111
task sequencing 236–7, 254, <u>405</u>; in collaborative conversation 251; in dictation 240; in dictogloss 241; in note-taking 248; in probing conversations 252; in selective listening 245
task support 218, 220
teaching listening 169, 195–6; default methodology for 206; historical approaches to 172–3; profiling approaches to 182–95; theoretical models for 176–82
teaching methodologies 171–2, 174, 182
teaching strategies 327
technological enhancements 337, <u>413</u>
technological mediation 169, 205, 218, 220–3
technology integration 231, 237–8, <u>405</u>; in collaborative conversation 251; in dictation 240; in dictogloss 241; in note-taking 247; in probing

432   *Index*

conversations 252; in selective listening 245
technology resources **237**
temporal lobe 11–12, 17, 19, 21
temporal processing 9, 378
test impact 263, 408; *see also* washback effect
test prompts 273, **275–8**, 408; composing 278–80, **279–80**
text classification 111, 393
text construction, variables in **217**
thalamus 13–16
themes 42–5, 382
theory integration 372
timbre 31, 33, 382
time frames 41, 306–7, 328
timed replays 221; *see also* technology mediation
Toulmin, Stephen 56
tokens 118, 393; *see also* AI, linguistic processing
tones, contrasting 45
tonotopic organization 10, 378
top-down bias 71, 239, 390
top-down processing 15–16, 29–30, 48–9, *49*, 55–6, 378
topic: as aspect of deictic framing 80; control, in power framing *84*; in semantic processing development 146; in pragmatic processing development 147; in comprehension building 192; in interactive listening tasks 193–4; in genre analysis 210
topical interaction 145, 398
top-level abilities 263–4, 408; *see also* assessment
total physical response (TPR) method 175–6
transactional conversations 94–5
transactional focus 158
transcription: and AI 110–11, 117–18, 286; analyzing 293, 297; and captioning 220; recall 313–15, **314**; research projects using 301–2; as research skill 369; variables in practices **298–9**
transduction 10, 378
transfer: of sounds *9*; of information in memory 70; of lexical mapping 155; of phonological strategies 153; of skills 189

transfer-appropriate processing (TAP) 189, 402
transformative experience 1, 159, 186
translanguaging 149, 184, 242, 248, 327, 335, 398
translation: in AI 108, 111–2, 115, 127; in simultaneous interpretation 68–9; in teaching methodolgy 172–3, 193, **262**; in technological resources 211, 297, 335, 365; in transcriptions 299
transliteration 156, 398
transmission in hearing 10–12, 378; individual differences in 22
transmission process *11*
transverse temporal gyri 11–12, 378
transvocalization 156, 398
triangulation 321, 370, 374–5
trochaically timed languages 153, 398
true/false statements (as a test prompt) 192, 280
truthfulness 87; *see also* communicative insincerity
t-tests 339, 371–3; *see also* quantitative research
Turing test 113, 303
turn-taking 83, 157; in transcription 297, 299

underextension 142, 398; *see also* lexical comprehension
understanding, mutual 63, 82
units of analysis (in transcriptions) 297, 318–19
universal grammar 144
unreliability blips 154; *see also* cognitive load
uptaking 89, 94, 96, 390
useable materials (in assessment) 273, 408; *see also* content validity
utility 174; *see also* biolinguistics

validity 170; in assessment 259–65; of statistical tests 371; *see also* assessment
Vandergrift, Larry 174, 181–2
variance 263, 408
verbal responsiveness 82; *see also* power framing, affective involvement
Verschueren, Jef 79, 81

vestibulocochlear nerve 8, 10
video: in AI training; in listening instruction 110, 180, 192, 205–6; 210, 220–3, 230, 235, 237–8, 241, 247–8, 334; in assessment 281; in listening research 297, 302, 309–10, 317; resources 357–364
virtual assistants 126
virtual reality (VR) 204, 222, 237–8; resources 365
visual aids 183, 220, 311; *see also* easifying input
visual information, integrating 17, 47
visual reinforcement 216, 220
visualizations (in research) 301, 371
vocabulary development 141, 149, 208–9, 233
vocabulary knowledge 190, 265, 337
voice80, 390; *see also* deictic framing
vowels: articulation of 34, *35*; centering and reduction 39–41, *41*, 382
Vygotsky, Lev 180

Wagner, Elvis 259, 273
warrants (in inferencing) 89, 390, 390

washback effect 263, 283, 287, 408
waveform 31, 33; *see also* timbre
Weizenbaum's simulator 112–13
while-listening activities 337, 346, 414
Wiio, Osmo 317
willingness to communicate 99; *see also* agency, attitudes and motivation
Wilson, Deirdre 14, 78, 93, 137
word boundaries 35–6, 39, 139
word knowledge 55, 58
word recognition 5, 36–9, *37*, 45, 195; by AI 118; and bottom-up listening 186–7; psychological effects (phonological, syntactic, lexical, schematic) 38–9; at hyper speeds 49; in L1 acquisition 140; in L2 acquisition 152; and lexical access 56–8; structured practice in 236
word segmentation 140, 272, 275
working memory *see* short-term memory

Xiaoice 126; *see also* chatbots

zone of proximal development 180, 402
Zwiers, Jeff 251, 253–4

Milton Keynes UK
Ingram Content Group UK Ltd.
UKHW022206220824
447265UK00011B/92